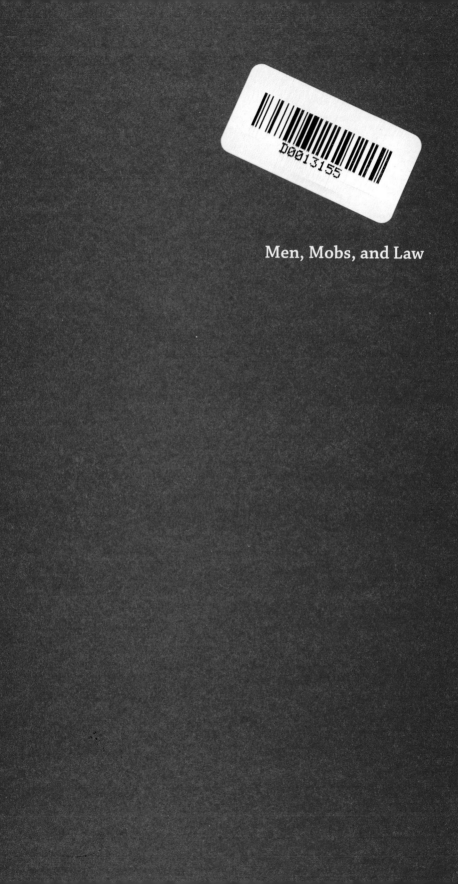

Men, Mobs, and Law

Rebecca N. Hill

Men, Mobs, and Law

Anti-Lynching and Labor Defense

in U.S. Radical History

DUKE UNIVERSITY PRESS   DURHAM AND LONDON   2008

Designed by C. H. Westmoreland
Typeset in Arno with Chaparral display
by Achorn International, Inc.
Library of Congress Cataloging-in-
Publication Data appear on the last printed
page of this book.

FOR MY MOTHER, IRIS TILLMAN HILL,

AND IN MEMORY OF MY GOOD FRIEND

JOSIE FOWLER (1957–2006)

Contents

Acknowledgments

Men, Mobs, and Law began as a dissertation, and in the intervening years I have managed to rack up many debts to friends, family, and colleagues. My adviser, Paula Rabinowitz, helped me define the project from its beginning in a seminar paper about Sacco and Vanzetti during my first year in graduate school. The rest of my committee at the University of Minnesota—Maria Damon, Douglass Hartmann, and David Roediger— provided tremendous guidance throughout the research and writing, and David Roediger continued to play a significant role in helping me move from dissertation to book. The Professional Staff Congress of the City University of New York's winning of release time for junior faculty made it possible for me to reduce my course load and spend more time in the library during the spring and fall of 2005. I am also grateful to Raphael Allen, who first took interest in the manuscript at Duke University Press, and to Valerie Millholland and Mark Mastromarino, who oversaw its completion. Peter Rachleff and anonymous readers for Duke helped me to tighten the manuscript and improve the scholarship. The staff at the Tamiment Library of New York University—particularly Evan Daniel, Peter Filardo, Erica Gottfried, and Gayle Malmgreen—helped me consistently over many years of research. Eugene Zapp and other librarians at the Boston Public Library helped me work with the difficult Felicani collection, and the staffs at the Harvard University Law Library, the Chicago and Wisconsin historical societies, and the University of Minnesota's Immigration History Resource Center were also helpful. Many conversations with my friend Josephine Fowler, who was finishing her book on Asian American communists, both motivated me to finish and informed me about the cutting edge in research on the international left. Her death from cancer in the summer of 2006 was a huge loss.

I have been lucky to have a mother, Iris Tillman Hill, who in addition to being a dedicated mom is also a skilled editor with a deep interest in American history. She read and made editorial suggestions for the first four chapters of the manuscript. Her help was immeasurable. I am also lucky that my stepmother, Penny Marcus, is a scholar of Italian studies. Her help with translating long handwritten passages in Italian made significant differences in chapter 4. My stepfather, George Entenman, provided computer advice and moral support. My aunts Lynne and Barbara Tillman; my brother, Andrew Hill; my sister-in-law, Kelli Souder; and my father, Robert Hill provided emotional, financial, and nutritional support. Susan Rios was also a big help.

During the revision process, a number of senior scholars read and commented on drafts of chapters. Readings and comments by Robin D. G. Kelley, Paul Gilje, Louis DeCaro Jr., and Nikhil Pal Singh helped me to define the argument and deepen the research. I also learned from conversations and comments at conferences where I presented pieces of the book. At the John Brown 2000 Conference in Harper's Ferry, West Virginia, I met and learned from Jean Libby and the Allies for Freedom, as well as from John Patrick McCarthy, John Stauffer, Asa Diggs, and Carol Lasser. Melanie Shell-Weiss, Leon Fink, Kathleen Brown and Steve Reich at the Southern Labor Studies Conference in Birmingham, Alabama, in 2004 made useful comments that helped with chapter 3. As part of a panel on the historiography of the Communist Party of the USA at the American Historical Association Conference in January 2005, I benefited from conversations with Bryan Palmer and Christopher Phelps. Another panel discussion, on Scottsboro, gave me a chance to discuss the ramifications of that case with James Miller, Lillian Robinson, and Jean Fagin Yellin. My participation in the panel "Was America Born in the Streets?" at the conference of the Society of Historians of the Early American Republic in the fall of 2002 led to a rollicking and informative discussion of early-republican urban politics with Graham Russell Gao Hodges, Peter Menlo Buckley, Timothy Gilfoyle, and Josh Brown.

Finally, over the years I have batted around ideas about the state, revolution, and prisons with a number of exceptionally smart activist friends and colleagues. Kai Barrow, Daniel Burton-Rose, Kathleen Cleaver, Sheila Cohen, Nina Dibner, Christopher Gunderson, Shaun Kershner, Jessica Klonsky, Kieran Knutsen, Carol Mason, Rachel Meyers, Kim Moody, Joel Olsen, Roger Peet, Juliana Pegues, Margrit Pittman, Charlie Post, Thomas Sabatini, Lee Schere, Frank "Big Black" Smith, Nikolas Stein, Leonard Weinglass, and Mike Whalen, all left some imprint on this project, whether they like it or not. The errors, of course, are mine.

Introduction

The dreams they dream in the *douars* or in the villages are not
those of money or of getting through their exams . . . but dreams
of identification with some rebel or another, the story of whose
heroic death still moves them to tears.

FRANTZ FANON

It has become a truism that activists on the left, particularly when on trial, seek heroic martyrdom.[1] Critics have suggested that the defense campaigns organized to save individuals from Joe Hill to Huey Newton were personality cults halfway to totalitarianism in their effort to deny the complexity of their heroes. Such critics might fear that these campaigns are practicing the kind of blind "loyalty to the leader" that Hannah Arendt argues is so central to totalitarian movements.[2] And in suggesting that people "seek martyrdom" for self-aggrandizing or cultish purposes, such critics argue that the left promotes the notion that individuals are superfluous, as they are in totalitarian states.[3] In such a worried scenario, every defense campaign—indeed, every leftist movement—is fascism in embryo.

However, the actual history of the defense campaign, one of the most popular elements of leftist politics, suggests otherwise. Since 1887, when Lucy Parsons toured the country trying to save the life of her husband, Albert, who had been condemned to death in Chicago along with seven other revolutionary labor leaders, radical socialists, anarchists, and union activists have campaigned to *prevent* the martyrdom of their comrades. As they have done so, they have created a new popular counter-history of the United States as a state of class war and have given the left its own canon of heroic martyrs who refused to be superfluous. Shortly after Lucy Parsons took to the podium, telling stories of justice outraged in Chicago, the Memphis journalist Ida B. Wells began what would become both definitive of American progressivism and the backbone of Black nationalist consciousness in the twentieth century with her campaign against savage "justice" in the South.

While these two forms of protest are different—one focusing on the need to prosecute, and the other on the need to defend—they are intimately related and have influenced each other substantially. Both labor-defense campaigns and anti-lynching campaigns historically have worked primarily through appeals to public opinion in the media, used stories of terror and heroism to build alliances across lines of class and race, and have been formative in the creation of radical political identities. They are united in proposing an alternative argument about power in contrast to the predominant liberal theories of the relationships between minorities and majorities or the interests of the individual in relation to the prerogatives of a state, assumed to represent the community as a whole. Finally, they have fundamentally transformed the notion of heroism itself, positing a dynamic relationship between the figure at the center of the campaign and the masses organized to save him. The characterization of the masses and of the law is the primary difference between these two types of campaigns, for while labor-defense activists began by drawing on populist logic, opposing the masses to the state in their campaigns, anti-lynching activists went in the opposite direction, castigating "the mob" and calling on the law. That difference has made for odd contradictions: White labor-movement activists have at times contrasted the "natural law" of the crowd with legality as a form, and anti-lynching activists have argued for bureaucratism as the solution to the problems of what they have defined as an exclusively working-class phenomenon of racial mobbing. For these reasons, the comparative study of anti-lynching organizing and radical labor defense reveals the complicated history of conflict and intersection between antiracist struggle and socialism in the United States.

Both labor-defense and anti-lynching activism were built in coalitions that united, however uneasily, radical critics of the American state with liberal reformers whose goal was to broaden the rights guaranteed in the Constitution. While the two main liberal groups to grow out of these traditions, the National Association for the Advancement of Colored People (NAACP) and the American Civil Liberties Union (ACLU) have been the subjects of academic study, there is no historical analysis that compares them.[4] Although there have been numerous studies of state repression of radicals, and of lynching, along with a huge number of books written about specific cases, no historian has looked at the history of the resistance to these types of repression. While many scholars using Friedrich

Nietzsche's and Michel Foucault's work have focused on the inner logics of state institutions, prisons, crime fiction, and prison-reform movements, my project is to examine the discourses involved in the resistance to these structures. At their most radical, defense campaigns did not seek to reform prisons, but questioned the fundamental justice of the system altogether.

That is the story I hope to tell in *Men, Mobs, and Law*, a history of both anti-lynching campaigns and radical defense from the era of abolitionism until the New Left. The first chapter describes the canonization of John Brown through the values of nineteenth-century romanticism and Western fiction. The second chapter describes how the socialists of the Haymarket defense and memorials at the turn of the century explicitly challenged the morality of the criminal law and created a new mass heroic ideal that challenged more conventional definitions of heroism while simultaneously mocking and drawing on tropes from crime fiction, sentimental Victorian literature, and images of "natural manliness" from Social Darwinist philosophy. In the third chapter, I describe the rift that divided the Industrial Workers of the World (IWW) and anti-lynching campaigns of the early twentieth century and explore the ways that these campaigns came together during the First World War. In chapter 4, I discuss how several different theories of heroism and terror among socialists, anarchists, communists, and liberals led to conflicts within the campaign to defend Nicola Sacco and Bartolomeo Vanzetti and how these conflicts predicted the collapse of revolutionary anarchist politics and shaped the direction of socialism and liberalism in the 1930s. The fifth chapter is a history of the Communist Party's International Labor Defense (ILD), whose merger between anti-lynching and labor-defense practices accompanied its journey from radicalism in the 1920s to bureaucratism during the Second World War. The final chapter describes how the Black Panther Party revived the revolutionary anti-police elements of the anti-lynching campaign and brought what had been a submerged "outlaw" hero in Black folk culture into the mass media, for the first time drawing white radicals into solidarity with carnivalesque attacks on the "pig" in support of a Black "lumpen" revolution.

Taken together, these campaigns form a popular analysis of failures of justice in America, historical narratives that question America's claims to democracy. Both the anti-lynching campaign and the labor-defense campaign have lent themselves to revolutionary discourses whose purpose is to challenge the legitimacy of the state and call for its overthrow. Producing a long train of "usurpations" and abuses of the people, these campaigns have done more than perhaps any other radical discourse within American political life to make a popular argument for revolution and have created a space for the articulation of oppositional ideals of revolutionary heroism and citizenship in contrast to those of the nation.

Neither campaign existed in a vacuum. While each may have argued for the overthrow of the state and the re-creation of America, both anti-lynching activists and labor defenders made these appeals in the realm of media and in the courts, and their appeals were directed to the public. For this reason, any analysis that attempts to unpack the history of such campaigns must be not only historical, but also literary. To an extent, labor-defense and anti-lynching activism are literary genres. To speak to the public, they have drawn on popular heroic literatures, creating a kind of radical parody of the major justificatory literatures of the modern American state. Rabelais, Mikhail Bakhtin tells us, "lived as did his contemporaries, in the world of these [popular-festive] forms; he breathed their atmosphere, he used their idiom with assurance." Similarly, anti-lynching and labor-defense activists have used the popular generic narratives of American heroic and popular culture in their stories of heroes in confrontation with forces claiming to act in the name of justice.[5]

Anti-lynching and labor-defense campaigners have created elaborate parodies of two of the most popular and influential literary forms in the United States: the crime story and the heroic soldier story. These narrative structures appear not only in the pages of popular literature, but also in the orations of prosecuting attorneys, congressmen, and presidents.

Parody I: Heroic Warfare and Labor Defense

A Long Train of Abuses and Usurpations   At the same time that they have made arguments for revolution against the national ruling class, labor-defense campaigns especially have portrayed themselves within the existing revolutionary tradition in the United States. America's own birth from revolution has preserved revolutionary action itself as a fundamental element in American nationalism. Thomas Jefferson was, and remains, the most famous critic of the potential danger in concentrated state power. As he asserted in the Declaration of Independence, "When a long train of abuses and usurpations, pursuing invariably the same object evinces a design to reduce them under absolute despotism, it is their right, it is their duty to throw off such government, and to provide new guards for their future society."[6]

The formulation of a list of wrongs is an essential part of the process of justification for armed struggle. These appeals are commonplace, because nations justify wars not as quests for dominance, but as self-defense. In his general attack on modern bourgeois morality, Nietzsche called the moral authority of the victim *ressentiment*. According to Nietzsche, the rise of Christianity led to a "slave revolt" in morality in which weakness was defined as good, and strength and power as evil. To legitimate itself in this moral system, Nietzsche argued, the state must present itself not as powerful but as a benign and benevolent protector of the weak and innocent.[7] No longer could war be fought simply as the right of the powerful; it had to be fought in defense against the power of another. In this way, "arms are defense against other nations—none admits the desire for conquest."[8] In his argument for modern warfare, *Just and Unjust Wars*, Michael Walzer demonstrates that the same belief holds true today, arguing that all wars must be explained in terms of the ethics of self-defense and must be seen as acts of punishment against aggression to be called "just."[9]

Rebels   Although it has become axiomatic that one of the modern state's definitive powers is a monopoly of legitimate violence,[10] the United States has traditionally legitimated certain varieties of non-state violence as part of the national identity of a nation of anti-imperialist rebels. The revolutionaries of the 1770s identified taxes and even England's participation in the Atlantic slave trade in the series of "abuses and usurpations" that justified the colonists' revolution. However, it was the Boston Massacre narrative whose colonial repetition galvanized the public against the violent acts of the British and thus helped build popular republican nationalism.[11] Just as nations must argue for prior attack before going to war, revolutionary labor-defense activists have called on the history of activists executed by the state as evidence that revolution is the only answer and to call the U.S. government a murderous enemy that is incapable of change by other means.

By the 1840s, when national revolutions against the Old World's empires rocked Europe, national heroism was defined as rebellion in the writings of such figures as Thomas Carlyle, George Wilhelm Friedrich Hegel, and Johann Gottfried von Herder. This same language was also used by Americans in the 1840s, some of whom, such as John Brown and Frederick Douglass, called for the battle of heroic slaves against Southern despotism, but also by the journalist John L. O'Sullivan, who urged the United States to follow its "Manifest Destiny" by attacking Mexico.[12] For John Brown, as I will argue in chapter 1, this belief in republican heroism meant that the path to liberation for the slaves was through armed rebellion. The fact that American courts declared slavery to be legal turned courtrooms into dramatic scenes of confrontation over the direction of the country during rescues of fugitive slaves and, finally, during Brown's own trial.

Defending the "right to revolution" as part of the American national identity was particularly important for those defendants who were charged with crimes because they had spoken forcefully about revolution. In 1886 in Chicago, eight anarchists were charged with conspiracy to kill a policeman because of articles they had written in newspapers. The Chicago anarchists used the platform that their public trials provided to argue that what they had done was inherently American. As they went to trial for endorsing the very actions that were celebrated in the historical legacy of the "Fathers of the Country," they also used the trial to challenge "American exceptionalism" —the idea that America is more democratic than Europe—as a myth.

In response to Daniel Shays' rebellion in 1787 and on the eve of the Constitutional Convention, called partly to create a government strong enough to suppress such actions, Thomas Jefferson wondered, "And what country can preserve its liberties if its rulers are not warned from time to time that this people preserve the spirit of resistance? Let them take arms. . . . The tree of liberty must be refreshed from time to time with the blood of patriots and tyrants. "[13]

Jefferson also endorsed a constitution that, according to some, significantly reduced the amount of democracy in America, but his remarks in favor of Shays have been recalled by many activists who argue that violent action against the forces of repression is an essential part of the American national tradition, valued and endorsed by its most brilliant founding father.[14]

American radicals' interpretations of the role of revolution in America's political history have occurred most explicitly, and have been argued most persuasively, not in treatises justifying revolution or in theoretical articles about the meaning of the law, but in the context of defense campaigns in which activists have faced death at the hands of the U.S. criminal-justice system and have been accused as outsiders and betrayers of the American way. Faced with such accusations of evil and betrayal of the American nation, activists have questioned the law's claim to be an enforcer of general morality and its claim to represent the American people as a whole. In their trials, the Haymarket anarchists compared themselves to the founding fathers and pointed to the many ways the American media celebrated violence in reporting actions perpetrated by the Reconstruction-era Ku

Klux Klan (KKK) or by police and military troops directed against dissidents such as themselves. Each public trial created another forefather; the Haymarket Martyrs also referred to John Brown. Another generation of radicals would point backward to the Haymarket anarchists at their trials. Activists from abolitionist times to today, when charged with breaking up the national community and disregarding law, have referred to the history of American mob violence and to the revolutionary tradition for authority, showing at least one overarching continuity despite the many schisms, conflicts, and changes over time in the history of U.S. radicalism.

When these defense activists drew on the legacy of American rebellion and mass violence, they were limited by a rhetoric that valorized certain kinds of mass action while demonizing others. The institution of republican whiteness allowed Americans to celebrate a group of white rebels "refreshing the tree of liberty," and, because of the racial divide in the working class, did not label them an undifferentiated, bloodthirsty, and chaotic mob, as they would when viewing European revolutionaries. Republicanism simultaneously championed revolution and rational manhood. Beginning particularly in the eighteenth century, republicans celebrated rebellion in the bourgeoisie, but rejected it in the property-less mob as a sign of chaos. European and American republican thinkers defined property holders as supremely disinterested and virtuous.[15] In contrast, they defined the poor as a "mob" driven by their bodies and therefore incapable of free thought, rational use of military force, or responsible use of political power. The masses were dangerous precisely because their hunger, their desire, made them incapable of the disinterestedness required for political virtue. In politics they might, as Madison argued in Federalist Number 10, in a reminder of the recent Shaysites, try to level property distinctions or pass laws in favor of paper money. They might, as the Paris masses did, pass a law capping prices on bread. Terrifying, indeed.

Such theories did not end with the revolutionary era, but remain influential today. Arendt generally associates mass politics with terror and articulates this republican philosophy in On Revolution, the comparative study of the French and American revolutions in which she describes the desiring masses as the source of terror. "It was the urgent needs of the people that unleashed the terror and sent the [French] Revolution to its doom," Arendt writes.[16]

Despite anxiety about the mob and its desires, white rowdies have often been depicted as spunky and heroic in America, where, as David Roediger explains, republicanism became "racial republicanism," and whites of all classes took on the character traits often associated with property owners in traditional republican theory.[17] Manly direct action is defined as a defense of manhood against oppression, as a vigorous protection of one's home or property, and can be seen in the image of the heroic crowds of the American Revolution—in the Boston Massacre and the Boston Tea Party. In contrast, mob action is defined as fundamentally irrational, driven by passion and bloodlust, during which the individual will succumbs to the pernicious influence of others. Instead of defining the difference in terms of the holding of property, Americans made whiteness itself into a form of "property." It allowed white men to vote and to bear arms. White men have been depicted as showing independence and strength when acting in groups, while Blacks in action (even alone) have been portrayed as dupes of others smarter than themselves and in the thrall of passions and misconceptions.

This double vision about group violence appears strikingly in Thomas Jefferson's writings on revolution. While Jefferson admired Daniel Shays, he described the French revolutionaries as a mob and imagined in a future slave rebellion the destruction of American society in a wave of bloodlust.[18] His fear of slave insurrection led Jefferson to argue that the slavery question would have to be settled with colonization, for he believed that the unique rage of inassimilable slaves would destroy America in a race war.[19] Jefferson, with his notion of an "empire of liberty," also made one form of white violence into the very salvation of America from the creation of a rebellious American working class. The white settler's right to use violence had been central to the expansion of the English colonies, and continued to be important to the nation after the Revolutionary War. Because American expansion initially required independent, violent action by settlers, the notion that the state had a monopoly on legitimate violence never fully applied in America, where settlers were the leading edge of the Indian wars.[20]

In *American Slavery, American Freedom*, Edmund S. Morgan explains how the conflation of property ownership and disinterest ultimately gave way to *Herrenvolk* democracy in America through the pressures of class conflict in the colonial period in Virginia, but it was Jefferson's articulation of decentralist democracy both during the Revolution and during his fight with Alexander Hamilton and the Federalists that maintained the idealization of manly violence in American politics after the revolutionary generation had died. Jefferson's supporters in the years prior to the "revolution of 1800" believed that they would have to take up arms to defend the republic from falling to tyranny.[21] Gabriel, a slave in Virginia, mistakenly believed that the calls for republican direct action against the Federalists meant that the Jeffersonians would take his side in a revolt, but the Jeffersonians, while rebellious, were fiercely proslavery.[22]

The differentiation between slave rebels, French mobs, and the debtors allied with Daniel Shays indicates the importance of slave rebellion as the force against which acceptable citizen violence was defined in revolutionary America. In fact, just as the exclusion of slaves from citizenship allowed the "pale-face poor" to vote, it also allowed them to riot. According to Arendt, Jefferson's belief that the mob would cause "the destruction of everything private and public" was essential both to the racialization of the mob and to the preservation of democracy in the United States.[23] For Arendt, white supremacy was fundamental to the stability of American democracy, because it eliminated sympathy from the founders for the most miserable layers of the population and therefore prevented the formation of mass politics. She argues that, in contrast to France's Jacobins, who initiated mob rule because of their pity for the poor, the American Revolutionary War generation's lack of interest in the plight of their African slaves meant that they were saved from succumbing to "compassion, the most devastating passion" in revolution. According to Arendt, it is sympathy for those at the bottom of society by those at the top that is most dangerous to democracy. She defines the French Reign of Terror as the model for totalitarian rule in socialism and argues that the terror occurred because Robespierre succumbed to pity for the masses, making victimization and misery into virtues, the goals for all to strive for in France. By doing so, Arendt maintains, Robespierre collapsed the division between the private and public and created terror by trying to make the poor happy, satisfying their bodily needs. In contrast, she argues, America's founding fathers succeeded in eliminating the terrible collapse of private and public by painting the mob "Black" and eliminating them from the legitimate, un-miserable, and potentially political working class.[24]

Arendt's critique of "pity" in the work of Robespierre in particular is persuasive, but it conceals a slippage between the notion of "pinning one's faith in the natural goodness of a class" and believing in the capacities of the poor for self-rule.[25] By defining true democracy as both sentimental and apolitical, Arendt implies that hunger and poverty make one incapable of rational political participation, so that the poor become a perennial source of terror. Such a division between the desiring body and the liberated mind is central to classic republicanism, and while it is not the same as fascism, it shares with fascism a fear of what the philosopher Giorgio

Agamben refers to as "bare life" —a kind of life that is without worth and can be killed, but not murdered.[26]

Morgan's work on the colonial history of race and the birth of democracy in Virginia exposes the violence involved in the elimination of what Arendt calls "pity" from American politics. As Morgan argues, whiteness was fundamental to the creation of the free subject in American democracy, and the early colonists did not ignore or forget Blacks (as Arendt suggests they did) but were quite intentional in shaping images of the slaves to create the possibility for white democracy. Morgan argues that the categories usually used to describe the same poverty-stricken hungry mob that Arendt and Jefferson rejected as politically incapable were projected on Africans and Native peoples in America. He writes, "Racism . . . absorbed in Virginia the fear and contempt that men in England, whether Whig or Tory, monarchist or republican, felt for the inarticulate lower classes."[27] The association of servile insurrection and uncontrollable desiring masses with Africanness became the logic behind Blacks' perpetual enslavement and the vehicle through which the pitiless "pale-face poor" in the United States came to be understood as free-minded, even when they were in a state of rebellion. It was the fear of servile insurrection, Morgan argues, that made

> slave owners court the favor of all other whites in a common contempt for persons of dark complexion . . . as men tend to believe their own propaganda, Virginia's ruling class, having proclaimed that all white men were superior to Black, went on to offer their social (but white) inferiors a number of benefits previously denied them.[28]

In Morgan's argument, Americans could only believe in equality because they had enslaved Africans, defined them as incapable of self-control, and thus removed them from consideration as citizens. When whiteness became a form of property in itself, and Blackness defined one as property, those whites in the working class would ally themselves with bourgeois whites and would never form a threat to the slave owners. Meanwhile, these whites would, Morgan continues, "absorb" as their inheritance the republican hatred, contempt, and fear of the canaille. Later, as I will show in chapter 3, they would develop a new act of mass terror designed to maintain boundaries between the newly created races: the lynching. Acts of violence against non-whites, particularly against Native Americans in early America, as Morgan shows, became significant in maintaining alliances between the pale-face rich and poor. Moreover, race became a determining factor in what was defined as violent or insurrectionary activity, as opposed to what was defined as popular justice, and the ability to use violence in an orderly way became evidence of whiteness itself.

One of the most important differences between anti-lynching campaigns and labor-defense campaigns originates from this racialized division in the perception of the use of force. Historians of mob violence in America have observed that slave rebels and riotous mobs of whites have received markedly different treatment by the criminal-justice system from the very beginning of the country.[29] The same could be said of popular culture. White individuals could be portrayed as capable of heroic violence, and myriad stories glorify white men who used violence: Kit Carson, Jesse James, and so on. The use of violence is part of the character's "manliness" and his disregard for the feminizing rules of society. As Richard Slotkin argues in his masterly trilogy about American Westerns, the story of "regeneration" of both men and the nation through acts of violence against non-white others is at the very center of American popular culture and American identity.[30]

Tales of slave rebellion, which, as the abolitionists pointed out, in many ways fit into nineteenth-century notions of heroic action, were not destined to become part of American popular culture. Instead, stories of slave rebellion were repressed and forgotten; they were stories that depicted the "land of the free" as a regime of oppression. The only people who made Nat Turner into a folk hero were Black, and they did not shout about this heroism to the wide world in the pages of popular fiction or even in popular song. Because of the racial divide that splits American popular culture (at least) in half, whites could call on a tradition of popular revolt that fit into a nationalist logic while Blacks could not. For this reason, as I will discuss in chapter 1, John Brown was depicted as "crazy" for trying to foment a slave revolt in Virginia but was seen as heroic for warring against "border ruffians" in Kansas three years before. The abolitionists who went to court during this time, however, reminded Americans by pointing out the hypocrisy of racial republicanism.

Parodies II: Crime

Victims   After the Civil War, the crime story replaced the story of the heroic rebel at the center of American popular-fiction heroism. Even white heroic rebels, while they still occupied a place in American fiction, became less celebrated. Increasingly, what Nietzsche called *ressentiment* became an ideology against revolutionary legitimacy, rejecting action in the name of liberation and embracing instead action in the name of law enforcement. As the nation's soldiers went to war, they acted less in the name of their own personal freedom and more in the name of outraged others in the triangular action that defines the genre of melodrama. In melodrama, three characters create the story line, and only two of the characters are actors in the true sense of the word. There is a chivalric hero who acts to preserve "good," and there is a base villain who threatens the "good." The good itself is an object, not an actor, and is usually represented by a white woman or an idealized female child.

In America, the traditional story line is racialized. Innocence and guilt are coded white and Black, and the white woman serves in the justificatory popular narratives of militaries, police departments, and courts. She is defined as "good" because of her separation from both economic and political struggles for power. This lack of participation in any quest for power or dominance keeps her hands clean of all forms of desire for power. Her innocence is complete—and impossible. The action done on her behalf undermines her agency. This kind of victim is not a republican citizen because she cannot act. Her elevation as a symbol of the citizenry, dependent on heroic leadership in a time of crisis, is a sign of the erosion of republican beliefs in American culture.

The symbol of this "white woman" is the ultimate embodiment of ressentiment. Stories about her wronged innocence serve to supplant the role of property in the heart of most actions of law-enforcement and military adventure. In her, the private sphere becomes the fetish for private property itself; at the center of the home, the innocent woman stands in for property and becomes an object whose relationship to labor and conflict is utterly erased and naturalized as outside the realms of human action. Instead of property, Nancy Armstrong argues, the "woman" at the center of domestic fiction defines bourgeois subjectivity (and property itself) as outside power.[31]

In the melodramatic stories told on the threshold of wars, the state is portrayed as the hero who acts only to protect women and children. Similarly, the expansion of the state's policing powers has been justified by appeals to the need to protect the same innocent and powerless group from the savage criminal classes. Such claims do not have to be accurate to work; it is easy to present acts of aggression as defense of the women and children of the nation. The United States, for example has gone to war under the slimmest pretenses of self-defense, whether raising the cry, "Remember the *Maine!*" or manipulating information about the Gulf of Tonkin incident, or, most recently in the use of the attack on the World

Trade Center on September 11, 2001, to justify an aggressive attack on Iraq in what those on the left know as the So-Called War on Terror (SCWOT).[32] The manipulation of September 11 in particular, which focused on the heroic firefighters and police killed by the terrorist attack, represented the mourning public through children's drawings pinned to police- and fire-station walls and created a story of military heroes defending an infantilized and helpless public.[33] In this pattern, the public is not allowed to question the chivalric hero. It can only be the grateful recipient of care.

In these melodramas, villains are totally savage. They are depicted not in a rational struggle for power, but in a senseless quest to dominate and hurt powerless women and children. The most common use of the racial melodrama is in the reports of crime that appeared in American newspapers in the 1870s–1900s, provoking lynchings by developing a generic image of a Black beast attacking white innocence.[34] This characterization of Blacks as beasts effaced the reality of racial conflict in the post-Reconstruction South. In a struggle that makes power itself the enemy, to define one's enemy as "in struggle" is a problem because it reveals one's own power. According to the philosopher Phillip Hallie, the victim's incapacity to struggle on her own behalf is necessary in order to identify the power that attacks her as "evil," and serves to define the action against villains as selfless, benevolent, and heroic. Thus, when the state acts to punish the cruel villain, whether through the military or the criminal-justice system, it portrays itself as a chivalric and disinterested hero, not as a force engaged in a struggle for power. As Hallie explains in his analysis of William Hogarth's series of paintings, "The Four Stages of Cruelty," the passivity and helplessness of the victim are necessary. Describing a dog pinioned by a crowd and being tortured by a cruel mob, he writes, "If that creature could get away, or get help, it would no longer be passive enough to be a victim, it would be an active enemy or an active, running prey, . . . an active victim does not have the passivity that slow maiming demands."[35]

If the dog were moving, we would no longer "be witnessing cruelty—we would be witnessing a battle." Hogarth's paintings depict helpless animals and women as objects of cruelty, while the actions of men, whether criminal or just, surround them. The difference between the two actors of power—criminal and judge—is that, while the first uses force as a means of gaining power over others, the second uses force in the name of protecting the society from "power" itself. In this way, the acts of the state against the criminal are not seen as elements of class struggle. They are, instead, an exercise of benevolent protection of the citizens, who are increasingly represented as innocent and helpless in times of great social conflict. The actions of rebels are defined as irrational and evil attacks on the innocent that necessitate the intervention of heroic protectors. Nat Turner thus becomes a mad child killer, bloodthirsty and irrational, instead of a rebel against a vicious despotic order.

Hogarth's final scene in the four-part series is the "reward of cruelty," an image of a criminal being dissected and studied by scientists, in which the artist displays not the power of the state, but the necessary destruction of threatening, selfish power. The dissection of the body is not done for the purpose of "cruelty," as Hallie describes it, but to destroy the power of the "cruel" villain by making him into an object of study. The dissection of criminals and the continuing practice of mutilation of Black men in twentieth-century America demonstrated the attempt to defeat the power of the "irrational" man by attacking power at its physical source. Similarly, following the revelation of acts of torture in Abu Ghraib and elsewhere, defenders of these actions have called them necessary to protect the American people from the "terrorist" and the "ticking bomb."[36]

Examples of this logic of transforming the perception of dissidents by portraying them as attackers of powerless women and children abound in contemporary discourse. The far right's attack on the women's movement has been most successful in gaining the moral high ground when it has transformed the target of feminist attack—the patriarchal family—into the ultimate innocents: unborn children. The fetus, because it has no personality and is completely incapable of any action at all, is the ultimate measure of good in the economy of ressentiment, as it exists only in the realm of the ideal.[37] Similarly, Blacks' struggles for social equality in the South were described as a quest to dominate helpless white women. It was against this portrayal of themselves as the powerful demons threatening "the good" that anti-lynching activists had to fight. As a result, they did not offer a simple counter-melodrama of Black innocence, because to do so would have undermined their own citizenship claims.[38] Instead, Ida B. Wells and others who followed her unpacked the mythology of rape that surrounded lynching and found that most people killed by lynch mobs had not even been accused of rape, as I will discuss in chapter 3.

In countering these melodramatic crime stories, labor-defense activists and anti-lynching campaigners brought the struggle for power back into the story, questioning the representation of the law as a disinterested tool of morality and naming it a weapon of the forces of power instead. In both types of activism, the police, courts and prisons become a force of "terror." Labor-defense activists called for mass demonstrations and class solidarity as the best weapon against the brutality of police and the cruelty of courts, making a hero out of the very "mob" that the capitalist press categorized as a source of terror. The labor-defense campaigns celebrated mass action as a joyful parade of liberation.

However, because of the centrality of race to the perceptions of "good" and "evil," and because of the role of extralegal white violence in enforcing the laws of race, the representation of this "joyful mob" would not make sense in the context of anti-lynching activism. Therefore, anti-lynching activists have made some of the most radical parodic commentary on American power. Whereas newspapers often described lynch mobs as acting on behalf of wronged innocents in the name of justice, anti-lynching activists have referred to the takeover of the law itself, from police to courts, by mobs. Not simply attacking "mobs" and calling for law and order, radical anti-lynching activists have pointed to police–mob collaboration or what I call "the police–mob continuum." As I will show in chapter 3, Ida B. Wells and other anti-lynching activists often emphasized manly resistance in their portrayals of the victims of lynch mobs, who stood proudly and rationally in contrast to the frenzied, savage mobs that surrounded them. Although unable to resist with force such large numbers, the victims of lynching in these radical campaigns were depicted not as victims, but as heroes dying with dignity. In addition, while labor-defense activists described the literal prison as the apex of capitalism, anti-lynching radicals who pointed to the real reasons behind mob killings demonstrated how public spaces, South and North, had themselves become prisons for Blacks: unable to leave ghetto neighborhoods, unable to exercise common freedoms.

Anti-lynching campaigns and labor-defense campaigns are different because of the role of race in shaping American justice and American popular culture, and because of the importance of mass action for the enforcing of racial norms. Nonetheless, both campaigns serve very similar functions for the groups they represent. Both are organized to defend and resuscitate people who come to symbolize their communities in the mass media and to criticize the moral systems of the law and the media. Anti-lynching campaigns are "defense campaigns" for individuals who did not receive trials, and, like labor defenders, anti-lynching activists compile lists of atrocities performed against their people. In the process of shaping the defense of the labor leader, the rank-and-file organizer, or the anonymous Black person killed by a racist mob, both types of "defense campaigners" assert the value and strength of their own people, their own ideas, and their own movements, and they create a popular history of America as a struggle between forces of repressive terror and heroic defiance.

Anti-lynching campaigns' analysis of white mass violence did much to inform labor-defense activists about the nature of American power, and ultimately their analysis of the "police–mob continuum" became central to the rhetoric of American labor defense. First, white labor radicals referred to the nativist prejudices of judges and juries in trials of immigrant radicals such as Sacco and Vanzetti as "legal lynching" and talked about the "mob atmosphere" surrounding their cases. The most important merger of the labor-defense and anti-lynching campaigns, however, came with the ILD's campaign against the executions of the "Scottsboro Boys" of Alabama, which I will discuss in chapter 5.

Defense Campaigns in Practice, Democracy, and Action: Who Is the Hero, the Man or the Mob?

As the campaigners studied the history of repression, whether legal or extralegal, they developed complex theories of how power works in the United States and how best to respond to it. Traditionally formations that united liberals and revolutionaries, both labor-defense and anti-lynching campaigns led to intense debates among activists about the best tactics to use to save their comrades, suggesting the use not only of legal arguments, but also of popular protests, alliances with others, and even revolutionary direct action. The history of these changing strategies shows the complicated arguments that went on between activists as they worked out their own theories of power and democratic practice in the context of resisting repression.

As I have argued, defense campaigns are the place where radicals most directly attack the power of the state and the representative claims of the mass media. In the United States, where the rhetoric of American exceptionalism depends on the belief in the unique fairness of the judicial system, this element of the defense campaign is particularly important. By describing America's legal system as a force of terror and repression, and by calling the mass media a "mob," defense campaigners and anti-lynching activists confronted what Theodor Adorno and Max Horkheimer refer to as the "candy floss of ideology,"[39] or what Nietzsche describes as "ressentiment," a smiling chivalric modern power that denies its own powerfulness.

Terror always leaves a body behind. It is the body that shows that a crime has been committed. So just as prosecuting attorneys talk about the victims of crime, defense campaigners and anti-lynching activists display the bodies of executed and murdered activists as evidence of the monstrous, murderous nature of the United States. They attempt to expose power through the marks it has left on their own collective body. Stories about the heroes of defense campaigns—John Brown, George Jackson, Nicola Sacco, Hoke Smith—show the figures at their center as wounded selves in defiance, exposing power as a force that wounds. Evoking America's own popular status as a democracy, they show these bodies and compare American society to infamous despotisms: ancient Rome, the Spanish Inquisition, Britain's star chamber, Russian czardoms, and, finally, the lynch mob, America's native form of terrorism.

In this dramatic parody of the American crime and solider stories, anti-lynching activists and labor-defense campaigners turn the melodramatic triangle into a story of power struggle between two forces. The characters in the story reflect a kind of dialectic process and are simultaneously weak and strong. Heroes such as George Jackson of the Black Panther Party appear wounded and defiant at the same time. Heroic agency passes between the "hero" at the center of the campaign and the campaigners who work to save him, so that one person is not the only source of power or redemption. During the campaign to defend the prisoner, to prevent his martyrdom, the masses become the hero. The hero depends on them as he waits in jail; he needs them. As the IWW said during its many defense campaigns, "We are in here for you, you are out there for us."

However, when the defense campaign has failed to save the hero, as in the cases that I describe in *Men, Mobs, and Law*, the hero at its center has become a martyr. To be a martyr, the condemned man cannot be a victim. He must be a hero. The only act that a condemned person can make is to choose his own death; his death must become a sacrifice for a higher purpose. When defense campaigns are unable to save the defendant, the moment of action flows back to him. In the last moment, he must choose martyrdom, never the humiliating gesture of confessing, "Tomming," or renouncing his revolutionary beliefs. He acts *for* the movement that he is part of and becomes the ideal "good" of that movement. In doing so, his last moments of life and death are crucial in the history of the literature of both anti-lynching and the labor-defense campaign.

In the tales of revolutionary defense campaigns, heroes die because they refuse to renounce their beliefs or their manhood, just as the early Christians died because they refused to renounce their faith. For example, George Jackson, who was killed during an escape attempt, was running toward the prison wall when he was shot and killed by prison guards. This act is seen by his supporters as his last symbolic rejection of the confines of the prison and as an act for his fellows, as he was "trying to draw the fire" of the guards away from the other prisoners in the yard.[40] In the act of running for the wall, despite the realities of the prison that surrounded him, he became a heroic metaphor for the entire Black Power Movement.

The martyr, in the defiant act of a chosen death, becomes the actor who takes power away from the state. Martyrs fling their corpses into public space as evidence of the states' illegitimacy as if wounded bodies are weapons, and movements recall in the dark hours before sunrise the speeches of their own dead heroes to gain further inspiration to act. As they do this, activists often speak in Hegelian terms, describing how revolutionary consciousness came to them in the moments of imminent death.

In *The Body in Pain*, Elaine Scarry argues that during torture, all agency moves to the hands of the torturer, who becomes the "world" for the prisoner.[41] By making the martyr's wound into a source of revolt, the heroic martyr story reverses this relationship. One of the most dramatic examples of such a reversal occurs in the Mahasweta Devi's story "Drapaudi," when a revolutionary woman, after being tortured for her role in the insurgency, confronts the official who ordered her torture. She stands before him, naked, and finally speaks, spitting a gob of blood on him in the process. " 'Come on, *counter* me,' " she says pushing him "with her two mangled breasts, and for the first time," Devi writes, "Senanayak [the official] is afraid to stand before an unarmed *target*, terribly afraid."[42]

This story of the defiant martyr was not so much invented by the defense campaign as it was drawn from an existing ancient folk tradition of ecstatic martyrdom. Literatures of religious and political martyrdom confound simplistic understandings of the body and the spirit. Graphic saints' stories often disrupted concepts of bodily prohibition in ascetic schools of Christianity. By making beautiful the "beastly interiors" against which Christian self-denial erected serious prohibitions, the stories of Christian martyrs depicted intestines, tears, blood, flesh, and muscle pouring out in demonstrations of the love of God, and reanimated the experience of the prohibited inner self, expanding the notions of the possible. Visual representations of acts of self-sacrifice and of miracles redeemed the self's own limitless desire by constructing it as a desire for the infinite, a desire for God, a source of rebirth.[43]

Revolutionary martyr stories have at times depicted their heroes pouring themselves on the gladiatorial floor in similar, limitless expressions of faith in the future uprising of the masses. Revolutionary tales of political martyrs, often compared to stories about saints, echo not only Christian mythologies but also Dionysian and pagan folk traditions, defined by Bakhtin in the concept of "blood as the seed." In popular grotesque imagery, Bakhtin argues, every death is a generative process, a "death giving birth" and martyrdoms work to point to historical transitions, as the "death of the individual is only one moment in the triumphal life of the people." That is, the story of martyrdom, in its most celebratory form, becomes an opportunity to proclaim the possibility of revolution, as the death of the martyr symbolizes the moment when the old world falls apart in a "pregnant death," and the martyr's death heralds the coming of the new age from the blood and tears of the old.[44] This trope is fundamental to stories of political martyrdom and appears in numerous guises—recently, for example, in the closing credits of the film *Lumumba*, which shows fire burning the murdered body of the anticolonial leader Patrice Lumumba as his words echo into the darkening theater.[45]

Stories of martyrs are critical to the formation of group consciousness; they are used to lead masses to challenge state power. Memorial rituals have tended to play a major role in the days immediately before revolutionary action takes place, just as they do in times of warfare between nations. E. P. Thompson's influential work on the formation of the working class in England makes clear that political consciousness often takes shape within cultural forms that are not clearly "political" in nature. This general point about political consciousness is true not only in the formation of class-consciousness, but also in the formation of most ideological positions. The cultural influences present in revolutionary politics may come from surprising places. For example, in 1998, while I was writing my dissertation, I went to a rally for Mumia Abu-Jamal, who had just lost an appeal before the Pennsylvania Supreme Court. At one point in the rally, a member of the Puerto Rican Political Prisoner solidarity committee stood up and spoke for Abu-Jamal and, in doing so, repeated century-old defense-campaign themes in the imperative language of contemporary sports discourse. In a style reminiscent of a high-school football coach, the speaker reminded his audience that Abu-Jamal, currently on death row in Philadelphia, had fought for environmental activists in Minneapolis from his prison cell by writing about their struggle to stop the expansion of State Highway 55. The crowd should return the favor, the speaker proclaimed, by struggling to keep him alive. In these last days before a death warrant was to be signed, he demanded of the crowd, "What are you going to eat for dinner tonight?" and knowing the answer, the crowd shouted," MUMIA!" What are you going to teach in your classes? And again the crowd shouted, "MUMIA!" "What are you going to talk about tonight with your friends on the phone?" "MUMIA!" the crowd roared back.

Although the speaker drew on a discursive tradition familiar to situations of male solidarity (winning one for the Gipper), the defense campaign is typically gendered female. Its work is supportive, reproductive, and, despite its importance for the shaping of revolutionary consciousness, often defined as "secondary" to and diversionary from "real" struggles over material issues. However, as I will show, rather than being incidental or obstructive of other goals, the defense campaign provides the moral and ideological discourse that is often missing in more pragmatic and localized struggles. The imperative to "free Mumia," or anyone else, calls us to the kind of activity that is routinely asked of women—and of mothers, in particular—and brings this emotional experience into the core of revolutionary solidarity.

When we are called to make Mumia Abu-Jamal's safety our first task, we are asked to incorporate the preservation of the life of one individual into part of our daily routine, making the reminder part of every activity in which we engage as activists. It has often been an active mother or wife who spearheads the popular defense campaign. From Lucy Parsons to Mamie Till, the wives and mothers of murdered or condemned men have participated in an activist tradition in which leftists focus on the role of the state and the mob in inflicting terror. The campaigns' concern with violence and repression evokes continuous debates about the preservation of democracy in mass action, as the rhetorics of the collective and the personal, political, and familial are used to explain why one life matters in a mass struggle and how mass struggle could matter to one life. In chapter 4, for example, Sacco's and Vanzetti's defense committee argued with more "heroic anarchist" critics of the campaign that they had not become so insensible to human relationships that they would sacrifice their friends and comrades on the altar of the ideal.

During the defense campaigns, when campaigners exhort masses to join them in protests, in acts of solidarity, the masses become the hero of the story. They must act to save the condemned man. In this way, the defense campaign creates a "mass hero," and the mass is knit together by its identification with and love for the comrade whose defense is the center of the campaign. The defense campaigns do not create ascetic heroes who are happy to give up their lives. They depict their heroes as men who love living and make their particular absence an irredeemable loss. Anti-lynching activists in the NAACP, as I will discuss in chapter 3, tirelessly investigated every element of the story of the lynching both to make the mob's terror visible and to bring the murdered men and women of the South back to life. The imprisoned and wounded heroes of labor-defense and anti-lynching literature are shown to be permeable, breakable, and subject to pain. Similarly, campaigns invoke an image of the crying masses not as weak or defeated, and their desire is not for material property. They desire connection and are depicted as beautiful and a source of power. Defense committees have demonstrated heroic love for stigmatized criminal defendants by working to save them despite the guilt by association that has attached to them as a result.

The passion and love the masses feel for this comrade becomes, in revolutionary campaigns, the source of revolution. Joe Hill, one such figure, famously commanded his comrades in the IWW: "Don't Mourn, Organize!" But at the end of a defense campaign, mourning *is* organizing. The heroes need the masses not only to organize, but to cry. It is their grief and rage that is supposed to bring on the revolution, in a flood of women's tears and men's blood. Recording the stories of murdered activists becomes the source of a popular history of struggle with power that motivates succeeding generations of activists, who make reference to the previous martyrs during their own experiences with the state.

Slavery, Solidarity, and Prison   It is important that the person defended at the center of the campaign is someone who has been outlawed by the powers of the society. He is not shaped into a passive figure of "good," such as the one that motivates the action of the lynch mob. The ideal embodied in the defense campaign emerged in nineteenth-century movements of Europe, Haiti, and America that championed the power of the human spirit in revolt against slavery, both chattel and waged. Abolitionist defenses of fugitive slaves and republican defenses of rebels in debtors' prisons still echo in both anti-lynching activism and labor defense. In the United States, labor activists called capitalism a form of slavery not because of the material issue of money, but because of the lack of real freedom. In the labor-defense campaign, this notion of capitalism as a force of domination appears in the fierce criticisms of police and prisons, identified as the iron hand of the new despotism. The revolutionary socialists of Chicago, who can be credited with creating the theories that would govern most labor-defense campaigns, argued along with Karl Marx that capitalist individualism is not freedom but creates "isolated individuals who live in relationships daily reproducing this isolation."[46] Black radicals questioned whether men were really free if they could not move into any neighborhood, walk down any street.

These campaigns are not prison-reform campaigns, but they often become arguments about the injustice of the prison, its techniques, and its attempts to impose capitalist value as the ultimate expression of all that is wrong with capitalism. More than simply preserving the life of the individual, the defense campaign, whether it addresses the prison or the scaffold, asks us to fight for the *freedom* of another, keeping freedom from confinement at the center of radical action. Similarly, anti-lynching campaigns continually pointed out that lynching was often the enforcement of unwritten laws against "sauciness" or "unruly" behavior by Blacks and argued for the right to "manliness" as the center of Black struggle in the South and North. Prisons and Jim Crow meant that the fight against slavery was not yet over. Both campaigns repeated the kind of arguments that had been made against slavery as confinement.

However, the latter campaigns, such as the antislavery activism of the nineteenth century, defined individual freedom within the context of a loving community that desperately worked to preserve itself in the face of an onslaught from above. In her "scare text" against mass politics, Arendt argues that love is a politically dangerous emotion, a force born of loneliness that erodes individual liberty and, hence, democratic politics.[47]

While the idealization of certain forms of self-sacrificing love does contain totalitarian capacities, which I will discuss in chapter 4, the most "totalitarian" period of the left's history—during the Second World War—was marked by a transition from the heroic story of the revolutionary defense campaign toward the elevation of the most bureaucratic elements of both labor-defense and anti-lynching activism, as I will discuss in chapter 5. But even during the Stalinist era, the practice of the defense campaign was a source that kept basic notions of participatory democracy in the center of the American left's imagination. The defense campaign uses the rhetoric of love as a weapon against the isolation of individuals from each other in a moralizing society; the practice of the campaigns asserts that individual lives are crucial in the struggle with the forces of power. Campaigners also argue that love will help them identify with the "pariah" figures attacked by the state. Assata Shakur expressed this sentiment in a poem written from prison, "love is contraband in hell / 'cause love is an acid / that eats away bars."[48] Love is depicted in the defense campaign as an attack on the isolating nature of the prison as a mode of punishment and criminalization in modern life. The contemporary Christian anti–death-penalty activist Sister Helen Prejean, while not a revolutionary seeking to overthrow the state, has worked with defense campaigners and has argued about the importance of love to the work that she does with death-row prisoners. Although she does not argue for their innocence in every case, Prejean's concept of Christian forgiveness especially for the guilty is a strong rebuke to the current use of legal execution in the United States.[49]

When lynching declined in the United States, anti-lynching campaigns did not end, but they attacked the use of the death penalty as lynching by other means. The prison in the United States has replaced slavery as a primary line of division between the worthy and unworthy members of the working class, and it, like slavery, has a racial and economic character. Labor-defense campaigners' attacks on the state have always pointed out the central role that the prison plays in upholding capitalism, particularly in its use as a container and its creation of a divided working class. Because the definitions of good and bad have been intensely racialized in the United States, the merging of anti-lynching and labor-defense activism that began with the Communist Party of the USA (CPUSA) and continued with the Black Panther Party in the 1970s, with their critiques of "good" and "bad" or "guilty and innocent," have been important for the challenging of "dominant values" of other kinds, as well. The recognition of the importance of this goal to further working-class action makes fights against the prison absolutely central to the process of working-class action in the United States.

In many defense campaigns, the prisoner, that person defined as the most evil and untrustworthy member of society, moves into a position of power and authority for other activists. While some may find this reversal a cause for concern,[50] the practice is part of the project of questioning the values of the state. American revolutionaries have long argued that attacking the values of the state is as important to working-class action as any other struggle. Big Bill Haywood implied in his instructions to the ILD in 1926 that getting people involved in a movement against a racially defined criminal-justice system was particularly challenging to those who thought of themselves as white men. "Members, more members," he declared, "get them, black, red, brown, and yellow, and white—if they are good enough to work for men behind prison bars and their needy mothers, wives, and children."[51]

As Haywood suggests, such campaigns can become challenges to working-class activists to expand their understanding of working-class politics beyond the immediate issues of free labor in the same way that Frederick Douglass suggested that the lives of white workers and Black workers were linked, or as Marx wrote that "labour in a white skin cannot emancipate itself where it is branded in a black skin."[52] Just as slave narratives and antislavery tracts mobilized people with stories of the pain of human isolation, so prisoner-support campaigns have focused on an extreme situation of capitalist isolation. The narratives produced during radical defense campaigns are revolutionary arguments that seek to expand the grounds of working-class politics by defining isolation as capitalism's primary form of terror. In defense campaigns, as it was in the antislavery movement, the creation of the boundary is the primary evil. The ruling power is a divider of families, a wrecker of communities, a squelcher of desire, an imprisoner of the lively spirits of men. Defense campaigners who argue for organizing in the defense of prisoners in jails have argued that lonely men in jail; crying wives, mothers, and children; floods; and wounds and blood are the products of capitalist rule and will be its ultimate undoing.

In telling these tales, leftists have drawn readers into sympathy with those they represent by engaging them in a story of personal triumph over power where the hero's alliances with others allow him to defy the law that is being enacted on him. In socialist and populist martyr legends, the state and the forces of order, constraint and control, are represented as villains, as symbols of capitalist machines that remove human interest from politics and thus go against everything that represents life and democratic participation. The worst thing about the cold state in these stories is its indifference to the tears of women and men who beseech it to release the prisoner. In populist martyr stories, the bodies of the masses mess up the works, calling for democratic action in the vision of a community of many races and genders and rejecting the permanence of existing reality along with the boundaries of the body in an ecstasy of lives joined up in struggle.

In the chapters that follow, I will discuss martyrs who were defended by wives, sisters, and mothers, whose heroic stories highlight the humanity of the prisoner by focusing on his attachments to the world and the flesh. These communities invoke the image of the fleshy human self as the most precious object that is ignored by capitalists' focus on property in the law. This ideal of interconnection as the source of transcendence, so fundamentally the primary source of power in socialism, also shifted the focus of power in the defense campaign from the individual prisoner to the defenders. Defense organizations made the participation in the politics of defense into a heroic act, as the ability to defend one's comrades made it possible for simple people—anybodies, not just heroes—to act in social movements. By speaking to the law, these campaigns celebrated difference and self-definition as heroic defenses of civil liberties for everyone. In all these ways, defense campaigns have had a profound impact on American political culture, informing the contemporary anti–death-penalty movement as well as liberal organizations such as the ACLU.

The defense campaign does not simply call people to "duty" but places a value on political participation and defines group obligations to individuals, imagining groups as dynamic and reciprocal entities. Defense campaigns have often argued that it is heroic to challenge the law, to question values, to refuse to cede authority to the law, to surpass the limits of the present, to invent new morals and define mutual obligations between communities and individuals by arguing that defending the rights of one's fellow workers is not only a duty but, actually, is critical to the maintenance of one's own rights and capabilities.

Rather than evoking totalitarian consciousness or advocating martyrdom for its own sake, stories of heroic defiance in court encourage citizens to question accepted values of law, define their own values, and argue for mass action in the name of preserving democracy. The engagement in politics is emancipating, challenging, and risky. If political action is by definition risky, it is doubly so for those whose status in an existing structure of power is already one of dependence. Workers who have lost jobs for joining or attempting to organize unions could testify to this truth. In the early twentieth century, IWW activists argued that defense campaigns for that reason were essential to their own practice, because they made action possible and because they are metaphors for the smaller acts of risk necessary for resistance. Defense campaigns have worked differently over time, but in that aspect they have remained remarkably consistent.

While the defense campaign as a whole cannot be condemned as some kind of fascistic personality cult, individual defense campaigns have been problematic in a number of ways. The biggest problem in labor-defense activism stems from the "racial republicanism" in American popular culture. In their popular arguments in defense of imprisoned comrades accused of violent acts against the bourgeois state, labor-defense activists have often relied on the popular antistatist elements of the American revolutionary tradition and have attacked not just the morality of specific laws, but the very concept of the court because they see it as an institution that removes decision making from the public's control. While one aspect of this argument is profoundly democratic, as legal scholars have described "labor's constitution of freedom" against a court that has undermined legislation aimed at ameliorating the worst ills of capitalism,[53] it has often been made with theories of "natural law" and simplistic arguments about the "goodness" of the people in action. In contrast to attacks on bourgeois morality and calls for mass participation in decision making, such popular appeals to "mass action" as essentially democratic overlap uncomfortably with popular arguments for vigilantism and lynching as practices of popular democracy that eliminate the "tiresome" procedures of the courtroom, suggesting not a system beyond good and evil, but a system in which good and evil are obvious and simple to behold.

This tendency in labor-defense campaigns to attack the "statute" law in favor of "natural" law and mass power is at the heart of the conflict between Black and white radicals in the United States. Inasmuch as labor-defense campaigns have resorted to glorifications of the "goodness" of the people, they run into trouble with the deeply racialized characterization of "good" and "bad" in the popular culture of the United States. Because racial divisions in American society are often most explicitly seen in the realm of criminal justice, the intertwining histories of anti-lynching politics and labor-defense campaigns expose the difficulty inherent in arguing for spontaneous mass working-class action in a society defined by a sharp racial division within the working class itself. These problems still plague us today, as can be seen in the paucity of Black heroes at the center of the stories of labor-defense campaigns that follow and in the continuing debates among factions of the left over the relevance of race to American power.

1

John Brown:
The Left's Great Man

Veneration of great men is perennial in the nature of man. . . .
Show the dullest clodpole, show the haughtiest featherhead, that
a soul higher than himself is actually here; were his knees
stiffened into brass he must bow down and worship.
THOMAS CARLYLE

This has been one of the saddest days Harper's Ferry has ever
experienced. This morning when the armorers went to the shops
to go to work, lo and behold, the shops had been taken possession of by a set of abolitionists and the doors were guarded by
negroes with rifles.   GEORGE MAUZY

Some doubt the courage of the Negro. Go to Hayti and stand on
the fifty-thousand graves of the best soldiers France ever saw and
ask them what they think of the Negro's sword.
WENDELL PHILLIPS

You see how war-like I have become. . . . Oh yes, war is better
than slavery.   ANGELINA GRIMKE

On the heels of the American Revolution, those who called most often
for the use of violence to overthrow American institutions were the leaders of American slaves. Gabriel Prosser, Denmark Vesey, David Walker,
Nat Turner, and Henry Highland Garnet all planned, engaged in, or called
for a violent overturning of the system of slavery. At times, they referred
to the example of the founding fathers in their efforts to mark their own
struggle as one that was within, rather than outside, the American tradi-

tion. Frederick Douglass did so often, noting American hypocrisy in his famous Fourth of July address and comparing the aptly named slave rebel Madison Washington to the founders.[1] David Walker demanded of white America, after quoting the Declaration of Independence in his *Appeal*, "Do you not understand your own language?"[2]

Just as frequent were appeals to biblical stories of justice and liberation. In his book *Exodus!* Eddie Glaude Jr. argues that the militant abolitionist Henry Highland Garnet said that the Bible did not just allow force, but actually demanded it.[3] Black abolitionists, particularly Nat Turner, read the Bible as a text of earthly justice; according to Sylvia Frey and Betty Wood, African Americans were drawn to evangelical Christianity because they saw salvation as "a spiritual revolution that would turn the moral universe upside down." At times, this longing was not just for a spiritual revolution, and men such as David Margate, a slave who came to envision himself as "a second Moses and should be called to deliver his people from slavery," alarmed whites.[4] Similarly, David Walker, who was influenced by the slave rebel Denmark Vesey, made slave insurrection a version of God's wrath in his famous appeal: "My color will yet, root some of you out of the very face of the earth!!!!! You may doubt it if you please. . . . So did the ante-diluvians doubt Noah, . . . so did the Sodomites doubt until Lot got out of the city and God rained down fire and brimstone from Heaven upon them, and burnt them up."[5] Such revolutionary readings of the Bible by Black evangelicals could be argued to be the first native American radicalism. Although some might argue that the belief in signs and visions from another world was an "obvious manifestation of madness," it was not only Nat Turner who followed seasonal patterns and eclipses when making plans. Farmers' religion was "full of mysticism" during the 1830s, and whites also used astrology when making important decisions about when to plant their crops.[6] While some aspects of African American Christianity bear the mark of Africa, these biblical interpretations endorsing slave rebellion were directly related to the experience of slavery, as Frederick Douglass once said to a white minister at an antislavery meeting: "If the reverend gentleman had worked on plantations where I have been, he would have met overseers who would have whipped him in five minutes out of his willingness to wait for liberty."[7] Many Black abolitionists saw violence as an acceptable tactic for liberation because they recognized slavery to be a system of terror whose authors were immune to moral arguments. Douglass's stories, whether told on the speaker's podium or in his writing, suggested that the use of brutality against slaves had perverted the souls of the slaveholders, destroying the womanhood of slave

REBECCA N. HILL

IS AN ASSOCIATE PROFESSOR

IN THE DEPARTMENT OF SOCIAL

SCIENCE, THE BOROUGH OF

MANHATTAN COLLEGE,

CITY UNIVERSITY OF NEW YORK.

*Library of Congress
Cataloging-in-Publication Data*

Hill, Rebecca Nell
Men, mobs, and law : anti-lynching and labor
defense in U.S. radical history / Rebecca N. Hill.
p. cm.
Includes bibliographical references and index.
ISBN 978-0-8223-4257-1 (cloth : alk. paper)
ISBN 978-0-8223-4280-9 (pbk. : alk. paper)
1. Lynching—United States—History.
2. Mobs—United States—History. 3. Riots—
United States—History. 4. Radicalism—United
States—History. 5. Labor unions—United
States—History. 6. Civil rights movements—
United States—History. 7. African Americans—
Crimes against. 8. United States—Race
relations—History. I. Title.
HV6457.H55 2008
364.4'045230973—dc22   2008041805

mistresses and hardening the hearts of slave masters. He emphasized the irrelevance of moral suasion in his description of the terrible beatings his aunt received from Captain Anthony in Maryland:

> I have often been awakened at the dawn of the day by the most heart-rending shrieks of an old Aunt of mine, whom he used to tie up to a joist and whip upon her naked back until she was literally covered with blood. No words, no tears, no prayers, from his gory victim seemed to move his iron heart from its bloody purpose. Where the blood ran fastest there he whipped longest, he would whip her to make her scream, and whip her to make her hush; and not until overcome by fatigue would he cease to swing the blood-clotted cowskin.[8]

By 1831, former slaves seemed to agree almost to a person that the slave-holders' religion was hypocrisy.[9] At the same time, shortly after Nat Turner's rebellion, slave masters in the South began to preach a particularly pacific brand of Christianity to slaves.[10]

White abolitionists, like Black abolitionists, reminded their countrymen of the American revolutionary tradition when they talked about slave rebellions, and in many cases they used the Bible to justify their cause. William Lloyd Garrison, who opposed violence in general, jocularly commented after hearing the popular song "Fall Tyrants Fall" sung on the Fourth of July with its lyric, "How noble the ardor that seizes the soul / how it bursts from the yoke and the chain / what pow'r can the fervor of freedom control / or its terrible vengeance restrain," that all Americans must be hoping and praying for the coming of slave insurrection.[11] Garrison also suggested that Americans were "patriotic hypocrites" in the days after the Nat Turner revolt, for writing panegyrics to "Frenchmen, Greeks and Poles" and yet reproaching Turner and his band.[12] The radical white abolitionists described slavery as a continuing state of war against slaves, distributing such striking texts as Theodore Dwight Weld's *American Slavery as It Is*, with its revealing lists of advertisements for runaway slaves.[13] In addition, white and Black abolitionists alike referred to America's frontier heroes when they looked for precedents to justify disobeying laws that supported slavery. How could Americans celebrate Davy Crockett and Andrew Jackson and yet demand that abolitionists follow the laws of slavery? they asked. For slaves and free Blacks, and for many white abolitionists, slave rebels were heroes.

However, the best-known white abolitionists, the Garrisonians, were dedicated to the philosophy of "non-resistance" and refused to extol the use of force against slavery.[14] For this reason, when many historians write

about John Brown, who became the most famous martyr of the abolition movement following his raid on Harper's Ferry and hanging by the State of Virginia in the fall of 1859, they have asked two questions: Why did this particular man turn to the use of violence, and why did non-resistant abolitionists celebrate him as a martyr?[15] However, for a man who chose to be a hero in a time of heroism, the choice to be nonviolent was more deviant from national culture than was the use of force. The unusual aspect of John Brown in the nineteenth century was not that he, a white man, chose to use force but, rather, that he, a white man, sought to organize a slave rebellion. Consequently, it was Brown's effort to raise a "slave rebellion" and not his use of violence in general that had to be expunged from his legend by the people who originally crafted him as a hero in the days before the Civil War.

Violence and Nineteenth-Century Heroism

John Brown lived in a time when America openly celebrated heroic fighters. From the 1830s to the 1850s, Americans celebrated violent acts as regenerative, and those who perpetrated them were the great heroes of republicanism. While western settlers championed their victories over Native Americans and Mexicans as evidence of their own natural superiority and destiny, revolutions rocked Europe, Africa, India, and the Caribbean. In the era of the 1830 and 1848 revolutions, romantic theorists argued that a nation's ability to win self-determination against tyrannical rule was the test of strength that proved a necessary prerequisite before any subjugated nation could argue for its independence as a natural right. Sam Houston, for example, "elevated the importance of freedom achieved through armed and willful action: the 'soldier-citizen,' like the 'pioneers' engaged in a contest against overwhelming odds that displayed 'unsubduable courage,' 'bold and generous daring,' and 'independent might.'"[16] Even as Americans subjugated their Native neighbors, they heralded European struggles against tyrannical regimes in the name of national self-determination as heroic. Just as Johann Gottfried von Herder, the German romantic, had heralded each nation's unique traits and tendencies, so Americans described each country and each race with its own unique character traits and argued that rebellions proved an actual genetic inheritance of freedom. In contrast, subjugated nations were deemed "dying races" doomed to extinction.[17] The American excitement for war, particularly in

the aggressive attack on Mexico in 1846, was striking enough that, according to one German observer in Chicago, "You Americans are the most ferociously warlike people that I have ever known."[18] Ned Buntline's and George Lippard's popular accounts of western adventures, argues Shelley Streeby, promoted "empire as redemptive, where damaged urban masculinity might be rehabilitated."[19]

In American cities, where rioting had long held a place in civic culture, the republican doctrine that physical courage was evidence of natural rights for white men made it difficult to oppose the continuation of the "politics out of doors," even following the extension of suffrage to all white men in the 1820s. In the "age of Jackson," American political life drew in masses through highly partisan agitation; popular, cheap newspapers with party affiliations flourished; voter turnout increased to 75 percent; and people attended political meetings, rallies, and lectures regularly. Religious revivals championed emotional experiences and led masses of people into political reform. Political parties inspired intense loyalty and castigated their opponents as dangerous to national safety, arguing that attempts to curb local self-determination were secretly efforts to reinstall the pre-1812 rules of Federalism.[20] Election Day thus became a major day for rioting. The riots increased in both frequency and ferocity to the extent that many called 1834 "the riot year."[21]

In 1841 in Rhode Island, mobs, while proclaiming themselves to be egalitarian, were often enforcers of existing hierarchies. Young working-class men terrorized houses of prostitution in "bully attacks" on brothels that reinforced gender hierarchies.[22] Antiabolitionist mobs attacked the abolitionists as "Jacobins" and race mixers. Such mobs were not that unusual, as the New York Sun editorialized: "It is not a difficult matter to get up in our city one of those elegant assemblages called a mob."[23] While Democrats such as Walt Whitman lauded nativist rioters in New York,[24] Whig activists referred to mobs as the mere weapons of ruling class demagogues, repeating a neo-Aristotelian conception of the link between masses and tyrants. Abraham Lincoln, a young Whig, spoke against popular violence, following the lynching of five gamblers in Vicksburg, attempting to replace the cult of rebellious violence with the political religion of law.[25]

Lincoln's argument did not immediately win everyone over, for, according to the western historian Richard Maxwell Brown, "During the nineteenth century and into the twentieth . . . Americans saw vigilante participation as an act of public spirit as important in its own way as election of public officials."[26] The use of violence to enforce order was especially

popular, and those who joined vigilante groups or supported them saw the use of violence to enforce community norms as part of their rights as citizens. "The people of this country are the real sovereigns," declared the Indiana Regulators in 1858. "Whenever the laws, made by those to whom they have delegated their authority, are found inadequate to their protection, it is the right of the people to take the protection of their property into their own hands and deal with those villains according to their just desserts."[27] George Templeton Strong, aristocrat of New York, seemed to admire the 1856 San Francisco Vigilance Committee and noted in his diary: "San Francisco is in anarchy. . . . The vigilance committee has acquired the highest office. . . . The committee treats habeas corpus as a nullity . . . but . . . claims to represent all the respectability, property and honesty of San Francisco, and if so, I hope its experiment may succeed. One like it will have to be tried in New York in ten years."[28] Ralph Waldo Emerson, too, approved of California's rule "by the bowie knife and the revolver."[29]

Even the seemingly rebellious crowds of New York, Philadelphia, and other major cities were more regulatory than rebellious in their energy. In *Gentlemen of Property and Standing*, Leonard Richards notes the preponderance of the well-to-do in the antiabolition mobs of the 1830s and demonstrates their role as protectors not of democracy, but of existing social structures. The most intense period of anti-abolition rioting was led by respectable town leaders and defended "the established order against the encroachments of internal subversives."[30] The riots' leaders attacked the abolitionists whose goal, they claimed, was to incite slave rebellions and compared them to French revolutionaries. In 1834, Ephraim Hart of Connecticut announced that if the abolitionists were allowed to speak, "The niggers will be excited to rise and murder their masters and the white population."[31] Cities maintained a racial double standard for rioters, demanding in Philadelphia, for example, that "Blacks should behave inoffensively and with civility at all times" to avoid making whites angry. Apparently, they were not docile enough, because in the antebellum North, Blacks were ten times more likely to go to jail than were whites.[32]

Although the historian of mass violence Paul Gilje argues that few would defend rioting after 1819, rioting continued to be part of urban politics well into the 1850s, even if Whig newspaper editors bemoaned it.[33] In his newspaper, the *Subterranean*, the Jacksonian Mike Walsh announced that he would "light upon" George H. Woolridge, the "pimp and brothel chronicler" like "an angel of God," proudly described his fistfights with "thieves and blackguards" who opposed his newspaper and, in the name

of white supremacy, threatened to "flatten" Rhode Island's State House and "pillage" Providence because it had awarded Blacks suffrage following the "Dorr War" of 1842. His "Spartan" gang played a pivotal role in New York election riots in the Sixth Ward in 1842, but this did not hurt Walsh, who won "overwhelmingly" there when he ran for Congress in 1854.[34] According to Sean Wilentz, who sees Walsh as a kind of anticapitalist hero, "His use of force was perfectly in keeping with the rough-house standards of the 1840s."[35] William Tweed (before he became "Boss" Tweed) was expelled from his fire company for swinging an ax at a rival fireman, but that did not end his political career. He won the alderman's position in the following election year. Similarly, the leader of the Irish street gang the Killers, William McMullen, became an important leader in Democratic Party politics in Philadelphia following his stint in the Mexican-American War.[36]

A certain sympathy for white rioters remained through the Civil War. The Democratic Party had prepared the ground for the Draft Riots of 1863 by depicting the Union Army as an occupying force similar to the British Redcoats and referring to Lincoln as a tyrant akin to Charles I.[37] During the riots, the Catholic church's most respected leader among New York's Irish, Archbishop John Hughes, spoke sympathetically to the rioters and declared that abolition was "a revolutionary violation of property rights."[38] By the end of the trials of the draft rioters, though, 443 rioters were arrested and only 67 were convicted, and of those, only one received a heavy charge for injuring a Black person.[39]

Abolitionists, ever unpopular, were among the harshest critics of vigilante attacks, since they were the attacks' frequent victims. Especially when the newspaper editor Elijah Lovejoy was killed by a mob in Alton, Illinois, his fellow abolitionists condemned the crowd violence that so many others justified. Said Edward Beecher, following Lovejoy's death, "There is no tyranny on earth so execrable as the tyranny of a mob."[40] However, the mass nature of riots cloaked these forces of reaction in the gown of a genuinely popular upsurge. As Gilje put it, urban rioters often "acted in the name of the people to deny others full participation in the American republic."[41]

Andrew Jackson had once said that such vigilantes and rioters were not acting in "opposition to the established laws of the country, but a supplement to them."[42] The truth of this statement is reflected in the fact that, instead of eradicating vigilantes and repudiating their goals, many cities incorporated them into their political systems. By 1845, in response to

Democratic Party mobs, Know-Nothings organized their own mob actions and would later form a critical ingredient in the Republican Party's constituency. By the mid-1850s, the leaders of immigrant gangs and Know-Nothing posses had become the vanguard of the new police departments and political parities in New York, Boston, Chicago, San Francisco, and Philadelphia.[43]

Vigilantes also filled fictional streets and western towns. Popular nineteenth-century fiction depicted the virtuous use of force by the lone man against the wilderness, a trope that easily transferred from tales of the "Wild West" to tales of the "wild city," whether it told the story of Deadeye Dick or Natty Bumppo. Fictional characters and mythologized "real" people, such as Davy Crockett and Kit Carson, transformed the ruthless killing of Native Americans into vernacular humor. Carson, for instance, proclaimed his willingness to scalp Indians: "Now we mountain men have got a right smart chance at scalping."[44] Richard Slotkin demonstrates in his frontier trilogy that the "western hero" could be retained and reshaped over and over again as long as he acted on the frontier, outside of civilization, and perpetrated his violence on racial others.[45] As Alexander Saxton argues, the western tales of Daniel Boone, Kit Carson, and Davy Crockett made Indian killing, white manhood, and democratic politics synonymous and increasingly defined partisan politics in the cities as a state of open warfare. At the same time, the Bowery B'hoy Mose, a "loveable criminal" who enjoyed a straightforward "punch up" much more than a shady backroom deal, became a popular hero on the stage and in stories and would serve as a model for the Horatio Alger series of the 1870s and 1880s.[46]

Mose and the b'hoys of New York, who broke laws because they could not get a fair shake in court, echoed the reality of vigilantes like the Indiana Regulators, who called community justice the last resort. Eventually, as Slotkin demonstrates, the vigilante hero replaced the revolutionary rebellious crowd as the chief hero in American popular fiction.[47] The man against chaos, rather than the mass upsurge against tyranny, increasingly came to redefine the ideal forms of "popular" violence away from the heroic protests of the revolutionary era and toward regulatory enforcement and community consensus, giving law enforcement the superficial appearance of populism. When they criticized such mob actions, abolitionists appeared all the more unmanly in the eyes of the public.

In the name of order, both Democratic and Whig newspapers justified most of the actions of anti-abolitionist rioters in New York in 1834, arguing that abolitionists had provoked the community into action. The

Evening Post, the Whig paper, damned the rioters, but blamed both the abolitionists and the Democratic *Courier and Enquirer* for provoking the crowd. "A mad spirit has gone abroad among our populace," a reporter wrote, "a spirit excited, no doubt, by the proceedings of the inflammatory publications of the abolitionists as they are called, but even in greater measure by the violent tirades of certain prints opposed to the abolitionists."[48] Historians of urban riots have argued that the Whigs described the rioters as ruthless and even devilish. However, newspaper accounts of anti-abolition riots still recognized them as members of "our populace," however misguided and temporarily insane they might be: "The fury of demons seems to have entered into the breasts of our misguided populace . . . like those ferocious animals which, having once tasted blood, are seized with an insatiable thirst for gore and kept going until they had destroyed as much as possible."[49] When they argued that the physical attacks on abolitionists were a justified reaction to their "incendiary" ideas, the newspapers undermined these condemnations.

Drawing the Line: Slave Rebellions

This ambivalent attitude toward popular violence does not appear in contemporary accounts of slave rebellions. As David Roediger has argued, republicanism in America became "herrenvolk republicanism" and associated "slavishness" with Blacks.[50] Whereas white manhood was defined by the will to fight for one's rights, the slaves were damned no matter what they did. If they did not rebel, they were unmanly; if they did rebel, they were beasts. Many antislavery activists argued that the slaves were basically of a slavish nature and would not revolt, just as proslavery whites did. In her *Key to Uncle Tom's Cabin*, Harriet Beecher Stowe articulated this philosophy clearly. According to her, Blacks were "more simple, docile, child-like and affectionate than other races."[51] In his Cooper Union address, Abraham Lincoln reflected the general attitude held by whites at the time, although in his case, the argument is tempered by an acknowledgment that the same behavior could be seen in Europeans:

> Much is said by Southern people about the affection of slaves for their masters and mistresses; and a part of it, at least, is true. A plot for an uprising could scarcely be devised and communicated to twenty individuals before some one of them, to save the life of a favorite master or mistress, would divulge it. This is the rule; and the slave revolution in Hayti was not

an exception to it, but a case occurring under peculiar circumstances. The gunpowder plot of British history, though not connected with slaves, was more in point. In that case, only about twenty were admitted to the secret; and yet one of them, in his anxiety to save a friend, betrayed the plot to that friend, and, by consequence, averted the calamity.[52]

Nonetheless, when slaves did revolt, most whites argued that they were being irrational rather than acting in the name of freedom. Slaves did not want freedom, according to slavery's justifiers, and it was only when stirred up by whites, free blacks, or mulattoes that they acted. Edmund Ruffin, for example, said that the slave revolt in Haiti happened the way it did because mulattoes stirred up the slaves. However, because slaves lacked manly self-control, according to these theorists, these same placidly happy slaves would become beasts immediately, in whom "natural ferocity is unleashed."[53] Slave insurrection was "bad violence," and, like the French Revolution's Jacobin revolt, it would terrorize and enslave everyone. Perhaps this image of ferocious revolt was a metaphor for a simpler reality. While white mobs' attacks on social outsiders might be frightening to the public, they did not seriously threaten the existing social order. The emancipation of slaves, whether achieved through slave rebellion or an act of Congress, would.

Blacks were incapable of self-rule, according to racist thinkers. In the *Niles Weekly Register*, Haiti's Christophe was portrayed as a "buffoon or an ape who mimicked the manners of royalty," and whites attacked free blacks in general with the minstrel character "Zip Coon," a cowardly and lascivious dandy.[54] When they revolted, slaves became not men, but "beasts," enslaved by unmanly rage and passion. Most historians of the time did not describe even the most successful slave rebellion, the Haitian Revolution, as a revolution on par with those of Europe.[55] The idea that slavishness was essential to the African character even in acts of violence appeared in the racial theories that held Blacks to be superior in physical strength, but subordinate in intellectual and moral power.

Victorian racial thinkers described the relative strengths of races in the realms of the brain, the sinew, and the spirit. The significance of the combined force of physical action and mental strength for the creation of the legitimate revolutionary appeared in the way that the authors at the *Atlantic Monthly* attempted to determine "to what race did Spartacus belong?" by comparing the physical strengths of the Thracians against the mental strengths of the Greeks. They concluded that Spartacus must have a mixture of both bloods in his veins. In contrast, Nat Turner was described as

"Frankenstein's monster" combining the physical passions of a man with the mental imbecility of a child. Even this published confession by Ralph Gray was condemned by the *Richmond Whig* as attempting to "give the bandit a character for intelligence which he does not deserve and ought not to have received."[56]

In contrast to Africans, Anglo-Saxons, according to these racialist thinkers, combined moral virtue, physical power, and rationality in such a way that they could control the savage passions within even when they were wielding force. A particular intolerance of subordination and love for freedom also came to them as a genetic inheritance. Thus, while white men's superior rational and spiritual power checked their savage physical impulses, actual "savages" could never bring that strength of mind or spirit to bear.[57] Blacks could not be trusted to revolt on their own.

Generally, slave rebellion was the negative limit of popular violence. While there were similarities between reports of the urban mobs of the North and Southern slave revolts, there were also subtle differences. Newspaper reports of Nat Turner's rebellion, like those that described the urban riots in the 1830s, described the violent group as driven and out of control, sometimes stirred up by the ideas of others. "The wretches who have conceived of this thing are mad—infatuated—deceived by some artful knaves" or "stimulated by their own miscalculating passions," the *Richmond Compiler's* report on Nat Turner's revolt suggested.[58] However, the Southern newspaper editors who described Turner's rebellion made it seem that the real cause was that the leader had been allowed to mull over ideas that were beyond his racially limited mental capacities. For example, another Richmond newspaper concluded that "no black man ought to be permitted to turn preacher."[59] Turner was "a bold fellow . . . of the deepest cunning who for years has been endeavoring to acquire an influence over the minds of these deluded wretches."[60] Perhaps they were "misled by some hallucination."[61] According to the *Richmond Constitutional Whig*, his band consisted of "deluded wretches [who] have rushed on assured destruction" and were "incited by a spirit of plunder and rapine," not by any threat, whether real or perceived, and certainly not by a desire for freedom.

Importantly, (white) abolitionists were ultimately to blame in both the descriptions of the Turner revolt and the anti-abolitionist riots. The white rioters who attacked abolitionists in New York were justified in horror at the abolitionists' provocative ideas, while Southern papers suggested that Turner's revolt would never have happened had not abolitionists stirred up the slaves. Although they were capable of such a temporary spasm,

Black rebels were hardly a long-term threat, the paper reassured its readers: "The ruin must return on their own heads."[62]

State responses to white and Black mobs or riots were more noticeably different. Even during the New York Draft Riots, speakers practically begged assemblages of rioters to disperse, and most white rioters were brought back into the fold of the community.[63] When Black slaves revolted, as they did in Southampton, the local militias did not plead with the rioters for peace, but shot immediately. As soon as they received news of the Turner rebellion, which involved sixty slaves, whites from the surrounding countryside and various armed forces from neighboring counties descended on Southampton. They did this quickly, despite poor communication and transportation, a feat achieved because, by 1831, Virginia was already practically an armed camp.[64] There was no hesitation in putting down the revolt. White militias shot bound prisoners and carried their heads away with them as trophies or placed them on pikes to intimidate others. They slaughtered at least one hundred Blacks who had nothing to do with the rebellion. Authorities had to order white citizens not to rush into the streets firing their guns. One newspaper warned any potential Black readers that a further insurrection would lead to the extermination of the entire Black race in the southern quarter of Virginia.[65] The level of preparedness in the South for dealing with insurrection contrasted sharply with white Southerners' efforts to convince themselves and their critics that they had nothing to worry about because their slaves were happy.

Servile insurrection scared the North, too. Following Nat Turner's rebellion, both Whig and Democratic Party newspapers simply printed Southern dispatches about the events and expressed sympathy for the white victims. Abolitionists who described slave rebellions differed from proslavery whites in that they saw the rebellions as a response to—and, therefore, evidence of—the brutality of slavery. Slave rebellion to them was a natural and uncontrolled force, a simple reaction to oppression, unified in its will. When Nat Turner rebelled in Southampton, William Lloyd Garrison's *Liberator* described it as "the first step of the earthquake which is ultimately to shake down the fabric of oppression," making rebellion similar to an uncontrollable natural force beyond human control.[66] Another writer saw the potential slave revolt as a volcano: "When the molten rock bursts forth in a torrent of burning lava, it will overwhelm those who may be in its way whether they had expected the explosion or not."[67] The "servile insurrection" while proof for white abolitionists of slavery's cruelty, was also a threat should slavery not be abolished immediately.

The antislavery workingmen's paper *Workingman's Advocate*, which argued that Turner and his band had acted as they did because they sought freedom and "there can be no security for any rights but by numerical and physical force," drew a limit at endorsing slave rebellion.[68] The Turner rebellion was a "melancholy affair" whose lesson was that gradual emancipation was necessary "if only to avoid a worse alternative."[69] After all, the editors asked,

> Does anyone believe that if they [the slaves] could, which God in his infinite mercy avert, obtain mastery as they did in St. Domingo, that they would stop at the Mason Dixon Line? Not they! Where there was plunder and victims, rich towns and fruitful fields there they would march if possible.... The most prompt and efficient means must be taken to prevent this servile war, and then decisive steps should be adopted by those whose duty it is for the gradual abolition of slavery throughout the land.[70]

In a similar warning, C. Camden wrote to the paper that whites had better proceed with education, emancipation, and colonization, or the South's whites would be defeated and the region would become "the black empire of the globe."[71] Similarly, the *New York Sentinel* printed that the Blacks, while justified in their anger, were "degraded, ignorant blacks" whose "absurd" and "foolish project" of trying to emancipate themselves from slavery was the product of their lack of education.[72] In her novel *Dred*, which is also fairly sympathetic to a slave rebel, Harriet Beecher Stowe vented a similar vision. The would-be rebel of her novel, who is not its hero, speaks convincingly to the whites who cannot see but can only hear him. His voice emerges from the dark at the camp meeting with terrible prophecy straight out of the white evangelical unconscious:

> Take away from me the noise of thy songs, and the melody of thy viols; for I will not hear them, saith the Lord. I hate and despise your feast-days!... for your hands are defiled with blood, and your fingers are greedy for violence!... Ye oppress the poor and needy, and hunt the stranger; also in thy skirts is found the blood of poor innocents!... Hear, O ye rebellious people! The Lord is against this nation! The Lord shall stretch out upon it the line of confusion, and the stones of emptiness!... Thou shalt be cast out as an abominable branch, and the wild beasts shall tread thee down.... Behold, I am against thee, saith the Lord, and I will make thee utterly desolate![73]

Like Thomas Jefferson, who wrote that he "trembled" at the thought that "God is Just," Stowe's novel dreads the coming of slave rebellion as

the act of an avenging God, scourging the white population. If all were guilty, perhaps all would be destroyed. Abolition would prevent this horror, as a Mrs. Sturges wrote to Theodore Dwight Weld: "Whites must either grant blacks freedom or find a horde of barbarians on our border sending their troops of bandits to make predatory incursions on all our villages."[74] Whites could take pride in defining their own capacity to enter and leave savage states at will; they even dressed as Indians and Blacks when they rioted. But slaves were not deemed capable of the transformation back from beast to man.[75] Slaves, it was presumed, would take as their enemies not just slaveholders, but all whites, and if slaves rebelled successfully, as they had in Haiti, the republic would not be refreshed; it would be destroyed. Just as unacceptable sexual desire was projected onto Blacks, so was uncontrollable rage.[76] If such a "savage" race were to defeat the Anglo-Saxons in America, racialists argued, it would bring the downfall of civilization similar to the Dark Ages after the defeat of the Roman Empire by barbarians. The *Atlantic Monthly* made detailed arguments based on the "truths" uncovered by a proslavery historian that the Union must break with slavery lest the Black race, more able to tolerate the heat of Southern climates than the whites, take over America, thus replacing the civilization of New England with the barbarism of "New Africa."[77] One of John Brown's funders, Thomas Wentworth Higginson, who is often remembered for his laudatory book on slave rebellions and his diary of a Black regiment during the Civil War, described how lack of physical exercise would cause the Anglo-Saxon to be too easily defeated by barbarous races. "The life of the literary man is more dangerous than the frontier dragoon," he claimed. Only a rigorous program of exercise could protect white Americans against the "prophecies of Dred."[78] Another of Brown's supporters, Theodore Parker wrote that, "with no white man to help," a Saint-Domingue-style revolt could occur in America.[79]

Abolitionist Martyrs, Heroes, and Fugitive Slave Defense

While the rest of the nation feared slave revolt or celebrated righteous white action, some abolitionists built and admired their own heroic pantheon, which included both noble slave rebels, such as Toussaint L'Ouverture, and American abolitionist martyrs. As Christians, radical abolitionists wrote a great deal about self-sacrifice and the dignity of suffering, describing both the slaves in bondage and the abolitionists who

were victimized by mobs. Some of the more notorious attacks on them did increase abolitionist popularity. Wendell Phillips, who would become one of the greatest abolitionist orators, was inspired to join the movement when he saw William Lloyd Garrison dragged through the streets of Boston in an ox harness.[80] There were many martyrs in the abolitionist movement, and the abolitionists championed these martyrs, holding them up as examples for others to follow. Harriet Martineau even titled her work on the American abolitionist movement *The Martyr Age of the United States*.[81]

John Brown would have seen many examples of abolitionist heroics. He was born in 1800, the year of Gabriel's conspiracy in Virginia, and was thirty-one at the time of Nat Turner's Southampton revolt. According to some, he pledged his life to antislavery after the death of newspaper editor Elijah Lovejoy at the hands of a mob in 1837.[82] During that same era, Brown would have heard of Prudence Crandall, persecuted for the crime of trying to educate Black girls. He definitely read the stories of the successful rebels Madison Washington, who had seized control of the slave ship the USS *Creole*, sailed it to Nassau, and was declared free by the British, and Sengbe Pieh (Cinque of the *Amistad*), whose rebellion on board the illegal slave ship similarly led to freedom after the celebrated case went to the Supreme Court. Following the passage of the Fugitive Slave Act in 1850, Brown read about and met people charged in court with violating the act and, in the spring of 1851, formed one of the many defense leagues dedicated to resisting it.[83] He inspected the coat worn by Charles Sumner when he was caned in the Senate by Preston Brooks. By the time his own day in court came in Virginia in 1859, Brown was already part of a lengthening chain of heroic resistance to slavery in the eyes of many of his contemporaries.

At least two cases of martyrdom involved major publicity campaigns. In 1837, Lovejoy, who some see as a kind of model for Brown, was widely celebrated as a martyr to free speech and an example of courage in the face of a savage mob, although some argued that his use of weapons to defend his printing press from the mob outside made him not a "true martyr" but the setter of a "dangerous precedent."[84] The *Amistad* case and the committee dedicated to funding the return trip to Sierra Leone for the ship's captives also gave abolitionists both a major slave-rebel hero in Sengbe Pieh (Cinque), who testified about the experience of the Middle Passage to a "packed courtroom," and a powerful legal and philosophical argument in favor of Africans' right to self-defense against kidnapping in an illegal slave trade. John Quincy Adams even argued that "self-liberation"

should be cause for the legal declaration of freedom, although he did not argue that point in court.[85]

The broad support for the *Amistad* captives among even relatively conservative abolitionists, such as Lewis Tappan, and the hagiographic treatment that Toussaint L'Ouverture received from Harriet Martineau, shows the level of interest in Black republican heroes among white abolitionists. Certainly, many Black abolitionists advocated that Blacks do more to fit into the model of republican heroics that Americans revered. Following his break with Garrison, Frederick Douglass argued that if Africans did not resist oppression with physical force, they were proving not their virtue but, rather, their slavishness. "That submission on the part of the slave has ceased to be a virtue is very evident," he wrote in response to the Fugitive Slave Act, and he endorsed killing fugitive-slave catchers, if necessary.[86] Douglass understood, as Garnet and Walker did, that only violence by Blacks would "wipe out" the notion of slaves as submissive and "fit for slavery" in the minds of whites. Indeed, Blacks' understandings of whites' admiration for violence as a measure of manliness was explicit in their writings. Douglass, for example, referred to antislavery resistance as an "appeal to the lynch code" that was so popular with whites in the 1850s.[87] To them, slave insurrections proved not only that slavery was not a benevolent system, but also that African Americans demonstrated all of the traits of republican manhood.[88] When the French, who since the early nineteenth century had defined their aristocracy's hereditary nobility through the Teutonic forests,[89] lost their battle to the Haitians, radical abolitionists like William Wells Brown and Wendell Phillips persistently referred to the revolt as evidence of Negro racial dignity. When the Hungarian Louis Kossuth visited Boston and thrilled abolitionist audiences, James McCune Smith, writing under the pseudonym Communipaw, made sure that his readers knew that "*Kossuth is not a white man!*"[90]

Frederick Douglass's most famous description of regenerative force came in the narrative of his life, which he delivered on speakers' platforms and twice in print before John Brown's 1859 raid on Harper's Ferry. In his description of his fight with the overseer Covey, Douglass argued that, although he was once broken in spirit by this master, his fight with Covey was a turning point in his life. For the first half of the narrative, the reader had seen "how a man was made a slave." During the fight with Covey, Douglass explained, "you shall see how a slave was made a man." With a "High John Conquerer" root in his pocket to give him strength, Douglass resolved to face his nemesis, and from that moment he was reborn as a

man and able to think again of freedom. Violence was no moral failing, no sin, but "a glorious resurrection,"[91] one that was strengthened by an African root, not diluted or destroyed by it, establishing Africa as a pan-ethnic member of the family of nations. Douglass drew on the transatlantic theories of national heroic power to make his claim for African manhood, and, as Paul Gilroy argues, he invoked Hegel's dialectic, showing how at the point of death, the slave rather than the master was the ideal subject of history. In formulating that very notion of the national heroic character, it was likely, as Susan Buck-Morss has argued, that Hegel himself was thinking of the actual, rather than the abstract, "heroic slaves" of Haiti.[92]

The African American militants Henry Highland Garnet and David Walker both indicate the importance of rebellion to definitions of manhood in their exhortations of slaves, and both demand more from slaves, with Garnet making the point that, "TO SUCH DEGRADATION IT IS SINFUL IN THE EXTREME FOR YOU TO MAKE VOLUNTARY SUBMISSION." In closing, he demanded, "In the name of God we ask, are you men? Where is the blood of your fathers? Has it all run out of your veins?"[93] John Brown, who was friendly with Garnet and Douglass, agreed with them that slave insurrection was the only force that would undo slavery. For this reason, his first biographer, James Redpath, saw that proving that slaves in Harper's Ferry had tried to revolt was the most important ideological task after the failed raid. Based on reports in Southern newspapers, he wrote that "slaves were in many instances insolent to their masters and even refused to work" in the days following the raid, and he highlighted any example of Black resistance that he could find, such as in this footnote in his biography of Brown:

> It is true that the slaves did not join John Brown. But why? Because they had not time to know his design, and to act, ere their heroic liberators were either killed or imprisoned. But one negro, I know,—a slave of Washington,—whom Governor Wise pretended had probably been killed by Captain Cook in endeavoring to return home, was shot in the river *as he was fighting for freedom.* I know this fact from one of John Brown's men who saw him. I have positive knowledge, also of sixteen slaves who succeeded in escaping from Harper's Ferry.[94]

The idea that this kind of heroism was what mattered both influenced and was influenced by the events of the 1850s. Following the passage of the Fugitive Slave Act, abolitionists throughout the Northern states defied the new law with daring rescue missions. The rescues of Jerry (also known

as William Henry), Shadrach Minkins, Anthony Burns, and John Price all involved two layers of conflict with the law. The first legal conflict was during the actual rescues. In the cases of Jerry and Shadrach Minkins, abolitionist groups actually entered the courtrooms where the fugitive slaves were being "identified" by slave catchers and owners and spirited them away. Free Blacks organized what they called "vigilance groups" to protect themselves from slave catchers following the passage of the new law, and white abolitionists joined them in the endeavor. Lewis Hayden formed the first league, which was responsible for the rescues of William and Ellen Craft, as well as the famous Minkins rescue and the failed Burns rescue attempt. James McCune Smith and Gerrit Smith were both members of the Syracuse Vigilance Committee, which rescued Jerry. In Christiana, Pennsylvania, the fugitive William Parker led a group that killed a slaveowner. He fled to Canada to avoid prosecution. In the last year before Brown's raid, a group of citizens of Oberlin, Ohio, followed a group of slave catchers to Wellington, the next town over, and managed to bring the fugitive John Price out of the hotel where the slave catchers were holding him. One of John Brown's men later took the fugitive to Canada.[95]

Because the law was so clearly stacked against accused fugitive slaves, who were not allowed to testify in their own defense, these kinds of dramatic actions were the only possible defense. And while middle-class abolitionists tried to control the groups and to discourage physical resistance, they were largely unsuccessful at stopping what one Black porter in New York's Vigilance Committee called "manly physical struggle" during the rescue attempts.[96] John Brown was close to McCune Smith and Gerrit Smith, and he knew Lewis Hayden well. In the spring of 1851, when he was living in Springfield, Massachusetts, Brown formed a less well-known vigilance group, the mysterious League of Gileadites, to whom he wrote "Words of Advice" suggesting the use of physical resistance. Brown delivered these words to the Gileadites just after the daring Shadrach Minkins rescue masterminded by Hayden of Boston, and it is likely that some of Brown's suggestions, such as bringing small amounts of gunpowder into the courtroom in paper packages, came from Hayden, who, after all, was famous for the large casks of gunpowder that sat in his basement, protecting his Underground Railroad station. Brown also knew William Wells Brown, who wrote in the 1870s that he had attended a meeting of the Gileadites.[97]

If physical resistance to slave catchers was the first line of defense, the second was the court cases that followed the rescues. Abolitionists used

the stage of the witness box to denounce the laws of the United States in these earliest and most revolutionary of political-defense cases. As John Brown put it in the "Words of Advice" to the Gileadites:

> The trial for life of one bold and to some extent successful man for defending his rights in good earnest would arouse more sympathy throughout the nation that the accumulated wrongs and sufferings of three millions of our submissive colored population. . . . No jury can be found in the Northern states that would convict a man for defending his rights to the last extremity.[98]

To a degree, he was right, although the men who defended their *own* rights, such as William Parker, fled to Canada rather than face the penalty for murdering a white slaveowner. The rescuers' trials were sensational. Held in abolitionist strongholds, they featured eloquent defendants whose defense attorneys were drawn from the ranks of the great antislavery politicians. Thaddeus Stevens was the lawyer for the thirty-eight Christiana rescuers, most of whom were acquitted. In the Oberlin–Wellington rescue, both defense attorneys and defendants, who were prepared, they had said, "to go to prison, or if necessary go out on the battlefield to meet the slave oligarchy," made arguments for the "higher law" position.[99] In asserting his obedience to a higher law, the defense attorney Albert G. Riddle argued that "*right* and its everlasting opposite *wrong* existed anterior to the feeble enactments of men, and will survive their final repeal" and proclaimed that the defendants were "guarded by fiery cherubim armed with the many-sided sword of the common law."[100] The African American politician Charles H. Langston defended his rights at length in his address to the court before sentencing, pointing out that he expected nothing from a court in a country set against Blacks:

> I was tried by a jury who were prejudiced; before a Court that was prejudiced; prosecuted by an officer who was prejudiced, and defended, though ably, by counsel that were prejudiced. And therefore it is, your Honor, that I urge by all that is good and great in manhood, that I should not be subjected to the pains and penalties of this oppressive law, when, I have not been tried, either by a jury of my peers, or by a jury that were impartial.[101]

He also pointed out the hypocrisy of a country that so admired rebellion and upright resistance to oppression in Europeans and yet would find him guilty for his role in rescuing a fugitive slave. In all of the cases, the rescuers proudly proclaimed what they had done and used their trials as a place to expose the injustice of the Fugitive Slave Act, and of slavery in general,

in ringing terms, expecting for the most part to pay the consequences for breaking the law. These proud statements of defiance of unjust laws are the paradigmatic expression of republican heroism in court. They defy the law in the name of right, proclaim the existence of a natural or divine law that supersedes the statute, and are prepared to face the consequences.

The more that Brown was involved in Underground Railroad activity, the more he came into contact with fugitive slaves. For many in the abolitionist cause, sympathy with the slaves was meant to go beyond distant pity. Brown often cited the passage from Hebrews 13:13: "Remember them in bonds as bound with them." Brown brought himself close to the suffering fugitives. He sought out opportunities to be among free Blacks. In 1847, the year Brown first met Frederick Douglass, he wrote a column for the Black newspaper the *Ram's Horn*, and in 1851, wrote to his wife from Springfield that he was upset by stories of fugitive slaves with whom he was working, who were "so alarmed they cannot sleep on account of either themselves or their wives and children. . . . I want all my family to imagine themselves in the same dreadful condition."[102] He moved his family to North Elba, New York, where Gerrit Smith had bought a plot of land for free Blacks, and lived among the freedmen, hoping to teach them how to be pioneers. He declared he would be a "sort of father" to them, exhibiting both paternalism and a commitment to the integration of freed Blacks into the American republic.

If Brown was tender and full of pity for the weak and enslaved, in practical politics he saw the solution to the problem of slavery in the fostering of republican manhood among slaves rather than by glorifying suffering.[103] Brown argued that slavery was wrong not only because it was violent and cruel, but also because it violated the basic principles of the producer ethic. Brown saw slaves as productive laborers, and, like his associate James McCune Smith, who argued that the land should belong to those who worked it, he told the journalist James Redpath: "The land belongs to the bondman, he has enriched it and been robbed of its fruits."[104]

Thus, when Brown chose to go into action on the slavery question, he worked primarily with those abolitionists who would coalesce around the Liberty Party, later the Radical Abolition Party, and Frederick Douglass, some of whom, such as Brown and Gerrit Smith, were Congregationalists who rejected slavery and the market economy in general.[105] But the slavery question took Brown away from his church's official policies. Jonathan Edwards had rejected "distressing manifestations of antinomianism, spiritual pride, immediate revelation, censoriousness and unregulated lay

exhorting." Confronted with a church hierarchy that was segregated and hypocritical, Brown broke these rules, joined independent antislavery churches such as the Free Church in Springfield, and held his own inter-racial prayer meetings.[106]

In 1847, Brown asked Frederick Douglass to dinner at his house. Douglass had heard much about Brown from Henry Highland Garnet.[107] At that dinner, said Douglass, Brown had told him that he had developed a plan for the "speedy emancipation of my race" and that Brown felt that no one would ever gain respect for the Negro until he took up arms in his own defense. Brown had told Douglass that "the practice of carrying arms would be a good one for the colored people to adopt as it would give them a sense of manhood."[108] Brown and Douglass remained connected, and Brown hoped to take Douglass with him to Harper's Ferry as a general.

Brown subscribed to *Frederick Douglass' Paper* when it first appeared in 1851, following Douglass's break with Garrison, and his letters appear in its pages more than once.[109] If Brown's son's explanations of the Harper's Ferry raid and the Missouri slave-rescue incident are any clue, Brown's strategies were at least as materialist as his inspiration was religious. At the first anniversary of John Brown's death, his son John Jr. spoke again of abolitionist strategy and goals at J. Sella Martin's church in Boston. John Jr.'s description of the goals at Harper's Ferry and his recommendations for further action were based on the idea that slaveholders were immune to moral suasion and that actions should strike at their interests as property holders. Compared to the slaveholding class, John Jr. said, "the tiger is a model of sympathy and love." Slavery had to be attacked materially, reducing the value of slave property and making slavery as terrifying to masters as it was to slaves.[110] "Give me liberty or I will give you death" should be the rallying cry of freemen and slaves alike, he said.[111]

Such tactics were acceptable for Brown, and for some others, because they saw the antislavery movement as part of a worldwide revolt for free-dom against tyranny. There was no difference, for Brown, between Eu-ropean revolutionaries fighting for independence from empire and the slaves held in bondage by the despotic South. From Troy, New York, Brown wrote to *Frederick Douglass' Paper* about Louis Kossuth, the Re-publican fighter who had come from Hungary to seek U.S. aid against the Austro-Hungarian Empire, but who had rejected appeals for antislavery statements from abolitionists, claiming that Americans needed no out-siders butting into their domestic affairs. Like many other abolitionists, Brown wondered at the hypocrisy and asked, "What is it that captivates

the bad and the good in that man so wonderfully?" But he echoed James McCune Smith in his assessment of Kossuth's strategy as a trickster:

> What, with all his talents as a speaker and writer, is it that gives him one particle of advantage over Frederick Douglass? It is *not* the color of his skin. If he *have* any, *it is* that he has had an opportunity to prove to the *wide world* that he has in possession the *true Philosopher's Stone* and that he will, if opportunity occur, make a most thorough and practical use of it. I think that, notwithstanding policy, prevents his opening all his batteries direct upon our accursed, hypocrisy, aristocratic feeling, injustice, God insulting, provoking ingratitude and most abominable cruelty and oppression, he is doing more to instruct our young people and indoctrinate them in the *true* republican principle than any has done since the revolution.[112]

Indicating his excitement about the growth in democracy all over the world, Brown continued to be excited by Kossuth's visit and by the revolutions of 1848. He wrote to his wife, Mary, about the exciting events occurring in New England's cities:

> There is an unusual amount of interesting things happening in this and other countries at present, and no one can foresee what is yet to follow. The great excitement produced by the coming of Kossuth, and the last news of a new revolution in France, with the prospect that all Europe will soon again be ablaze seem to have taken all by surprise. I have only to say in regard to these things that I rejoice in them.[113]

Brown made close allies of several German "1848ers" who had emigrated to America following Germany's failed revolution and became involved in antislavery activism. Like Brown, these men rejected pacifism, and several 1848ers, including the Jewish abolitionists August Bondi, Joseph Benjamin, and Theodore Weiner, fought with Brown in Kansas. Ernst Schmidt, another 48er, became a financial contributor to Brown's cause in 1857, and who would later be a major figure in the defense of the Haymarket anarchists, held meetings for Brown in Chicago, denounced pacifism, and proudly displayed a signed picture of Brown in his home.[114] The experiences of antislavery settlers in Kansas only increased the abolitionists' sense that their freedom and lives were threatened by slavery—that they had a self-interest in opposing slavery as well as a moral obligation. As they saw it, the existence of slavery had created a despotic slave power that threatened to take over the entire United States.[115] In his opposition to the slave power's cruel assault on genuine republicanism and godliness, Brown again displayed sympathy with the ideas of his

friend Frederick Douglass, who described the "slave power" as a problem affecting every American individual:

> The evils overshadow the whole country and . . . every American is responsible for its existence and is solemnly required, by the highest convictions of duty and safety to labor for its utter extirpation from the land. . . . Slavery is a pestiferous breath that taints the whole moral atmosphere of the North and enervates the moral energies.[116]

Thus, for Brown and his allies, although the American republic had begun with the goals of freedom and revolution, the institution of slavery had plunged the entire nation into a state of despotism. Brown saw it as a civic responsibility for Americans to fight slavery. In the eyes of Brown and his fellows, to see heroic republicanism as the property of whites only was not only small-minded but also a distortion of reality. Because he took on the cause of the slave as his own, Osborne Perry Anderson, a free Black man who fought with Brown at Harper's Ferry, saw Brown as an inheritor of a heroic tradition that transcended race. For Anderson, freedom's

> nationality is universal, its language understood everywhere . . . coming down through the nations . . . regardless of national boundaries or particularities— there is an unbroken chain of sentiment and purpose from Moses of the Jews to John Brown of America, and the Denmark Veseys, Nat Turners, Madison Washingtons of the Southern slave states.[117]

The Construction of Brown as an American Hero

Would John Brown and his troop succeed in putting the "heroic slave" in the center of national consciousness with the Harper's Ferry raid? The answer is no. Daniel Littlefield has argued in a persuasive essay that Brown was a paternalist who sought to help Blacks, whom he saw as beings beneath him.[118] However, I will argue here that it was not Brown himself who was paternalist and racist. He was, rather, portrayed that way by the people who crafted his image while he was on trial and awaiting execution and who later memorialized him. Because in many ways he closely fit into the mold of existing republican heroism, John Brown has come to be seen by the American left as the most "American" example of revolutionary action. He earned his reputation as a hero in the American media during the border wars in Kansas, three years before his raid on Harper's Ferry. There he was depicted as genuine "western hero" in the style of such famous

figures as Kit Carson and Davy Crockett. As David Reynolds explained in his sympathetic biography, Brown "filled a need for Northerners who were looking for a hero to admire in a time of immoral laws and spineless politicians."[119] That his eulogizers could not see Black heroism as equal to white was not Brown's fault. To an extent, heroism in the era was defined more by style and means than by ends. Just as Brown was in Kansas, fili-busterers such as William Walker, who attempted to expand the territory for slavery, were celebrated as frontier heroes. As Richard Slotkin's work on the myth of the frontier has shown, "a common concept of heroism" was used to "rationalize opposing ideologies."[120]

Rewriting Harper's Ferry: From Rebellion to Rescue   Immediately after the Harper's Ferry raid, many of those sympathetic to Brown de-scribed what he was doing as something quite different from inciting a slave insurrection. Shortly after Brown's arrest, the explicit goal of slave rebellion was converted into a *rescue* attempt. Redpath complained fruit-lessly in letters to newspaper editors and biographers that Brown had in-tended rebellion and not rescue, but even Brown contradicted Redpath. On the first day of his trial, Brown denied that he was guilty of "conspiring with slaves to commit treason and murder" and said instead that he had gone only to rescue slaves—this during a time when daring slave rescues were seen as heroic by many abolitionists.[121] On being confronted later with the contradiction, Brown corrected himself, commenting, "[I] did not consider the full bearing of what I then said" and explaining that "it was my object to place the slaves in a position to defend their liberties, if they would, without any bloodshed."[122]

To make John Brown a republican hero America could love, Brown's supporters cast his October 19 raid on Harper's Ferry as a "rescue at-tempt" for helpless others rather than as an attempt to encourage slaves to defend themselves. This characterization required erasure, for Brown had prepared for the raid by having several iron pikes made, imagining that these tools would be easier to use without training. He recruited an integrated troop of eighteen men to go with him to Virginia. There is evi-dence that Brown did gain supporters among Blacks in the Harper's Ferry region, who set fires around the mountains in the days that followed.[123] Blacks freed during the raid did join his troop, and recently the famous "Washington gun" confiscated during the raid was found in the attic of a Black family in Harper's Ferry. Before he set out, Brown had taken special pains to find black officers, asking both Frederick Douglass and Harriet Tubman to serve as generals, although neither showed up.[124] The most

important documentary record of the raid is Brown's provisional constitution, which suggested the formation of a kind of maroon colony of guerrilla warriors in the Virginia mountains.[125]

To describe the Harper's Ferry raid as a rescue attempt would make Brown a model of chivalric heroism instead of making Blacks into republican subjects. In the tributes written to him in abolitionist periodicals after the trial, Brown's actions were justified by representing the slaves as the "weak victims" of a tyrannical power. Such a chivalric hero could be represented as paternal and disinterested. A rescue could even be consistent with a plan for Negro removal or with a paternalistic, gradualist plan for blacks within a post-emancipation America. The creation of a slave army, however, spoke not just for immediate emancipation, but also for the immediate capacities of formers slaves for citizenship.

The (few) Republican Party newspapers that defended the Harper's Ferry raid did so by comparing it favorably to the "savagery" of Turner's rebellion in Southampton, thereby casting the "white" Brown as a moderating influence. In its eulogy to Brown on December 3, 1859, the Republican *Chicago Press and Tribune* remarked: "The way for the emancipation of the American slave and the civilization of the South lies not in the incendiary fires, the brutal ravishing of delicate womanhood by untamed beasts upon whom slavery has fixed its impress, The braining of children against the father's dwellings and the nameless midnight horrors and atrocities which a revolt would be."[126]

Lest the readers think that Brown was some kind of maniac, the writer argued that he had made his raid in the northern section of the South because "the ferocity of the slaves further south could not have been checked," suggesting that Brown's true goal was to contain the emancipation of Blacks without threatening white supremacy.[127] The Anti-Slavery Society's report of the "John Brown Year" said his war was fought "as humanly as warfare can be" and specifically drew a contrast between Brown's and Turner's rebellions.[128]

Whites were not the only ones to express dismay at Brown's notions about Black mass action. Reverend James Newton Gloucester, for example, urged Brown not to have too much faith in the masses, "You speak in your letter of the people. I fear there is little to be done in the masses: The masses suffer from want of intelligence and it is difficult to reach them. . . . The colored people are impulsive—but they need sagacity—sagacity to distinguish the proper course."[129]

Just as important as the notion that Black rebellion was animalistic and savage was the perception of white Southerners as part of the national

family, despite their sinful practice of owning slaves. The abolitionists' greatest crime, as it was decried by others of the period, was their dis-Unionism, their incapacity to solve the slavery question in a manner that would take into account the rights and interests of both the South and the North. Garrison's burning of the constitution was the most dramatic example, along with John Brown's willingness to use force—not against racial outsiders in protection of the nation but against white American citizens. But, as Garrison and Brown saw it, to be in a union with slaveholders meant that the national identity itself was compromised and irreparably damaged by the anti-republican exclusion of Blacks from citizenship.

Garrison's opposition to the use of force made him appear unmanly and ridiculous to his contemporaries, even as Brown's enemies admired him *because* he had used violence. However, their admiration depended on the belief that Brown had gone to Harper's Ferry not to arm slaves, but to rescue them and thus *prevent* the inevitable slave insurrection. As the historian Bertram Brown-Wyatt noted, it was John Brown who "endowed anti-slavery with a virility that its long association with Sunday school ethics, missions to the heathens, and women's causes seemed to deny."[130] Nat Turner, no matter how virile he was, could not do this for them, but as long as Brown's ideology was separated from "slave rebellion," his use of force made him simply "a *man* in comparison to non-resistants," the one whose capacities of manhood enabled him to successfully lead Blacks to freedom. George Templeton Strong, no friend to abolition, said of Brown, "His simplicity and consistency, the absence of fuss, parade and bravado, the strength and cleanness of his letters, all indicate a strength of conviction one does not expect in an abolitionist."[131]

In contrast, those who tried to use the Harper's Ferry raid to fulfill its initial promise of Black heroism—Redpath, Osborne Perry Anderson, Frederick Douglass, and the Langston brothers of Ohio—all emphasized the military contributions of Brown's Black comrades in arms. Both white and Black members of the troop, Shields Green, John Cook, Andrew Hazlett, John A. Copeland, Aaron D. Stevens, and Barclay Coppoc, were hanged after Brown on December 16 and February 2, but neither they nor the men killed in the Harper's Ferry fight, including two of Brown's sons, nor Ben and Jim, two slaves who had joined the raid, joined Brown as heroes in a national fable. As Littlefield noted, Black abolitionists chafed at the erasure of Black men from the record of the Harper's Ferry raid, asking, "Were they not men?"[132] Just as what W. E. B. Du Bois called "The myth of Reconstruction" erased the role of Black soldiers and Black refugees in the Civil War to define Lincoln as the Great Emancipator, so Brown's

status as abolition's Great Man or abolition's ultimate fanatic erased Black agency in the militant abolition movement.

Osawatomie Brown: Western Hero   John Brown first became a nationally known figure through his involvement in the Kansas Border Wars in 1855–56. During the Border Wars, Brown oversaw the summary executions of five proslavery settlers, going to their homes in the dead of night and killing them on the spot in an event now known as the "Pottawatomie Massacre." While these actions made him popular with Republican Party members at the time (negative versions of the massacre did not emerge on a wide scale until Brown made headlines in Harper's Ferry), contemporary historians see them as the primary moral argument against Brown's heroism. Although many Free Soilers opposed Brown's abolitionism in Kansas, they praised his courage. Charles Robinson, for example, wrote Brown a "heartfelt thanks" for his "efficient and timely action against the invaders of our rights and the murderers of our citizens" shortly after the Pottawatomie killings—although Robinson later repudiated them.[133]

Later antislavery and Republican depictions of the Kansas civil war became a crucial element of Union identity.[134] In these tales, Brown was a champion not because he was an emancipator of Blacks, but because he represented Anglo-Saxon manhood, a force for order in the Wild West. Transforming the story of Brown in Kansas into a battle of political parties divided between the English and the Irish, the stories of Missouri's "border ruffians" (proslavery forces who rushed across the Kansas border to vote in the elections in Kansas) resembled contemporary nativist representations of Irish Catholic immigrants and Indians as "savages" or the "mob."[135] All three groups were defined as whiskey-swilling hordes not yet ready for citizenship. Mirroring accounts of urban politics, newspapers described the men from Missouri as "riff raff" and "scoundrels" who followed the whims of demagogic leaders. Gunja SenGupta describes how Free Soilers and abolitionists alike joined to "civilize the west" with their vision of a free republic.[136] The call for the use of "Beecher Bibles," the common slang for Sharps rifles, appeared openly in the *New York Tribune*.[137] Richard Slotkin's chapter on Brown as a western hero shows how the series of articles by William Phillips in the *New York Tribune* that later became the book *The Conquest of Kansas* portrayed Brown as a hero of the Wild West and transferred tropes of Indian war to this "white-on-white" terrain. Instead of depicting the "border ruffians" as simple scoundrels, Thomas Wentworth Higginson portrayed the free-state settlers as the

"Kossuths of Kanzas," while one *Tribune* article referred to the border ruffians in alignment with the "mailed hand of federal power raised to destroy."[138]

Following the Harper's Ferry raid, this portrait was adjusted. Kate Edwards Swayze's play "Osawatomie Brown," first performed in New York City's Bowery Theater in 1859, demonstrates how Puritan and western heroic ideals came together to make Brown a hero in Kansas, but how the advocacy for slave rebellion undermined his heroism in Virginia. Like many theatrical productions of that same era, Swayze's play included blackface characters as servants in the Brown's home, capering, eating cake, and engaging in sexual banter. Brown's heroic actions occurred in Kansas, where "border ruffians" were gathered in a "rude tavern or ranchero, drinking and gambling." In this part of the play, slavery is never mentioned as an issue. However, in this tavern, "Black Jim," a (white) foreigner and a border ruffian, kills Brown's son Frederick after he refuses to join in the sinning. On discovering the deed, Brown gets his entire family to swear revenge on the ruffians, and the Kansas border wars begin. During that scene, Brown is a hero, responsible for saving women from lustful attacks on their virtue by the evil Black Jim.

When the action in the play moves to the scene of Harper's Ferry, however, Brown's actions appear motivated out of fanaticism, not heroism. Swayze has Brown's Black servant Jeptha denounce him as a ringleader of rebellion, and the play announces that Brown has fallen from a "martyr" to "grovel among the lowest felons of the earth, driven mad by his son's death."[139] This representation of Brown's use of force as heroic in Kansas, but insane or criminal in Virginia, was only the most extreme of the "Free Soil" visions of the "mad old Brown," which typically displayed admiration for his use of violence against border ruffians and condemned the attack on Virginia as the result of personal revenge and unmanly passion. Vigilantism in the name of order was acceptable; revenge for a death in the family was understandable. But slave rebellion was insane: Such a call for mass action by a truly "undifferentiated" mass of slaves challenged the basic rules of American citizenship.

Brown's role in Kansas was recalled when he was on trial in 1859 and served to mitigate his representation as a simple abolitionist Jacobin. His Kansas story fit into an existing Wild West literary market. J. B. Jones, for example, added the book *Wild Southern Scenes: A Tale of Disunion and Border War* to his previous *Warpath and Wild Western Tales* shortly after Brown's trial in 1859. Just under the advertisement for the forthcom-

ing *Wild Southern Scenes* appeared the *Tribune*'s announcement of James Redpath's forthcoming biography of Brown.[140] Like Swayze's play, the Republican *New York Tribune*, in 1859, praised the efforts of border warriors in Kansas but found the raid on Harper's Ferry to be a "deplorable affair." Instead of defining the slave revolt as a republican exercise of freedom that was in keeping with Brown's politics, Free Soilers insisted that the Harper's Ferry raid was entirely personal, motivated by uncontrollable grief and anger over Brown's son's death in Kansas. Characterizations of his grief as a motivating factor in the raid on Harper's Ferry gave Brown an excuse for hating slaveowners as personal enemies without having to show him as an advocate of Black equality. Thus, the *Tribune* retained the possibility of admiring Brown as a purely free-soil figure rather than as an antislavery one, as Richard Slotkin points out, fitting him into the character of a frontiersman who "acts out of an immediate sense of grievances and persecution and usually with the aim of protecting his settlement from raiders or rescuing captive members of his family from ruffian hands."[141] Such representations preserved the possibility of Brown as a hero, if a flawed one, and erased the importance of slave self-activity to Brown's own goals.

John Brown: Puritan

Like the image of Brown as a western hero, the image of Brown as an old-school Puritan, a Calvinist, made particular sense in the political context of the 1850s, when Transcendentalist writers seeking an American hero found one in Brown. The Transcendentalists glorified the Puritan past, claiming it as an antidote to the cheapness of experience during the "market revolution."[142] In praise of Thomas Carlyle and Oliver Cromwell, for example, one New Englander wrote that "religion is serious, not second hand or ready made. . . . This world is a serious world and human life and business are serious matters."[143]

Comparing Brown with Cromwell helped define heroism itself as both otherwordly and part of an Anglo-Saxon tradition. Transcendentalists, who looked to the spirit as an answer for the problems of capitalism, found their hero in the figure of English revolutionary and scourge of the Irish. Cromwell went through a revival in America beginning in 1837—interestingly around the time of increased Irish Catholic migration.[144] Nine years before Thomas Carlyle's popular biography of Cromwell was published in

England, American Transcendentalists referred to Cromwell as the kind of Great Man of history who had been lost in the present age of commercial interest, faddish hysterical religion, and hollow speculation. Margaret Fuller remarked on Carlyle's influence in her review of his history of the French Revolution and numerous articles about Carlyle, Calvin, and the Puritans appeared in Transcendentalist publications.[145] In an 1842 essay in the *Dial* Magazine, Charles Lane argued that Cromwell stood for Puritan values that America had only so recently lost as part of its lifeblood when it surrendered itself to commercial capitalism.

Cromwell was a particularly good symbol for the possibilities of Anglo-Saxon free labor to achieve greatness in America. He inspired Lane because he came from the "artisan" class and was "able to climb to the top despite being in his education dissipated, his fortune mean, his dress slovenly, his speech disagreeable, his person coarse." Cromwell's fanaticism was an inspiration. "How deep must be that feeling," Lane wrote, "how sincere those convictions, how lively that indignation, which permit men having the Christian scriptures in one hand to take up the sword with the other."[146]

When Carlyle wrote of Cromwell in 1845, the Great Man's authority stemmed from scriptural devotion. For Carlyle, it was interaction with the divine that allowed a Great Man to spring past ordinary political debate, legality, and print culture. Among a "book ridden people," wrote Carlyle to Emerson, "the only hope of help . . . for this wretched generation of ours [is] new Cromwells and new Puritans."[147] Carlyle and the Transcendentalists found solace neither in the actions of the mob and the multitude nor in attacks on property, but in the spiritual transcendence of natural great men. Certainly, their racial and religious mysticism was antidemocratic. For Carlyle, the goal of all revolutions had not been the leveling of men, but the replacement of false rulers with true ones. "All this liberty and equality, electoral suffrages, independence and so forth we will take therefore to be a temporary phenomenon," he wrote.[148]

Carlyle's Puritan hero was anti-mass and antipolitical. The hero depended on an opposition between God and science, man and mass, speech and physical forcefulness; Cromwell was an inarticulate prophet whose "rude passionate voice . . . disregarded eloquence." He was driven by divine inspiration, not petty ambition, and would have been "content to plough the ground and read his Bible" had he not been called to serve out of moral need.[149]

When John Brown arrived on the scene, the Transcendentalists immediately portrayed him as a Cromwellian hero. Franklin Sanborn was among

the first to make a comparison between Brown and Cromwell in a lecture at his Concord School in Massachusetts in 1857. In the lecture, Sanborn defined Puritanism as the source of American democracy. It was through John Calvin that "the peasant and the prince met on the level of common belief and were treated with a certain impartiality."[150] In Brown, Sanborn announced, he had "recently met a person who so illustrates himself the Puritan of Cromwell's time that he seems to me worth describing as the type of chap which has almost wholly disappeared."[151]

Henry David Thoreau, an admirer of Carlyle and a friend of Sanborn's, also compared Brown to Cromwell in his address "A Plea for Captain Brown," the very first speech given in New England about Brown after his arrest in Virginia. Quoting Carlyle directly by commenting that Brown, like that great leader, disdained eloquence and would rather "plough his ground and read his bible" than enter the world of politics, Thoreau not only praised Brown but lampooned other abolitionists. Thoreau spoke little of pikes and slave revolt. Instead, he defended Brown as a counterexample to reform organizations, which he characterized as talk without action. This general attack on talk and writing and the conflation of action and "direct action" dismissed the efforts of abolitionist political organizing. Perhaps it was a symptom of what Ann C. Rose has described as the frustration of some Transcendentalists by the 1850s. When Emerson finally summed up Fuller as an "eloquent talker," he indicated what he "saw as the movement's failure to produce anything of lasting artistic or social value and instead only magazine literature, series of lectures, and short-lived utopias."[152] Thoreau not only supported Brown. He supported him as an exemplar of physical force in contrast to what he described as a flawed republic of talk and writing.

Like Carlyle describing Cromwell, Thoreau detached Brown from his historical context and attached him to an Anglo-descended world-historical destiny. Thoreau wrote that it was "no abolition lecture that converted" Brown and described Brown's years in abolitionist Ohio as a stint in the "great university of the West."[153] He also made Brown manlier by erasing his sentimental qualities: He was no Little Eva. When Brown and his wife cried before the execution, Thoreau wrote that it was "as if the rocks sweated."[154]

While Thoreau's disgust with the daily concerns of Boston's propertied classes was understandable, his representation of Brown had more to do with his own philosophy than with Brown himself. His attacks on abolitionism and deification of stern manliness were antidemocratic. Thoreau's effort to define Brown's influences as external to society has led to a

pervasive sense of Brown as an otherworldly, biblically driven individual that has been hard to shake.

This transcendental image of Brown as motivated mostly by religion has influenced the contemporary interpretation of him as a religious fanatic. The notion that Brown was ultimately motivated by religious ideas is probably the most dominant element of contemporary historiography. In their quest to explain John Brown's violence, most contemporary historians, like the Garrisonian abolitionists, find the use of force morally problematic, even indefensible, and in the quest for the cause of Brown's use of it, they read his writings in search of ideological symptoms or critical moral errors. For such interpreters, Brown's ideas become not just an explanation of his actions, but a cautionary tale about extreme ideology in general. The religious theories range from finding Brown's motivations in Calvinism, as Stephen Oates does, to antinomianism, as the more recent book by John Stauffer does.

Those who see Brown as an "antinomian" argue that he was able to justify his actions in Harper's Ferry because he believed that he was an "instrument of God." Scholars writing about Brown in the 1970s connected his disturbing use of violence to the revolutionary left. Today's historians are just as likely to compare the "antinomian" Brown to right-wing evangelical Protestant militants, as represented by the antiabortion terrorist Paul Hill. In each case, antinomianism as a way of thinking, rather than the context and complicated events of the time, is described as the reason for the use of political violence by everyone from Brown to Al-Qaeda. Scholarship from the 1970s and more recently describes Brown as an undemocratic political figure and emphasizes religion as a motivation. Oates's 1971 biography of Brown, *To Purge this Land with Blood*, which remains the most cited work in current accounts, attributes most of Brown's ideology to a particular reading of the Old Testament's Book of Judges.

Oates argues that Brown used force because he was a Calvinist who believed that he was acting on God's behalf. "His conviction that he was an agent of God, that a sovereign and wrathful Lord was working through him to punish sinful men, was an outgrowth of Calvinist faith," Oates asserts.[155] This reading of Brown as a monomaniacal Calvinist appears again in Richard Ellis's recent *The Dark Side of the Left*. Ellis, who relies heavily on Oates's biography, writes that Brown "took his inspiration from the remorseless, vengeful scriptures of the Old Testament" and suggests that Brown was one of abolition's many "charismatic leaders who disregarded institutional restraints . . . that are essential to ensure the

sort of limited and predictable government that is the foundation stone of liberal democracy."[156]

Bertram Wyatt Brown, expressing a more direct concern about current radicalism, compared the Weather Underground and Brown, finding antinomianism to be the shared psychology of both generations of antiracist revolutionaries.[157] John Stauffer has also defined Brown as an antinomian and compared him to Captain Ahab in his "monomaniacal pursuit of the white whale," leading his friends in the Radical Abolitionist Party to destruction the way Ahab bewitched the crew of the *Pequod*.[158]

A recent dissertation on Brown argues that leftists should not be surprised to find civil disobedience appropriated for use by the far right and argues that the concept of "higher law" was a form of antinomianism that could only bring on an endless cycle of anarchy and vengeance. Another historian referred to Brown's statements after his arrest as comparable to those of the accused during Watergate and theorized that Brown had lied and made denials because of a need to defend his "assaulted reputation and character."[159] Conservative and liberal scholars alike may compare Brown to terrorists in general—to militia members and Christian, right-wing militia activists.[160]

To be an "antinomian" is to claim that one has access to God's plan and can act outside the usually accepted moral rules of the society. Antinomianism was associated not only with German dissent and with Anne Hutchinson, who challenged New England's clergy, but also with the movement of the Levellers in the English Civil War, who made such statements as "all things are lawful for me" in a society where religious law actually played a role in the state. While it seems potentially dangerous, this antinomian claim to access God's plans, also made by Nat Turner, is the principal claim to authority for people who are excluded from the process of lawmaking and legal participation in any society in which religion plays a significant role in politics.[161] While it is commonsensical that placing oneself above the law, particularly when justifying the use of force, can lead to terrible consequences, the labeling of such resistance as by definition antidemocratic carries its own risks. Those who level such charges as the "antinomian heresy" against antislavery activists of the nineteenth century not only must wonder at taking sides with the church authorities against Anne Hutchison, but also should grapple with what it means to call for the rule of law in an era when slavery was officially legal. As such, attacks on Brown's violence rest on the continuing erasure of the fact that slavery was a reign of terror.

As William Lloyd Garrison and Brown both knew, for slaves in 1859, liberal democracy, despite its grounding in law, did not rest on the "consent of the governed" and represented a power that was neither limited nor predictable. For abolitionists who lived during the period of slavery, the violence done to slaves was an ongoing reality, not an abstract question. James L. Huston points out that attacks on Northern antislavery activists as "overwrought moralists driven by evangelical religion" rely on erasing the connection between the Southern institution of slavery and the motivations and behavior of abolitionists.[162] Louis De Caro, whose *Fire from the Midst of You* is the most sympathetic biography of Brown and the first since Du Bois's to follow up on Brown's connections to Blacks in the Underground Railroad, asserts that "even his nineteenth century opponents had a better understanding of his religious world view than do many biographers and scholars today."[163]

These accounts of Brown as an "antinomian" may also be the inheritance of the image of Brown as created by Thoreau and Emerson, whose accounts have been the most widely reread, although they were not the only people to memorialize Brown during his trial. Wendell Phillips, as an abolitionist activist, was closer to the events surrounding Brown than was Thoreau, and he offered an alternative vision of Brown in his eulogy. For Phillips, Brown's raid was not a response against democracy, but the fruition of "unbridled democracy." Instead of higher law, Brown showed that the law of the sidewalk was threatening slavery. "It seems to me," Phillips told his audience, "that the idea of our civilization is that men do not need any guardian . . . the best power this side of the ocean is the unfettered common sense of the masses." The "talk of the sidewalk today is the law of the land," he argued, and "law is nothing unless close behind it stands a warm public opinion."[164] Implying that Brown was a product of the masses rather than a force of divinity and comparing Brown's act to earlier rebellions against law that democrats had described as "spunky," Phillips challenged his audience to remember its own respect for the "rule of the bowie knife."

Arguing against the idea that true manhood was determined by an ability to go it alone, and thus making some of the claims that would later characterize militant defense campaigns for political prisoners, as will be clear in later chapters, Philips argued that American slaves could not revolt successfully in America without aid from those outside the South. Instead of making this observation into an argument for white superiority, Phillips pointed out that the Anglo-Saxons, in contrast to their own mythologies, had *not* won their own liberty but, rather, that serfdom had "crushed

out our manhood so thoroughly that we had not vigor left to redeem ourselves." The only race that ever redeemed itself, explained Phillips, was
that group in "Saint Domingo," who "with their own hands wrested chains
from their own bodies."[165] Mere mortals should have no shame in needing
help from elsewhere, and it made them nonetheless men. By challenging
independence in revolt as a standard of manhood without rejecting violence, Phillips in his speech—and Brown by his revolt—challenged the
underlying basis of white-supremacist attacks on slaves' manhood. Both
men, more than any other whites of their own era, made the argument
for the solidarity of the free and the enslaved as a moral obligation and
a political necessity and suggested that the need for aid from outside did
not disqualify Blacks from potential citizenship. This major challenge to
independence as an ideal was perhaps the most radical challenge to the
ideal of republican manhood during the abolitionist era.

Brown neither independently reached his conclusions, nor did he im-
pose ideals of complete independence on others to see their manhood.
He was quite a sentimental fellow. Although Brown, like many of his
contemporaries, saw the Bible as an instruction book for daily life, he
stood on the ground and took his inspiration from those around him.
As W.E.B. Du Bois and others have shown, among those influences were
Black radicals such as Thomas Thomas, who worked for Brown in Springfield at Perkins and Brown, and recalled Brown's early morning discussions of the slavery question with several fugitives. These men told him
personal stories about slavery that horrified him enough that he wrote letters home to his family about them. Brown sent Thomas Thomas to "look
up" Madison Washington, whose rebellion on the slave ship *Creole* had
so impressed him.[166] During those years in Springfield and North Elba,
Brown was surrounded by fugitive slaves whom he sought to help but
from whom he also learned.[167] When Thoreau made Brown into a Cromwellian hero, he detached Brown from these former slaves and from the
democratic aspects of his revolutionary vision, which involved handing
out pikes to an unknown group of slaves in the hope that they would rise
up in revolt against their masters and in the faith that they might do this
without the shedding of too much blood.

Instead, to promote his own philosophy of personal example and spiritual transcendence, Thoreau made Brown a Great Man of history, a man
above his time, rather than a man of his time. In doing so, Thoreau created
a "type" for American heroes. This model of the abstemious hero, imper-
vious to his surroundings, continues to shape not only Brown but also

heroes who mold themselves similarly, if unknowingly, in concert with the "anti-mob" ideals of the elite in the 1850s.

Brown at His Trial

Thoreau did not produce this heroic image alone. Brown's self-presentation also contributed. During his last days, and particularly on the day of his hanging, he acted out a role in facing execution quite similar to ones shown in the popular work of English nationalism, *Foxe's Book of Martyrs*, and as David Reynolds, who has also noticed the Transcendentalists' fixation on Cromwell, notes, Brown counted J. T. Headley's *Life of Cromwell* among his favorite books.[168] Making rebellion against the tyrannical Catholic church into a sacred act by drawing on representations of first-century Christian martyrs, John Foxe defined the first Church of England as a democratic rebellion against Spanish Catholic tyranny. A typical martyr from the book, Philpot, met his death with courage. Appearing before Catholic bishops, he stated, "Your idolatrous sacrament which you have found ye would fain defend; but you cannot and never shall. . . . God give you grace to repent your wicked doings; and let all men beware of your bloody church." At the grief of his servant, who sighed at seeing him before the stake, Philpot was the consoler: "I shall do well enough; thou shalt see me again." As he was readied for burning, he said: "I am ready; God grant me strength and a joyful resurrection." Noting that execution had been good enough for Jesus, Philpot said he would not "disdain to suffer at this stake" and wished his tormentors repent.[169]

In almost all of their communications from jail, Brown and his comrades strove for a similar representation of forgiving Christian courage in confrontation with a counterfeit Christianity. All of the men who died with Brown refused to acknowledge the authority of their persecutors, wished God's forgiveness on their enemies, and told their friends and families not to mourn, for they would all meet again in Heaven. Brown told his daughters not to worry at seeing him in jail, as Christ, too, had been a prisoner and was hanged as a felon.

In their letters to Brown's daughter Annie, all of the men mitigated their complaints and miseries. Hazlett wrote that he was "cheerful and happy, patiently waiting the hour of my departure," and gladly anticipated "what joy there must be when meeting with friends in the other world."[170] Stevens, also writing to Annie, similarly remarked that "it is always best not to give up to sorrow and sadness. I am quite cheerful and happy, never felt

better in my life. We may never meet again, but we will meet in the spirit land."[171] In his words from prison, which were reprinted in the *Anglo-African*, John A. Copeland, a freeborn Black Methodist and Oberlin College student, reported that he was happy to be dying in a great cause and doing honor for his race, and he advised his parents not to mourn.[172]

In court, Brown took the position of the true republican hero. He did not seek to be rescued, and even rejected a proposal for a jail break from his allies in the North.[173] He denounced the authority of the court, saying:

> If a fair trial is to be allowed us, there are mitigating circumstances, that I would urge in our favor. But, if we are to be forced with a mere form—a trial for execution—you might spare yourselves that trouble. I am ready for my fate. I do not ask for a trial. I beg for no mockery of a trial—no insult— nothing but that which conscience gives or cowardice would drive you to practise. I ask again to be excused from the mockery of a trial. I do not know what the special design of this examination is. I do not know what is to be the benefit of it to the Commonwealth. I have now little further to ask, other than that I may be not foolishly insulted, only as cowardly barbarians insult those who fall into their power.[174]

When he was sentenced to death, he again defied the court's moral authority but accepted his coming execution just as earlier martyrs had: "Now, if it is deemed necessary that I should forfeit my life for the further-ance of the ends of justice, and mingle my blood further with the blood of my children, and with the blood of millions in this slave country whose rights are disregarded by wicked, cruel, and unjust enactments—I sub-mit: so let it be done."[175] Stoic behavior at the moment of execution was so critical in the proof of manliness that newspapers went out of their way to ridicule the behavior of the Black prisoners as they marched to the scaf-fold. While the march of Brown and his white comrades was described even in Southern newspapers as an example of manliness, the Black mem-bers of the guerrilla band were described as "downcast." The Republican *New York Tribune* also reported that the Black men "wore none of that calm, cheerful spirit evinced by Brown under similar circumstances."[176] When Virginia's Governor Wise described Brown and his comrades as "cool, collected and indomitable," he made an exception for "the free Ne-groes with him."[177]

Black abolitionists and some whites did their best to redeem the reputa-tions of Green and Copeland from the blight cast on them by those who were able to witness the executions. Reporting on the funeral of Cope-land, which was attended by three thousand people at Oberlin, the *Weekly*

Anglo-African reported that "no less God inspired him to nobly represent a race and how worthily did he represent them."[178] Given the importance of armed resistance as proof of manhood in the early republic, Black memorialists did not so much focus on Brown's actions as they looked for proof of Black involvement in the raid. The Harper's Ferry raid was a test not of white abolitionism's manhood after, but as a test of Black manhood, and Southern detractors had proclaimed it as proof of the slaves' contentment. Brown's African American comrades-in-arms, Dangerfield Newby, Shields Green, John Copeland, Lewis Leary, and Osborne Perry Anderson, who were often ignored or maligned in white newspapers' accounts of the events at Harper's Ferry, were at the heart of Black memorials of the raid. The *Anglo-African* admonished its readers to, "beside the captain's name serene with Leary, Stephens, Copeland, Green, Inscribe upon your banner's sheen."[179] Anderson, the one Black man who survived, made sure to describe the heroism of Black men who had participated. He also rejected the "Puritan" theory of Brown's origins and placed him in the Black abolitionist tradition of biblical interpretation that embraced slave rebels of all races.

Although free Blacks were not able to travel southward to visit Brown in prison, African American church members continued to make chivalric pledges to uphold Brown's memory and the memory of his compatriots and to support his family financially immediately after the execution. Black activists saw Brown in particular as a man who should be looked on with awe and even gratitude because he was the first "disinterested martyr"[180] in the antislavery movement who had died for Black freedom as if defending his own. By defending Brown and providing financial support for his widow, Black churches reversed the relationship of paternalism that appeared in many whites' descriptions of Brown's raid. William Wells Brown declared that "colored patriots" will "teach our children to revere his name," and a group of Black women set up a subscription service to fund Brown's widow and surviving children. Samuel Jackson of Ohio, despairing that he could not travel south, wrote to Lydia Marie Child declaring that, if he could, he and other colored men would "go all the way on foot to Charlestown and pick a hole through the jail if permitted and take up that old man Brown, and carry him on our shoulders through the glittering bayonets, and past the troops of the national guard, not firing or fearing a leaden ball."[181]

Though such a procession never formed, when Brown's body was transported for burial, the *Liberator* reported that "a great crowd of colored people follow[ed] Brown's casket on its way to Philadelphia,"[182] and in

Haiti, citizens wore mourning badges for three days in Brown's honor.[183] For longer than anyone else, Black communities across America upheld Brown's memory with "John Brown Pageants," "John Brown Days," and pilgrimages to the Brown gravesite in North Elba. These memorials remained contained within the Black community.[184]

Brown as National Hero: The Biographies

During the Civil War, Brown became a symbol of the Union—most famously, in the Union Army's marching song "John Brown's Body" and its transformation into the "Battle Hymn of the Republic" by Julia Ward Howe. The first biography about Brown was an attempt to set the record straight on his true goals. Brown's family chose James Redpath, the *Tribune* reporter, over Lydia Marie Child.[185] Redpath's biography was distinguished by its attempt to describe Black heroism and its rejection of the Republican Party's claims to Brown. Redpath was the only white writer of the time who endorsed Brown's actions not as an attempt to rescue slaves, but to incite rebellion and slaves' self-defense in the South. Like Brown and Douglass, Redpath believed that a "forcible separation of the connection of master and slave was necessary to educate the Blacks for self government."[186] Traveling in the South and interviewing slaves while under the English nationalist pseudonym of "John Bull Jr.," Redpath concluded that "Negroes have all the fierce passions of a white man" and uttered this proclamation: "Let races be swept from the face of the earth. Let nations be dismembered. Let dynasties be dethroned, let laws and governments be cast out and trodden under the feet of men."[187]

Although Redpath saw slaves as men, he still created Brown as an American national hero, whose greatness came from his genetic inheritance. The book began with an assertion of Brown's Mayflower lineage.[188] Redpath argued that the love of freedom was inherited through family bloodlines, of which Brown's ancestors, killed in the American Revolution, were evidence. Redpath criticized less radical abolitionists by arguing that Brown's insistence that Negroes were men had set him apart from other abolitionists, who were "alarmed and disgusted" at his suggestions of Negro equality.[189]

Redpath's assertion of Brown's alliances with Blacks remained unique among white writers. Brown's manhood, rather than African manhood, became the subject in most depictions of the "old man." A series of post-Reconstruction-era hagiographies, just as Thoreau's and Emerson's

essays and Swayze's play had, ensconced Brown in a national heroic tradition that combined western battle, Anglo-Saxon lineage, and New England Calvinism and ignored his commitment to African American agency.

The first of these was written by another of Brown's funders, Franklin Sanborn. Sanborn's biography of Brown carried with it the transformations of national ideology in the postwar years toward a vision of the need for savage warfare between races and professional leadership in all elements of society. Sanborn entered explicitly into the new scientific racism of the era and referred to the genealogy of Brown's "Saxon sense," which, he argued, the old man had received as a biological inheritance from a long line of English and Dutch ancestors. Brown's racial genealogy was backed by a political ideology, but, wrote Sanborn, Brown was not a "Garrisonian" or a Jacobin but a "Saxon follower of Calvin and Augustine." As Southerners brought up the evidence of Brown's killing of proslavery settlers at Pottawatomie Creek in a midnight raid during the Kansas Border Wars, his defenders justified his acts not by arguing that these settlers had owned slaves and violated the free-speech rights of abolitionists in Kansas, but by comparing the "border ruffians" to various savages of the time. Declaring that because Brown's troop was "elite" like Garibaldi's and did not have Black officers, Sanborn described the raid as paternalistic. Border ruffians were like immigrants, Indians, and drunken mobs, and the story of their role in the fight over Kansas displaced the Republican critique of Southern planters and the "slave power" with an attack on "crackers," or working-class whites, as the primary perpetrators of racism, just in time for the alliance of Northern and Southern white capital during the end of Reconstruction. In this account, as in others, Brown's heroic character was maintained by distancing him not from violence but from the "mob."

Brown as the Great American Hero The Brown legend we hear most often today is as much part of the American mythology of the Great Man and mid-nineteenth-century mass culture as is Davy Crockett, to whom Brown was once compared by James Newton Gloucester.[190] In John Brown, the New England Transcendentalists, in the thrall of German and English romanticism, found a way to connect antislavery radicalism, which was often described as a "dis-unionist" and anti-American form of religious hysteria or fanaticism, to ideals of manly action in their effort to create an antislavery version of American nationalism. Defending Brown became a way to defend the manly identities of those whites who supported the abolitionist cause. As he was associated with those three great signifiers of American nationalism—

Puritanism, Anglo-Saxon ancestry, and Manifest Destiny—and dissociated from both feminine sentimentality and Black insurrectionism, Brown became a man above the mob, a romantic individualist hero. The Brown legend became part of the popular understanding of both the Civil War and Reconstruction as he helped bring whites into a central position in the story of emancipation from slavery and turned abolitionism into a story of Anglo-American nationalism. In this tale, Brown was America's Cromwell, to whom Black America owed an unpayable debt. This myth of Brown was part of what Du Bois calls the "Myth of Reconstruction," and it was Du Bois's still mostly underrated biography that used Brown as an entry point to his own alternative history of Black agency and heroism turning the tide of the Civil War.

By the end of the century, Brown was canonized in a series of biographies, poems, plays, and children's books that replaced his close connections to Black radicalism with celebratory stories of Anglo-Saxon blood and divine inspiration. Such literature led the African American newspaper editor T. Thomas Fortune to write that Black Americans would do better to revere Nat Turner than Brown, whose "memory is part of the history of government . . . embalmed in a thousand songs and stories."[191] The replacement of Black influence with divine inspiration and Calvinist orthodoxy, understood as genetically inherited Anglo-Saxon traits, along with the description of Brown's motives as disinterested chivalric action on behalf of victims, constructed Brown's acts as heroic rather than mad. Later, when socialists revered him, they did so to connect themselves to an Anglo-Saxon past. They noted always Brown's manhood, as Eugene Debs described it in 1907: "His calmness upon the gallows was awe-inspiring, his exaltation supreme."[192] However, the abolitionist nationalism of the 1860s did not survive Reconstruction, and to make this man who had promoted slave rebellion into an American national hero was not easy, and it did not last. By the 1930s, Brown's soul was not marching on in national legend; he had been kicked off the heroic pedestal, and, according to the most recent survey of literature on him by Merrill Peterson, "It is clear that Brown will never again knock at the door of the American pantheon."[193] If that is so, it is because many whites still refuse to see what Douglass, Du Bois, and, finally, Malcolm X would when they looked at the old man: someone who was exceptional not because he used violence, but because he believed the best role that a white man could play was to aid a Black man to stand up for himself.

As the nation emerged from the Civil War, mass action would again threaten when industrial workers rebelled against low wages in the Great

Railroad Strike of 1877 and rose up in a general strike for the eight-hour day in 1886. With that action, the left would gain eight martyrs whose self-presentation, while drawing on the story of John Brown, also challenged the Republican heroic ideal with a glorified representation of mass action.

2

Haymarket

If you are men, if you are the sons of your grandsires who have
shed their blood to free you, then you will rise in your might,
Hercules, and destroy the hideous monster that seeks to destroy
you. AUGUST SPIES

The true anarchist labors not, he drinks beer and wears long
hair. *New York World* (November 14, 1887)

If John Brown's legend followed the tropes of the Great Man, the defense
campaign waged in Chicago for eight anarchists who were accused of
conspiring with an unknown man to throw a bomb at a crowd of charging police on May 4, 1886, created a new type of American heroism.[1] The
defense and memorial campaigns for the Haymarket Martyrs introduced
the concept of the executed men as fallen heroes in the class war and argued that, rather than allowing them to be sacrificed, it was both the duty
and the ultimate destiny of the passionate masses to save them. In making
the hero's salvation into the responsibility of the masses, the anarchists of
Chicago went against the notion of martyrdom as a necessity for heroism
and reversed the roles of the crowd and the "Great Man."

At the time of their sentencing, the Haymarket anarchists—George
Engel, Samuel Fielden, Adolph Fischer, Louis Lingg, Oscar Neebe, Albert
Parsons, Michael Schwab, and August Spies—predicted that an uprising
would follow their executions, and Dyer Lum, one of their closest allies,
spoke of their deaths as the "dawn of a new era." In what would become
one of the most quoted passages in U.S. radical history,[2] Spies addressed
the court:

If you think that by hanging us, you can stamp out the labor movement—
the movement from which the downtrodden millions, the millions who
toil and live in want and misery—the wage slaves—expect salvation—

if this is your opinion, then hang us! Here you will tread upon a spark, but there, and there, and behind you and in front of you, and everywhere, flames will blaze up. It is a subterranean fire. You cannot put it out. THE GROUND IS ON FIRE upon which you stand. You can't understand it. You don't believe in magical arts, as your grandfathers did, who burned witches at the stake, but you do believe in conspiracies; you believe that all these occurrences of late are the work of conspirators![3]

Of course, Spies was making the argument that revolutions were the product of social conditions, not the acts of conspirators. This was a point he made often, but this particular image of the revolution as a "subterranean fire" surrounding the feet of the bourgeoisie and beyond their control lent a more mystical and ancient power to the bodies of labor's martyrs. With this pronouncement, Spies brought an ancient popular heroic tradition into the culture of early American socialism to challenge the impermeable body of the Republican hero. In his book on medieval popular folktales, Mikhail Bakhtin writes, "Death, the dead body, blood as the seed buried in the earth, rising for another life—this is one of the oldest and most widespread themes [in popular folklore]." This death–birth relation is an important mark of the unity between what Bakhtin calls the popular folktale's "grotesque body" and the world, as every characterization of the grotesque body emphasizes its orifices and insides to disrupt the boundaries between the self and its surroundings. When the Chicago anarchists talked about the future that would follow their deaths, they spoke of their own deaths as the seed of a great uprising, and their supporters continued to pronounce this prediction for years after their executions in gatherings at the graveside.[4] With this metaphor, the anarchists had brought into contemporary American political life not a displaced notion from established Christianity but, rather, the ghost of an ancient folk story: "The events of the grotesque sphere are always developed on the boundary dividing one body from the other, and as it were, their points of intersection. One body offers its death, the other its birth, but they are merged in a two-bodied image."[5] Here was the "many-headed hydra" that the bourgeoisie feared and loathed, but in this story, the hydra became the hero. When the anarchist August Reinsdorf pronounced, in a German court, "If I had ten heads, I would sacrifice them all!" what other image could have come to mind?[6]

There were precedents for mass defense actions for people deemed political prisoners prior to the Haymarket campaign. Michel Foucault notes the importance of the "disturbance around the scaffold" during which

"criminals were transformed into heroes" to popular consciousness in France, and of the relationship of these disturbances to a shift in Europe from public execution to the regime of the prison. Peter Linebaugh has described the heroic representation of the escape artist extraordinaire Jack Shepherd, as well as the figures of Dick Turpin and other heroes who fell among London's hanged in the eighteenth century. These men were held dear by those close to and far from them, as seen in the attempts of relatives of hanged prisoners to get their loved ones' bodies home, by the powers attributed to their relics in popular folklore, and by the profusion of popular ballads celebrating their deeds.[7] During the English Civil War, protest against the court and efforts to overturn its rulings were critical to the political development of Leveller consciousness. The supporters of the Leveller John Lilburne rioted outside the prison where he was kept in the 1630s on the brink of the war, and in 1642 his wife petitioned the House of Commons, ultimately winning a reprieve because of her repeated visits to the Royalist Parliament. When Oliver Cromwell sent Lilburne to trial for treason in 1649, his arguments in self-defense convinced the jury to acquit him.[8] Such practices continued in the eighteenth century and appeared in America, as well, where Paul Gilje notes a number of mass actions to release prisoners from jail.[9]

The rescues of fugitive slaves of the 1850s also qualify as mass defense campaigns. The vigilance groups that rushed into the courtrooms to "spirit away" prisoners took mass defense literally, and these extralegal defense actions led in turn to legal appearances. When they went on trial, the abolitionist rescuers' supporters filled the courtrooms, and they hired politicians to be their lawyers. Charles H. Langston, John Brown, and others all used the courtroom as a political platform during their trials and defied the law in the name of divine law. Despite this proud history, most Americans were not whistling the tune of "John Brown's Body" in remembrance of that populist folk hero by the 1880s. Rather, one of Brown's old enemies from the Kansas wars came to national prominence as a "Robin Hood" against the railroads, and Americans read about and sang the song of the outlaw legend Jesse James, a Confederate counterrevolutionary who sought legitimacy as a popular symbol by associating himself with the old British folk heroes, even when he dressed in a Klansman's robe.[10] The model of the hero against the law and for the common man crosses times, nations, and even ideologies.

What made the Haymarket defense campaign of 1886–87 unique was the way that the old heroic tradition of the man on trial before an unjust court interacted with the burgeoning modern socialist movement and

the new spirit of unionism, with its "distinctive working-class subjectivity" created in America's first industrial union, the Knights of Labor.[11] That organization's slogan, "An Injury to One Is an Injury to All," took on a special meaning during the trial and execution of the most famous popular labor leaders in Chicago following the incident of the bomb throwing in Chicago's Haymarket Square. Members of the mostly moderate Knights of Labor, as well as of the International Working People's Association (IWPA), a radical split from the Socialist Labor Party that was loosely affiliated with members of the "Black International" headed by Mikhail Bakunin in London, Chicago's anarchists challenged capitalism not only in material terms, but also in moral ones.[12] Capitalism's notion of the self was all wrong, they suggested in their newspapers, and instead they celebrated the very unbounded "mob" that had been such a problem for some of the most devout abolitionists, who maintained a Mazzinian concept of revolution. The Chicago social revolutionaries called for the "coming storm," the uncontrollable fire, and the irresistible flood of mass action, and ushered a new hero onto the scene.

Not only did the Chicago anarchists literally mix their critiques of the state with popular folkloric imagery, but they did so in more modern terms. In a society that was increasingly nativistic, despite its dependence on immigrant labor, they took on a cosmopolitan internationalist identity; in a society in the midst of police professionalization, prison reform, and frightening tales of urban criminals, they mocked bourgeois law and morality and questioned the division between the honest worker and the tramp.

They celebrated some of the things that most horrified the American bourgeoisie: the French Revolution and the Paris Commune, and they called dynamite a great equalizing weapon. They also invoked the old republican opposition to royalist courts, most alive in American nationalist memory in the attacks on the pre-Revolutionary British law and the abolitionists' attacks on "the slave power." However, they went beyond republicanism to argue that the entire foundation of the American government, as exemplified in the courts and the "rule of law," was merely a sham to be manipulated by the wealthy. Like Karl Marx, they argued that the state was a tool of the ruling class, and they said that their own deaths were the illustration.[13] Their deaths, if nothing else, should prove that the early republic's belief in equal justice through equal suffrage could not survive the industrial capitalist order.

The anarchists' main strategies at their trial could not have surprised anyone familiar with their ideas about American law, police, and the criminal-justice system. These ideas appeared in the IWPA's newspapers

the *Alarm* and *Die Arbeiter Zeitung*, which responded to the impact of big business on the American republic in the form of Pinkertons, police, and prisons.

Context

By the end of the Civil War, American industries had become both more sophisticated and more concentrated. Corporations grew in size and in importance, dramatically affecting Americans from the streets and shops to the courts. Industries recruited immigrants to fill their factories, and by the 1880s, 75 percent of the industrial workforce was either foreign-born, first-generation American, or African American.[14] Between the time of the Great Railroad Strike of 1877 and the beginning of the twentieth century, big business often won the class war in the courts, defining which forms of worker action were acceptable, whether this meant outlawing sympathy strikes, boycotts, and workingmen's militias, overturning local and state laws such as Illinois' eight-hour rule, or using injunctions to stop job actions in their tracks. Beginning with the Slaughter-House Cases in 1873, the Supreme Court interpreted the Fourteenth Amendment to mean that no state law could interrupt freedom of contract between a worker and his employer.[15]

When businesses pushed in one direction, workers resisted, and the 1870s and 1880s saw waves of violent strikes. Because most newspapers were also in the hands of the wealthy, their response to worker action was generally negative. European class conflict worried the American bourgeoisie. When the Paris Commune rose in 1871, some American Southerners saw it through the frame of the ongoing Reconstruction and pronounced the French as incapable of handling liberty as the "Negro slaves." Like the freedmen, one Southerner argued, the communards "interpret it as license and all manner of idleness and wantonness and freedom to insult all that is good and worthy of distinction."[16] While some Americans celebrated the communards as exemplars of republican manhood,[17] the vast majority of the reports in American papers were negative. Northerners compared them to the disloyal, treasonous South, and Southerners compared them to freed blacks. In the aftermath of Reconstruction, the American Bourbons had won the ideological battle. In 1877, workers and citizens together confronted the hated railroad corporations, and the fear of an American commune grew. Some even suggested that the Great Fire in Chicago was the fault of the working class.[18]

Thus, both the Civil War itself and the growth of American industry worked together to undermine the traditional American view of (white) violence as a characteristic of manliness and politics "out of doors" as a virtuous practice. As industrial society was increasingly incapable of containing or managing "tumultuous politics" of the antebellum type, and slaves were emancipated, the old bogey of insurrection appeared in the popular media. Realism replaced romanticism as the aesthetic mode. In his novel of the same era, *Billy Budd*, Herman Melville seemed to comment on the switch from romance to realism, as the handsome, stuttering sailor Billy Budd, a natural-born romantic hero, met the stern reality of Captain Vere on the ship *Bellipotent*. Eerily, Melville describes the tale's hero, who says "farewell to the Rights of Man" and consents to his own hanging, killing republicanism itself to save the republic.[19] Although radicals saw the Russian nihilists and the Paris communards as brothers, the bourgeoisie no longer admired foreign rebels as they had Kossuth. As one newspaper writer expressed it after the railroad strikes, "There is too much freedom in this country rather than too little."[20]

W. E. B. Du Bois lamented in his masterwork *Black Reconstruction* that the radical republican vision of the abolitionists glimmered for a moment and then was lost with the betrayal of Reconstruction by the alliance of Northern and Southern capital. With the rejection of Black freedom as railroads consolidated and the nation turned a blind eye to the forces of white terror that attacked Southern Black voters, "white men" suffered, as well. While fraud and terrorism replaced Southern republican governments with white "home rule," the national media blamed strikes and unrest in the North on the cultural idiosyncrasies of immigrants. Forgetting the rowdy nativist crowds of the 1840s and 1850s, the leading thinkers of the 1880s now argued that rebellion and riot were European and not part of the American tradition. As the *Atlantic Monthly* put in 1886, "If we are to avoid the necessity of putting down anarchist riots, we must see to it that the dissemination of Anarchist doctrine is prevented. . . . The anarchists are not to be regarded as fair material for citizenship. . . . They come from the old world's revolutionary muckheap and all their instincts and tendencies are aggressive, subversive and destructive."[21]

The national media refused to define strikes or workers' complaints as legitimate protests against injustice and instead described the labor movement as selfish, criminal, or lazy—or all three. Representations of immigrant criminals as threats to social stability drew little distinction between strikes and crime, and the largely immigrant, urban labor movement became the new "canaille." According to Paul Boyer, "Melodramatic tales of urban crime became increasingly popular after 1880," and the stories depicted the city as "reeking of blood and violence."[22] Not even Northerners considered John Brown a symbol of American manhood anymore. They compared him instead to Russian terrorists.[23]

While fear of working-class uprisings grew, traditional republican fears of excessive police power diminished. By 1885, the year before the famous "riot" in Haymarket Square, the nation was in the midst of a crime panic, as the number of arrests went from 32,901 in 1870 to 59,258 in 1880 and increased again each year. Police forces increased in size and "professionalized" to deal with the social problems of poverty and organized labor, despite some old republicans' fears of despotism. Regardless of the hopes of prison reformers to create institutions of rehabilitation and therapy, prisons in the post–Civil War era were characterized by overcrowding and brutality.[24] In Chicago, according to Bruce Nelson, the public police force grew from 473 men in 1880 to 637 men in 1884 and had increased to 1,000 men by 1886, the year of the Haymarket incident, despite stressed city finances. By 1890, the force had nearly doubled in size, to 1,870.[25]

The influx of new immigrants into the country's prisons, where they quickly became the dominant population, was accompanied by a remarkable change in the attitude of middle-class prison reformers, some of whom, like John Brown's old pal Franklin Sanborn, were old abolitionists. Although the National Prison Association (NPA) began in the 1870s as a Quaker reform organization dedicated to eliminating harsh corporal punishments and viewing prisoners humanely, by the mid-1880s, when unemployment wracked the country and workers struck for the eight-hour day, criminals were described by prison professionals as "pirates on the high seas" and "Commanches." Laws similar to those for controlling recently freed slaves appeared in the North during economic crises. In 1877, Chicago passed an anti-vagrancy law that made unemployment nearly illegal. It was "broad enough to cover pretty much all varieties of the dangerous and vicious."[26] Tramps, unemployed men who traveled the country looking for work, were outlawed and described as a "menace to farmers, robbing and plundering the premises, outraging the women and children."[27]

The group of wardens and sociologists who attended NPA meetings in the 1870s and 1880s, whose penal reforms dominated prison administration until the 1960s, blamed the increasing number of youth in prison on the labor movement's successful campaign against child labor. Unions, the "great evil of our time," they argued, encouraged idleness and thwarted individual autonomy and advancement by workers.[28] The reformers looked for ways to influence prisoners with proper attitudes toward work by developing contract labor projects, claiming that idleness was the product of a character disorder. One prison warden speculated that "unwillingness to make a living by manual labor is the chief cause of crime."[29] As a means of therapy, reformers suggested, "you must first beget in the prisoner a love of work and then you must furnish him while in the prison with opportunities of work."[30]

Manliness and wage work had come together in the free-labor ideal in antebellum racial formation, and slaves were imagined as living a life of leisure on the "pastoral" plantation.[31] In post–Reconstruction America, criminals and paupers on relief represented those who had failed as men because they were too lazy or arrogant to work. Instead of hating slaves for their luxurious lifestyles, Americans could now look with a mixture of envy and contempt on the "criminal classes"—those too lazy to do honest work. Again, the simultaneously attractive and repugnant figure of leisure was characterized by racial difference, whether he was a rural Black "jumping Jim Crow" or a recent European immigrant dwelling in the lower depths, swilling beer and talking revolution.

Prison professionals theorized new methods of discipline, and the mass-circulation media helped to popularize the new sciences of criminology and penology whose definitions of racially deficient urban malcontents blamed poverty and social conflict on the deranged personality structures of the poor. Tramps, vagrants, drunks, brigands, strikers, and anarchists mingled together in international social-psychology texts as well as in popular fiction during the 1870s and 1880s. As immigrants occupied a tenuous racial status, the characterization of the mob remained tinged by race. When not combated by working-class activists, it remained a powerful weapon against the "European" socialists even among the working class. As Du Bois had argued, the contempt for the work of Blacks had led to a general "animus against all unskilled labor" in parts of the labor movement. Anti-mob sentiments bolstered the turn toward craft-unionism and reliance on arbitration. For example, the St. Louis General Strikers' executive committee in 1877 agreed to terms set by the anti-labor business leaders of the town at least partly out of fear of a multiracial rank-and-file upsurge, going so far as to cancel strike-support parades.[32]

The similarity of anti-immigrant anarchist and anti-Black stereotypes reflects their common source in republican conceptions of the undeserving poor. As Edmund Morgan argued, stereotypes directed at African slaves originated in stereotypes of Irish and English paupers. Many of the distinctions between the European lumpen proletariat, or "mob," and the

mythical American honest workers were the same ones that had led to the definitions of "Blackness" and "whiteness." In the seventeenth century,

> according to the men who wrestled with the problem of England's poor, half the English population consisted of wage earners and all of them would rather drink than eat and rather starve than work. Worse than the wage earners were those who had never learned any trade but lived by begging and stealing. . . . The English poor were "vicious, idle, dissolute." They were addicted to "laziness, drunkenness, debauches and every kind of vice . . . to mutinous and indecent discourse."[33]

The English had suggested "some form of involuntary servitude" was the best means for controlling these urban populations, who expressed their antisocial behavior and lack of self-control alternatively through individual crime and collective "vices" such as strikes. In Europe, the state created workhouses, or "houses of correction," to put beggars to work. Morgan writes, "Imprisonment became the mode of extracting work from the criminal, the insane, and the poor alike. . . . Work was the proper cure for all and could best be administered by incarceration."[34]

These stereotypes of the urban poor were directed with vigor at immigrant workers in the United States during the post-Reconstruction era, particularly those from eastern Europe and southern Europe, who were also seen as racially different from Anglo-Saxons during the early twentieth century.[35] However, with the rise of the United States as an imperial power, Americans came to see themselves as part of a family of civilized nations; wealthy Americans celebrated Italian and German high culture but attacked Italian and German immigrant workers as the rabble. By the time of the Haymarket riot, Germans were definitively white, upstanding members of the Republican and Democratic parties—indeed, by the end of the century, the "Teutonic" race would compete with the Saxon in American theories of racial superiority.

If the anarchists were bad, the police were good. Not only in fact, but also in fiction, police action replaced the republican crowd as the ultimate defender of American ideals. When urban police departments were characterized as too close to workers, Alan Pinkerton's detective agency moved from its specialty in the labor-spying field to lead the movement for national police reform.[36] In truly "magical narratives" that brought together opposing ideas to resolve ideological contradictions, mass-media sources depicted police in a pseudo-populist vein. They became the hardest workers of all, defending unorganized workers against their "real" enemies: the tyrannical and bloodthirsty unions.[37] Described in Michael Denning's

Mechanic Accents, the stories of the Molly Maguires, "The Terror of the Coal Mine," suggested that radical union organizers were in league with the bosses and that the honest worker's real allies were the cops.[38]

Anarchist Tales

While capitalists developed their morality tales, popular writers in Europe and the United States offered a counter-melodrama. Albert Parsons's *Alarm* and August Spies's *Arbeiter Zeitung*, both anarchist newspapers, were full of references to popular and "high" literature and they used both to inform their own analysis of society. Victor Hugo's *Les Miserables*, with its cruel police and suffering poor, was a special favorite in the *Alarm*. The anarchists named the poor "*les miserables*," and following in Hugo's tradition, described all the men in prison as men like themselves who had fallen into misfortune.[39] While Hugo's portraits of the poor rarely depicted anyone working,[40] the anarchists' versions of Chicago's "miserables" emphasized the relationship between the unemployed and the workers, rejecting the notion that the two were in separate categories and thus challenging one of the fundamental elements of bourgeois ideology. Throughout the 1880s, both the *Alarm* and the *Arbeiter Zeitung* remarked on the media's characterization of the poor. In popular tracts, common vices or misfortunes became crimes and signs of deep character flaws. The anarchist press commented explicitly on the social construction of the poor's immorality, even as the change in attitude happened before their eyes.

"We used to be just tramps," one writer commented, "People looking for work, but now since 1873, the capitalists label tramps vagabond, idler, thief, loafer."[41] The *Alarm* contested the view that people chose to "loaf" and described unemployment as an "enforced idleness" brought on by the irregularities of capital and its need for surplus labor. This enforced idleness and accompanying poverty, and nothing else, anarchists argued, caused crime. If crime was caused by poverty, its solution was socialism, not law and order. In response to the growth of the police force in 1884, the anarchists observed, "Anticipating that the miseries of the working-class from enforced idleness will drive many of them into an attack upon the divine right of property the privileged class are crying aloud for an increase of the police force of the city."

Disputing the image of police as defenders of freedom, they argued that such measures did not bode well. "People will learn," the writer explained, that when the winter sets in, "law and order" will mean the "club and the

revolver."[42] In denying the middle-class reformers' views of tramps as a unique class, the *Alarm* carried a number of maudlin stories describing unjustly arrested and imprisoned tramps who, they argued, were driven to crime, drugs, and drink by poverty, hunger, and cold.

The IWPA members attempted, at a time when drunks were so often represented as villains, to portray drug users and alcoholics as society's victims who came from the ranks of the working class. One writer for the *Alarm* noted that a woman who had drifted into a passive death from an overdose of laudanum had died of "poverty and despair."[43] The anarchists argued that crime was created by the criminal-justice system, which outlawed poverty and, by fining and imprisoning the poor, drove them into ever more desperate circumstances. Under the headline "Who Is Guilty?" they asked whether it was the man whose empty belly made him get drunk without meaning to or the makers of the law and the institution of wage slavery who were to blame for the fact that he went to prison because he could not pay the fine he received after getting caught drunk in public.[44] Proclaiming "every worker is a tramp in embryo," the anarchists argued that tramps were the result of the whim of the boss, and the *Alarm* cautioned, "The day your boss can discharge you, you will be a tramp."[45] At the same time that sociologists developed elaborate systems of classification, and newspapers contrasted honest workers with criminals, the anarchists' forcefully depicted the fundamental connection of unemployment to capitalism and disputed the idea that there was such a thing as a separate "criminal" class.

Because they viewed tramps as the products of capitalism, they saw prisons that way, too. "It is a lie to say that a person is punished for his own good," wrote one contributor to the *Alarm*. "He is punished for the sole purpose of sustaining the position of those who punish him. The last instruments to sustain the infernal system are the prisons and only a bitter use of dynamite will blow these infernal things from the face of the earth."[46]

Criticizing capitalism as a system of robbery, the anarchists celebrated certain criminal practices as examples of class warfare. In the tradition of those who had celebrated figures such as Dick Turpin and Jack Shepherd, the anarchists made criminals at least as manly as "honest workers" and politicized individual acts of expropriation against wealthy hypocrites. In a brief report, a writer for the *Alarm* noted: "A minister of the gospel was sandbagged on the corner of Lincoln and Ohio and robbed of his diamond ring, gold watch and chain. Perhaps the cold had something to do with this matter? Perhaps not?"[47]

This minister's gold watch and chain begged to be stolen for sheer material value; they also exposed the hollowness of his Christianity, thus making his robber into a social critic as well as a desperado. Not only did the
anarchists pity tramps. They also saw these victims as the source of revolutionary power. Even for the lumpen proletarians, redemption was to be
achieved not through moral reform, but revolution. The Paris Commune,
with its prostitute heroines, was the model for a new form of revolutionary subject, and Lucy Parsons's appeal "To Tramps" showed that the anarchists firmly believed in the potential of society's "dregs to act in their own
interest." Addressing unemployed men, who, she said, "had been used by
the capitalists until over production [caused the] iron horse to which you
had been harnessed" to be stilled, Parsons told the tramps to go to the
homes of the rich and "let your tragedy be enacted there! Awaken [the
wealthy] from their wanton sports at your expense! Send forth your petition and let them read it by the red glare of destruction."[48]

Like his wife, Albert Parsons also refused to make a moral distinction
between the unemployed and the workingman, and he criticized the divisions between men upheld by more traditional trade unionists. In a speech
at the Haymarket rally, Parsons had urged workers to look beyond the
"scab" to see the larger problem:

> The Unionist fights the scab. What is a scab? A man as a usual thing that has
> been out of employment, who is destitute and whose necessities drive him
> to go to work in some man's place who has employment, and of course he
> can only get the employment because he will take the work for less than the
> man who is employed is working for. He is at once denounced as scab by
> the Unionists, and war is made on him. . . . Gentlemen, socialism don't do
> this thing. They regard these men as the victims of a false system, and to be
> pitied.[49]

There were other differences between the anarchists and other labor
activists of the time. Many in the labor movement fought representations
of the working class as a "mob" by demonstrating their own adherence
to the work ethic and republican manliness. Temperance activism played
an important symbolic role in proving the sobriety of new working-class
organizations. The Knights of Labor, for example, encouraged members
to take the temperance pledge. Although support for temperance did not
immediately signal a middle-class sensibility, the attribution of acts of
labor violence to drunkenness played into popular stereotypes of strikers
as irrational drunks, and drunkenness was a characteristic often attributed
especially to Irish and German immigrants. So when the Knights' leader,

Terence Powderly, blamed the "liquor trade" for Molly Maguire violence in 1877, he diminished the legitimate grievances of the miners.[50] In contrast, the Chicago anarchists defiantly drank beer. With their consistent challenge to the representation of the urban criminal and castigation of the hypocrisy of prison reform, police, and criminology, the anarchists exposed the bankruptcy of "free-labor" ethics.

The anarchists' definition of wage labor as slavery aided their attempts to gain sympathy among the last holdouts for American radical republicanism. The original antebellum labor unions had described the North's workers as "wage slaves" and said that they deserved the rights of "white men." Such men made up the ranks of the American Federation of Labor (AFL). There were also those, clustered around various reform societies and in the ranks of what Timothy Messer-Kruse refers to as the "Yankee International," who went from Quakerism and abolition to a form of individualist anarchism that had much in common with the values of antebellum republicanism.[51] If the republic was in a state of degeneration in the 1880s, it was not because of foreign workers, the anarchists and their friends argued, but because of the encroachment of police on the democratic rights of America's workers. One of the chief elements of the anarchists' attack on industrial slavery focused on the role of police terror in suppressing workers' freedom. For despite the growth of support for larger police forces, not all middle-class Americans embraced the new state. Some prison reformers saw the growth of prisons and the centralizing police forces in the 1870s and 1880s as signs of encroaching despotism. In 1874, prison reformers warned each other that they should avoid emulating the French, whose "police powers are annoyances fit only for a nation of children or enemies," and worried about how to create a professional, centralized police force without creating a police state. Police states, they argued, reigned in Russia and France, societies characterized by "a chronic state of discontent and suspicion and fear of internal disorder, not a fear of foreign insurrection but a fear of one's own disaffected population."[52]

The anarchists' rejection of parliamentary methods was built at least partly on a critique of the role of police. If police could legally kill workers and escape punishment, was there any point in trusting the state as a means to justice or fairness, particularly when police played such a key role in corrupt political regimes? In 1886, the *Alarm* had described a terrible massacre in which police fired on strikers in Lemont, Illinois. Decrying the bandits of law and order, the paper described women who were "bayoneted" and called "termigants" and quoted "little Mary," a nine-year-

old girl the reporter found crying over the corpse of her brother, as saying, "Oh sir, they killed my poor, poor brother! He did no harm to anyone."[53]

Like John Brown's comrade-in-arms Osborne Perry Anderson, who had attacked the manliness of Virginia's slaveholders, the anarchists made sure to point out that members of the middle class were not manly, for they performed their dirty work "not by their own dainty hands forsooth! Oh no, but by the hands of hirelings!"[54] Using traditional republican language that found "hirelings" less than manly, the anarchists proclaimed that the police were merely a "hired band of assassins" doing the bidding of the wealthy.[55] The rest of the state, with its fraudulent elections, was hardly different. With their descriptions of "Pinkerton Monsters" and police action called "Murder Most Foul," the anarchists satirized the descriptions of beastly, gothic crimes in popular fiction and tabloid newspapers and exposed the hypocrisy in bourgeois claims to refinement and civilization. In the pages of the *Alarm* they decried the police as "the banditti of armed outlaws, a new monster from the dark ages" and called capitalists "ghouls" and "vampires," echoing the excessive mode of contemporary melodramatic fiction and drama, in which the use of hyperbole suggested a cosmic morality beneath the banal surfaces of things.[56]

Despite their valorization of some criminal acts and their scorn for the police, the anarchists did not adopt a Nietzschean attitude toward morality. Rather, they reversed the classes to whom definitions of wickedness and goodness should be applied. They defended those defined as criminals while referring to the police as "bandits," "drunks," and "thugs." August Spies theorized that he was to be hanged because his newspaper was "the only paper in the city that dared to expose the outrageous villainies and criminal practices of these drunken and degraded brutes [the police]."[57] In September 1885, the *Alarm* carried an article headlined, "Our Civilization: The Bullet and the Policeman's Club." The German anarchists had gone after the police before, running a petition against Police Captain John Bonfield in July 1885 that one thousand people had signed.[58] The police officer was a "blue-coated, brass buttoned, black belted, wooden clubbed bandit" and did not just beat strikers, but participated in other outrages.[59] In one particularly daring move, Spies went to the aid of Martha Seidel, a working woman who had been raped in jail by a policeman. Spies heard of the woman's imprisonment through the press, went to her father, and received a warrant for the arrest of the policeman who had raped her. "Outrage!" cried the *Alarm*'s headline over an article that suggested the police officer be brought to public justice by "Judge Lynch" in

Chicago now that "the law and order beast Patton has been triumphantly acquitted owing to the employment of the whole police force in hunting up evidence against the girl, the victim of his cruel lust. . . . Such are the ways of justice."[60]

During the trial, Oscar Neebe declared that "the police hollered and hurrahed just like a lot of wild Indians."[61] The police, rather than the anarchists, took on the stereotypes usually applied to the lumpen proletariat. German socialists, who followed the case closely through the newspapers, soon concluded that Chicago's police were composed of the "scum of worthless loafers and street toughs for whom there is no better pleasure than to bludgeon down the defenseless."[62]

Defending Violence, Defending the Bomb Thrower

Given their attitude toward police and law, it is not surprising that the anarchists argued that armed action was the only tool that would be effective in changing the balance of power between labor and capital. Most troubling of all to Chicago's leaders, the anarchists praised dynamite, referring to it as the great leveler. It was cheap; it was easy to conceal; and it could raise havoc in the ranks of the police.[63] When there was a "dynamite scare" in Denver, the St. Louis branch of the Knights of Labor publicly distanced itself from such actions. The *Alarm's* writers castigated their brothers: "The St. Louis dynamiters should be defended regardless of what Powderly says!"[64]

Following the Haymarket events, the anarchists maintained their argument that revolutionary solidarity required that they support armed struggle. Thus, the Chicago anarchists' most ardent supporters distinguished themselves from the rest of the labor movement by refusing to repudiate the unknown person who threw the bomb. "Beware!" read Joseph Labadie's headline in the Detroit *Labor Leaf* shortly after May 4. "The use of the death dealing bomb in Chicago will have done good if it enforces a more humane treatment of mobs by the police."[65] Similarly, the *Labor Enquirer's* writers were unwilling to condemn the bomb thrower, noting that "the militia and police are brave and reckless when they feel safe." As a result, they found that "the dynamite bomb was terrible and yet it will make people think."[66] Both papers celebrated the act, with the *Labor Leaf* commenting that the "beastly police" had gotten their comeuppance. "Instead of cracking heads," the paper crowed, "they got cracked!"[67] William Holmes—an IWPA member, the husband of Lizzie Holmes, and a close

friend of Parsons and Spies—escaped the final indictment and wrote under the name "Cato": "Lo! the tables have been turned! They may have learned that there is virtue in a dynamite bomb when thrown by a practiced hand!"[68] In Detroit, even a lawyer argued that "the bomb thrower was justified under law in attempting to prevent the police from committing a felony."[69] According to M. C. Kovens, another *Labor Leaf* correspondent, the main tragedy was that the Haymarket bomb tossers had "only one poor pitiful handmade bomb among them. . . . I don't believe in force as a remedy, but if we're going to use it, do it in such a way not to render ourselves balls for the police and militia to shoot at."[70]

The idea that revolutionary action was a fundamental component of American identity was at stake for these activists during the Haymarket trial—and, indeed, valuing the use of force appealed to some workers who responded with revolutionary republican rhetoric to the story of the case. In an article titled "A Little Haymarket," William Holmes reported that a Kansas City group had resisted a police attempt to disperse it in the fall of 1886. As one man shouted, "I am an American working-man, I am a mechanic! I say that we will have Sunday meetings here if we so desire, whether or not the police say otherwise," the police attempted to pull him off the platform, but the workers defended him. According to Holmes, "Large crowds lingered round for an hour or more, excitedly discussing whether or not the time had come to defend the principles of liberty and free speech for which our fathers died or whether we should longer submit to being ground in the dust."[71]

A European Revolutionary Working-Class Identity   While they often remarked on Americans' right to bear arms and tried to maintain the legitimacy of violence in America, the Chicago anarchists did not generally make their arguments in the name of U.S. nationalism unless they were pointing out its hypocrisy. One of the ways they demonstrated their support for the use of force against capitalism was in their celebration of Europe's revolutionary heroes and in their argument that it was time for Americans to join them in revolutionary practice. The heroic actions of the Russian populists and nihilists, the stories of heroic political prisoners in France, and the triumphant speeches of Germany's social revolutionaries who defied the courts—all reported in the *Alarm* and the *Arbeiter Zeitung*—created an international "imagined community" of transatlantic working-class radicals. The anarchists were not concerned by racial differences applied to Europeans. Their canon included Socrates, the Paris Commune,

the Spanish Black Hand,[72] Irish rebels against England, and Russian populists as members of a heroic international working-class community.[73]

In 1884, August Reinsdorf, a German revolutionary who was a friend of Louis Lingg's, was executed in Germany for "plotting against the Kaiser and other dignitaries." The anarchists in America followed his trial, and the *Alarm* praised him for his "bold demeanor" and his "unqualified support for anarchist principles" when he said in court that he would rather die than renounce his beliefs. Reinsdorf, creating the model that the Chicago anarchists would follow a year later in their own trials, admitted his use of dynamite and refused to betray any of his companions. He was, they noted, gentle with women and children and demonstrated "great strength of character and kindness of heart."[74] As a figure, Reinsdorf was a romantic hero much like John Brown in his self-presentation. He paid little attention to his legal defense and used his trial primarily as a forum in which to declare his political beliefs. The *Alarm* reprinted his final speech, in which he called the accusations against him "sheer falsehood" and, evoking the image of the hydra, declared, "If I had ten heads I would sacrifice them all."[75] Anarchists in New York, Denver, Chicago, and St. Louis held events to commemorate Reinsdorf's death. Comrades in St. Louis wrote that "Reinsdorf was most disinterested, he sacrificed himself for manhood. Faithful to his principles he died for his fellow workers."[76]

In addition to following the exploits of German revolutionary socialists, IWPA members all over the United States celebrated the Paris Commune every year as a "complete overthrow, for the time being, of all existing institutions, a protest of robbed against robbers, and an attempt to found a social and industrial republic based on the rights of man."[77] The images of the "stern unflinching Decleuze," who spent two-thirds of his life in prison, and the noble Louise Michel, who had to receive a special permit to go from prison to her mother's funeral, all appeared in detail in the *Alarm*'s pages. Signing his letters from prison, "From the Bastille," Albert Parsons explicitly drew connections between the Chicago anarchists and the Communards and between the government of the United States and the undemocratic regime in France.[78]

Anarchy on Trial

The anarchists saw the defense of revolution as their fundamental right, and when they were tried for what they had said about dynamite and

the law, they defended—to the death—their right to say it. In both their responses to prosecutors' cross-examinations, which involved the repetition of speeches and newspaper articles, and in their speeches to the court before sentencing, the anarchists were defiant. Spies, Parsons, Lingg, Fischer, and Engel made outright arguments in favor of the use of violence as the right of the working class in self-defense against capitalist militias and police, whom they described alternatively as despots and bandits during the trial. They argued that even though they had not done it, the bomb throwing at the Haymarket rally was justified because it had been done in self-defense.

They did have lawyers and a team of people to support them. Immediately, although the anarchists repudiated social democracy, their case became a "popular front" between revolutionaries and parliamentarians. Ernst Schmidt, a friend of August Spies and a socialist who had supported John Brown in the 1850s, brought people together to raise money for lawyers as soon as he heard about the arrests. He and George Schilling, another social democrat and friend of the defendants, canvassed "liberal minded humanitarians" throughout the world, winning international support for the internationalist defendants.[79] With the money they raised, they hired the lawyers Moses Salomon and Sigmund Zeisler, two young Jewish men who worked for Chicago's Central Labor Union. The lawyers also argued that the rush of the police on the demonstration had provoked the bomb thrower, although they did not quite call the act justified.[80]

Parsons described the actual bomb throwing as a police plot, but in the same eight-hour speech to the court, he also described dynamite as "the diffusion of power" that made everybody equal because it destroyed the power of the Pinkertons, the police, and the militia. Dynamite was, he said, "the abolition of authority" and the "dawn of peace."[81] Parsons also appealed to the American tradition of valorizing a republic of armed citizens. "Does not the constitution of the country under whose flag myself and my forefathers were born for the last 260 years provide that protection?" he asked. "[Does it not] give me, their descendant, that right, does not the constitution say that I as an American have a right to bear arms?[82]

Spies also appealed to America's aspirations to republican freedom in his speech to the court:

We have preached dynamite. Yes we have preached the lessons history teaches, that the ruling classes of today would no more listen to the voice

of reason than their predecessors; that they would attempt by brute force to stay the wheel of progress. Is it a lie or the truth we told? Are not already the large industries of this once free country conducted under the surveillance of the police, the detectives, the military and the sheriffs. . . . American citizens, think of it, working like galley convicts under military guards.[83]

In their speeches in court, the anarchists did as much as possible to identify themselves not as individual exemplars of republican manhood, but as representatives of a mass uprising that would continue beyond their lifetimes, as Spies did in his reference to "subterranean fire." The anarchists' refusal to deny that they were revolutionaries made them not just victims, but heroes, because in refusing to repudiate revolution, and even by insisting that revolution was part of the American tradition, they did in fact stand up for the rights of the people who followed them in future generations. The brave stance of all eight men despite the penalty they faced simply because they refused to disavow revolution may explain why they received such enthusiastic support from people who did not agree with them. Even Samuel Gompers, whose businesslike AFL benefited tremendously from the Haymarket executions and the subsequent collapse of the Knights of Labor, understood the importance of the case for the future of free speech and assembly in the United States. While he and the anarchists were "fighting for labor upon different sides of the house," as Gompers put it, he did ask himself, "What good can come to the people of the State of Illinois; what good can come to the people of our country . . . if these men are executed? . . . Hundreds of thousands of laboring men all over the world would consider that those men had been executed because they were standing up for free speech and free assemblage."[84]

Two Defense Campaigns

After the last of the men had given his speech, all of the anarchists except Neebe were sentenced to death. Almost immediately, their friends began organizing a campaign to save them. The anarchists' most tireless defender was Albert Parsons's wife, Lucy, who toured the country speaking to Knights of Labor assemblies during the time between the sentencing and the execution. The anarchists predicted in court that their judicial murders would provoke an uprising. Lingg, standing before the judge during the trial, said that he was "confident that hundreds of thousands

to whom I have spoken will remember my words . . . and when you shall have hanged us then, mark my words, they will do the bomb throwing!"[85] Rather than putting this uprising off until after the deaths of the heroes, the anarchists' defense campaign hoped to put the mass uprising to work to save the defendants. In doing so, Lucy Parsons and her allies created the modern tradition of labor defense. The goal was literally not to mourn, but to organize.

Clemency   Schilling and Schmidt organized the social democrats and liberals, who disagreed with the anarchists but did not want to see them hanged, beginning a pattern that would characterize almost every future labor defense. Despite its sympathy for the condemned, the clemency campaign for the anarchists departed from most of the anarchists' heroic representations of passionate mobs, bomb throwers, and European revolutionary heroes as the agents of social change. While Spies and Parsons told Schmidt to give the money collected for the appeals to their soon-to-be widows, Schmidt argued that a defense was a necessity, "if only to expose jurisprudence in America for what it is—neither better nor worse than in the old capitalistic countries of Europe which we had abandoned in the hope of finding a land where justice prevails for all classes of society."[86]

Although Marx had argued that the "well-meaning bourgeois" was the type "best suited" to fund raising for the legal defense of radicals, the alliance had its pitfalls.[87] The most obvious way to defend the anarchists through the press and among middle-class reformers was to describe them within the image of chivalric manhood or to argue that they were absolutely innocent. Above all, it was necessary to separate them from the stigmas of mob violence, criminality, and foreignness by defining them as American, gentle, and law-abiding. A week before the scheduled executions, the defense committee convinced Fielden, Schwab, and Spies to ask the governor for clemency, commuting their sentences to life imprisonment. In their letters to the governor, the anarchists repudiated their advocacy of violence, Fielden and Schwab calling their own speeches at the Haymarket "irresponsible" and "injudicious." Spies initially wrote a letter as well, but following outcry from other revolutionaries that he was a coward who had betrayed the cause, he retracted it and offered his life in place of the others.'[88]

The defense attorneys, like the post-trial defenders of John Brown, emphasized the loving and selfless nature of the anarchists' beliefs, denying the selfishness of motive, distinguishing the anarchists from criminals, and

attributing to them great powers of sympathy that would associate them with non-resistant abolitionists rather than with radical slave rebels:

> Now these defendants are not criminals; they are not robbers; they are not burglars; they are not common thieves; they descend to no small criminal act. On the contrary this evidence shows conclusively that they are men of broad feelings of humanity, that their only desire has been and their lives have been consecrated to the betterment of their fellow men. They have not sought to take the life of any man, or any individual, to maliciously kill or destroy any person, nor have they sought to deprive any man of his property for their own benefit. They have not sought to get McCormick's property for themselves; they have not sought to get Marshall Field's property for themselves and to deprive Marshal Field of it feloniously, but they have endeavored to have a different social system. . . . They have stood by the man who has the le[a]st friends.[89]

Where the bourgeois press had called the anarchists criminals, driven by desire for material goods, the reformers in their defense campaign described them as chivalrous and self-sacrificing, Christian heroes who acted not on their own, but on behalf of others who were weaker than themselves. Thus, not only were the anarchists not "criminals," but they were chivalrous, acting on behalf of the friendless poor and downtrodden. At the same time, like heroes of realist fiction, they suffered from a tragic flaw: Their sympathies caused them to commit excesses.

Responding to the nativist attacks on the defendants was a much more difficult task. In the group, only one of the men—Parsons—was a native-born, Anglo-Saxon American. Lingg, Spies, Engel, and Fischer were German; Neebe was an American-born German; and Samuel Fielden was English. To emphasize the "Americanness" of the anarchists, the defenders engaged two different rhetorical strategies. Some who advocated labor rights attempted to defend the men by referring to the republican tradition that made revolutionary violence a regenerative force. Those who argued for the Americanness of violence focused attention on Parsons. The most popular pamphlet sold during the trial, by General Matthew Trumbull, referred to Parsons as an "indomitable puritan."[90]

Although Parsons was just as enamored of dynamite as his fellows had been, and although he quoted freely from European thinkers and had married a woman of unknown racial background whom some described as a "Negress," in most descriptions of him his ideology was made to conform to his racial heritage.[91] Parsons was American because of his American racial genealogy and his agrarian past, and both of these characteristics

suggested that he was peaceful and conservative rather than wild and militant. The California Defense Fund assured readers that Parsons was a "conservative Anarchist" and "an American by birth whose forefathers fought in the revolutionary war and whose brother fought in the civil war."[92] The California Defense Fund did not mention, of course, that both Parsons and his brother had fought on the Confederate side in the Civil War or that Parsons had left the Southern cause to become a radical Republican before he went to Chicago.[93]

The defenders did their best to distance the rest of the group from Lingg, the most recent immigrant of the group, who had manufactured bombs and belonged to a secret conspiracy of men who advocated street fighting with the police. In their defense of Spies, the two Germans from the Socialist Labor Party—Schilling and Schmidt—worked to disassociate Germanness from revolutionary violence by drawing a sharp contrast between Spies and Lingg. Unlike the anarchists, Schilling and Schmidt did not describe law and order as tyranny or the police as "bandits." Schmidt recalled in his memoirs that

> Lingg was a brute of a man . . . trapped by the police in his landlord Seliger's house, where he put up a fierce fight for more than an hour, he was finally captured by one of the bravest men I have ever known, Inspector Hermann Schuettler. . . . I never knew much about Lingg. Seeing him in jail I took him for a surly sort of fellow, wild eyed at times, somebody with whom you do not care to become acquainted.

In contrast, Spies, according to Schilling, was "a man of intellect and cultivation and of tender feelings for all poverty and distress."[94]

The third element of the defense was to point out that the anarchists had not thrown the bomb or approved of the act of the bomb thrower and that prosecuting them was simply a violation of freedom of speech and the trial, a miscarriage of justice. There was considerable merit to this claim. Most of those who were finally convicted were newspaper editors or editors' assistants, and they were chosen as defendants out of a pool of thirty-five largely because of their influence as speakers and writers. Some of the defendants were not even present at the Haymarket gathering when the bomb was thrown. Nonetheless, the articles they wrote in newspapers were used as evidence of their participation in a conspiracy. Thus, instead of making reference to John Brown as historical precedent, the defense attorney compared the anarchists to the non-resistant news editors who dominated the memory of abolitionism in liberal communities after 1877: "What would now be said of a proposal to indict Horace Greeley, Wendell

Phillips, Gerrit Smith, William Lloyd Garrison and the host of immortals whose names were then a reproach and a byword, but are now honored in all lands, under the charge of murder . . . because of the act of John Brown?"

The lawyers also compared the anarchists' case to other examples of popular violence. While the anarchists had focused on the calls for death to strikers that had appeared in the national newspapers, the clemency campaigner Captain William Black raised the issue of anti-Chinese violence and the legend of the Klan to legitimate the use of calls to violence:

> What about in the South—domination after war by colored race, whites with shotgun policy, and press advocates that whites should dominate, massacres by KKK which are excused by the press, was it ever pretended that the these newspaper editors and stockholders could be made liable upon indictments for murder for the lawless conduct of these night-riders? And the denunciation by entire western press against the Chinese—are they then arrested when Chinese are murdered?[95]

Because the anarchists were newspaper editors and because the police attack on a legal demonstration arguably had provoked the bomb thrower, the men's liberal defenders argued that the anarchists should be defended for practical reasons, but they also defended them as if they stood above the working masses. Because of the likely effects that the prosecution might have on other citizens, particularly those in the labor movement, it became an issue of great self-interest for laborers and labor leaders to become involved in the defense. The obvious biases of the judge, the provocation of the bomb thrower by police officers who attacked a peaceful demonstration, and the unfairness of the procedures during the trial made this a fight for democratic rights, regardless of the ideology of the defendants.

One of the many local defense committees invited "all friends of impartial administration of justice" to join and reminded them, "Don't think that participation in the defense makes you an anarchist or that others are."[96] Similarly, Samuel Gompers argued that it was important to defend the anarchists, despite their views, to maintain the rights of laboring men to free assembly. In doing so, he explained that the bomb had been thrown not only because of radicalism, but also because the police had trampled on a legal assembly. His participation in the defense was not sentimental; it was a move of self-interest, for a conviction could hurt the rights of all in the labor movement. Gompers called for legal action to stop police violence as superior to direct action by workers, simultaneously

defending labor's right to assembly and establishing a standard of control for mass demonstrations that undermined their radical potential. Gompers defended the Haymarket anarchists but criticized revolutionary self-defense as against working-class interests.

Although Gompers was the principal labor leader to get involved in the clemency campaign, it was the more inclusive Knights of Labor whose members joined the campaign in large numbers, as individual locals responded to the anarchists' speaking tours. Terence Powderly's refusal to support the anarchists hurt his position, and eventually one of his men was removed from the Knights' newspaper in Chicago in favor of an ally of the Haymarket martyrs.[97]

Although the clemency activists repudiated *revolutionary* criticisms of the police, they did criticize them. They used the rampaging police not as evidence of American despotism but, rather, as a sign of police anarchy and unmanliness. They especially hated the Pinkertons, a "private army" of hirelings comparable to the private armies of feudal lords. The Pinkertons bore the brunt of the progressive attack, and both the AFL and, later, the Populist Party of the 1890s especially following the battle with Pinkertons during the Homestead steel strike of 1892 called on the state to regulate "business anarchy" by outlawing or getting rid of the private cops.[98] Descriptions of police by anarchists and their supporters as "ruffians" became a motivation for increasing professionalism of the police, who were seen as too much like the drunken ruffians they were supposed to keep in order. Governor John Peter Altgeld of Illinois, who pardoned the anarchists in 1893, noted that police brutality was the best organizer of anarchists:

> Resorting to tactics of 1886 and planting evidence of bombs, and anarchy, bad behavior by police will cause people to revolt. What is far more serious, no course could have been pursued that would so certainly make converts to the cause of anarchy among ignorant men, for a thousand loud-talking agitators could not sow as much anarchi[c]al seed in a year as your officers have done in a week.[99]

In their criticisms of wild anarchists and wild police, the middle-class reformers who joined the clemency campaign defined both sides of the debate as wild and anarchistic and argued that social reform was necessary to moderate each side to save the state from anarchist revolution, the product of the anarchy of capitalism as well as the anarchy of the working class. The blood lust of anarchist bombers, described so well by Edward Bellamy in his influential novel *Looking Backward*, became a metaphor

for the social chaos that both robber barons and anarchist revolutionaries represented to middle-class Americans, labor leaders, and parliamentary socialists. The defense attorneys—and, increasingly, the anarchists themselves—defined the bomb thrower as a police agent rather than as a disgruntled worker who was defending himself against an unlawful attack. The story of the bomb thrower as a police agent, which began as an ironic anarchist conspiracy theory comparing the bomb thrower's behavior to articles that had appeared in the capitalist press, effectively united "anarchy" and "capitalists" in the socialist theory of the Haymarket affair.[100] These two forms of "anarchy" were ultimately in league with each other, as Bellamy's Dr. Leet put it in *Looking Backward*, written that same year: "No historical authority nowadays doubts that they were paid by the great monopolists to wave the red flag and talk about burning, sacking and blowing people up, in order, by alarming the timid to head off any real reforms."[101]

Bellamy's definition of anarchism as chaos echoed statements made by the anarchists' own clemency campaigners. Social democrats sought clemency for the men as a way to preserve American democracy and maintain social peace and presented themselves as the middle ground between the twin evils of police and anarchism. Henry Demarest Lloyd, a progressive activist and muckraking journalist who was active in the Haymarket clemency campaign, referred to preservation of free speech for workers as a way to maintain peace against the outrages of anarchists and police.[102] In his 1888 speech to the workers who had been assaulted by police in Greif's Hall in Chicago on the anniversary of the Haymarket anarchists' hanging, Lloyd complimented their moral superiority because they had not defended themselves against the attack.

The rejection of revolutionary socialism and anarchy as forms of childish romanticism was also a defining element in the realist movement in fiction. William Dean Howells sympathized with the anarchists and asked for clemency—but he also rejected their political ideals as the product of a tragic character flaw. His faith in the American justice system was deeply shaken by the case, and yet in his novel *Hazard of New Fortunes*, whose character Mr. Lindau was reminiscent of Ernst Schmidt, Howells ultimately showed that the chaotic responses of the anarchists to the social conflict, even when provoked by great sympathy, were as dangerous and hurtful to the cause as were the unregulated actions of monopolists and their police forces.

By the 1890s, anarchists had become the foil against which social democrats and others defined their own legitimacy. Anarchism became something of a psychological disorder in their eyes. Indeed, Cesare Lombroso,

the father of criminal psychology, was also a significant figure in the Italian Socialist Party. Lombroso not only included anarchists as a group in his dictionary of "criminal types," but he also wrote an entire book dedicated to their study at the same time that he was creating a new racial theory to explain the inferiority of southern Italians.[103] Socialist battles against revolutionary anarchism in Europe, part of the struggles in various labor parties there, entered the literature of American criminology and penal reform in the 1890s. Anarchists also featured prominently in the 1895 work of the French syndicalist Augustin Hamon, who wrote *Psychologie de l'anarchist-socialiste*. Gustave Le Bon's two influential works of mass psychology, *The Crowd* and *The Psychology of Revolution*, proved formative study guides for leaders interested in taming crowds and identifying pathological revolutionary personalities and racial types. According to Le Bon, who wrote *The Crowd* in 1895, the power of crowds was determined by the racial spirit of its members, and the Anglo-Saxon crowd was the least de-individualized, while the Latin was the most dangerous.

The crowd theories that emerged in the 1890s actually racialized the emotional state that was fundamental to collective action. Sigmund Freud's *Group Psychology and the Analysis of the Ego* extended Le Bon's analysis of the masses, and his allegorical *Totem and Taboo* made the reassuring argument that all opposition to political authorities, despots, and the like came from unresolved oedipal conflicts that united childish/primitive groups around charismatic patricides.[104] Le Bon and Freud agreed that people in groups literally became "savages." Groups, they said, were dangerous because in their quest to topple political leadership, they conquered the internal despots that governed and regulated each individual mind and let loose the savagery within. If every person's unconscious was "savage," it was only individualism that kept this savagery in check. In groups, the governing superego of each person was subsumed into the reign of unconscious drives that characterized the mob. Groups, Freud argued, "show an unmistakable picture of a regression of mental activity to an earlier stage such as we are not surprised to find among savages or children."[105] Blending theories of infantile subjectivity with primitivist interpretations of non-European cultures, these authors gave antirevolutionary arguments a newly scientific veneer and brought imperialist philosophy into the analysis of mass protest. To be a member of a "mob" was to be a savage. Social democrats would thus spend a good deal of time in the twentieth century establishing the boundary between anarchic and civilized forms of public protest.

The Nativist Mob

Anarchists completely rejected this notion of the savage mob as bad and continued to celebrate mass action as the instrument of redemption. But when the masses did not rise up sufficiently in their defense, anarchists began discussing why they had not. When finally pushed to explain what made American workers submit to such despotism, the anarchists argued that the American dream of "exceptionalism" was the principal obstacle to the formation of a radical working-class movement in the United States. As industrialism eroded American democracy, the Chicago anarchists argued, patriotic mythologies about American republicanism prevented American workers from joining Europe's workers in revolt. In his speech to the court, Samuel Fielden described nationalism as a capitalist trick that hurt the working class. Instead of appealing to the nationalist sympathies of his audience, he directly confronted Americanism, claiming that

> the patriotic tricksters who have been telling the people to worship the American flag while they quietly put their hands in their pockets and robbed them, they have said that this is merely a European question. It is an American question, and the close contact of nations cemented by the facilities of civilization is bringing all the questions that affect one people to affect all people equally all over the world.[106]

Because it was similar to executions and jailing of radicals in Europe, the hanging of the Chicago anarchists was the ultimate evidence of America's similarity to other industrial nations, and anarchists continued to emphasize this point throughout their defense campaign as they compared American despotism to czarism or to the reign of Bismarck. Thus, when their comrades were hanged, the anarchists argued that it would expose America's hypocrisy to both the American workers and to the international working class. By dying with honor, and by refusing to kowtow to the morality of America, Chicago's anarchists hoped to demonstrate that the United States had revealed its inner despotism, publicly executing American sovereigns for espousing the doctrines of liberty and had done so under the eyes of the world. With America's mythologies exposed, they imagined that American workers would rise up and reject their timidity, and revolution would follow.

Because the anarchists celebrated the "mob"—the idea of spontaneous, unfettered revolutionary action—the most crushing element in the Haymarket tragedy for them was not the police attack on the workers

during the May Day strikes, which they had expected, but the attacks hurled at them, they imagined, as they read the newspapers, by the people in whose name they had spoken. In most accounts of the Haymarket tragedy, supporters of the Chicago anarchists and the labor movement describe the hysteria that struck Chicago after the throwing of the bomb. Lucy Parsons wrote in her foreword to the collected writings of her deceased husband, "The people of the nineteenth century have committed the hideous crime of strangling their best friends."[107] While the anarchists attempted to see in the executions the heralding of a moment of triumph, the dawning of a new era, the times appeared desperate, indeed. Before the trial, the anarchists had generally agreed that more workers did not come to their side in the cause because they were deluded by capitalism. After the deaths of the anarchists, the remarks about the masses grew bitter. As the national newspapers clamored for blood and Chicago's police both planted bombs and searched for them, the anarchists and their supporters described the frenzy for their lives, it appeared, using the same terms that had been used to attack them. They went after the mob.

As they did so, passion was no longer an uncomplicated benefit. Reflecting on the way the trial had gone, Parsons said at the opening of his speech to the court: "If there is one distinguishing characteristic that has made itself prominent in the conduct of this trial it has been the passion, the heat, the anger, the violence both to sentiment and person, of everything connected with this case."[108]

General Matthew Trumbull's pamphlet "Was It a Fair Trial?" which the anarchists sold on street corners and in union halls, described the enemy as "King Populus":

> When king Populus is in his humor he can be as bigoted, irrational, and despotic as any King Henry, King James or King George. When King Populus gets drunk his judicial servants must make the law drunk too. When he demands a bloody sacrifice, they must provide the victims. He can exact illegal judgment from his court of law with as much intolerance as any king of England ever did. . . . How interesting the resemblance between the judicial appointments of King James . . . and the appointments of King Populus today![109]

August Spies's recognition of the American masses' hatred for the German anarchists led him to claim that, if it had been left to them, "The people would have lynched us long ago."[110] Voltairine de Cleyre, who recalled having been initially convinced by the mass hysteria after the Haymarket bombing, also laid the anarchists' death at the feet of the

masses.[111] However, while other immigrant labor activists of the day described the "mobbism" of Blacks and savages, Chicago anarchists said that nationalist ideology, not racial identity, created mobs. Ultimately, they blamed the new corporate mass media as the purveyor of nativistic mob spirit. The newspapers duped the workers, leading them to believe that they shared capitalist interests that masqueraded as Christianity, Americanism, and civilization. "How did the anarchists meet their doom?" Fielden asked. "We have but to refer to the columns of editorial streetwalkers who represent Christian civilization to find the answer." He attacked the newspapers in his speech to the court before his sentencing:

> The reporters have been depended on to provide a conviction in this case. There is not a public speaker in this country but what has had cause to complain of the reports of his speeches in the newspapers. So intolerable has this become that the chief magistrate of this country, less than a year ago, stated . . . that there never was an age in the world in which newspaper lying existed to the extent that it does now; and there never was a country in which it existed to the extent that it does in this. A man whose life is placed in jeopardy on the bare report of a newspaper reporter is as liable to be murdered as not.[112]

Thus, although the anarchists asserted a kind of natural up-swelling of popular feeling as an alternative to tyranny in their celebration of natural law as the source of revolution, their critiques of the newspapers led them in the opposite direction, suggesting that the masses' feelings were not natural at all. Their attacks on the media's influence on the masses created an avenue for a critique of nationalism as a form of hysteria and provided the basis for a working-class celebration of cosmopolitan values. When they promoted the international ties between workers as the reality that national feeling masked, the anarchists were true "Marxists." Their primary method for countering nationalist propaganda was with counter-education: radical newspapers, conferences, and counter-culture. The celebration of the Chicago anarchists as part of a transatlantic pantheon that included the Paris Communards and German assassins was part of the formation of this counter-hegemonic community.

However, the anarchists' need to defend themselves to the existing American public and their rejection of American nationalism led to contradictions in their literature. Like the clemency campaigners, they referred to the American Revolution and the Puritan hero John Brown to show that violence was inside the "American" tradition. John Brown's son helped them establish their connection to the Old Man by sending them fruit baskets in prison and asserting that the Old Man would have

approved of their actions.[113] At the same time, the anarchists tried to convince the masses that such national traditions were illusions fostered by the capitalist press. This ambivalent attitude toward American nationalism, which could lead either to attempted appropriations of American revolutionary heroism or to direct challenges that exposed the limits of the American revolutionary legacy, would come to typify immigrant socialist approaches to heroic self-representation.[114]

Particularly during the defense campaign, the anarchists discussed the role of the burgeoning capitalist press in representing the labor movement. Because they identified the national press as a primary tool of the bourgeoisie to dupe the workers, the anarchists' defenders and memorialists argued that it was imperative that the labor movement create its own history of the Haymarket Martyrs. Thus, the obligation to memorialize the heroes of the working class remained central to early American socialism, as Eugene Debs proclaimed in 1907. If he could not make things right by restoring "the flesh to their skeleton bones," he would make sure that "the stigma fixed upon their names by an outrageous trial can be forever obliterated and their fame be made to shine with resplendent glory on the pages of history."[115]

The martyrs became the lesson. Instead of describing their deaths as a defeat, the men's friends wrote that the Haymarket Martyrs had become ghosts who would haunt the American bourgeoisie and inspire the working class. Their memory would always expose the brutality behind American Anglo-Saxon patriotism and its judicial mythology. Dyer Lum wrote that, in dying proudly, they had become "immortal souls, marching on in the hearts of the downtrodden to animate, inspire, and encourage in the path of duty."[116] As such, they represented the deification of values antagonistic to those of the mainstream culture. Defiance of the law was a critical position in the campaign. The anarchists appealed to the masses to free them in a general upheaval but refused to sign on to the clemency campaign organized by their social-democratic supporters. They refused to hide their ideals to save their necks and proudly praised dynamite in the courtroom.

The memorials dedicated to the anarchists were quite different from those of the 1850s and 1860s for the martyrs of abolitionism. In an explicitly secular and anticlerical movement, the anarchists replaced religious concepts of sublimity that had surrounded the abolitionist martyrs with stories of romantic, sexual love. Anarchist newspapers published the love letters of the Chicago anarchists and their wives and girlfriends, another practice that was taken up by most socialist defense campaigns. This near-

fetishizing of the anarchists' frustrated desire for their wives and girlfriends during their imprisonment made these heroes more embodied and more vulnerable in appearance than the republican heroes of the earlier era, and this was in keeping with the socialists' deification of the passionate mob. In building the anarchist "counter-memory" of the Haymarket affair, the anarchists' families and friends organized mass actions, giving the expression of emotions—particularly the emotions of love, rage, and grief—an important role in radical politics. Passionate stories of husbands and wives were a metaphor for the glue that held masses of individuals together in struggle, and the prison, which dramatically refused admission to Albert Parsons's wife, Lucy, as a visitor on the day of the execution, became the archenemy of such family values. The togetherness of husbands and wives made women and their grief public at the same time that the hero's own desires were a cause for celebration. In this way, the anarchists sacralized the activists' private selves so that the preservation of (heterosexual) intimate connections between people became central to the experience of socialist politics.

Industrial capitalism had brought men and women of the working class close together; the "mobs" of the industrial era were not manly. Women had played a critical role in organizing local communities behind striking militants earlier in the industrial era. In the first and most celebrated battle between industrial labor and capital, in 1877, as men struck the railroads,

> The wives, mothers, children and friends of the strikers . . . thronged the vicinity of the Baltimore and Ohio depot . . . pleading and begging with babes in their arms for the moral support of the community on behalf of a husband, a brother, and lover . . . calling upon husband and father to submit no longer to what they consider the grinding into dust of those near and dear. Sweethearts swell the crowd with a delicacy and feeling of expression seldom brought to light among those who do not stand high in the scales of aristocracy, beg their lovers to be men and stand firm.[117]

Not only in the railroad strike, but in many actions labor activists in the 1870s and 1880s emphasized the power of female sentiment in the class struggle. The anarchists' mass defense campaign and memorial tradition went even further than this impromptu act in 1877 and made the display of dramatic female sympathy into a means for achieving a national movement based on the Knights of Labor's slogan "An injury to one is an injury to all." After the executions, the *Alarm* went on a campaign to rehabilitate the memory of Louis Lingg. Its first step was to demonstrate his connection to women, particularly to his girlfriend and his mother. In

one article, Dyer Lum skillfully repudiated not only the attack on Lingg's character, but also the moral order from which that attack emanated, in the name of "natural" manliness defined in sexual terms rather than racial ones. Lingg's critics, for instance, referred to him as a "tiger," implying in an era of imperialist racism that he was a "beast." Lum responded by making Lingg into the first "lover and fighter "of the anarchist tradition. In an age in which Teddy Roosevelt and other "natural men" prided themselves on their capacity to call on and then squelch their "savage" masculinity, Lum reversed the epithet to champion Lingg's sexual virility, for he was a "lion . . . on the dance floor." He published Lingg's letters to his girlfriend Elsie, and many were decidedly sexually suggestive. Telling her that he kissed and embraced her in dreams every night, Lingg made a running commentary on popular fiction in these letters. After reading one novel in which a monk whose awkward behavior and bad skills as a lover toward his would-be mistress made him a fool who did not know the "eleventh" commandment—"Thou shalt not get caught"—Lingg ended one letter wryly: "I dreamed I was with you and that I was more clever than the monk. Now lovely maid, do you picture to yourself the lovely and blissful embraces and endearing kisses I gave you?" If this was the happy tale of young love, the *Alarm* could not leave it at that. The story, and the letters, ended with Lingg's last words to Elsie before his death:

> I know now that I don't need to analyze for you the reasons why and wherefore I cannot and dare not beg for mercy. Your sweet mouth explained it the day before yesterday with the words that "this would resemble a confession." Your noble, proud words, my dear angel, have gladdened me more than dozens of resolutions passed in various cities and by various labor mass meetings. I am proud, ineffably proud, dearest of my heart, to possess your heroic love.[118]

Such private correspondences were typical inclusions in the *Alarm* when Dyer Lum was its editor.[119]

Like Elsie Friedel, the lovers of the other men—Nina Van Zandt-Spies and Lucy Parsons—shared their intimate expressions of love for their husbands with the public, not only humanizing the anarchists by showing their closeness to their wives and children, but also inviting others to participate in this loving relationship vicariously, first by joining the defense campaign in solidarity, and after the executions by maintaining their memories. Both women edited their husbands' autobiographies, and Van Zandt-Spies, who had fallen in love with August Spies while attending the trial and married him while he awaited execution, included

his letters to her from prison in her book, along with her own criticisms of the press's representation of her relationship with the German anarchist. Although the *New York Times* had depicted Nina Spies as crying over her husband's refusal to sign the appeal, asking, "Why should he want to die?" Van Zandt-Spies herself was angrier about the depiction of her love affair with Spies in the national press than she was with her husband. "If I had married an old, invalid debauche with great riches, those moral gentlemen who assail me now would have lauded me to the skies as a very sensible girl," she wrote.[120]

After the hangings of the revolutionaries, the continued elaboration of the story of the Haymarket Martyrs served both to reaffirm the solidarity of the "left" wing within the labor movement and to increase its alienation from the rest of the U.S. working class. By 1887, the replacement of the industrial organization the Knights of Labor with the craft-unionist AFL led some immigrant anarchists to attack the native-born American working class for its nativist stinginess, its cowardice, and its Protestant provincialism.

Mourning and memorializing the Haymarket anarchists played major roles in defining American anarchist politics and in establishing group identity and values among radical socialists for the twentieth century. The Pioneer Aid Society, organized to fund the Haymarket anarchists' widows, sold small trading cards with images of the hanged men, which could be collected in scrapbooks or affixed to walls. Ernst Schmidt included in his scrapbook an entire "memorial" section that included cards of the Haymarket Martyrs interspersed with other popular images of martyrs: Jesus, Socrates, and Jan Hus burning at the stake.[121] By creating memorial images and poems and by celebrating the anniversaries of the martyrs' deaths every November, socialists and anarchists turned the remembrance of the victims of capital into a political act and affirmed their own legitimacy as a separate culture. They had their own heroes, men whose stories dramatized the conflict between the American people and the ruling class and between immigrant radicals and the conservative leadership of the American labor movement. In addition, the linkage of these martyrs to the great martyrs of European free thought and philosophy (Galileo, Socrates), along with John Brown, established the "martyrs of Chicago" as figures in a long-running Euro-American tradition of libertarian martyrs murdered by the institutions of church and state. The Haymarket memorials thus folded American republicanism back into its international community and created continuity between Jeffersonian secularism, liberalism, and radical socialism.

The Haymarket anarchists symbolized the left's opposition to bourgeois morality and nativist definitions of the U.S. working class well into
the twentieth century, challenging the characterization of rationality and
self-restraint as the key elements of manhood. Increasingly, anarchist
memorial literature, rather than selecting Parsons as the figure of greatest heroism, made Louis Lingg, the pariah of the original group, into an
important figure. As his legend grew, Lingg became the first hero of a socialist revolutionary bohemia, that community of radicals who defined
their opposition to the United States in cultural as well as in class terms
and who were most closely identified with the circle surrounding Emma
Goldman. While Parsons and Spies were the heroes most cherished by
the members of the clemency campaign who later joined the American
Anti-Imperialist League, the Sunset Club, and the Populist Party, Lingg
was especially beloved in anarchist and syndicalist movements in the
twentieth century.

In his 1907 novel *The Bomb*, Frank Harris celebrated Lingg because,
he said, "The higher the tide of execration rose against the other anarchists, as foreigners and murderers, the more the American mob desired
to make an exception in favor of Parsons." In his short essay on Lingg,
Franklin Rosemont explains his particular attraction for counter-cultural
activists: Lingg was only twenty-one years old, handsome, and something of a "hipster." His defiance made him an appropriate symbol for
youth in revolt.[122] In addition to making bombs, Lingg participated in
popular cultures of the city that were frowned on by older socialists, enjoying dancing and cheap sensational fiction, which he discussed with
his sweetheart in racy letters that were published in the *Alarm* after his
death.

Harris's work helps demonstrate how increasing alienation from mass
culture, labor unions, and social-reform movements intensified the anarchists' bonds to each other as members of a unique and increasingly
sectarian faction within the left. He argues, "It seemed well to me to demonstrate that love between social outcasts and rebels would be naturally
intenser and more idealistic than among ordinary men and women."[123]
Harris wrote of the transcendent experience of bonding to Lingg
through the eyes of Lingg's lover, Elsie Friedel, or "Ida," who in one out-
burst shouted to the book's narrator:

> Oh if you knew how I love him! And how happy I've been in his love. It's
> nothing to say "I am his." I am part of him, I feel as he feels, think as he thinks;
> he has given me eyes to see with, and courage to live or die with him; but not

without him. If you knew where I was when he met me. Ah, what a man! I had been fooled and deserted, I didn't care what became of me, and he came and oh, at first I scarcely hoped for his love, and he gave like a King. How kind he is and strong. . . . The flesh in woman is faithless as in man . . . but since I met Lingg my flesh even has been faithful to him.[124]

This expression of sexual love between the anarchists was a means of bonding readers to the subjects. It was not unique in Harris's book but mirrored the approach that characterized a good deal of the anarchists' memorial literature, which gave a central role to women's expressions of passion. The effect of these public intimacies was to strengthen the bonding between anarchist newspaper readers and the martyrs and their families. These emotional stories dramatized both the readers' alienation from the reactionary media and state that had separated the tragic lovers.

Women who were not intimately connected with the men became the carriers of their legend in later years and helped build an aesthetic for revolution that was markedly different from earlier visions of heroism that had focused on "Great Men" who died solemnly apart from their wives and without emotion. The anarchists around the Haymarket Martyrs adapted the Victorian tropes of sentimental culture and heightened emotion in the name of revolution. Lizzie Holmes, Emma Goldman, and Voltairine de Cleyre all wrote about their personal feelings of loss after the hangings as part of a political consciousness and served to symbolize the experience of sympathy with the lowly as a moral choice in opposition to capitalism.[125]

Lucy Parsons inspired this correspondence from Seward Mitchell, a ninety-three-year-old man from Newport, Maine, who was a regular *Alarm* reader. "My Dear Sister," the letter began, "No one but myself will know my feelings when I read your letter in the *Alarm* of April 2. My heart was sad and full of tears. O man, is there no animal so cruel to his kind as you? You and your husband are helping to work out the world's redemption. It is a fearful price you are paying, but so it has been with all holy souls in the ages."[126]

Jack London's *The Iron Heel*, while featuring an ultra-masculine hero in Ernest Everhard of "the Chicago Commune," kept up this tradition by telling the story in the voice of Avis Everhard, a Nina Van Zandt-like character who, in the first pages of the novel, laments the loss of her "eagle . . . the flaming ideal of human freedom," and who throughout the book remarks on the working-class rebel's sexual prowess in contrast to that of the unmanly bourgeois characters.[127]

The Haymarket anarchists' trial and the anarchists' public mourning rituals were important for not only their material effects but also for their legacy of symbols and their influence on the transition of concepts of gender and individualism on the left. Instantly after the deaths, rich descriptions of women in passionate mourning created emotional bonds among sympathizers, stretching the experience of personal loss across the entire socialist movement. As they cried over the men and wrote sentimental articles about them, the anarchist mourners rehearsed the continual debate in which they responded to capitalism's valorization of the individual will with an argument for the necessity of the collective struggle for freedom.

By stressing the passion, physicality, and sexual frustration in their publications of left-wing prisoners' correspondence with their wives and lovers, and by developing "cults of personality" for Albert Parsons, August Spies and Louis Lingg, the (primarily) female memorialists gave shape to a group of heroes who were loveable and vulnerable and with whom all anarchists and social revolutionaries could imagine themselves in personal relationships. While they might have been personality cults, the figures the anarchist memorialists shaped were not the invulnerable, untouchable, and awe-inspiring men typical of later leader cults. Readers of the Haymarket correspondences would find instead men in mourning for their own lives and friends, as Louis Lingg wistfully wrote to Elsie Friedel about hearing waltz music through the prison walls and wishing he could go to the dance hall.

Most important of all, the idea of the defense campaign itself went against the idea of a traditional martyred hero. When Lucy Parsons toured the country demanding that the workers band together to save her husband, she broke with the heroic tradition of the "great man" and defined egalitarian personal relationships in collective struggle as central to libertarian socialist politics. Rather than being entirely negative, then, the creation of these "personality cults" showed the value that this group of revolutionaries placed on individuals. The stories of the Haymarket widows preserved the private selves of the anarchists as a legitimate part of revolution, and the defense and clemency campaigns made the saving of individuals into a vital task of working-class radicals.

The notion of the "blood as the seed" became central to the mourning by anarchists who saw in the executions the unveiling of capitalist terror that would eventually lead to revolution. One letter writer's poem to Lucy was published in the *Alarm* three days after the execution, exhorting, "Let their tears in crystal flood / mingle with our martyrs' blood."[128] Voltairine de Cleyre repeated this hope in many of her poems. In one, she depicted

the blood of the dead and the tears of their mourners as the source of revolutionary action, writing about how, from the grave of the revolution's martyrs one day, a "thousand voices rise / where the words of the martyr fell / the seed springs fast to the skies / watered deep from the bloody well."[129] This passionate representation of women and men together in the shadow of the scaffold was new because it defined grief and sadness not as a political problem leading to the "un-manning" of the movement but as a positive part of the revolutionary process. The publication of the private grief of the various anarchists and the interspersing of such private experiences with larger political commentary indicated a changing depiction of the forms of emotion that were appropriate in politics.

As they addressed themselves to the police and the state, and to nativist workers, members of this passionate community contrasted their own demonstration of feeling with the coldness of the law and its representatives. In a rejection of chivalrous codes, women became the best people to attack the state's cold law. Instead of arguing that they attacked the police because the police were "savage," the anarchists who came after the eight Haymarket Martyrs described the police as representatives of law and order whose primary characteristic was a deficit of basic sympathy. The funeral for the anarchists combined the connections of anarchists to workers' institutions and to the women in their lives. The procession was carefully planned to include each of the five men and their comrades in the history of the affair. It began with a group of women from the Lassalle Society who met in Thalia Hall (a beer house) and then went to Adolph Fischer's house, where they were in turn met by Fischer's local of the Typographica Union to stand in "solemn quiet around the little house which held the precious remains in an open casket." They were joined by another group composed of the *Arbeiter Zeitung* Typographica Union Local 7 of New York, several women's societies, and the women's singing society, whose rendition of "Good Night" caused the women to break into tears.

"After the murdered man's tender wife had been led, or practically carried to the waiting team, the procession assembled and set off to Milwaukee Avenue." From there, accompanied by Gounod's funeral march, the group went to August Spies's house, on to Parsons's home, and then to Aurora Turner Hall, where his body was held. From there, they went to George Engel's house, sang the Marseilles, and all shouted, "Hurrah." In the midst of this combined sadness and celebration, the *Arbeiter Zeitung* reporter rounded out his story with a note of triumph, for the police were temporarily unmanned by the emotional force of the crowd: "The

police stood there, looking on in terror. Faced with this huge crowd, which expressed its sympathy with the murdered men in such a demonstrative manner, they didn't dare intervene. They stood there with horrified looks on their faces and watched as the procession reformed and set out once again."[130]

Following the executions, and as a direct response to ongoing repression of labor by Chicago police, several new institutions were created: the Chicago Workers Legal Aid Society, the Pioneer Aid Society, the Personal Rights League, the Amnesty Association, the Alliance Bureau of Law, and the Arbeiter Rechtsschutz-Verein (Worker Rights League).[131] These organizations were the first ongoing legal-defense committees created by radicals that would take up the defense of labor agitators on a consistent basis, and they were among the earliest manifestations of civil-liberties organizations in the United States.[132] Such organizations were not simply for legal defense; they became the sites where labor activists and radicals defended their ideology in popular and personal terms and argued for the international solidarity of workers as an alternative to American nationalist subjectivity. Such groups, in addition to fighting legal battles for workers, were central in challenging the definitions of "American heroism" and as such constituted an important reproductive force on the left. That is, the left would not continue to exist in the face of state repression if it did not defend itself. The defense campaign was also reproductive because it created a popular historical record of the left for future generations of activists. Engaging in both memorial activities and civil-liberties organizing, such groups performed an educational function, writing an alternative history of the "character" of the American working class that attempted to promote cosmopolitanism and reshape class alliances along internationalist lines and away from nationalism, individual manliness, and omnipotence.

The Haymarket Martyrs' story addressed and confronted directly what it meant to be an American worker by using the story of the execution to create the beginning of a counter-culture that would tie American workers, both immigrant and native-born, to the European industrial working class. This alternative history of America and its masses was complicated by the executions and the popular hysteria that surrounded them. Although the anarchists of Chicago had first celebrated the "mob" in unqualified expressions of hope, the trial itself and the response of the American public following the bombing tempered the anarchists' celebration of the "mob."

However, in neither their glorifications of the revolutionary mob nor in their critiques of the hysterical nativist mob did the anarchists acknowledge anti-Black racism or the rule of Judge Lynch in the South. Because of this blind spot, the anarchists' continued celebration of "natural law" and the enraged fury of the passionate mob could blend all too easily with the discourses of "heroic" white vigilantism that were simultaneously developing in the post-Reconstruction South, even as the anarchists' attacks on nativist spirit were similar to arguments about the masses made by anti-lynching activists. Even though the anarchists defended the manhood and rights of Chinese workers and cast their lot with the American Indian, and even though Albert Parsons gave speeches on the evils of imperialism in Asia, the models the anarchists chose to define themselves fit within the boundaries of whiteness and, in fact, created an "alternative" Euro-American cosmopolitan white identity for the working class, in contrast to the more limited Anglo-Saxonism of the bourgeoisie.

The anarchist newspapers included no manly descriptions of Black rebellions against whites to show the legacy of slave revolt. Instead, like other white working-class publications, the anarchist publications cast African manliness in doubt. Even as the anarchists wrote that Blacks and Chinese workers were men and should rise up and revolt, they underestimated the repression those workers faced and blamed them more than they did others for failing to fight back on their own. In fact, the anarchists equated all nationalist movements with capitalist ideology, regardless of whether they were oppositional. Thus, although many of Chicago's Irish workers were sympathetic to the Irish Home Rule movement, English-born Samuel Fielden wrote that Irish and British masters were the same and that nationalist activists against British imperialism were duped by patriotic tricksters.[133] Despite this rejection of nationalism, anarchists did not hold white racists to the same standard, and the IWPA sections on the West Coast joined in anti-Chinese activism. A visitor to that group, although initially against the "anti-Coolie movement," wrote that the Chinese needed to be taught solidarity by being beaten.[134]

As Saidiya Hartman and many historians of subterranean Black resistances have argued, because of the illegal use of mob violence to control Southern blacks, the type of heroic self-representation that anarchists championed as evidence of manhood would have been nearly suicidal for Black workers, and when such resistance did occur, the anarchists did not refer to it.[135] Particularly as immigrant socialists advanced into the middle-classes, fin de siècle Marxism's transatlantic community was constructed

through the national heroic mythologies of English, French, German, and Russian workers' heroism. The alliance with social democrats increased this tendency.

During the defense campaign, Ernst Schmidt used references to German high culture to prove the civilized character of his friend August Spies, liberally quoting from Goethe and Gissing in his descriptions of the German Socialist Party's origins. Spies's own German nationalism got the better of his cosmopolitan arguments, as when he described how "Polish Jews" guarded the scabs during the strikes.[136] Just as the anarchists defied the dominant ideology of American exceptionalism, their use of entirely European examples of revolutionary manhood let them fit in with an increasingly cosmopolitan culture of industrialized western nations.

If German workers described Jews as potentially traitorous racial others, for many nineteenth-century socialists, Black men in America appeared to be "docile" laborers, dupes of the Republican Party who were not helping the class war in a significant way. Because the anarchists did not acknowledge any significant difference in their own position as "wage slaves" from that of the former slaves in the South, they implied that both Black subjection and Chinese servility were the result of subject behavior. It did not help that some Southern Black leaders and Republicans argued that Blacks should be hired because they were "good Americans" who were better and more diligent workers than foreign immigrants. Observing the furor over the upcoming anarchists' hangings, some Black Republicans fought for nativism as an alternative hierarchy to racism, noting the hypocrisy of the supposedly nativist republic that let admitted insurrectionists sit in jail writing letters while innocent Blacks were massacred in the South.[137]

Lucy Parsons (herself probably a daughter of a former slave) argued that Black rebels in the South should stop depending on the help of the Republican Party and instead help themselves by sending messages to the ruling class with bombs. She also argued that it was their mistaken belief in racial oppression (rather than white terror) that stood in their way.[138] Although the Parsonses had once been members of the Texas Republican Party, both of them ignored the role of the white working class in anti-Black violence and mitigated the relevance of the struggle for voting rights in the struggle for Black freedom, calling the vote itself irrelevant and useless as a tool.

Chicago's anarchists might not appear to have had any specific privileges in relation to African Americans. After all, they were hanged and reviled as savages. However, even these European radicals had access to citizenship,

to industrial jobs, to union membership, and to the European "imagined community" of republican revolution, in which they, unlike John Brown, did not include Blacks. They and their allies could also vote, a fact that helped the clemency campaign when labor leaders and political activists sought the sympathy of Illinois's Governor Altgeld. Most significant, at least a few of the anarchists had the ability to portray themselves to white heroes of republicanism and to call on a presumption of innocence that was unavailable to Black rebels. The Socialist Labor Party, while disagreeing heartily with the anarchists' politics, immediately argued that Spies and Parsons were innocent.

In the context of Southern mob terror against Blacks, the Chicago anarchists' adherence to antipolitical and anti-legalist theories of popular justice was problematic.[139] Herbert Spencer's theory of natural law had a huge impact on anarchist theory. In their discussions of justice, anarchists who saw economic laws operating elsewhere often replaced social theory with a purely juridical interpretation of power and defined due process as an unnecessary mediator in conflicts. Instead of "statute law," which they defined as the product of a corrupt civilization, the anarchists defended "natural law." A belief in natural law did not mean a mild and peaceful society. Echoing the theories of Spencer, many of the *Alarm*'s subscribers argued that in a lawless society, the fear that any man would face swift retaliation for any act of violence would be more effective than the existing legal system, which was flawed because "lawyer's tricks" often allowed guilty people to escape justice. This belief in a "natural law" that would be revealed once the tricky "statute law" was abolished by revolution exemplified the generally apolitical vision of most nineteenth-century revolutionary socialists that the working class was homogeneous. Importantly, this critique of "statute law" as less effective than popular justice also connected fin de siècle anarchist politics to lynching and Social Darwinism.

By 1887, the phenomenon of lynching had not made African American leaders, even those friendly to the labor movement, well disposed toward the use of political violence by white Americans, whether they were native-born workers or "in-between" immigrants. T. Thomas Fortune, who supported unions and demanded Black self-defense in some contexts, also noted the racism of craft-union organizers and the hypocrisy of the nation's reception of militant white labor. He noted the betrayal of Black workers by whites in 1877, commenting that the "colored men who were boisterous between 1877 and 1878, were hunted down, arrested, tried, punished in the courts and kept out of employment by the same white working men who had inaugurated the strikes." He saw the great

bomb scare of Chicago not as un-American but as an example of American assimilation, as chickens coming home to roost:

> When white foreigners arrive at Castle Garden they are taught and disciplined by white Americans to hate the native born colored man, to oppose him in everything he attempts. They also read that shooting, torturing, burning, and mobbing colored men and women is a common thing. . . . These anarchists, communists, socialists and nihilists have concluded to try their hands at it, commencing on their white teachers first.[140]

Even as white activists saw themselves persecuted and excoriated by the law for practicing what they defined as their American rights to political self-determination and citizenship, some Black activists looked at the movement to defend Chicago's immigrant socialists as an example of racial privilege.[141]

Thus, although the anarchists were able to sympathize with Mexican workers, to criticize anti-Chinese bias, and to defend Italian brigands—as long as action by the people was manly but not tyrannical—lynching became an exercise of "popular justice." In the case of the rape of Martha Seidel, the anarchists publicly advocated the verdict of Judge Lynch. Because of the flexibility of the theory of "natural manhood" and the deification of passionate direct action by workers as an example of manly self-reliance, both of which had a much holier position in American popular culture than did theories of class warfare, anarchism could easily lead away from socialism and toward the right. For example, Dyer Lum, once a stalwart supporter of European anarchism and industrial unionism, would later move into the AFL and (albeit privately) defend the lynching of Blacks in the South as an exercise of natural justice.[142] Because natural-law theories did not define any forms of power except the opposition of "the people" to the state, they also left the anarchists at a loss in explaining why the workers did not rise up with them against the police, except to say that they were duped by the media.

It was in this one space, this official distrust of the media and the efforts to combat it with a counter-culture, that the anarchist defense campaign left an avenue open for an alliance with Black activists. Racial exclusion from "the American people" and alienation from the mass media were intimately connected, and by the 1920s, immigrant radicals and African Americans were defining the combination of state violence and mob action in very similar ways.

However, the alienation between the far left and "the people"—defined as the consumers of Indian hating, pietistic, and nativist mass media—

remains a point of contention within the contemporary American left. Adherence to a left-wing counter-culture has been called the socialist left's major flaw. For example, in a column in the *Nation* in 1997, the popular left–labor filmmaker Michael Moore described the supporters of Mumia Abu-Jamal as the "nutty left" who were "completely out of touch with the American people," because they were incapable of joining his friends at Cleveland Indians games.[143] In more scholarly historical work, supporters of working-class consumption of mass culture as a viable site of resistance have described Marxist and feminist critiques of the mass media and white racism as moralistic, anti-working class, and connected to European elitism.[144] The history of this counter-culture's origins in the context of violent repression of the immigrant left should give Moore and others some perspective. The anarchists' critiques of American mass culture were based on the serious negative effects that the promotion of a "white working class" in the culture industry had on immigrant workers, and on radical labor organizations. The Haymarket anarchists, even before their own defense, would have argued proudly that their ideology was neither American nor foreign but a proud part of the historic international movement of the industrial proletariat. The task was to educate the workers out of their patriotism, not join them in it. Rather than being a progressive or liberating move, the attempt to bring the defense campaign into the fold of American republicanism only served to forge an imaginary alliance between working-class radicalism and the Southern lynch mob, as I will discuss in the next chapter.

3

Anti-Lynching and Labor Defense: Intersections and Contradictions

Lynch law has become so common in the United States that the finding of a dead body of a Negro, suspended between heaven and earth to the limb of a tree is of so slight importance that neither the civil authorities nor the press agencies consider the matter worth investigating. IDA B. WELLS

Tell the boys I died for my class. WESLEY EVEREST (1919)

As urban Americans turned increasingly against "tumultuous politics" and toward the use of professionally managed police forces, defining both manhood and democracy through concepts of rationality and self-restraint, Southern politicians and newspapers continued to defend passionate extralegal violence against African Americans as a form of chivalric manliness. America responded to the Paris Commune of 1871 with terror and described immigrant anarchists as a bloodthirsty mob. In contrast, during the 1871 Ku Klux Klan trials, a federal judge sympathetically described Klansmen on trial for beating and murdering Blacks who had been trying to vote as the "ignorant dupes of designing men" and handed out light sentences. The court stenographer in the case showed little pity for the victims, recording the courtroom's laughter during one Black man's description of a vicious beating as the white audience's response to what she interpreted as "the ludicrous gestures of the witness."[1]

This complete difference in perception of men and the law also appears sharply in the popular literary heroes of the time. Outlaw ballads and dime novels made defiance of the law heroic for whites such as Jesse James, who continued to be a central character in American mythology. However, the heroes of Black outlaw ballads, the chief one being Stagolee, the lawbreaking, woman-chasing, gambling man who remained a folk

hero for working-class African Americans, did not become part of mainstream popular culture. Even jazz greats compromised. Jelly Roll Morton told Alan Lomax that he used to sing the "Robert Charles song," about the distributor of Bishop Henry McNeal Turner's newspaper who had shot a police officer in New Orleans, but he stopped singing it to remain on the "peaceful side."[2]

In the years between 1877 and 1920, an era that one historian has described as "the nadir" of African American history, the middle class sent one eye on a "search for order" while the other winked at lawlessness and celebrated "natural manliness."[3] In 1971, Mary Frances Berry explained that courts had justified this contradictory behavior with a duplicitous use of the constitutional principle of federalism since the era of slavery, when federal troops were sent out almost informally against slave rebellions, but not against marauding whites who attacked African Americans.[4] The inconsistency continued and expanded in the modern era. Beginning in 1877, federal troops were regularly used to quell labor disturbances while federal authorities claimed constitutional powerlessness to stop lynch mobs. Predominantly white working-class organizations and African Americans both faced government and extralegal repression; they had much in common. However, the importance of race in defining one's relationship both to law and to mobs at the turn of the century meant that the institutions and philosophies of labor defense as created by a mixture of socialists that included the boisterous and mostly white IWW, the community of American anarchists surrounding Emma Goldman, as well as Clarence Darrow and other liberal and progressive supporters of labor, differed from the strategies adopted by anti-lynching activists, best represented by the largely middle-class professionals of the NAACP.[5] Although they often faced the same enemies, they developed different strategies for representing and resisting repression and crafted different kinds of heroes and villains when they depicted the ideal forms of responding to repression.

Middle-class Black anti-lynching activists identified white mob terror as their primary opponent, describing crazed white mobs acting irrationally in anarchic orgies of blood: "merciless maniacs swooping down on one defenseless creature just because they have the power."[6] Playing on progressive fears of mob hysteria, they contrasted such mobs with rational, heroic Black manhood. In some cases, progressive anti-lynching activists appealed to the party of order's hatred of urban incendiaries and compared anarchists and lynchers. Booker T. Washington referred to Leon Czolgosz as a "lyncher" after he assassinated President William McKinley and

thought it would be a good national lesson if he were "put to death through the majesty of the law."[7] Walter White, one of the NAACP's most important anti-lynching activists, said that if white America could see lynch mobs as "anarchists," the federal government would not hesitate in intervening to stop them.[8] The NAACP advocated the use of federal law against lynching and in one case considered a bill that would have defined a mob as "any assemblage or gathering of three or more persons for the committing of any act, the commission of which would be or is a violation of the criminal law of the state" and that would hold each individual member of that mob liable for any crime of murder committed by it.[9] In a 1920 press release titled, "Anti-Red Bill a Blow at Lynching?" the NAACP suggested that a new sedition bill introduced by Representative George S. Graham of Pennsylvania would make lynching a federal crime.[10]

Labor-defense practices, in contrast, emphasized direct action in response to restrictive law at the turn of the century. The labor-defense campaigns spanning the years from the 1890s to the 1920s emerged from within a labor movement and radical culture that encompassed a multitude of political views. The liberal Clarence Darrow, the defense lawyer who represented labor in three of the most important trials of the era—Eugene Debs in the Pullman Strike; Bill Haywood, Charles Moyer, and Edward Pettibone in the murder case of Idaho Governor Frank Steunenberg in 1906–1907; and the McNamara brothers in 1911—is the best-known labor defender. But anarchists and other revolutionary socialists played an equally important role in crafting a tradition of defense that went far beyond legal arguments. Finally, the IWW, the target of many mob attacks and hundreds of legal prosecutions, built what would become the institutional model for labor defense in its General Defense Committee.

Emma Goldman, Alexander Berkman, and the immigrant anarchists of Russia, Italy, and Spain who shared their general philosophies advocated the use of revolutionary violence and often rejected the reliance on lawyers for defense in court.[11] When Berkman went on trial for his attempt to assassinate Henry Clay Frick in 1892, he told Emma Goldman, as she recalled in her autobiography, "I will kill Frick . . . and of course I shall be condemned to death . . . but I will die by my own hand, like Lingg."[12] Later, Berkman would be a major organizer of popular defense campaigns, including Tom Mooney's. In 1902, Goldman was one of a small number of American radicals who defended Czolgosz, arguing that he had been driven to the assassination of McKinley because he was a "supersensitive being" and could not "supinely witness the suffering of others."[13] Going

against Berkman's heroic methods, Goldman even sought a lawyer for Czolgosz.

Berkman and Goldman saw themselves as in the tradition of the Haymarket anarchists and developed their own complex anarcho-communist ideology in the 1900s. While they generally opposed the use of lawyers as a waste of time and a demonstration of a false faith in the courts, the twentieth-century anarchists participated in most of the other defense campaigns of the era, including those for birth-control activists and sexual dissidents.[14] In doing so, they created their own tendency within the labor-defense tradition that simultaneously called for "direct action" and forged alliances with middle-class progressives and cultural and intellectual radicals.

The group that did the most to create a tradition of radical labor defense practice was the IWW (or Wobblies) founded in 1905 in Chicago. They, too, maintained a strong connection to the Haymarket Martyrs. Lucy Parsons spoke at the IWW's founding convention. As IWW members faced countless trials for their activity in organizing unskilled immigrant workers, they organized mass defense campaigns that championed direct action. They differed from the more absolutist anarchists by hiring lawyers who became specialists in labor-defense cases. Their innovation was to take the Haymarket defense strategy of organizing solidarity for fallen members through the labor movement and make it into a mass organizing strategy. In a way that Lucy Parsons had begun, but that the Chicago anarchists had not fully followed, the IWW intentionally organized masses for the defense of prisoners, masses intent not on revolution in the future but on the practical task of saving the individual worker in the here and now. Members of the group did not always agree with this tactic, some finding it naively hopeful about the capitalist courts and a diversion of energy and resources from labor organizing. But building defense became an organizing strategy in itself. The IWW used the defense campaign to expose the fallacy of American exceptionalism. Because the IWW did not believe that the law was written to work in its interests, but was merely a tool of the capitalist class, it argued that mass action, whether in a general strike or in massing in courtrooms and outside, was the best method of saving comrades in a way that echoed the Haymarket anarchists' invocation of the passionate mob. The union also believed in the "spirit" of the Bill of Rights, as it demonstrated in its "Free Speech Campaigns" in the early 1900s. Both through these campaigns and in its opposition to the U.S. military draft during World War One, the IWW inspired the creation of the ACLU.

Regardless of their individual ideologies, labor-defense activists from Debs and Darrow to Goldman and Berkman appealed to traditional American populist antistatism. Often, the new corporate-friendly state was depicted as a fall from the early republican ideals of the revolutionary era and a betrayal of Jefferson's ideals as put forth in the Declaration of Independence. The Wobblies as well as the Goldman–Berkman anarchists depicted the court as cloaked bourgeois power. In labor-defense literature, locks, bars, uniformed officers, and cold buildings represented the law as a destructive machine run by capital; the prison, as a tomb for the souls of lively men. The law's complicated rules became a sticky, tricky spider's web. Against these deadly forces, labor activists pitted the breathing, lively bodies of workers who, joined together, formed the mass of natural men. When the IWW attacked state control and repression in the name of freedom and mass direct action, it was responding not only to the state, but also to the rise of the AFL's "business unionism."[15] Between the trial of Eugene Debs in 1895 and the trials of hundreds of draft resisters during the First World War, radical labor activists responded to legal repression with mass protest and calls to general strike, and at least until 1911, they argued that violence was a legitimate strategy for resisting a law that failed to represent them. What good was the law if, as the syndicalist paper the *Agitator* put it in 1911, it was a web designed to catch workers—"1,600 laws and ignorance no excuse for breaking them! Get it? See how they catch us coming and going?" As radical workers saw their comrades imprisoned by the hundreds, the "fair trial" became a "somber robed lie."[16]

The IWW's defense campaigns also shaped the heroic representation of the radical labor movement in the 1900s. The Wobblies' own roots were in the American West, in the Western Federation of Miners, and in some cases members embraced the West's mythology to define themselves. As it did in the Haymarket era, the radical labor movement's attack on law and order often came close to replicating the tropes of romantic literature that defined American manliness with settler vigilantism and lynching. However, the IWW was also a victim of western vigilantism, and it eventually argued that these supposedly "popular" actions were often simply the work of "thugs" hired by the bourgeoisie; thus, the vigilantism was just another version of bourgeois law and order. As both the NAACP and the IWW confronted the wave of reactionary violence and increasing government repression between 1917 and 1920, their explanations of repression in America came closer together. The antiradical repression between 1917 and 1920 made the connection between the state and the mob clear in

both the rise of a second Ku Klux Klan and the creation of the Federal Bureau of Investigation (FBI) that attacked both "reds" and Blacks.[17]

This same rise of vigilante attacks coupled with state suppression of activism also motivated the "New Crowd Negroes," whether they were the socialists associated with A. Phillip Randolph's paper the *Messenger* or the nationalists of the Marcus Garvey movement, to criticize the NAACP's legal tactics and to argue for direct action against lynching more openly.

In the Beginning: Ida B. Wells and the Fight against Lynching

The New Crowd Negroes were not the first people to praise the use of self-defense against lynch mobs. As anarchists, socialists, and labor organizers fought against the lawless police, in 1892 Ida B. Wells began her newspaper campaign against Southern white anarchy and maintained a delicate balance between an appeal to white Americans' beliefs in "law and order" and an attack on the apparatus of law enforcement. When she inaugurated a major publicity campaign against the criminalization of Black men, which in addition to strewing the South with the broken bodies of its "citizens" also filled Southern jails and chain gangs, Wells faced a legal system that criminalized behavior among Blacks that would be defined as manly when exercised by whites and that, like Southern slave-patrol regulations, encouraged white volunteers to practice "informal" law enforcement. As Glenda Gilmore explains, even for well-to-do Blacks, the South's concept of "place" was, as the novelist Charles Chestnutt had described it, like Procrustes's bed, "a confining space in which Blacks were to remain, not rising so high as to threaten whites."[18] Lynching was not directed simply at working-class Blacks. Middle-class Blacks could also be victims of lynching, as they had clearly violated white concepts of place. Drawing on the abolitionist tradition of heroic discourse, Wells made sure when she described horrible lynching scenes to note the superior manhood of the victims at the pyre, focusing especially on elements of calm, unflinching rationality, resistance to pain, and religious faith in her descriptions of lynching victims.

In Wells's writing, which is foundational to modern Black radical critiques of the American caste system, the description of the encounter between the victim and the lynch mob was a metaphor for the larger problem of African Americans in a lawless white society, where lynching was not an aberrational event but an attack on all Blacks by the whole

white population not just in the South, but in the United States more broadly. After all, as Christopher Waldrep notes, even the *New York Times* described "people who are lynched as if they were convicted murderers."[19] Wells described the lynching as endemic to white supremacy, an irrational institution that dissolved the separation between men and law and denied the legitimacy of Black agency and social mobility.[20] Although Wells was not the first person to oppose lynching publicly, her strategy set the methods that would be used by the NAACP when it began its anti-lynching campaign, and for that reason her ideas and methods are critical for understanding later developments.[21]

Wells's anti-lynching campaign allowed for a double reading. On one level, it appealed to Black nationalist opposition to white state power and endorsed armed self-defense and the withholding of labor. Wells also appealed to white progressive opposition to Southern working-class savagery. However, even as she did so, Wells made the proto-revolutionary point that the entire American legal system was illegitimate. For in her writings, she consistently defined white mobs as part of the criminal-justice system of the post–Reconstruction South. The physical attacks on the African American population were part of an attempt by whites to maintain white-only citizenship, Wells argued, by marking African Americans as a race of criminals. Lynching was not simply a white mob out of control or a practice of law enforcement, but a use of criminal accusations as a form of propaganda against Blacks in general. As she wrote in *Mob Rule in New Orleans*, "It is now, even as it was in the days of slavery, an unpardonable sin for a Negro to resist a white man, no matter how unjust or unprovoked the white man's attack may be."[22]

In her descriptions of white monopolies on law, Wells did not offer law as an alternative to the courts of Judge Lynch but noted the identical makeup of the lynch mob and the state, defining a police–mob continuum. "All the machinery of white law and politics is in the hands of those who commit the lynchings," she wrote. Lynchings, as Wells described them, brought white mayors, crackers, gentry, police, and even small children together. It was not the act of "the lawless element upon which the deviltry of the South is usually saddled," she argued, but simply the "whites" of Southern cities who gathered for lynchings across class boundaries.[23] Thus, Wells recognized what the historian Richard Maxwell Brown argued in his important early book on vigilantism: that extrajudicial action is not law enforcement's opposite but has often been the leading edge in U.S. criminal law.[24]

Because lynching was a form of propaganda, Wells systematically disputed its claims. Just as political trials of labor activists made "examples" that affected the larger group, and therefore required a political defense, so did lynching. The anti-lynching movement was a "defense campaign" organized to defend the innocence of Black people as a group from extralegal prosecutions that carried the weight of law and order. Like labor-defense activists, anti-lynching activists confronted a mass media that depicted their own group as a threat to the rest of the community. Wells explained in her autobiography, "We should be in a position to investigate every lynching and get the facts for ourselves. If there was no chance for a fair trial in these cases, we should have the facts to use in an appeal to public opinion."[25]

Also like the Chicago anarchists, anti-lynching activists rejected dominant definitions of guilt and innocence, identified the arbitrary behavior of the officials in charge of law enforcement, and created heroic images of resistance to the law. However, anti-lynching activists had to recognize something that labor activists often did not: the role of extralegal mass violence as a unique element in maintaining the status quo and cementing white opinion behind the caste system. Lynching's simultaneous call to populism and law and order was exactly what brought working-class whites together with the bourgeoisie in a permissible exercise of power that unified whites across classes as a community protecting its boundaries. The fact that the law was enforced not simply by jackbooted jailers was an act that forged white solidarity. In lynchings, as Wells argued, groups of whites acted together in a carnivalesque atmosphere; terror did not come from outside or above but was part of the popular culture of the white South. For this reason, anti-lynching activists would be leery of populist opposition to the law and would never define mass action by whites in and of itself as "good" or natural.

Wells showed the continuity, rather than the division, between the police and the mob. In her pamphlets "A Red Record" and "Mob Rule in New Orleans," Wells made sure to point out that it was not simply "the lowest element of the white south" who "turned loose to wreak fiendish cruelty on those too weak to help themselves." This was particularly terrible because they were joined and abetted by "white men who controlled all the forces of law and order in their communities and who could have easily legally punished rapists and murderers, especially Black men who had neither political power nor financial strength with which to evade any justly deserved fate."[26]

Moreover, the fact that lynchings occurred despite a racially biased justice system made them ironically unnecessary and, thus, irrational. Wells's theory of the mob actually reversed the image of the envious, hungry mob of traditional republican theory. She described the irrationality of the crowd in her writing as the product of power rather than powerlessness. The rulers of the society, holding all the reigns of order in their hands, had an unjustified fear of people they already dominated. While the press claimed that lynching was a tool used only because the law failed to work, Wells, like the anarchists of Chicago who remarked on the leniency of the law towards the wealthy, argued that it "is only the wealthy white man who the law fails to reach. In every case of criminal procedure the Negro is punished."[27] Whites feared and attempted to control even the most innocent and inoffensive Black people.

When the NAACP began publishing the *Crisis*, W. E. B. Du Bois continued Wells's general depiction of the mob–law continuum, maintaining a regular column devoted to recording lynchings. As local branches grew, the investigation, description, and prosecution of lynch mobs *and* brutal police officers as partners in crime became a central focus of activism for the NAACP in the North and South. As African Americans were killed— spectacularly by large crowds or casually by police—news of the identities of the victims reached a national community of African Americans who read eyewitness accounts from across the country, creating an emotional alliance between Black readers, lynching victims, and their families.

The articles describing the incidents worked to defend the character of the mob's victims and thus served as the only form of "defense activism" that was available to people who had never had a day in court. These descriptions sometimes highlighted innocence and inoffensiveness to expose the irrationality and cruelty of the forces of power; at other times, they emphasized heroism rather than victimization. Claims of outraged Black innocence responded to an existing discourse of white innocence and Black power.

Lynching was initially explicitly political, an attack on Black political power during Reconstruction.[28] The use of the "rape myth" during the 1890s displaced political conflict and was harder to contest than a political accusation. The racial depictions of Blacks' crimes against whites in the South were melodramatic, showing irrational superior physical power and eros out of control in acts against weak, white female victims, of whom the lynch mob became the heroic savior. Before Wells began her crusade, even Frederick Douglass, she reported, had "begun to believe it true that there was increasing lasciviousness on the part of Negroes."[29]

Wells did not begin her crusade against lynching until her good friend Tom Moss, a well-liked Black shop owner, and his business partners were murdered by a white mob in Memphis in 1892. The lynching of these men, Wells recalled later, "opened my eyes to what lynching really was." Before that time, she had believed, "like many another person who had read of lynching in the South . . . that although lynching was irregular and contrary to law and order . . . perhaps the brute deserved death anyhow."[30] The breaking of this "big lie" was the first essential task of Black journalists who wrote about lynching. When she went to England, Wells wrote, "The hardest part of my work was to convince the British people that this [bestiality] was a false charge against Negro manhood."[31]

In the effort to show Blacks' innocence and to win sympathy, many descriptions of lynching victims emphasized their vulnerability and terror. In her description of Moss's death, for example, Wells appealed to pity, noting that as the lynchers came at him, he "begged for his life for the sake of his wife and child and unborn baby."[32] Like earlier abolitionist writings, such descriptions of vulnerability humanized Blacks who had been stereotyped as unfeeling and animalistic. This focus on innocence was effective because Southerners had argued that enslavement was essential for African Americans, who otherwise would revert to savagery.[33] Wells traced lynching to these kinds of beliefs, quoting a famous South Carolinian who had argued:

> Since the emancipation came and the tie of mutual interest and regard between master and servant was broken, the Negro has drifted away into a state which is neither freedom nor bondage. Lacking the proper inspiration of the one and the restraining force of the other, he has taken up the idea that boorish insolence is independence and the exercise of a decent degree of breeding to white people is identical with servile submission.[34]

To reverse this perception, Wells and other activists sometimes showed the victim's total weakness in the face of brutal and unnecessary expressions of power. Lynch law, Wells wrote, "was directed against those persons very largely defenseless and more or less under social ban, afflicted by disability and always under the fatal disadvantage of race prejudice."[35] For example, the Black-run newspaper, the *Springfield Weekly Republican*, which reported extensively on white savagery against Blacks in the Progressive Era, reported that Sam Hose had "pleaded pitifully for mercy and begged his tormenters to let him die."[36] In a similar rhetorical appeal, the *Crisis* in 1916 published an editorial cartoon satirizing police brutality and media representations of Black criminals. Rather than speaking of

the rage of the Black race rising up in revenge against the lynching, Wells, in *Southern Horrors,* praised Black men who refused to riot, showing "obedience to the law which did not protect them."[37] Wells, of course, was not advising quiescence, just strategy. For such hands to be raised required a voice like Wells's—one that was far removed from the scene. Not simply a fight for life, the anti-lynching campaign tried to win the basic right of resistance for American Blacks in the Jim Crow South. These portrayals suggested that Black men needed women such as Wells to advance the interests of the race.[38]

However, in other descriptions of lynching Wells portrayed heroic resistance. The most consistent characteristic that Wells praised was not fierce passion, but extreme coolness and rationality in contrast to the frenzy of whites. For example, when she praised Robert Charles for defending his rights against the police and the mob, she pointed out that he had "deadly aim"; she referred to the cowardice of the police; and she argued that, despite what the newspapers said about his being a "desperado," the only evidence that Charles was a desperate man was that he "refused to be beaten over the head by officer Mora for sitting on a step quietly conversing with a friend."[39]

Wells also fought images of Blacks as servile by compiling statistics on people who were lynched for such crimes as "being saucy" or for attempting to join farmers' cooperatives. The absence of legal protection for Blacks, and the availability of whites for mob action, made anti-lynching activism more difficult than labor-defense activism. Attempts to resist or speak out against lynching while it occurred were dangerous. A Reverend King, for example, came in close contact with white terror and lived to tell the tale to a New York newspaper: "I was ridden out of Paris [Texas] on a rail because I was the only man in Lamar County to raise my voice against the lynching of [Henry] Smith." After watching the burning and mutilation of Smith, King wrote that finally, "I could stand no more and with super human effort dashed through the compact mass of humanity and stood at the foot of the burning scaffold. 'In the name of God,' I cried, 'I command you to cease this torture.' The heavy butt of a Winchester rifle descended on my head and I fell to the ground. Rough hands seized me and angry men bore me away, and I was thankful."[40]

Affronts to white superiority could result in murders—or, worse, wholesale race riots. When it could not kill Robert Charles, the New Orleans mob attacked helpless old people, women, and children instead. In another example, Wells described how all those who might be brought in for questioning in a court of law were simply killed if they refused to

OUR BRAVE POLICEMEN

"After a terrific struggle the burly Negro was finally subdued."

Lorenzo Harris, "Our Brave Policemen," *Crisis*, June 1916, 96.

John Henry Adams, "Women to the Rescue," *Crisis*, May 1916, 43. As the woman hits the vultures of Jim Crow with her club labeled "Federal Constitution," the fleeing man says: "I don't believe in agitating and fighting. My policy is to pursue the line of least resistance. To h— with civil rights. I want money. I think the white folks will let me stay on my land as long as I stay in my place (shades of Wilmington, NC). The good white folks ain't responsible for bad administration of the law and lynching and peonage—let me think awhile, er—"

provide information about their accused relatives. "During the search for Julian on Saturday," Wells reported, "one branch of the posse visited the house of a Negro family in the neighborhood of Camp Parapet, and failing to find the object of their search, tried to induce John Willis, a young Negro, to disclose the whereabouts of Julian. He refused to do so, or could not do so, and was kicked to death by the gang."[41]

Like Reverend King, Wells risked life and property when she spoke out against the great Southern taboos. She was lucky enough to escape being murdered by a Southern mob because she was out of town when her article describing consensual sexual relationships between white women and Black men was published in her newspaper, the aptly titled *Free Speech*. When she defended the right to self-defense, directing criticism at Booker T. Washington, she wrote that "the more the African American yields and cringes and begs, the more he has to do so, the more he is insulted, outraged and lynched."[42] Wells's attacks on lynching, regardless of how they depicted its victims, indicated a refusal to abide by white definitions of good and evil. Moreover, like Frederick Douglass, who described his battle with his master Covey, Wells's work argued for Black manhood and citizenship rights rather than simply against lynching as a form of barbarity. Thus, she could not stop with images of pure victimization and meekly borne suffering or moral superiority of the kind that appeared in Harriet Beecher Stowe's *Uncle Tom's Cabin*. Instead, she depicted African Americans' valiant and reasonable struggles with the forces of irrational, wild white mobs as an argument for the possibility of Black participation in American political life on the basis of superior rationality, bravery, and skill. It was a fight that showed the relationship between democratic rights and access to due process and equal protection of law, as men such as Charles were driven to defend themselves because the law would not:

> Betrayed into the hands of the police, Charles, who had already sent two of his would-be murderers to their death, made a last stand in a small building . . . and, still defying his pursuers, fought a mob of twenty thousand people, single-handed and alone, killing three more men, mortally wounding two more and seriously wounding nine others. Unable to get to him in his stronghold, the besiegers set fire to his house of refuge. While the building was burning Charles was shooting, and every crack of his death-dealing rifle added another victim to the price which he had placed upon his own life. Finally, when fire and smoke became too much for flesh and blood to stand, the long sought for fugitive appeared in the door, rifle in hand, to charge the countless guns that were drawn upon him. With a courage which was

indescribable, he raised his gun to fire again, but this time it failed, for a hundred shots riddled his body, and he fell dead face fronting to the mob.[43]

Writing about another event, Wells reported the speech of C. J. Miller, who addressed the lynch mob before it killed him:

My name is C. J. Miller. I am from Springfield, Ill[inois]. My wife lives at 716 N[orth] 2nd street. I am among you today, looked upon as one of the most brutal men before the people. I stand here surrounded by men who are excited, men who are not willing to let the law take its course, and as far as the crime is concerned, I have committed no crime, and certainly no crime gross enough to deprive me of my life and liberty to walk upon this green earth.[44]

No matter how inoffensive or manly the depiction of Black victims of lynching, progressive whites remained doubtful of these stories of virtue. Even Northern white progressives had fallen for the myth of Black criminality, regardless of their opposition to the savage practice of public burning. At least one NAACP leader, Oswald Garrison Villard, demanded that Blacks' crimes be printed alongside the record of lynchings that appeared in the *Crisis*.[45] Ray Stannard Baker's stories on lynching in the *American Magazine* described both Black criminals and lynch mobs.[46] Wells reported on the many debates she had with progressive white women over the Southern rape myth. These debates extended into her settlement-house work in Chicago, where she fought with Frances Willard and Georgia Plummer, the Chicago reformer. Willard, a proponent of the Populist Party, friend of Tom Watson, and leader of the Women's Christian Temperance Union (WCTU) had disputed Wells while she was on tour in England and won support for the American racial-caste system by comparing segregation to British imperial policy in India. Willard asserted that it was true that Southern white women were afraid to leave their homes at night for fear of rape.[47] To stop lynching, Plummer had argued after the Atlanta Race Riot, Blacks should "drive the criminals out from among you."[48] At the same time that progressive women focused on criminal elements in the Black community, some of the Populist Party's leaders turned to racism to defend their party from the Democrats, abandoning earlier attempts at interracial organizing.

As Gail Bederman argues, when Wells addressed whites, she urged them to act in the name of law and order against Southern anarchy. Although she had argued that lynching was a form of unofficial "law enforcement" that worked through police collaboration with mobs, it made sense for Wells to appeal to progressive women through an attack on the barba-

rism of public hangings as an atrocity, as a barbaric *form* of punishment connected to backwardness and savagery.[49] The anti-lynching movement, particularly among white progressives, echoed the civilizing anti–death penalty movements that had already taken hold in a much earlier era, as English, French, and American activists organized against public executions because of their infectious and socially corrupting nature.[50] Like the anarchists, Wells used her stories of mass terror to question American claims for exceptionalism. She reported that her audiences wanted to know "why the U.S.A. was burning human beings alive in the nineteenth century as the Red Indians were said to have done three hundred years before."[51]

For this reason, Wells's anti-lynching campaign succeeded in winning over prominent Republicans such as William Howard Taft and Theodore Roosevelt, who denounced lynching as a form of savagery. Wells also played directly to fears of anarchism and working-class disorder. That Wells was not unaware of the impact of class issues on lynching was evident in her comment on why the leaders of Louisiana eventually intervened to stop the New Orleans Race Riot:

> The killing of a few Negroes more or less by irresponsible mobs does not cut much figure in Louisiana. But when the reign of mob law exerts a depressing influence upon the stock market and city securities begin to show unsteady standing in money centers, then the strong arm of the good white people of the South asserts itself and order is quickly brought out of chaos.[52]

When Wells "inverted" the Progressive Movement's discourse of "civilization," she struck a chord with white middle-class progressives, who were ashamed of the image of America as "savage" that Wells created during her two speaking tours in England.[53]

From Wells's campaign to the NAACP's, the anti-lynching movement was a defense of the manliness of all Black Americans in the face of an increasingly rigid ideological system that excluded Blacks from citizenship by defining all Black agency as criminal, racializing conceptions of guilt and innocence at their very cores. That is, as Saidiya Hartman argues, the code of race relations made "self-abasement" into virtue for Blacks, excluding them completely from the manliness ideals of the era.[54] The efforts to remedy the imbalance between the treatment of whites and Blacks before the law, and to establish the innocence and humanity of individuals who were lynched, jailed, and executed, were central to the attempt to gain Black citizenship in an era when the convict camp became the new plantation. Despite its appeals to middle-class respectability, the use of

lynching as the ultimate sign of Black valuelessness in the heart of white America was a powerful emotional attack on white America as a heartless beast. That attack was similar to the one that the abolitionists had made during slavery. It was also similar to the attack on capitalism by the anarchists of Chicago—except that while anarchists drew the line between classes, anti-lynchers drew it between Blacks and whites.

The NAACP, Du Bois, the *Crisis*, and the Twentieth-Century Anti-Lynching Crusade

Wells's anti-lynching campaign set the pattern that would be adopted by the NAACP when it formed in 1909 in response to the Springfield Race Riots. Echoing Civil War–era fugitive-slave-rescue groups, the local branches were called "vigilance committees."[55] These groups attacked not just lynching, but other "problems of legal redress."[56] Perhaps continuing the work of such groups as New York's Citizens Protective League, which held a 3,500 person forum on anti-Black police brutality in Carnegie Hall in 1900, the NAACP made little distinction between lynching and police brutality.[57] When Du Bois began editing the *Crisis*, he developed the "police–mob continuum" further. In his columns, he speculated about the causes of anti-Black violence and often argued that mobs lynched and police shot Black men not for "nothing," but for violating the subtle racial codes of place in the South. His column "Along the Color Line" celebrated everyday acts of manly defiance against Jim Crow and defended the rights of Blacks to resist while depicting acts of violence by police and mobs. Du Bois pointed out that following the "law" was not always the answer: In describing one legal death sentence, he noted that "it may not go down on the lynching record, but its difference from lynching is not large enough to cause us any feeling of uplift."[58]

The behavior for which men were attacked might be a response to existing unprovoked violence, as the *Crisis* reported: "Police murderously assaulted Dr. Thomas G. Coates for remonstrating against the beating of another colored man."[59] Police killings appeared in the lynching column, challenging notions of law and order as the solution. "Policemen have killed their usual quota of colored men," Du Bois reported one week.[60] Or, to put it even more simply, "The police *is* the mob. The courts *are* the lynchers."[61]

Like Wells, writers for the *Crisis* directly confronted the representation of Black criminality not only by attacking police, but by humanizing those

defined as criminal, describing killings inside prisons and corruption in law enforcement. The *Crisis* exposed the prison's role in maintaining divisions in the working class and creating a super-exploited layer of workers within the prison and contract-labor system. The system of convict leasing encouraged the random arrests of innocent African Americans. The sheriff in one county, according to a reporter, acted as a "recruiting agent for the employers of convict labor. . . . About 87% of the convicts of the state are Negroes, many of whom, arrested for trifling offenses have drifted into crime because of ignorance and the neglect of the state to properly educate them. Life in the convict camps of the South is more degrading and cruel than it ever was under slavery."[62]

It was not an empty "conspiracy theory": Police and state governments did act in concert with New South businessmen looking for ways to cut costs and achieve greater control over labor.[63] In another case, according to a column reprinted from the socialist *New York Call*, sheriffs encouraged crime in order to make arrests. Provocateurs, the *Call* reported, would "get stout, husky niggers into crap games . . . then report them to the sheriff who promptly arrests them and sends them off to work."[64] Not all those captured were guilty—even of trifling crimes. As an article in December 1912 issue of the *Crisis* remarked, "All the women sent to convict farms are not prostitutes. Hundreds are honest, self-respecting, law abiding women who do not have the opportunity to prove their innocence in the courts." Sometimes the prosecutions were the result of resistance to racism; one girl, the reporter noted, "protested her innocence so vigorously that she was arrested for resisting the officer."[65] The *Crisis* showed how Southerners victimized Blacks through the use of police, courts, prisons, and mobs and thus profited from the subjection of Blacks as cheap labor. Like mobs, police were hysterical and out of control. In one tragic incident, Du Bois described how a policeman had killed a child because "he didn't stop when called."[66] In another, "a police inquiry nearly killed a man," whom "Atlanta tried to lynch."[67] When police acted as judge and jury, the NAACP's local branches fought lynching and police killings as related acts of lawlessness, pressing suits against police officers in several Northern cities during the 1910s.[68]

The NAACP's national anti-lynching campaign, begun officially in 1916, was similar to Wells's in that it stressed investigation, research, and publicity above all. In addition to traveling to regions where lynchings occurred, NAACP officers hired a clipping service and wrote letters to people they knew in locales to find out the story behind the mass media's representations. Field Secretary Chapin Brinsmade wrote to one person from whom

he sought news, "We make it a practice to get all possible information about lynchings at first hand from people in the neighborhood."[69] The NAACP also circulated shocking photographs of victims of lynching as the bodies that bore the signs of Southern savagery. Following Jesse Washington's lynching in Waco, Texas, the *Crisis* ran a photograph of his charred body on the cover an eight-page supplement titled "The Waco Horror."[70] These images, sent to Congress and national news publications, were not the first images of lynching to be published. Whites who participated in lynchings made photographic postcard souvenirs that they circulated as trophies of the events, and a Black newspaper in Topeka published a photograph of the victim of an Oklahoma lynching in 1911, calling on other Black newspapers to do likewise.[71]

Not everyone agreed on which cases merited attention. For example, in one case in Oklahoma, Scott Brown Jr., a Muskogee attorney, wrote to the national office of the NAACP and to a women's club in San Diego that the lynching of Marie Scott "isn't the one" to make a special case. First, he wrote to NAACP Secretary May Childs Nerney that the case had arisen as part of an attempt to "clear the red light district," and that he would not say anything about the rest of it to a woman because Scott's crime was so revolting. In his next letter, he told Ms. Anderson of the Friday club: "A complete investigation into the facts will not result in obtaining public sympathy for the victim, because her character [is] as bad as possible and because the circumstances of her crime [are] revolting and shocking."[72]

However, the national office wanted to know more and kept searching for direct eyewitness accounts. It got one from J. H Coleman of Blackdom, New Mexico, a Black town that was awaiting the arrival of the victim's brother from Clovis, to which he had fled after being "smuggled out" of Muskogee by a group of porters. Despite the NAACP's reputation as a rigidly middle-class organization, this account of the Muskogee lynching, which described the rape of Marie Scott by two white men and her brother's killing of one of them, is the one that Du Bois published in the *Crisis*, the one that was picked up by the all-female "anti-lynching crusaders" who publicized the lynching of women, and the one that survives today.[73] As W. Fitzhugh Brundage argues, such "exposes enabled blacks to compile their own collective history of white repression."[74]

These representations of Black innocence and white arbitrariness reached a dramatic climax in the Harlem Chapter of the NAACP's silent march against lynching following the St. Louis race riots in 1917. Demonstrating mass power and respectability, they protested the massacre of "honest toilers." The NAACP analyzed the criminal justice system's op-

pression of Blacks as fundamental to the status quo in the racially divided labor market and indicated the often sympathetic relationship between Black middle-class activists and Black workers.[75] What made the NAACP's strategy for dealing with the problem of combined extralegal and state repression different from the simultaneous labor movement's attack on the state's iron heel was faith in the courts and the use of federal law. The NAACP relied on a staff of mostly elite white lawyers with "impeccable" credentials to press their cases in court and strove for an image of middle-class propriety.[76]

White Progressives and Socialists in the
Anti-Lynching Campaigns

While for Wells and Du Bois the cause of lynching was white supremacy, which was endemic to the entire United States, most of the white Americans who opposed lynching saw the problem differently. Often, early-twentieth-century studies of lynching depicted the South's violence as part of a backward rural culture. Progressives' explanations of white Southerners' behavior made implicit connections between the perpetrators and the victims of these crimes and described lynching as a regional and economic phenomenon.[77] Here, white progressives implicitly accepted the logic of white racist populists, such as Mississippi Governor James Vardaman, a prison reformer and advocate of lynching between 1900 and 1910 who argued that Blacks were in league with "feudal lords," and Tom Watson, who presented lynching as a form of direct democracy.[78]

Northern progressives, who fought lynching and immigrant lawlessness because they were related forms of chaos, were thus not unlike the white Southern bourgeoisie: Both worked to reduce the number of eligible voters. Their anxieties about the disruptive effects of class violence, their faith in modernization, and their association of lynching with industrial labor violence made them a perfect audience for Wells's critiques of Southern lynching as an anarchic and "uncivilized" practice. For progressives, the problem was not the murder of African Americans per se, but the mutilations and illegal mob attacks on Black workers by what the white progressive Ray Stannard Baker referred to as the "lowest element of the white population."[79] The progressives saw both the victims of lynching and the lynchers as part of the anarchy of Southern life, and their anti-lynching strategy of choice involved the use of federal police and federal law. This white–Black progressive alliance at the heart of the NAACP's anti-lynching

activism prevented more radical and confrontational anti-lynching strategies from being voiced in the national political discussion.

The Black middle class also had a stake in preserving order, believing that behavior by rowdy working-class Blacks would reflect badly on them and jeopardize their positions. Thus, the author Fenton Johnson told the cautionary tale of working-class violence in his story "Call of the Patriot," published in the *Crisis* in 1917. In it, Johnson depicted an aristocratic hero named Garrison who had modeled himself after Toussaint L'Ouverture. The hero's knowledge of French and his mulatto status, his partial whiteness, made him a superior leader. The story reached its climax when a parlor maid named Hagar killed her mistress with a broom, leading to the arrival on the Black college campus of a posse of whites to kill the hero, Garrison. A hero for social equality, or a paragon of assimilation, Garrison dies in the arms of a white female teacher, who had been impressed by his recitations from classic works of European literature.[80] This cautionary tale against working-class action cannot be defined in terms of class conflict alone. Class mobility for Blacks in America has consistently been linked both to light skin color and to the adoption of "European" manners. As Michael Gomez argues, class divisions among African Americans have always been defined through race, since house servants have tended to have lighter skin and greater economic mobility than fieldworkers after emancipation.[81]

Despite the NAACP's insistence on court cases, others did call for the use of force against lynchers. The *Topeka Colored Citizen* recommended, for example, that whites involved in lynching "should be burned while sleeping with their families around them dreaming of the terror they have scattered among the colored people."[82] W. Fitzhugh Brundage has made an effort to unearth the "informal, unorganized resistance by blacks during the era of Jim Crow" and has found several incidents of Blacks resisting lynching with calls for popular retaliation, although these calls had to toe a careful line to avoid the massive retaliation from whites that might meet even measured Black resistance. Terrence Finnegan also notes a number of cases of Blacks' using violence or threats of violence in response to white attacks, particularly in the earliest years of Jim Crow. In 1883, one thousand armed Blacks were able to force justice out of a white court system following the murder of a Black man by a white clerk. Blacks who faced mob attacks in Leflore County because of their efforts to organize a farmer's alliance in 1889 burned down a white businessman's store after he refused to sell them ammunition. A group of Black women called on people to

"burn Barnwell [South Carolina] to the ground" at the funeral of two men lynched there in 1889.[83] In 1899, in Darien, Georgia, "hundreds of blacks, many armed, surrounded the jail" that held a man threatened with lynching. Instead of causing a full-scale race riot, the defense prevented the lynching and led to a "biracial effort" to ease the "clearly volatile situation." Nonetheless, the long-term impact of the "post-insurrection" effort was to suppress Black protest by jailing the jail's defenders as "rioters" and to maintain the leadership positions of prominent Blacks in Darien.[84] In their study of Black-on-Black lynching,[85] the sociologists Stewart E. Tolnay and E. M. Beck found that in a small percentage of the cases, Black mobs lynched Blacks for "collaborating with whites in the prosecution or persecution, of blacks."[86]

Just as there were real incidents of violence, a few Black authors envisioned a revolutionary response in works of fiction. Sutton E. Griggs's *Imperium in Imperio* depicted a set of brave "race men" fighting militantly in an underground army. But the most prevalent critiques of both criminal law and extralegal action in fin de siècle African American culture appeared in the blues. In 1892, the peak year for lynching in the South, the ballad of Stagolee, a super-manly gambler, first emerged. The real Stagolee was Lee Shelton, and he had killed Billy Lyons, a "bully" from a wealthy Black family. At his trial, Shelton's lawyer argued self-defense, and Shelton was the subject of two defense petitions—one by his allies in the Democratic Party, and another by middle-class Blacks associated with the *Negro World* newspaper.[87]

In song, Stagolee became "the man who never died." He was loved by women and fought and killed death itself. The character drew from African traditions and stories that challenged Christian morality as well as the authority of legal systems. The Stagolee ballads defined eros as power and questioned the dualism of good and evil as defined in Christianity. Like the immigrant anarchists' tales of Louis Lingg, the Stagolee ballads represented the "law" as an oppressor and manly rebellion as a good and made Stagolee's successful evasions of legal repression super-heroic. He was so strong, for example, that in one version of the song, "his neck refused to crack" when the state tried to lynch him.[88] Although he never appeared in anti-lynching literature, Stagolee was remembered through the informal networks of local communities who had lost members to lynch mobs, police, and official courts. In the 1930s, the convict Roy Williams, defined as a "bad Negro" by whites, was heralded in Black folklore because his refusal to confess made him akin to Stagolee, and some legends described

Williams "bustin down the door to hell and breakin' off de Devil's horns." But as Cecil Brown points out, "Stagolee was not the kind of song that decent people heard."[89]

Natural Law and Natural Men: The IWW, Labor Defense, and Lynching

Labor activists had their own experiences with vigilantism. The IWW activist Eugene Barnett would recall growing up in West Virginia, where the mining camp

> was honey-combed with Pinkerton and Baldwin Felts detectives—[a] union organizer would come in, they'd find out and then they'd find him hanging on a beech tree out in front of the company store.
>
> Or knock him on the head out on the railroad tracks, kill him.
>
> If in broad daylight, [the] detective would probably have to leave camp for two or three weeks and then come back. No one was ever arrested for it. No trials were ever held.[90]

However, theories of direct action, manliness, and natural law nonetheless separated labor radicals from the white–Black progressive alliance that shaped the anti-lynching campaign. Labor organizations and civil liberties groups were profoundly influenced by the vision of the state as the "iron heel," as shown in Jack London's novel of that title. They revered the Haymarket story as an example of American despotism and worker agency, identifying the "juridical" power as the primary locus of terror and depicting the militant (white) masses as the agent of justice. Just as Spies, Engel, Fischer, and Lingg had compared America's police state to Bismarck's, Russian radical groups who had immigrated to the United States in 1905 compared the U.S. government to the despotism of the Russian czar and the Cossacks when they met with repression. As Emma Goldman argued in 1907, after the arrest of Haywood, Moyer, and Pettibone of the Western Federation of Miners, "We see in the state the mailed fist, the executioner's sword that flies from the scabbard the moment the rich feel the possession of their stolen property endangered."[91]

These activists had good reason to criticize the state as a "mailed fist." As anti-lynching activists denounced mob justice and police violence, members of the labor movement faced legal repression. In 1892, the Pennsylvania Supreme Court chief justice, Edward Paxson charged strikers at the steel plant in Homestead with treason for using force to resist a boat

landing of Pinkertons. In 1894, workers of the American Railway Union (ARU) struck the Pullman Palace Car Company and then boycotted Pullman cars. The attorney-general and president sent in troops to stop the boycott, and the result was a riot. Following this mayhem, the federal government charged the ARU's leader, Eugene Debs, with conspiracy to interrupt the mail. The result was a defeat for labor unions: The Supreme Court upheld the use of the federal injunction, which remained a major weapon of capital against striking workers until 1932. When martial law was declared in 1899 in Coeur d'Alene, Idaho, the president sent in federal troops, including the Black Twenty-Fourth Regiment, dubbed the "Buffalo Soldiers," to guard the strikers, who were held in an infamous "bullpen."[92]

When Leon Czolgosz assassinated President McKinley, the federal government passed a new "anti-anarchist" law that required immigrants coming into the country to swear an oath that they were not anarchists and that they did not believe in overthrowing the U.S. government.[93] In 1906, when Governor Frank Steunenberg was assassinated with a bomb, the Pinkerton National Detective Agency, with funding from the mine owners, led the prosecution of three major leaders of the Western Federation of Miners as conspirators.[94] In 1913, Mother Jones and several miners were court-martialed in association with violent conflicts between miners and guards during the Cabin Creek and Paint Creek strikes in West Virginia.[95] In Colorado in 1914, private police and the Colorado National Guard (along with private detectives and company goons dressed in National Guard uniforms) slaughtered striking miners' families in a tent colony during the infamous Ludlow Massacre.[96] And from 1909 until 1920, members of the IWW faced a flood of legal attacks from state and local governments, as well as the federal government. The attitude of the labor movement toward the U.S. government was shaped by these experiences.[97]

Like the trial of the Haymarket anarchists, the Pullman trial played a formative role in shaping labor defense. The case radicalized both Debs and his lawyer, Clarence Darrow, who would become organized labor's most famous legal advocate in the early twentieth century. During Debs's conspiracy trial in 1895, Darrow traced the origins of American conspiracy law to the English Court of Star Chamber, evoking popular representations of the American Revolution as a revolt against English tyranny and revealing the clandestine cabals of the railroad managers' association in attacking the ARU.[98] This description of the conspiracy law as creating a direct line between royal despotism and management tyranny was an important theme both in labor trials and in the antimonopoly movement.

The argument made its way into IWW as well as AFL trials that had wide labor support and major newspaper coverage. These references to capitalists as "royalty" implied that the labor unions were the inheritors of the Jeffersonian revolutionary tradition and fit into republican versions of heroism.

In 1903, Darrow defended an AFL union man, Thomas Kidd, accused of "conspiring to injure the business of the Paine Lumber Company" in Oshkosh, Wisconsin. Darrow again drew on popular republican language, painting the company's owner, George Paine, as a money lord, a "misfit in Republican institutions and in democratic days," and comparing Thomas Kidd to Jesus, sacrificing himself on behalf of his brethren. Darrow made union organizing a sign of democratic liberation in the tradition of Protestant Christian revolt and American revolutionary manhood as he described why the laborers had revolted after the boss turned down their demands by throwing them in the garbage:

> I know every American that had a spark of manhood left in his body would have sworn that he would give up his life if need be, unless those just demands were answered. You cannot build a great country out of citizens that would not have done it. You cannot make a free people out of citizens that would not have spurned with contempt an employer like this.[99]

Darrow also defended the first major IWW activists in the first year of the new union's existence. Following the accusation that they had conspired to kill the governor of Idaho, Charles Moyer, Bill Haywood, and Edward Pettibone, leaders of the Western Federation of Miners, went to trial in 1907.[100] Major newspapers covered the trial daily for its entirety, and the reports ran alongside coverage of another "trial of the century"—that of Harry Thaw for killing the architect and sexual libertine Stanford White in New York. The charismatic Haywood, who was known as "Big Bill," was offered a three thousand-dollar advance for his story by *McClure's* magazine,[101] and parts of the trial were filmed and featured in "Hale's Touring Car."[102]

The trial also became the IWW's, and the radical labor movement's, major cause. Debs's "Arouse Ye Slaves!" a call to action that appeared in his newspaper, *Appeal to Reason*, in March 1906, immediately after Haywood and Moyer were abducted from Colorado and taken to Boise to stand trial, set the tone for the defense campaign by comparing the new trial to the Haymarket tragedy. Referring to the mine owners as "gory beaked vultures" who were "ready to pluck out the heart of resistance to tyranny and robbery," Debs saw the case in the American labor tradition:

Nearly twenty years ago, the capitalist tyrants put some innocent men to death for standing up for labor. They are now going to try it again. Let them dare! There have been twenty years of revolutionary education, agitation and organization since the Haymarket tragedy, and if an attempt is made to repeat it, there will be a revolution, and I will do all in my power to precipitate it.

Recalling the earlier united effort to fight the Haymarket executions, and drawing on what was left of the progressive–populist antimonopolist alliances of the previous decade, Debs, who had become a socialist as a result of his own trial during the Pullman Strike, predicted the unity that could be created by such a trial placing freedom against tyranny and argued that it was not simply a sentimental call, but the duty of the working class, whose manhood would be measured by their solidarity with the men:

> Upon the issue involved the whole body of organized labor can unite and every enemy of plutocracy join us. From the farms and factories and stores will pour the workers to meet the red handed destroyers of freedom, the murderers of innocent men and the arch-enemies of the people. Moyer and Haywood are our staunch allies and true and if we do not stand by them to the shedding of every last drop of blood in our veins, we are disgraced forever and deserve the fate of cringing cowards.[103]

Debs linked the fate of the three men with that of the entire working class. The defendants also adopted the roles taken by previous defendants in such trials. Haywood, Moyer, and Pettibone published statements declaring their innocence and proclaiming their willingness to give up their very lives for the cause of labor, with Haywood echoing the cry of Spies that others would follow him if necessary: "They may murder me by law, but there are a thousand Haywoods and Moyers in the [W]estern Federation of Miners to take our places and push the work."[104]

The trial united radicals against both the governor and the conservative AFL, who were deemed betrayers of the working class. But while anarchists, syndicalists, and liberals all supported the three men, they disagreed about the best means to free them. Emma Goldman's journal *Mother Earth* admonished Samuel Gompers of the AFL for his failure to support the defense, remarking that his "cowardly manner" was truly despicable. Voltairine de Cleyre went on tour to speak about the upcoming trial. Italian anarchists also covered every detail of the Haywood trial in their newspapers.[105] Arguing for what would become the "far left" position in labor defense, the anarchists advocated defense strategies of

direct action and denounced the use of the law and lawyers to defend the labor movement. Protest meetings and fund raising for legal fees were not enough, they insisted, and would not save the men. There was no way a trial would succeed, because the jurors were clearly chosen by the prosecution and were a "bunch of simpering idiots." Economic pressure in the form of a general strike was the only solution.[106]

Others in the labor movement chose more conventional means to appeal to the public. When Big Bill was on trial, the IWW member J. T. Doran wrote a song with the chorus, "Oh ye lads of Fair Columbia / listen to the cry! / hear that fair-haired babe of Haywood's Ask / Will Papa Die?"[107] Socialist Party activists, rejecting what they called the "hysterical" approach to the defense, argued instead for rationality and reminded their comrades that "it is not emotion which accomplishes these things." They called for political action rather than a general strike, arguing that court cases gave solidarity workers great amounts of time to make their cause known through legal channels.[108]

Darrow, by now a superstar of labor defense, wooed the jury with appeals not only to freedom against tyranny and descriptions of the mine owners' war against the Western Federation, but also to nativism and Protestant morality, painting Haywood as an old-style republican hero. "Haywood was born here in Utah," he said in his address to the jury, "he is not a foreigner. His ancestors came here before the revolution. He does not know a jack from an ace, he did not know how to make a living except by work, poor fellow. He is a plain, blunt, courageous, able fighting man."[109]

Workers across the country apparently identified Haywood's liberation as connected to their own. When Big Bill was acquitted, labor activists all over the country celebrated. According to the *Chicago Tribune*, workers in Chicago "paraded the streets, wearing in their hatbands 'Haywood acquitted.'" In Butte, Montana, "a cheering mob of men, women and children" could be seen "parading in celebration." In New York, activists held a "jubilee" at the labor temple.[110] Anarchists celebrated and sent a telegram to Teddy Roosevelt in defiance, although they insisted that the verdict was not a vindication of American justice but a fluke produced by the clearly venal character of the prosecution's primary witness, Harry Orchard.[111]

Hoping to have another such success, Samuel Gompers hired Clarence Darrow four years later, in 1911, to defend two AFL workers, J. J. McNamara and J. B. McNamara, who had been accused of conspiring to bomb

the anti-labor *Los Angeles Times* building in which twenty-one people had been killed in 1910.

J. J. McNamara was the treasurer of the Structural Ironworkers Union, the men who were building the new skyscrapers. After McNamara's arrest, Gompers declared that he was "confident that secretary McNamara is innocent" and ran a massive national campaign on the brothers' behalf, raised a large sum of money to finance Darrow's defense, published buttons with J. J. McNamara's picture on them, and sponsored a "McNamara Day" shortly before the trial was scheduled to begin.[112]

Although the McNamaras were neither socialists nor IWW members, IWW activists and anarchists—and even the socialists who opposed the use of direct action—immediately became involved in the campaign out of basic class solidarity. Bill Haywood argued, "We are all defendants in every case where a worker is to be tried and a capitalist is the plaintiff." As in the Haywood case, the manhood of the men, and the American man's right to use violence in defense of his manhood rights, was a significant part of the defense. Haywood said that the McNamara brothers were manly because their work was among the most dangerous in the country. Ironworkers were "men with iron in their blood, men who shake hands with death many times in the course of a day's work, men the very nature of whose labor develops an individualism, a spirit of self-reliance, and independence," Haywood wrote as he traveled across the country to speak for the defense campaign.[113] Like the anarchists who had worked to defend him, Haywood argued for the general strike as the best means of solidarity and said that violence was an acceptable form of manly resistance.

When the McNamaras shocked everyone by confessing to the crime in December 1911—J. B., on the condition that his brother would not be charged, and J. J., on the condition that his brother would not be executed—Gompers and the AFL denounced the men, but the IWW and the anarchists still defended them. Debs called Gompers "cowardly and contemptible" for disowning the McNamaras, whose crime, he said, was only the logical outcome of "the policy of Gomper's craft unionism." Rather than being unmanly, their efforts to save each other by confessing put their detractors to shame and demonstrated that superior love had governed their actions.[114] The weakness of the AFL was to blame for the desperate acts of the men, Debs argued, and Frank Boehn of the IWW agreed: "Old antiquated unions fought one tenth of the war against the enemy and nine tenths of the war against unorganized workers." Debs and Boehn both compared the McNamaras to John Brown (even though

the brothers had participated in the Asiatic Exclusion League of California) because of their use of manly force, but Boehn made clear that "the McNamaras were just as misguided, but more so, than John Brown."[115] Unlike Debs, who had admired the men for confessing out of love and fidelity for each other, Boehn asked why they could not have been men and died without confessing. Jay Fox, editor of Seattle's *Agitator* newspaper, asked the same question, denouncing Gompers and criticizing the McNamaras along with him.

The McNamara confession crystallized divisions between the Socialist Party and the IWW. While socialists officially broke with the IWW in 1912, IWW members, particularly Bill Haywood, made the defense of manly force and the rejection of confession into critical characteristics of revolutionary labor defense. Interestingly, although Haywood explicitly rejected nativism and racism in his 1928 autobiography, he used American racist vigilantism to justify the McNamara's actions in 1911. While he at one time had argued that race-conscious craft unionists were "soft, spongy souls, halting and timorous who cannot be trusted to guide the social craft through the stormy waters of class conflict," he rounded out his defense of labor militancy with a list of atrocities against western workers that built to a bloody climax. He told the audience about the miners of Colorado. "A thousand working men, just as good as you are, who were surrounded by Black troops in a stockade."

> While those young miners were fighting for the flag, for their freedom the Black soldiers were at home outraging, ravishing their wives, their sisters, and sweethearts. So you understand that we know the class struggle in the West, and you realize having contended with all these bitter things that we have been called upon to drink to the dregs, do you blame me when I say that *I despise the law*? (tremendous applause and shouts of NO!).[116]

At this crucial moment in the history of the labor movement, Haywood had collapsed the vigilante tradition with working-class direct action. Along with the celebrated western labor trials in which Clarence Darrow appealed to the nation, drawing as they did on populist attacks on money lords, evocations of masculine strength, and boisterous resistance to the trappings of law, the radical labor movement took advantage of the legacy of both lynching and Indian fighting when pleading the case for direct action as part of American citizens' natural rights. In the early 1900s, men of the American West were definitively manly, as they had been in the 1850s; they were traditionally "fighters," whether in actual street scuffles, in politics, or in journeys from one career to the

next. The muckraker Lincoln Steffens described political reformers who were out to bust railroad monopolies as "insurgents" and "guerrillas in the hills" of the West.[117]

The IWW's highly publicized "free-speech fights" manipulated this romantic view of the West in an interesting way. In the national media, migrant laborers had been negatively defined as "tramps," as the Haymarket anarchists had complained in Chicago, and as a major threat to peaceful society. The IWW had set out to organize these "tramps" who were not simply the rootless unemployed but, rather, seasonal labor in oil fields, harvest hands, and timber workers.[118] One of the IWW's early tactics in this campaign was soapbox speaking in the hub cities where migrants went between jobs.

As soon as the IWW began such a public organizing drive, cities passed laws banning street speaking. The Wobblies responded with the free-speech fights, holding at least twenty-one between 1909 and 1913. Although some IWW members, such as Fred Thompson, saw the struggles as diversionary, the free-speech fights not only forced the IWW's interpretation of the Constitution into the U.S. courts, [119] but made the point that "direct action" against legal repression was more effective than a legal argument made in court. When confronted with an ordinance banning speech, the Wobblies would call on the "overalls brigade": migrant workers who would ride boxcars to the town to give "read-ins" of the Declaration of Independence and the First Amendment from soapboxes. Following their arrests, IWW members typically sang IWW songs in jail and behaved boisterously, aggravating their jailers. These campaigns were hugely popular and reportedly brought Joe Hill into the group for the first time.[120]

As Lucy Ann Cloud described in an interview, the free-speech fights reinforced solidarity, as Wobblies in the West came to the defense of the right to organize. "When they send a call, 'Spokane is having a free speech fight, send fifty men here,' they dropped whatever they were doing and get on— that impressed me about as good as anything," she said. "When my very own husband walked off the job, he said, 'I've got to go to Spokane.'"[121]

These drives expanded the rights to speech in the West and defined free speech in broad terms, as David Rabban has pointed out, making many of the arguments that would later show up in Supreme Court decisions. Especially important in these free-speech fights was the assertion that particular ways of speaking should be part of accepted public political discourse. IWW free-speech fights enacted the right to public assembly, using the streets, courts, and even prisons as public spaces for protest. On soapboxes the speakers regularly insulted the police, calling them "dogs" and

"pimps."[122] The direct action in these campaigns literally pitted the "noisy masses" against both the formal structures of the law and its enforcement agencies.

Anti-speaking ordinances were not the IWW's only problem. In 1914, Joe Hill, the IWW's most popular songwriter and cartoonist, was arrested in Utah and charged with the murder of the grocery owner John G. Morrison and his son, Arling. Hill had not wanted the union to get involved, and at first the IWW did not. However, when the publicity grew around the trial, the IWW claimed Hill and started a defense committee, announcing in *Solidarity*, "THE MAN WHO WROTE MR. BLOCK AND CASEY JONES CAUGHT AND HELD ON TRUMPED UP CHARGES."[123] The campaign to save Hill became a cause célèbre, with Debs's *Appeal to Reason*, liberals, and radicals all joining together to save the Wobbly songwriter. Hill questioned whether the whole thing was worth it, arguing, that "the organization should use its resources to keep the live wires on the outside, I mean the organizers and orators. When they are locked up they are dead as far as the organization is concerned. A fellow like myself, for instance, can do just as well in jail. I can dope out my music and poems in here and slip them through the bars and the world will never know the difference."[124]

The IWW organized a defense for Hill on the basic principle of solidarity, saying that a movement that let its members die was no movement worth mentioning. The IWW's insistence, against Hill's own directives, on the defense campaign as solidarity was, like the free-speech fights, a critical turning point in the history of the defense campaign strategy. The idea that organized mass defense was a form of class solidarity and that organization was a process of reciprocal obligation between individuals pulled the IWW activists away from a simplistic valorization of self-sacrificing individual manliness and the dream of spontaneous mass revolt.

Elizabeth Gurley Flynn's visits to Joe Hill in jail and her articles about them helped shape not only Hill's image and her political career, which increasingly focused on civil liberties and defense work, but also the Wobblies' general practice of prisoner defense. Combining sentimental representations of prison visits with revolutionary evocations of manly power, Flynn commented on Hill's constant manly good cheer and selfless concern that his case not drain funds from Wobblies' coffers.[125] Describing Hill's spirit of life that defeated the prison in spite of his incarceration, Flynn used the story of one man in prison as a metaphor for the heroic fight of the working class against state repression. As she contrasted the beautiful air of Salt Lake City in spring with the "familiar fetid jail odor,"

Flynn described the tragedy of the prison that held Hill, who was "tall slender, very blonde, with . . . deep blue eyes." As they sat in the sheriff's office, "looking out the open barred door at the wide expanse of beautiful lawn," Flynn noted, Hill joked with her. "He's lucky, Gurley," he said pointing to an old bearded man outside who was mowing the grass. "He's a Mormon and he's had two wives and I haven't even had one!" Drawing on Hill's sexuality to connect him to the natural world and associating his blue eyes and blonde hair with the sun, grass, and snow-capped mountains of Utah, Flynn's descriptions presented "life" as the value that would surpass and defeat the somber, disinfected air of prisons. She recalled, "I can see him standing behind the barred door, 'smiling with his eyes' as the modern song describes."[126] In describing this tragic attack on the working class in Hill's person, Flynn did not depict Hill as a defeated victim but made his desiring body into a challenge to the prison itself. Like Stagolee, Hill became the "man who never died" following his execution.

The representations of Hill in prison continued the tradition established during the Haymarket defense of reinforcing solidarity of the group by publicizing the relationship between the imprisoned man and women in the organization. Like Spies and Hill, dozens of IWW activists who wrote public letters from prison to IWW publications reassured their visitors with arguments about the value of struggle and argued that prison was but an extreme version of capitalist everyday life. These comparisons between prison and life under capitalism illustrated industrialism's oppression of the individual spirit, just as August Spies had in his descriptions of factories as similar to prisons in his address to the court in 1886. Representations of both prisons and factories as spirit breaking bolstered arguments that risk taking in the name of freedom was not a form of self-sacrifice or martyrdom, but a fulfillment of one's true self and an escape from slavery.[127] The literal division of Hill's ashes among the IWW's members made the community around Hill even more explicit.[128]

Following Hill's execution came the charges against IWW members Tom Mooney and Warren Billings, accused of bombing the Preparedness Parade in San Francisco in 1916. Although it was revealed in 1918 that the charges against him had been cooked up, Mooney would spend nearly twenty years of his life in prison. Thus, not only defense before conviction, but support for prisoners afterward, became an essential aspect of labor solidarity in the 1910s as more and more IWW activists languished in prison.

Like women in the anti-lynching movement, female activists in the labor movement were significant to the early work of defense and prisoner support. Mother Jones had played a maternal role in relation to her

K., "The Prison of Wage Slavery," *Industrial Worker*, April 15, 1916, 1.

"boys" of the coalfields, and both Elizabeth Gurley Flynn and Ella Reeve "Mother" Bloor built on this tradition when they toured the country speaking for the Workers' Defense League. In addition to their public activities as speakers, Flynn and Bloor, who would become Communist Party members, took principal responsibility for visiting IWW prisoners as an important element of women's political work that blended old Quaker traditions with newer socialist ones.[129]

Calls to support class-war prisoners stressed the helplessness of the prisoners, the power of those outside, and the importance of human connections to the maintenance of political activism. All IWW publications

Bingo, "Remember: We Are In Here for You, You Are Out There for Us," *One Big Union Monthly*, vol. 2, no. 7, July 1920, 38.

related to defense showed the image of the prisoner reaching out from behind bars with the slogan, "We are in here for you, you are out there for us." [130] IWW activists in prison also organized their fellow prisoners, particularly when large numbers of Wobblies were incarcerated together in Leavenworth for resisting the draft. The Wobblies in Leavenworth took part in the 1919 general strike of prisoners led by a combination of war resisters and gangsters. According to the communist Carl Haessler who looked back on the strike in the 1920s, by organizing around a program of amnesty, better conditions, and release of gangsters from solitary confinement, they were able to transform a "mere heedless destructive mob," which had been attacking Black prisoners, into an "organized, disciplined, and completely unified body of men" with a set of demands that led them to victory over the prison administration. [131] In Leavenworth Ben Fletcher brought the Black prisoner Joseph J. Jones into the IWW, and Jones went on to organize for the IWW following his release. [132] In addition to challenging the lines between inside and outside by organizing in the prison, the Wobblies on the outside called for general strikes with the release of political prisoners as principal demands.

The letters and poems from inside the prisons that appeared every month in the IWW paper blending political ideology, personal regards, and effusive thanks to supporters revealed the vulnerable humanity of

the incarcerated men, countering heroic mythologies of individual power and voluntarism with stories of mass interdependence. Because these letters were often written to female audiences, they gave male socialists an opportunity to engage in a confessional discourse about loneliness that rarely appeared elsewhere.

Sometimes it might have been easier to describe feelings of loneliness by portraying them in the voices of children and wives, as one prisoner wrote in the voice of a son missing his "Dada" who "hasn't kissed me for a hundred million years." In a similar move, Kate Richard O'Hare organized a "children's crusade" of the children of imprisoned First World War resisters to Washington, D.C., during Christmas of 1921. Carrying posters reading, "Debs Is Free, Why Not My Daddy?" the children shamed capitalist prisons as a wicked destroyer of the family.[133]

Vigilantism

Finally, the Wobblies were targets of armed vigilantes in attacks that seemed only to escalate. Individual Wobblies were roughly instructed to leave town, and whole groups were "deported" en masse from Aberdeen, South Dakota, and Bisbee, Arizona. At times, mobs did more than usher organizers to the county line. The Everett Massacre of 1916, like Hill's execution, was galvanizing. It also demonstrated the impact of the anti-lynching movement on the labor movement. The massacre emerged from a free-speech fight that followed the banning of IWW members from the town of Everett, Washington. To get into the town without encountering an armed citizens' association, the IWW (some of its members armed) boarded a boat. When they arrived at the dock, the sheriff and his lieutenants had already gotten word and met them with guns. During the fire-fight, five Wobblies were killed.

Perhaps influenced by the NAACP's use of photographs, the *Industrial Worker* showed large photographed images of the men killed in Everett lying barely draped with sheets in the morgue, emphasizing the cruelty of the killers. It was unusual in a paper whose images were usually cartoons.[134] In a special issue dedicated to mourning the Everett martyrs, the paper featured the dramatic last moments of Abraham Rabinowitz, who died on the boat. As a Jew, the paper said, he was "born of a race without a flag—a race oppressed by the intolerance and superstition of the ages," and he "died a martyr to the cause of liberty." According to the article, his last spoken words were, "I am dying boys, but do not give up, lift me

I want to sing the Red Flag." He and his fellow martyr Hugo Gerlot, who also died singing, were inspirations for workers of the future, because Rabinowitz, "with the song of revolt against industrial slavery on his lips, . . . died countryless, homeless that the workers of the world might have a country."[135]

The vigilante attack became a defense case, and the IWW hired Fred Moore and George Vanderveer, who had become its regular lawyers, to defend them in court.[136] When the men were acquitted, local papers threatened lynch law.[137]

By 1917, IWW activists were working more and more in mining and timber regions, where they frequently met vigilante action. Frank Little was threatened with hanging while he tried to organize men in Michigan; a lawyer for the Everett defendants was also threatened. Wobblies who tried to organize oil-field workers in Tulsa, Oklahoma, were forced to run a gantlet in 1917. Little was lynched in Montana in 1917 and was memorialized as a martyr to the rule of copper bosses. Centralians lynched Wesley Everest, a First World War veteran and IWW member, in 1919, after the IWW's local defended its hall in Centralia during a raid by the American Legion on Armistice Day. The men arrested with Everest became the "Centralia Victims," sent to prison for conspiracy to shoot the head of the American Legion local, Warren Grimm. One of the men died in jail, and the last of them was finally freed in 1936.[138]

Thus, the IWW grew to have a complicated relationship to Western mythology and the practice of vigilantism. They used the idea of themselves as rough-riding "pioneers in boxcars," as footloose men with few attachments, and at the same time decried the mobs of the West. Covington Hall referred to the Bisbee Deportation of July 1917 as the "Most Cruel Crime in History of Peonage and Slaughter" and called it a "pogrom."[139] In November of that year, Charles Ashleigh compared the persecution of the IWW to that of Elijah Lovejoy, who had been killed by a "blood drunken mob."[140]

At the same time, the IWW claimed the legacy of the Wild West for itself. In his popular pamphlet about the Centralia lynching of the Wobbly Wesley Everest, Ralph Chaplin referred to the struggle between labor and capital in the western states as part of the new, living West, claiming that "the present day pioneers ride in boxcars." Chaplin wrote that the first explorers of the Western woods were heroes who had cooperated for "settlers must be made secure from the raids of the Indians and the inclemency of the elements."[141] In those early days, "the lynch mobs of the lumber trust were still sleeping in the womb of the future," and "opportunity was open

for everyone." It was not until the "plague center in Wall Street" sent its germs out west that inequality and danger arrived. For Chaplin, the timber worker had a special character, "a tang and adventure to his labor in the impressive solitude of the wood that gives him a steady eye." He stood in contrast to the "conservative home-guard" of the sawmill workers (a large percentage of whom were African American)[142] and to factory workers who were also conservative, for their labor was dispiriting. "Out of the labor ghettos they swarm and into their dismal slave pens," he wrote.[143] Vera Moher compared the lynching of the IWW activist Wesley Everest ("Only a body hanging to a bridge") to the killing of a pioneer by Indians ("Only a skeleton pinned down with arrows").[144]

The characterization of the Wobblies as traveling western hoboes, which was promoted in the free-speech fights, drives to organize agricultural workers, and the Joe Hill trial all led to an image of white masculine individuals in the far West as the primary constituency of the One Big Union in the nation's media. As Debs put it in an interview with his biographer David Karsner, he liked Tom Mix movies because they reminded him of the IWW and the Western Federation of Miners.[145] The huge figures of bare-chested white workers in natural settings that adorned IWW publications; the comparison of labor leaders to the Protestant heroes of the English Civil War and to America's forefathers in Darrow's orations; and the defense of violence as definitive of manly labor radicalism were significant not only in shaping the IWW, but also in conflating democracy, masculinity, whiteness, Protestantism, and violence in the theory of working-class radicalism in the United States.[146]

The major exception to this type of representation came when the IWW defended two of its Italian members following the multinational strike in Lawrence, Massachusetts. As Sal Salerno has shown, the IWW has been depicted as a mostly native-born western organization by historians such as Melvyn Dubofsky, who refers to the IWW's "Anglo-Saxon origins in Western mining communities."[147] However, the group was multiethnic and associated with counterculture anarchists. The Greenwich Village radicals of the 1900s included labor activists and free-love experimentalists. In Chicago's "Hobohemia," the IWW's rootless men rubbed shoulders with all manner of literati at the Dill Pickle club.[148] Even in the West, IWW activists included counter-culture activities and sexual freedom in their political work. IWW activists in Seattle, for example, held an annual party to which the hosts came dressed as police and priests and forced partygoers into either "jails" or "marriage" as part of the entertainment. Making "marriage" a punishment for "spooning" the party's "outlaws" (a set of ri-

diculous guidelines prescribing and proscribing various activities) determined "what God hath joined together, let no man put asunder, divorce
is immoral and sinful. The only cure for marriage is more marriage. Marry
another, marry again." Following these instructions, Annie Grosmutz
won a prize because she "got married" 160 times during the evening.[149]
Showing an interest in the most proscribed of western cultures, Joe Hill
was known to be a good cook of Chinese food.[150]

In the East, the Wobblies promoted their defense through an alliance
with the counter-culture world of the *Masses* magazine. Two of the IWW's
biggest successes in gaining public sympathy were in the massive textile
strikes in Lawrence, Massachusetts, in 1912, and in Paterson, New Jersey,
in 1913. During the trial of two Italian IWW organizers, Arturo Giovannitti
and Joe Ettor, who were charged with murder as a result of the Lawrence
strike, some have speculated that the IWW's threat of a general strike won
their freedom. Giovannitti, as a result, became a "familiar figure in the bohemian leftist world of Greenwich village."[151] The Paterson strike of 1913
had tremendous significance in shaping the alliance of New York's literary
bohemia with the labor movement, as John Reed and others from Greenwich Village organized a pageant in Madison Square Garden where workers reenacted the events of the strike. Interestingly, although the IWW had
used the reputation of the fighting men of the West in the defense cases
there, in the East the union's approach to the use of violence was quite different. Italian anarchists, who supported "propaganda of the deed," came
into conflict with IWW leaders. During the Lawrence and Paterson strikes,
Haywood and Ettor discouraged violence.

Newspapers in Lawrence had described the strikers as Italian men
armed with "race weapons," and some strikers in their later recollec-
tions referred to the fight to change the public image of the group from
"blood-stained anarchists."[152] While the rejection of such claims might
seem commonplace, it is nonetheless interesting that the use of violence
was seen as "threatening" and un-American in an Eastern industrial and
immigrant context but could be rehabilitated in the West as an emblem
of Americanism. Instead, during defense campaigns in Lawrence and
Paterson, where the large textile mills had huge masses of female workers, women and children were in the spotlight. Whether it was because
the visible face of the strikers was female or because the IWW moved
away from public endorsements of violence following the McNamaras'
confession of 1911, or because of the questionable racial status of Italian
and Portuguese workers, IWW speakers did not call for "direct action"
there. Instead, groups of children who were taken from Lawrence before

Cover of the pamphlet "Direct Action and Sabotage,"
by William Trautman (Chicago, 1912).

the strike substituted the concept of the family for the image of the strikers as "violent revolutionaries."

The women of Lawrence were central to the image of the Wobblies on
the East Coast, but it was the men of the West who took center stage in
the stories of the IWW's most heroic conflicts with the state, when the
IWW could build an association between its members and the western
and Southern mythologies of manly direct action. In the era of the "natural man," IWW members also compared themselves to animals, a strategy
that would have been problematic for Black activists of the same era.

When Ralph Chaplin wrote the song "That Sabo-Tabby!" to the tune of "Dixie," he combined the image of France's "wooden shoe" with a more problematic American rebellion. The song's lyrics, "The tiger wild in his jungle sittin' / Never fights like this here kitten / Hurry Now, Wonder How, Meow, SABOTAGE," could make playful references to Wobblies as wild jungle animals partly because very few Americans would take the message literally. Similarly, one Wobbly artist depicted the organization as a ferocious bulldog, indicating the ability of IWW activists to claim beast-like strength without being seen as terrifying beasts out of control. The IWW's heroic imagery showed that its members never lacked the ability to use white "natural" manhood to their advantage.

As the burgeoning socialist media made white workers into icons of masculinity, the most striking images of working-class Blacks that appeared in the socialist press were of brutalized, mutilated, burning bodies—like Jesse Washington's body, which was photographed to shock and horrify. Max Eastman, editor of the popular magazine the *Masses* and a close friend of Claude McKay, whose poem "If We Must Die" was one of the most profound responses to the Red Summer of 1919 (during which there were more than twenty race riots), discussed the need for Black heroes to help the Black race. Whites, and some Blacks, still relied on Victorian images of manly heroes and, without them, perceived Blacks as passive. It was time for a new Toussaint L'Ouverture, but where was he? Eastman had wondered in 1913, suggesting that Blacks still waited for heroes to arrive, as if from on high.[153] The mighty image of the IWW's gigantic white male workers also could be seen to represent the (white) labor movement as the potential "savior" of Black America, much as John Brown could be shown as the rescuer of enslaved blacks. Such images not only portrayed white workers as strong and Black workers as helpless, but they also neutralized violence in the national imagination by removing it from the modern urban context. Manly direct action could be portrayed as heroic in western scenes, where the struggles of labor and capital could be incorporated into the story of the frontier. Representation of violence against Blacks focused primarily on Southern rural "backwardness."

With World War One, these representations began to change. When it was raided and persecuted, the IWW formed the General Defense Committee (GDC) to support members charged with espionage, criminal anarchy, sedition, and other crimes. Forrest Edwards, whose authority to speak might have stemmed from the fact that he was a "twenty year federal prisoner in Leavenworth," sharply disagreed with the idea that the

"Christmas in the USA," *Industrial Pioneer*, October 1924.

defense campaign was retrogressive or unmanly. Organized legal and mass defenses were not only the source of good publicity, he argued, but important in terms of winning recruits who did not see manly self-sacrifice as the central characteristic necessary for labor organizing: "Can the IWW appeal to a man by saying, 'We stand for solidarity of Labor everywhere, except when you are arrested? An injury to one is an injury to all, except when you are arrested and brought into court'? Not very encouraging to a man willing and anxious to become active."[154]

Challenging ideals of superhuman, manly self-sufficiency, the GDC, which went to work in earnest after 1919, often highlighted interdependence and personal vulnerability and emphasized the ties of activists and women, as the memorial literature for the Haymarket martyrs had. IWW activists made defense work a special job and codified it with organizations. Activists assisted in defense campaigns by making financial contributions, striking in solidarity, or holding demonstrations, and even by writing letters to prisoners. In addition, the support in the IWW for particular labor lawyers made it clear that, because of the ever changing nature of the law, each individual case was significant for all workers. Liberal allies became essential to the work, as the bureau to defend World War One draft resisters, led by Emma Goldman's friend Roger Baldwin, simultaneously took on more and more IWW cases and became the ACLU.[155] Although many criticized the IWW for its focus on defense—as did the historian William Preston, who wrote that "the IWW became a defense rather than a labor organization, and drained off its leadership, militancy and finances in a fruitless resistance"[156]—the group's defense strategy would create as much of an institutional legacy within the left as would its industrial unionism.

The Great Migration and the Great War

In the early 1900s, labor activists and anarchists had fought the law as the symbol of ultimate evil and defined mass action as the ultimate good while simultaneously attacking the mass media's attempts to stir up hysteria against them. By the late 1910s, the labor movement was beginning to focus on lynching as a major problem. Its concern increased during World War One, as the "patriotic mob" gained influence and as Blacks became more militant in their anti-lynching protests, taking up arms in self-defense in a few public incidents. The movement of Southern Blacks to northern cities, known as the Great Migration, led to an urban concentration of African Americans and the growth of dynamic organizations and newspapers, such as the African Blood Brotherhood (ABB) and its newspaper the *Crusader* and A. Phillip Randolph's and Chandler Owen's *Messenger*. Black nationalism also emerged in the public eye with the mass organization the Universal Negro Improvement Association (UNIA) and its leader, Marcus Garvey. Anti-lynching politics would become more militant, and labor defense, more complicated.

When IWW members wrote about lynching, they explained it as the outgrowth of class conflict. Shortly after race riots of 1917 in East St. Louis, Illinois, during which AFL activists called on their national organization to get rid of Black workers, Covington Hall (who a week later would call the Bisbee Deportation a "pogram") wrote in the *Industrial Worker* that what had occurred in St. Louis was not actually a "race riot" but a "clash over scabbing." Although Hall decried the riot and declared that workers got nowhere when they mobbed other workers, his description of the riot as simply a "scab" issue and his claim that the government was "partly responsible" for what had happened because militia men had been "assaulting speakers, breaking up meetings and raiding union halls" could be seen to let rioters off the hook and to miss the point.[157] Later, when he described the white mob that had attacked Blacks who had formed the Progressive Farmers and Household Union in Elaine, Arkansas, Hall again argued that this was really a class conflict and that the "Elaine Riot" only had the appearance of a "race war" because the "tenants happen to be colored."[158]

Black radicals offered a different explanation. Garvey had famously frightened the FBI by suggesting that Blacks should kill a white person in the North in retaliation for every Black person lynched and called for Blacks to band together as a separate nation.[159] Garvey also claimed that "lynching mobs and wild time parties are generally made up of 99 percent of such white people" as filled the Communist Party and the trade unions, while the whites of the NAACP were trying to fool the Negro and hold him in check.[160] Neither the established Black leaders nor the white left could ignore Garvey. W. E. B. Du Bois, while critical of Garvey, nonetheless wrote approvingly of his idealism. Cyril Briggs, one of the significant influences on communist thinking about Black rights, had tried to gain access to leadership in Garvey's association. Many other future Black communists and socialists spent time in Garvey's ranks.

In this same moment, A. Phillip Randolph and Chandler Owen supported the IWW and urged Blacks to form mass working-class organizations. Briggs, of the ABB, seemed to suggest forming a clandestine militia for the self-defense of African Americans and reveled in the publicity that came his way when the FBI suggested that his organization had been behind the use of guns by Blacks in Tulsa. The New Crowd Negroes were threatening to the federal government, who spied on and infiltrated every Black organization in the United States during and after the First World War, all the while claiming that the groups were secretly controlled by white anarchists or communists. Riots in Tulsa, where Blacks de-

fended themselves against mob action; in Houston, where Black soldiers took military action against a would-be mob and where several soldiers were executed after court-martial; in Elaine, Arkansas, where both local whites and federal troops attacked Blacks who joined a union; and, later, the defense of the black homeowner Ossian Sweet who had fired into a mob that had surrounded his house, led the NAACP into campaigns during which it argued for the rights of armed self-defense against terror. In the case of the Elaine rioters, it scored the important legal precedent of *Moore v. Dempsey* in 1923.[161] In these cases, NAACP activists such as Carrie Shepperson pushed for more action from the NAACP's rank-and-file. Shepperson, a teacher in Arkansas, stood up and spoke for the Elaine campaign at the state teachers' meeting only because several women had pleaded that she be allowed to speak. Frustrated with decreasing participation in the Elaine cases, she urged "the men to get more backbone," only to get the response that they would not, because men had lost their jobs over the riot case.[162]

Although IWW activists and communists paid attention to the cases in Arkansas and Tulsa, they offered their own organizations as a better solution to white violence than Black organizations, whether the NAACP or the UNIA. In one example, the IWW circulated a flier with the picture of Jesse Washington that had appeared on the cover of the *Crisis* supplement in 1916 with the messages that "protests, petitions and resolutions will never accomplish anything" and that "the government is in the hands of the ruling class of white men," so "no appeal to the political powers will help the Negro." The only power for the Negro was his "power as a worker," and the IWW was the only union to admit Blacks to full membership; not until "workers of every race" joined together would a stop be put to lynching.[163] Repeating the canard of the early white working men's associations, another IWW pamphleteer even asserted, "We who have worked in the south know that conditions . . . are such that the workers suffer a more miserable existence than ever prevailed among the chattel slaves before the civil war."[164] The words were always the same. "The only power of the Negro is his power as a worker," Frederick A. Blossom argued in the IWW newspaper. "If they form separate racial organizations, they will only encourage race prejudice and help the master class in their effort to divide the workers along false lines of color and set one race against the other, in order to use both to their selfish ends."[165] Whites who insisted on cross-racial organizing as the only way to achieve group solidarity defined Black self-organization as traitorous to working-class solidarity and drew parallels between white lynch-mob misleaders and

Black nationalist misleaders or between the Black middle class and the white ruling class.

Legal Lynching   Despite their scorn for race-based arguments, when they started calling attacks on immigrant labor activists in court "legal lynchings," labor-defense activists showed their complicated reaction to the increasing tide of Black protest. At the same time that Wobblies called lynchings examples of class prejudice, they argued that nativist attacks on immigrant radicals were equivalent to the lynchings and persecutions experienced by Blacks and drew from the caste analysis of anti-lynching campaigns. Rather than associating the actions of police with "brigands," American socialists increasingly referred to the law's attacks on European immigrant workers as racially defined nativist "legal lynching." Like the Black activists who attacked lynching, immigrant socialists described the mob in specifically racial terms, noting the Anglo-Saxon backgrounds and nativist prejudices of frenzied and irrational prosecutors, judges, juries, and newspapers during the trials of mostly immigrant or first-generation labor activists. When Attorney-General A. Mitchell Palmer attacked Russian and other immigrant workers, raiding organizations and jailing or deporting socialists, anarchists, and communists at the end of the First World War, liberal lawyers and organizations used the language of the progressive anti-lynching campaign against him: He was hysterical, prejudiced, and driven to excess.

The anti-lynching movement's discussion of race helped socialists and liberal allies of immigrants to identify American nativism, imperialism, and nationalism with white mobs and thus bolstered the cosmopolitan modernism in the left that had been first raised by the internationalists of the Haymarket campaign and had been continued in the rise of urban bohemian communities that brought middle-class intellectuals together with labor sympathizers such as Emma Goldman. The discourse against lynching that had been created by Blacks and progressives in the 1890s joined with Haymarket-type critiques of the Americanist media in Euro-American socialist discourse by the 1910s as a way to describe the nativist ruling class as irrational, hysterical, and undemocratic. This tendency was most clearly exemplified in the defense of Nicola Sacco and Bartolomeo Vanzetti, the subject of the next chapter. The increasing comparison of Anglo-Saxon juries and courts to irrational lynch mobs brought the IWW closer to the anti-lynching movement's analysis of the police–mob continuum.

When they made these critiques, the radicals included racial prejudice in their analysis. They never said that workers "just happened to be immigrants" but argued against American nationalism, sometimes calling American native-born workers small-minded and petty. In one IWW article urging emigration of immigrants away from the United States, an author removed himself and his fellow Europeans from the white race and described whites as lazy people who did not work as hard as foreigners.[166] The IWW and all-Black workers' organizations made common cause in a few fights against repression in the late 1910s and early 1920s. Covington Hall at least nominally supported the NAACP's defense campaign for the rioters in Elaine, Arkansas, printing notices from the People's Freedom Union in the *Industrial Pioneer* about their initial (three-day trial) in 1919 and seeking financial support.[167] Following the Tulsa riot, in which Blacks had resisted white violence, both the IWW and the nascent Workers (Communist) Party circulated literature directed at African Americans, voicing their support for the Blacks of that city.[168] Meanwhile, the ABB, which was not the source of the Tulsa riot, nonetheless profited immensely from the government's assertion that it was.[169]

The victimization of Wobblies by American legionnaires and other vigilantes led them increasingly to borrow from African American critiques of mob violence. As labor-defense institutions became more codified in the following decade, they began to articulate a relationship between mobs and the defense of property rights. Instead of appealing to populist understandings that pitted the individual against the state as the primary contradiction in power, the IWW began to talk about a "secret government" of business interests that hid behind the "fake government" in Washington, D.C. As Vandeveer put it at the IWW trial in 1918, corporations were "the invisible government of your country."[170] When fascism began to develop in Europe, immigrant socialists, who still looked primarily across the Atlantic for their intellectual guidance, began to develop the analysis of Klan violence that African American activists had already identified in the years before.

Italians in the IWW contributed significantly to the analysis of fascism in Europe and America, as they suffered from American racism as "in-between people" and as they watched fascism in Europe. In 1923, Italian anarchists described how fascism relied on the "pathology of the crowd" and claimed that, through this method, "the dominant classes are able to send their collective psychosis in the direction of the interests of tyranny and tyrants."[171] In 1924, Elizabeth Gurley Flynn, who had become increasingly

identified with civil liberties and defense organizing—and with Italian radicals because of her close relationship to the Italian syndicalist Carlo Tresca—gave a speech comparing the KKK and the Italian fascist movement.[172] This relatively new understanding of the danger of vigilantism would lead to increasingly close relationships between white communists and African American antiracist activists, leading to the famous Scottsboro trial that began in 1931.

However, while Blacks had argued that the lynch mob's psychology was collective and not the product of one class or another, the socialists and anarchists argued that the mob was driven by a conspiracy of property owners. Anti-lynching advocates stressed the way that fears of rape and outraged innocence might seize a whole town in a frenzy, uniting people across classes. White socialists portrayed racist mobs as manipulated by capitalists but also held on to the concept that lynching was a traditional expression of working-class direct action. For example, in 1934, Al Weisbord, a radical socialist and anti-Stalinist organizer from the textile strike in Passaic, New Jersey, of 1926, equated lynching with direct action, arguing: "What is wrong with lynching is not the act of lynching itself, but the reactionary direction which lynching generally takes." Although Weisbord saw the Negro as the heart of the working class, claiming that "THE NEGRO IS LABOR AND LABOR IS THE NEGRO," he also claimed that "lynching is too old and important an American custom for us to scold at it like fishwives." Instead of condemning it or recognizing, as Black activists did, that lynching was usually created in alliance between white workers, white law men, and white bosses in a kind of pathological frenzy, Weisbord still saw the white lynch mob and popular justice as equivalent, arguing, "We must use the direct street action of the masses for our own purposes."[173]

Weisbord's interpretation, like that of many of his generation, protected a romanticized concept of white working-class direct action as a source of revolutionary liberation, equating white mass action with working-class action in general. When they used their power the wrong way, they became not the workers anymore but, like the KKK of 1871, the "ignorant dupes of designing men." The contradictory, complicated image of the mobs as at once working class and not, as pliable and yet ready to act in the name of revolution, turned the white working class into a tool over which competing leaders must do battle. This contradiction enabled radicals to retain an image of the working class as (morally and literally) white and helped bolster support for intellectual vanguard leadership. As Carl

Haessler has argued, the alliance of political prisoners and gangsters who led the Leavenworth strike did not "produce the mob" that had initially attacked Black prisoners, and might have attacked the radicals next. Instead, they had "supplied the direction" for the mob. Haessler's hope was that in a national revolutionary upheaval "men of national calibre" would produce similar results.[174] The resistance to seeing motivations for white working-class participation in lynch mobs, and the celebration of working-class unanimity in "direct action" and natural law in the mob, thus paved the way for Stalinism and social-democratic bureaucratism in the 1930s and 1940s.

The importance of the use of the courts for political ends that began with Ida B. Wells and continued with the work of the NAACP suggested that it was not primarily the state that was responsible for repression of African Americans but state-sanctioned lawlessness by the white "settler" population. The idealized vision of "the people" against the state that dominated anarchist politics in the 1880s and early 1900s had in some ways been an adaptation to Jeffersonian ideals that were implicated in both capitalist exploitation and white supremacy. This definition of American freedom from the law was simply not appealing to Black reformers, who created institutions of self-defense because the concepts of mass, mob, and riot—which appeared to white labor activists as democratic expressions of working-class power—were among the principal forces of white terror against Blacks.

During her tour in London, Wells noted that the supporters of the white working class could mourn the losses of their "own" and fail to feel the loss of Black lives in the South. This made any sincere coalition between the groups seem unlikely: "The American dispatches in the English press tell how members of congress, prominent citizens and legal authorities are exercising themselves on behalf of the Coxeyites and other agitators. Nobody is moving a finger to stay outrages upon Negroes."[175]

It was possible for the white working class not only to see white lynchers and Black nationalists as equally duped by mis-leaders but also to retain the image of Joe Hill as *the* great martyr of labor in 1915, the same year in which between eighty and ninety-six African Americans were killed for a variety of small affronts to white supremacy in the South. Labor's history, most of its icons, and a good deal of its folklore remained much whiter than its membership. It was for this reason that Du Bois, who was sympathetic to the goals of the labor movement, still felt disconnected from it in the end. Even after he had become a communist, Du Bois wrote

of that period in his life, when he was continually disappointed by social-ists, progressives, and union members, and it was to the images of defense campaigns that he referred:

> Although a student of social progress, I did not know the labor development in the United States. I was bitter at lynching but not moved by the treatment of white miners in Colorado or Montana. I never sang the songs of Joe Hill and the terrible strike at Lawrence, Massachusetts, did not stir me, because I knew that factory strikers like these would not let a Negro work beside them or live in the same town. It was hard for me to outgrow this mental isolation, and to see that the plight of the white workers was fundamentally the same as that of the Black, even if the white worker helped enslave the Black.[176]

By the early 1920s, the major legal-defense institutions to fight labor prosecution and lynching were all on the way to solidifying. The First World War had produced a new form of anti-lynching activism and labor defense, as liberals and radicals united against deportation and nativist mobbism that reached its apogee in the Palmer raids. Black radicals who had moved into cities in large numbers during World War One moved away from the politics of respectability, and as Black working-class orga-nizations formed—whether through Garvey, A. Philip Randolph, or the African Blood Brotherhood—they began to develop more militant re-sponses to racial violence. Garvey, for instance, went against the NAACP's traditional respect for the law by refusing to use a lawyer in his defense dur-ing his deportation trial and by questioning witnesses. He created "sensa-tion after sensation in the court room," where every session was "crowded with negroes."[177] These groups would maintain a consistent argument that Black caucuses and Black organizations were central to the fight against white supremacy, and some, such as Briggs, would also maintain a heroic tale of secret, underground Black armies proudly acting in defense of the Black community.[178] The IWW's General Defense Committee, established through the early criminal trials and codified during the mass trials of the IWW draft resisters, continued to argue for mass organizing, publicity, and legal action as "class struggle," and they generally attacked both courts and vigilantes as agents of class power while defending immigrants from nar-row nativist definitions of Americanism.

The ACLU, associated with the intersection of the IWW and bohemia, made the ideological rights of political dissidents its central focus. While they publicized trials, the ACLU's lawyers often argued for the expertise of progressives as an answer to hysteria and "delirium" to which Palm-

erism and other temporary spasms subjected the populace, just as the progressives of the NAACP argued for federal law and order in response to Southern mob law. These sometimes similar, and sometimes contradictory, logics characterized most defense campaigns against American terror until the late 1960s.

4

No Wives or Family Encumber Them:
Sacco and Vanzetti

He painted Vanzetti as the patient, tireless labor organizer. He
had to be careful . . . he skipped over the Anarchist philosophy,
for he addressed an audience that mostly despised Proudhon and
knew Marx's polemics on the subject by heart.
RUTH MCKENNEY, *Jake Home*, 1943, 275

Association with criminals is an important feature in the history
of Anarchists.   DAVID FELIX, *Protest: Sacco and Vanzetti
and the Intellectuals*, 1965, 141

Most liberals described the "Red Scare" of Palmerism, which came to its
end in 1920, as a temporary abuse of the law that was quickly remedied
with the attorney-general's fall from grace. However, the work of both
labor-defense activists and anti-lynching activists continued well into the
1920s. For labor defense, the most celebrated case was that of Nicola Sacco
and Bartolomeo Vanzetti, which began with their arrest in the spring of
1920 and lasted until their execution in August 1927. Anti-lynching activists spent the 1920s trying to get the Dyer Bill passed, which would have
made lynching a federal crime.

The Sacco and Vanzetti case was pivotal for all those organizations
and individuals who were involved in any form of labor activism. It was
also wracked by the moral and tactical conflicts that always occur during
defense campaigns, as advocates of heroic values, individual rights, and
group solidarity such as anarchists, liberals, communists, and syndicalists
fought with each other over the best methods to save the two obscure
Italian anarchists from execution. During this period, when international
fascism was on the rise, an unparalleled sense of urgency permeated the

campaign. Occurring in a period marked by repression, the defense of Sacco and Vanzetti was in many ways an early (and unsuccessful) attempt at a popular front against fascist reaction. The case became a stage on which different parties of the left argued with each other over the role of the individual in society, the meaning of law, the use of violence, and the method of organization. Although all of the defenders made the two men the center of the campaign, it was clear soon into the case that Sacco and Vanzetti had come to represent something beyond themselves. The two anarchists, unknown prior to their arrests to anyone except a small circle of Italian anarchists, came to represent the fate of the left altogether, and because of that importance, anarchists, socialists, and communists struggled almost as much over who Sacco and Vanzetti were as they struggled over how they should be defended. The two questions are related, and each group's version of Sacco and Vanzetti mirrored its own vision of history's vanguard.

Sacco and Vanzetti were arrested in Massachusetts on May 5, 1920, and charged with robbing a payroll truck and killing its guards. This event might not seem to qualify for a major labor-defense campaign. Unlike previous heroes of defense campaigns, the two men were unknowns who had been accused of a crime unconnected with a strike or ongoing action. However, they had been active in labor struggles in Massachusetts and were members of a small revolutionary anarchist circle around Luigi Galleani, a major figure in individualist anarchism in both Italy and the United States. According to Robert D'Attilio and Paul Avrich, they may have been connected—at least through association—to the bombers of A. Mitchell Palmer's house.[1] Whether they were connected with the bombing or not, Sacco and Vanzetti were clearly connected with people who had been accused of the bombing. Andrea Salsedo and Roberto Elia were their comrades and were being held for questioning in connection with the bombing in 1920.

As Boston's anarchist newspaper *L'Adunata dei Refrattari* (Call of the Refractories) described it, Vanzetti was a member of Salsedo's group and had sought to investigate his mysterious death:

> The defenestration of Andrea Salsedo happened the morning of May 1920 and brought together the survivors of the companions of faith, a tiny number, but not lacking audacity, who decided to denounce the crime that was denied. One of this small handful was the good Bartolomeo who again took up agitation in New England. . . . His worthy companion Nicola Sacco, the ardent anarchist idealist that does not know renunciation.[2]

When Salsedo and Elia were arrested and held incommunicado in New York, anarchists in Galleani's circle had gone to Carlo Tresca of the iww.[3] Tresca got them together with the ACLU lawyer Walter Nelles. Shortly afterward, Salsedo mysteriously jumped (or was pushed) out of a window at the Justice Department, where he was being held and questioned. Shortly thereafter, Sacco and Vanzetti were arrested. Perhaps thinking that they were being arrested for associating with Salsedo, they lied to the arresting officers. Vanzetti was quickly convicted on an additional robbery charge in Bridgewater, and a trial date was set for the two men to face a murder charge in South Braintree. The anarchists and iww activists who had already become involved in the defense of Roberto Elia immediately began organizing in Sacco's and Vanzetti's defense.

By 1920, the anarchists were an embattled minority even within the labor movement and radical circles. Following the McNamara brothers' confessions in 1911 and the Palmer raids in 1919–20, most of the socialist left backed away from heroic ideals and revolutionary violence. This fundamental strategic disagreement made it difficult for the anarchists and the iww's General Defense Committee to work together. In the first four years of Sacco's and Vanzetti's case, the iww lawyer Fred Moore (who had defended a number of iww activists in the West, winning acquittals for Charles Kreiger and the Everett Massacre defendants) battled intensely over defense strategy with Sacco's and Vanzetti's closest comrades, leading to insults and finally a death threat against Moore.[4] While the anarchists argued for heroic direct action, Moore wanted the case to have mass appeal, along with accountability, discipline, and organization. After four years as the primary legal defender and organizer of popular protest, Moore was fired from the case in 1924. That was also the year in which the iww split over issues of centralization and decentralization, and a year later the Communist Party's International Labor Defense took with it much of the membership and methodology of the iww's General Defense Committee. Hating communists, the anarchists chose the ACLU as Sacco's and Vanzetti's primary popular defense strategist. This split between anarchists and radical labor defense was part of the ongoing process that made anarchism as a philosophy less and less connected with the left wing of the labor movement.

How could revolutionary anarchists make a more successful alliance with liberals than with revolutionary syndicalists, with whom they had so much more in common in terms of strategy? The answer stems both from the individualist elements of the anarchist movement and from the generally reactionary nature of American politics in the 1920s. The early

years of the Sacco and Vanzetti defense campaign were very grim. It might have been possible to win a case with a general strike in 1912, when Fred Moore ran the successful defense of the IWW activists Joe Ettor and Arturo Giovannitti, the major labor leaders accused of the killing of Anna Lo Pizzo during the Lawrence textile strike.[5] Moore's efforts were successful that time, despite the fact that, as Elizabeth Gurley Flynn recalled, "It was a dangerous gamble never tried in this country as far as we knew, a political strike directed not at the employer, but at the state."[6] There was an Ettor and Giovannitti defense fund in every major city in Italy during the trial, but it was hard to build a mass labor-defense campaign in the 1920s.[7] The mass arrests and deportations of radicals between 1917 and 1920 had decimated the left. Socialism was in a state of global fragmentation; union membership in the United States was in decline, and the majority of existing labor unions were dominated by nativist "business unionism." When Congress passed the KKK-backed Johnson–Reed immigration act in 1924, which set up strict quotas for southern Europeans and eastern Europeans and, by extension, explicitly asserting the racial inferiority of Jews, Italians, and Slavs, Samuel Gompers "reluctantly embrace[d] the idea that European immigration endangered America's racial foundations." He also wholeheartedly endorsed the continued exclusion of Asian immigrants.[8] The KKK grew to great popularity, comprising two million members at its peak in 1925,[9] and in even less clandestine circles the pseudo-science of eugenics gained wide audiences among the elite. In Italy, the Fascist Movement took power in 1922, and Benito Mussolini gained prestige in the American press and support from the American government, which agreed with the dictator's claim that "Italians have not the self-control . . . of the Anglo-Saxons."[10] In America, Italians held on to marginal jobs in American industry and were stereotyped as bootlegging gangsters in the Prohibition-era mass media. In the midst of worldwide reaction, socialists were in conflict as well, following the failed revolution in Germany in 1919. The Bolsheviks of Russia cracked down on anarchists, and Joseph Stalin spent the mid-1920s clawing his way to power within the Bolshevik party. It should be no surprise that Italian anarchists in America saw themselves under a worldwide siege, and not only because of fascism. Of all revolutionaries, anarchists were the most critical of the communists.

In 1921, the Red Army put down the rebellion of anarchist sailors at Kronstadt. International anarchists who initially had supported the Russian Revolution now denounced Lenin's Bolshevik party as the "Judas Iscariot" of the working class, describing the Kronstadt rebels as the "Paris Commune of Russia."[11] Alexander Berkman's and Emma Goldman's

writings from exile, in addition to reports on Nestor Makhno, the Ukranian anarchist who went into exile in 1921, persuaded international anarchists that the communists were as much their enemies as were the capitalist class.[12] Relief for the anarchist prisoners in Russia became a major aspect work for both anarchists and liberals. Roger Baldwin raised funds and interest in anarchist prisoners, as did Alexander Berkman.[13]

Anarchists and syndicalists also split in Europe. These international divisions spilled into the IWW, whose members decided whether to ally themselves with French syndicalists, Italian anarchists, or Russian Bolsheviks after 1919. In Italy, Mussolini's fascists, who had split from left socialists by supporting Italian participation in World War One, began attacking anarchists and socialists on the streets. The paths of Italian syndicalists were complicated. Some became communists, and others remained independent, while still others became fascists. Anarchists, too, like the futurists to whom they were close, in some cases became fascists. In other cases, they became fascism's victims.[14]

When Lenin died in Russia in 1924, *L'Adunata dei Refrattari* trumpeted the "death of the dictator." That same year, the IWW split over factional differences. Many IWW members became Leninists, moving into the ranks of the Workers (Communist) Party and the Trade Union Educational League.[15] The U.S. communists attracted adherents. By 1928, a year after Sacco and Vanzetti died, Stalin had consolidated his power in the Soviet Union.

In this period of sectarian competition, the expression of anarchist ideology was very important to those in Sacco's and Vanzetti's circle. They were anarchists who identified with a long tradition of European forebears. Sacco wrote from prison that he followed in the sensibilities of "Bakunin, Carlo Cafiero, Reclus, Fanelli, Bruno, Arnaldo de Brescia, Francisco Ferrer, Spartaco, the martyrs of Chicago, the nihilists of Russia, Ravachol, Henry, Caserio, Angiollo and Bresci." This international political identity was important to him, he explained, and it did not matter what his friends did to defend him as long as it was done through the principles and in the name of his "immutable faith in Anarchism."[16] Sacco and his comrades on the defense committee of Boston would work to maintain their understanding of anarchist philosophy and practice at the campaign's center for the duration of the trial.

The anarchists in Sacco's and Vanzetti's circle believed that revolution would be achieved through the spontaneous action of the masses, much as the anarchists of Chicago had believed about forty years earlier. Sometimes this spontaneous action might be inspired by a single act of vio-

lence, the "propaganda of the deed." When Gaetano Bresci, one of the heroes cited in Sacco's speech, left Paterson, New Jersey, to assassinate the king of Italy, he was first cursed by his comrades for taking off with their money but later hailed in the anarchist newspaper *La Questione Sociale* as a martyr, and a circle of New York's Galleanists named itself the "Bresci Group."[17] Although Bakunin, the most prominent theorist of anarchist revolution by mob action, had died in 1876, he left a profound legacy, particularly in Italy. Bakunin, who had worked with many Austro-Hungarian activists in eastern Europe and central Europe before going to Italy, glorified the revolutionary mob, arguing that revolution would be created by the unleashing of the "brutal passions" of the people, who would destroy public order. Like other theorists of the revolution as a natural, spontaneous act of the "people," Bakunin also defined those people as potential dupes. For, he argued, without the leadership of "enlightened democrats," the masses would be "betrayed by political swindlers." He tended to organize by forming small bands of conspirators and both proclaimed the need for unfettered mass action and promoted a vanguard of intellectual leadership and heroism for world revolution. Vanzetti, who remarked in his letters from prison that the "[h]umbles" were capable of sentiment, but not cogitation, voiced a similar notion.[18]

Bakunin's theory of the crowd also foreshadowed the writings of Gustave Le Bon, whose work was replete with racial essentialism to explain which masses, based on national characteristics, were the most advanced. Arguing that the state was the product of the "Yids"; that Chinese workers demonstrated "primitive barbarism"; and that ideas of revolt were "natural" to particular individuals and nations, Bakunin also loathed the "herd like activity" of the people and argued that intellectuals must create a "unified popular consciousness."[19]

The attempted revolutionary actions of Bakunin's disciple Errico Malatesta indicate some of the problems in the effort to create a revolution through spontaneous mass action with an inspiring deed. Because this theory of revolution relied on such a voluntarist definition of action, the Italian anarchists, like the Haymarket anarchists, could easily come to define the masses with contempt as less than manly when they encountered them in the flesh. Take, for example, an attempted revolutionary act by Malatesta's circle with Carlo Cafiero in 1877. On April 8, they arrived in the village of Letino, burned all of the state documents in a bonfire in the town's central square, and distributed weapons, declaring, "The rifles and axes we have given you, the knives you have, if you wish to do something. If not, to hell with you."[20]

"Salve O Bresci," *La Questione Sociale*, July 9, 1905. In the original newspaper, directly underneath Bresci's portrait are the words, "Salve O Bresci [Hail, O Bresci]" and a celebratory poem that begins with the stanzas:

Hail, hero of human vengeance	How many tears did fall on your breast!
Hail to you, who boldly struck	What a deep, awful pain
the tyrant of the Italian shore	Tormented your fervent heart
what a fatal unexpected blow	At the massacre of the outcast people

(Translation by Lucy Hill)

Anarchists in Italy and in the United States memorialized these revolutionaries for decades to come, naming study circles after Cafiero and republishing Bakunin's work in Italian.[21] But these anarchists were not the only Italian radicals in America. During the massive wave of European immigration to the United States between the 1880s and 1919, Italian syndicalists also played a critical role in the radical wing of the U.S. labor movement, forming revolutionary syndicalist groups long before the creation of the IWW and maintaining mass heroic ideals within the left as they did so.[22] They influenced the Wobblies and worked in most IWW industrial organizing drives as well as within the AFL's United Mine Workers of America. In many cases, the syndicalists and individualist anarchists traveled in the same circles and worked on the same causes. Malatesta edited a newspaper in Barre, Vermont, for a short while, and Luigi Galleani, the principal voice of individualist anarchism,[23] started the newspaper *La Cronaca Sovversiva* (the Subversive Chronicle). Anarchists and syndicalists held study groups from Paterson, New Jersey, to Boston and brought their ideas of direct action and spontanaeism into the major strikes in those cities. Sacco and Vanzetti both participated in the important IWW strike in Lawrence, and in other New England uprisings, although they were critical of the leadership. The closeness of the two tendencies in the Italian left was indicated by the fact that, despite their association with individualism, Sacco's and Vanzetti's circle went to the syndicalist Carlo Tresca when they got in trouble with the law.

The two shared the principles of Emma Goldman and Berkman, and as they did, the Italian anarchists combined class-consciousness with Nietzschean philosophy. The columns of *L'Adunata dei Refrattari* combined the theories and practices of Eugene Debs, Errico Malatesta, Galleani, and Bakunin to arrive at a form of revolutionary socialist anarchism that endorsed worker action and the propaganda of the deed but rejected labor leaders and organizers who emphasized "discipline," whom they attacked as "*duci* [leaders]," "*crumiri* [Algerians, or scabs],"[24] and "*castroni* [castrated men]."

The use of the term "*crumiri*" for scabs, which originated in Italy as a racial epithet against Algerian workers, points to the complicated way in which the Italians' experiences as racialized workers shaped their interpretations of power and their strategies in the United States. As members of an "in-between" category—white according to the interpretation of naturalization laws, but with their racial identity up for debate by their Nordic contemporaries[25]—Italian radicals made alliances with both "white" and "non-white" workers and mixed up race and class in their

definitions of the American power structure. At the same time, however, they also seemed to regard southern Italians as "illiterate ragamuffins."[26] Perhaps applying Bakuninist anti-imperialism to their own experiences in America, the new immigrant radicals denounced "the crimes of the white race"; scorned American Fourth of July celebrations; and made alliances with Spanish, Argentinean, and Mexican radicals, forming a pan-Latin anarchist movement within America's radical labor organizations.[27]

These ideas not only came from an intellectual legacy but were developed in the material realities of anti-Italian racism and class oppression in America. The AFL remained the primary voice in organized labor from 1900 into the 1920s, and the hostility of its craft unions to both radicals and unskilled immigrant workers fed anti-organizationalist tendencies among Italian radicals.[28] However, the Italian anarchists were not nationalists; they also attacked Italian fraternal organizations, particularly as fascism grew in popularity. Like other socialists, Italian anarchists and IWW members explicitly rejected race and nationalism. Race, they said, was a fiction produced by "the astute to confound the stupid," and in the place of nations, they imagined a solidarity that united all nations, including the Zulu, against the "stingy sentiment" of patriotism.[29]

Because of America's own racial character, despite official pronouncements that class was the only real source of alliance, the experience of what they called "*italianofobia*" influenced the way these anarchists described power. For example, Vanzetti testified in court in 1920 that the First World War was not "like Abraham Lincoln's and Abe Jefferson [*sic*] ... to give chance to any other peoples, not to the white people, but to the Black and the others because they know they are mens [*sic*] like the rest, but they are war for the great millionaire."[30] He saw the interpenetration of race and class in American society, regardless of the official ideological positions his comrades might take. In the midst of the Sacco and Vanzetti case, *L'Adunata dei Refrattari* called on the workers to "remember the Italians of Louisiana" who had been lynched there "in the name of the law."[31] Nonetheless, like the IWW activists, and the Haymarket martyrs, the anarchists argued that the white working class was the victim of manipulation by ruling-class racists and that "class was behind all racial prejudice."[32]

This class-based analysis did not mean that the anarchists were narrowly focused on "bread-and-butter" economic issues. More so than many American-born radicals of the era, the internationalist Italians were staunch antimilitarists. As a result, they suffered disproportionately during the Palmer crackdowns of the war era. Hundreds of Italians were deported, sometimes to face execution or assassination by fascists when

they arrived in Italy. As the Palmer raids continued, anarchists' portrayal of American law as an absolute tyranny against the working class, and against Italians in particular, increased in urgency. While the IWW began to moderate its position on direct action and use legal defense more frequently, Italian anarchists became more dramatic and confrontational in their stance toward the legal apparatus and more adamant in their critiques of other activists in the face of repression.

Paul Avrich's research indicates that a small group of Italian anarchists calling themselves the "American Anarchist Fighters" decided to defend their ideals by sending a batch of package bombs to police and officials.[33] This small group's actions, its support for similar ones, and its critiques of statute law placed it beyond the pale for the IWW. Carlo Tresca, Joe Ettor, and other members of the Italian American syndicalist party, the Federazione Socialista Italiana (FSI), as well as Italian socialists, vehemently rejected the propaganda of the deed, as did Italian socialists in Italy. Bombing was associated with provocateurs. The IWW's *One Big Union Monthly* described the 1919 bombing as a police plot. "Whenever you hear of any 'revolutionary' act somewhere," the article's authors wrote, "don't ask us as they used to do—'*ou est la femme?*' But ask, where is the Palmer Stool Pigeon?"[34] Kate Richards O'Hare, socialist and prison reformer, was also convinced that the bombings were the work of police agents after she met one of the accused Galleanists, Ella Antolini, in the women's federal prison.[35] Tresca, who represented the IWW among Italian New Yorkers, denounced anyone who advocated the use of direct action as a police agent and called for the expulsion of agents provocateurs from political groups.[36]

In contrast, the Galleanists celebrated assassination, crimes against property, and bombing as signs of working-class heroism. The anarchists had previously split with Ettor and Big Bill Haywood and vociferously defended Arturo Caron, an anarchist who was killed while building a bomb with which to avenge the workers killed in Colorado's Ludlow massacre.[37] As it had been for the Chicago anarchists, the concept of revolution as basic class justice, "an eye for an eye and a tooth for a tooth," was central to Galleanist rhetoric; capitalist law was described as a system of hypocrisy that decried worker violence while supporting the mass violence of exploitation.[38]

The Galleanists' depictions of natural justice, like Bakunin's, were based on the notion that the working class was incapable of tyranny. This antipolitical belief in the working class's inherent virtue, like the natural-law theories of the Haymarket anarchists, placed the mark of evil on the

man-made state as a source of hypocrisy, artificiality, and intrigue. The law was bad partly because its power was hidden. It was a "monstrous political conspiracy" that spread "tentacles around the throats of innocents." Drawing simultaneously on images of the Inquisition and bestial savagery, the anarchists described the court as a "cannibalistic, Torquemadist" scene of intrigue, contrasting the modernity of anarchism with the grotesque majesty of Old World institutions.[39] The court was a "medieval inquisition." It was not modern but had "revised with the progress of time through esoteric laws and procedures, in its essence, a fierce institution of a barbarous epoch. All the human passions which revolve in the human heart are hidden under a robe of human hypocrisy."[40] Both individual acts of heroic resistance and spontaneous mass uprisings were defined in contrast to this manipulative and deceptive institution of the bourgeois court.

Like Goldman's newspaper *Mother Earth*, Sacco's and Vanzetti's circle published articles about Nietzsche's superman and promoted the work of Georges Sorel. As they did so, their rivals in organizationalist circles criticized them.[41] They always insisted that the spirit of the individual revolutionary was to be revered, and they publicized and marveled at the acts of heroes. Syndicalists, too, celebrated revolutionary violence as "beautiful in its disarray."[42] In *L'Adunata dei Refrattari*, one author argued that there were two reasons to defend terrorism and individual expropriation. The first was that the social order itself was so unfair that any act of individual rebellion was justified, even if it was simply criminal. The second was what the author called the "heroic" reason: "There is this small exuberant and audacious minority of Dionysian nature, now satanic, now divine, always aristocratic and unassimilable, contemptuous and anti-social, who possessed by the flame of anarchy, constitute the grand perennial rogues who obviate every form of slavery, who burn to ashes and die."[43]

Thus, as others on the left became more enamored of "social realism" and discipline in the 1920s, Sacco and Vanzetti and their friends held on to the romantic concept of spontaneous mass uprising fueled by acts of individual heroism. Rather than being a product of workplace collectivity, it seems that the revolutionary impulse came from inside the spirit of each individual.[44] Like those IWW members who called the GDC's fund raising a waste of time, these individualist anarchists believed only in direct action in response to state persecution and tended to repudiate the use of lawyers entirely. The only use for the courtroom was as a stage on which to articulate one's political vision and take the consequences, as Louis Lingg, Alexander Berkman, Gaetano Bresci, and Emma Goldman had. Shortly before his death, Sacco rejected parliamentary socialists as

"legalitarians" who stifled revolution and refused to sign the appeal, warning his friends of "the illusions of legalism."[45]

Self-sacrifice and martyrdom were indeed ideals in this movement, and this applied to women as well as to men. The individual spirit that was most glorified in anarchist literature was a self-sacrificing one, burning to ashes and dying in the interest of the masses. Thus, despite their own interest in spontaneous mass action, the Italian anarchists' heroic ideology worked both in response to and in conjunction with the moves of syndicalists toward fascism in the 1920s.

Tina Cacici's short piece "Profilo Muliebre [Feminine Profile]" indicates the more problematic elements of this type of heroism and its relationship to democratic organization.[46] In her description of the "new woman," Cacici, who was an organizer for the syndicalist Amalgamated Clothing Workers Association (ACWA), a participant in the Sacco and Vanzetti defense campaign, and an associate of the IWW organizer Arturo Giovannitti, focused almost entirely on isolated experiences of spirituality and emotion. Cacici made the anarchist "Idea" into a god capable of redeeming women in a new era of peace and internationalism, but it is not clear how different the experience of political ideology was from the solitary religious experience of prayer. Cacici replaced the sublime romantic love that had united Chicago's anarchists in joyful masses trying to keep themselves alive with an image of heroic asceticism and transcendent political idealism:

> I am new in sentiment, in the unspeakable expression of love and the ineffable expression of grief. I am new because I ignore happiness. . . . I cried when a grand and infinite love smiled in the bright morning of my youth, when I felt certainly loved because I had loved truly. . . . I wanted to smile at love and joy but sadness and silence crashed around my ears and opened the doors of my eyes to the fleetingness of joy and the eternity of grief. I am new because my spirit, devastated by the tempest of grief, is pleased by the devastation and does not permit anyone to rebuild it. I am new because I suffer my grief in silence with the stoicism of a martyr, and in the supreme grandness of this martyrdom I redeem my faith in the goodness of life and the goodness of things. . . . I am new because no one at my level feels so penetrated by the love of this vision, which is the beautiful, ardent offspring of my powerful woman-spirit. I am new because I sacrifice my youth and my future on the altar of one grand, immortal goddess, because I burnt on her altar all that is generous, all that is noble, all that is excellent, all that which vibrates, palpitates, and trembles in the soul of woman—the wife, the mother.[47]

Although Cacci was an internationalist, her principal difference from nationalist concepts of the cult of state motherhood that would arise under fascism was her claim to worship the heroes not only of Italy, but of all nations. "I do not have a fatherland, nor do I bend my knees at the altar of its martyrs," she wrote. "My fatherland is the world and its heroes will be those who will destroy frontiers and will elevate humanity to the heights assigned to them by nature." Cacici's portrayal of the "new" woman, like other representations of heroic, self-sacrificing female ideals, associated political dedication with the rejection of happiness. Instead of placing women in dynamic action, which filled so many descriptions of heroic anarchist men, Cacici's joy came from spiritual fulfillment as she embraced the collapse of her own joy into grief. In her description of the "ideal," the international mother would burn herself up on the altar of world socialism.

Ultimately, such images of self-sacrificing heroism as a means to mass identification could serve to replace all ideals of private attachment with a complete bond between ascetic revolutionaries and an idea of the "good" masses, so that the dissolution of the private self became a precondition for revolutionary commitment. Such a complete conflation of the undivided self with an idealized "mass spirit" that rejected desire entirely made divisions within the working class appear to be the product of selfishness or the aspiration for power. Hannah Arendt argues that this kind of love for an abstract notion of the masses and belief in the "natural goodness of a class" is the source of attraction in totalitarian ideology.[48]

Such a belief in sacrifice might also lead to a rejection of the defense campaign as a strategy. These seductive notions of self-transcendence and heroic sacrifice worked against maintaining an active campaign for Sacco's and Vanzetti's survival.

Anarchists who supported Sacco and Vanzetti explicitly challenged this belief system. Many Italian anarchists (including Cacici) worked on the men's defense from beginning to end. Despite their disdain for law and their distrust in lawyers, they raised three hundred and sixty thousand dollars for the legal defense between 1920 and 1925.[49]

When Sacco and Vanzetti were sentenced to death, several in the Galleanist circle criticized the romantic heroic elements of their own doctrine. Because Sacco and Vanzetti had risked their lives by stating their political beliefs in court, "they have a right to our solidarity and gratitude," one of their defense organizers explained. "They have testified, under infamy, to the beauty of our ideal, of the purest aspirations of all humanity for freedom. And we, who are free, must especially liberate and defend

them . . . for us, Sacco and Vanzetti, of all the political prisoners, are the most precious."[50]

Those who tried to mix the ideals of propaganda of the deed with the defense campaign argued that action, whether by the proletariat or by daring individuals, was the only acceptable strategy for the defense. Instead of advocating that Sacco and Vanzetti die as martyrs, they called for a dramatic act of retaliation that would free the men, proving the power of the masses, but again calling for the masses to sacrifice themselves for Sacco and Vanzetti—who were noble because of their sacrifice for the ideal. It was not necessary, however, to view this act as a negation of desire, as a sacrifice for others. It was also possible to define Sacco and Vanzetti's testimony in court as a choice to maintain their own integrity despite the consequences, and thus a heroic and brave stance in the name of anarchy.

Because Sacco and Vanzetti were willing to die for their beliefs, it made sense that many on the defense committee insisted that anarchism itself was essential to the defense. Sacco and Vanzetti should be held up as symbols of anarchism; they had to be saved with anarchist tactics, and it was critical to clarify that they were anarchists, not criminals. The Galleanists, who formed the core of the defense committee from its very beginning, saw their comrades as representatives of international anarchism. They continually identified Sacco and Vanzetti as political prisoners who were anarchists, not simply workers or Italians. In every description of the case, both the reason that Sacco and Vanzetti should be defended and the reason that they were being persecuted was their activity on behalf of Andrea Salsedo, the anarchist whom they said was murdered by the U.S. Department of Justice. It was because they were valiantly standing by Elia and Salsedo and exposing the crimes of the Justice Department that Sacco and Vanzetti were heroes of anarchism. The anarchists held up Sacco and Vanzetti as the special exemplars of anarchist ideology, a strategic answer to the problem of both fascist reaction and communist dictatorship. "We the anarchists," they announced, "have the most direct interest in Sacco and Vanzetti through the communication of the idea and aspirations."[51]

However, the organizers who got involved in the defense were not individualist anarchists but IWW members. When Aldino Felicani, editor of *L'Adunata dei Refrattari* and head of the Boston Defense Committee, called on Carlo Tresca for help, he immediately brought into the case the entire burgeoning IWW mass defense tradition, which had been honed during the mass trials of the 1910s. It was Tresca who chose Fred Moore. For a time, the Galleanists and Moore worked together. The Boston

anarchists began publishing *L'Agitazione*, a news bulletin dedicated to re-porting on the defense, on Moore's suggestion. *L'Agitazione* critiqued the legal system and its relation to capitalism. It described multiple methods of frame-up, remarking on the new use of the label "criminal" to attack political prisoners, and described the spiritual torture of prison.

L'Adunata dei Refrattari, to Moore's and Tresca's apparent dismay, also continued to put out calls for workers to take direct action for Sacco and Vanzetti. In 1926, for example, an anonymous author in the paper an-nounced, "The hour of action has come! The verbal protests have not impressed the hearts of certain hard people, abandon all moral scruples towards the enemy . . . in the name of God Pluto and Lex Talionis, im-pose force on the heads of those responsible!"[52] In the summer of 1927, *L'Adunata dei Refrattari* saluted "Bresci of Today and tomorrow" and re-ferred back to the original Galleanist terrorist handbook *La Salute è in voi!* (Health Is in You!).[53] On September 16, 1921, someone set off a bomb on the corner of Broad and Wall streets in New York City, killing three people and wounding more than two hundred. Immediately following the Wall Street bombing, the FBI believed that Galleanists who supported Sacco and Vanzetti were responsible, and when an article appeared in the news-papers, Moore responded: "I do not know a single person who is con-nected with any such alleged group."[54] In 1921, an FBI agent reported on a meeting in Philadelphia during which one speaker apparently said that if Sacco and Vanzetti were not released, the Italian masses would liberate them by breaking down the jail's doors. This could have been standard metaphor, but given the possible involvement of Sacco's and Vanzetti's defenders with bomb plots, it may have been meant literally. The FBI did actually infiltrate the defense committee and were continually on watch for any proposed act of terror among Sacco's and Vanzetti's supporters.[55]

Sacco's and Vanzetti's friends argued that acts of personal sacrifice such as hunger strikes and dramatic bombings would not be individual acts, but would awaken the spirit of manly revolt in the working class. For example, *L'Agitazione*'s writers argued that the workers would have an immediate understanding and be inspired by Sacco's 1923 hunger strike. Writers for *L'Adunata dei Refrattari* claimed: "Only the workers can understand the desperate cry of Sacco from the House of Justice," because "people who have no heart cannot understand the beauty of the heroic act of protest."[56] Implying that workers had more "heart" than the middle class, such com-ments again suggested that the source of revolution was in the natural im-pulses of the "good" masses. As the anarchists argued that the workers' main reasons for refusing to revolt came from the union bosses who con-

trolled them or from the committee work that slowed them down, their evocations to direct action argued that, given freedom from all constraint by labor leaders, members of the working class would embrace anarchist principles themselves.

Throughout the campaign, Sacco expressed revolutionary romantic heroic ideals of anarchist direct action, describing his struggle for freedom as one pitting the forces of life against death and declaring defiance more valuable than life itself:

> The tenth of July, the electric current will be burning our bodies, the machine is the horrible imaginative instrument that the capitalist uses to frighten the working class into a slave and blind man. But nevertheless, today is the first of May of 1927 and the flowers, the trees, and all the creatures have come back from the storming of life more vivid, and bloom in perfect harmony with mother nature. . . . After the capitalist court of Massachusetts has crushed us every day and night, devouring the flesh of our bodies and torturing our souls for seven years, and finally deals the last vicious heartless blow, they send us to our graves as red handed felons and murderers. . . . I did refuse to sign my name into petition to the Governor Fuller and I will refuse any other request or legal procedure.[57]

Vanzetti had gone in the other direction. By the end of their time in prison, he had joined the liberals and intellectuals in hoping that shifting popular opinion would succeed, but Sacco wrote, somewhat suggestively, in a letter delivered through Felicani that the workers should save him now, before it was too late, "with the formidable cry of the oppressed, like dynamite that shatters the house of the magistrates, and all the tyrants of yesterday and today."[58]

The defense became a test of the anarchist idea not only in the United States, but internationally. Describing the failures of the Sacco and Vanzetti movement in the mid-1920s as the result of their "castration" by the slow-moving legal defense, the anarchists viewed other political groups' interest in the case with suspicion.[59] They also rejected organizational discipline and authority as ineffective and crippling, continually arguing that spontaneous and dramatic action in revenge by the masses was the only thing that would save the lives of the men. As the campaign's end drew near and the masses did not revolt, individual action would work just as well. As one writer, calling himself "Prometeo," put it: "It is time to finish it! If the proletarians won't, the anarchists will!" But again, views were divided. Some on the committee responded that this desperate cry only indicated the sad state of affairs and said, instead, that "[we] must

rise and coordinate all the forces into one force for the grand work of liberation."[60]

Although many of the anarchists objected on philosophical grounds to the use of lawyers, in contradiction to these pronouncements they raised large amounts of money for legal defense efforts. In calls for action that appeared in 1922, 1923, and 1927, the editors at *L'Adunata dei Refrattari* insisted: "Although we are in agreement in recognition of the fatuity of the law and equality before the law," defending Sacco and Vanzetti, even with lawyers, was the responsibility of the anarchists. Here *L'Adunata dei Refrattari*'s writers echoed Forrest Edwards's comments on legal defense from a few years before:

> Listen, it's not possible to be heroes every day of your existence, and a few of us love the quiet life. I am not justifying anything, but . . . even if I must tread on someone's corns, who believes that an anarchist must automatically be a hero and not a man like all the other mortals? We are just a few, and to a large part of the few, life is still beautiful even with all the oppression and the pain. . . . When we find one of ours trapped by a filthy accusation, held in infamy with all the victims of the movement for the ideal of emancipation, it becomes almost a duty to unmask the frame-up. . . . Considering also that the arrested ones are our dear comrades. And we have not yet come to such an insensibility that we neglect the people to exalt the ideal on an altar of rigid coherence.[61]

In other notices, anarchists on the defense committee took those comrades to task who had time for recriminations against the defense committee but had done little work for Sacco and Vanzetti.[62]

Although the IWW did not approve of the anarchists' calls for violence, they also saw heroism in primarily masculine terms, and the rhetoric of masculinist self-sacrifice dominated much of the IWW's defense rhetoric during the trial. Moore built Sacco's and Vanzetti's case as a mass campaign, combining legal action, mass-media appeals, and working-class mass action that he hoped would appeal broadly to the Italian working class, to middle-class Italian progressives, and to liberals.

Without regard for the political ideals of the defendants, Tresca, Moore, and Flynn, from the beginning of their involvement in 1920, treated the Sacco and Vanzetti trial as they would any IWW case and proceeded in what had become the usual way, calling on a collection of liberals, intellectuals, and labor activists to organize mass meetings, fund raising, and appeals for their defense and making particular criticisms of the role of

nativism in oppressing working-class radicals. When Moore took charge of the defense, he did not simply hunt evidence and write motions but immediately began a broad propaganda and fund-raising campaign among union activists, particularly focusing on the most racially diverse union of the AFL: the United Mine Workers. Working the IWW–socialist–liberal alliance built by the GDC during World War One, Moore sent a letter to Flynn stating that he wanted to get in touch with Roger Baldwin (head of the ACLU and a supporter of Russian prisoners) and, further, that he wanted her to help him "get in touch with Felix Frankfurter and anybody else here in this city who may be of value at the earliest possible moment."[63]

As a result, political conflict arose almost immediately between IWW and anarchist activists. Moore was "disgusted" with the group of Galleanists and wrote to Flynn in August 1920, shortly after he had arrived, that the committee was "perfectly willing that someone else should do all the work providing that they can control all the expenditures." Furthermore, Moore did not agree that the defense should be driven by the principles of anarchy that motivated Sacco, Vanzetti, and their friends. He complained that the defense committee was both too Italian and too anarchist. He wanted Flynn to send him someone who spoke and understood English and had "some responsibility to the organized labor movement." He wrote, "There is no one here with any sense of responsibility to anyone other than themselves. I trust you will understand that there are a great many times when a fellow gets simply desperate."[64]

In September, the committee chose Aldino Felicani to go to New York to talk to Tresca's group and asked Flynn to go on a national speaking tour.[65] In November, Moore began asking for mailing lists of unions with large numbers of Italian members.[66] Despite his zeal, Moore worked without any understanding, it appears, of the complexity of Italian politics and seemed to assume that all Italians would automatically agree with each other. Such was not the case. Money conflicts soon erupted between the New York syndicalists and the Boston anarchists, as L'Agitazione's editors failed to publish financial contributions made by New York and implied that Tresca's group were thieves.[67] The New York committee at some point "refused to give any more money to Felicani," because L'Agitazione basically made it clear to its readers that people should send money only to Boston,[68] even though several members of the New York group were on speaking tours for Sacco and Vanzetti.[69] Meanwhile, in Boston Moore reported to Flynn that several other Boston committee members who

were hard workers were "disgusted" with the sectarianism,[70] but he still saw the case as an opportunity to attack the entire "frame-up" system and continually defined the efforts of the Boston committee as a hindrance to that end.

On July 14, 1921, Sacco and Vanzetti were found guilty of a crime that carried the death sentence. After the verdicts, more appeals to the public began. Moore got the ACLU and IWW member John Beffel to work with him on an article that would be the first to publicize Sacco's and Vanzetti's story in the liberal English-language press. Moore was impassioned about the case when he wrote about it to Art Shields, an IWW activist who was working on what would become the pamphlet "Are They Doomed?"

> We have a terrific battle on our hands. We have got to save the lives of those two boys. The trial has only served to confirm my absolute conviction of their innocence. . . . All of us here appreciate fully the burden that the IWW is carrying. We do not want you to sacrifice anything that may be vital to your own boys on behalf of the case, but if you can give us any space [in *Solidarity*] then we will appreciate it.[71]

Shields's article on the trial, which appeared in several IWW publications, was radically different in emphasis from those accounts of Sacco and Vanzetti that had appeared in the Italian anarchist propaganda. The philosophies of anarchism and antimilitarism disappeared in Shields's account of the case, and instead of representing the two men as unique political prisoners, Shields focused on their experiences as victims, as foreign-born workers laboring under a racial stigma. He represented Sacco and Vanzetti as rank-and-file labor activists who rejected craft unionism and supported cross-ethnic organizing, exemplars of the IWW's own philosophies.

In New England, he explained, the foreign-born population "finds itself as badly off as in the Europe of yesterday." National divisions among the workers were the biggest obstacles to unity in this multiethnic workforce, he argued. Shields described Sacco's status as a skilled edge trimmer in a shoe factory, going into detail about his craftsmanship and his role as a leader who "explained to his fellow workers the advantage of being their own masters . . . instead of laboring for wage lords who lived far away from the scene of their workers' toil."

Because of his militant activism against the no-strike alliance of bosses and craft workers, Shields said, Sacco was a "marked man" in New England. Like the anarchists, Shields argued that Vanzetti was prosecuted because he had been involved as a leader in the strike against the Plymouth

Cordage factory and had worked to bring Portuguese and Italian workers together. Comparing Vanzetti to Debs, Shields argued that Vanzetti had been forced to work as a fish peddler because he was blacklisted.[72]

Despite these differences, the IWW papers and the *L'Adunata dei Refrattari* shared notions of heroism as a form of masculine self-sacrifice. Carlos Tresca's syndicalist paper, *Il Martello* [The Hammer], and *L'Adunata dei Refrattari* drew tight bonds between Sacco, Vanzetti, and a predominantly masculine image of the working class. Although some articles highlighted the judge's cruelty by emphasizing that Sacco's wife, Rosina, had a new baby, such sentimental appeals were much more common in the liberal press's coverage of the case than they were in *L'Adunata dei Refrattari*. Most of the letters about the two men published in the anarchist press were written by and to male comrades, and the touring speakers were almost all men. Although Michael Miller Topp remarks on the "enormous emphasis on masculinity among Italian radicals in the US," this was not simply an Italian phenomenon but was characteristic of the IWW, as well, which, despite its vulnerable image in prison correspondence during the war, still retained a firmly masculine image of working-class militancy.[73] conflicts between revolutionary and parliamentary socialists the IWW explained in gendered terms.

Moore, who was responsible for a good deal of the English-language publicity, made sure that the working class would be represented as masculine. In a letter to the socialist writer and Bolshevik sympathizer Eugene Lyons in 1924, he specifically requested that the pamphlet to be written by former anarchist Rob Minor, who had become a communist, compare Sacco and Vanzetti to Tom Mooney, the Irish American union activist in California, commenting that he needed a *man* to write the story and draw the pictures. "I'm afraid of [the journalist] Mary Heaton Vorse because the slant of her mind is largely sob stuff," he wrote.[74] Tresca, who edited *Il Martello*, may have had similar fears. When that paper reprinted Vorse's article, the passage in which she described her visit to Rosina Sacco at home was excised.[75] When the IWW opposed the war, it had to make it clear that this did not mean that its members were pacifists. Femininity and pacifism, even as elements in opposition to the war, were dangerous to the radical movement:

> We submit the proper way to deal with this question (war) is to directly attack it from the economic approach instead of merely appealing to the pacific interests of women. Unless these instincts are led into the channels of practical economic effort with a view toward making war impossible, it seems to us

that they will merely lead to a sex conspiracy against warlike men of proletarian instincts.[76]

Perhaps for the same reasons, descriptions of women pleading with the court against the foul hand of judicial revenge rarely appeared as part of the Sacco and Vanzetti case. It was not that the descriptions of the workers were not romantic. Sacco, Vanzetti, and their supporters all used the language of family and love to describe men's activities in public life. Vanzetti was portrayed, for instance, as "having made a marriage to the cause" when he joined the striking workers of the Plymouth Cordage factory in defense speeches by Enrico Albertini for the defense committee.[77] Similarly, marriage and love among men abounded in the work of the popular poet and IWW organizer Arturo Giovannitti, who wrote of "America, where men never kiss men, even when they march forth to die," in his description of the lynching of Frank Little.[78] The anarchists used romantic love as a metaphor for political solidarity. Sacco could easily say of the international proletariat as he explained why he would not fight in the war, "I love them people just as I could love my wife," or, as Vanzetti put it, "The anarchism is as beauty as a woman for me . . . perhaps even more."[79]

The IWW's construction of male prisoners who depended on their defense committees turned them into the possessions of the people who contributed to their cause. This dynamic repeated itself in Sacco's and Vanzetti's case, as the two men were depicted as vulnerable within the grasp of the state. When Luigi Quintiliano of the IWW's Italian Political Victims Committee went on a speaking tour, calling for dramatic acts from the workers, he referred over and over again to "our two martyrs" or "our two prisoners" who "depend on us in their final hour."[80]

As the IWW activists showed Sacco's and Vanzetti's helplessness and their great sacrifice, they also insisted on the power of the masses to free them. As the two became ever more representative of the international working class in a time of reaction, it became crucial that the working class be the agent to free them. It was at this moment that sacrifice was demanded—not from Sacco and Vanzetti, but from the masses, who must act in a moment of crisis to save these heroic, self-sacrificing men.

The defense campaigners also included the most democratic elements of the defense campaign's logic in their appeals. The anarchists who worked to free Sacco and Vanzetti opposed jail on principle because they "loved the life and the freedom of life,"[81] and they clearly spoke in favor of working-class self-activity as the most important power in the case. Like other socialists, they said that bodily love was central to their politics and

insisted that they had not yet come to exalt the ideal over the individual. At the same time, they relied on intensely ascetic and masculinist notions of revolutionary action, displayed a self-destructive distrust of organization, and expressed a belief that all failures of the working class were the fault of bad leaders.

Moore, too, saw Sacco and Vanzetti as symbols of the labor movement in a moment of danger. By December 1921, he had become ambitious and began to define the campaign to save Sacco and Vanzetti as a means for saving the entire labor movement from the frame-up. The way to accomplish this goal, he decided, was to find the guilty culprits. Although Elizabeth Gurley Flynn and the Italians had argued that the men themselves should be the central focus of agitation, Moore argued that "sooner or later the broader implications of this case and many allied cases of the country must be met." The case should be addressed, he argued, in a "big program" so as not to have one's view of "the tree obscured by the twigs and leaves." He went on, "I realize that right now the problem is to save the twig. But some day I have a devout hope that I will have some part in the process of taking care of the trunk."[82] Flynn replied that she feared with his strategy, Sacco and Vanzetti themselves would be "lost in the shuffle."[83]

Despite this warning, Moore began what would be an incredibly expensive and time-consuming mission to prove the men's innocence by finding the real killers, contrasting the concept of socialism and the ethics of the working class with the meaningless acts of criminals. The new strategy, which demanded both delay and money, was not popular. In early 1922, Flynn reported that, as she toured the country, she was finding people angry with the national headquarters of the defense committee. Activists were burning out. Flynn wrote that "local groups feel that the Sacco–Vanzetti case is taking all their time, all their money, stultifying their efforts along every other line and that it is just a small group in Boston who are isolated, extravagant, and incommunicative. . . . Radicals are only superficially interested, Communists are putting all their time and money into Russian relief work. The IWW is doing the amnesty campaign for federal prisoners."[84] Viewing the field from the perspective of a touring speaker, Flynn remarked on how "few people know about the case and how many Italians (especially the close comrades of the Boston group) say they are innocent with their tongues in their cheek and don't believe it themselves. This must be stopped. Does it come from the Italian publicity? We must know what is the cause."[85] Conflicts within the defense committee continued. Vanzetti was disgusted with his comrades and wrote to Moore: "There is not a single one intelligent enough to really help you

and I must stay in jail probably be kill[ed] only because those who could save me with the truth have no courage or intelligence to tell it."[86]

In May 1922, addressing the "so-called Sacco Vanzetti Defense Committee [SVDC]," Moore complained of a general lack of cooperation that was expressed in the failure of the group to meet, in lack of coordination between English and Italian activities, and in the absence of fund raising.[87] In July, he helped to send out a circular to organized labor, which complained that "the lack of funds is seriously hampering the defense." For the Italians, as well, the struggle for the defense of the two men had become a heroic one, and now the "honor of the labor movement" and the American working class was itself at stake.[88] Saving Sacco and Vanzetti was no longer simply a humanitarian duty, or even a fight for the ever dwindling civil liberties of the immigrant working class, but a test of the working class's power. For both Moore and the anarchists, the confrontation between the state and the masses over the fate over these two men expressed in microcosm the conflict between the state and the workers in general. To lose this struggle would be to lose everything.

As expenses continued to mount in Boston, Flynn, who was in New York and was living with Carlo Tresca, joined in the criticisms of Moore. Moore protested to Flynn that the expenses involved in the investigation were great because of the strategy he had adopted, but rumors about Moore's squandering of money on wine, women, and cocaine began to circulate. Felicani saw Moore sitting exhausted in the office and was convinced he was taking dope. The anarchists generally distrusted Moore. Constantino Zonchello, one of the most active members of the Boston committee, complained to Vanzetti about Moore's expenditures, and Vanzetti, at the end of his life, wrote to Mary Donovan that "Moore had built an office harem with two or three young ladies employed, automobiles, etc."[89]

Moore's expenses were, in fact, huge. At one point, he was paid three hundred dollars a week by the committee, an astonishing sum in 1923, but the biggest problem between Moore and the anarchists probably stemmed from ideological differences and the stakes in the case, not from drug addiction or irresponsibility. Moore had a reputation for emotional instability, but he had been a good lawyer on a number of very difficult political cases in the past. He was upset about the fact that the Mooney case, as he put it, had destroyed people's faith in legal institutions, leading many radicals to abandon defense activism. To continue along that path, Moore argued, would lead to desperate acts of violence. He wrote, "I want to prove that the law is still a remedy that can be, when appealed to intel-

ligently and honestly, made to avail." If he won, Moore believed, Sacco's and Vanzetti's case would be "a turning point in the struggle of American labor in the U.S. courts."[90] For the anarchists, whose most immediate enemies were the twin devils of corporate power and business unionism, the attempt to work in closed committees and with the slow speed of the law must have seemed dubious indeed. When Moore wanted to spend money and time, and asked the anarchists to help him find the people responsible for the South Braintree robbery, this offended the anarchists' notions of justice. Even if their concepts were "elastic" as one writer for *L'Adunata dei Refrattari* had explained in justifying the use of a legal defense committee, they did not want to become "gendarmes," handing over offenders against the laws or private property.[91]

Moore also blamed the failure to build a mass movement of labor on the defense activists. The organizing failures of the Italian defense committee, Moore believed, resulted from the fact that it was sectarian and dogmatic in its rejection of legal methods, unions, and progressive allies. To an extent, Moore's criticism seems valid. However, if Sacco and Vanzetti were willing to risk death to defend anarchism, it would hardly make sense to run a defense that did not mention, or blatantly betrayed, anarchist politics. Moore also minimized the significance of political conflicts between Italians. Political prisoners in Italy dominated the interests of many of the Italian Americans, who had family members suffering under Mussolini's iron heel. The Italian American syndicalists had split, with one branch turning to fascism. But while Arturo Giovannitti spoke on platforms about the need to fight fascism and Italian labor activists fought pitched battles with fascists and mobsters over union control, Moore wondered why the Italian defense committee had not tried appealing to the middle-class progressives among the Italian community.[92] He read their political conflicts as petty and unimportant, but at least one former syndicalist, who had become a fascist, led the FBI to Aldino Felicani.[93] Flynn had to remind Moore that, with the ascendancy of Mussolini, the scene had changed. "There *are* no Italian progressives, Fred!" she exclaimed in one letter.

By 1923, according to Flynn, all of the committees were falling apart. The New York committee was "for all purposes dead," partly due to internal factionalism, and Flynn remarked that the Boston anarchist Zonchello "had thoroughly damaged the work of the committee" so that "to say that the case needs money is simply to invoke abuse at the present."[94]

Although Moore hoped to slow down the legal process to get a fairer hearing, the anarchists were exhausted by the delays in the trial. Sacco,

who was being held in solitary confinement, went on a hunger strike in March 1923 to pressure the judge into deciding on the defense's evidentiary motions. Moore's response was to send Sacco to an insane asylum, where he was diagnosed as suffering from sensory depravation. As a result, *L'Adunata dei Refrattari* declared Sacco's internment a "victory for the legal defense" and a "disaster for anarchism."[95]

The defense campaign had thus begun to split into two factions. The socialists and IWW activists began organizing a new committee in which to carry on the work for Sacco and Vanzetti, which they called the Labor Defense Committee (LDC). The anarchists were suspicious of the LDC and described it as "communist," much to Flynn's consternation. Even Roger Baldwin and Norman Thomas were LDC members. Flynn exclaimed in a letter to Moore, "They can't afford to antagonize all these people!"[96] While Sacco and some on the SVDC railed against the "communist" LDC, Vanzetti moved away from the most anarchistic on the committee and began advocating popular-front strategies rather than partisan organizing in the name of anarchism.

In April, as he read Errico Malatesta's writings on fascism in Italy from his prison cell, Vanzetti remarked that political factionalism was making fascism's victory easier. In a letter to Elizabeth Glendower Evans, a prison reformer and liberal who had been corresponding with both him and Sacco since early in the case, he wrote that everyone in the antifascist faction in Italy was hampered by dissension. They were united only in necessity, and the anarchists, to his dismay, "distrust all the others."[97] Here, even Galleani was in agreement with Vanzetti and was writing in favor of a popular front of the working classes by 1926. [98]

In 1924, the liberals who had become interested in the case organized under the name of the New Trial League, sponsoring an English-language bulletin to build broad support for Sacco and Vanzetti in contrast to the revolutionary campaign sponsored by the anarchists. The bulletin reported on the league's first major activity, a "monster benefit" under the joint auspices of the fascist-friendly newspaper *Corriere D'America* and the New York Committee for Sacco and Vanzetti. According to the bulletin, the benefit involved the joining together of Italian businessmen and anarchists in a display of unified support for Sacco and Vanzetti while a sixty-piece Italian band played under the direction of Giuseppe Creatore.[99]

The creation of the New Trial League prompted an immediate reaction from inside the Charlestown jail by Sacco, who denounced Fred Moore and his "philanthropistic friends," including Evans, whom he had once addressed as "mother" in his letters from prison. Soon after, the Italian

committee held a conference, splitting Fred Moore from all political activity and restricting him to legal work. Moore was prohibited from pursuing further investigations, and his salary was limited. The new agreement seemed to clear things up for a time. The IWW advocates in the SVDC soon wrote to Moore that they had no objection to the new group and specifically said, "between us and the American friends can't be any intentional misunderstanding."[100]

With the organization of the New Trial League, Moore again tried to invigorate a mass labor campaign for the defense, requesting new pamphlets by Rob Minor and Eugene Lyons. Again, the newly harmonious relations masked continuing tension. In a letter to Matilda Robbins, Moore complained that the Italian committee, now responsible for all the publicity, was doing 95 percent of it only within its own circles. The majority of the men connected with the Italian committee, he wrote, are "utterly unorganized, I mean by that they are not members of organized labor bodies."[101] In contrast, the anarchists had long found it "strange how Moore always showed up to ruin everything."[102]

Finally, Moore resigned from the case, enraged when Felicani refused to pay him:

> I call you a committee . . . but I do this out of courtesy. As a committee you have existed solely on paper. As a committee you have never functioned. Sacco and Vanzetti are entitled to the unswerving loyalty of those who pretend to be their friends. A committee that would serve them must be broad gauged enough and intelligent enough to act in such wise as to permit all shades of political and industrial opinion to cooperate freely in the struggle for justice. I am compelled to believe that your committee is not actuated by such motives. . . . All but Guadagni are of one political faith and you have looked askance and with disfavor upon the aid or assistance of anyone unless they accepted your political dogma. Members of your committee are not even affiliated with organized labor. You have never made any sincere or honest effort to reach even the Italian public of America. It is impossible to secure a decision from you which is abided after being made. At the so-called convention of last February you created a committee of members of the same political faith as yourself and all Italian. Arbitrarily and by your own action you have cut yourself off from all contact, moral and racial, with all other groups in America. Now you are bankrupt.[103]

In response, all of the Italian newspapers published editorials denouncing Moore's legal strategy and demanding that immediate legal action be forced from Judge Webster Thayer.[104] Flynn defended the criticisms of

Moore in a letter to John Codman of the ACLU and argued that, in contrast to Moore's attacks on them, the Italians on the committee had "done so much" and that Moore's expenses were simply too heavy.[105] Flynn also suggested that Codman should approach the Italians as amicably as possible. Italians as a group might be "temperamental, inarticulate and difficult to work with," she said, but they were certainly not fools. Four days later, Sacco denounced Moore and the New Trial League, making a direct threat on Moore's life by closing his letter with the words, "I will not be surprise if somebody found you some morning hang on a lamp-post."[106]

After Moore's departure, the anarchists were surprisingly happy to be working with a much more conservative lawyer whom Moore had hired to assist him: William Thompson.

Despite Moore's absence, the case did not fall into the anarchists' hands.

Another Popular Front: The Anarchists and the Progressives

The creation of the New Trial League in 1924, the firing of Moore, the continued incarceration of Sacco, the anarchists' satisfaction with the new lawyer, and the breakup of the IWW indicated the beginning of a shift in the anarchists' strategies of defense. Roger Baldwin of the ACLU made a suggestion that the anarchists agreed with: to form a Boston defense committee.[107] The Boston committee became an anarchist–liberal alliance that defined Sacco and Vanzetti through their beliefs and personalities rather than primarily through their class status. The liberal literature replaced capitalism with nativism as the source of terror.

Like the progressive anti-lynchers, the liberals in the anti-Palmer alliance of the World War One era had focused on cultural and psychological elements of the nativist reaction. Louis F. Post's *Deportations Delirium* stated their position by title alone. The progressive campaign against Palmerism had described the First World War crackdown against aliens and radicals as a spasm of hysteria that would soon be corrected by a return to rationality. Other liberals came to see the nativist reaction not as a momentary element, but as a pathological and persistent aspect of nationalism itself. Osmond Fraenkel argued, "If psychopathology should seriously concern itself with the study of nations, national hysteria and its causes, manifestations and results would come under close scrutiny."[108] Like the anarchists, who rejected patriotism as stingy, many liberals and

socialists in the 1920s embraced cosmopolitanism and defined nationalism, including Anglo-Saxon, 100 percent Americanism, as irrational.

Once admired as the heritage of manly individual freedom, Puritanism in the 1920s became associated with the Ku Klux Klan, along with fundamentalism, racism, capitalism, and prohibition. Clarence Darrow advised that no one should ever seat a Calvinist in the jury box and claimed, "The Mayflower descendents are the most of devoid of human sympathy as any people on the earth today."[109] However, although these members of the Sacco and Vanzetti defense attacked the hysteria of nativism, the liberals were different from the anarchists because they also argued that "hysterical" working-class protests in Sacco's and Vanzetti's name were the reason for the nativist reaction against the two men.

Why, then, did the anarchists continue to work with the liberals and eschew the IWW? Most important of all, although the communists and anarchists both identified capitalism as a system of tyranny, pooh-poohed the efficacy of law, and advocated mass action instead, the anarchist groups' leaders and the liberals bonded over anticommunism and a belief in the importance of individual ideas—and individualism—to the defense. What Fred Moore had seen as the "twig," the anarchists and liberals saw as the trunk: The close friends of the men and the liberals in the ACLU united to make Sacco's and Vanzetti's characters and political ideals—rather than their status as workers—into the focus of the defense. The alliance also worked because by 1924, as saving Sacco and Vanzetti began to look increasingly impossible, the power in the Italian defense committee shifted. After Sacco's incarceration in the mental hospital and deterioration after years of solitary confinement, Vanzetti, who was already a popular speaker and writer among Italian anarchists, became the campaign's most significant figure.

In particular, after the criminal Celestino Madeiros confessed to the robbery, exonerating Sacco and Vanzetti, and implicated the "Morelli Gang" of Providence, liberal support for Sacco and Vanzetti grew. Nonetheless, *L'Adunata dei Refrattari* continued to denounce the liberal propaganda about the case until 1927. By 1926, however, Vanzetti was arguing that the liberals were doing a fine job. He wrote to Alice Stone Blackwell:

> The indolence, incapacity, the inexactness of those who have willingly or half-willingly wrote on our case has always caused much disgust and often, indignation and wrath in me. I am sorry to say that the writings of conservative or of the liberals have shown much more competence, sense of measure and of responsibility, than those of the more near to me. . . . Someone of

our comrades made big errs and blunders. . . . Of all this I have spoken and lamented with one of the *Masses* staff who was here a few days ago.[110]

As Vanzetti's letter indicates, there were grounds for alliance between the liberals and the anarchists. One of the most important aspects of Sacco's and Vanzetti's symbolic power stemmed from the old Haymarket counter-culture alliance of European immigrant radicals and leftist intellectuals that had continued with Emma Goldman's circle and with the IWW. Intellectual bohemians had connected with the labor movement during the famous Lawrence, Massachusetts, strike of 1912, during which twenty-five thousand textile-mill workers of twenty-five different nationalities struck for ten weeks with the help of the IWW leadership. The American-born writers who helped the strike created a romantic image of the working-class melting pot as the real America. In her 1955 memoir, Elizabeth Gurley Flynn, one of the organizers, recalled: "It was internationalism. . . . It was also real Americanism. . . . One nation, indivisible, with liberty and justice for all. They hadn't found it here, but they were willingly fighting to create it."[111]

Progressive and socialist writers were charmed by the singing Italian workers. "Lawrence was a singing strike," wrote Mary Heaton Vorse. "The workers sang everywhere, at the picket line, at the soup kitchens, at the relief stations, at the strike meeting, there was always singing."[112] Ray Stannard Baker was particularly taken with the Italian women who "burst into the Internationale" while peeling potatoes.[113] The interest in the Italian singing strike led by women reappeared with the celebration of the Paterson Silk Strike in the 1913 Madison Square Garden pageant created by John Reed and strike participants. That this image of singing Italian workers has struck a chord in American labor mythology is clear not only in early labor writings in which the song "Pane e Rose" (Bread and Roses) is a familiar refrain, but in more recent works, as well. Singing Italian workers have even appeared on film, in John Sayles's story of coal miners in *Matewan*.[114]

Since Italianness was associated not only with criminality in the United States, but also with beautiful singing, Sacco and Vanzetti could already be symbols of the special benefits of cosmopolitan Americanism, an alternative America to the one envisioned by the narrow-minded Anglo-Saxon nationalists of the 1920s. Many "white" activists in the 1920s maintained an interest in distinct national cultural characteristics, in some ways repeating Woodrow Wilson's Fourteen Points plan for national self-determination as the new model for national pride. Rather than being in service of white-

ness, attention to ethnic differences played an important role in building cross-ethnic alliances, as well as white–Black alliances in Southern labor organizations, and may have worked against the binary logic of whiteness in some areas.[115]

Moreover, it made sense to approach the prosecution of the two men as motivated by racial stereotypes. Sacco's and Vanzetti's status as racial others was very important to the case. Criminal stereotypes dominated the prosecution's case against Sacco and Vanzetti, which equated criminality, Italianness, and anarchism and defined the men as "un-American" slackers driven by bloodlust and laziness. The two anarchists were accused of a gang-style payroll-truck robbery, not a political crime. During the trial, witnesses indicated their inability to tell Italians apart, and the prosecuting attorney continually referred to the defendants as "bandits," a common epithet used to describe Italian criminals.[116] For W. E. B. Du Bois, Thomas Dabney, and William Patterson—Black activists who became involved in the fight to save Sacco and Vanzetti—the status of the men was similar to that of Blacks. They saw the prosecution of Sacco and Vanzetti as racially motivated. What was described as a shock for many of the nation's liberals, Thomas Dabney of the American Negro Labor Congress saw as "business as usual" in America.

> Of course this is no new thing: Negroes have been lynched, burned and murdered both North and South ever since the civil war. America is a land of oppression, murder, lynching, and crude civilization. Nowhere, so far as I know, are police so ignorant, arrogant, crude and uncivil as in America. For my own part I have long lost faith in America to lead the world in anything except mob rule, murder, race prejudice, and oppression.[117]

However, many of the men's Italian defenders downplayed this issue and focused instead on the fact that the two men were political prisoners, not criminals. They argued that Sacco's and Vanzetti's political activism was the real reason for their prosecution. In a way that distanced the two Italians from Blacks, other defenders argued that anti-foreign discrimination was based on ideological, not racial, differences. Thus, the Italian anarchists and liberals on the case kept pointing out the distance between the high ideals of political activists and the lowly activities of bandits. Because they saw the charges as a holdover from the Palmer era, rather than as a symptom of the Prohibition era, many socialists and liberals were sure that, if they could win clemency until the "anti-radical" frenzy of the war era died down, Sacco and Vanzetti would be given a fair trial.

Such hopes ignored the context of the 1920s. Although the Palmer raids were over by 1920, that decade was a conservative era in the history of labor, race, and criminal justice. While Freudian theories helped spur the "new penology" of the 1920s that emphasized rehabilitation and reform of individuals rather than punishment, there was also "a loud clamor for reversion to more punitive forms of treatment for law breakers," according to prison reformers in the 1920s.[118] Prohibition did not help. In the context of a rollicking, unregulated economy, fears of working-class crime, and racialized theories of immigrants' criminality only grew in intensity while Sacco and Vanzetti hoped for release from prison amid report after report of Italian bootlegging and mobsterism.

During the last weeks of Sacco's and Vanzetti's trial, members of the American Legion marched in Milton, Massachusetts, armed with guns, and the Ku Klux Klan held a rally "in full regalia with pistols and cartridge belts" demanding that the executions proceed. "There was no disorder" at the armed right-wing rallies, according to a reporter for the *Boston Globe*, but at the unarmed pro-Sacco and Vanzetti rally on Boston Common, "a thousand turned into a yelling, cheering mob."[119] Although Sacco's and Vanzetti's supporters traced the source of anti-foreignism to antiradicalism, in several important moments criticisms of basic anti-Italian racism made their way into the publicity about the case. Felix Frankfurter publicized the racial impulse behind the statement of one witness in the trial who said, "I could tell he was a foreigner by the way he ran," by comparing the statement to the popular song lyric, "All coons look alike to me."[120]

While the Haymarket anarchists had attacked the morality of the criminal-justice system in a systematic way, all of Sacco's and Vanzetti's defenders drew a line between Sacco and Vanzetti and the criminal type. Even Vanzetti contrasted himself and Sacco to the confessed criminal Madeiros, commenting to Virginia MacMechan, "Just compare his case to ours: he is an habitual robber; we were two real workers enjoying a good reputation. His record is most taint: ours were spotless. His conduct in prison was bad; we were publicly declared model prisoners. There is no possibility of doubts on his guilt[i]ness; there is at worse, many doubts on us."[121]

Defining Sacco and Vanzetti as "political" prisoners rather than as "class prisoners" increasingly distanced their defense campaign from the working class. Their Italianness, when described as a European national identity through high culture had the same effect. In the spirit of cosmopolitan opposition to Babbitry, instead of making Sacco and Vanzetti less Italian

and more "native-born," their defenders argued that Sacco's and Vanzetti's Italianness made them culturally superior to many Americans.

Those who wrote about Sacco's and Vanzetti's Italianesss emphasized Italian high culture to show their distinction from other workers. Commenting on his chats with Sacco and Vanzetti about good wine and the Italian countryside as they sat in the prison yard, Bruce Bliven wrote in 1927, "You must not be deceived by an accent, or by the workingman's easy way of sitting on a hard bench as though they were used to it. These are book men. Their faith is philosophic anarchism, and they know its literature from Kropotkin on down. In this year's graduating class from Harvard there will not be twenty men who on their own initiative have read as many difficult abstruse works as these gray clad prisoners. "[122]

Bliven made the Italian anarchists appear to be relatives of the cosmopolitan, educated upper classes. Similarly, the IWW activist Jim Seymour attacked the ignorance of white Americans. In 1921, long before most liberals were involved in the case, he imitated the voice of a typical, 100 percent ignoramus: "They're only a couple of God Damn Dagoes! / I don't see how anybody can expect white people / to do anything for the likes of them!" Allying Sacco and Vanzetti with Italian art and Italian republican revolution, Seymour highlighted the irony of any American who looked down on Italians as culturally inferior, "As fer arky—arky / fine building / why you'd think they never looked / at our office buildings. . . . They can talk about 1776 instead of yellin' their heads off about Garrybaldeye and Spartycuss. . . . They don't only have nothing about books 'n' music and invention and science, 'n' makin purty pictures and such things, but they don't even know how to talk the American language right. "[123]

As they defended Sacco and Vanzetti against mob hysteria, liberals echoed the principles of the progressive anti-lynching activism, but instead of defining the judicial response as "Southern," they now defined it as an outgrowth of conservative Puritanism against the forces of free thought and modern cosmopolitanism. Because of the trial's location in New England, defenders made comparisons between the jury and the Salem Witch Trials, describing "anti-alien hysteria" that had taken over the Cape Cod jury just as it had once made "godly folk of New England" see "a witch in every old woman. "[124]

The alliance that defended Sacco and Vanzetti saw a conflict similar to the polarization among Southerners that was revealed during the so-called Scopes Monkey Trial (*State of Tennessee v. John Thomas Scopes*), which was occurring at nearly the same time.[125] The jury and Judge Webster Thayer

represented country backwardness within Massachusetts. George Kirchwey, prison reformer and writer for the *Nation*, for instance, described how the clever prosecuting attorney had "cunningly invoked against the defendants all the fears and prejudices of the mob spirit that was running through the community from which the jury was drawn." Felix Frankfurter, who had published an extremely influential article in the *Atlantic Monthly* in March 1927 attacking the manifest personal prejudices of the trial judge, was, in contrast, a "still small voice of reason."[126]

Individual character and personal emotion on the part of both the accusers and the accused was central to liberal arguments about the defense strategy. Instead of focusing on the institutions of power, liberals derided the character of the trial judge, and they were hopeful that saner heads in government would appeal the verdict. During the last year of the case, Governor Alvin T. Fuller and President A. Lawrence Lowell of Harvard organized a committee to hear the merits of the defense and decide whether clemency should be granted to allow time for a new trial. The liberals believed that this review would be a fairer hearing than Sacco and Vanzetti had received before a jury. The *Nation* had "high hopes that Governor Fuller [would] make the right decision" at the impending meeting at Harvard.[127] As they organized support, the liberals emphasized the fact that Sacco and Vanzetti were "men of intellectual gifts and of fine character, honest, industrious, and generous in their social interests."[128]

The liberals tried to make Sacco and Vanzetti into less threatening figures. They portrayed them as pacifists and characterized them (and, by association, other Italians) as charming and quaint instead of ferocious. According to a pamphlet by Elizabeth Glendower Evans, Vanzetti demonstrated the "exquisite courtesy characteristic of the South Latin race, and his interests are philosophical and humanitarian. . . . He is much esteemed among his fellows as a thinker." No proletarian born and bred, Evans pointed out, Vanzetti "comes of highly respectable people," of "refined quality" whose house was filled with "beautiful antique furniture."[129] Sacco was a swift worker, a well-paid craftsman, whose family life was more important to him than anything else. "No one knows Sacco," Evans wrote, "who has not seen him with his family nor heard in his ingenuous talk about the happy days of home." When his wife came to visit him in jail with their new baby, Evans reported, "with the lack of self consciousness so foreign to northern races, he would toss the little one and fondle her as if he were in the privacy of his own home."[130] Through her well-meaning and paternalistic pamphlet, Evans erased the men's political activism, depicting them as victims rather than as heroic enemies of the

law. As Vanzetti pointed out, the pamphlet robbed them of working-class manhood. "I feel sure that she is animated by good will," Vanzetti wrote, "but I have to speak. My doctrine is heroic, has heroic traditions and to win it must have heroic fighters. The truth must be shown. "[131]

Many of the liberals who defended Sacco and Vanzetti were opposed to the anarchists' principles. Evans and George Kirchwey were both members of the National Prison Association (NPA), which met in Boston in 1923, in the middle of the Sacco and Vanzetti campaign and was addressed by Governor Alvin T. Fuller, who four years later would reject the merits of the appeal at the Harvard meeting. At its 1923 conference, the NPA was clearly influenced by the popular eugenics movement. Defining criminality as a form of insanity, the NPA recommended the sterilization of the insane, alcoholic, and syphilitic, arguing that "the contamination and debauches and deadly forces that are destroying our national life, putrefying our social life, and working death and ruin among us may be compared to a mighty waterfall with a swallowing current just above it. "[132]

Both in their representations of Sacco and Vanzetti and in their criticisms of the communists on the defense campaign, the liberals continually rejected mass action. Norman Hapgood, whose nephew Powers became dramatically involved in the case, argued that "mentally ill equipped Communists" were ruining the chances for justice in the case and argued that Evans, Frankfurter, and Thompson, as well as "trained lawyers," were the best elements in the defense campaign because they had "no interest, or else positive distaste for the mental processes of the noisy foreigners. "[133]

Sacco's and Vanzetti's new lawyer, unlike Fred Moore, did not try to mobilize the masses in their defense. Instead, he and other liberal advocates referred to spontaneous actions of irresponsible Italians and the machinations of scheming communist demagogues as the primary obstacles to the appeal process. The slip from the anti-mob argument to the unstated racial anxiety of floods and hordes was, as usual, easy enough. Describing a rally on Boston Common when the police attacked the crowd, liberal supporters writing for the *New Republic* made a direct connection between "Italianness" and violence, claiming, "It needed only some impulsive gesture on the part of an excited Italian in that crowd and Boston Common would have been the scene of another Boston massacre. What saved the assembly was a law abiding assembly of citizens. "[134]

Persistent rejection of working-class action underlay the liberal opposition to both the communists and their efforts to hide from view and redefine the "excited Italians" both in jail and on the committee. This same distaste for the masses also appeared in both the opposition to the

newly formed International Labor Defense (ILD) and to descriptions of Moore's previous efforts as destructive to the cause. The new lawyers in the case saw the anti-Sacco and Vanzetti agitation in the mid-1920s as the direct result of the "foul" work of Fred Moore. Herbert Ehrmann wrote,

> A grave disqualification of Mr. Moore as defense counsel . . . lay in his hostility to the existing social order. . . . Mr. Moore proceeded to blow up the trial into worldwide prominence among left wing groups. For this purpose he won the support of the communists, labor unions, and radicals everywhere. The swelling denunciations of the purposes of the prosecution produced the inevitable reaction.[135]

Arguing that "the judicial institutions of our country recognize the possibility of judicial errors and provide machinery for their redress," the liberals on the defense committee like the lawyers counseled patience. Contradicting years of boisterous Americanism, one article in the *Nation* rejected violence as the action that would bring down the movement, arguing that it was "the American way to accept such a defeat in peace," even if the men were executed.[136] Regardless of their criticisms of the judge, most of the liberals had faith in the court. Felix Frankfurter wrote to Herbert Ehrmann in July: "I cannot believe they are ruthlessly determined to have those men go to the chair no matter what."[137] During the last days of the case, *L'Adunata Dei Refrattari* was bubbling with calls for heroic action, but *The Nation*'s editors hoped the two defendants would dissuade such moves: "There is one other word from these men that we wish we might record from their lips before they step over into eternity. That is an appeal to all their fellow workers of the world to refuse to be goaded by their deaths into any violence whatever." When the Lowell Commission at Harvard rejected the appeal, the ACLU attorney Paul Kellogg argued that Sacco and Vanzetti were executed not because of class antagonism, but because the Lowell group had failed to apply "the techniques of the social science professions at arriving at the truth in the face of hysteria."[138]

The ILD: Communists for Sacco and Vanzetti

As the liberals counseled caution, many of the radical labor activists who had originally been drawn into the case by Flynn, Tresca, and Moore took part in the newly organized ILD. In 1925, the organization was not yet exclusively communist, and it attempted to organize mass protests through the Trade Union Educational League and other labor groups. As the Gal-

leanists had, the ILD argued that "only fools put faith in the courts of the enemy."[139] Like Moore, the ILD claimed that "all forces must be united without delay into the broadest possible basis in the struggle to free Sacco and Vanzetti."

When the ILD took up Sacco's and Vanzetti's cause as a workers' struggle and called for a general strike as the only means to fight for class justice, the liberal defense committee in Boston vehemently objected, calling it an attempt to exploit the case for communist ends. However, the anarchists were themselves calling for a general strike in the pages of *L'Adunata dei Refrattari*.[140] Both Sacco and Vanzetti were impressed with the working-class campaign of the ILD. Vanzetti subscribed to the *Daily Worker* and the *Labor Defender* in prison and wrote several letters to the *Labor Defender*. He celebrated the fact that proletarian support for the case was growing,[141] but he was frustrated and surprised by the communist attack on Russian anarchist prisoners that he read in the *Daily Worker*.[142]

As the ILD became more clearly communist and less an extension of the IWW, many anarchists joined the liberal criticisms of the group, but Vanzetti did not. He argued that it did not matter which people defended him or why; all efforts were welcome. Again arguing for the importance of the popular-front strategy, Vanzetti suggested to Roger Baldwin that he should tone down the anticommunism of his committee, commenting, "As for the communists, or whoever wants to do something, somehow in our behalf, let them do what they deem best. To base their defense on the principles and aims of their own parties is perfectly logical and natural, therefore not objectionable or harmful, provided good will and faith."[143]

Vanzetti demurred from making decisions about defense-committee strategy when asked, remarking that, because he was in prison, he had no ability to decide about what was going on outside.[144] He reiterated this point in a letter to the socialist Mary Donovan after he had met with another of his anarchist comrades, who had regaled him with polemics, observing, "I am sick to death of the sectarianisms, narrow-mindedness, personalisms, groupisms and so forth that deform and sterilize such a great cause."[145] Nonetheless, Vanzetti was frustrated by his inability to make his own politics more explicit during the case. After a "good communist girl" wrote to him in support, he asked Alice Stone Blackwell, "How can I say to her that at the very thought of the Russian Revolutionary's failure all the sores of my heart open themselves, and all the anguish of my soul arises? Without hurting, or maybe offending her?"[146]

The failure to which Vanzetti referred did affect the ILD's participation in the last months of the Sacco and Vanzetti agitation, which coincided

with a major factional struggle over the direction of the Communist Party. James Cannon, head of the ILD, was central to the fighting, and his group sent a memo to the Communist International (Comintern), dominated by Nikolai Bukharin and Stalin, under the name National Committee of the Opposition Bloc. Immediately following its receipt, the Comintern denounced the bloc in a cablegram printed in the *Daily Worker* while Jay Lovestone's group, which sided with Bukharin, maintained favor. A month later, with only weeks to go before the scheduled executions, the American group voted down the proposal by Foster and Cannon to postpone the national worker's party conference in order to concentrate all forces on the Sacco and Vanzetti defense.[147]

Although they were similar in many ways to the anarchists in their rhetoric and strategy, the ILD disagreed with them on certain basic principles. It not only renounced individualist ideals; it also renounced those anarchist tactics that did not appear publicly in English language newspapers. Evoking the references to bombs left on doorsteps of judges and magistrates, one writer explained, "We are knocking on the door, not with the hands of irresponsible individuals, but with the titanic fist of the workers of the world."[148] Like the IWW activists, the communists defined Vanzetti's and Sacco's speeches in court as signs of their class (and not their political) loyalty.[149] Rather than a spontaneous uprising, the communists said, only the "organized might of the working masses" could save Sacco's and Vanzetti's lives. Here, they criticized both anarchists and liberals, saying that "the liberals with their counsels for moderation, have accomplished nothing but the weakening the movement. . . . They have spread illusions in the ranks of the workers . . . kept them in acquiescent leash until the last moment when the executioners reach out to turn the electric switch."[150] As liberals fought the moment of reaction and denounced Judge Thayer, while hoping that justice would prevail, James Cannon echoed the Haymarket defense, claiming that in killing Sacco and Vanzetti, "America shows its real face to the world and the mask of democracy is thrown aside." The ruling class was a "vengeful, cruel murderous class which the workers must fight to conquer before the regime of imperialism, torture and murder can be ended." The ILD argued that the movement among some liberals for commutation of the death sentence to life in imprisonment was a conscious effort to destroy the movement, and reminded readers of the fate of Tom Mooney and Warren Billings who still languished in prison; "after ten years there remain only a few who still keep alive the memory of these buried men."[151]

The ILD and the anarchists shared the combination of class solidarity and manly ideals that had defined the work of the IWW's GDC. Eugene Lyons described how Sacco and Vanzetti, instead of being passive in court, "strained at their chains, proudly, defiantly, exposing their beliefs and their hopes instead of concealing and ingratiating themselves." They went to their deaths with "noble dignity and courage, calmly, bravely, without fear or embarrassment."[152] And like the IWW and the anarchists of the 1920s, the communists emphasized self-sacrifice and repudiated mourning. In contrast to the Haymarket anarchists who had described women's grief as the moving force of revolutionary action, Ella Reeve Bloor celebrated ascetic versions of heroic stoicism, commenting that Rosa Sacco, "one of the brave heroes of our class war, . . . kept her personal grief in the background and with the spirit of her husband said, 'they belong to the working class of the world, not to me.'"[153]

In the wake of the executions, intellectuals reversed the lesson of 1887, arguing that the liberals' strategies in the end had proved ineffective. The executions of Sacco and Vanzetti shook the liberals' faith in the judicial process and the reign of expertise, pushing many of the intellectuals toward communism and mass politics in the 1930s.[154] Shortly after the executions, liberal periodicals displayed outrage at what had happened. The *Nation*, which had excoriated protest in the weeks and days before the executions, proclaimed afterward that "issues of classes are as significant in the Sacco Vanzetti case as the issue of slavery was in the John Brown case."[155] They compared Governor Lowell to Governor Henry Wise and suggested that the verdict of history would be upon him. Rather than describing mob hysteria in his analysis of the psychological foundations of the execution, John Dewey criticized the use of legalism as a strategy that had allowed the Lowell Commission to avoid responsibility rather than face the moral issues in the case, and like many anarchists and socialists, Dewey now defined the coldness of the law and lawyers as a pathology.[156] The *New Republic*, which had been arguing for the rule of experts for years before the Sacco and Vanzetti case, now saw the problems of a bureaucratic order that worked against democratic participation. The editors declared after the "Ominous Execution" that "an America in which prolonged and full public discussion fails to influence opinion and guide official action has become a dangerous and unstable America." Still, most liberal voices sought to define the limits of what was acceptable as public opinion. The *Waterbury* [Connecticut] *Republican* printed an editorial that drew the line carefully: "The majesty of the law is upheld when it proves itself

inflexible against the winds of passion and prejudice, but when it proves itself impregnable to the criticism of the public conscience. The law waxes in power when it withstands the shouting of the mob, but it wanes in authority when it will not heed the sober reasoning of good and wise men everywhere."[157]

For the communist Mike Gold, among the lessons to be learned was that the lawyers in the case were not to be trusted. "They are as infatuated with their jobs as are policemen or society women," he said, and "there is no white virgin daughter of platonic protection living in this bad world named justice. There is a bloody battle between classes and one side wins or the other. In Soviet Russia the workers imprison businessmen and their military allies, in America rebel workingmen are burned in the electric chair. This must go on until there are no more classes."[158] There was no other need to be concerned with civil liberties or law, as far as Gold was concerned, and after the revolution there would be no need for lawyers or defense committees.

This analysis clearly was different from that of the liberals. Two years after the executions, several prominent liberals contributed statements on the case to Gardiner Jackson's *Lantern*, whose introduction defined fascism as the "growing denial of common fairness in America to people whose opinions, race, religion, or color are disliked by the authorities and by the majority which allows the authorities to hold power." Mentioning the cases of Tom Mooney and Warren Billings in California and of the communist defendants in Gastonia, North Carolina, the writers urged that everyone "prevent this country from taking its place alongside Mussolini in absolute violation of the instinct of civilized human beings."[159]

The Literary Legacy

Making the agitation around Sacco and Vanzetti a major media event, the leftists had helped raise concern about the fairness of criminal procedures and began the first popular literary representations of the great "frame-up." In 1930, as part of a series on great modern mysteries, *Liberty* magazine published "The Mystery of Sacco and Vanzetti," offering a ten-thousand-dollar reward to the contestant with the best solution.[160] Maxwell Anderson, who wrote two different plays based on the case, one of which drew on Herbert Ehrmann's book, also wrote the screenplay for Alfred Hitchcock's film *The Wrong Man*, which featured Henry Fonda as

an Italian misidentified by several witnesses because of police methods similar to those used in the Sacco and Vanzetti case.[161]

Although the Sacco and Vanzetti defense campaign did evoke an alternative "melting pot" Americanism in contrast to Anglo-Saxonism, the literature inspired by the case suggested that to be "American" still required some Anglo-Saxon ingredients. Almost all of the fictional accounts of Sacco and Vanzetti established the separation of the two men from the Italian community and revolutionary action and connected them to the Anglo-Saxon women on the defense committee. The majority of narrative accounts of the defense committee replaced the vision of the Italian anarchist community with the story of the defense campaign as a dramatic encounter between ragged Italian workingmen with "Boston's Blue Blood Ladies" —Alice Stone Blackwell, Elizabeth Glendower Evans, and Cerise Jack—to whom the men wrote letters while they were in prison, which were later published.

It would have been easy enough to make grammatically correct English translations of Sacco's and Vanzetti's Italian writings to their comrades. However, these writings showed the men in their actual political context, as advocates of working-class revolutionary action and opponents of imperialist war. Vanzetti's *Story of Proletarian Life* and *Events and Victims* both depicted the world of the Italian working class in America in detail, along with an articulate version of Vanzetti's proletarian internationalism. Sacco's letters to Felicani and to the radical papers indicated that he wrote in the ornate tradition of Galleani. His articulate letters disprove the persistent representation of him as a simple-minded southern Italian worker—but they also indicate that he believed in the propaganda of the deed.

Instead, *The Letters of Sacco and Vanzetti*, published in the year following their deaths, presented the two from the point of view of the women who visited them in jail, erasing their many other correspondents, including labor activists and Italian anarchists. The publication played a significant ideological role in the years after the campaign in fusing images of anarchism and liberalism. Henry Ward Dana, who had been a close friend of Vanzetti's, wrote to Felix Frankfurter criticizing his wife's choice of letters and the exclusion of letters he had received from Vanzetti. He also criticized the "Americanism" of the defense. "Many in the defense committee urged me not to do anything to stir up protests abroad," Dana wrote, "but Sacco and Vanzetti both wanted them because they hold the "cause [of proletarian internationalism] dearer than their lives."[162]

Even as the ghost of Lawrence's singing women haunted Sacco's and Vanzetti's defense in English-language accounts of their defense story, the substitution of the blue-blooded women of Boston as the major defense activists worked to characterize the Sacco and Vanzetti defense campaign as a battle of liberals and distanced Sacco's and Vanzetti's anarchism from working-class activism that took place during their seven-year agitation. This substitution aided both the communists' and the liberals' ideological agendas, because the telling of the case's history moved toward an increasing split between civil-libertarianism and revolutionary socialism. It allowed liberals to argue that free thought and rationality were incompatible with mass action and allowed revolutionary communists to depict American socialism before Stalin as a failed combination of childish European anarchists and bourgeois women.

Liberal women were not the only ones involved in the defense, and they were certainly not the only recipients of letters written by the two anarchists. When Sacco's wife, Rosina, wrote to *L'Adunata dei Refrattari* in 1928, she participated, as most widows have, not only by giving an emotional response, but by making a political point as she described the "assas[s]ination of my husband and Vanzetti by the reactionary detritus concentrated in the state." She then (heroically) requested that no more funds be sent, as she no longer needed financial contributions, which should really go on to other, more troubled workers' families.[163] Other Italian anarchist and socialist women were prominently involved in the defense campaign. Tina Cacici of the ACWA worked for the defense among textile workers. Aurora D'Angelo, a young anarchist from Chicago, was arrested and incarcerated in an insane asylum shortly after the verdicts were delivered, shouting, "All you cops are bums!" as she was dragged off to the police wagon. Ella Antolini, who may have been part of the Galleani group, helped raise money for Sacco and Vanzetti in Detroit and sent frequent letters to *L'Adunata dei Refrattari* using the pseudonym "Linda J." Selma Maximon, an IWW organizer, played a significant role in the defense campaign in Chicago, because her sentimental appeals were popular in mass meetings.[164]

However, by replacing Italian women with native-born inheritors of American traditions, the English-language literature about Sacco and Vanzetti was able to reinvent the men by redefining their mourners. The erasure of Nicola Sacco's wife, Rosa, broke the primary ties between Sacco and Vanzetti and the Italian anarchist community: As Rosa's mourning quickly disappeared from the story, so did the Italian anarchists' claim on the men's interpretation. It was no longer the case, as the anarchists

had argued in 1920, that "we, the anarchists" held the reigns of the publicity. With no wives or children to encumber them, Sacco and Vanzetti became more easily assimilated into an image of a unified American culture. Instead of tying the men to an anarchist community, as the literature about the Haymarket Martyrs did, the literature about Sacco and Vanzetti bonded the audience to the men through identification with the emotions of bourgeois, white, female reformers who stood for the traditions of Boston abolitionism. The fact that Emma Goldman once expressed a wish to adopt Sacco's son, Dante, while he was living with his mother and sister indicates that this blindness to the existence of Rosa Sacco influenced even the most radical elements of the English-speaking left.[165] In this way, Sacco and Vanzetti literature sustains the idea not only that all Italian anarchists were men, but also that all female activists were bourgeois, and that all liberals were Anglo-Saxons, thus subtly reifying the notion of racial democratic heritages precisely at the moment when the conflation of Anglo-Saxonism and democracy was being cracked open by the working-class immigrant communists, avant-garde thinkers, and antifascist critics of American nativism.

In the two most popular American novels that describe the Sacco and Vanzetti trial, John Dos Passos's *USA* and Upton Sinclair's *Boston*, the protagonists in the story are all native-born socialist or liberal women. In both novels, the women act as the interpreters of Italian culture for the unknowing reader, who accompanies the female guide on a voyage of discovery into Italian mill towns and back-alley political meetings.

Boston's blue-blooded heroine, Cornelia Thornwell, a figure similar to Elizabeth Glendower Evans, acts as an ethnographic observer, moving into Vanzetti's boardinghouse just in time for the Plymouth Cordage strike, when Vanzetti first became a popular speaker. Through her we learn many important details about the Italian anarchists' world. She goes to hear the Italian anarchist leader Luigi Galleani speak; uncovers Vanzetti's boxes of anarchist literature; and hears Vanzetti refer to social democrats, and even IWW organizers, as reformist traitors to the working class.

Regardless of this attention to the details of Vanzetti's politics, Sinclair allows Cornelia and her niece Betty to stand in the places of Italian matrons of Plymouth, at least one of whom "was keeping a lamp lighted to her Saints and Gods and Madonnas for six consecutive years in her home" to support the atheist martyr.[166] The Italian women who appear in *Boston*, like the strikers of Lawrence, Massachusetts, rarely speak. More often. they sing, cry, or scream. In this story of Italian workers, the first encounter with Italian life occurs in the kitchen of the boardinghouse,

where Cornelia first meets the anarchist woman Alfonsina Brini, in whose home Vanzetti lived. "Before Cornelia had been in the house half an hour, Beltrando had produced a big red record, 'You listen to Carroos,' said the little boy, and Mrs. Brini stopped washing the vegetables for the salad and stood with her hands wet and rapture in her eyes while a mighty voice spread and bore her soul to Italy."[167]

That Alfonsina Brini named her daughter La Fevre and was one of Vanzetti's primary correspondents while he was in prison disappears. Much later in the novel, Italian women become hysterical in the courtroom, with "screaming" and "wailing" emerging from their bodies "like a contagion."[168] Rosa Sacco appears only a few times, and her words are rarely discernible. She "chats" with Nicola during courtroom breaks, tries to persuade him to sign papers in the jail, and finally screams exactly the words that appeared in the court transcript following the death sentence: "You bet your life! . . . You take-a my man! I got two children—what I do?"

The same records of the case demonstrate that Rosa Sacco was active in her husband's defense. Before Nicola Sacco was charged with murder, Rosa burned all of the anarchist literature in the house, anticipating a deportation case.[169] When it became clear that this was not another "Red Scare" case, Rosa rushed to Boston with her grocery receipts to meet a man who was later to become an important member of the Italian defense committee, Felice Guadagni. When Rosa found Guadagni, she immediately began the search for Sacco's alibi. "Don't you remember that Sacco was with you and he was to the consulate?" she asked him and urged him to go with her to Baldina's grocery, where Sacco had shopped on the day of the robbery.[170]

By concentrating so much energy on the ties between Vanzetti and Cornelia Thornwell, Sinclair avoids telling this story of Rosa Sacco, who later married a man she met on the defense committee.[171] For Sinclair, Rosa and her children become victims of the execution rather than members of the political community who would carry on the struggle afterward. The anarchists' words live on in the socialist world of Betty and Cornelia, but not in the anarchist collectives and newspapers that still existed in Boston and Plymouth after the men's deaths. In Sinclair's account, Sacco in particular was identified as a "brown and excitable" southern Latin, in contrast to Vanzetti's more sober "northern" personality.[172]

For John Dos Passos, the execution of Sacco and Vanzetti was also final. His WASP heroine, Mary French, begins as the classic example of the young American socialist woman. She is raised in a conservative Midwestern family, reads *The Jungle*, goes to college, works for Jane Addams at

Hull House, and falls in love with a variety of exotic immigrant labor organizers, who educate her about the meaning of the working-class struggle. When she joins the Sacco and Vanzetti defense campaign, she tells us almost nothing about them—only that they are good men who "must not die."

Like Dos Passos, French receives a political education during the case. She has little political experience and no previous knowledge of the Italian community and views the iww as too violent and disorderly. French's experience, however, is so central to the story for Dos Passos that Sacco's and Vanzetti's execution becomes an element in her development. Their politics are almost completely absent from the story, and their death is viewed as a defeat for anarchism rather than a survival of it. For Dos Passos, and perhaps for many of those who became communists, working on the Sacco and Vanzetti defense campaign proved the failure of both anarchism and liberalism; the defense's defeat helped people decide to abandon the iww–socialist alliance of the 1920s and join the Communist Party.

It is through the trial that French loses the qualities of middle-class intellectualism and idealistic naivete that Dos Passos longs to leave behind, along with the "near-beer" socialism of the 1920s. By the end of the novel, French has finally repudiated her criticisms of the iww but has become hard and unsympathetic, turning away a friend's plea for emotional support with the comment, "I have too much to do to spend my time taking care of hysterical women on a day like this," then busily rushes off to yet another meeting.[173] Thus, Dos Passos dispenses with the two most vexing problems of leftist politics: effeminate intellectuals and unkempt bomb-throwing foreigners. He also dismisses before the book even starts the reality that a great many of the Italian workers of New England were women, many of whom had their own political ideas. All of this would fade into the background as the western wanderer "Vag" (to whom Steinbeck's Tom Joad bears a resemblance) takes over as the voice of the "people" at the novel's end.

Dos Passos's embrace of "Vag" was not a complete rejection of ethnic difference, but an embrace of the internationalist working-class alliance that juxtaposed the iww's image of the western hobo against the institutions of Anglo-Saxon law with the cosmopolitan anti-lynching ideals. When he compared Sacco and Vanzetti to Boston's founders and the ideals of Americanism in his famous "Two Nations" section, Dos Passos argued that the working-class immigrants, with dreams of a better life, constituted the "real" America in opposition to the betrayed ideals

of the "sticky spiderwebs" of state and law as represented by Judge Webster Thayer. Dos Passos abandoned the Anglo-Saxon hero of the working class by declaring, "This fish peddler you have in the Charlestown jail is one of your founders, Massachusetts," giving a messianic role to the immigrant working class.[174]

Dos Passos's legend of the creation of the communist melting pot is similar to the representation of Sacco and Vanzetti that Eugene Lyons created in his story of the American immigrant experience, as well. Preceding Oscar Handlin's *The Uprooted* by several years, Lyons described how immigrant workers became separate from their roots and wandered, helpless in America, confused by noise and industry until they discovered politics among American workers. Rather than describing Vanzetti's politicization in Italy among socialists there, which Vanzetti described in his autobiography, Lyons's popular story of the trial again evoked antiracist discourse by describing how Vanzetti came to political consciousness in America because he was "hardly reckoned a white man." At first implying that class-consciousness was formed in the context of American racial prejudice, an interesting point to make at this precise moment in Italian American radicalism, Lyons backtracked and made sure to stress that Sacco and Vanzetti had learned about socialism from more manly native-born American workers.[175]

Ruth McKenney's *Jake Home* also profoundly expresses communism's criticisms of anarchism as passé and liberal. Her narrative presents outdated, black-suited, first-generation immigrant anarchists whose efforts to save Sacco and Vanzetti fail, in contrast with the actions of the hearty second-generation communists in the book's second half. Her story of the rise and decline of Jake, as he mistakenly marries a middle-class, feminist, bohemian woman from the defense committee and, as a result, collapses into alcoholism, provides the most striking ideological argument against Old World anarchism and feminist socialism as the twin evils that led to Sacco's and Vanzetti's deaths.[176]

Communist accounts of the defense campaign, while eulogizing Sacco and Vanzetti as noble, continually told the Sacco and Vanzetti story as a defeat of the liberal–anarchist alliance, just as the social democrats of the 1890s had subtly blamed the Haymarket anarchists for their execution. Elizabeth Gurley Flynn in particular would play a significant role in creating the Communist Party's version of the Sacco and Vanzetti story, writing about the men regularly in her columns in the *Daily Worker*. As Flynn described it in her 1955 memoir, *The Rebel Girl*, Sacco's and Vanzetti's defense was important in her own life, politically and personally, because

the deaths of Sacco and Vanzetti coincided with the end of her relationship with Carlo Tresca and with her temporary retirement from politics when she went to live with Mary Equi in Portland for several years.

Describing herself as brooding unhappily, Flynn remembers that Fiorello LaGuardia "suddenly made a most penetrating and unexpected remark": "'Elizabeth,' he'd said, 'why don't you stop mixing up with all these Italian anarchists and go back to the American labor movement where you belong?'"[177] The fact that Flynn's own descriptions of the early labor movement show that it was dominated not by "Americans" but by immigrants is lost as Flynn comments that she heeded LaGuardia's advice by joining the Communist Party in 1936. To what "America" was she returning?

Although all of the literature about Sacco and Vanzetti seems to celebrate immigrants' contributions to American culture, both liberal and communist stories about the case revived the story of Italian color and song only to assign them a place in the past. Instead of memorializing and maintaining a vision of a pluralistic working class, the popular-front story of the case actually helped bury the diverse past of the immigrant working class and to integrate these workers into "whiteness." Whiteness for immigrants was achieved through the relinquishing of distinct and unpopular aspects of their national identities. The experience of the pain of that transition is articulated over and over again in the representation of Sacco's and Vanzetti's story as the end of nationally specific radicalism. Theirs was no carnivalesque "death giving birth." It was, quite simply, an end. In the literature of Sacco and Vanzetti, Rosa Sacco, Alfonsina Brini, and other anarchists neither mourned nor organized, but disappeared, and the "marriage" of Sacco and Vanzetti and "Boston's Blue Blood Ladies" led to the figurative second-generation communists and liberals. According to Flynn, Dos Passos, and Sinclair, this unruly and ideologically diverse immigrant community had no place in the new American movement that was being born in 1928. As a result, Sacco's and Vanzetti's case ultimately came to mean not a glorious martyrdom, but a closed chapter—a static point from which to look back nostalgically on immigrant radicalism in the United States as if it were truly a thing of the past.

Thus, by 1927, the communists attacked anarchism and liberalism as unrelated to working-class action, and liberals opposed communism as a form of hysteria similar to fascism. For liberals, anarchism was also divested of its association with mass politics. With the alliance of anarchists and liberals during the defense, anarchism ceased to be the primary representative of irrationality, Old World radicalism, and violence, and was

replaced with an image of communist mob rule. Anarchism, now safely buried with Sacco and Vanzetti, came to represent pacifist individualism and anticommunism. Precisely at the moment that the CPUSA was embracing Black radical agency, Carlo Tresca marked his own anticommunism with opposition to the actions of the Gastonia strikers, and some individualist anarchists moved ever closer to Bakuninite rejections of the mob as a "herd." In the pages of *L'Adunata dei Refrattari*, Paulo Scicchi declared that Mussolini had turned Italy into "Africa," the land of "Tippu-Tip," filling it with slave drivers and cannibals.[178]

By the mid-1930s, communists would form an alliance with liberals, abandoning their own sectarianism to form a popular front. While the liberals and communists disagreed on the nature of popular action, they came to agree on the benefits of assimilation. For both sides, the Sacco and Vanzetti story served as an origin point. Instead of excluding the history of anarchism in the United States, both groups appropriated Italian anarchism as an early and dead childhood out of which their own groups had grown and matured.

With the Lawrence strike and the executions of Sacco and Vanzetti, the pan-European identity politics of the Chicago anarchists became the dominant characterization of the American working class. The hagiography about them indicated that the labor movement had moved away from the Anglo-Saxonism and western ethos that had bedeviled earlier labor mythology and expanded the boundaries of American identity to include southern Europeans. At the same time, the Italian radicals who defended Sacco and Vanzetti were largely erased, as were the political views for which Sacco and Vanzetti had sacrificed their lives. Was this the price of immortality?

5

...❦...

The Communist Party
and the Defense Tradition from
Scottsboro to the Rosenbergs

You are blind like young kittens. What will happen without me?
This country will perish because you do not recognize enemies.
JOSEPH STALIN

Stand up for your rights, even if it kills you. That's all that life
consists of. CLARENCE NORRIS

Following the Sacco and Vanzetti defense campaign, the Communist
Party's International Labor Defense became the most significant partisan defense organization in the United States and organized some of the
most important defense campaigns of the next twenty years. According to
the communist organizer James Allen,[1] the CPUSA "perfected the policy
and technique of mass defense on behalf of labor leaders and activists
prosecuted for their activities."[2] Not only did communists continue the
IWW's project of building an organization and method for labor defense,
but they changed the definition of labor defense itself by including in the
ILD's work the defense of working-class African Americans accused of
nonpolitical crimes—most notably, with the Scottsboro case in Alabama,
when the ILD led a national movement to free nine young black men who
were convicted of raping two women on a train. Later, it continued that
work in the 1940s and 1950s with a number of popular criminal defenses
of Blacks through the Civil Rights Congress (CRC). However, as a civil-
liberties organization, the ILD was also different from every previous
labor-defense group in U.S. history because of its ties to the Soviet Union.
Not only did the Communist Party continue and build on the tradition
of labor defense, but it also defended the Soviet Union's show trials;

endorsed the internment of the Japanese; and did nothing when in 1940 the Smith Act (also known as the Alien Registration Act of 1940), against which the party itself had campaigned in 1939, was used against American Trotskyists. Instead, as the civil-liberties historian Michael Belknap comments, communists "watched with delight while the government used that law to harass their enemies."[3]

In recent years, it has become impossible to discuss the history of the CPUSA without entering into the contentious debate between contemporary historians about the relationship of the organization to the Comintern, the KGB, and espionage. This issue is particularly important for anyone studying the history of state repression of the American left. The conservative standard-bearers Harvey Klehr and John Earl Haynes, and their followers, argue that the state's actions against the Communist Party were not political in nature; rather, they were acts of justice against a criminal and traitorous organization.[4] As the title of one of their recent books suggests, Klehr and Haynes deem anyone who regards members of the CPUSA as anything but a Stalinist puppet to be "in denial." Such accusations ignore the complexity of contemporary leftist scholarship. While some historians might celebrate the Communist Party as if it were just an offshoot of New Deal politics, most scholars on the left are increasingly interested in studying the relationship of the CPUSA to the history of the Comintern and the Soviet Union. This recognition need not mean that the CPUSA's members were merely tools of the Soviet party, much less criminal conspirators. The study of the complicated interactions between Soviet directives and American adaptations to them has long been central to some of the best American scholarship on the CPUSA even before the release of documents from the KGB and Comintern archives.[5]

The history of the ILD and its many mass defense campaigns has been as divided as every other aspect of the history of the Communist Party. On one end of the spectrum, Michael Denning describes the ILD as "perhaps the most effective part of popular front public culture" and celebrates its contribution to the American civil-liberties tradition, calling it "the earliest popular front organization."[6] On the other end is Theodore Draper's formulation of the ILD as simply an American version of the MOPR, the International Society for Relief of Revolutionaries, or more commonly, the "International Red Aid."[7] In this chapter, I will strive to sort out the relationship between indigenous political conflicts and Soviet directives as they influenced the defense campaigns of the ILD, whose methods played a significant role in shaping mass defense strategies into the 1960s.

Generally, it is clear that the Comintern's shift in analysis of fascism, world revolution, and the role of bourgeois parties from the Third Period to popular front had a dramatic impact on communist defense strategy. During the Sacco and Vanzetti case and the defense of the textile-mill strikers in Gastonia in the 1920s; during the defense of the Southern Black communist Angelo Herndon in the early 1930s; and in the first years of the Scottsboro trials, the ILD invoked mass heroic ideals, celebrated a multiethnic working class as a vehicle of liberation for the imprisoned, and called for popular mobilization as opposed to "legal maneuvering" to defend "class-war prisoners." However, by the end of the 1930s, and especially during the Second World War, the ILD's calls for mass action receded. The CPUSA's compromise with the New Deal, mandated by the Stalinist strategy of forming a popular front with bourgeois democracies, undermined the traditional defense of heroic rebellion, increased the reliance on lawyers, led to the adoption of legislative action as a major element of defense strategy, and supported Franklin D. Roosevelt's expansion of executive power, including the use of wiretapping, most dramatically during World War Two. In other words, during the popular front, the ILD differed from liberal organizations through its positions on racial justice, its call for mass rallies on behalf of defendants, and its support for even the most egregious policies of the Soviet Union, but not in the defense of revolutionary socialism.

In its early years, the ILD picked up and developed the IWW's arguments about the connections between vigilantism and state repression and increasingly labeled vigilantism "fascism," emphasizing connections between fascist groups and the state. For the IWW in the 1920s, and for the communists who came from that group, this "fascism" had to be understood as a tool of the capitalist class. For liberals of the same era, fascism was usually represented as a form of mob hysteria best controlled by the application of law. By the 1940s and 1950s, the communists' definition of fascism had become similar to that of the liberals; one could thus say that the popular front had a dramatic effect particularly on the left's efforts to combat both legal and extralegal forms of repression and that it became difficult to maintain a significant leftist response to McCarthyism. The difference between the Communist Party's defense campaigns in the Third Period and its post–World War Two approach to defense work also reflects the conflict within the party over the nature of the American state and American nationalism. African American communists and those closest to them tended to make pessimistic arguments about America,

while European immigrants and their children tended to identify with a multicultural New Deal Americanism.

Popular Fronts and Labor Defense

As I have argued in the preceding chapters, U.S. labor-defense campaigns were always fought by a "popular front" of liberals and radicals, and these alliances have always been fraught with conflict. Anarchists and progressives fought over the approach to the Haymarket defense, and anarchists, IWW activists, and communists had all attacked the liberals in the Sacco and Vanzetti defense for their "legalism" and "bureaucracy," even in those cases when they worked closely with them on committees. It is therefore interesting that the person who advocated most vociferously in the Comintern for the popular-front strategy was at the center of the most famous communist popular legal defense ever: Georgi Dimitrov, the defendant in the Reichstag fire trial.[8] Although the Soviet Union's own fluctuating attitude toward fascism was based on Stalin's perceptions of national self-interest, communists from different nations within the Comintern also had reasons to agree with either the Third Period line on "social fascism" or the popular-front argument for an alliance with liberals and social democrats, and they had their own experiences with each strategy. U.S. labor-defense activists had made both arguments long before existence of the Comintern. Antifascism as a philosophy was born in the context of a history of organized self-defense to the capitalist state repression of the left that preceded the rise of fascism.

Defense in the Workers Party's Early Years

There was no way the Communist Party could have avoided doing defense work. From its very inception, it was a target for law enforcement. In 1919–20, states sent nearly three hundred political dissidents to prison through state anti-syndicalism laws, while ten thousand radicals, whether anarchists, socialists, or communists, were arrested during the federal Palmer raids.[9] Benjamin Gitlow, a leader in the early Communist Party, was sentenced to five years in prison for the crime of distributing the newspaper *Revolutionary Age* in 1919, and the Supreme Court upheld the conviction in 1925, arguing that speech advocating revolution was not protected by the First Amendment. In the summer of 1922, fifteen of the

Workers (Communist) Party's leaders were arrested following a conference in Bridgeman, Michigan, during which they agreed to become an above-ground organization. William Foster, one of the principal defendants, went to trial, which according to the party was an opportunity to present "the communist idea . . . for the first time . . . on a nation-wide scale to the people of the United States."[10] Because of his reputation in the labor movement, not only communists, but also local civil-liberties activists and the Chicago Federation of Labor were "instrumental in setting up a defense committee for Foster."[11] According to one of Foster's recent biographers, Edward Johanningsmeier, communists were so dedicated to defending their leadership and to defending IWW members that they asked for one hundred thousand dollars from the Comintern for defense cases in 1921, but only asked for ten thousand dollars for union organizing.[12]

Bail Jumping

Although political trials might provide an opportunity to speak directly to the public, their primary impact was to hinder activism and annoy individuals. No one likes to spend a long time in court, much less in jail, and in the beginning the Soviet Union seemed to provide an entirely new line of defense for activists facing charges in the United States. Many communists and anarcho-syndicalists jumped bail in the early 1920s and left for the new workers' state as a safe haven from anticommunist prosecution. Communists as famous as Big Bill Haywood, as well as more obscure activists, engaged in the practice in the 1920s, and it was to the ILD that they turned in seeking help. Letters requesting repatriation to the Soviet Union pepper the correspondence files of the ILD.[13] Big Bill Haywood was the most famous bail jumper to go to the Soviet Union, and his action created even more controversy between the various socialist and civil-liberties groups that had worked together so fitfully to begin with. The IWW vainly sought to get either the American party or the Soviet party leadership to reimburse it for the money it had lost when Haywood left. As the attorney Frank Walsh put it in one letter to the party: "It was members of the communist party who induced Haywood to jump his bail and leave the Industrial Workers of the World holding the bag."[14] The ACLU also complained.[15]

However, as much as an American patriot might think that American communists should "Love it or leave it!" bail jumping could not be sustained on a broad scale either politically or economically. In response to legal persecution and to Soviet strategy, the communists founded the

International Labor Defense in 1925 as a division of the International Red Aid, or MOPR, of the Soviet Union. Despite its connection to the MOPR, the ILD, even Draper admits, was the brainchild of James Cannon and William Haywood and initially was the locus of Cannon's factional power, staffed by his closest allies.[16] The ILD's basic strategy was very similar to that of the General Defense Committee of the IWW, only it tried to do something even more difficult. Cannon wanted to create an organization that would not be obviously dominated by the Communist Party, that would attract a wide and diverse base of members from the trade-union movement, and that would argue for the most radical version of labor defense. In the beginning, despite its connection to the Soviet Union, the ILD was heavily influenced by the IWW and the GDC, five of whose members were on the ILD's executive board.[17] Letters from prisoners, defense organizing strategies, and exhortations to workers dominated the official journal of the ILD, the *Labor Defender*, often written by former IWW members. Elizabeth Gurley Flynn, who had been a pioneer in IWW defense, was on the ILD board, which also included Norman Thomas, Ralph Chaplin, and Big Bill Haywood. Carlo Tresca wrote for the *Labor Defender* on Italian fascism. Cannon, who continued to praise the ILD even after his expulsion from the Communist Party, defined the ILD's task early on as

> unifying on a non-partisan basis the forces of labor defense. We built an organization not on the personal basis for this or that individual or group, but on the class basis of extending aid and defense to all workers who were in need of it. Anarchists, socialists, communists, IWW, members of the AFL, and workers without affiliation have found the hand of the ILD ready and able to aid them at all times.[18]

Chaplin and Haywood had emphasized the importance of a general defense strategy rather than reliance on ad hoc committees. As Chaplin put it, the ILD would be a form of "liberty insurance": "Past experience has taught us that the sporadic form of defense organization is ineffective. . . . The technique of defense is almost as necessary to the working class as the techniques of combat. It should be studied carefully. . . . These cases are a menace to the life and liberty of any worker with dissenting opinions or the wrong color in America."[19]

In these first few years, the ILD defended a variety of activists, regardless of their political affiliations. Unlike previous defense organizations on the left, the ILD also made it a point to defend people whose victimization was based on being "the wrong color," and not only those who had been active in labor struggles. In addition to its defense work for American laborers,

the ILD maintained an international solidarity program with communist victims of fascism in Europe. At their first conference in June 1925, ILD members discussed strategies for freeing the IWW activists imprisoned for their opposition to the First World War, followed the progress of the civil war in Russia, and emphasized the importance of labor defense for the writing of a popular history of the United States as class struggle. By writing about the "historic struggles of the working class in the past," ILD organizers argued, they would "help build up in the minds of the coming generation of workers a regard for the tradition of the movement and the spirit that enabled the men and women of those days to see their lives and liberties in the struggle."[20] That year, ILD activists supported Sacco and Vanzetti; Calogero Greco and Donato Carillo, anarchists who were charged with murder in New York; and three Portuguese anarchists from Fall River, Massachusetts. They also continued to participate in the effort to free Tom Mooney from prison. In many defense cases, a key aspect of the campaign was to draw connections between different examples of persecution: Sacco, Vanzetti, and the Gastonia strikers were connected; later on, so were Angelo Herndon and the German Communist Party leader Ernst Thälmann. Rather than being the quirks of judges or prosecutors, the ILD argued, trials that railroaded labor organizers and communists were part of capitalist class warfare. These mass campaigns served a purpose beyond defense:

> We must not get the idea that we are merely defense workers collecting money for lawyers. That is only a part of what we are doing. We are organizing workers on issues which are directly related to the class struggle. The workers who take part in the work of the ILD are drawn, step by step, into the main stream of class struggle. The workers participating begin to learn the A,B,C of the labor struggle.[21]

To accomplish this goal, the ILD championed mass action by the workers, including general strikes; argued against legal efforts as a bourgeois illusion; and advocated that the workers use the courtroom as a podium. In 1928, the organization issued a pamphlet titled, "Under Arrest! Workers Self-Defense in Court," that outlined a legal strategy not for lawyers, but for workers. "Be prepared," warned the pamphlet. "Don't depend on your attorney. . . . The real burden of presenting class issues will fall on you." In court, workers were representing the "entire working class" and should realize that the charge of the court was merely a smoke screen for the "real working-class activities" that were the reason for the arrest." It claimed that "not even the police are interested in the technical crime." Workers

should not deny crimes but should argue forcefully for the right of worker self-defense against bourgeois law. "Don't say no to force and violence," suggested the pamphlet, but remind the jury of the "right of revolution" as guaranteed in the Declaration of Independence and question the jurors about their prejudices against the working class. The worker must not stand for "pussyfooting" by attorneys or comrades who might advise "opportunistic and legalistic tactics to avoid the real issues." Above all, it said, "The trial is a place to expose to their fellow toilers the true nature of the courts in the bosses' political and economic oppression. . . . A courtroom packed to the doors with workers serves for the masses of workers as a practical study of class justice."[22]

The ILD's practice and philosophy in all of these cases was very similar to the old IWW's, and in the case of the courtroom presentation, it was similar to the anarchists' self-defense. They refused to pay bail to capitalist courts, organized mass meetings, distributed literature, packed courtrooms with workers, rejected clemency appeals, and called for heroic revolutionary proclamations from the accused. During the Sacco and Vanzetti case, the ILD even called for a general strike. Like the IWW and the anarchists before them, the ILD attacked "legalism" and defined the dignified procedures of the courtroom as signs of bourgeois trickery. Continuing Cannon's argument that the bourgeoisie preferred to defend workers with "respectability" and the "soft-pedal" instead of "vulgar" and "noisy" working-class protests, the ILD warned of falling for the stratagems of liberals who would simply try to bring the "right way" of justice into a court gone off track instead of using the trial to expose bourgeois justice as class warfare.[23]

However, while the Italian anarchists who supported Sacco and Vanzetti had attacked the "deluded" liberals who helped them, they often did so in Italian-language newspapers that their liberal friends did not read. The Communist Party's contempt for liberals was easier to see. In addition, while anarchists might have championed notions of mass justice and criticized the courtroom as a stage for bourgeois power, they—and the IWW—had also championed the Bill of Rights and offered an alternative American tradition of collective popular justice. Communists seemed to go further, arguing that in the class war all weapons were equally fair, and when fighting over defense strategy, they seemed as hostile to the ACLU as they were toward the reactionary bosses.

Conflicts between communists and liberals grew harsh during the 1920s and early 1930s. Following the Makhno revolt and the Kronstadt rebellion, it became clear that anarchists rejected the Soviet Union as a revo-

lutionary paradise. Many in the IWW were also disillusioned with Lenin. The conflict between communists and the ACLU came to a head when Roger Baldwin supported a tour of the Menshevik Rafail Abramovich to talk about political repression in the Soviet Union. In the spring of 1925, communists heckled the Abramovich meetings, and, according to Socialist Party members, CPUSA members led by Juliette Stuart Poyntz threw "bricks and other missiles through the windows when Abramovich came to speak.[24] This event led Baldwin and the ACLU to say that the CPUSA was concerned only with "civil liberties for us [communists]." Baldwin wrote to Earl Browder, who was then William Foster's protégé and editor of the *Labor Herald*:

> It is intolerable that the workers party should solicit and accept aid in its own efforts for the right of free speech and free assemblage and deny it to its opponents. I cannot understand how the party can continue to talk about free speech, to sponsor organizations of the labor defense council, to accept the help of the American Civil Liberties Union, to retain William Z. Foster on our national committee, and at the same time to approve of tactics such as these. The party must either stop soliciting or accepting the help of liberals outside, or it must indicate some respect for the principle it invokes.[25]

The Communist Party's response indicated that only state power mattered when it came to civil liberties, and that only the ruling class was capable of oppression: "The workers communist party of the US is not yet the ruling party in the US. On the contrary, it is the most outrageously persecuted and oppressed section of the American labor movement. Consequently, to demand as you do that we respect the civil rights of our opponents or that we concede them such rights, is ridiculous."[26]

This debate had gone on for some time and led Baldwin to request that the CPUSA send him its official position on the question of free speech for what he called a "debater's handbook."[27] Ironically, Browder's response was that if Baldwin wanted to understand the communist position on civil liberties, he should read Trotsky's *Dictatorship versus Democracy*, probably the "best thing available on the Communist Party's position on free speech." In addition, Baldwin would probably also want to see Bukharin's pamphlets "The Communist Program" and "The ABC of Communism."[28] The ACLU's founder was convinced to an extent by the arguments and, following his trip to the Soviet Union in 1927, held that "repressions in Soviet Russia are weapons of struggle in the transition period to socialism."[29]

Nonetheless, the CPUSA's behavior toward political opponents in the 1920s alienated many American intellectuals and socialists from the

party, including Upton Sinclair, who refused to speak on communist platforms following the disruption of Abramovich meetings.[30] The other, most problematic aspect of the 1920s ILD for liberals was its method of working in cooperation with groups such as the ACLU. According to one memorandum, those ILD members who participated in ACLU groups should always be "representative of the ILD, fighting for the interest of the ILD, and . . . shall not bind themselves to any decisions made by the committee which may be contrary to the policy of the ILD."[31]

Forrest Bailey of the ACLU wrote to the *Daily Worker*, "I will venture to make one more suggestion" and defended himself against charges that he was a "liberal":

> Instead of sneering at liberals at this time you would do well to recognize that they can be very helpful to you. I do not consider myself to be one, despite your opinion, so I can speak with impartiality, What I mean is that the liberals are a potential source of support to the cause of the Gastonia defendants, whose cause is so just that even a liberal can see it. Liberal sentiment can do much more there; liberal cash can do more.[32]

The new ILD drew criticism because it explicitly competed with the ACLU, the NAACP, and the IWW over strategy and members, and IWW members were later bitter about what they called the party's "take-over" of their defense organization. Indeed, early in its career, the ILD was a competitor to the IWW's defense work. While communists attempted to create "communist nuclei" within the IWW, with the goal of "placing . . . communists in important appointive and elective positions in the IWW" to combat "the syndicalist error," in New Orleans the IWW successfully took over the ILD chapter, much to the communists' dismay. Harry Glickson, the organizing secretary of the New Orleans ILD, wrote to the ILD head Louis Engdahl that "threats are being made to organize every Wobbly, Anarchist, whatnot to join the ILD and take control."[33]

Despite political disagreements, the ILD did join successfully in the liberal–syndicalist defense campaign coalition for two members of Arturo Giovannitti's and Carlo Tresca's Anti-Fascist Alliance of North America, Greco and Carillo, who themselves endorsed the ILD's work on their case. The two men had been accused of the murder of two Italian American fascists, Joseph Carisi and Nicholas Amoroso, at the Memorial Day fascist demonstration in 1927.[34] Although Clarence Darrow and Arthur Garfield Hayes were their lawyers, and Norman Thomas was credited with "organizing their defense," the ILD did most of the mass defense organizing for them and resolved to "defend workers irrespective of their political and

labor affiliations."[35] Following their acquittal, Greco and Carillo publicly announced in a letter to their supporters that the ILD—and its movement to save them—was the best thing to come out of the Sacco and Vanzetti defense movement. Both this endorsement and Vanzetti's approval of the ILD's methods of action suggest the similarity between the ILD in the 1920s and syndicalist notions of labor defense, which endorsed large demonstrations and the use of the political strike.[36]

Although they might have financed good lawyers, liberals did not agree with anyone on the socialist left about the importance of mass demonstrations, political strikes, and the making of political speeches in court. On these points, anarchists, syndicalists, and communists agreed with each other more than they did with the members of the ACLU. The ILD also showed its ties to the IWW's history of labor defense through its continuous activity in several of the cases begun by the IWW. Tom Mooney's was among the most significant, although it became entangled with the quarrels between the IWW and the Communist Party. At the January 1930 bureau meeting, it was resolved that Tom Mooney must know that

> we fundamentally disagree with the purely legalistic policy in labor defense cases, and disagree as well with those who hold that the freedom of Mooney and Billings be obtained by bringing influence to bear upon the authorities who are keeping the prisoners in jail. Only an aroused and militant working class can free class war prisoners and save them from imprisonment.[37]

In addition to demanding activist defense work, the ILD was trying to change the way that labor defense was done in general. The organization rejected "the bad traditions of the labor defense movements of the past," which was based on committees and "little groups of workers." Instead, the ILD attempted to create a "stable mass movement of workers which would develop into an instrument of the class struggle by drawing thousands of workers into its ranks and activities."[38] This meant that, while labor defense was a product of necessity, the ILD would try to make it a means for building class-consciousness, an end in itself.

While the ILD was successful in institutionalizing the "mass defense" strategy, its leaders found it short of the mark of a "stable organization" a good deal of the time. It is difficult to know whether internal communications at the time reflect the kind of frustrated reminders that leaders of organizations often send out to their members, whether members of the group were attacking the leadership in connection with factional struggles of the 1920s, or whether the organization really was on the brink of failure for the most of the decade. For instance, George Maurer criticized Rose

Karsner and James Cannon for having "neglected the ILD" and for the too obvious connection between the Communist Party and the organization. If the ILD met at the same time and place as the Communist Party's branch meeting, for example, would that not suggest that there was no difference between the two groups?[39] Despite popular tours and open meetings to build the ILD, the organization's real dues-paying membership was always in flux, and at one point so much of the ILD's membership was unemployed (66 percent) that it had difficulty collecting dues.[40] In addition, the ILD faced exactly the problem that promoted defense work in the first place: a mounting number of legal cases and the effort to respond to them without running out of money or becoming completely diverted from the original project that led to the arrests and jailing of members. In Passaic in 1926, for example, as the Workers' International Relief (WIR) and the ILD sorted out their respective roles in relation to an ongoing strike,[41] there was a concern that "pushing the defense angle too hard" would interfere with the effort for strike relief and that the growing national movement for Sacco and Vanzetti would actually hurt the Passaic defendants unless it could be turned "to account by attempting to divert the connections we establish in the Sacco and Vanzetti campaign into the movement for the Passaic comrades."[42]

High levels of activity did not translate into membership. Despite the popularity of the campaign on behalf of the Scottsboro Nine in Alabama, for instance, the ILD actually had fewer members on its books in 1932 than it had in 1929, although it had an "enormous agitational gains strengthened by fine, concrete accomplishments in the cases of the Scottsboro Nine, Oprhan Jones, and the Imperial Valley defendants."[43] In the early 1930s, the national office's assessments were generally critical. For example, the author of one "directive letter to the ILD of the USA" suggested that "there is something radically wrong with an organization that gains 5157 new members in 1921 [sic] and its gain at the end of the year was 696."[44] In October 1932, leaders warned that the ILD might become "a small and helpless sect" in the call to action for a conference in Cleveland.[45]

George Maurer wrote to the ILD's district organizers that they should send the national office all reports of arrests and defense cases. He also wrote:

> We are opposed to the hiring of expensive lawyers. . . . Now there are so many cases that we cannot afford to rush into extensive obligations to attorneys. We haven't the money and we must make a sharp and nation-wide turn to much greater economy. The same thing applies to fines. We are opposed to

the payment of fines in all but very exceptional cases—workers will have to be prepared to serve sentences that are imposed on them in terms of days. . . . We are trying to refund money given in the 1922 Michigan cases, but the recent arrests of Beal, Raymond and ten others in Michigan, against the same criminal syndicalism law will probably make it difficult for us to have any success in this regard.[46]

In a similar letter, written in April, Maurer again emphasized:

We cannot continue to handle cases throughout the country this way. It is wrong from every standpoint. We cannot continue to undertake to pay thousands upon thousands of dollars in exorbitant fees to lawyers for unnecessary and expensive appeals, for the fines when short sentences could be served. . . . A frantic cash approach to the mass arrest . . . prevents the building up of a mass ILD and defense movement.[47]

These communiqués suggest that the notion of "mass defense" had not filtered down through the membership and that the hostility to lawyers, and the favoring of mass organizing, was not only ideological but a practical necessity if the ILD was not to rely on the funding of more liberal organizations, such as the ACLU, for its legal defense.

Despite every call to use radical self-defense and eschew connections with liberals, local defense activities continued to rely on exactly the same patterns that had already been established from the days of 1919: the coalition of liberals and radicals using a combination of legal arguments based on the Bill of Rights and mass defense tactics. For example, following an attack by John Lewis's "thugs" and police on a meeting of the National Miners' Union in Pittsburgh in 1928, the Pittsburgh ILD first hired lawyers and later organized a "delegation of liberal elements, preachers, lawyers, doctors, professors and other forces who would visit the director of public safety and demand the right for the convention to hold its conference and to receive the fullest protection from the police. This of course was not to be organized in the name of the ILD." The resulting cost was more than six hundred dollars when lawyers' fees and fines were all added up. "Could the national office please send the money?"[48]

Making Anti-Lynching Activism a Part of Labor Defense

Although there was a dramatic increase in the advocacy of anti-lynching activism in the ILD after the Comintern's 1928 plenum, the idea that white

workers should defend Black workers victimized by lynching did not originate in Moscow, nor was it a cynical attempt to bring Blacks into the CPUSA, as has been argued by right-wing historians. Rather, white radical opposition to lynching emerged during labor-defense struggles in the South even before the Communist Party became involved there. IWW activists, inspired by the militancy of northern Black labor, began challenging segregation in the movement and recruiting Black organizers in the 1920s. In 1924, the IWW activist Vern Smith, who would later join the Communist Party and become an ILD organizer, specifically argued that white workers had for too long aided in the subjection of Blacks. The burden of fighting racism belonged to whites. To "make the Negro an ally," Smith argued,

> The radical portion of the white proletariat must at once sharply define its break with the white bourgeoisie and the ideology of the "superior races." The only way we can do this is to emphasize and over-emphasize the fact that we have absolutely no part in the discrimination against the black skin. . . . We will have to sit with the Negro on the street car by choice, and not by necessity, and we will have to be even more polite to his women than we are to those of fairer skin. And we must add to such examples as these a vigorous, defiant defense of all Negro workers in whatever trouble they find themselves, and never tire of protesting against, striking and struggling in every possible way against, Jim Crow laws, lynchings and every other vicious attack on the Negro as a race.[49]

Because it would lead to struggles that directly addressed the bogey of "social equality" in the South, an anti-lynching campaign would be an important way to act on Smith's suggestions. However, communists debated the anti-lynching campaign in the 1920s. Leading followers of Jay Lovestone, William Patterson, and Lovett Fort Whiteman criticized the American Negro Labor Congress (ANLC) for "concentrating on racial abuses, such as lynching, Jim Crowism and other social evils which at once renders it a rival org[anization] to the NAACP." They found this to be an "incorrect policy," as lynching was a "sporadic and spontaneous act of violence striking terror only in Negroes of the community where it occurs."[50] However, others in the organization maintained that lynching was precisely the fight. What hurt the party's work among Blacks, they said, was the "failure to develop concrete struggles of Negro masses on the basis of immediate practical issues. Little if any use has been made of such burning issues in the life of the Negro masses as repeated lynchings, residential segregation and discrimination, the cotton crisis and the plight

of the Southern Negro farmers, the struggle against war and imperialism, the relief for flood victims, etc. "

These workers, who sought to link the "recent outrages and discriminations against Negroes" to "more general struggles of the Negro race" were the ones who ultimately succeeded when the Communist Party turned its eyes to organizing the South after 1928.[51]

Gastonia

Like other ILD campaigns, the Scottsboro case had antecedents in the years of repression in the 1910s and 1920s. Just about anyone who wanted to fight repression in the United States ultimately would need to respond to vigilantism in general, and anyone who wanted to address the repression of Blacks could not just ignore lynching. While the ILD was formed during the Sacco and Vanzetti campaigns of the 1920s, its first independent defense case was in Gastonia, North Carolina. Communists had come to organize workers at the Loray Mill in their own union, the National Textile Workers Union (NTWU) in opposition to the AFL's United Textile Workers.

When a strike began in April of 1929, strikers immediately faced both police violence and arrests, but in June the violence came to a climax. When armed police came to the union hall following a demonstration during the day, shooting broke out, and the chief of police, Orville Aderholt, was killed and four officers wounded. Following the incident, fourteen strikers were charged with his murder and faced the death penalty.[52] Lucy Parsons saw the frame-up in Gastonia as "so similar" to the charges against her own group following the Haymarket bombing that she also wrote about it. She saw the key issue as the press attack on communism during the strike as the primary danger to the "Gastonia victims," whose prejudiced jury would be forced upon them, and said that "it is going to take hard work, good lawyers and plenty of money if their side is to be brought out properly."[53] The Gastonia strike led to a major defense case for the ILD, but factions within the party could not decide how to conduct the defense. The leftist faction argued for the most difficult of all positions—the right to armed self-defense "against the illegal armed raid by the police and mill owners' thugs" —while others called it a "frame-up." The threats in Gastonia were so great that it was difficult to keep organizers there. As lynchings and threats of lynchings occurred, one man at a fraction meeting in the summer of 1929 called the region "a howling

wilderness of hysteria."[54] That summer culminated in the shooting of the balladeer and union activist Ella May Wiggins in September while she was on her way to a union rally. The communists credited Wiggins for her ability to organize Black workers, and race permeated the interpretation of the Gastonia strike. When she was killed, the Black communist Otto Huiswood wrote, "today the lynch rope is no longer held in reserve for the Negro masses. This vicious system of murder, the chain gang and other methods of torture are being utilized by southern bosses against the white workers who dare challenge the whole system of robbery and plunder, and attempt to organize the white and black workers of the South on the basis of equality."[55] Although the strike, trials, and Wiggins's murder galvanized national support among liberals and radicals alike, the leadership remained highly critical at the ILD's national convention in December 1929. The group had failed, according to conference minutes, to "mobilize its own membership" and to "link up the Gastonia campaign" with other local problems. Despite journeys of Gastonia organizers to such places as Winston-Salem, where they canvassed mill workers and organized multiracial meetings against a local lynching,[56] the leaders judged that the ILD left particular cases isolated in neighborhoods or regions and that, as a result, the Gastonia trial did not "attain the mass character of which it was capable.... The workers did not relate the Gastonia attack to their own problems."[57]

In the spring of 1930, a number of the Gastonia defendants, including the strike organizer Fred Beal, going under an assumed name, skipped bail and went to the Soviet Union. According to the ILD's records, the defendants were "new members of the Communist Party, unknown to the local ILD," and it was suggested that this new trick was the work of agents-provocateurs.[58] Building a national organization, as opposed to an ad hoc group of workers around a local struggle, had its own special problems. For example, the ILD's national office noticed that party papers in North Carolina tended to "minimize or completely ignore" news stories sent from the national office and printed only those written in Gastonia.[59] Thus, even as some in the party argued for a less obvious relationship between the party and the ILD, the national fraction decided to relocate the ILD's office even closer to the Communist Party office so that the ILD could "render effective aid and guidance to the ILD in the South."[60]

Lessons learned in Gastonia may have informed the way that the ILD organized for the Scottsboro defense two years later. In the same discussion of the shortcomings of their defense work on this case, communists

commented that the Southern lawyers had controlled the case too much. In addition, discussions of ILD work in general between 1925 and 1929 reflected a frustration with the lack of Black participation, and two of the primary problems faced in Gastonia had been both the rejection of interracialism by white workers at the Loray Mill and the reprisals the communists met when they attempted to have interracial meetings.[61] Despite some arguments to the contrary, lynching was high of the list of issues for Black Americans, and at the 1929 ILD convention in Pittsburgh, where the number of Black members was the largest, Louis Engdahl suggested that the "need to engage in the fight against lynching burst with full force."[62] Despite this reported need, George Maurer's report on the Southern ILD conference of 1929 said that it was "generally very good," except that there was only one Negro delegate. We have the "merest beginning in work among Negroes," said the conference report, "the most oppressed section of the American population."[63]

As a solution, the conference report suggested that the ILD work more closely with the ANLC, that all the branches of the ILD must be "interracial," and that there should be a special "Negro department" of the organization. Again, the party was critical following the district conference of the ILD in Philadelphia, finding that there were "no Negro delegates" and that there was "no union support, and no money."[64] As Communist Party organizers sought to include Blacks in the party's work in greater numbers and to build the ILD, the Gastonia experience suggested to Bill Dunne that "it is possible for the ILD to become a real mass organization of the Negro workers and the exploited farmers here. Especially is this true immediately here in this sector. The International Labor Defense can be built up into the defense organization of the Negro masses."[65]

Dunne's comment suggested that the Negro masses needed their own "defense organization" beyond the usual type of ad hoc defense, and that building an interracial working-class movement in the South would happen more easily through anti-lynching activism than through union-organizing drives like the one in Gastonia. Given the heavy level of repression that Blacks faced, as was evident in the response to the initial formation of the Sharecroppers' Union in Alabama, the party had to engage not only in legal defense for its own members but also in more general anti-lynching activism. Immediately following their efforts to organize Southern Blacks, the communists met repression. On May 22, 1930, the ILD national office received a notice that six party members in Atlanta had been arrested at a meeting of the ANLC and charged with inciting insurrection. The group immediately resolved to respond by

holding an "anti-lynching conference" to "place the white terror in the South in the foreground." In late 1931, Black sharecroppers in Tallapoosa County, Alabama, who were organizing a union with the communists faced horrific violence. When their group, the Croppers and Farm Workers Union (CFWU) held a meeting about union issues and the Scottsboro case in Camp Hill, an armed mob of sheriff's deputies attacked. The union activist Ralph Gray retaliated, shooting the sheriff. Dispersing only to return with reinforcements and vengeance, the mob killed Gray, mutilated his body, and burned down his house. Initially, between thirty and forty Black union activists were charged with conspiracy to murder the sheriff, but following ILD organizing the charges were dropped. Later, in the same region, the sharecropper Ned Cobb was imprisoned for his role in attempting to protect his comrade Cliff James when a mob came to steal his mule. When the outspoken young Black communist Angelo Herndon organized a march of the unemployed in Atlanta in 1932, he was arrested and charged with inciting insurrection. Despite an able defense from the Atlanta lawyer Benjamin Davis, who would later become a leader in the CPUSA, Herndon was sentenced to death.[66]

Cobb and Herndon, as well as Hoseah Hudson, and other Southern Black communists who fought to organize unions in the South in the early 1930s faced not only the danger of arrest, but also possible lynching, putting them in a position different from that of white workers facing "legal lynching" or imprisonment for activism. In many cases, Herndon claimed that he was lucky when sent to jail, because it saved him from being lynched.[67] Because these activists really were political prisoners, their cases fell squarely into the traditional work of the ILD. Herndon's case was especially important, featuring an explicitly revolutionary Black communist activist on the witness stand who declared "you cannot kill the working class." As the ILD activist Sasha Small put it, Herndon was threatening to white Southerners who were "haunted by the vision of the wrath of the Negro masses when they are organized and launched against those who have for centuries crushed them under the hell of terror, poverty, misery, ignorance and dread." However, it was the immediate eruption of extralegal violence against Black organizers that made the special conditions of the South visible to white organizers in a way they had not been before. As Robin Kelley has argued, "Violence compelled local communists to make antiradical repression and the denial of civil liberties a central issue on their agenda."[68] The work of the ILD was significant enough that, by the mid-1930s, a party leader argued that "in some regions (the Northwest and South) the ILD actually takes on the functions of such organizations

as the League against War and Fascism, the Communist Party, the LSNR [League of Struggle for Negro Rights], and the Unemployment Councils," but its weakness was that it functioned outside of the shop committees, thus separating civil liberties and antiracist work from direct connections to union struggles.[69]

As communists called for the outlawing of the KKK in Alabama in 1934 and refused to advocate anti-lynching bills unless they carried a mandatory death penalty for lynchers,[70] they also had their eyes on fascism in Germany and Italy. The Communist Party and the broader labor left focused increasingly on vigilantism as a form of repression against the working class while simultaneously attempting to identify the relationships between property owners, hysterical mobs, and the institutions of law and justice in the United States. ILD activists in the 1930s challenged liberal theories about the individual and the state and were able to identify a broad pattern of class terror that worked both legally and illegally, announcing at the beginning of 1930:

> We are faced with increasingly great tasks. . . . Three to four thousand workers have been arrested since January first because of their class activity or opinion, dozens of Negro and some white workers have been murdered or lynched by the boss class. Hundreds face long terms in prison. . . . The total number of class war prisoners actually serving sentences increases from day to day at an even faster rate.[71]

The Communist Party's international ties and the influence of the Sacco and Vanzetti case, with the growing discussion of Italian fascism, were integral steps on the way to the Scottsboro mass defense. Still, the organization was not what it wanted to be. Just a month before the arrest of the nine young men who would become known as the "Scottsboro Boys," George Maurer remarked at the National Bureau meeting of the ILD that "the party is of the opinion that the ILD is in bad shape politically, organizationally, financially, with 40% of its money going to mail campaigns. "[72]

From 1929 to 1930, the ANLC was caught in the party's factional conflicts, and its role in relation to the ILD was in flux. In February, the Guianese communist from Harlem, Otto Huiswood, went on tour to build the ANLC, seeking members in unions and attempting to build "bridge organizations" that maintained a separation between the Communist Party and the ANLC. However, the organization was not thriving. Cyril Briggs wrote to George Padmore that "even the Negro department does not function properly because of the failure of most of its members to

attend meetings."[73] In June, the ANLC was to hold a conference in St. Louis at which its lack of a mass base was to be discussed. Members of the organization defended the ANLC, saying that the group's Crusader News Service and its journal, the *Negro Champion*, did have an influence on the "Negro masses."[74] According to its leaders, the ANLC had helped the ILD with Negro contacts and had brought Blacks into the Young Communist League (YCL).

The situation grew worse when the entire Negro department was suddenly reorganized from above in July 1930 as a result of the shift in the Comintern's analysis of the "Negro Question." At a meeting that month, William Patterson proposed that the party clarify to the comrades "why there has been so many drastic changes made in the Negro department." Huiswood complained that the "party did not think it necessary to tell the comrades about proposed changes." He continued: "Somebody can tell me that I made a speech at the party convention which was interpreted as being against the [Comintern] line, but I know this to be a lie, because the stage scenes were set. My remarks were already planned beforehand. No one knows the reason for my removal." Briggs, too, had been removed, and it was either he or Huiswood who commented, "This is ridiculous."[75] As "K. Kratov" would put it,[76] the handling of Huiswood's case by the Communist Party was "inexcusable and caused three Negro leaders to drop out altogether." Anger over the liquidation of the ABB continued to fester. From this point on, Kratov argued that the disgruntled members of the ABB were agitated by a white comrade named Pollack against the party and created an "anti-party group" that had to be liquidated.[77] By December 1930, the ANLC's liquidation was a fact, and the LSNR had come to take its place. Here, the relationship between Negro work and the ILD was formalized, and in the winter of 1931, Richard Moore was asked to come to the national office to become the Negro organizer for the MOPR (ILD). At this point, the organization was small, with no affiliate unions, no Negro members, no proposals for future work, and no sufficient literature.[78] In addition, the ILD's leadership struggled with the most common view of the organization as primarily a "legal-aid society to take care of the struggle's victim after the struggle is over."[79]

The Significance of Scottsboro

When nine young men were arrested and convicted of raping two women on a train in Scottsboro, Alabama, in March 1931, it would be a new kind

of case for the ILD. Immediately, the organization decided to "make a big issue of the case and get an attorney down there."[80] This action created a major turnaround both in the party's work with Blacks and in the history of labor defense. First, alliances with local liberals were unlikely, so the old methods of labor defense could not work in the South. The organizer Jane Dillon wrote to George Chamlee, the Southern lawyer that ILD lawyer Joseph Brodsky had hired to help him, rejecting the suggestion that she "get in touch with prominent southern liberals," arguing that there was "no way . . . we can appeal to our outright enemies in this case without compromising ourselves and the boys also."[81]

Second, when the Communist Party entered the anti-lynching movement by taking up the Scottsboro case, the work immediately contrasted with the traditional methods of labor defense and anti-lynching activism. The most obvious difference from labor-defense work was that the Scottsboro Boys were not political activists. Unlike mass defense cases of political prisoners, when the defendants themselves chose to become heroic spokespeople for their class—as Angelo Herndon would in his 1932 trial—the Scottsboro Boys became subjected to a tug-of-war among multiple organizations and individuals. The arguments for the mass defense strategy were more difficult to make when the defendants were not themselves politically committed. They had gotten into a fight over a boxcar with some young white men and beaten them. In retaliation, the whites accused the Scottsboro Nine of rape. The fact of their innocence and their racial persecution exposed Jim Crow in a way that no case of a political prisoner could.

To some, it did not make sense to make the Scottsboro case part of the ILD's work, and, in fact, the Communist Party's Political Bureau (or "Polburo," as it was known) voted to shift the project out of the ILD and into the LSNR. Max Bedacht, a former party leader once associated with Jay Lovestone, wrote in a complaint to the Polburo early in the campaign to oppose this decision:

The argument was advanced by practically all comrades that because the Scottsboro cases grew out of the national oppression of the Negroes, therefore they cannot be considered labor defense cases. Their argument is advanced in order to minimize the role of the ILD as a labor defense agency in this case. To achieve the desired aim, the comrades conveniently replaced the term "victims of capitalist class justice" with the term "labor case." In doing so, the Polburo obviously disregards its own urgent instructions of some two years ago to the Communist fraction of the ILD. In these instructions it categorically demanded that the ILD must treat all cases of Negro persecution

as manifestations of capitalist class justice which fall within the sphere of activity of the defense of victims of this justice. Now, when in the Scottsboro case the ILD, really for the first time, acts in accordance with this policy, the Polburo interprets the Scottsboro cases as not belonging to labor cases and therefore no longer a primary concern of the ILD. [82]

As Bedacht pointed out, the party's official position was that lynching was a part of capitalist class justice, and most ILD publications argued that lynching was a capitalist phenomenon. Therefore, this case should be fought by the ILD. This analysis of lynching as class justice, and the idea that the case should be fought by an interracial working class, made the ILD's Scottsboro project different from progressive era anti-lynching activism. It was, in other words, a case of "legal lynching," making the actions of the state and the "respectable community" rather than "mob violence" the target of attack. The "legal lynching" concept allowed the Scottsboro activists to point to the connections between lynch mobs and the institutions of law. These aspects of the case put it outside the traditional "anti-mobbism" of the progressive anti-lynching movement but within the logic of the radical "police–mob continuum" identified by Ida B. Wells and taken up most programmatically by the NAACP in the Arkansas, Tulsa, and Houston riot cases of the First World War era.

These innovations, along with the ILD's willingness to defend working-class Black men accused of rape, opened new avenues outside the highly charged area of access to jobs for collaboration between white and Black working-class activists. It also led to the important legal decision of *Norris v. Alabama*. In addition, the ILD promoted individual Black masculine heroism during the Scottsboro, Herndon, and Camp Hill campaigns and glorified multiracial masses in action, envisioning "hosts of dark, strong men, the vast army of rebellion" rising up in the South.[83] In keeping with their valorization of the multiethnic masses as the heroic agent for change, the party called for the breaking of boundaries between national groups as a practical requirement for ending lynching and liberating the working class.

However, while Wells had defined the "police–mob continuum" in racial terms so that working-class whites and the white bourgeoisie were united in an undifferentiated "mob" against Blacks, the communists described lynching—both legal and illegal—as an exercise of class power. The ILD writers argued that it was white bosses rather than white workers who were the primary agents of lynching. Lynching was not worker direct action. It was the "white ruling class" or the "white bosses" or the "mobs of landlords, store-keepers, and bossmen" or the AFL labor fakers who

used lynching to squelch the united struggle of Black and white workers.[84] Even if bosses were not doing the lynching themselves, the ILD argued, lynching fever had been created by the attempts of bosses and the "boss press" to whip up, distract, and divide workers who were becoming united by conditions brought about by the Depression.[85] They also suggested the opposite: that immediate conditions led working-class whites to lash out against Black scapegoats. One writer argued that the "relationship between mass unemployment and the activities of the lynch-noose and the burning stake is as close as the union between Wall Street and the Whitehouse." As James Allen saw it, looking back, the 1930s created a somewhat paradoxical dynamic. First, the Depression led to an increase in the number of lynchings in the South, but he said "impulses" of solidarity arose between whites and Blacks because of shared misery. Either way, the communists argued, antiracism was imperative for the working class, while the fight against the boss was essential to the fight against lynching. They suggested that, to succeed, workers needed to build "a workers' defense corps against this lynching epidemic of the bosses!"[86]

Scottsboro, unlike Gastonia, also had the capacity to appeal to a national Black movement. Harlem Blacks immediately connected their own experiences of police repression in the North to the experiences of Southern Blacks. Scottsboro revealed not only the special repression of Southern Blacks, but also the unique way that the state and the mob came together to enforce racial norms in the United States more generally. Communist Party activists tried to take up a 1930 rape case in Delaware before the Scottsboro case began, and numerous "little Scottsboro" cases were fought in the North in the 1930s and 1940s.[87]

The drawback was that the party's attack on lynching as a "boss phenomenon" or simple reaction to economic deprivation minimized differences in legal status between white and Black workers and failed to explain white working-class identification with racial hatred. By interpreting racism economistically, the CPUSA's official position preserved the innocence of the white working class. This evasion of the issue of working-class responsibility implied that white workers were weak and vulnerable, the dupes of bad leaders, victims who were not capable of making political decisions in their own interest.

To point to the real use of racial power by the working-class whites on the train from which the Scottsboro Boys were ejected would have contrasted with the Communist Party's argument that the case was caused by bosses. Scottsboro highlighted effective differences in status between poor whites and Blacks, and Elizabeth Lawson, one-time editor of the

Liberator, came close to pointing them out in her illustrated Scottsboro pamphlet, "They Shall Not Die." She wrote, "All of the workers, white and Negro, would be branded by the bosses as bums. But so rigid is the system of Jim Crowism in the South, that even on freight trains 'niggers' must 'keep in their place.'"[88] It was not the case that the Southern police viewed these bums as the same: The white men and women who made the accusations, regardless of their poverty, had more power than the nine men they sent to jail. However, the notion that the bosses branded them both as bums better fit the picture of the white working class as simply "poisoned" by bosses, and fit into the Communist Party's dependence on the "correct leadership" to prevent the masses from going astray.

The Scottsboro case did expose the racism of the South, and it was a major step forward because of its advocacy of mass protest against lynching instead of the use of courts. As James Allen put it, the case revealed "the whole system of vicious repression of Negroes in all its nakedness." The young men, who had been riding in a boxcar and were seeking work, were a "symbol of the oppression of the Negro people." The jury in the case "took it for granted that all Negroes are rapists" because of "decades of deliberately built prejudice and division between white and black."[89]

The ILD also exposed the connection between the South and the federal government. While building the ILD in the South, James Allen had drawn connections between the Klan and the federal government, arguing that the 1920s Klan leader Joseph Simmons had "used the secret service to build the klan" and that later, the leader Hiram Wesley Evans was "consciously a fascist" and an "undercover agent for Hooverian imperialism." In the early years of the Scottsboro case, Theodore Dreiser wrote a pamphlet on the Scottsboro Boys for the ILD, denouncing Roosevelt for not intervening in the case and arguing that his failure to do so "showed his collaboration with the frame up." President Roosevelt's willingness to leave it "up to Alabama," Dreiser claimed, showed his direct aid to the "Alabama lynch terrorists." The delegation to Washington demanding that Roosevelt free the Scottsboro Boys included Dreiser, the former prosecution witness Ruby Bates, and Mary Church Terrell.[90] They argued that a "small but powerful ruling class of white landlords and capitalists ruthlessly maintain this frightful system of slavery and exploitation in order to wring super profits out of the toil of the downtrodden Negro masses" and compared the Scottsboro trial to the Nazi frame-up of Dimitrov during the Leipzig trial in Germany.[91]

Heroes or Victims?

As it characterized its enemies as the federal government in collaboration with the "bosses' lynch law," the Communist Party also depicted the Scottsboro defendants. Like other lynching victims, the Scottsboro Boys could be defined almost as entirely "innocent victims." They had not been heroically fighting the class war when they were arrested; they were targeted simply because they were Black. In one ILD pamphlet, Isidore Schneider referred to the case as a "lynching [of] Negro children in Southern courts,"[92] even though several of the defendants were in their late teens or early twenties.[93] The image of the Scottsboro Boys as children was reinforced by the fact that, while white men's wives and girlfriends fought for them, the female speakers for the Scottsboro Boys were their mothers. If the staple image of the Haymarket and Joe Hill defenses had been scenes of flirtation and sexual longing across prison bars, such images of imprisoned sexuality were scrupulously avoided in communist literature about Scottsboro.

In continuation of the mass defense tradition, the organized masses, rather than the defendants, were shown as powerful. James Allen described how Blacks who previously had been distrustful of whites "solidly lined up behind the defense movement" and who would not stop "until they [had] ousted the white landowners, bankers, and credit merchants both from the land and from the government." The ILD also publicized the joining of whites and Blacks in marches for the Scottsboro Boys, bringing Blacks into the Haymarket notion of the mass hero. Because the party did not define the original actions of the nine young men—fighting against white hoboes in a boxcar—as heroic and instead focused on the false accusation of rape, they missed an opportunity to actually address intraclass conflict in the South. Instead of admitting what their internal documents said—that the white and Black working classes were not uniting in the South—the party trumpeted that the Scottsboro Boys were being victimized because of growing interracial class solidarity.

The political-defense trials of Southern Blacks in the 1930s stood in contrast to Scottsboro. Jane Dillon wrote in the summer of 1931 to Gertrude Akerman in the ILD's national office about the case in Camp Hill, complaining that it was "politically far more important than the Scottsboro case" but that it did not receive comparable attention.[94] However, the storm over Scottsboro did lead to the quiet dropping of the charges in the Camp Hill case, as the community did not want that kind of national

attention.[95] Angelo Herndon's trial, based on an old statute from the era of Reconstruction, which became the center of a major national campaign that involved financial contributions of Blacks from all over America, was hugely significant in promoting a Black hero as part of the tradition of political defense, and the Communist Party even referred to him as a "young Dimitroff."[96]

However, with the embrace of the popular-front strategy, the promotion of heroic figures such as Herndon and Ralph Gray of Camp Hill diminished, and a legislative campaign against sedition laws took over the focus of the ILD's national office. In 1937, the ILD in Alabama disbanded, and local Blacks were encouraged to join the NAACP.[97] When liberals took over the popular-defense efforts in Scottsboro, they represented the Scottsboro Boys almost exclusively as "innocent victims." In his book on the case, the Southern liberal Allan Knight Chalmers, who handled the case at the end, referred to "those boys" as like a "rabbit" and a "mouse." The difficulties of organizing Southern whites against racism, along with major changes in international Communist Party policies, led the Communist Party to compromise its organizing strategy in the ILD dramatically to build an interracial alliance not with white working-class Southerners, but with the middle-class interracial committees that they had once castigated. While in the early 1930s communist organizers had described lynching as a technique of bourgeois terror that the president actually supported, in the late 1930s, the rhetoric began to describe lynching as an "un-American" practice that was unique to the South. Instead of attacking Roosevelt's complicity with lynchers, communists after 1936 attacked the enemies of the New Deal: Senator Theodore G. Bilbo, Senator James Eastland, and Senator Martin Dies. The party also compromised on the issue of working-class militancy as the best means for self-defense. The Scottsboro Defense Committee, headed by Chalmers, dropped the incendiary rhetoric of Negro masses at war with landlords and bosses and instead appealed to "Alabama citizens of standing and influence," who wanted to save Alabama from "the stain on her honor" created by the terrible persecution of innocent boys.[98] When right-wing opposition to Roosevelt grew, the Communist Party adopted the white progressives' old argument that lynching was an un-American phenomenon that could be fought through federal courts in the name of national unity and law and order. By 1935, the official policy of the ILD had become "the best legal defense together with the broadest, most powerful mass protest." The organization even went so far as to endorse "following the policy of selecting the best attorneys for the specific legal defense task."[99]

From its beginnings, the ILD had argued that labor-defense cases were not merely a sideline, but were organizing opportunities in their own right. Scottsboro, a case in which there was no automatic call to defend a fellow party member, tested this notion of the mass defense as an organizing tactic and showed that, indeed, the mass defense could pull people into radical analysis of American power and into the Communist Party itself. The case pulled Northern white and Black radicals into the work of achieving racial justice in the South. Not only did the ILD make lynching, both legal and illegal, into a class issue, but they argued that it was the responsibility of white workers to build unity across race in the working class by organizing in defense of Blacks instead of wondering why Black workers had failed to join their movements in larger numbers. Asking white workers to engage in the defense of Black victims of the law was a crucial step forward in bridging the gap between anti-lynching activism and labor defense.

Fighting for the Scottsboro Boys was a way for white activists to take a stand against many manifestations of whiteness. At its national plenum in December 1931, the ILD took the official position that "only defending Negroes in strike situations is a bourgeois, social-reformist anti-working class, chauvinist attitude which must be rooted out ruthlessly and immediately. We must have a mass defense of all racist prosecutions." This philosophy was applied to many Northern "Scottsboro" cases that did bring working-class Blacks and whites together. Party members might even be overzealous. One New York neighborhood club was admonished by the ILD that it should not sue a white driver who had gotten into a collision with one of its Black members.[100] The Scottsboro campaign, in the context of the history of labor defense, was a major turn for the socialist left, which finally came to address the mob intimidation of Blacks as central to the overall repression of the working class. However, the Communist Party's refusal to address the power difference that allowed poor whites to turn to the law for revenge on the Scottsboro Nine showed the limits of the party's capacity to attack the reality of white privilege. For it was not so, as Lawson claimed, that the bosses saw all the boys on the train as "bums," but that even for bosses, perhaps some bums were more equal than others. This failure to attack white privilege, simultaneous with the growing recognition of the role of mob violence, contributed to the party's continual portrayal of the working class as a cognitively or morally fragile and yet physically powerful group, capable of using its might either for good or for ill. That portrayal fit in well with the notion that even the "good" working class would easily go dangerously wrong

when led by the wrong people. Those misleaders could just as easily be Black nationalists; finally, the "young Dimitroff," Angelo Herndon, was kicked out of the party in 1944 because of his arguments for "black nationalism."[101]

International Solidarity and the ILD

While all socialists had included international protest in their defense campaigns as they attempted to create an international working-class community that superseded national loyalty, the Communist Party's internationalism was different. Everything in the ILD was more programmatic than previous defense work in the United States had been. One aspect of this work was solidarity with international victims of fascist terror. The ILD was officially part of the MOPR, and contributed both money and action to the efforts to defend communists against Nazis in the 1930s. Money raised for these political prisoners was to be sent to the MOPR directly.[102] The campaigns for those such as Ernst Thälmann included not only letter-writing campaigns to Hitler and public protests on Thälmann's behalf, but also the effort to link local U.S. defense cases to an international phenomenon of anticommunist attack. Thus, William Patterson argued in 1934 that the "Herndon campaign [should] be made the center of a campaign against developing fascism in the US, linking it with Thälmann and against fascism abroad."[103]

At the same time, communists organized "Patronati" societies—immigrant groups that supported compatriots in countries where fascists had taken over. These were to be built in the party's foreign language groups, with money to be collected through the MOPR.[104]

The most important labor-defense case internationally inaugurated the popular front against fascism and acknowledged an already established set of radical procedures in a labor-defense case. Georgi Dimitrov defended himself in court during the Reichstag Fire case, and during his interrogation of the self-confessed fire starter Marinus van der Lubbe, pointed out his lack of revolutionary mettle: "As was already said, he was not alone. His conduct, his silence makes it possible for innocent people to be accused along with him. I would not ask van der Lubbe about his accomplices, had his act been revolutionary, but it is counter-revolutionary."[105]

In his closing statement, Dimitrov returned to this point of van der Lubbe's conduct in court as evidence of his status as the fascists' puppet:

What is van der Lubbe? A Communist? Inconceivable. An Anarchist? No. He is a declassed worker, a rebellious member of the scum of society. He is a misused creature who has been played off against the working class. No, he is neither a Communist nor an Anarchist. No Communist, no Anarchist anywhere in the world would conduct himself in court as van der Lubbe has done. Genuine Anarchists often do senseless things, but invariably when they are hauled into court they stand up like men and explain their aims. If a Communist had done anything of this sort, he would not remain silent knowing that four innocent men stood in the dock alongside him. No, van der Lubbe is no Communist; he is no Anarchist; he is the misused tool of fascism.[106]

Largely because communists were persecuted around the world during the 1920s, making the case for the Soviet Union as a bulwark against bourgeois reaction could not have been hard for an audience used to the stories of American repression of radicals. Labor-defense activists had portrayed working-class interests as unitary and following "natural laws," thus diminishing the importance of procedures for protecting individual freedom as part of the definition of democracy. When presented with clear breaks within the working class, such as the racial fault line revealed in lynch mobs and race riots, the Communist Party's tendency was to assign responsibility to the ruling class. ILD organizers argued that American struggles against the Ku Klux Klan and the American Legion were part of an international defense of communism, and all efforts to stop fascists in all guises helped the struggles for civil rights of the working class against the capitalists.

During its first five years, the ILD in the United States thus organized campaigns in defense of European workers: to defend the communist leader Mathias Rakosi in Hungary in 1925; to defend "victims of Capitalist persecution" in Poland, Lithuania, and Italy; and to fight "against mass slaughter of peasants in China. "[107] Before the entry of the United States into the Second World War, the Communist Party encouraged the growth of a Black international against imperialism, as they argued that America's Black workers should form an alliance with Indian, African, and West Indian workers against British imperialism.[108]

The impact of Stalinism on the ILD appeared after 1928. First of all, the ILD abandoned work for anarchists and other socialists, declaring that "no member of the ILD can be opposed to the Soviet Union. "[109] The defense of the right to revolution eventually disappeared from most of the ILD's rhetoric, although individual defendants made revolutionary arguments

in court, as Angelo Herndon did in his trial for inciting insurrection in Georgia.[110] Even during Herndon's case, during the ultra-revolutionary Third Period, his lawyers depicted him as an "organizer" rather than a revolutionary. The erosion of heroic ideals in the ILD's rhetoric over the 1930s was connected to the increasing support for the repression of dissidence in the Soviet Union. During the Soviet purge trials, Stalin argued that political opposition would destroy the Soviet state. Dimitrov, whose "Reichstag Fire" speech had done so much to define the power of the Nazi state, recalled a speech by Stalin in 1937:

> Anyone who attempts to destroy the unity of the Socialist state, who aspires to detach from it individual parts and nationalities is an enemy, a sworn enemy, of the peoples of the state, of the peoples of the U.S.S.R. And we shall destroy any such enemy, even if he is an old Bolshevik, we shall destroy his kith and kin. Anyone who encroaches on the unity of the Socialist state in action or thought, yes even in thought, will be mercilessly destroyed. To the final destruction of all enemies! (cries of approval: to the Great Stalin!)[111]

However, the presentation of the Communist Party and the ILD as the last line of defense for the working class was not cynical. During the 1920s, American communists saw themselves as in the vanguard of defense for a truly international movement, as the last holdouts in America for revolution in the face of a bureaucratic reform movement of socialists and a disintegrating anarchist movement. They were, in fact, the primary defenders of German, Italian, and Russian workers against fascism. As they publicized the links between anticommunists in different countries, ILD activists brought American cases to international attention. They took part in an organization that included thousands of members who formed an international—as they called it, "behind-the-lines"—corps that gave aid to those who had fallen and suffered "in the front line battles."[112] Like the IWW, the ILD operated on the principle of "class defense" rather than defending an amorphous "people" from the institutional power of the state and the legal bureaucracy. However, the communists differed from other groups on the left when they began to define defense against "capitalist reaction" and the battle against enemies on the left as identical. They could make this leap because they defined any conflict inside the class as traitorism that would lead to vulnerability when the class was under attack, to the extent that labor defense and the defense of the Soviet Union became the same thing. E. H. Carr argues that this idea went back to the earliest institutions of the Soviet Union, as Bolsheviks believed that "the notion of an anti-thesis between the individual and the state was the natural

assumption of a class society, but that it was illogical to set the interest of the worker against the worker's state. "[113]

Not only communists but, later, liberals supported the seemingly heroic Russian regime. The *New Republic*'s Malcolm Cowley would defend the Moscow Trials of 1938 and denounce Trotskyism as a menace because, unlike the Stalinists, Trotsky supported international revolutionary action. Similarly, Powers Hapgood, a Socialist Party member who was close to the Communist Party in the 1930s, pooh-poohed the concerns of IWW organizers living in Siberia when he visited the Soviet Union.[114] As Alan Wald had explained this, "Some of the liberals sympathetic to Stalinist Russia had worked out complicated rationales that enabled them to tolerate undemocratic judicial procedures and other drastic measures in the Soviet Union that they would find totally unacceptable in the United States. "[115]

Like many liberals before them who had opposed revolution, New Deal–era liberals balked at the radicalism of the "left opposition" and joined the communists in arguing that it was completely reasonable for the state to repress anarchists, as well.[116]

A history of opposing frame-ups in the U.S. context did not seem to make a difference, as Max Shachtman noted in a letter to the *Nation*:

> The execution of the sixteen men [as a result of the Moscow Trials] on August 24, 1936, was the result of the biggest frame-up in history! In cases of Dreyfus, Mooney and Billings, Moyer–Haywood–Pettibone, or Sacco–Vanzetti, the frame-up involved only one, two or three men, in the present case, not only are dozens of individuals involved, but an entire section of the revolutionary movement.[117]

In the American context, this could make for even stranger arguments. The party leader Earl Browder argued against every lesson ever taught by American labor defense when he supported the Moscow Trials. "It is in the great American tradition," he said, "to wage uncompromising struggle against traitors, and to preserve eternal vigilance against the secret agents of reaction. "[118] While most of the publicity of the ILD concerned lynching, trials, and letters from American class-war prisoners, by 1929 a few articles describing the enemies of the Soviet Union had also appeared in the *Labor Defender*. For example, although it was a defense organization, the ILD heartily approved of the methods of rehabilitation described in D. Zaslawasky's "A Trial in a Soviet Prison." This particular trial was part of the rehabilitation of S. Broide, whose principal crime was the publication of a book that attacked Soviet prisons as havens of degeneracy.[119] Forgetting anything they might have learned from years of prisoner-

support work, the editors printed an article that cheerfully described as part of this rehabilitation all the prisoners in the jail joined in denouncing the new inmate in a mock trial, under the watchful eyes of political authorities. The author noted, "Involuntarily one forgets that these are people deprived of liberty, that not so long ago they themselves were the object of no less thunderous orations." This "trial" was almost identical to the "kangaroo courts" that had once been denounced in the IWW defense bulletins by Wobblies jailed for First World War draft resistance as a clever method of destroying prisoner alliances.[120]

In January 1931, Henry Hall of the *Labor Defender* reported on the trials and executions of a group of engineers inside the Soviet Union as "plotters against the U.S.S.R." whose projects of swamp drainage were interpreted as preparing paths into Russia for French invaders, and whose failed attempts to build good machines were described as intentional efforts to drain Soviet resources and "disrupt industry."[121]

Thus, while the ILD defended American comrades who were victims of racism and state repression of labor and communist activism, they supported the trials, convictions, and executions of party members within the Soviet Union. William Foster, for example, "ardently supported the various show trials and executions of Stalin's political opponents."[122] The longtime communist Steve Nelson justified his support of Stalin's no-strike rule, with the question, "How can you strike against yourself?"[123] Similarly, Nelson's understandings of both the Japanese internment and the Hitler–Stalin pact reveal a connection between the support for Stalin in the Soviet Union and the CPUSA's analysis of issues within the United States.[124]

State heroism and chivalric discourses about the Soviet Union came hand in hand with a decrease in the images of militancy by defendants in individual trials. In tension with depictions of heroic workers facing the capitalist judge with scorn was the image of the working class as the victim of capitalist or fascist evil who awaited help from the forces of the ILD and its lawyers. This representation of the ILD and the helpless worker coincided with the representation of the Soviet state as the embodiment of the united masses, the heroic savior of victimized workers, so that the ultimate working-class heroism became loyalty to the Soviet state.

National Heroes

Russian heroic literature during the Second World War, like their stated policies, championed absolute unity as the primary virtue. The Soviet

Union's heroic tradition stretched back to the days of Narodnik and nihilist revolts of the nineteenth century and Russian workers of both genders had a solid following in America among Communists and liberals alike. During World War Two, the Russian War Relief organization, not all of whose members were communists, published a magazine that celebrated heroes of the Russian Army like "the poet with a gun," and in numerous poems and songs leftists and liberals celebrated this girl hero, Liudmila Pavlichenko, who had toured the United States and described how she had "mowed down Hitlerites like ripe grain, as drunk with blood as with vodka."[125]

Soviet and American communist propagandists used stories of Soviet women's loyalty to the army as an example of model citizen unity. Oakley Johnson reported an anecdote of a Soviet couple registering to fight "side by side" in the Red Army.[126] Readers of the women's page in the *Daily Worker* were reminded of heroines such as Praskevoya Zrereva, widowed mother of two sons, a People's Guard member and trade unionist, who after being captured by the Germans disguised herself as a peasant, escaped, and returned to Russia, where she rebuilt a textile factory with other women to give more help to the war effort.[127] They were told of the "firm and burning courage that has fused the women of the Soviet Union along with the entire population in the unbreakable unity for the defense of their socialist country against the Nazi invaders."[128]

Stories of families acting together contained the strength of "new women" within the family and the state, and created a metaphor that associated support for the state with loyalty to the family. When American Communists reported on the unity of husbands and wives they made similar arguments.[129] However much it may have enjoyed the Soviet propaganda of families at the barricades, the American party did not embrace the popular Soviet stories of loyalty to the state over loyalty to the family. One major Soviet martyr whose story did not make the American party's papers was Pavlik Morozov, a "legendary child who turned his father in as a hoarder" and was then killed by his relatives. He was listed as a martyr in the Soviet Union in 1937, but this "squealer's" story did not make it into the American communist's martyrology.[130]

ILD and Popular History

While it did not champion children who ratted out their parents, the American communist movement did valorize American nationalism in

ɪɪs own defense stories in the 1940s. The CPUSA insisted increasingly on its sole claim to the mantle of the working-class movement, and ILD activists made the writing of working-class history part of their work. Not only did the Communist Party collaborate in the suppression of rival leftists in the 1930s in Spain and in the 1940s in the United States, but the Communist Party's major labor-defense historian, Elizabeth Gurley Flynn, marginalized other leftist groups as she crafted the history of American class warfare in the context of popular-front politics.

The change in position toward the U.S. government was accompanied by an increasing tendency to identify communism's "native" American roots. By the time the fiftieth anniversary of Haymarket rolled around, Flynn was describing the "mistaken" ideas of the anarchists and referring to Albert Parsons (who opposed electoral politics as useless) as an "eloquent advocate of full suffrage for the Negroes," while the other seven defendants disappeared. Milton Howard, also writing about the anniversary of the executions, described how "the kid who ran with Texas Trappers and Indian raiders grew up to be a leader of industrial strikes."[131] He used Parsons's story to repudiate the "charge that we [communists] are foreigners." Similarly, Alan Calmer's *Labor Agitator* recorded only Parsons's history, mentioned Spies briefly, and denounced bomb throwing.[132]

Howard Fast also told the story of the Haymarket affair by focusing on the American origins of Albert Parsons while simultaneously regretting and criticizing the mistaken and "wild" ideas of the primitive era of the movement as the product of a left-wing childhood. The primary character in Fast's 1947 novel *The American* was John Peter Altgeld, the governor who later pardoned the anarchists. The drama in the story focuses on the social democrat George Schilling's appeal to the governor, describing him and Altgeld together in the parlor of his home in Chicago. In his appeal, instead of discussing Spies, the fictionalized Schilling decided to talk about Parsons as a metaphor for America itself. The tragedy was not just in killing a man but, Schilling argued, in killing a tradition in America by killing this son of revolutionaries, whose entire life had been dedicated to liberty.[133] Like the others, Fast's story served to "Americanize" socialism with references to a white, native-born radicalism and the American Revolution and by attempting to minimize the significance of the immigrant backgrounds of much of the American working class.

These popular-front-era memorialists also conceded the Chicago court's point by concluding that the anarchists' rhetoric had caused the bomb throwing, and they described self-defense as dangerous, claiming that anyone who threw a bomb was actually a police agent. Parsons's "mis-

taken theories of Anarchism," according to Milton Howard, "made the frame-up against him easier to arrange." These communist erasures and repudiations of the Haymarket anarchists did nothing to counteract the ideas put forth by those such as Morris Hillquit, who argued that revolutionary anarchism was "a gospel of violence, a philosophy of despair," and that it appealed only to Germans and Russians, who were inspired by their false ideals borne of experiences under despots in Europe.[134]

While many of the Communist Party's ideas about African Americans had come from its associations with Black radicals such as Cyril Briggs and Richard Moore, its emphasis on interracialism also meant that it saw Black nationalism as divisive. By the time of the Second World War, Black nationalists were being called "disloyal." Thus, when the Communist Party revived John Brown's heroic legend during World War Two, it focused not so much on his individual manhood as it did on the interracial character of Brown's troop during a time when many Blacks rejected participation in the war. Explaining how Negroes had fought to get into the Union Army during the Civil War, Eugene Gordon wrote, "The Negro today can think of Harper's Ferry and events that followed as links in the historic chain leading to complete emancipation. Today anti-fascist war breaks the last of the bonds which Brown and his compatriots struck so valiantly eighty-three years ago. "[135]

The tendency to celebrate national unity and loyalty in the ILD during the popular-front era eroded political power for the working class as the primary goal of the labor-defense campaign. This celebration of unity and state power also changed the definition of the international enemy. By the mid-1940s, communists were defining fascism as a form of mass hysteria or as an insidious and un-American "fifth column" rather than as an expression of class interest. From 1939 on, the ILD maintained a campaign against the forerunner of the House Committee on Un-American Activities (HUAC), the anticommunist Dies Committee, which it called a tool of "reactionary un-American forces" and "part of a fascist coalition. "[136] The group took equivocal stances on the wiretapping bills introduced by congressmen Samuel Dickstein, Horace "Jerry" Voorhis, and Emmanuel Cellar, the last of which the ILD officially supported, and proclaimed that it would "cooperate with the government in winning the war and combating fifth column activities. "[137]

The view of fascism as a form of "hysteria" made it easy for many supporters of the New Deal to compromise on civil liberties. In 1941, members of the National Lawyers Guild were not sure how to oppose the FBI's wiretaps on their offices. Writing to another guild member, Richard

Gladstein equivocated that "wiretapping as such is not a bad thing, since it has been used and can be used for purposes of which we approve, such as the present trial against the Nazi spies." The Guild's compromise on the wiretapping was a product of the relationship the organization sought with the Roosevelt administration, a Stalinist strategy that was easier than upholding revolutionary aims.[138]

The Communist Party also abandoned its traditional anti-imperialist politics after Roosevelt and Stalin's meeting in Teheran. In 1944, numerous speeches made at a memorial tribute dinner for the longtime ILD organizer Anna Damon equated the work of the ILD with the support of the United States against internal enemies, as one speaker joined what would be the AFL's postwar position that the expansion of the U.S. economy overseas was a great benefit to the U.S. working class.[139] The party even abandoned the argument that the federal government was complicit with Southern violence—an argument that had been so fundamental to its earliest activism against lynching.

The danger of these liberal antifascist arguments was that they could so easily be reversed and applied to any popular working-class movement. Liberals, neglecting the anticommunism of fascists, had defined fascism as a largely mob-driven hysterical psychological phenomenon that was similar to the French Reign of Terror. Much popular antifascism was already based on anti-mob theories that were first used against the left. Second World War–era descriptions of fascists had been drawn from previous progressive arguments that lumped lynchers and socialists together as hysterical examples of working-class fanaticism or premodern barbarism. These liberal theories were based on the presumed creation of fascism through the duped, hysterical masses and their demagogic and charismatic leaders. In addition, the liberal theories were Orientalist. The epithet of "Asiatic" despotism, which implied that, because of the history of serfdom, Russians were a racially slavish Oriental people, was used to characterize the Russian Revolution and the Bolshevik party from its earliest days.[140]

Like the progressives of the 1920s, the liberals in the Cold War era located the sources of political repression not with the state's defense of itself and of capitalist business owners against popular opposition, but with the masses and demagogues. The terror came not from the needs of the capitalist class to protect its interests but, instead, from the hysterical masses who, in literary representations of the McCarthy era by both Lillian Hellman and Arthur Miller, were feminized. With this powerful image of hysterical feminized masses misled by demagogues, it was possible to attack

communists and anticommunists at the same time by arguing that both were essentially incorrectly applying a conspiratorial theory to a history in which power simply did not exist, as Richard Hofstadter did in his classic book *The Paranoid Style in American Politics*. The theory of "hysteria" as the source of terror in the 1930s had serious consequences for liberal civil-liberties activism in the 1950s. In their focus on hysteria as the root of the problem of authoritarian rule, the liberals ignored other instruments of American power. The definition of "totalitarianism" as a form of populism in the 1950s served to justify the use of repression of civil liberties in America through the building of what William W. Keller describes as an "internal security state" based on professionalism, clandestine policing, and surveillance, of which most liberals heartily approved.[141] Morris Ernst of the ACLU developed a close relationship with the FBI Director J. Edgar Hoover, seeing him as an ally at the top who would help the cause of freedom, and Gardiner Jackson, the former head of the Sacco Vanzetti Defense Committee, assured his friends among the anarchists that the "J. Edgar Hoover of today" is not the "same man he was during the Palmer era. "[142] Since the liberal understanding of "fascism" connected it with the masses, the maintenance of professional and expert surveillance operatives did not appear to liberals to be threatening to democracy. In their attempts to achieve a rational policy against communism, liberals "contributed to a universal anti-Communist consensus that placed the FBI beyond the reach of responsible criticism as well as higher executive or constitutional controls. "[143]

Capitalists and communists attacked each other by association with "fascism" as the ultimate political evil. However, since communists had spent the 1930s and 1940s supporting spectacular trials against Trotskyists and other political dissenters in the Soviet Union who had confessed to terrible crimes of disloyalty and then were forced to name their associates to further consolidate the authority of the regime, the CPUSA's claim to be an advocate of civil liberties appeared disingenuous to the liberals with whom it had come into such conflict during defense cases in the 1920s and 1930s. Defining themselves as the vanguard of American patriotism during the Second World War, communists had shared opposition not only to Nazis, but also to other socialists whom they described as subversive, fifth-column threats to the nation and the war effort. Similarly, they obliged the prosecution of Black draft resisters and the imprisonment of Japanese Americans in internment camps and kicked Black nationalists, Japanese activists, and gays and lesbians out of the party as security risks and betrayers of the working class.

Thus, when the forces of reaction attacked the CPUSA in the post–World War Two era, their primary rhetorical response was not to a class analysis of power, but to the progressive vision of a multiethnic America born in the liberal wing of the Sacco and Vanzetti defense campaign. Since the 1920s, liberals and the radical right had struggled over the definition of American cultural identity. In 1938, two years after the American far right began to reorganize under the influence of European fascism,[144] the arch-conservative senators John Rankin of Mississippi and Martin Dies of Texas led HUAC to attack the New Deal under the name of rooting out subversion by naming communists inside the government. While HUAC claimed to stamp out communism, it seems clear from the committee's own rhetoric that it was attacking the definition of multiethnic American-ism that the progressive–labor alliance of the 1920s had championed. The Communist Party had promoted this same version of Americanism in its efforts to build the Congress of Industrial Organizations (CIO), promote social-welfare legislation, and act against segregation and lynching in the Deep South.[145] Where the popular-front communists and their liberal allies saw a united movement of immigrant workers and Blacks to cre-ate unions and a social democracy through a labor–government alliance, Dies imagined Mongol hordes at Red Square preparing to send a "Trojan Horse" to America to destroy its national integrity.[146]

By attacking the New Deal and multiethnic coalition as an Oriental, slavish tool of Stalin, himself the reincarnation of the "demon soul of Genghis Khan,"[147] the American far right tried to disassociate American nativism and racism from the now "anti-American" taboo of fascism. Indi-cating the importance of racial identity to the Dies Committee's concept of Americanism, the committee defined the KKK as an "American" orga-nization rather than as a subversive group because it had its origins in-side the United States and had established a long tradition.[148] Given such claims, it is not surprising that communists and many liberals believed by the 1950s that the right wing in America had formed a new "popular front" with fascism against the New Deal and all its goals. As Elizabeth Gurley Flynn argued, the Dies Committee and other anticommunists were calling for a return to the 100 percent Americanism championed by the American Legion and the KKK in the 1920s. Communists called it a fascist popular front.[149]

Throughout the war, the ILD described fascists as a fifth-column threat to the internal stability of the United States and argued that the Com-munist Party's goal was to preserve the rights of immigrants and workers "of the wrong color" against fascist reaction. Rather than being a revo-

lutionary organization that challenged the legal apparatus of the United States, the ILD had become a very effective progressive organization that combined expert legal work with mass pressure to help white and Black workers in the courts.

The ILD's defense of constitutional rights of free speech, campaigns against lynching, and descriptions of prisons were important foundations for civil-rights activists in the 1950s and 1960s. The ILD described bad prison conditions and chain gangs in the South based on correspondence from the Scottsboro Boys and Angelo Herndon. Communists did pioneering work fighting prison segregation, particularly in the landmark legal struggles when Ben Davis and Angelo Herndon exposed racism in prisons in the 1930s and 1950s. As the ILD's founders had argued back in 1928, struggles for individuals were meant to be stepping stones into more general activism dealing with issues of criminal justice. As the ILD activist Sasha Small urged her readers, the point was not just to "free Herndon . . . but [to] become active about chain gangs." In their daily correspondence with prisoners, prisoner-relief activists fought convict labor, opened prisons to radical newspapers, and conducted direct aid with families of prisoners, in many cases bringing families into political action and, generally, according to Small, "let jailers know they were under constant surveillance."[150]

The beginning of the Cold War led to a left turn in Communist Party policies, particularly in terms of race and imperialism. At the war's end and with the revolt by Black activists against "Browderism" in the Communist Party in the late 1940s, activists in the party again connected the Southern "KKK spirit" with the U.S. racism, which they frequently described as "fascist."[151] After the United States abandoned its wartime alliance with the USSR, the ILD dissolved and merged with the National Negro Congress to form the Civil Rights Congress. In the late 1940s, the Communist Party adopted the position that the United States was on the road to fascist takeover and called for mass defense as a supplement to legal action in cases for Black civil rights. "Dixiecrats and planners of concentration camps," wrote William Patterson, leader of the CRC, "can be stopped by democratic action but they will not voluntarily end their terror. They are not to be persuaded of the error of their ways by arguments alone. Those who would save democracy must mobilize and unite and formulate a militant democratic program of action if they would unite and really win the battle for freedom."[152]

The communists' vigilance toward American jails, courts, and police, joined with a growing class of Black radical leaders, was essential to the

growth of Black resistance in the South and in Northern cities during the 1940s and 1950s. After 1945, the Communist Party's anti-police brutality, anti-jail, and anti-death penalty campaigns drew on strong defense work with Black activists in the South and in Harlem—and, like previous Black radical organizations, it identified racial violence along a police–mob continuum. Local organizing campaigns that put police on the defensive continued throughout the 1950s, bringing white and Black activists together against police brutality and racist trials in countless campaigns in California, Harlem, Detroit, and the South.[153] These ties, formed by National Lawyers Guild lawyers and CRC activists, would contribute significantly to early urban civil-rights activism in the anti-prison movements of the 1970s and to the Black Panther Party's legal defense in California, where Charles Garry, a former lawyer for the California Longshoreman's union and a veteran of the ILD and National Lawyers Guild, would adapt the methods of the ILD for Huey Newton's trial. Black Communists would play a critical role in the Soledad Brothers Defense Committee and would later form the National Alliance against Racist and Political Repression.[154]

Continuing the basic policies of the ILD as a mass-based organization in the postwar era, the CRC leadership continued to promote mass organizing, commenting in 1952 that "legal action alone can never go over to the offensive in the fight to preserve the people's interests."[155] The people were to be won for long-term participation in the struggle; they were not simply to be "used" for demonstrations but encouraged to join the CRC and later, perhaps, other political organizations, making political participation into a front line of defense against persecution. People who began as defense organizers soon went on to other forms of activism. For example, Black communist women and the wives and sisters of Black men defended in anti-lynching and anti-death-penalty campaigns formed the backbone of the early feminist group the Sojourners, which organized the first anti-rape speak-out (by Black women) in the 1950s.[156]

However, while they defined these battles of the 1940s and 1950s as part of a conflict between fascism and Americanism, communists did not defend communism. They were thus left in the odd position of being incapable of doing the one thing that had characterized the entire history of radical defense: making dramatic speeches in the name of their movement and using their trials to critique the dominant ideological frameworks of their time. As if they were only defending liberalism, and not communism, the Communist Party members on trial constantly pointed to an imminent hostile fascist takeover of the U.S. government by some

alien force rather than addressing what was actually happening. For example, communists tried to make headway with liberals by arguing that participating in the defense of Julius and Ethel Rosenberg was "not communism, it is democracy against fascism."[157] The argument that the defense of radicalism was impossible because of the context of the times neglects the history of revolutionary socialists who braved execution and prison to defend their ideas in previous eras.

When describing fascism, most popular literature by communists in the 1950s characterized it as mob hysteria. Communist Party writers described the battles of "McCarthyism versus Americanism" in the pages of the *Daily Worker* every day. These descriptions were far milder than those of the late 1920s, when Elizabeth Gurley Flynn had denounced the courts as "dignified tailors who drape the vicious persecution of an oppressed class with legal finery."[158]

Legal finery itself did not carry the negative connotations that it had during the militant years of the ILD. While earlier defense activists had once preached against "legalism" and distrusted lawyers as middle-class lackeys who thwarted mass energy, the CRC championed progressive lawyers. In one pamphlet explaining why party members should contribute to the defense of the party's lawyers when they were charged with subversion in 1952, the party contradicted its earlier analysis of worker action in the court and argued, "Our system of justice is much too complicated" to allow legal defense to fall to the workers themselves in absence of a lawyer.[159]

The CPUSA's abandonment of revolutionary politics was explicit in its responses to the Smith Act prosecutions in the 1950s. In her 1951 history of the Smith Act, Elizabeth Gurley Flynn, who had been thrown out of the ACLU in 1940 because of her communist sympathies, argued that the Smith Act had not directly attacked civil liberties but, instead, had made a "sneak attack on the Bill of Rights."[160] In three particularly interesting moments, Communist Party members explained that they were not revolutionaries and that the Smith Act just did not apply to them. In May 1951, Elizabeth Gurley Flynn commented on the unfairness involved in dragging up documents from 1919 to attack the Communist Party of the 1950s. The party of 1919, she explained, "Was a lusty newborn infant. The Communist Party of 1951 is a mature, balanced, responsible organization. It's no more the identical party than a 32 year old man or woman of today is the infant that gurgled in 1919. The party has changed, learned from experience. . . . It has shed infantile leftism, it has coped with adventurism and opportunism in its ranks."[161]

A little more than a year later, Herbert Aptheker made a similar point, arguing that communists should be honored and respected as good citizens. Communism, he told the anticommunist McCarran Commission, was the most law-and-order ideology around, having been "born in the nineteenth century in struggles against Anarchist and Terrorist doctrines of Bakunin, Most, Blanqui and Sorel."[162]

Even after they had repudiated "Browderist" revisions of Marxism, the communists' most fervent goal during the 1950s was not to cancel the Smith Act entirely, but to "knock out" the membership clause, leaving only the charge of fomenting violence and subversion as legitimate reasons for imprisonment. Rather than arguing that the advocacy of revolution was legitimate free speech, as they had in the cases of Benjamin Gitlow and Angelo Herndon, the McCarthy-era communists said that there was simply no way that they could be found guilty of advocating revolution because they were not revolutionaries. The Smith Act defense committee's own bulletin stated, "It would be strange indeed if the Communist Party should be found to be an 'action inciting' organization."[163] Steve Nelson did not want to defend revolution, either, and argued with one of his major character witnesses, Herbert Aptheker:

> I wanted to make the point that we did not favor force but preferred to reach our goal by democratic means. Herb was afraid he would be distorting the classical formulations. I said, "Look, I'm on trial, we're not writing the program of the Communist Party with the jury. We're trying to win the case without compromising on principles."[164]

Later on, Nelson's emphasis on social-democratic and parliamentary politics held firm. He argued about the trials that "we made it far too easy for the right wing to focus exclusively on the rhetoric of revolutionary violence." As the appeals wore on, Nelson relates, "Rob Minor kept urging me to have confidence in American democracy despite its nightmarish appearance."[165]

In 1948, Elizabeth Gurley Flynn was struck by the lackluster efforts of the party in the defense of its leadership after members of the Communist Party's central committee were arrested and charged under the Smith Act with conspiring to overthrow the government of the United States by force and violence. Shortly after twelve CPUSA leaders had been arrested under the Smith Act and charged with membership in a subversive organization, Flynn, the party's staunchest civil libertarian, told her fellow leaders that she was "frankly surprised" by their reaction to the trials. "This is our party," she said. "These are our leaders. No one else will

defend them unless we do. It cannot be left to specialists in defense who are very scarce today."[166] Some in the party were reluctant to get involved with defense work. According to William Z. Foster, defense organizing had "led to the collapse of the i.w.w." and should be avoided.[167]

When the popular Communist Party defense campaigns did begin, they emphasized the normal character of the families of party members. Even as Julius and Ethel Rosenberg sweated in prison, women wrote to the *Daily Worker* during a feminist renaissance in the Old Left, demanding attention to "housewives who work" and other issues facing working-class women.[168] Although the Communist Party had gone through a radical rethinking of the "woman question" and the role of domesticity in the late 1940s, when the red-baiting era began, communists demonstrated their similarity to other "regular people" during defense campaigns by appealing to domesticity.[169]

Rather than describing masses of union members or workers of the world coming together around them in a fraternity of struggle, the communists of the 1950s—in the Rosenberg case, as in others—described how *families* were the base of the movement. The Smith Act defendants also organized a "families committee," making private and personal ties the most important bonds of solidarity in their most public self-representations. "FBI Takes Vengeance on Mother of 8 Year Old Child!" one headline announced in 1953.[170] Defense-committee pamphlets for several different communists emphasized family ties. "They are family men with at least twelve young children dependent on them," Elizabeth Gurley Flynn said about the twelve leaders of the Communist Party who had been jailed under the Smith Act.[171] When Peggy Wellman was threatened with deportation, a pamphlet appeared with a family portrait and the caption, "This is the family the government is trying to destroy—Why?"[172] In story after story, articles exposed the Cold War government as betraying American domestic life by invading, spying on, and destroying American families. An attack by Albert Kahn on the Smith Act in 1951 paid special attention to the harm done to families by the Red hunts:

> More than 60 homes in New York, San Francisco, Los Angeles, Baltimore, Cleveland, Pittsburgh, Philadelphia and Hawaii have been invaded in the past two months. Over fifty children have had their fathers or mothers, and in some cases both, taken from them and now live with the knowledge that their homes are threatened.[173]

The "normal" part of the family cannot be overemphasized. Because of the increasing pressure on communists as "anti-Americans" in the postwar

years, the Communist Party was vigilant about maintaining domestic conformity. Each local organization had a review commission that could be used either by an individual to file a grievance against another member or by the group to "protect the organization from any alien elements who may enter to disrupt or hurt the organization in any other manner." Charges could be brought for any of the following crimes:

> Bureaucratism, white chauvinism, breach of democratic process, violations of party discipline, male chauvinism, strike-breaking, financial irregularity, immoralities, drunkenness, quarrelsomeness, favoritism, violations of constitutional principles and program of the party, factionalism, stoolpigeoning within the party or other organization, refusal to carry out assignments, and all other kinds of conduct generally recognized as unbecoming a member of the party inside or outside the organization and the labor movement as a whole.

> Also for security—to prevent people who had been expelled from entering the party in other cities—the names of a few categories of people were published as "enemies" in the party's press. They included "spies, provocateurs, political adventurers, factionalists, absconders of funds, sex perverts and similar elements."[174]

The Rosenbergs

The democracy–fascism division dominated the defense campaign in one of the most dramatic and terrifying political prosecutions in American history: the execution of Julius and Ethel Rosenberg, two Jewish communists from the Lower East Side. The Rosenbergs were executed for "stealing the secret of the atom bomb" on June 19, 1953. This event preceded another dramatic incident in the history of the CPUSA. Three years after Ethel and Julius Rosenberg were executed, Nikita Khrushchev announced to the communists of the world that Stalin had for a long time been killing loyal Russian citizens and political dissidents, falsely accusing them of being traitors. We do not know what political direction the Rosenbergs would have taken in later years, had they lived. They were not alive in 1956 to hear the devastating revelation that "terror was actually directed not at the remnants of the defeated exploiting classes but against the honest workers of the party and of the Soviet state; against them were made lying, slanderous and absurd accusations, concerning 'two-facedness' 'espionage,' 'sabotage,' preparation of fictitious plots, etc."[175]

Part of the continuing importance of the Rosenbergs as symbols of American communism may stem from the fact that their prosecution preceded the revelations about the Soviet party that devastated the party's ranks. The Rosenbergs represent the innocence of American Stalinists. They also stood for a Communist Party in which race became at least as important in class. William Patterson argued that the CRC should "fight anti-Semitism as an anti-racist ideal, because where you find an anti-Semite you find an enemy of the Negro people, labor and the foreign born, and usually an aggressive war-monger—and vice versa."[176]

While Jewish identity was central to the Rosenbergs' defense, class warfare was barely mentioned. The Rosenberg defense campaign depicted the couple as victimized innocents, an anonymous Jewish couple in the hands of a hysterical anti-American conspiracy that had somehow grabbed the reigns of government after Roosevelt's death and the end of the war. Instead of defining the Rosenbergs as martyrs for communism and class struggle, the defense campaign made them heroes of liberal multiracial Americanism so that the ultimate revelations about the Rosenbergs in the 1990s were shocking and terrible to some of their own champions.[177]

Initially, there was no political defense at all for the Rosenbergs. Ethel Rosenberg was arrested after she testified to a grand jury about her husband on August 16, 1950. No story covering Julius's arrest or Ethel's grand jury testimony appeared in the *Daily Worker*. The *Daily Worker* did discuss Soviet heroism, however, and on the day of Ethel Rosenberg's testimony, an editorial by William Z. Foster mentioned the heroism of the Russian people as a model for communist Americans to follow. "Communists in the Soviet Union have passed through a thousand crises that try men's souls and have faced innumerable Valley Forges," he wrote. They had "set an example of sheer courage and unbreakable fighting spirit." To brave the period now ensuing in the United States, American communists would need "an ample supply of grit."[178]

Instead of arguing a government frame-up against his clients, as he might have done in another time, the Rosenbergs' lawyer, Emanuel Bloch, presented the case as a purely interpersonal conflict between the Rosenbergs and the Greenglass family and referred to it as a "routine 5th amendment case" in its initial stages when he discussed the case with Jack Aronson and Cedric Belfrage, editors of the *National Guardian*.[179] The Greenglasses, Bloch argued, were the real communist spies, while Julius and Ethel were simply innocent idealists caught in their net. Thanking the prosecutors and judges profusely, Bloch's closing argument indicted the other couple of the crimes of spying—and of communism.[180]

The CP's first reaction to the Rosenberg trial was a defense of the party, not the Rosenbergs. Shortly before the sentencing, the *Daily Worker* declared that the trial had happened "to foment the pretense that espionage and the political platform of the Communist Party have something in common. "[181] The paper reminded its readers that the Rosenberg trial would have a negative effect on other legal proceedings involving the leadership of the Communist Party. After the death sentence was passed, the CPUSA, along with liberal activists, argued for the commutation of the sentence. The *Daily Worker* quoted the anticommunist *Jewish Daily Forward*'s response that the sentence had been "horrible" and "cruel" and called it a "pogrom tactic," reiterating that "it is a lie that the CP encourages espionage. "[182]

During the early period following the sentence, not everyone trying to save the couple argued that the Rosenbergs were completely innocent. The first campaign to save the Rosenbergs was merely a plea for clemency in sentencing based on the notion that the sentence was cruel and unusual in the history of espionage prosecutions. The first person to be caught in the investigation of the KGB's spies in the Manhattan Project, Klaus Fuchs, had actually confessed to trading atomic secrets, but because he was arrested in England, he was jailed rather than executed. He finally got out of prison and went on to live in East Germany as a respected citizen. Thus, for most of the Rosenbergs' first defenders, the issue at hand was not the conviction, but the sentence.

The communists noted that spies and traitors who allied with Germany and Japan, or former Nazis from those countries, had either received light sentences or were pardoned entirely. One of the most powerful arguments by the Rosenbergs' defenders was to note the preferential treatment given former Nazis over communists at the beginning of the Cold War, both in the United States and in postwar Germany. Far from naive or sentimental, the defenders argued about the realpolitik involved in both the prosecution and the sentence. The *Guardian* writer William Reuben's *The Atom Spy Hoax* suggested that the search for a scapegoat for the Soviet Union's development of atomic technology in 1949 was primarily a propaganda strategy to resuscitate the reputation of the United States as a world power.[183]

The defense was far from programmatic. In New York, several local groups, all with differing positions on the guilt and innocence of the Rosenbergs, formed to oppose the death sentence and demanded either clemency or a new trial.[184] The journalist Carl Bernstein has described his mother's setting up a local Rosenberg committee with a friend in Wash-

ington, D.C., even after her Communist Party local had ceased to exist because of fears of anticommunist persecution.[185] That ad hoc committee was emblematic of the Rosenberg defense. In their book on the history of the *National Guardian*, Cedric Belfrage and Jack Aronson described receiving contributions for the Rosenberg defense soon after the publication of William Reuben's story "The Rosenbergs: An American Dreyfus Case?"—before any defense committee existed.[186]

The ILD had done its job. Communists were by now familiar with the stories of "frame-ups." They had read of Sacco and Vanzetti, Tom Mooney, Scottsboro, and the Haymarket affair year after year. Maxwell Anderson, who had already written two plays about Sacco and Vanzetti, wrote a film showing the unfairness of the justice system called *The Wrong Man*. Ben Hecht's stage play *The Front Page*, based loosely on Leon Czolgosz's assassination of President McKinley, and the 1930s adaptation of it, *His Girl Friday*, starring Carey Grant and Rosalind Russell, made the "frame-up" into part of mass cultural consciousness. "It is a curious thing," John Wexley wrote, "that we can see the subject of frame-up used as the prevailing theme in popular fiction, in the movies and over radio and television but we refuse to recognize it when we see it in real life. . . . The common charge is to view the flat charge of frame-up as too pat an explanation."[187]

As the mass defense campaign assembled around the *National Guardian*, the dominant argument ultimately became that the Rosenbergs were innocent—and not only were they innocent, but they were "ordinary people." In the words of the National Committee to Secure Justice for the Rosenbergs and Morton Sobell (NCSJR), "We cannot have two kinds of justice in this country, one for convicted Nazi traitors who received ten year sentences and another for ordinary people like the Rosenbergs."[188] The Rosenberg defense committee was composed primarily of progressive Jews who were not necessarily affiliated with the Communist Party. The Communist Party became involved in the campaign only after the national movement had gained considerable momentum. Although the prosecution was denounced as political, the descriptions of the Rosenbergs depoliticized the couple—Ethel, in particular—to demonstrate their normalcy.

In 1952, for example, a group of "wives and mothers" wrote a letter to Ethel Rosenberg in which they declared: "We want you to know that we believe in your innocence. We are determined in the long months ahead that while your innocence is established that a more humane relationship shall be arranged for you and your children. We take deep pride as women

and as mothers in your inspiring courage and strength in spite of death house solitude."[189]

By dramatizing the ordinariness of the Rosenbergs, the people defending the remains of the popular front also defended the popular front's "Americanism." Although some basic strategic imperatives were involved in the Rosenbergs' legal defense, the insistence on their Americanism and normalcy hinted at the ideological core of the latter half of the popular-front left.

The Private Lives of Regular People

Virginia Gardner's *Rosenberg Story* places the Rosenbergs in the daily life of New York's Lower East Side, experiencing small degrees of upward mobility, ethnic assimilation, and the growth of socialist sympathies in the midst of settlement houses, Hebrew schools, and political lectures. Ethel Rosenberg showed her innocence by not being a serious political activist. As a young, ambitious girl, she became interested in politics, to the surprise of a more serious and committed friend. The Rosenbergs' political commitments, as Gardner saw it—and as their early defense campaign put forth—were emotional, an expression of love for each other and for others. They joined organizations out of a desire to "help people."

The Rosenbergs, whose most enduring literary monument is the series of letters they wrote to each other and to their children while in jail, saw themselves, and wanted to be seen, as family people. The people they spoke to were their sons and their friends, not their comrades, their fellow Soviets, or even any union members with whom they had fraternal ties of shop-floor loyalty. They represented a Jewish progressive community that idealized the nuclear family as a bulwark against fascism. They were modest—reformers, not revolutionaries. They were, as Elizabeth Gurley Flynn had described the CPUSA of the popular-front era, mature. They were parents who from their jail cells wrote letters to each other about their children's welfare and the state of their family business. As Julius Rosenberg put it, "I am just a plain, ordinary guy and I don't profess to be anything extraordinary or special. I feel my greatest accomplishment is being a successful father to my two boys."[190]

The Rosenbergs also became symbols of Jewish progressive life. They were "two Eastside parents." The Black poet Beulah Richardson compared them to the revolutionary nationalist Macabees.[191] The Rosenberg committee sought support from rabbis and Christian clergymen, all of

whom opposed the death sentences, regardless of the pair's guilt or innocence. Meetings held throughout New York emphasized the need for "clemency" and, with the Jewish leaders from many anticommunist newspapers, the committee opposed the execution as a barbaric excess, particularly in the wake of the Holocaust.[192] "When we heard that Julius and Ethel Rosenberg were sentenced to death, a shudder passed through all of us. . . . We are certain that every Jew who read this sad news felt this way. From our hearts came the words, 'death sentence, too horrible.' . . . Every Jewish home will be shattered by this tragedy."[193] However, for some, the accusation of the prosecution's anti-Semitism rang hollow. After the execution of eleven Jewish Communist Party officials in Czechoslovakia in the middle of the Rosenberg defense efforts, it was hard not to notice the contradiction within the Communist Party's statements. In December 1952, days before a delegation visited the Rosenbergs in prison, the *Daily Worker* announced, "11 Confessed Czechoslovak Traitors Hanged." These former leaders of the Czech secret police and ministers in the Czech government were mostly Jewish and were considered criminal because of their sympathies with Zionism. Thus, anticommunist Jews had a convincing argument when they claimed that the Soviet Union's attack on the Rosenberg execution as anti-Semitic was merely a tactic intended to deflect international attention from the Soviets' actions in Europe.[194]

The Rosenbergs Defend Themselves

In their own defense in court, the Rosenbergs presented themselves as progressives who were opposed to the "Hitler Beast." In their letters from prison, they described their political beliefs as based on their love for their fellow men, their loyalty to each other. The exchanges of words of longing and separation presented their living, ordinary desires as the primary energy that endangered the fascist persecutors who wanted to destroy them. This prison correspondence, more than any other aspect of the Rosenberg defense, maintained the traditional leftist defense campaign's critique of the state as a tool that coldly separates families and destroys human relationships.

But while the Rosenbergs denounced their own imprisonment, they did not argue that this was the punishment meted out to the working class. They did not have much to say about the "ruling class" and the "working class," or about the prison as an institution. Instead, they denounced the "jackals of hysterical reaction" whom they saw as responsible for their

sentencing. They did not denounce the prison or the justice system itself as a class institution and rarely complained about or analyzed the conditions there. Julius Rosenberg even entertained his son with a story of boss-robbing outlaws being brought to justice by cowboy heroes who then heroically saved their bosses.[195]

Unlike political defenses that used the moment of a trial to expound on the political views of the accused, the Rosenberg defense committee sought to mitigate the political views of the defendants, stressing the ideological nature of the prosecution by presenting the Rosenbergs as politically neutral humanitarians and progressives. The Rosenberg defense, like Cold War liberalism, defined ideology as "bad" and said that only the prosecutors, not the defendants, displayed it.

When the Rosenbergs' defense committee was charged with communist subversion in 1957, the married women who were called before the Senate criticized the senators for taking them away from their homes. Those who announced their occupations as "housewife" spent the least time of all those called during the hearing on the stand, because, like Mildred Rothenberg, they were able to make the committee look truly evil. Complaining that their trips to the Senate had taken them away from their homes and children, where, they told the senators, they "should be right now," Sylvia Freedland, a mother of three, and Adelaid Riskin were questioned very briefly, and then dismissed.

The Communist Party's critiques of the McCarthyites were accurate. The government did destroy families. The only reason to arrest Ethel Rosenberg at all was to use her as a "lever" to make her husband confess.[196] Not only did the government orphan the Rosenbergs' sons Michael and Robby, but they even pursued the boys after their parents were killed, threatening to remove them from the left-wing community to reorient them to proper citizenship.[197] It was also a family betrayal that brought the Rosenbergs into court. Julius Rosenberg brought Ethel's brother David Greenglass into his spy network in the last year of the war. Greenglass informed on Julius to protect his wife, Ruth, who lied about Ethel to protect herself.[198]

However, as the Rosenbergs provided the model of heroism for 1950s communists, not defying the courts openly but quietly facing death to defend their ideals, the representation of Ethel Rosenberg primarily as a housewife neglected the struggles of women to stay in the industrial labor force during the 1950s. Virginia Gardner portrayed Julius Rosenberg as a sentimental and emotionally vulnerable family man. Gardner described Julius as breaking down in prison when his mother visited, crying out:

"Momma I don't feel good. . . . Oh Momma where is my wife! Where are my children? I am sick. If only I were home you and my wife Ethel would take care of me."[199] Similarly, in one of the letters published during the wait before the execution, Ethel Rosenberg described her "pale and wan" husband. In his letters to her, Julius expressed sincere loneliness and longing. More intimate letters were suppressed, however; one that declared, "Who ever invented celibacy should be shot!" was excluded from the couple's published correspondence.[200] American communist representations of heroism during the popular-front era centered on respectable images of unity and family togetherness and drew a picture of McCarthy's victims as ordinary working-class families who worked for the simple causes of survival, community, and togetherness, in opposition to the stresses of unemployment, war, and, finally, government repression.

The broad front for the Rosenbergs was not divisive at all. Those involved in the case argued that it should be fought "on a broad, non-sectarian united front basis, presented in human terms and never in words that would alienate those shocked at the barbaric death sentence."[201] In his memorial speech to the Rosenbergs on June 19, 1974, Reverend Amos Barstow recalled that the old committee had been successful, and would continue to be successful, because "love" was the motivating factor in the campaign: love that allowed the forces advocating a new trial and those advocating clemency to work together; love that allowed communists to talk to anti-Rosenberg hysterics and win them over; love that could be represented by the ability of the organizer to thank a governor for governing. Insistence on one's own ideological view, Barstow argued, was a symptom of "liberalism."[202]

Emily and David Alman, both of whom worked as social workers within the criminal-justice system, were central to the founding of the NCSJR. They had lived in the same neighborhood as the Rosenbergs, Knickerbocker Village on Manhattan's Lower East Side, but they did not actually know them.[203] When HUAC accused David Alman and the Rosenberg committee of the attempt to "dishonor the United States," Alman responded,

> That is a terrible mis-statement. We were concerned with the honor and integrity of our country. An injustice had been done by people who we felt were unscrupulously using the courts to fulfill their own political or private ambitions. I don't regard the case as an imperfection in the justice system, I regard the error made in the courts as an imperfection in the behavior of some individuals who were connected with the attorney general's office.[204]

Even if they defended the ordinariness of the Rosenbergs, the couple's supporters attempted to redefine political action as ordinary and good. In doing so, they developed a powerful critique of the passive consumer culture of the 1950s. "As you quietly draw the curtain on the day's activity / and reclining / contemplate the fertile promise of unborn time," wrote Edith Segal, urging her readers to fear the coming fascist storm, "WILL THEY KILL YOU WHILE YOU SLEEP IF YOU SLEEP WHILE THEY KILL US?"[205] Ann Rivington, who in the 1930s had promoted domesticity in peace propaganda for women, now remarked,

> Listen
> You who walk unhindered on the streets
> Do you think you can live if these two die
> Julius and Ethel Rosenberg
> You who go to work on the bus each morning
> who drink beer at your kitchen table on Saturday night
> —or watch TV
> Who tuck your children in bed with a song
> Do you think you are free?[206]

In their letters and poems to the *Daily Worker* and the *Masses and Mainstream*, progressives and communists who defended the Rosenbergs defended Americanism as active participation in political life, in contradiction to the apolitical, privatized consumer culture of the 1950s. "Freedom's not something you carve from a hillside / Or build on a plain with a spire to the sky / Freedom's a letter you write to the president / telling him firmly these two must not die," Matthew Hall's poem "Personal" explained to the addled Americans of the day.[207] Another poem warned readers about the lies of the American media, to the tune of a song straight out of the hit parade: "Don't let the stars get in your eyes, don't let the moon break your heart / not if the stars are glassy lies, spit like poisoned fire flies / saying the Rosenbergs are spies."[208] Twenty years later, the Rosenbergs' supporters continued to ask, "Will America survive, or die?"[209] The preservation of an America where political activism was possible was the issue at stake for those at the grassroots level who came to the defense of the Rosenbergs. Communist Party activists, in defending their right to civic participation, argued for the basic commitment to participatory democracy and the freedom of speech as inherently American values, as the self-presentations by the Rosenbergs' defenders before HUAC in May 1957 demonstrated. As they were called before the Senate, numerous members of the Rosenberg defense committee were attacked

in predictable ways. The senators told them that they "didn't give a hoot about the Rosenbergs, and never gave a hoot about any of the individuals whom they allegedly supported" but merely used these campaigns to recruit followers.[210]

Such accusations distorted the concept of mass defense, and the respondents met them with testaments to their individual interest in the couple. Faced with the accusation that he "had as much interest in the Rosenbergs as the man in the moon," Dan Rothenberg let out an outraged, "How dare you impugn my motives?" As he was questioned further about his activities in the case, Rothenberg wondered aloud, "I don't know how many other aspects of the constitution you are going to take care of in one afternoon."[211] Phillip Koritz also showed his familiarity with the principle of labor defense that the jailed man is often a hero rather than an outlaw. He had spent much of 1948 on a chain gang in the South because of his participation in a strike, he told the committee. He went on to say that he had supported the strikers, and the Rosenbergs, because, "Ever since I was in high school, you know, educated in high school under the great traditions of our country, I have been interested in civil rights of myself and all people. I have done as much as I possibly could, under the circumstances to fight for and promote and advance civil and democratic rights."[212]

Suggesting that popular-front communists, such as IWW members, saw those in jails as allies in class struggle, Koritz also embraced the criminal's code of class loyalty and told the committee that he had learned "in jail that [informers] are the worst sort of people." For that reason, he said, he refused to name any names. Instead of referring to his former prison comrades as his source of moral authority, John Gilman, another member of the Rosenberg defense committee, turned to popular culture and remarked that he would not inform because he had learned about the evil of "stoolpigeons" as characters from "cowboy and Indian movies."[213] Bringing up another symbol of Americanism, Emily and David Alman, the chairs of the committee, who had retired from their jobs presumably because of the blacklisting of Red sympathizers, when asked their occupations, remarked, "presently we are farmers."[214]

The Rosenbergs' defenders described their enemies as a cabal against Americanism. The illustration by Hugo Gellert showing the Statue of Liberty in the electric chair and the clemency campaign that featured letters begging President Dwight Eisenhower and President Harry Truman to intervene continued to express the idea that Americanism and fascism were diametrical opposites. When Julius and Ethel Rosenberg's *Death*

House Letters was published, it included a plea for clemency that praised the history of American justice, claiming, "It is in the interest of the United States not to depart from its heritage of open-heartedness and its ideals of equality before the law by stooping to a vengeful and savage creed."[215]

While the Rosenberg defense and Smith Act cases offered an ideal of progressive multicultural Americanism in contrast to the far right's 100 percent Americanism displayed in the McCarthy campaign, they did not until the very end make a revolutionary critique of the American state. As a party, the communists argued that they were Americans, and not only that, but the best Americans, the vanguard of Americanism.[216] The Rosenberg defense was, indeed, as many activists argued, similar to the Sacco and Vanzetti agitation. It was an attempt to promote the rule of law and presented immigrants and African Americans as the "real" America whose ethnic differences should be considered valuable in the nation's political and cultural life. The Rosenbergs' Jewishness, like Sacco and Vanzetti's Italianness, was symbolic of the multicultural ethic of the New Deal–era progressivism, and the prosecution of the Rosenbergs was defined not in class terms, but in racial ones, as anti-Semitism. The party and its adherents cast themselves as the voices of law, modernism, and multiculturalism against racist mob hysteria, nearly replicating progressive liberal antiracist arguments of the 1920s.

Thus, despite the nightmare scenarios of revolutionary conspiracies described by the American anticommunists in the late 1940s and 1950s, the growth of the Soviet state served to replace revolutionary socialism with liberal multiculturalism at the center of the American left. The turning of the radical defense campaign into the liberal progressive one was part of a larger pattern. The Spanish independent communist Fernando Claudin has argued that, had the Soviets taken a different position during World War Two, they could have encouraged socialist revolutions in France and Italy. He explains: "From the point of view of the international aims of the war, the Soviet leaders did not add a comma to the aims proclaimed by the Allied capitalist powers, national liberation for the peoples of Europe and democracy."[217]

The Rosenbergs' Execution

If the communists had become like the liberals of the Sacco and Vanzetti defense, the liberals had become something worse. As Andrew Ross points out in "Reading the Rosenberg Letters,"[218] the *New Republic*, which later

would become the central liberal journal arguing for the Rosenbergs' guilt, had taken this position from the beginning of the agitation, referring to the communist uproar about the case "nonsense." "The Rosenbergs are guilty," announced the *New Republic* on the day of the execution. "They have had two years to exhaust every resource."[219] Continuing with a familiar accusation, the magazine insisted that the Rosenbergs were "willing to be martyrs" and that the communists "secretly prefer it that way." The *Nation* was the liberal journal that favored the Rosenbergs and placed the execution in the context of Europe, saying that "a moral gulf" would open between the United States and Europe if the Rosenbergs were executed.[220]

Although it was very similar in its opposition to nativist hysteria, the Rosenberg defense was starkly different from the Sacco and Vanzetti defense when it came to theories of class. The Rosenberg defense's anti-fascism emphasized ethnic identity rather than class. Few of the appeals made reference to the working class, and the workers' struggle, instead of being especially heroic, was described as ordinary and unthreatening. People were called out to demonstrations not as "fellow workers," but as fellow Jews. Rather than addressing people through workplace alliances, appeals were made to neighbors, families, and fellow people of decent values.

Public appeals and middle-class avenues of political action were the most prominent defense strategies. There was no critique of legalism or lawyers, and no refusal to bow, scrape, and beg for mercy, no search for the most radical point at which to move the people to free the Rosenbergs. There were no advocates of bomb throwing or general strikes, even in the last days of the Rosenberg defense movement. In early 1953, George Morris, a columnist at the *Daily Worker*, wondered why the leaders of labor were "still timid" in speaking out against the case while one thousand five hundred clergymen had signed an appeal for clemency. Although the anti-labor and anti-Rosenberg forces were one and the same, Morris argued, labor (from which communists had long been purged) had yet to distinguish itself at the vanguard of the Rosenberg struggle.[221] After the Rosenbergs had been executed, the role of labor was only a might-have-been. "Victory could have been the result if the labor movement had supported the struggle," Morris argued, also stating that, despite the execution, the popular outrage generated by the case was a victory for the people. Noting the complicity of the national labor leadership with U.S. foreign policy, Morris theorized that the government would ultimately betray labor in the sphere of domestic policy, despite this temporary Cold War allegiance.[222]

But the CPUSA, until the Cold War, had gone along with that policy. As Cedric Belfrage argued, the Soviet Union and the United States were each other's mirror images. National loyalty was critical in a time of war, and the loyalty oaths, confession rituals, and executions were part of attempts to build national unity in both the Cold War United States and the Stalinist Soviet Union. Many American communists would become disillusioned as tanks rolled first into Hungary and later into Czechoslovakia, and many American liberals would lose their faith in American Cold War mythology after the lying and scandals of the Vietnam War. For American communists, some of that disillusionment with Americanism came earlier, during the repression of communists. When the Supreme Court met in a special session to overturn a stay of execution, facilitating the deaths of the Rosenbergs on June 19, 1953, Emanuel Bloch stood in front of the court to ask, "What kind of animals am I dealing with?"[223]

This pronouncement signaled—at least, for one man—the second rejection of both faith in American innocence and faith in the law on the American left. As American communists turned increasingly to anti-imperialism in the 1950s and 1960s, America would be defined more often as a corrupt land of slaveowners, Indian killers, and repressors of the working class than as a land of democratic promise. It was not actually a new interpretation but one that revived earlier revolutionary socialists' and Black nationalists' definitions of American law. After the killing of the Rosenbergs, W. E. B. Du Bois wrote, just as he had in 1927, that the awful decision was not new but part of a pattern—one that Black supporters of Sacco and Vanzetti had also pointed to at a similar moment years before. Of Americans, he said, "We are the murderers hurling mud / We are the witchhunters drinking blood / To us shriek five thousand Blacks / Lynched without trial. . . . Hail Hell and glory to damnation, O blood stained nation."[224] It would be from the anti-lynching movement that the next major revolutionary defense campaigns would emerge.

6

Born Guilty: George Jackson and
the Return of the Lumpen Hero

Man, the first thing a guy starts thinking about when he is busted
if he is black is, can he make a deal? Can he cop to something
lower? Because there is no possibility of him getting off completely or pushing it all off him. He's born guilty, that's the way
it is.   GEORGE JACKSON

Many literary men have often dwelt on the idea of bands. The
country was said to be infested by them. You then imagine
rough bandits united by a will to plunder, by cruelty and hatred.
... It seems hardly probable that such men can organize themselves. . . . In prison every criminal may dream of a well-knit organization, closed but strong, which would be a refuge against
the world and its morality, but this is a reverie. Prison is that fortress, the ideal cave, the bandit's retreat against which the forces
of the world beat in vain. No sooner is he in contact with them
than the criminal obeys the banal laws.
JEAN GENET, *The Thief's Journal*

Everyone I know has been hit by a cop.
JAMES S. KIENEN, *Berkeley Barb*

In the 1960s, the old revolutionary heroes of the American left returned
with a difference: Whiteness—within the left, at least—had ceased to be
the emblem of manhood. With both the Civil Rights Movement and the
upsurge of Third World liberation movements, Blackness became the primary sign of resistance, replacing the European internationalism of the

nineteenth century. After the imprisoned Black Panther George Jackson was murdered by guards at San Quentin, James Baldwin used the label "Black" to explain the position that all the world now held in relation to America:

> George remained in prison because something in him refused to accept his condition of slavery. This made him a bad example for the other slaves, because the Americans still believe that they are running a plantation, and that this plantation is now the world. In the eyes of America all of us are Black today, and if you think I am exaggerating take a look at the results.... [F]rom this point on, every corpse will be put on the bill that this civilization can never hope to pay.[1]

In the 1960s, it was whites who had to prove their revolutionary manhood. First Malcolm X recalled John Brown to life in the popular imagination with his comment that white liberals should aspire to be "John Brown liberals," thus reversing the connection of Brown, Puritanism, and über-Americanism.[2] Following similar comments about Brown by the leader of SNCC and Black Power advocate H. Rap Brown and calls for revolutionary solidarity with Black radicals by Eldridge Cleaver of the Black Panther Party, white radicals, particularly those who would become the Weather Underground, embraced John Brown as their model. In their early years, Weather Underground activists argued that the use of violence against the imperialist United States would both separate them from their own white privilege and prove their toughness, destroying the "honkiness" that had "emasculated" the CIO.[3] Prior to the rise of Weather Underground, Noel Ignatiev had urged the New Left to identify with "moralistic John Brown," who made a "greater contribution to the struggle for liberation than all the sophisticated Marxists in the pre-civil war period."[4] Brown's bearded face was blazoned across the masthead of *New Left Notes* just before the Days of Rage in Chicago, accompanying headlines from the Rolling Stones song "Street Fighting Man."[5] Although Brown may have agreed with the Weather Underground about the proper role of whites in the struggle for Black liberation, he undoubtedly would have disapproved of Mick Jagger and balked at the fact that some of the people acting in his name had also claimed the moniker of the "border ruffian" of Missouri, Jesse James.[6]

The same group that emulated John Brown also evoked the memory of the Haymarket anarchists, announcing a "declaration of war" on the Chicago police by twice blowing up the statue memorializing police officer Degan—once before the Days of Rage in October 1969, and again the following year—leading to its eventual storage at a police academy.[7] Here

the New Left demonstrated the return to the revolutionary symbolic attack on law enforcement of the Haymarket days.

The most controversial hero revived during this era was not Brown but, rather, the folkloric symbol of Black manhood, Stagolee. The un-killable ragtime hero was hidden in organized anti-lynching activism; the blues songs that evoked him, an embarrassment to the Black middle class. But Stagolee songs were sung by prisoners across the country and by poor Blacks, becoming nearly a rite of passage for young Black men. The Stagolee concept of manhood, created in juke joints, gambling dens, and houses of prostitution, made him the perfect symbol for a party that would argue that the vanguard of history was not a unified working class but a resistance movement whose ideal base was defined as the "brothers off the block." Stagolee arrived on the national stage as a political icon in the writings of Black Panther Party activists, even as he became more visible in popular culture through recordings of "Stagolee" by James Brown, the Isley Brothers, Wilson Pickett, and Bob Dylan.[8]

The Black Panther Party demonstrated continuity with an underground past not only in its evocation of this folk hero, but also in its analysis of the police and the prison as primary elements in the oppression of African Americans. The Black Panthers' activism against police and for political prisoners began to address prisons as central to the maintenance of American capitalism and, to a much greater extent than any previous group on the left, made prisoners themselves into the base of grassroots activism.

After the Second World War, unemployment reached a crisis among Blacks as wartime production ended, and white GIs returned to "white jobs," while "deindustrialization" and white flight to the suburbs began. An increasing number of primarily white police patrolled the ghettoes of America's major cities. As they turned up the pressure on unemployed Black and Latino youth, labeled "delinquents," the police had become a primary target of Black community activism.[9] In California, where the Black Panthers began, the postwar rise in Black unemployment had serious results. Between 1944 and 1969, the prison population in California increased 505 percent, with the Black population increasing from 17 percent to 28 percent of the prison's total population.[10]

While unemployment was a continuing problem, major uprisings such as the Watts Riot of 1965 were sparked by conflicts with white police. The eruptions in America's cities in 1965, 1967, and 1968 made it appear to some that the unemployed of the cities were a powder keg of revolutionary potential. In the spring of 1962, six years before he would participate in the reports on race riots by the National Advisory Commission on Civil

Disorders (also known as the Kerner Commission), James B. Conant had given what must have been an alarming address to a meeting at the California Youth Authority titled, "Social Dynamite in Our Large Cities." Noting the high unemployment among Black youth in American cities (59 percent), Conant predicted that communism would become a serious threat in the near future and recommended flooding urban ghettos with even more police.[11]

It was in this context that the Black Panther Party put the "lumpen proletariat" of America's ghettoes into the center of its political mission. Doing so put the party outside the Marxist tradition. Not only had Marx rebuked both Eugene Sue and Victor Hugo for their sentimental form of socialism that focused on the virtuous criminals in their struggles with police, but he had defined the lumpen proletariat as the shock troops of reaction during the failed French Revolution of 1848 and wrote about them negatively in a number of texts. Their class position outside the social environment of the industrial workplace, their poverty, and their contingency led them to be vulnerable to temptation from the bourgeoisie. The "rogues, prostitutes and thieves" represented the lowest level to which a proletarian could sink under the pressure of the bourgeoisie, Marx argued.[12] The lumpen proletariat, he wrote,

> in all big towns forms a mass sharply differentiated from the industrial pro-
> letariat, a recruiting ground for thieves and criminals of all kinds living on
> the crumbs of society, people without a definite trade, vagabonds, *gens sans
> feu et sans aveu* [men without hearth or home], varying according to the de-
> gree of civilization of the nation to which they belong, but never renouncing
> their *lazzaroni* [rascally] character—at the youthful age . . . thoroughly mal-
> leable, as capable of the most heroic deeds and the most exalted sacrifices as
> of the basest banditry and the foulest corruption[13]

For late-twentieth-century activists and thinkers confronting what some sociologists referred to as a racially "split labor market" and an "aristocracy of labor" produced in the unionized workers of the developed countries,[14] this category of permanently unemployed and underemployed people took on significance as the victims of empire and as an anti-imperialist vanguard. Lenin's "Imperialism, the Highest Stage of Capitalism," had presented the notion of the tendency in imperialism to "create privileged sections among the workers, and to detach them from the broad masses of the proletariat."[15] Third World Marxists took Lenin's notion as the starting point. Frantz Fanon argued further that, in the colonized world, trade unionists were trapped in "anachronistic programs" that

neglected the revolutionary potential of the peasantry and the lumpen proletariat, who "won't become reformed characters to please colonial society," and constituted the "gangrene ever present at the heart of colonial domination."[16] The Black Panthers similarly saw the lumpen proletariat as a class formed by defiance to colonial morality and applied Fanon's vision of the colonized town to the American ghetto, which they defined as an internal colony. They saw the lumpen proletariat as the vanguard also because they saw the class itself, which they defined as Black, as the product of American racism, and they defined the division within the working class as a central contradiction in American capitalism.[17] The Black Panther Party founders Huey P. Newton and Bobby Seale saw the accusation of criminality as fundamental to American racism, and both accused criminals and prisoners were a focal point in the Black Panthers' Ten Point Program, the eighth point of which demanded the release of all Blacks from America's jails: "We Want freedom for all Black men held in federal, state, county and city prisons and jails. We believe that all Black people should be released from the many jails and prisons because they have not received a fair and impartial trial."[18] Fanon had explained in *The Wretched of the Earth* that the assumption of depravity also dogged colonial subjects who lived behind a veil of distrust and viewed the laws of the society as those imposed on them by conquerors. "Confronted with a world ruled by the settler, the native is always presumed guilty," he wrote. "But the native's guilt is never a guilt that he accepts; it is rather a kind of curse, a sword of Damocles, for in his innermost spirit the native admits no accusation."[19]

Thus, instead of calling for one innocent man's freedom as a political prisoner, when Black Panthers were arrested (and they were in very large numbers), their defense campaigns ultimately led to a mass movement for prisoners' rights that, at its most radical, demanded that prisons be abolished. The Black Panther hero who brought these ideas together, and the man who would become one of the most significant martyrs of the Black Power Movement and the New Left, was George Jackson, a politicized prisoner who had been accused of killing a guard in Soledad prison following the killing of three Black prisoners by guards. As a hero, Jackson was doubly guilty in the eyes of many whites, even those who were sympathetic to other prisoners. Racial assumptions about Black guilt created an increased level of distrust of Black prisoners even within the world of prison reform, whose definitions of "redeemable" and "incorrigible" prisoners often had racial implications. In the 1960s, these racialized assumptions about different prisoners remained intact.

Because the Black Panthers challenged the legitimacy of white law enforcement and the courts in general, and because targeting both police and courts was central to their party from its beginnings, their practice was closer to the anti-lynching tradition than to left-wing political-prisoner defense, despite their sometimes Marxist vocabulary. In addition, as Blacks already in the prison system became active in the Black Power Movement of the 1960s and were then punished, the Black Panther Party's campaigns for prisoners eroded the distinction between the "political prisoner" and the general population of prisoners even further. From the starting point of patrolling the police, the Black Panthers made a revolutionary critique of the American justice system as a whole and challenged both traditional prison reform and political-prisoner defense.

When they attacked the legitimacy of the law, the Black Panthers presented themselves not as virtuous innocents or icons of masculine respectability, but as defiant revolutionaries who rejected bourgeois morality in the image of Stagolee. Like the early Chicago anarchists who had used Victor Hugo's concept of the "*miserables*" as much as they did Marx's industrial proletariat, the Black Panthers brought together concepts from both political theory and popular fiction as they built their revolutionary organization.

Their version of Stagolee had multiple roots. He was a character based not only on the song, but also in late-nineteenth-century anarchism and the urban guerrilla. That guerrilla fighter, while clearly influenced by the ideas of Regis Debray, Che Guevara, and Carlos Marighela of Brazil, also had earlier roots in African American literature. As early as 1899, Sutton E. Griggs had imagined a Black underground army in his novel *Imperium in Imperio*, and the notion of this kind of subterranean armed resistance had surfaced in the South during the communist organizing drives, as well as in the work of Robert F. Williams and the Deacons for Defense and Justice.[20] The Black Panthers' representation of heroic lumpen characters was an attack on both material and moral definitions of bourgeois subjectivity, work ethics, and whiteness. They challenged the moral basis of capitalist law and the heroic character of the "free laborer." They also, more so than any other group in the socialist left's history, challenged the idea that the white working class was the revolutionary vanguard. As part of the Black Panther Party's effort to address divisions within the working class, the New Left prisoners' movement fundamentally questioned the "freedom" of the wage worker. The party's defense campaigns, both because of their defendants' status as people already under the veil of doubt and because

of their triumphant celebration of the "Stagolee" heroism, are among the most controversial in the left's history.

George Jackson's case was an even bigger challenge than other Black Panthers' cases because it necessitated a redefinition of the term "political prisoner." Jackson and his co-defendants in the Soledad Brothers campaign began and ended their political careers inside the walls of California's prisons. Within a party already stigmatized by many sensationalist writers as nothing but a group of street thugs,[21] Jackson, as a representative martyr, was even more stigmatized. Unlike Huey Newton, whose "Free Huey" campaign brought the group international attention, Jackson was not incarcerated for political activism but for serving as an accomplice in a seventy-dollar robbery. Unlike Eldridge Cleaver, Jackson was never released. The Soledad Brothers campaign was not created to save free men from prison but to save incarcerated men from execution.

In such desperate straits, Jackson became the ultimate embodiment of the lumpen-hero-turned-guerrilla-warrior ideal in the Black Panther Party's last days and one of the few figures who seemed to unite the warring sides of the divided group: a hero to both the Black Panther 21 in New York (associated with Eldridge Cleaver) and to Huey Newton in Oakland. He was also a close associate of the Communist Party member Angela Davis, who called him "a symbol of the will of all us behind bars of that strength which oppressed people always seem to be able to pull together."[22] Jackson's experiences in prison tied him to earlier representations of police and lynching victims as heroes against Jim Crow's laws of place and to the legacy of slavery. Jackson had never been paroled, and his supporters explained that this was because of his manly defiance of prison rules. Thus, he brought inside and outside together, because the weight of accusation occurred not just in prison but also in the "minimum-security" world outside.

Despite his widespread appeal and his ability to make connections between people on the outside and inside prison walls, Jackson was not an easy hero to incorporate into the American national tradition. Sentimental portrayals of Jackson as an innocent victim would be unlikely to succeed—not only because of his status in society, but also because, as a hero, Jackson was "born guilty."[23] Most people outside prison view those inside as criminals and assume they are fundamentally bad characters. In 1966, before Jackson rose to national prominence through his trial, the distrust of prisoners as liars worked effectively to shield prisons from criticism most of the time. The events leading up to the Soledad Brothers case began with a 1966 suit against the prison by a group of mostly Black

Soledad convicts who had spent inordinate amounts of time in the prison's "strip cells." The case was resolved when the judge decided that the prison administration had "abandoned elemental concepts of decency by permitting conditions of a shocking and debased nature." Despite this legal victory, little changed at the prison. Robert Jordan, the inmate who had brought the suit, commented later to the journalist Min S. Yee, "For some reason that I really don't understand, the masses of the American people disbelieve the reports that come out of prisons about the treatment we receive."[24]

The rise of the Black Panther Party and the birth of the prisoners' movement were simultaneous but not directly connected. At the same time that Robert Jordan sued Soledad prison for its disciplinary procedures, Huey Newton and Bobby Seale officially founded the Black Panther Party, basing the party's early analysis largely in the discourse of the Black nationalist anti-lynching campaign's critique of the law as "white." The party attacked police repression as part of a police–mob continuum that drew whites together across class and regional boundaries. Prison activists, motivated by both Malcolm X and the Watts rebellion, charged the prison administration with running the prison like a slave plantation and organized Blacks to fight both white guards and white prisoners.

The Black Panther Party was similar to previous urban Black movements and had its most direct antecedents in Black communists and Black nationalists who fought against police brutality in the 1940s and 1950s. As Malcolm X's own story indicates, the Nation of Islam also made the organization of prisoners a major focus. In the 1950s, Nation of Islam members became leading jailhouse lawyers, writing writs against unfair disciplinary procedures and organizing Black prisoners against crime and for Islam.[25] As he developed the power of the Nation of Islam as a mass organization with a militant agenda, Malcolm X described Harlem as "a police state."[26]

Communists, organized through the Civil Rights Congress in the 1940s and 1950s, fought police brutality and defended Black men accused of crimes as victims of racist persecution. They also provided prisoner support for imprisoned comrades, who themselves pointed out racism within the prisons. The communist Earl Conrad, despite the disapproval of the CRC head William Patterson, published the book *Scottsboro Boy*, the story of Haywood Patterson, who had escaped from prison and to ILD supporters in Detroit in 1949. The most politically minded of the Scottsboro boys, Patterson hid neither his experiences with prison crime nor his sexual experiences with "gal-boys."[27] While the CRC was ultimately defeated by McCarthyism, the National Lawyers Guild, a popular-front

organization from the Depression era, continued to function, and its lawyers both served the Civil Rights Movement in the South and tracked police violence in Northern ghettoes, offering legal representation to youths charged in riots in Detroit and Newark.[28] In June 1964, as the nation waited for the discovery of the bodies of James Chaney, Andrew Goodman, and Michael Schwerner, communists waged a campaign in support of the defendants in the Harlem "Fruit Riot" case.[29] During this period, W. E. B. Du Bois and William Patterson both defined the imprisonment of Blacks as an ideological and economic problem, Du Bois referring to the "national railroading to jails" of Black youth, and Patterson describing Black youth as political prisoners.[30]

What made the Black Panthers different from the Muslims was their open challenge to white police authority, their celebration of desire, their admiration for Black popular culture, and their categorical rejection of racial theories of power.[31] They differed from the communists, as well, because despite their arguments for white–Black unity, the Black Panthers called for direct action against police, made conflicting arguments about innocence and heroism, and rejected labor unions as a major force for change instead arguing that the conflict between the Black community and the police was the primary point of revolutionary contradiction.

The Black Panthers defined unemployed Blacks not as impoverished victims in need of service, but as a revolutionary anti-imperialist vanguard. As he looked at the unemployment crisis in American cities, Huey Newton came to believe that Blacks were becoming "valueless" even as surplus labor to American capitalism.[32] He was especially interested in recruiting "brothers off the block," with whom he identified, having been a young man with a criminal record himself. According to Bobby Seale, Newton admired men who had spent time in prison.[33] He saw them as exemplars of street manhood and had promoted Alprentice "Bunchy" Carter, once of the Slausons street gang into an important position of leadership. Carter, who brought many former Slausons, including Elmer "Geronimo" Pratt, into the party with him, wrote that Newton's genius was in his ability to talk to these "BAD niggers," his ability to "TAP this VAST RESEVOIR of revolutionary potential."[34] In the first years of the party's life, Newton had argued for arousing the masses through the "propaganda of the deed," for, he said, Black people were "not a reading community"; rather, they learned by observation or activity. "When the masses hear that a Gestapo policeman has been executed while sipping coffee at a counter, and the revolutionary executioners fled without being traced," he wrote, "the masses will see the validity of this type of resistance."[35] Eldridge Cleaver,

who joined the Black Panther Party when he was released from prison, where he saw himself following Malcolm X out of the Nation of Islam, gave the most complete explanation of the party's theory of the lumpen proletariat as a vanguard. "The key area of confusion," Cleaver wrote, "has to do with falsely assuming the existence of one All-American-Proletariat; one All-American Working-Class, and one All-American Lumpen Proletariat." Like Bakunin and many Italian radicals of an earlier era, Cleaver argued that revolutionary action would come not from solidarity among the masses, but from manly voluntarism, which he saw in the lumpen proletariat but not in the industrial working class. He first argued that the lumpen proletariat, who rejected work discipline and defied the rules of labor and had the fewest interests in the system, were the revolutionary vanguard, the "left wing of the proletariat."

Whatever its flaws, Cleaver's theory was based partly on the peculiar nature of American racial capitalism and the identification of much of the industrial working class with whiteness. Cleaver attacked the "bought off labor movement," which had "abandoned all criticism of the capitalist system of exploitation," and referred to it as a "new industrial elite" comparable to the craft unions and guilds of the nineteenth century. As a result of being shut out of industrial work by racist white workers, Cleaver argued, Black people on the whole could be said to have a "lumpen relationship to the means of production." This lumpen relationship made it impossible for Black rebellion to occur within unions, he explained, because Blacks were locked out of the system of production. The tactics of even people in Black labor activist groups such as the Dodge Revolutionary Union Movement (DRUM) and the Fair Share committees of steelworkers, according to Cleaver, would always leave the Black masses outside the boundaries of struggle. "The lumpen has no institutionalized focus in Capitalist society. It has no immediate oppressor except perhaps the Pig police with which it is confronted daily," he said. "The lumpen is forced to create its own forms of rebellion that are consistent with its conditions in life and with its relationship to the means of production and the institutions of society."[36]

Rather than noting the overlapping character of workers and accused criminals, Cleaver divided the interests of the lumpen proletariat and the working class, erasing Black workers as a group, erasing the complexity of a "lumpen experience" that included casual and occasional employment, and turning the working class into a virtual antagonist of the Black masses. Rather than attempting to coordinate the efforts of the unem-

ployed with radical Black workers in factories and service occupations, Cleaver argued that the lumpen masses should act against capitalism by attacking police from the streets, their own location of contradiction with American power.

Cleaver, Newton, and many others in the Black Panther Party also reveled in the cultural symbolism of the lumpen proletarian as the essentially masculine and lawless rebel that was described in the ballads of Stagolee. With this militant posture based on the ideals of the "Stagolees" and "brothers off the block" in the ghetto, the Black Panthers gained immediate national attention from media when they appeared in the California Legislature carrying shotguns to protest a change in gun-control laws, evoking long-standing anxieties about Black men and revolutionary violence.

The glorification of the symbolic prisoner or criminal was part of the Black Panthers' attack on the racism of the criminal-justice system, bourgeois morality, Keynesianism, and Stalinist social democracy in the 1960s. As Nikhil Pal Singh put it in *Black Is a Country*, the Black Panthers' celebration of the gun was a "dramatic performance of Black anti-citizenship" that "made a spectacle of government authority," so that they both "performed and deformed the state's reality principle."[37] Some Black Panthers drew from earlier socialist representations of heroic criminals. Newton wrote in his autobiography that he had read Hugo's *Les Miserables* three times while he was in high school, and George Jackson's favorite book in prison was Stendhal's classic work of proto-nihilism *The Red and the Black*. The Black Panthers also drew from ideals of masculinist "street" culture as a salvation from the concept of Blacks as docile. According to the Panthers, those who had done prison time had been tested as men, as if they had undergone the ordeals of slavery and emerged as rebel heroes. Some criminals had a particular place of honor because their rejection of the rules of the labor system was based on defiance of racial norms. Criminality kept people from playing what the ex-con and author Claude Brown called "the boy role."[38]

Rather than being an endorsement of crime, admiration for the lumpen hero was both a rejection of Black subjection and a celebration of desire—two fundamental elements of New Left politics. In a capitalist society, most of the sanctioned desire is for material goods. Thus, the lumpen proletariat for the Black Panthers became a set of "illegitimate capitalists" described in ambivalent terms. As Newton described them in *Revolutionary Suicide*, those who

drove big cars, wore beautiful clothes, and owned many of the beautiful things that life has to offer had a special status. Almost without trying they seemed to have gotten the things for which the rest of the people were working so hard. Moreover, they were having fun in the process. . . . They opposed all authority and made no peace with the establishment.[39]

George Jackson, who had come into conflict with the law at least once because he slashed his boss's leather car seats after he had been called a racist name, was a perfect example of the argument that many men in prison had turned to crime because of their unwillingness to humiliate themselves in white-dominated workplaces. Like Cleaver's theories, these arguments made the lumpen status racial, creating a reverse notion of the "culture of poverty" thesis that would become popular later in the decade by rejecting the rules of work as racially humiliating for Blacks. The sociologists Jay MacLeod and Pierre Bourgeois have both found that the rules of work in the United States in fact do disadvantage Black men and require performances of subservience. As MacLeod argues, the new service economy of the post–Second World War era puts young Black men at a special disadvantage, forcing them to "rub elbows" with white supervisors and customers. Unlike the disappearing manufacturing jobs with their culture of the shop floor, the service sector required them to "cultivate a style of interaction that puts employers and customers at ease."[40] In addition, even those Black workers who were in industrial jobs, such as the legendary League of Revolutionary Black Workers in Detroit, had to struggle against union-supported seniority, disproportionate white power in union elections, and other obstacles within the union.[41]

However, Black Panthers did not generally equate crime with revolution. In practical terms, they defined criminals as potential revolutionaries who would be transformed into political activists through participation in political-education classes and survival programs. Black Panthers declared that crimes against other poor people were basic violations of solidarity. Above all, the lumpen hero was a *symbol* of power rather than an actual practical political guide in the 1960s movements. Bobby Seale, who was reading "Black folkloric history" when he and Newton came up with the program for the Black Panthers,[42] was one of the most explicit exponents of the rejection of white "innocence" in the creation of the Stagolee hero. Arguing that revolutionary action was always rooted in people's "basic desires and needs," Seale attempted to be an antiauthoritarian guide when he worked at the Poverty Program in Oakland while simultaneously teaching kids about the perils of crime with humorous tricks rather than

moralizing sermons. Moralism was the enemy. Lynching, Seale argued, was created by the obsessive purity of monotheistic Christianity. "If you weren't pure, you were a witch" back in Europe, he said, "and you were burned at the stake. Europeans were a lynching people."[43]

Robin Kelley's work, which describes the infrapolitics involved in rebellions of zoot suiters, Saturday night partiers, and hip-hop artists as critical aspects of Black working-class resistance, indicates a basis for political action in the rejection of the "labor identity" that remains critical to Black folk heroism.[44] The Black Panthers' glorification of the lumpen hero was not only an economic analysis, but also a cultural redemption of eros and Black folk tradition as viable elements for building new heroic images for Black manhood that were explicit rejections of the ideal of the "honest worker" as the fulcrum of radical identity. These celebrations of the revolutionary as desiring self were self-conscious rejections of white authority as well as rebellions against religious and middle-class expectations of good behavior, and they worked for men as well as for women. They also rejected asceticism as necessary for revolutionary manhood. From Oakland, for example, "Brother Jimmy" wrote that "the people who look contemptuously on the lumpen are the same people who attempt to emulate the lifestyles of 'Leave It to Beaver' and 'Donna Reed' in vain efforts at transcending racial and class barriers rather than eradicating them."[45] As Arna Bontemps commented when W. E. B. Du Bois criticized him for writing the novel *God Sends Sunday*, which made his Uncle Buddy, a drunkard steeped heavily in Black folk stories, into a problematic hero, "White people have been enjoying the privilege of acting like Negroes for more than a hundred years." According to Bontemps, it was unfair to hold Blacks to a standard of hyper-respectability that required that they "not act colored," as Bontemps's father had advised him before he left for school.[46]

Black Panthers occasionally suggested that, since property was theft, taking from the rich and the owners was not immoral but an act of justice, a case of "chickens coming home to roost." Like the Haymarket anarchists and Italian radicals of previous generations, the Black Panthers described some street crime as "class justice." In June 1970, for example, the party's newspaper described the arrest of "three lumpen brothers shot in the process of taking what was rightfully theirs." They went on to say that "any act of violence upon you (the rulers) is right on. It's the people's duty to attack and destroy any symbol of oppression within the colony. We are POWs and anything we do to break out of what we're under is right on."[47] Panthers also saw it as a victory when police were killed, because it "destroyed the image of police indestructibility."[48]

The Pigs of Discipline   The Black Panthers used two primary modes of attack to describe the evil of the power structure. Rather than referring to tyranny and despotism, they called their enemies fascists and pigs. Recalling older representations of white irrationality in anti-lynching discourse, the attacks on pigs were hyperbolic and filled with ridicule that emphasized the animalistic wildness of the police. Newspaper articles referred to "Gestapo fire pigs" who attacked students with bayonets, and the kangaroo courts of "Harvey Hitler Bacon Brown." These pigs were often seen "running amuck" and terrorizing Black families in their homes.[49] In the prisons, the terms used to describe guards were also related to animalistic behavior, which had so often been applied to African Americans.

In one essay about a prison entitled "Sty Runs Amuck," the New Haven Black Panther George Edwards,[50] who was imprisoned in the crackdown on that party branch, described how the "pigs went insane" when Panther sisters refused "to become dehumanized and act like a bunch of mindless, wandering, robot idiots." "Wallowing in the mud and manure beneath the slimy hoofs of this fascist racist pig lackey McDougal, came the most foul degenerate, and criminally sadistic perverted pigs in the whole pig sty, the wardens and the guard-goons at the bottom of this slime pit."[51]

His description of the guards and cops relied on some of the same dehumanizing imagery that had been directed at Blacks, creating an opposition between the "slimy pigs" as unmanly lackeys and the activities of the sisters they wanted to reduce to "mindless robotic idiocy." As police models of good behavior for Blacks were actually "robotic," and the pigs demonstrated slavishness in their own relationship to administrators and bosses, it was the Black Panthers who demonstrated proud behavior, as the Panther 21 denounced courtroom decorum and their judge and rejected respectability as a tribute to the white power structure that they were unwilling to give.

Police Repression   Both their verbal attacks on police and their organizing efforts brought down the wrath of federal, state, and local police forces upon the Black Panthers, and the direct confrontation between the party's members and police only escalated as a result. The repression also drove the Black Panther Party into prison organizing by default as large numbers of its leaders were incarcerated between 1968 and 1970. When Eldridge Cleaver wrote in 1970 that the "pigs are carrying out a genocidal conspiracy of extermination against our people," it was not an exaggeration.[52] As has now been documented, the FBI organized a Counter-Intelligence Program (COINTELPRO) in the early 1960s and made

the Black Panther Party into its prime target in 1968.[53] Before the FBI declared the Black Panthers the most dangerous group in America, it had targeted Black militants more generally. Early COINTELPRO memos directed that agents "frustrate any plans they may have to consolidate their forces." The program worked by sewing discord within organizations. By 1964, Hoover had noted that "no opportunity should be missed to capitalize upon organizational and personal conflicts of their leadership," and in 1967 he advised agents to "be alert to determine evidence of misappropriation of funds or other types of personal misconduct . . . and prevent the groups from gaining respectability."[54]

Black Panthers were the targets of outright shootings and legal conspiracy charges. Huey Newton was arrested in October 1967 following a shootout during which Police Officer John Frey was killed. During the riots that followed the assassination of Martin Luther King Jr. in April 1968, Eldridge Cleaver and L'il Bobby Hutton, the sixteen-year-old student in Bobby Seale's summer-poverty-program group who was the first Black Panther recruit, were involved in a shootout with police. To protect himself, Cleaver stripped off his clothes and surrendered naked. Hutton surrendered with his clothes on, and police killed him as he walked toward them with his hands up.

The murder of Bobby Hutton by the police so soon after the killing of Martin Luther King increased the level of militancy. As Huey Newton claimed, "When L'il Bobby was killed the rage in me was enough to destroy everything in blue." Sonia Sanchez's "Death Poem (Unless We Wake Up)" gives a clear indication of the effect of the outright shootings of Black activists by police in the 1960s:

he was
part of a long
term
plan
for black
people.[55]

After the police riot at the 1968 Democratic Convention in Chicago, Bobby Seale was charged with conspiracy along with Jerry Rubin, Abbie Hoffman, and several other leaders of Students for a Democratic Society (SDS) and the Yippie movement—some of whom he had never met. In January 1969, two major killings of Black Panthers were a direct result of FBI infiltration. In a fight at the University of California, Los Angeles (UCLA), that was initiated by false memos sent from FBI offices to the

Black Panthers and to Malaunu Ron Karenga's U.S. organization, U.S. members shot and killed the Black Panthers John Huggins and Alprentice "Bunchy" Carter.[56] In Chicago, Fred Hampton, who had just been acquitted of stealing several gallons of ice cream, was killed in his bed by police in a raid planned and organized by Chicago police in cooperation with the FBI informants George Sams and Cotton Smith, as a federal investigation ultimately revealed. In New York City, twenty-one members of the New York Black Panther Party were facing trial on conspiracy bombing charges. In Los Angeles, police agents organized an attack on the party's headquarters, initiating a shootout with the Black Panthers inside who defended themselves. In New Haven, Bobby Seale and Ericka Huggins faced murder charges in the death of the suspected informant Alex Rackley (whose primary killer was George Sams, the FBI infiltrator).[57] This was only the party's national leadership. In Berkeley, the party's local organizer Charles Bursey was jailed in 1969, and numerous other Black Panther activists were either shot or imprisoned by 1969. Every issue of the *Black Panther* newspaper reported on arrests, shootings, and beatings of Black Panthers by police.

Defense Campaigns

When they went on trial, the Panthers presented themselves as heroes and did not make simple claims of absolute innocence. The defense campaign for Huey Newton in particular shaped the image of the Black Panther Party in the national media and led to the controversial alliance of the party with white students and liberals. It was Eldridge Cleaver who organized Newton's defense as a national campaign. Neither Newton nor Cleaver objected to lawyers on principle and hired the National Lawyers Guild activist and former communist Charles Garry to handle Newton's defense, Newton explaining that he would rather have a white political leftist than a Black lawyer who was simply acting out of careerist self-interest.[58] Cleaver made the "Free Huey" campaign into the center of Black Panther organizing efforts. According to Panther Earl Anthony, "Huey's personal well-being was uppermost in the minds of fellow panthers," but another important goal was to make his trial "a showdown with the racist forces of America who had killed countless Black leaders, or incarcerated them, or made them fugitives when they became too dangerous."[59]

When he sought to publicize "Free Huey" as a national organizing campaign, Cleaver appealed to students, white liberals, and the counter-culture. He chose the image of Newton in a rattan chair framed with a spear that became an icon.[60] The poster, as Leigh Raiford points out in her essay on the imagery of Black nationalism, emphasized leadership and glamour, placing personality rather than mass action at the core of the Black Panthers' national image. However, in other representations, Panthers did reach out to the masses, as Newton did in his address to his own defense campaign, calling for unity between two revolutionary groups in the United States: "the alienated white group and the masses of Blacks in the ghettos."[61]

This student–lumpen alliance of the New Left was symptomatic of the postindustrial trends in the American economy of the 1960s. Both the students of the New Left and the "lumpen" were rebels whose class position did not directly engage them with the forces of industrial production. Both had a primary locus of rebellion that involved them in different conflicts with capital from those of industrial workers. They were, like the councils for the unemployed of the 1930s, engaged primarily in neighborhood resistance to state organizations. The "brothers off the block" were in conflict with New Deal–derived bureaucracies that controlled their spaces and communities. They fought management and control on the streets and in hospitals, prisons, welfare offices, and universities. White students were also in conflict with bureaucracy through their experiences in corporatizing universities. White student activists and Black street radicals agreed that these institutions had been created to control, manage, and remedy the worst ills of capitalism.[62] White student radicals questioned the Old Left's focus on the industrial working class, to a degree following Herbert Marcuse, who questioned the capacity of the industrial working class for revolt. They also wrote in the context of the religious spirit of the early Civil Rights Movement and expressed their own experiences of empty affluence and called for a cultural revolt against professionalism and consumer society.[63]

Jean Genet, the former French prisoner, like many cons and ex-cons was inspired to political activism for the first time by the Black Panthers. After meeting the Black Panthers in Chicago in 1968, he toured with them and argued that white students could make themselves significant in the struggle against American racism only if they fought for Black Panther defense campaigns. Just as previous defense activists had called on the working class to save their comrades to prove their own power, Genet

told whites it was their duty to free Huey Newton. They must declare which side they were on, as Dreyfusards had in France. The campaign to "Free Huey" hit at the center of racial formation: the perception of guilt and innocence. As Genet put it, "White people need to adopt a mode of behavior which will eliminate their own privileges," and supporting "the guilty man" was one way to do it. "There was a time," he wrote, "in France, when the guilty man was a Jew. Here there was such a time, and there is still, when the guilty man is the Negro."[64] Genet's concept of the need to defend "the guilty man" echoed the general discourse of socialist labor defense, which always argued that fighting for the pariah was central to working-class solidarity. However, instead of coming out to defend Newton because they were the same as him, they were to do it because of difference. The act of joining the campaign itself, Genet and the Black Panthers suggested, would eliminate that difference. It would move the white students unequivocally away from their own privilege. Participating in the campaign gave whites the chance to transcend racial boundaries by siding with the stigmatized Black man. While they did so, the white students were also to acknowledge the Black Panther Party's leadership, with Newton and Seale as the vanguard of the movement.

Both the left and the right have strongly criticized all of the Black Panther's defense campaigns. The right-wing attacks, which the former Panther Reginald Major refers to as "stealth history," are a testament to the challenge to American racism that Black Panther defense campaigns presented. If placed in the context of the history of left-wing defense campaigns as a whole, the "Free Huey" campaign and other defense campaigns become tremendously significant. "Free Huey" was the first Black-led defense campaign that promoted a Black revolutionary nationalist hero to a white audience. Never before had an organization completely run by African Americans involved whites in a campaign to free a Black person. Participating in a campaign that associated whites with the bogey of "Black criminality" was an attack on white privilege, and some whites, such as the actress Jean Seaberg, paid the consequences for their support of the Black Panthers.[65] Writers have expended a great deal of energy in undermining the seriousness of whites' participation in the Black Panther defense campaigns, arguing that this participation was laughable and trivial rather than an early attempt to forge a meaningful alliance between white and Black revolutionaries. Those on the right have argued that the white defense activists were being cynically manipulated by a gang of thugs. Self-identified liberals, progressives, and radicals are also critical. In their book on the Bobby Seale–Ericka Huggins trial in New Haven,

Connecticut, for example, Paul Bass and Douglas Rae refer to the whites' attitudes toward the Black Panthers as "perverse white fantasies of the noble savage."[66] Judson L. Jeffries, while not as sensational, argues that the white left involved the party in "irrelevant" issues and that the party would have done better by being closer to Black cultural nationalists and Pan-Africanists, while Yohuru Williams argues that "the left manipulated the BPP during the New Haven trials" by turning the protest, which occurred on May 1, 1970—the day of the national student anti-war strike—into an antiwar demonstration.[67]

Because of the perception of Blacks as the embodiment of the category of manly eros itself, the Black Panthers' embrace of cultural rebellion made them extremely popular with white radicals and members of the counter-culture. Indeed, as Seale and many current scholars of racial thought based in psychoanalysis argue, much of American white racial identity had been structured through the rejection of eros and the projection of it onto the image of American Blacks.[68] Because of this use of an imaginary "Blackness" in the construction of whiteness, "Blackness" has also played a consistent role in the formation of white counter-cultures. White Beatniks and white jazz fans had developed an interest in African American folk culture in their own revolts against American middle-class morality, as had white fans of rock and roll in the 1950s.[69] While the imitation and mockery of "Blackness" in the blackface tradition has worked to reinforce whiteness as a system that minimizes the reality of Black victimization while indicating its own ability to know and control "the other," counter-cultures have also been productive spaces for "race traitorism." White counter-culturalists have sought out alliances with Blacks and "Blackness" in the name of self-interest, defining whiteness as a psychological prison that thwarts their ability to relate to themselves or to other people. It should not be surprising, then, that by the late 1960s white leftist activists would make solidarity with the Black Panthers into a vehicle for attacking white middle-class morality and models of "being" and would gravitate to them when the Panthers welcomed whites' support in their defense campaigns. White radicals who supported the Black Panthers, unlike white music fans, did not simply appropriate Black Panther style but were actively supporting Black political leaders and faced consequences for doing so, regardless of their complicated and fumbling psychological understandings of who those leaders were. White allies of the Black Panthers described their attempts to free Huey Newton as their own redemption from association with the white power structure.

To write off the Panthers entirely because some white sympathizers within the movement would confuse stereotypes of "Blackness" with actual African American people is too easy. The major example of this criticism of white supporters of the BPP came from Kai Erikson's description of white student reaction to Huey Newton's talk at a seminar led by the psychologist Erik Erikson at Yale in 1971. At the seminar, Newton lectured for an hour about his new ideological theories, and the students tried to "lure him down from the high cerebral plane he had chosen so he could be the political activist they thought him to be." Judson L. Jeffries uses this incident as evidence for the overall shallowness of white radical support for the Panthers.[70] However, the white students at Yale were not the only ones to be "turned off" by Newton following his release from prison. Many in the New Left did not understand the new intercommunalism theory when he first introduced it, and Newton himself, who had spent three years in solitary confinement, had problems with the movement that had grown while he was incarcerated. George Katsiaficas, a white radical, remembered finding the intercommunalism speech alienating at the Revolutionary People's Constitutional Convention in Philadelphia in 1970. Elaine Brown, Newton's top ally, found the theory befuddling, as well, as did David Hilliard. To judge the entire white left based on comments of one observer of one Yale seminar seems problematic, to say the least.[71]

Furthermore, not only does the rejection of "Blackness" as an imaginary category deny eros as a part of life that Black people can engage in as easily as whites, but it treats metaphorical representations as literal and reinforces Eurocentric Christian morality as normative. The frequent argument that the Black Panther Party met its downfall because of its interest in lumpen heroism devalues Black folk traditions, reifies a fetishized system of work discipline as the apex of revolutionary action, and treats the Black Panthers' imagery as if it were a direct representation of their political practice, failing to recognize the complexity and irony in Black Panther literature. The attack eliminates eros as an option in Black politics by replacing it with firm discipline and moral prohibitions only to be found in organizations modeled on the Nation of Islam and free-labor ethics.

The principal problem in Cleaver's representation of "lumpen" vanguardism was his rejection of solidarity, ethics, and interdependence as "unmanly," and this concept of revolution was the weakest element of his argument. Instead of depicting Huey Newton as a vulnerable prisoner in need of the power of the masses, the campaign promoted Newton as a "messiah" and the center of a personality cult, which contributed

to the disorganization in the party when Newton went to prison and to even greater problems when he left. Don Cox recalled that Newton was "smothered" with money, love, and attention when he was released from prison and referred to Newton's response to the New York Black Panthers' decision to buck his authority as "megalaomaniac perverted rage."[72]

This Nietzschean heroism contributed to an essentialist definition of Blackness as "lumpen" and masculine and made the Black Panthers easy objects of white-male fantasy, as Michelle Wallace argued in her landmark work *Black Macho and the Myth of the Superwoman*. In addition, the attack on the labor movement as "white" erased the revolutionary actions of Black workers and reified the image of them as docile and unmanly, as slaves. Like many whites, Cleaver depended on a simplistic vision of heroic individual agency in his definitions of revolutionary action. As later studies and current observations revealed, criminals and street people did not make up the majority of the Black Panther Party.[73]

Before Jackson's case, Charles Garry had developed a winning strategy for both courtroom and mass political defense for explicitly political prisoners. Explaining his strategy to the National Lawyers Guild in 1969, Garry argued that "we have to project certain images and issues into the courtroom. Ghettoes are the Colonies of the U.S., Huey [Newton] can't get a fair trial." He would also "present Huey as I saw him," he said. "Selfless and beautiful"[74] Garry's tactics, which relied on a division between the image of the criminal and the selfless political prisoner, worked for Newton: He was found guilty of a lesser charge and sentenced to a short term in the penitentiary instead of going to his death. In New York, the Panther 21 used a different strategy, disrupting the courtroom in a manner more comparable to that adopted by the Chicago Eight, and were acquitted by the jury. When the Panther 21 were acquitted in June 1971, *Newsweek* remarked on the new phenomenon, commenting that "broad gauge conspiracy charges appear to be causing more trouble for the prosecution than the defense." The magazine also noted the "difficulty of dealing with a new breed of Black revolutionaries."[75]

Political Prisoners and the Prisoners' Movement

When they were incarcerated, Black Panthers continued their campaigns behind bars. Organizing among prisoners allowed them to make arguments about the relationship between slavery and contemporary wage labor. Black men in chains and behind bars conjured up images of

chattel slavery, as did the splitting off of an entire section of the work-ing class from the opportunities of "Americanism." This paralleling of the prison and slavery focused on the elements of capitalism that limited free-dom rather than its immediate material inequities.

"A Man's got a right to be free / he can't be caged up like a dog," Afeni Shakur wrote in a prison poem dedicated to Jonathan Jackson after his death in August 1970. In the poem, Shakur charted the movement of an-ger and rage into action: "I know I can't take this trap no more / the walls are too close, the windows too small / but if we take the Warden we'll get through the door / I'd rather be dead and in my grave, than live this life as a slave. / there's nothing left but to die/FREE!"[76]

Shakur's poem, like Jackson's letters, spoke not simply of confinement in prison, but also against confinement in general—whether in the ghetto or in the middle-class home—as reminiscent of slavery. This redemption of the prisoner as the second coming of the heroic slave not only was an attempt to expand the definition of the working class, but it emphasized the importance of personal freedom as the primary goal of 1960s activism. If Genet had constructed the saving of Huey, Seale, and Huggins as work-ing against white self-interest, Jackson's definition of prison as a node from which everyone's slavery followed exposed the pettiness of white privileges and the bankruptcy of racism as a means to whites' advance-ment. Like antislavery activists who pointed to the use of slavery as an undercutting of white wages, the prisoners' movement, as Jackson saw it, was a way to challenge fundamental divisions among the working class.

As they were arrested and sent to prison, as George Jackson recalled it, and as was apparent in the Black Panther Party and prisoners' movement newspapers, the Black Panthers brought their community organizing programs into the prisons with them. White radicals also began organiz-ing as they were sent to prison for draft resistance. The New York Panthers Afeni Shakur and Joan Bird and the California Panther Charles Bursey were among the first to make a political issue out of prison conditions and prisoners' rights. Activists in the prisoners' movement described the crime of prison as its disruption of relation and unity. In 1968, Bursey attacked the indignity of solitary confinement as "isolation within isola-tion" used to prevent prisoners from acting in their own interests. He defined men held in solitary confinement as "political prisoners" within the prison.[77] As they were arrested and charged with extra crimes that got them sent to the hole, Black Panthers made solitary confinement into a sign of honor, describing it as a place for "the most recalcitrant slaves,"[78] and forged alliances between prisoners in the hole and those in the

general population. Because prison was reserved for the poor, and because within prison people were punished harshly for violating rules of racial deference, Shakur critiqued the class inequalities of the criminal-justice system and argued, "The Prisons and Jails Are Filled with Political Prisoners."[79]

In September of the same year, prisoners in the Tombs, New York's city jail, where Shakur was awaiting trial in the Panther 21 case, rebelled, taking several hostages. Demanding bail review for all those in jail awaiting trial, but for Shakur in particular, the rebels spoke in the name of unity and insisted "we are not animals."[80]

White draft resisters also wound up in prison, along with white pot smokers and militants. Sam Melville was sent to Attica on bombing charges in 1969 and began organizing for the New Left inside, playing a critical role in organizing whites in solidarity with Blacks in the prison before the Attica rebellion.[81] Like white activists who had gone South to witness racism, white student activists began choosing to go to jail rather than to post bail. Some wrote about the experiences to expose the terrible prison conditions and racism within prisons for their readers. Letters from prison appeared in all kinds of New Left papers after 1968 because of the popularity of Black Panther defense campaigns with white leftists and because of large numbers of draft resisters now held in prison. One *Village Voice* writer described his experience of going to jail for a routine traffic violation, and in San Francisco a writer calling herself "Sweet Judy Blue Eyes" went to prison on parking warrants in order to write a story about life inside for the *Berkeley Barb*.[82] Between 1968 and 1971, the pages of almost every New Left newspaper—from the Minneapolis newspaper *One Hundred Flowers* to Harvard University's *Old Mole*, Berkeley's *Tribe*, and the *Ann Arbor Argus*—were filled not only with the arrest reports of the Black Panther Party and continuing updates on the trials of the Panther 21 in New York, Bobby Seale and Ericka Huggins in New Haven, and the Chicago Eight Conspiracy trial in Chicago, but also the reports of the white underground activists John Sinclair and Pun Plamondon. The regular and routine police attacks on student demonstrations, the arrests of successive waves of white youths for dope smoking, and the arrests of suspected Weather Underground activists created an atmosphere of hostility toward state power and a sense of shared interest across factional lines in the left. Even *Newsweek* noted the paranoia and published a story about the "dope bust" from the perspective of a young white teenager.[83]

White radicals' rejections of whiteness, as indicated in their alliance with the Black Panthers, in their physical marks of membership in an

outsider culture, and their sympathy with the National Liberation Front (NLF) in Vietnam, made them much more vulnerable to police attacks in the late 1960s. The police attacks on Black Panther supporters, hippies, and white radicals during the antiwar movement, particularly after 1968, created greater sympathy among whites for the Black Panthers and broke down the threshold of suspicion that characterized white attitudes toward Blacks who described criminal activities by the police. For example, after he was physically beaten by police, who raided his home in Chicago during a cocktail party in support for Fred Hampton, Robert Gaylord Donnelly wrote, "I never believed most of the things I read about the tactics the police use. Most of the people I know still don't believe it. If this is an example of the type of thing that is happening to Black people, then I can appreciate the feelings and their reactions."[84]

After the Telegraph Avenue riot in Berkeley, when police grabbed hippies and verbally and physically assaulted them, one white college student remarked to a reporter, "Everyone I know has been hit by a cop."[85] When white radicals proclaimed, "We are all outlaws in the eyes of Pig America!"—first after the deaths of Weather Underground activists in an accidental explosion in their New York townhouse and again after the shootings of students at Kent State and Jackson State—they had plenty of evidence to support their claim.[86]

As historians of the prisoners' movement have argued, the influx of New Left radicals into prisons dramatically changed the nature of political activism around issues facing prisoners. Early activism by leftists had focused on campaigns for individual prisoners facing execution, such as Caryl Chessman. Prison reformers organized in efforts to increase the use of treatment programs as alternatives to harsh punishment models. From the 1920s until the 1950s, progressive theories of penology had created a system of control based on a combination of treatment models and convict hierarchy. A good deal of the activism directed at prisons in the 1930s and 1940s was led by semiprofessional prison reformers, not by organized groups of convicts. According to John Irwin, a white ex-con, prison reformer, sociologist, and prisoners' movement historian, "Soledad in the 1950s was a very peaceful and orderly institution. . . . The general mood was tolerance and friendliness. The races were somewhat hostile towards each other and followed informal patterns of segregation, but there was commingling between all races and many prisoners formed close friendships with other racial groups."[87]

However, during this same period, many prison administrators thought that the treatment model and the presence of communists in the prisons

had created mayhem, creating what Irwin describes as the "custodial" wing of the prison administrators against whom the more liberal criminologists were fighting. There was a difference between guards who made arguments as early as 1957 that "the thing that's wrong with this place now is that discipline has gone to Hell," and people like Donald Cressey, a liberal prison official who wrote the foreword to Irwin's book. However, the two wings of the prison administration had much in common. Guards and liberal reformers agreed that the people in prison were basically guilty, that the laws were basically fair, that people in prison were there because of their own bad actions, and that prisoners could be divided into the categories of "incorrigible" and "redeemable."

While criticizing members of the custodial wing of the criminology group for their poor educations and lack of professional training, Cressey also argued that "the saturation of neighborhoods with police, and the new techniques of surveillance in prisons" were both positive developments. After all, it was a mistake to believe that the "healthy personality should be allowed to express itself in numerous alternative ways."[88] While the liberal wing of the corrections industry argued for new methods of discipline that relied more on therapy and prevention than incarceration, they also were among the early proponents of the "culture of poverty thesis." Irwin, for instance, blamed the trouble in prisons in the 1960s after the arrival of Blacks on the disorderly and dishonest criminal culture of "hustling" associated with Black ghetto dwellers, in contrast with the more honest and straightforward "thieves' culture" of white cons in the 1950s.[89]

Irwin seems to suggest that conditions in the prisons began to go downhill when the racial balance in the prisons began to shift. However, African Americans who have written accounts of their experiences in prison give different descriptions of the prison environment from Irwin. In his memoir of California prisons, James Carr described a world of intense racial conflict in which Blacks were continually on the bottom of the prison hierarchy as white cons buddied up with prison officials. Similarly, in Manchild in the Promised Land, Claude Brown described two different kinds of prison time in New York State prisons: "The niggers get all the shitty jobs and the white boys, man they live good. It's just like it is out here. . . . Everybody isn't doing the same kind of time. There's white time in jail and there's nigger time in jail, and the worst kind of time you can do is nigger time."[90]

George Jackson also described conflicts and hierarchies among whites and Blacks in the prison in the early 1960s, as prison-based Nazis known

as "Hitlers' Helpers" fought Black prisoners defined as "extremists" at the goading of guards. Charles Manson, a longtime white con in California's prisons, made paranoid, anti-Black statements in the 1960s that marked him as having had contact with prison Nazis.[91]

According to Jackson, some of the racial conflict in the prison was the fault of Black convict activists, because the primary organization for Black prisoners before the arrival of the Black Panther Party was the Nation of Islam, which, Jackson said, treated white cons and guards as if they were the same. However, Jackson recalled the presence of "Hitler's Helpers" in the California prisons as early as 1961, as did his fellows, who wrote that Jackson had helped them form the "Capone Gang" to defend themselves against attacks by white Nazis.[92] In another testimony to racist organizing in California, the author Nathaniel West argued that Southern California bred more white-supremacist groups than the rest of the country and that there was considerable Nazi activity in Los Angeles in the 1960s, where a number of Los Angeles Police Department were members of the nearly Nazi John Birch Society.[93] As racial hierarchies were promoted by the "clique-controlled" underground convict economies that had long existed in the prisons, violence erupted as Blacks and Chicanos attempted to gain control of illegal drug dealing and gambling, challenging the existing distributions of economic power among the prisoners.

When Blacks and whites got into fights, regardless of who had provoked them, they could expect to be treated differently by white guards. For example, after a fight in Soledad's yard in 1970, Blacks for no apparent reason were put in solitary confinement for a period of nine days longer than the whites. According to Jackson and others, adjustment centers and solitary cells across the country tended to be filled with Black and brown prisoners, rather than with whites.[94] In the 1950s, before the advent of the prisoners' movement, tensions created by convict-run hierarchies had already instigated a series of riots and violence. Riots shook Jackson Penitentiary in Michigan, and Arkansas's vicious system of convict hierarchies was exposed by the prison reformers Tom Murton and Joe Hyams after protests led by the prison activist Richard "Dickie" Coombs.[95] In the late 1960s, the violence among prisoners led to demands among some prison activists to create a tighter system of segregation within the prison. Activists at Folsom State Prison demanded segregation during mealtimes, and prisoners in New York made similar demands. Ronald Reagan, in statements after a race riot in Soledad, agreed.[96]

Jackson and his friend W. L. Nolen argued that, rather than fighting each other, the men in prison should unite as a "convict class" to fight

the guards, whose use of racial terror was part of the strategy against the prisoners as a group. In 1966, Jackson was a leadership figure among Black prisoners at Soledad prison and had created a group dedicated to "the survival of the Black and some other sectors of the convict class against the prison administration and often their convict allies who quite openly demonstrated a desire to strip us not only of our self-respect, but in many cases of the last of our human rights—our right to live."[97]

After abandoning the philosophies and activities of the Nation of Islam, Jackson and Nolen were coming to the conclusion that "Marxism–Fanonism," as Jackson described it, offered a better analysis and strategic plan for social transformation. In their study group, the men came to decide that one of the principal strategies of control in American prisons was the fomenting of racial conflicts among inmates, which had a parallel in the wider society. "With history and class struggle complicated by the existence of overt and deeply rooted racism," Jackson concluded, America was a fascist state that used racism to maintain class supremacy. He argued that the fear of slave revolt was the "linchpin" of U.S. history, whose national ideology was based on counter-revolution. "We had concluded that the U.S. had developed because of its unique historical fear of revolution which must be accredited to the presence and always threatening black revolutionary potential."

The movement that Jackson and Nolen hoped to build was based on many of the same political principles that Eldridge Cleaver had outlined, but prisoners, unlike the disorganized brothers on the block who were unemployed, could be organized as masses. They also had a clear object to attack and a basis for cross-racial class unity that did not exist in most urban ghettos. Jackson also saw the Blacks in prison as allies of the Black workers. He did not separate the lumpen proletariat from the working class in any characterological or essentialist way but argued that changes in industrial capitalism had changed the structure of American labor, by creating "automation, military-corporate elitism . . . the new class of National Guard pigs . . . government controlled unions, right to work laws, etc." Beyond this, "Nearly six and a half million of them (the workers) can't find work."[98] He also described white convicts as fellow victims of the prison administration, concluding that unity within the "convict class" could be achieved by organized, disciplined cadres led by Black revolutionaries. He, Nolen, and several others formed a study group in San Quentin and began trying to talk to white prisoners about ending racial conflict in the prison and joining together to fight for better conditions.

Like so many other 1960s radicals, Jackson wrote of love as the motor of revolution. Three days after Nolen's death in 1970, Jackson said of Nolen, "Though the victim of countless racist attacks, he never once changed his position that under Black vanguard leadership in a socialist revolution, even the most vicious redneck could be redeemed from his delirium."[99]

Jackson and Nolen were well positioned to organize among Black convicts in 1966. Nolen was the prison boxing champion, and Jackson had status because of his long history of "manly" behavior in the prison: He was known as a character who refused to kowtow and was able to hold his own in the violent world of conflict and competition. In 1969, Johnny Spain recalled, Jackson was trying to unite Black prisoners in Soledad across old neighborhood gang loyalties, and in doing so he demonstrated a force of charisma and love that made prisoners proud of themselves and loyal to him. As he began discussing unity among convicts and moving toward political rather than criminal actions, Jackson not only became a hero among other convicts but also drew higher levels of surveillance from the administration than ever before. If the guards hated him, other prisoners did not. According to Spain, to hear other prisoners speak of Jackson in the late 1960s, it was as if he "walked on water."[100] Jackson taught several prisoners how to read and ran study groups on Marx and Fanon in the prison. According to one white prisoner, whom Min S. Yee interviewed during the writing of his well-researched *The Melancholy History of Soledad Prison*, the guards "tried to tell us that the Black Panthers were going to kill us," but the prisoner disputed this because Jackson had told him that "all the poor folk are oppressed." That, the prisoner said, was "why Jackson was a revolutionary person."[101]

However, when Black prisoners began organizing around issues of race and racism, reading political books, and standing up to guards, the guards wrote them up as "Black extremists" and "white haters." Such people spent large amounts of time in the hole or were treated with "bus therapy," being moved from one prison to another. In February, Nolen was transferred from San Quentin to Soledad; in April 1968, another Black nationalist prisoner in Nolen's group, Clarence Causey (also known as "C.C.") was killed by a gang of white convicts in Soledad. According to other convicts, the guards had orchestrated the killing. In October of the same year, guards beat to death the Black inmate William A. Powells in full view of other prisoners.[102] Nolen and several others, including Alvin Miller, began filing a suit against Soledad prison, charging the administration with fomenting conflicts between prisoners and organizing killings. In January 1970, with tensions at a high point, Nolen, Miller, and Cleve-

land Edwards, all described as "Black extremists" by the prison administration, were released on to the Soledad yard with several white cons who described themselves as "white racists" and "nigger haters." A fight ensued, and Prison Guard Opie Miller shot Nolen, Miller, and Edwards. As prisoners attempted to get help for the bleeding men, everyone (including the white racists) agreed that the guards refused to come, leaving the three Black organizers to die in the yard. An inquiry into the killings ended with the claim of "justifiable homicide," and white prisoners later told outside investigators that the guards had encouraged them to fight and to lie in their testimony about what had happened. A few days later, a prison guard was killed, and a note was found on his body reading, "One down, two to go."

Immediately, the prison was locked down, keeping all of the prisoners incommunicado from their families. Eventually, George Jackson, Fleeta Drumgo, and John Clutchette were charged with the murder of the guard. Although the murders of prisoners had gone unpunished, murders of guards mattered immensely to the media and to the state. In California, any prisoner who killed a prison guard faced a mandatory death sentence. Two weeks after the men's first hearings, where they appeared with no legal representation, Clutchette's mother received a note that read, "Mother! Help! Won't let letters get out. Send Lawyer! Might not let you come in. Life in danger. Hurry, Speedy."[103] Taking the advice of the three defendants, Clutchette's mother called Charles Garry's assistant, Fay Stender, and the Soledad Brothers defense campaign began.

The Soledad Brothers

The Soledad Brothers Defense Committee (SBDC), like many other committees that the Communist Party had organized on behalf of Black men, relied largely on the men's mothers to carry out publicity actions. Jackson's mother depicted him as the ultimate innocent, in some reports even denying that he supported prison activism and riots. Like many defense campaigners, lawyers defined Jackson as a victim of the prison system, describing how he had to appear in court in chains, and emphasized the need for mass action to save him. Angela Davis recalls that the Soledad Brothers Defense Committee was immensely and immediately popular in Los Angeles. As Davis was organizing what was meant to be a small planning meeting that had not been advertised, well over fifty people arrived at her office at UCLA to get involved with the defense of the three

men. Not students but working families and some friends, a few of whom were old prison and reform-school buddies of Jackson, Drumgo, and Clutchette, got together and began to raise money and organize. The campaign's rhetoric followed in the tradition of the methods the communists had used during the Scottsboro case, as the mothers made passionate pleas about their sons and described the men they knew as children who had been taken away from them years before.[104]

Fay Stender and the SBDC planned to use the same strategy in Jackson's defense that they had used for Huey Newton. The SBDC repeatedly told the story of the violence at Soledad and described the Soledad Brothers as political prisoners because they were leaders in the growing prisoners' movement. In the descriptions of prison life written by Stender, it almost seemed that no one in prison had committed a crime. She had become involved in prison activism while she worked on Newton's case and became intensely self-sacrificing in her approach to prison defense, constructing prisoners as fetishized innocents. She argued that lawyers should demonstrate total commitment to their prisoner clients and claimed that she felt "more alive" in prison than anywhere else. In an essay in the collection *Maximum Security*, Stender proclaimed, "I certainly felt that, person for person, prisoners were better human beings than you would find in any random group of people. . . . They are more loving. They have more concern for each other. They have more creative human potential."[105] As Jessica Mitford put it, Stender depicted prisoners as the "salt of the earth" because of the suffering they had undergone. Stender's images of prisoners replicated the trope of the suffering innocent created by white abolitionists. Many of those who responded to the SBDC donated money and effort because of these same images of prisoners' innocence. That Jackson had not killed the guard—indeed, could not have killed the guard—was part of the image to which they responded.[106]

This defense campaign, Stender did not seem to recognize, had an immediate logical problem at its core. Jackson was not, and did not claim to be, an "innocent," and he was not a "political prisoner" in the conventional sense. Although Jackson's situation appeared to be the same as Newton's because he was in prison and charged with a crime inside, he faced a different set of problems from activists on the outside and lived in a world where acts of violence in defense of one's manly identity were not only accepted but often seemed necessary for survival. Even if he was acquitted of the killing of the prison guard, Jackson would still be in prison, and he seriously doubted that he would ever be paroled. Between 1962 and 1970, Jackson had racked up forty disciplin-

ary charges and had been turned down for parole ten times. Many of these had nothing to do with politics, he readily admitted to his editor, Greg Armstrong, who did not understand why Jackson felt so remorseful about his previous "evil" actions toward other prisoners. However, Jackson felt the brunt of discipline more as a political activist than he did for mere criminal activity. Jackson told Armstrong that he had heard of twenty attempts to set up his assassination. At least two white convicts said that they had personally been offered money to kill Jackson by the guards at Soledad.[107]

I Won't Be a Good Boy Ever! The representations of George Jackson by Stender and by his own mother during the campaign clashed with Jackson's efforts to create his own heroic image, which he portrayed in *Soledad Brother*, edited and published by the SBDC. Drawing public attention to the petty indignities of life in prison, *Soledad Brother* discussed ideals of individual freedom of self-expression, described the exploitation of prison labor, and theorized unwritten codes of racial deference, using the prison as a metaphor for American society as a whole. Inspiring white and Black prisoners alike, as well as those outside, Jackson described how the prison demeaned manhood through race baiting and violence. He discussed the relationships not only between the imprisoned man and the state but also between Black and white convicts, and between white guards and Black guards, describing the prison as a system of total control. Jackson's work addressed both the world of the prison and contemporary global politics: The prison, with its racially defined prisoner–guard alliances, threats against resistance, and subtle daily insults to dignity became a metaphorical expression of the rules of Jim Crow capitalism.

As Jackson described them, white cons were pivotal in prison dynamics as both victims of the system and oppressors. Should one white man enter prison without showing racism, Jackson argued, other white cons would pressure him "to join their racist brand of politics," while white guards pressured him to become an informer.[108] The prison as the embodiment of the division of white and Black workers and as a scene of economic exploitation, surveillance, and humiliation—as well as the product of New Deal Keynesianism—served as the perfect microcosm for what Jackson described as American fascism.[109] Through Jackson, the prison became a metaphor for the outside world and undermined the underlying assumption in organizing among political prisoners that focused on the distinction between free workers and prisoners.

As August Spies had in 1887, Jackson described the similarities of prisons, streets, and workplaces in America—but Jackson's critique dealt with racial rather than class forms of social control, examining the ghetto instead of the factory. The concept of the ghetto as a "concentration camp" showed the similar techniques of control used in the prison and the street and forged a spiritual identification between Jackson and all urban Blacks by describing modern America as a "police state." Like Nicola Sacco, George Jackson struggled with his own defense committee. Jackson participated in a collective struggle, but his effort to redeem the image of Black manhood led him to valorize individual heroism in ways that at times conflicted with the practices of mass defense organizing. This quest for heroic redemption may also have been one of the causes of his death.

In early letters in *Soledad Brother*, Jackson complained about his mother's ideas of goodness. Long before he had made his direct contacts with the Black Panthers, he confounded conventional confessional discourse, rejected Christianity, and refused to apologize for anything he had ever done. Responding to his mother's letters to him in prison, Jackson told her, "I won't be a good *boy* ever" and demanded to know, "Why did you allow us to worship at a white altar?"[110] He complained about the Easter cards his mother sent him and constantly told her to stop holding him back. Like Louis Lingg, Jackson responded to the prison administration and to all attacks on him by white racists with defiance. Because he had an "indeterminate sentence" that connected the length of his prison term directly to his compliance with prison rules, he spent ten years in prison for a minor property crime that would normally have carried a sentence of only six months to a year. These disciplinary violations alarmed his mother, but they earned Jackson a heroic stature among prisoners and Black radical activists that was similar to the status Newton and Seale had achieved by going to the capital with guns.

Jackson's refusal to confess and his explanations of that refusal in *Soledad Brother* inspired the young Michel Foucault to think about the relationship of the reform of the soul to the maintenance of power.[111] Jackson's rejection of the white law broadened the extent of working-class revolutionary ideology in the United States by reviving the notion of spirit as an aspect of working-class struggle. By validating desire and promoting the image of the heroic slave who would rather die than live in psychic bondage, Jackson provided a way to connect rather than divide the problems of despotism and white racism in American society. The Black radicals who were at the heart of the prisoners' movement made the Black freedom struggle against slavery in the present day part of a continuing battle for

Black manliness that had begun in the days of slavery and Reconstruction. They also put Black manhood at the center of human liberation. Because Black men had been brutalized and criminally sanctioned for years for crimes of "social equality"—whether they involved "speech acts" that defied unwritten rules of deference to white authority or individual behaviors—it remained important for the many Black activists who admired Jackson to make a defense of individual Black manliness a way to argue for Black leadership ability. Through Jackson's eloquent writings in *Soledad Brother*, the prison emerged as an institution that supported a soul-killing form of racism and cheap labor. His writings and actions in the prisoners' movement against the divide-and-conquer tactics used by the prison administration to prevent class unity between Blacks and whites not only highlighted problems within prisons but made the prison into a microcosm of repressive techniques in America and resistance to them. Jackson's self-representation was essential to this fight because it identified the humanity of the lumpen proletariat and identified both white racists and Black criminals as redeemable—even as potential leaders. Identifying political activism with practices rather than with fixed internal essences or class locations, Jackson's descriptions of prison life and his letters to those on the outside were a potentially radical critique of vanguard politics and historical determinism.

Through Jackson's writings, leftists came to see the prison as a central element in American life precisely because of its role in racial formation in the denial of Black male agency and citizenship. The intellectual and political impact of Jackson's book and his defense campaign was widespread and changed the character of prison-reform activism. It paved the way for the revolutionary critique of social institutions most frequently credited today to Foucault, who spent critical years in the mid-1970s in Berkeley during the height of the prison-activist movement and wrote an early pamphlet about George Jackson that was published in France.[112]

Masculinity was a critical element in Jackson's heroic self-representation, as it was in the Black Panther Party, in the revolutionary white left, in the Nation of Islam, and in the Southern Christian Leadership Council. Jackson's war against the confinement of his manly spirit attacked not only the prison, but also the Black family—particularly the mother–son relationship—as an element in the system of repression. Jackson was nineteen years old when we went into prison, and he spent his early twenties demanding independence from the rule of his mother, whom he could not forgive for raising him to be a "good boy" and a "respectable" Negro like his father. Both Jackson and his father described Jackson's childhood as

a form of confinement, remarking that the boy had been incapable of escaping outside to play because his mother watched him so vigilantly and refused to let him play with other Black children.[113] *Soledad Brother* was a book that a generation in revolt could easily take up as their own attack on the conventional morality of the 1950s. Jackson's words show him to be a youthful rebel, attempting to move through adolescence and into adulthood, defining himself against his parents, and then begging their forgiveness, only to turn on them again in subsequent letters.

Other books of the era show a similar combination of rebellion and dependence on the older generation. In *Coming of Age in Mississippi*, Anne Moody describes intense struggles with her mother over proper ways to behave and rebel, as does Endesha Mae Holland in her recent autobiography, *From the Mississippi Delta*. However, while Moody and Holland described their battles with their mothers as a generational conflict, Jackson gendered his attacks on his mother, making the tyrannical reign of his mother into a critique of Black womanhood in general as the Black man's first encounter with racial law in the United States. This element of Jackson's rebellion drew questions from feminists, including Angela Davis, who during her correspondence with Jackson urged him to rethink his understanding of Black women's role in the revolutionary struggle. She finally appeared to have convinced him to modify some of his harsh criticisms of the "Black woman's" role in keeping Black male rebels inside the womb when she convinced him to apologize to the women in New York's House of Detention for things he said about his mother in the book.[114]

Jackson's mother had criticized him for this behavior, and many of the fights between Jackson and his parents stemmed from the letters they wrote to the prison administration. The worst letter sent to the prison was not written by Jackson's mother, however, but by his father. The letter described Jackson as "bent on violent self destruction" and resulted in his being sent to solitary confinement. Calling his father a "sick man," Jackson said the letter was like something written by Harriet Beecher Stowe.[115] However, after her first son's death, in an attempt to free his brother by taking hostages in the courtroom in San Rafael, Jackson's mother and his sister Penny had both joined the SBDC. Jackson told Greg Armstrong to take anything out of the book that made his mother sound like she was not a "revolutionary mama." Nonetheless, on first reading *Soledad Brother* in October 1970, Jackson's mother attempted to stop the publication, calling it "lies put out by white people." She did not like the book, Armstrong argues, not because of the letters written to her and about her but because of what Jackson said about himself, particularly in the autobiographical

introduction, in which he describes his criminal activities as a teenager. Georgia Jackson was trying to defend her son's innocence, but he did not want to be defended that way.

According to Georgia Jackson, her son, as he always did, was putting too much guilt on himself when he was actually innocent.[116] In August, after Jackson's death, she told the *New York Times* that the lawyer she had talked to during her son's attempts to gain parole had told her that her son "spoke out too much in his own defense and if he would learn to keep quiet more and just be humble when he went before the board, take everything they accused him of, not say anything back, he would be better off."[117] Jackson's mother and the Black Panthers shared a disgust with this system of plea bargaining and acquiescence, but they responded to it in radically different ways.

Guerrilla Heroes and the Sense of Revolutionary Crisis in 1970

George Jackson, in prison in Southern California, had joined an increasingly divided Black Panther Party. Although he had joined with loyalty to Huey Newton, Jackson's strategic ideas were similar to those of the "Cleaver faction" of the party. Members of that group tended to advocate not a care-free "lumpen" image of manhood but that of the disciplined soldier. When they later formed the Black Liberation Army (BLA), this was the kind of manhood that they would celebrate as the sense of revolutionary crisis within the party grew during the period of repression and FBI infiltration. The New York Black Panthers, who later went into action to fight drug addiction, described how "capitalism + dope = genocide."[118] As the level of danger from infiltration and uniformed police increased, the Panthers advocated a new level of discipline, and military models of manhood came into competition with the celebration of lumpen individualism. According to the BLA member Geronimo Pratt, "All the nickel and dime games that you play on other oppressed people must stop. All the red devils, trues, and drugs must go. Those El Dorados will have to turn into tanks, and those bad rags into guns and ammo. You must understand that you're going to be on the front line, whether you like it or not."[119]

The first theories of urban guerrilla strategy had emerged among Black separatists who had been influenced during the Southern Civil Rights Movement and the Nation of Islam. Robert Williams, writing from exile in 1964 about his short-lived group, RAM, argued that mass organizing

was a worthless strategy. "The Revolutionary Action Movement doesn't attempt to project itself publicly using the oppressor's mass media" he wrote, arguing that there should be no more martyrs in the Black struggle but only victories. He promoted two main elements: a "welfare corps" to be recruited on a public and humanitarian basis, and a cold, sober, secret cadre organization that would have "no meetings, no discussion" and that would take Nat Turner as its model. Turner, Williams wrote, knew the "psychology of white America," and they would adopt his strategy: "Strike by night and spare no one."[120]

Williams gave up entirely on whites' ability to reform. Claiming that "minority revolution is possible," he outlined a plan of urban guerrilla warfare supported by an influx of Third World revolutionaries in support of the American struggle that would eliminate white people entirely.[121] Beginning in 1967, strategic discussions of urban guerrilla tactics appeared in rigorous detail in the Black Panther Party's newspaper when it was still largely influenced by the Revolutionary Action Movement.

Militants had also described guerrilla action as an alternative to disorganized and spontaneous mass action after the 1967 riots in Newark, N.J., and Detroit. *Black Panther* newspaper cartoons of 1967 suggested that sniper activity and small groups of "twos and three" were preferable to the massive urban rebellions that had resulted in police repression and death. The same theory became the advised guerrilla strategy in Sam Greenlee's 1969 novel *The Spook Who Sat by the Door*, which portrayed a Black man as an "infiltrator" of the police force who would become the leader of gangsters-turned-revolutionaries in Chicago.[122] All of these theories of guerrilla warfare defined manhood in strict, almost puritanical terms as the only way to beat the ruling class, and they emerged in response to extreme situations of police infiltration and outright terror. It was these ideas of military leadership, more than "lumpenism," that led to the most disastrous actions in the Black Panther Party, such as the torture and murder of Alex Rackley.

Jackson, who did fingertip pushups in his prison cell and worked on a rigorous schedule of reading, advocated extreme levels of discipline and centralized leadership. As feminists from within the party have argued, these attempts to create discipline within the party as a military unit often resulted in promoting masculine authority and unity at the expense of internal democracy. They also made criticism of serious problems within the party very difficult.[123] Conflicts between discipline-oriented male activists, feminist activists (of both genders and multiple ethnic groups), and anarchists characterized several battles in multiracial organizations

in the 1960s. The splits between Jackson and white cons in San Quentin over methods of anarchy and Maoism mirrored conflicts that had erupted earlier over gender, democracy, and multiracialism in the Student Non-violent Coordinating Committee (SNCC) and again in SDS.[124]

Critics of the left often define the turn toward celebrating what the Weathermen referred to as the "heroic guerrilla" as "crazy," but they do so only after taking those activists out of their historical context. Other incidents of violence during the era—particularly the violence of the United States in Vietnam and Cambodia—are erased in sensationalistic representations of U.S. radicals' relatively minor assaults on property.

The year of the Soledad Brothers campaign, 1970, was a particularly violent one. Throughout the spring of that year, Lieutenant William Calley was being court-martialed for atrocities at My Lai in Vietnam while American Legion activists demonstrated in his favor and government officials argued for leniency. President Richard Nixon removed Calley from the military stockade, and news sources suggested that he would serve no more than seven years of his twenty-year maximum prison sentence before being paroled. In May 1970, the National Guard shot and killed four students at Kent State and killed two more students at historically Black Jackson State in a similar attack that received much less public attention. Following these killings, Nixon and Vice President Spiro Agnew went on a publicity campaign to define students as violent and initiated a counter-revolutionary strategy on university campuses across the country.[125]

In contrast to Nixon's defense of the U.S. military, radicals celebrated the efforts of the Vietcong in fighting American imperialism, and during the spring and summer of 1970 they described the actions and strategies of the Tupamaros of Uruguay and the urban guerrillas of Brazil, whose successful kidnappings of diplomats had appeared on newspaper front pages across the United States. Student radicals who resisted the draft were sent to prison, and the level of militancy increased with the level of repression. A few weeks after the killings at Kent State and Jackson State during nonviolent antiwar protests, the Weather Underground Organization proclaimed a state of war in America and adopted what they called the "urban guerrilla strategy of the Tupamaros."[126] At a protest memorializing the students killed at Kent State, New York building-trades workers, in a demonstration organized by CIA agents, physically attacked peaceful student demonstrators.[127]

Leftists, mainstream newspapers, and political leaders were defining the United States as on the verge of a major revolutionary crisis in the

spring and summer of 1970. Spiro Agnew argued that Americans would prefer the "policeman's truncheon" to the "anarchist's bomb," and Richard Nixon used inflammatory rhetoric to increase levels of police in major cities, set up a surveillance commission on college campuses to redesign buildings to foil future revolt, and initiated the drug war in a massive publicity campaign targeting "the young, the poor, and the black."[128]

It was not really so "crazy" or surprising that a large number of young antiwar and Black Power activists believed that the time was right for the guerrilla struggle to move from the cities of Brazil, Vietnam, and Uruguay into Watts, Berkeley, and Harlem. With Nixon, fascism had apparently arrived. The guerrilla-warfare theory was a response to an increased level of violence and repression against the left and was quite similar to the catastrophic thinking that appeared among the Italian anarchists in the 1920s.

The Black Panthers publicly celebrated killings of prison guards and police in their newspapers, even as the defense campaign argued that Jackson was innocent. In one issue of the *Black Panther*, the cartoonist Ralph Moore depicted a bespectacled Black convict killing a prison guard right near an article on the Soledad Brothers defense. As Erika Doss argues, Emory's image of the revolutionary figure celebrated a mostly masculine concept of the urban guerrilla hero.[129] Similarly, white New Left supporters, such as the Ann Arbor *White Panther Community News Service*, readily allowed that Jackson might have killed the prison guard. Describing the "Soledad incident" in which three Black prisoners were killed from the guard tower and the killing was judged a "justifiable homicide," the *Ann Arbor Argus* reported that "a white prison guard was offed when the jury's verdict was announced."[130] Although many radicals rallied to the defense of the Soledad Brothers, it appears that they did so not because they thought Jackson and the others were innocent of killing the guard, but because they believed that such killings were justified.

The San Rafael Courthouse

While Fay Stender, George Jackson's mother, and Angela Davis organized a mass defense campaign, Jonathan Jackson, George's seventeen-year-old brother, convinced that the legal strategy would not work, joined with agent provocateurs and Black Panthers to plan a hostage exchange modeled on the actions of the Tupamaros.

On July 9, 1970, Jonathan Jackson walked into a hearing with a gun, handed guns to the two defendants on trial—William Christmas and

WE WILL FIGHT WITHIN THE PRISON WALLS UNTIL WE ARE MURDERED OR VICTORY OF THE PEOPLE IS WON!

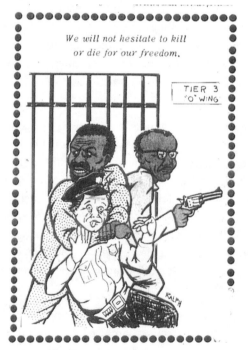

Two cartoons by Ralph Moore from *Black Panther*: (a) August 29, 1970; (b) two men dragging guard with "O Wing" sign, February 6, 1971.

James McClain—and took three hostages. The group jumped in a van that was waiting. Surprisingly, despite the presence of hostages, the police fired on the van, killing Jonathan and many of those inside. Jonathan's fatal attempt to free his brother in July 1970 brought national attention to the California prisoners' movement and attention from prisoners nationwide to the Soledad Brothers as ultra-revolutionaries. The first stories about the Soledad Brothers in the national leftist press appeared not early on, when Jackson was first charged with killing a guard at Soledad, but after Jonathan's action, which inspired many activists and terrified others. However, according to the self-identified FBI agent Louis Tackwood, who was the brother-in-law of Jackson's prison buddy James Carr, the attack on the courthouse had been organized at least partly by police, who by the summer of 1970 had created havoc in the Black Panther Party. Through Tackwood and agent Cotton Smith, the police maintained complete knowledge of underground activities during the summer of 1970 and encouraged and fomented further confusion and conflict among the Panthers. Jonathan Jackson's escape attempt was the product of intentional miscommunication by agents within the Party in Oakland. Huey Newton, who had just been released from prison in June, cancelled the plan, calling it crazy, but the agents involved "forgot" to tell Jonathan Jackson about the change of plans, leaving him alone in his attempt.[131]

With this story kept behind the scenes, prisoners, Black Panthers, and white radicals defined Jonathan Jackson's act as the beginning of a new level of struggle:

> The attempt at freedom was an attempt for all Black men, their murder is the murder of all oppressed people trying to throw off the bonds of imperialism and their blood running in the streets of Marin County is our blood flowing through the streets of every city and every county of imperialist America where men have stood up to fight this avaricious beast who has been sucking the blood of impoverished and economically exploited people all over the globe. . . . the destruction of your beautiful Black bodies have become the creation of hundred of revolutionists who will step in your place and carry on the struggle until every fascist swine is swept from the face of the earth. Rest easy Black brothers, the fight is ours now, it will continue either until we are all murdered or victory is won[132]

Instead of seeing Jonathan's murder as a tragedy or defining the moment as one of decline, the Black Panthers saw themselves in a revolutionary crisis, imagining that Jonathan Jackson's action would be followed by more heroic efforts that would finally result in victory.

The SDS activist Tom Hayden stated, "It has taken a seventeen year old warrior with guns to bring justice to an American courthouse at last" and speculated that if the guards had not been willing to kill the judge and the hostages as well as the hijackers, the attempt could have been successful.[133] Shortly after the shootout, the repression escalated yet again. Angela Davis was arrested and charged with procuring the arms for Jonathan Jackson. The prosecution at Davis's trial argued that she had been driven to acts of desperate violence by her mad passion for George Jackson. The Communist Party mounted a large, broad-based mass defense for her, and her defense drew more attention to the Soledad Brothers case, making Jackson's story more prominent in white communist circles. In October 1970, *Soledad Brother* was released and sold three hundred thousand copies.

The emphasis on direct action in the guerrilla-warfare section of the movement was, as far as both Davis and Stender were concerned, destructive to Jackson's defense campaign. Jackson himself was also being influenced by militants and misinformation. He railed against the defense committee, writing in his last letters from prison that he did not believe that pamphlets or other forms of "talk" would work to liberate him. He said that he did not like being represented as a victim, and he wanted his brother's attempt celebrated, not decried as an adventurist tragedy. Davis argued with him about his defense strategy, and communist pamphlets denounced the San Marin takeover.[134]

Jackson's growing concern for his safety and his need to protect his manly identity led him into disagreements with Fay Stender and his defense committee that erupted angrily into the streets and into the columns of the newspapers. Adopting a heroic position, Jackson made his defense subordinate to the larger cause, writing in the *Black Panther* in July 1971, "The goal is not acquittal, but formation of a revolutionary army." He further described his San Francisco defense committee as "one long ego trip" and defended his brother's action at the San Rafael courthouse, saying, "You took the wrong position on August 7th both publicly and privately. I don't want to be represented as a helpless victim. . . . You cannot save me with reformist, reactionary steps backward to the techniques of the 1930s." Jackson went so far as to state, "My life means nothing; our individual lives mean nothing—no individual's life has value outside the totality of the interrelationships of the commune."[135] Jackson fired Stender from his defense, isolating himself from the defense committee. By this time, he was getting all kinds of misinformation from a variety of sources, including rumors that his friend Jimmy Carr, who had become Huey Newton's

bodyguard, was a police agent. Despite the circulating rumors and hostility, Jackson divided his personal and political conflicts. He sent a message through another convict telling Fay Stender that he "still loved her, no matter what."[136]

It was as if the conflict between Fred Moore and the anarchists was happening all over again. In her book *If They Come in the Morning*, Davis argued, "It is the mark of the immature revolutionary to dismiss such actions [mass organizing] as reformist or liberal. Such an attitude confuses the subjective consciousness of a minority of individual revolutionaries with objective development of the masses of people." She asked people in the movement to "lay aside sectarianism and reject personality cults."[137] Davis and the communists argued for mass strategy, claiming that acts of terrorism were anarchistic, adventuristic, and dangerous. In contrast, Jackson, from a position inside a prison where he frequently discovered that his white allies had been offered money to assassinate him, thought that guerrilla warfare was the only path to freedom. For radicals in prison, the guerrilla-warfare strategies were appealing because prison was already a world in which everything had to be done underground, in small, tight, clandestine groups.

After Jackson's death, the Black Guerrilla Family (BGF), a group he initially had organized, became more and more like a gang. It also got involved in the embittered warfare within the Black Panther Party in the 1970s. According to Hilliard, who had taken Newton's side in the factional dispute, the BGF decided that its members were being killed off by Huey Newton's faction within the party, beginning with James Carr and continuing with Popeye Jackson, who was killed in 1976. Following Jackson's death, prisoners more amenable to prison administrators rose to power in the BGF.[138]

Jackson demonstrated his attitude toward the dangerous factionalism within the Black Panthers during the conflict between Eldridge Cleaver and the Oakland Black Panthers over the Angela Davis defense campaign. In January 1971, the *Black Panther* published a letter by Eldridge Cleaver titled "On the Case of Angela Davis," arguing that the defense committee, run by sinister Soviet communists in collaboration with the ruling class, was using that trial to distract national attention from Bobby Seale's (and Ericka Huggins's) trial in New Haven. Both George Jackson as an individual and the group of prisoners in Soledad calling themselves the August 7th Movement in honor of Jonathan Jackson's revolt, put messages to Cleaver in the *Black Panther*. On March 13, Jackson wrote that Angela Davis was no one's "darling liberal," and that it was important to criticize

Cleaver, "but not in unprincipled terms."[139] On the same day, the August 7th Movement sent in an anonymous letter reading, "You know our language and we know yours; if you get sent to Quentin or Folsom, you're never going to leave here again. . . . The grapevine has your name on it. You need to be dead. You're trying to kill Bobby and Ericka in a sick, cunning way."[140] Jackson seemed to be having trouble with his group shortly before his death. He wrote to an anonymous comrade:

> I was hoping that you wouldn't get trapped in the riot stage like a great many other sincere brothers. I have to browbeat them every day down here. They think they don't need ideology, strategy or tactics. They think being a warrior is quite enough. And yet, without discipline or direction they'll end up washing cars or unclaimed bodies in the state morgue.[141]

Further conflict was ahead. During the summer of 1971, Penny Jackson, James Carr, and Georgia Jackson went to the San Francisco office of the SBDC after hearing about misappropriations of funds. They took it over in the name of the Black Panther Party and locked all the doors, keeping the old defense committee out.

On August 21, 1971, under circumstances that have never been fully explained, Jackson was killed during an escape attempt that the former FBI agent Louis Tackwood argues was set up by prison guards in concert with the FBI. After the killing, guards locked down San Quentin, and information could not get out. Multiple contradictory stories appeared in the press. In one particularly unbelievable story, prison officials said that Jackson, after a visit with his lawyer, Stephen Bingham, pulled a gun from under an Afro wig and began an escape. Jackson's trial was to have gone forward in a matter of weeks and would be at the center of a massive publicity campaign. Had it occurred, it would have brought into the open the entire history of guard-inspired violence at Soledad and would have featured several witnesses to murder attempts and false-confession stories, as several prisoners had told defense organizers about how the prison guards had threatened or favored them and other prisoners to get them to testify against Jackson and to cover up the shooting in which Nolen was killed.

The reports that emerged from the prison were inconsistent. The gun the police said Jackson had been holding changed several times in the accounts, but police eventually settled on a 9 mm Aftra, a very large gun. The *San Francisco Chronicle* tried to fit such a gun under an Afro wig and published the pictures in the paper, indicating the impossibility of the scenario. The *New York Times* printed Georgia Jackson's theory that her

son had been killed in his cell and dragged into the yard. Six other prisoners were charged with the escape attempt and with stabbing three white guards and two white tier tenders during the attempt. Very few people, whether liberal or radical, now believed that George Jackson had been guilty as charged. In the *New York Times*, Roger Wilkins and Tom Wicker both eulogized Jackson. Wilkins argued, "Perhaps he killed a man or more, but if he did, he did it inside an iron circle of hell where the agents of a careless people have almost unlimited sovereignty over the bones and spirits of the men they keep."[142]

Whether he had killed the guard or not, Jackson's power as a symbol of Black resistance to white power remained immense in the years after his death. When Jackson died, the Black Panther Party mourned him both as a man and as a revolutionary. Although some vowed that they would carry on, it must have been difficult in 1971 to see Jackson's death as the beginning of a new revolutionary wave in America rather than as a failure of the minority-guerrilla-army strategy for Black rebellion. If Jackson, whom Huey Newton eulogized as almost a superman, had not been able to escape the prison on his own, it would be hard to imagine that anybody else would.

The August 7th Movement's tribute to Jackson described his death as the loss of a leader. He had taught them everything—how to read, how to organize. He "gave us our manhood, showed us our creed through his every day actions and teachings."[143] The Folsom cadre sent a message to the funeral, as well, speaking of Jackson's "determination, will, and undaunted spirit. . . . He was a true warrior, honed to perfection, and he instinctively performed with the nature of a Panther backed against the wall."[144]

Before he was killed, Jackson had run from the yard, and several witnesses saw his act as an attempt to "draw the fire" away from other prisoners at whom the guards were shooting, giving Jackson's death a heroic and selfless meaning.[145]

Revolutionary toughness gave way to tears. As Jackson's allies saw his murder as one more in a long line of assassinations, they protested that he should be mourned, as Black men were not mourned enough in America. "We as a people have historically allowed our leaders to be swept away with only a nod of the head or forced tears in supplication, we have become victims of murder . . . too timidly."[146] Bert Small of Oakland wrote a letter to George Jackson's mother, proclaiming, "Let us mourn him, let us love him, let us miss him. Let us do as he did in the name of freedom." Clutchett, Drumgo, and Maxwell wrote of their "pain and heartbreak."[147] Angela Davis described his loss as a personal one, the loss of an "irretriev-

able love." Convicts from all over the country wrote in to express solidarity with the Jackson family and swore to be true to Jackson's memory.

Jackson's impact on convicts as a symbol was finally expressed in the series of events that occurred at the Attica Correctional Facility in New York State shortly after his murder in San Quentin. On the day following Jackson's death, prisoners at Attica who had been discussing his writings in study groups mounted a silent protest, organizing hundreds of prisoners in a hunger strike in his honor. The organized memorial was successful, and in the huge dining hall on the day of the strike, says Frank "Big Black" Smith, who would become the prisoners' head of security during the Attica rebellion, it was frighteningly quiet: "No one picked up a spoon."[148] The rebellion at Attica that followed on September 9, just two weeks later, brought the spirit of the prisoners' movement that had been defined largely by George Jackson to international attention.

Jackson was a loss not only to the Black Panther Party and the California left, but to the Black Panthers' ethos of cross-racial, anti-whiteness organizing in the prisoners' movement. After Jackson's death and the crushing of the Attica rebellion, the prisoners' movement split along racial lines, and the category "prisoner" became the one used to define all convicts as equally oppressed within the prison system. This was an increasingly white-dominated, colorblind prison organizing strategy that led to splits in the prison union between "class" and "race" groups.

Whites whose writings appear in prison anthologies drastically exaggerated the percentage of Blacks in prison. One widely read anthology edited by the sociologist Robert Minton featured writing from whites that claimed "the Negro is king in the pen" and that white officers' hands were "tied with red tape." Thus, claimed one prisoner, "The Negro is free to agitate all whites day and night. He preaches 'Black Power' at will for hours on end with only slight resistance from officers." Attributing numerous familiar traits of irrationality to these Black kings, the white prisoner claimed that Blacks would "rather be King inside than get paroled," and described how noisy Blacks tormented quiet white students by singing and hollering during the night, as "packs" of Black gang rapists who would surround their "white prey."[149]

White prisoners organized racial hate gangs with visions of racial Armageddon under the power of Black Panthers just at the moment when Black activists began organizing in the prisons—and just as guards tried to convince many white prisoners that Black Panthers were out to kill them. This same representation of racial Armageddon fuels the Aryan supremacist groups that continued to move from the prisons back into the

population in the 1990s, and collaborations between white prison gangs and guards' unions continue to be revealed, just as they were in the 1970s. Charles Manson, who was released from San Quentin in 1967, immediately went into San Francisco's Haight-Ashbury neighborhood with a vision drawn straight out of white supremacist prison discourse, describing how Black Panthers were going to take over the country and saying that the only hope for whites was to fight back in a conspiratorial "biker–dune buggy army" that would retreat underground, as if they were going into protective-custody cells back in the joint. The later killers of James Byrd Jr. in Jasper, Texas, had also been involved in the Aryan prison gangs.[150]

By the late 1970s, guards' unions had organized against prisoners' unions, and much of the momentum of the prisoners' movement had been neutralized by the involvement of prison reformers who used the violence in the prisons to argue for a renewed division of prisoners into incorrigibles and "redeemables," setting up new classification systems and "prisons of last resort." Although prison-reform efforts had attempted to close large prisons and replace them with halfway-house systems and a few small, "last-resort" maximum-security facilities, the effect of prison reform was to contribute to the prison-building boom of the 1980s and 1990s.[151]

In 1980, Edward Brooks, a member of the BGF, shot Fay Stender and accused her of betraying George Jackson, making her sign a statement that she was a traitor. Although the event happened nine years after Jackson's murder, the attack has been described as the logical outcome of Jackson's politics and the Black Panther Party's ethics. In 1989, Huey Newton was shot and killed by another BGF member in what was called a drug robbery. In both cases, these events have been read backward to find messages about the character of the Black Panther Party and its heroes.

Jackson's past, before his political conversion, as a street hood and rebel who was mad at his mother, and the way that these teenage behaviors appeared under a cloak of demonic evil Blackness, made his legend vulnerable to puncturing in the years following the era of revolt. Instead of looking at the complex interaction of the Black Panther Party with the criminal-justice system and the FBI's COINTELPRO, popular authors have used the stories of Jackson and Newton to arrive at the conclusion that the party was simply a group of "criminals."[152]

In the 1980s, anti-Jackson biographies and anti–Black Panther histories began to appear in histories of the 1960s that claimed to have new "inside" information on the "truth" about Jackson, based on anonymous interview

sources, police, mainstream newspapers, white former prisoners, prison psychiatrists, and prison officials. One of these was the autobiography of James Carr published posthumously and edited by his brother-in-law, who apparently had been "making the ultra-leftist infantile critique of the left for years."[153] Viewing Jackson as a criminal who had slyly manipulated white activists, many of these historians have discounted Jackson's own writings as inauthentic and claimed that they were either written by white editors or plagiarized from other writers. They consistently rely on Carr's account, on the other hand, as the unvarnished truth.[154] Carr's autobiography, however, should be treated as a dubious source. Carr did not see Jackson after 1966, the moment when he described Jackson as "going soft" after he became involved with Marxism. When he was released from prison, Carr became Huey Newton's bodyguard and, according to his own account, began dealing drugs and had contempt for many in the left. Carr's sister was married to Louis Tackwood, and it was from Carr's pants pocket that Jackson's San Quentin "escape plan" was supposedly taken.

It has been easy for people to believe attacks on Jackson's character even from such a problematic source, because Jackson embodied the biggest challenge the (white) left would face in a hero since the days of Nat Turner. This man, who saw himself standing in Turner's footsteps; whose favorite novel was *The Red and the Black*; and who, according to Carr, loved pirate novels and as a teenager had romantic ideas about "killing people right," would test the left's ability to trust Black men, to believe in imperfect heroes, and to define itself without the long-standing and comfortable logic of white rebellion and Black victimization. What we know for certain about Jackson's political ideology appears in *Blood in My Eye* and *Soledad Brother* and in numerous articles Jackson wrote for the *Black Panther*. To discount these works as a mask covering Jackson's inherent criminality, as the anti-Jackson books do, is nothing but an assertion of the presumption of guilt.

As Frank "Big Black" Smith of the Attica Brothers put it, the contemporary attack on Jackson is a failure to see the complexity of human experience. "That is hogwash about George as violent and manipulative," he told me when I asked him what he thought of some of the recent books. "Everybody got a past, a present and a future. . . . Racism is the whole backbone of this thing."[155] To understand Jackson as a heroic figure, people on the left had to abandon and reject the absolute innocence that had often been central to even the most radical definitions of heroic identity in the American left's history. They also had to abandon the

demand for confession as a purgative act and, most of all, they had to trust the word of a Black convict who was not political before he went to prison against the expert opinions of police, prison officials, and a few white convicts.

The difficulty of this task, and the ease with which Black heroes became "criminals" again in the popular media of the 1980s, explains the centrality of the anti-Jackson argument to some of the most bitter critiques of the 1960s Black liberation movement. David Horowitz, whose attack on the Black Panthers, *Destructive Generation*, has been remarked on as the ur-text of post-1968 whiteness,[156] uses Fay Stender's death at the hands of disaffected members of the BGF in the 1980s as the parable explaining the truth of the prisoners' movement, George Jackson, and the revolutionary politics of the 1960s in general. Rather than attempting to understand this tragic and specific event in its own historical context, Horowitz, perhaps channeling Thomas Dixon, uses the Stender story to rewrite the 1960s revolt as the victimization of white women by Black men.

Like the 1974 film *Death Wish*, which depicts a liberal "bleeding heart" turned vigilante after the murder of his wife and rape of his daughter by graffiti-slinging, hippie-like hoodlums who are too powerful for a lenient justice system to punish, Horowitz's writings depict an omnipotent Black Panther Party whose massive support from delusional, sentimental political activists left police forces "powerless" to stop their criminal acts. It was these defense campaigns and high-powered lawyers, Horowitz wrote, that made it impossible for the courts to "sustain a single legal conviction against the Black Panthers."[157] In these campaigns, which he once supported, the Black Panthers, Horowitz now believes, "used my generation's idealism in the 1960" just as Stalin had used his parents' idealism in the 1930s to commit crimes against humanity. Both Stalinists and Black Panthers, Horowitz wrote, were "ruthless exploiters of the radical dream, just like our forbears, my comrades and I were credulous idealists who had served a criminal lie."[158]

Stender's tragic death cannot be separated from the decline of the radical left in the 1970s, from the FBI's war on the Black Panther Party that left a chain of interparty murders in its wake, or for that matter, from Stender's own romanticizing of prisoners as angelic victims. Horowitz's version of the Black Panthers transforms a complex historical reality into an old racial melodrama that allows white men to emerge as the heroic saviors of virtuous female victims who are perennially at risk from the vicious Black villains who prey on their fragile bodies.

Contemporary Praise for Jackson:

Despite such "debunkings," Jackson's memory continues to inspire contemporary activist youth, who have joined an older generation of activists in the contemporary prison-abolition movement. When the popular
hip-hop group Digable Planets sang, "My heroes died in prison: George
Jackson," and in the same song intoned lyrics that are slogans of the
largely incarcerated Black Liberation Army—"One love, gun love, come
'n free the land with us (pigs they cannot stop this project's creamy lavish-
ness)"[159]—they demonstrated the continuing intersection of Black popular culture, Black radicalism, and the prison experience in the United
States. Similarly, when Tupac Shakur signed off a rap with a salute to
Sekou Odinga, Mutulu Shakur, Mumia Abu-Jamal, and Geronimo Pratt
as the "real OGs [Original Gangstas]," and Sanyika Shakur, the former
gang member "Monster Cody," refers to the "George Jackson phenomenon," they indicate that today's youth still see in Jackson a sign of heroism and redemption as they attempt to find a way to make contemporary
Black youth culture into a source of radicalism and rebellion.[160]

Angela Davis also invokes Jackson's spirit in her activism. She spoke of
him in her remarks at the opening of the Critical Resistance Conference
in Berkeley in 1998 and in her talk on prisons at the American Studies
Association that same year. However, Davis sustains the capacity to be
inspired without succumbing to blind admiration. When one enthusiastic
student approached her after a talk, cheeks aglow with excitement about
Soledad Brother, Davis asked her about the Panthers' most famous female
hero, Assata Shakur: "Did you read Assata's book?"

With this question, Davis acknowledged that the most troubling elements of Jackson's heroic legacy have to do with those in the New Left
and the Black liberation movement who have lost activists to masculinist
voluntarism. Folk heroism and Nietzschean philosophies that celebrate a
joyful and manly, lively, defiant life and early death as preferable to slavery
characterized the spirit of George Jackson, but such celebrations have an
edge.

Jackson's rejection of mass organizing toward the end of his defense
campaign indicated that his own fears of being represented as weak rather
than strong were a product of multiple factors, including the atmosphere
of prison violence in which he had come to political consciousness. The
conditions of competitive manly identity inside the prison were unde-
niably a hindrance to the building of a workable alliance in his defense.

Jackson's story, as it appears in his own writings, exposed his vulnerability in relation to his parents and friends, as well as his flaws and insecurities. It also included numerous declarations of desire for connection with others that helped to break the boundaries and definitions of manhood inside the prison—Jackson's own life and writings reflect not simply one story of violent denunciation, but a position that fluctuated between a desire for unity with a mass movement he imagined beyond the walls, as embodied by Angela Davis, and the notion of clandestine armed revolt. He did not live long enough to resolve the questions, and the prison abolition movement that has followed him has not resolved them fully, either, although they have made some efforts.

Some of those who took up that piece of Jackson's activism were the members of the George Jackson Brigade, a group of prisoners turned revolutionaries from Seattle. Inspired by *Soledad Brother*, they formed a multiracial guerrilla faction intent on bombing capitalist institutions without causing death or injury. When they were captured and returned to the prisons, members of the George Jackson Brigade continued as prison activists for antiracism, feminism, and gay liberation and broke the divide between the politics of masculinity and revolution, proclaiming, "We are cozy, cuddly armed and dangerous, and we will raze the fucking prisons to the ground." Ed Mead, who later organized Men against Sexism at the Washington State Prison at Walla Walla, instituted armed self-defense of gay men against prison rape and created a prison activist group that would inspire others all over the country.[161] Rita "Bo" Brown, a former member of the George Jackson Brigade who now works in prison organizing for the Lesbian Out of Control Committee to Free Political Prisoners, advocates Native American sovereignty and described Jackson's book as her first political awakening.[162]

Abandoning both the "feminine" politics of *ressentiment* and its flip side in Neitzchean masculinism, these activists have found ways to shape the politics of revolt around their own complicated identities. But the building of a mass movement around prisoners remains difficult because of the nature of prison itself. That fortress, as Jean Genet has described it, is designed to frustrate and divide. The relationships between those on the "inside" and those on the "outside" continue to be fraught with anxiety, as both prisoners and their "outside supporters" wonder about the "truth" on the other side of the wall.

Conclusion

As I was finishing the second revision of this book, I awoke late in the morning to hear the voices of Rachel Corrie's parents emerging from my radio alarm clock. Three and a half years after her death in Rafah, on March 16, 2003, the play about her life and death, *My Name Is Rachel Corrie*, was being performed at New York's Minetta Lane Theater.

At twenty-three, she left her home in Washington State to join the International Solidarity Movement (ISM) in a project in the occupied territories of Palestine and died protecting the home of the Palestinian pharmacist Samir Nasrallah from the bulldozer that killed her. Corrie's writings, circulated through thousands of forwarded e-mails, and now put together in a moving play about one young woman's growing consciousness of her own place in the world, reveal her to be an unusually careful thinker who was concerned with her own complicity, as a citizen of the United States, in global inequality. She wrote to her father from Rafah that, if she went to France, it would be a transition to too much opulence: "I would feel a lot of class guilt the whole time."[1] It's hard to imagine a person who more fits the classic definition of a martyr: She saw other people suffering and in danger and rushed toward them, despite the personal risk involved. About the Israeli occupation of Palestine, she wrote, in her last e-mail, "I think it is a good idea for us all to drop everything and dedicate our lives to making this stop. I don't think it's an extremist thing to do anymore."[2]

When Corrie died and her words showed up in my e-mail, sent by a friend who was not even an activist, I was overwhelmed by the commitment that can still appear in the words of people who know that they are risking their lives because of their desire not for an abstract God, but for earthly justice. It is hard to write a book on martyrs and victims because there are so many, and I can safely predict that there will be more. It would be impossible to include an in-depth discussion of every single martyr of the American left or to expand this book to include a discussion, as some asked me to, of the martyrs of struggles in Ireland, the Middle East,

or Latin America. Even in America, it is hard to contain the material. So many people died in the Civil Rights Movement, and have been written about at such length, for example, that I finally decided that the story of Civil Rights Movement martyrs was just beyond the scope of this project.[3]

There is nothing to help a person recognize the magnitude of death, victimization, and violence that we live with every day, as well as the seemingly limitless insights that people have come to about these realities, than to try to master the avalanche of articles, books, plays and poems written by or about John Brown; the Haymarket anarchists; the thousands of victims of lynching; the IWW; Sacco and Vanzetti; the Scottsboro Boys; the Rosenbergs; Malcolm X; Martin Luther King Jr.; James Chaney, Andrew Goodman, and Michael Schwerner; and members of the Black Panther Party, not to mention some of the more recently executed or incarcerated people around whom movements have sprung up while I have worked on this project: Karla Fay Tucker, Stanley "Tookie" Williams, Wanda Jean Allen, Tyrone X Gilliam, and, of course, Mumia Abu-Jamal, whose defense campaign originally motivated my research into the history of the defense of political prisoners. Someone asked me once, did I sort of hope that Mumia would die so I could write about his execution? The answer has always been no, and the problem with this project, sadly, was never the shortage of deaths, campaigns, and memorials about which to write. I would like nothing better than to see the entire genre of plays, movies, books, and stories of executed prisoners come to an end. But one thing that seems not to die is the will to kill people who get in the way of profits and power.

Activists have responded to that repression with tremendous creativity, and even with humor. One of the funniest successful defense stories that I came across during my research was that of the socialist Bernard Chazanow, who arranged to have a strikebreaker who was going to testify against strikers from the Ladies Garment Workers Union taken to Turkish baths on the eve of the trial "and make him so drunk he shouldn't be able to come in court."[4] While American activists have responded in different ways to the reality of repression over time, they have continually represented their allies in struggle as heroes: whether they see them as heroic masses in revolt, heroic individuals facing the mob, or heroic lawyers protecting the "average everyday people" who themselves become heroes in their encounters with state power. Even Chazanow's "frivolous" strategy succeeded in keeping his friends out of prison.

If winning a case against the state has been cause for celebration and laughter, anticipating death can bring on profundity, and in any number

of cases that I have not written about here, I have been struck by the power of the words of martyrs and families in a way that goes beyond academic questions. Rachel Corrie risked her life knowingly in a place where death still comes randomly and arbitrarily in a long war against a civilian population. It led her to reflect on the nature of her life and her values:

> There are no rules. There is no fairness. There are no guarantees. . . . It's all just a shrug, the difference between ecstasy and misery is just a shrug. And with that enormous shrug there, the shrug between being and not being—how could I be a poet? How could I believe in truth? And I knew, back then, that the shrug would happen at the end of my life—I knew. And I thought, so who cares? If my whole life is going to amount to a shrug and a shake of the head, who cares if it comes in eighty years or at 8 P.M.? Who cares? . . . Now I know who cares. I know if I die at 11:15 P.M. or at 97 years—I know. And I know it's me. That's my job.[5]

Here, Corrie indicates that her decision to risk her life was not about self-sacrifice or treating herself as "superfluous," but about living with integrity, which to her meant stepping in front of a bulldozer.

However, shortly after her death, which was first publicized by the ISM, the quotation marks had already sprung up around the word "martyr" as it was used to describe her. It is no surprise that a right-wing, radical radio commentator and columnist such as Dennis Prager called her a "fool" and said she should be viewed with contempt for choosing sides with a country that had bred "the cruelest murderers of innocent people in the world."[6]

Four days after Corrie's death, the United States began bombing Baghdad in a campaign it named "Shock and Awe." No one in the national media questioned the heroism of the American troops, and anyone—academic or otherwise—who unwisely questioned the virtue of the victims of the September 11 bombing would be disciplined rather intensely.[7]

The debate over Corrie, whose memory was not sacrosanct, continued as the war went on. The liberal magazine *Mother Jones* printed an article in October 2003 suggesting that Corrie was a pawn, a fool, and that the ISM was a host of naifs, at best, and charlatans, at worst.[8] Corrie was first killed, then heralded as a martyr in Palestine, then attacked from the right, then attacked again from those on the "left" who claimed to seek a more complex reality behind the "simplistic" story of the heroic martyr.

It is a common pattern, and the skeptical accounts from the left have critiqued the memorials written about executed left activists from John Brown to George Jackson and beyond, sometimes suggesting that

movements that memorialize such figures are really sly manipulators, that the martyrs they celebrate are victims not of the state but of the movements from which they came. It is not only from the right but also from the left that we are told that the story of the martyr is a simple one, a melodrama that does not capture the full story. Wise and knowing articles and commentaries again and again insist on the importance of the campaign against making left-wing idols. In *Labor: Studies in Working-Class History*, Timothy Messer-Kruse presented himself as a scholar bravely standing against the tide of "historical orthodoxy" by suggesting that the prosecutors of the Haymarket anarchists were right.[9] The real problem, he suggested, is that people on the left just are not self-critical enough; they depict their canon of martyrs as saints, immune from criticism. The irony of such criticisms, whether they are about Rachel Corrie's standing in a crowd next to some member of Hamas or Nicola Sacco's possible guilt— or Mumia Abu-Jamal's, or John Brown's, or Julius Rosenberg's—is that they claim to speak in the name of complexity but argue that the presence of inconsistencies, failings, and imperfections in the left's heroes should push them off the heroic pedestals of memory. The left either should not have heroes or it should find better ones.

In some cases, critics do not go so far as to attack the martyrs of the movement. Instead, they attack the movement for which they died, and which remembers them. Take, for instance, the response to Nathan Schwerner, when he sent out a SNCC fund-raising letter to the mailing lists of Amnesty International and the New York ACLU telling the story of his son's murder in Mississippi. One of the hundreds of hate letters that Schwerner got back in reply told him that it was his "responsibility as a Jew" to share his feeling that Schwerner's son Mickey had "died in vain." Protesting such pronouncements, Schwerner took out a full-page ad in the *New York Times* that contained the text of the statement that he would read at the National Mobilization Committee to End the War in Vietnam in August 1967:

> Despite my personal views, I will defend SNCC's right to speak out against the policy of any government which it believes to be racist and imperialist. I wish to record that my immediate family and myself deeply resent the use of my son's name in the publicized castigation of SNCC. How indecent and contemptible of those who did not even know him or his thinking to cite his death in bolstering their views.[10]

From what I have seen, then, it is not criticism of movements and their martyrs that people seem to shy away from but, rather, the recognition

of martyrdom itself. The way that the word "martyr" itself shows up in quotation marks suggests that there is something inauthentic and embarrassing about making the claim at all. However, if Hannah Arendt, no radical leftist, is right, the continuing disavowal and dismissive attitude toward "martyrs" is cause for alarm. In *The Origins of Totalitarianism*, she writes:

> The next decisive step in the preparation of living corpses is the murder of the moral person in man. This is done in the main by making martyrdom impossible. "How many people here still believe that even a protest has historic importance?" This skepticism is the real masterpiece of the ss. Their great accomplishment. They have corrupted all solidarity. Here night has fallen on the future. When no witnesses are left, there can be no testimony.

Although Arendt was writing particularly about the way that the concentration camps obliterated individuals' deaths from view, her more general point about the importance of mourning and remembrance are well taken. She continues that the banning of act of grief and remembrance extended beyond the immediate victim to family and friends in both Stalinist and Nazi German societies and notes that the granting of the slain enemy the "right to be remembered," was a "self-evident acknowledgment that we are all men (and only men)." [11]

In the preservation of memories, in martyrologies, stories of heroes, social movements preserve their own history. In the efforts to save individuals from death, they preserve the importance of the individuals who make up their movement and attempt to tell a different story of justice from the one promoted by the courts. My point is not that scholars and journalists should not criticize social movements or even the martyrs of social movements. Obviously, I have criticized both movements and martyrs here. However, the last thing we should be doing is undermining the legitimacy of the arguments of heroism and martyrdom altogether. That gesture of denial is simplistic. It is a serious project to look at actual defense campaigns and memorials as strategies, but it has to be done in the context of understanding where the strategy comes from, from looking at the creation of the martyr in the original context of repression that makes such defense campaigns necessary in the first place.

Trials compress events and exclude historical conditions as much as possible from the events in question. The structure of the trial itself forces polarities. Presentations during political trials have allowed activists to represent their movements in concentrated bursts, creating images of villains and heroes, as life-and-death choices that face those who represent

themselves before the bar of judgment to reduce complexity even more. The pressure to simplify is not the product of radical ideology. Simplification originates in the law itself, when acts of violence are read purely within the law's definition of "wrong." A crime becomes an isolated moment outside of history.

As Herman Melville's Captain Vere asserts in *Billy Budd*, "The prisoner's deed, by that alone we have to do."[12] Melville's story draws out some of the most significant problems of the presentation of the American innocent in confrontation with the law from the perspective of both the defender and the accuser. In the story, a young, handsome sailor, Billy Budd, well liked by all, not too clever, and with a terrible stutter, boards a ship as a crew member. The ship's master of arms, Claggart, who is something of a ship's policeman and, Melville indicates, an all-around wicked man, develops an aversion to Budd and frames him for fomenting mutiny. Confronted with the accusation, Budd, who is innocent but unable to speak in his own defense, strikes the man down and accidentally kills him. Captain Vere (who is called "Starry" Vere because of his contemplative and abstract nature) has to try Billy Budd according to the rules of law and nothing else.

Despite his pretensions to viewing Budd's deed in isolation and the abstract, Starry Vere's readings of the law and the event, the story shows, are based on his own position on the ship. His decision about what to do with the handsome sailor preserves the law, not the good, above all else. Rather than being abstract, H. Bruce Franklin argues, Vere lives up to the nautical term from which his name originates and "shifts in the wind." [13] Far from an objective judge, Vere makes his decision with the memory of a recent rebellion on another ship in mind, so that "a sense of urgency overruled in Captain Vere every other consideration."[14]

Although he was strangely attracted to Budd, there was little Vere could do, for his duty to order had to overcome his personal judgment. He could see why Budd had reacted as he had, because the young could not utter his response. Nonetheless, since Claggart's accusation was not a crime, it could not be helped, and Vere hanged the handsome sailor. Despite the tremendous virtue of Budd, and the widely recognized venality of Claggart, newspapers later reported on "the depravity of the criminal" and the "respectable and discreet" victim.[15] Although that was the only published record of the event, Melville points to the history and monuments to Budd maintained by the sailors themselves, for whom the spar from which Billy Budd was hanged became "as a piece of the cross" that "traveled from ship to dockyard and again from dockyard to ship."[16] It was the sailors, too, who in their songs about the execution for years afterward

gave Billy Budd a voice at last, having him sing, "O 'tis me, not the sentence they'll suspend."[17]

American social movements have told countless versions of this classic story of the frame-up, exposing again and again the drama of the individual confronted by the state. All too often, as with Budd, the hero of the story is delineated also by those narrow constraints that make rosy cheeks and a pale complexion into the primary signifiers of innocence and natural nobility. For this reason, perhaps, Melville assured his readers at the beginning of his tale that Englishmen alone did not claim the title of "handsome sailor," and in what appears at first to be a strange digression, he notes, just after describing the natural regality of some sailors who are widely honored by their shipmates:

> A somewhat remarkable instance recurs to me. In Liverpool now half a century ago, I saw under the shadow of the great dingy wall of the Prince's deck (an obstruction long since removed) a common sailor so intensely Black that he must needs have been a native African of the unadulterate blood of Ham—a symmetric figure much above average height . . . in jovial sallies right and left, his white teeth flashing into view, he rollicked along, the center of a company of his shipmates. These were made up of such an assortment of tribes and complexions as would have well fitted them to be marched up by Anarchasis Cloots before the bar of the first French Assembly as Representatives of the Human Race. At each spontaneous tribute rendered by wayfarers to this Black Pagod of a fellow . . . the motley retinue showed that they took that sort of pride in the evoker of it which the Assyrian priests doubtless showed for their grand sculptured Bull when the faithful prostrated themselves.[18]

Melville defines Budd by his natural innocence, not his rebellious nature; he was innocent even of the act of rebellion of which he was accused, and he was so innocent that he could not even speak when the law addressed him. To a degree, the handsome sailor was struck dumb because he spoke the language of law itself, so innocent that he went to his death without a murmur of protest. Like a force of nature, his arm rose up and smote the evil man down. This reflection on the impossibilities of romantic innocence's capacity in confrontation with the law of the industrial era could leave only one alternative in Melville's story: a rejection of innocence and embrace of slave rebellion as the historical model that could speak without a stutter and would overturn Vere's boat.

With this set of limitations on us even today, the future for organized mass action in relationship to the criminal-justice system remains unclear.

David Feige, a public defender in the Bronx, writes in his recent book on his work defending indigent Americans:

> Oddly, no one has trouble understanding the humanity of white crooks. We mythologize them all the time—Bonnie and Clyde, John Gotti, Carolyn Warmus—all our complex people we find ways to relate to and even admire.... But put a black face on Gotti and no matter how dapper a don he is, the press, the prosecutors and the public only read menace.[19]

Angela Davis and other female veterans of the Black Panther Party have initiated a new abolitionist movement directed against prisons as a fulcrum of racial formation in America. Before the attack on the World Trade Center in 2001, this activism against the so-called prison–industrial complex had come to the forefront of the American left's consciousness. More than just one campaign among many, the contemporary prison-abolition movement forces us to grant Black people the presumption of innocence and to recognize Black agency, and thus determine the future of today's left on the side of either socialism or *Herrenvolk* republicanism. By dividing the prison question from labor issues, or by describing activism around prisoners as sentimental and insufficiently radical; by saying that we need "perfect victims" around whom to organize instead of rallying around the real people who are actually in prison; by saying that sympathy with such people is possible only for sentimental women and drug-addled youth, contemporary critics of the left's martyrs are the ones who take the easy way out. As Bill Haywood said in the 1920s, and as Jean Genet said in the 1970s, it is not that easy to sympathize with the "guilty" man. As Rachel Corrie, who died defending the "unsavory" characters of occupied Palestine, might have argued, putting yourself on the side of people who are under attack can do more than damage your reputation.

As I hope I have shown, evocations of love and passion and the embrace of apparently unsavory figures has been at the base of the most successful democratic movements in American history. The capacity to imagine a different world might begin with the ability to refuse to accept the characterizations of people who were willing to recklessly go against the rules of the society in which they lived as wicked, misguided, wrong, foolish, or criminal. It is much harder to see the face of the "handsome sailor" on an imperfect human than it is to accept the underlying message of the modern-day nation-state that the only real heroes are the cops and soldiers who protect "us" from the rest of the world.

Notes

Introduction

Epigraph: Frantz Fanon, *The Wretched of the Earth*, trans. Constance Farrington (New York: Grove Press, 1963), 114.

1 See, e.g., Hazel Catherine Wolf, *On Freedom's Altar: The Martyr Complex in the Abolition Movement* (Madison: University of Wisconsin Press, 1952); Robert Penn Warren, *John Brown: The Making of a Martyr* (New York: Payson and Clark, 1929); Wallace Stegner, *Joe Hill* (New York: Doubleday, 1950); Francis Russell, *Tragedy in Dedham: The Story of the Sacco and Vanzetti Case* (New York: McGraw Hill, 1962); Gail Sheehy, *Panthermania: The Clash of Black against Black in One American City* (New York: Harper and Row, 1971); Ilene J. Philipson, *Ethel Rosenberg: Beyond the Myths* (New Brunswick, N.J.: Rutgers University Press, 1993); Daniel Williams, *Executing Justice: An Inside Account of the Case of Mumia Abu-Jamal* (New York: St. Martin's Press, 2002).

2 Hannah Arendt, *The Origins of Totalitarianism* (1951; New York: Harcourt Brace Jovanovich, 1976), 385–86.

3 Ibid., 457.

4 On the NAACP, see Manfred Berg, *Ticket to Freedom: The NAACP and the Struggle for Black Political Integration* (Gainesville: University Press of Florida, 2005); Gilbert Jonas, *Freedom's Sword: The NAACP and the Struggle against Racism in America, 1909–1969* (New York: Routledge, 2004); Charles Kellogg, *NAACP: A History of the National Association of Colored People* (Baltimore: Johns Hopkins University Press, 1967); John Hope Franklin and Genna Rae McNeill, eds., *African Americans and the Living Constitution* (Washington, D.C.: Smithsonian Institution Press, 1995); on the ACLU, see Diane Garey, *Defending Everybody: A History of the American Civil Liberties Union* (New York: TV Books, 1998); Samuel Walker, *In Defense of American Liberties: A History of the ACLU*, 2d ed. (Carbondale: Southern Illinois University Press, 1997); William Preston, *Aliens and Dissenters: Federal Suppression of Radicals, 1903–1933* (2nd. ed.; Urbana: University of Illinois Press, 1994); Zechariah Chafee, *Free Speech in the United States* (Cambridge, Mass.: Harvard University Press), 1948.

5 Mikhail Bakhtin, *Rabelais and His World*, trans. Hélène Iswolsky (Bloomington: Indiana University Press, 1984), 212.

6 Thomas Jefferson, "A Declaration by the Representatives of the United States of America in General Congress Assembled," in *The Life and Selected Writings of Thomas Jefferson*, ed. Adrienne Koch and William Peden (New York: Modern Library, 1998), 24.

7 Friedrich Nietzsche, *On the Genealogy of Morals and Ecce Homo*, ed. Walter Kaufman (New York: Vintage, 1989), 34.

8 Idem, "The Means to Real Peace," in *The Portable Nietzsche*, ed. and trans. Walter Kaufman (1954; New York: Viking, 1977), 71–72.

9 Michael Walzer, *Just and Unjust Wars: A Moral Argument with Historical Illustrations* (New York: Basic Books, 1977), 12, 21–22, 52, 59.

10 Max Weber, "The Profession and Vocation of Politics," in idem, *Political Writings* (Cambridge: Cambridge University Press, 2002), 316.

11 Alfred F. Young, *The Shoemaker and the Tea Party: Memory and the American Revolution* (Boston: Beacon Press, 1999), 33–41.

12 Eric J. Sundquist, *To Wake the Nations: Race in the Making of American Literature* (Cambridge, Mass.: Belknap Press, 1993); Shelley Streeby, *American Sensations: Class, Empire, and the Production of Popular Culture* (Berkeley: University of California Press, 2002); Eric Foner, *Free Soil, Free Labor, Free Men: The Ideology of the Republican Party before the Civil War* (New York: Oxford University Press, 1970); Georg W. F. Hegel, *The Phenomenology of Spirit* (1807), trans. A. V. Miller (New York: Oxford University Press, 1977), 111–19.

13 Thomas Jefferson, letter to Colonel William Smith, Paris, November 13, 1787, in Koch and Peden, *The Life and Selected Writings of Thomas Jefferson*, 403. Shays was a farmer who led a rebellion of debtors against Massachusetts in 1787.

14 Edward Countryman, *The American Revolution* (New York: Hill and Wang, 1985). On the historiography of the American Revolution more recently, see Edmund Morgan, "The Other Founders"; Staughton Lynd, "History from Below"; and the reply by Edmund Morgan in *New York Review of Books*, September 22, 2005, December 1, 2005.

15 On Republicanism as a paradigm in American history, see Daniel T. Rodgers, "Republicanism: The Career of a Concept," *Journal of American History* 79 (June 1992): 11–38.

16 Hannah Arendt, *On Revolution* (New York: Viking, 1963), 65.

17 David R. Roediger, *The Wages of Whiteness: Race and the Making of the American Working Class* (New York: Verso, 1991); Cheryl Harris, "Whiteness as Property," *Harvard Law Review* 106 (June 1993), 1707–91.

18 Mary Frances Berry, *Black Resistance, White Law: A History of Constitutional Racism in America* (New York: Penguin, 1994).

19 Thomas Jefferson, "Notes on the State of Virginia," in Koch and Peden, *The Life and Selected Writings of Thomas Jefferson*, 238–43, 257–58.

20 Patricia Nelson Limerick, *Something in the Soil: Legacies and Reckonings in the New West* (New York: W. W. Norton, 2000).

21 See Richard N. Rosenfeld, *American Aurora: A Democratic Republican Returns* (New York: St. Martin's Press, 1997).

22 Douglas R. Egerton, "The Empire of Liberty Reconsidered," and James Sidbury, "Thomas Jefferson in Gabriel's Virginia," in *The Revolution of 1800: Democracy, Race and the New Republic*, ed. James Horn, Jan Ellen Lewis, and Peter Onuf (Charlottesville: University of Virginia Press, 2002).

23 Arendt, *On Revolution*, 55, 62.

24 Ibid, 65–66. On the historical inaccuracies of Arendt's version of American and European history, see Eric J. Hobsbawm, "Hannah Arendt: On Revolution," in idem, *Revolutionaries: Contemporary Essays* (New York: Pantheon, 1973), 201–208.

25 Ibid., 70; quoting J. M. Thompson, *Robespierre* (Oxford: Basil Blackwell, 1939), 365.

26 Giorgio Agamben, *Homo Sacer: Sovereign Power and Bare Life*, trans. Daniel Heller-Roazen (Palo Alto, Calif.: Stanford University Press, 1998).

27 Edmund S. Morgan, *American Slavery, American Freedom: The Ordeal of Colonial Virginia* (New York: W. W. Norton, 1975), 386.

28 Ibid., 344.

29 Paul A. Gilje, *Rioting in America* (Bloomington: Indiana University Press, 1996), 87–115.

30 Richard Slotkin, *Regeneration through Violence: The Mythology of the American Frontier, 1600–1860* (Norman: University of Oklahoma Press, 2000); idem, *The Fatal Environment: The Myth of the Frontier in the Age of Industrialization, 1800–1890* (Norman: University of Oklahoma Press, 1998); idem, *Gunfighter Nation: The Myth of the Frontier in Twentieth Century America* (Norman; University of Oklahoma Press, 1998).

31 Nancy Armstrong, *Desire and Domestic Fiction: A Political History of the Novel* (New York: Oxford University Press, 1987).

32 Edward Hallett Carr also notes this phenomenon in *The Twenty Years' Crisis, 1919–1939: An Introduction to the Study of International Relations* (London: Macmillan, 1946), 71–74.

33 In New York City during the months after the September 11, 2001, attack, the public mourning of the loss of the World Trade Center began as a spontaneous outpouring of support for the families of both firefighters and civilians in public places, particularly Union Square. The attack was interpreted by New Yorkers, who sported "I Love New York" T-shirts just as much as American flags, as a personal attack on their city. However, these spontaneous memorials in public parks were torn down by the city so that eventually the only places to memorialize the trade center were on police and fire stations. Increasingly, children's drawings became the primary images that could be seen in the city's

public spaces. The earliest mourning ceremonies emphasized messages of peace.

34 George M. Frederickson, *The Black Image in the White Mind: The Debate on Afro-American Character and Destiny, 1817–1914* (Middletown, Conn.: Wesleyan University Press, 1971); Jacquelyn Dowd Hall, *Revolt against Chivalry: Jessie Daniel Ames and the Women's Campaign against Lynching)* New York: Columbia University Press, 1974); Glenda Gilmore, *Gender and Jim Crow: Women and the Politics of White Supremacy in North Carolina, 1896–1920* (Chapel Hill: University of North Carolina Press, 1996); Bruce Baker, "North Carolina Lynching Ballads," in W. Fitzhugh Brundage, ed., *Under Sentence of Death: Lynching in the South* (Chapel Hill: University of North Carolina Press, 1997), 219–45.

35 Philip P. Hallie, *The Paradox of Cruelty* (Middletown, Conn.: Wesleyan University Press, 1969), 22.

36 Mark Danner, *Torture and Truth: America, Abu Ghraib and the War on Terror* (New York: New York Review of Books, 2004).

37 For a thorough discussion of pro-life narratives, see Carol Mason, *Killing for Life: The Apocalyptic Narrative of Pro-Life Politics* (Ithaca: Cornell University Press, 2002).

38 This argument goes against that made in Linda Williams, *Playing the Race Card: Melodramas of Black and White from Uncle Tom to O. J. Simpson* (Princeton: Princeton University Press, 2002).

39 Max Horkheimer and Theodor W. Adorno, *The Dialectic of Enlightenment,* trans. John Cumming (New York: Continuum Books, 1995).

40 Safiyah Bukhari, telephone interview by the author, Minneapolis, April 1999.

41 Elaine Scarry, *The Body in Pain: The Making and Unmaking of the World* (New York: Oxford University Press), 1985.

42 Mahasweta Devi, "Drapandi," trans. Gayatri Chakravorty Spivak, in Spirak, *In Other Worlds: Essays in Cultural Politics,* (New York: Routledge, 1988), 196.

43 Georges Bataille, *Visions of Excess: Selected Writings, 1927–1939,* ed. Allan Stoekl (Minneapolis: University of Minnesota Press, 1985), 134; David S. Potter, "Entertainers in the Roman Empire," in *Life, Death, and Entertainment in the Roman Empire,* ed. David S. Potter and D. J. Mattingly (Ann Arbor: University of Michigan Press, 1999), 303–325.

44 Bakhtin, *Rabelais and His World,* 327, 341, 408, 412.

45 Raoul Peck, dir., *Lumumba* (Zeitgeist Films, 2000).

46 Karl Marx, *The German Ideology,* pt. 1, ed. and trans. C. J. Arthur (New York: International Publishers, 1989), 79, n. 1.

47 Arendt, *On Revolution,* 65; Corey Robin, *Fear: The History of a Political Idea* (New York: Oxford University Press, 2004), 101–106.

48 Assata Shakur, "Love Is Contraband in Hell," as quoted in H. Bruce Franklin, *Prison Literature in America: The Victim as Criminal and Artist* (New York: Oxford University Press, 1989), xxi.

49 Austin Sarat, *When the State Kills: Capital Punishment and the American Condition* (Princeton: Princeton University Press, 2002); idem, *The Killing State: Capital Punishment in Law, Politics, and Culture* (New York: Oxford University Press, 2001); Helen Prejean, *Dead Man Walking: An Eyewitness Account of the Death Penalty in the United States* (New York: Vintage, 1994).

50 See, e.g., Eric Cummins, *The Rise and Fall of California's Radical Prison Movement* (Palo Alto, Calif.: Stanford University Press, 1994).

51 Bill Haywood, "A Message from Bill Haywood," *Labor Defender*, June 1926, 86.

52 Karl Marx, *Capital: A Critique of Political Economy*, vol. 1, trans. Ben Fowkes (New York: Penguin, 1990), 414.

53 J. G. Pope, "Labor's Constitution of Freedom," *Yale Law Journal* 106, no. 4 (January 1997): 941–1031.

1 John Brown

Epigraphs: Thomas Carlyle, *On Heroes and Hero Worship in History*, ed. Michael Goldberg (Berkeley: University of California Press, 1993), lix; George Mauzy to Eugenia Burton, October 18, 1859, in the online exhibit "The Mauzy Letters on John Brown's Raid," Harper's Ferry National Historical Park, available at http://www.nps.gov/archive/hafe/mauzy.htm (accessed February 16, 2008); Wendell Phillips, "Toussaint L'Ouverture," in idem, *Speeches, Lectures and Letters* (Boston: Lee and Shepard, 1870), 491; and Angelina Grimke to Gerrit Smith, November 10, 1862, quoted in Robert H. Abzug, *Passionate Liberator: Theodore Dwight Weld and the Dilemma of Reform* (New York: Oxford University Press, 1980), 279.

1 Madison Washington was a slave who led a successful revolt on board the USS *Creole* as it sailed from Richmond, Virginia, to New Orleans in 1841. Taking advantage of the abolition of slavery in the British colonies, Washington directed the ship to Nassau, where he and the rest of the former slaves on board were declared free. On the *Creole*, see Edward D. Jervey and C. Harold Huber, "The Creole Affair," *Journal of Negro History* 65, no. 3 (Summer 1980): 196–211; George Hendrick and Willene Hendrick, *The Creole Mutiny: A Tale of Revolt aboard a Slave Ship* (Chicago: Ivan R. Dee, 2003).

2 David Walker, "Appeal to the Colored Citizens of the World" (1829), in *Pamphlets of Protest: An Anthology of Early African-American Protest Literature, 1790–1860*, ed. Richard Newman, Patrick Rael, and Philip Lapsansky (New York: Routledge, 2001), 108–109.

3 Eddie S. Glaude Jr., *Exodus! Religion Race and Nation in Early Nineteenth Century Black America* (Chicago: University of Chicago Press, 2000), 143–59.

4 Sylvia R. Frey and Betty Wood, *Come Shouting to Zion: African American Protestantism in the American South and British Caribbean to 1830* (Chapel Hill: University of North Carolina Press, 1998), 98, 112–13.

5 Walker, "Appeal to the Colored Citizens of the World," 106–107. On David Walker's connection to Vesey and the African Methodist Episcopal church in Wilmington, North Carolina, see Peter P. Hinks, *To Awaken My Afflicted Brethren: David Walker and the Problem of Antebellum Slave Resistance* (University Park: Pennsylvania State University Press, 1997).

6 Douglas R. Egerton, "Nat Turner in Hemispheric Context," in *Nat Turner: A Slave Rebellion in History and Memory*, ed. Kenneth S. Greenberg (New York: Oxford University Press, 2003), 135–37.

7 From *Annual Report of the American Anti-Slavery Society* (New York, 1853), 51, 55, as quoted in Benjamin Quarles, "Frederick Douglass," in *The Antislavery Vanguard: New Essays on the Abolitionists*, ed. Martin B. Duberman (Princeton: Princeton University Press, 1965), 127.

8 Frederick Douglass, *Narrative of the Life of Frederick Douglass, an American Slave, Written by Himself* (New York: Penguin, 1986), 51.

9 Michael Gomez, *Exchanging Our Country Marks: The Transformation of African Identities in the Colonial and Antebellum South* (Chapel Hill: University of North Carolina Press, 1998), 257–61.

10 Ibid., 255–59.

11 *Liberator*, July 9, 1831. The song "The Triumph of Freedom" is British and first appeared in the *Cambridge Intelligencer* in 1794.

12 Ibid., September 3, 1831.

13 Theodore Dwight Weld, *American Slavery as It Is: Testimony of a Thousand Witnesses* (New York: American Anti-Slavery Society, 1839); an online edition is available at http://docsouth.unc.edu/neh/weld/menu.html (accessed February 16, 2008).

14 The best source on non-resistance is Lewis Perry, *Radical Abolitionism: Anarchy and the Government of God in Anti-Slavery Thought* (Knoxville: University of Tennessee Press, 1995).

15 See, e.g., John Stauffer, *The Black Hearts of Men: Radical Abolitionists and the Transformation of Race* (Cambridge, Mass.: Harvard University Press, 2004); David S. Reynolds, *John Brown, Abolitionist: The Man Who Killed Slavery, Sparked the Civil War, and Seeded Civil Rights* (New York: Alfred A. Knopf, 2005); Paul Finkelman, ed., *His Soul Goes Marching On: Responses to John Brown and the Harpers Ferry Raid* (Charlottesville: University Press of Virginia, 1995). Some are concerned with different questions, such as Louis A. DeCaro Jr., *"Fire from the Midst of You": A Religious Life of John Brown* (New York: New York University Press, 2005).

16 Nancy Isenberg, *Sex and Citizenship in Antebellum America* (Chapel Hill: University of North Carolina Press, 1998), 138–39.

17 Slotkin, *The Fatal Environment*; Streeby, *American Sensations*; Reginald Horsman, *Race and Manifest Destiny: The Origins of American Racial Anglo-Saxonism* (Cambridge, Mass.: Harvard University Press, 1981); David Levin, *History as Romantic Art: Bancroft, Prescott, Motley, Parkman* (Palo Alto, Calif.:

Stanford University Press, 1959); Richard White, "*It's Your Misfortune and None of My Own": A New History of the American West* (Norman: University of Oklahoma Press, 1993). For an insightful commentary on the influence of this theory on German socialists, see Warren Breckman, "Diagnosing the German Misery: Radicalism and the Problem of National Character," in *Between Reform and Revolution: German Socialism and Communism from 1840–1890*, ed. David C. Barclay and Eric D. Weitz (Providence, R.I.: Berghahn Books, 1997). For a discussion of the "myth of the vanishing Indian," see Robert Berkhoffer, *The White Man's Indian: Images of American Indians from Columbus to the Present* (New York: Alfred A. Knopf, 1978); Alexander Saxton, *The Rise and Fall of the White Republic: Class Politics and Mass Culture in Nineteenth Century America* (New York: Verso, 1990); Roediger, *The Wages of Whiteness*; Gordon Wood, *The Creation of the American Republic, 1776–1787* (Chapel Hill: University or North Carolina Press, 1969); Winthrop Jordan, *White over Black: American Attitudes toward the Negro, 1550–1812* (Chapel Hill: University of North Carolina Press, 1968), 512–69.

18 *Chicago Press and Tribune*, July 11, 1859.

19 Streeby, *American Sensations*, 153.

20 Joel H. Silbey, *The American Political Nation, 1838–1893* (Palo Alto, Calif.: Stanford University Press, 1994); Paul A. Gilje, *The Road to Mobocracy: Popular Disorder in New York City, 1763–1834* (Chapel Hill: University of North Carolina Press, 1987); William Gienapp, "Politics Seem to Enter into Everything," in *Essays on Antebellum Politics, 1840–1860*, ed. William Gienapp (College Station: Texas A&M University Press, 1982).

21 Philip Hone, *The Diary of Philip Hone*, vol. 1, ed. Allan Nevins (New York: Dodd and Mead, 1927), 109, 134; Carl E. Prince, "'The Great Riot Year': Jacksonian Democracy and Patterns of Violence in 1834," *Journal of the Early American Republic* 5 (Spring 1985): 1–19.

22 Patricia Cline Cohen, *The Murder of Helen Jewett* (New York: Vintage, 1998), 82–85; see also Gilje, *The Road to Mobocracy*; Timothy Gilfoyle, *City of Eros: New York City, Prostitution and the Commercialization of Sex, 1790–1920* (New York: W. W. Norton, 1994).

23 Christopher Waldrep, *The Many Faces of Judge Lynch: Extralegal Violence and Punishment in America* (New York: Palgrave, 2004), 27–28.

24 Anthony Gronowicz, *Race and Class Politics in New York City before the Civil War* (Boston: Northeastern University Press, 1998), 88; editorials from the *New York Aurora*, April 9, 13, and 15, 1842, in Walt Whitman, *The Collected Writings of Walt Whitman: the Journalism*, ed. Herbert Bergman (New York: Peter Lang, 1998).

25 Waldrep, *The Many Faces of Judge Lynch*, 36–37.

26 Richard Maxwell Brown, *Strain of Violence: Historical Studies of American Violence and Vigilantism* (New York: Oxford University Press, 1975), 148–50, 162.

27 Indiana Regulators, January 1858, in Gilje, *Rioting in America*, 80.

28 George Templeton Strong, entry dated June 29, 1856, in idem, *Diary, Volume 2: The Turbulent Fifties*, ed. Allan Nevins (Macmillan, 1952), 282.

29 Emerson, as quoted in Reynolds, *John Brown, Abolitionist*, 228.

30 Leonard Richards, *Gentlemen of Property and Standing: Anti-Abolition Mobs in Jacksonian America* (New York: Oxford University Press, 1971), 69.

31 Ibid., 90.

32 Noel Ignatiev, *How the Irish Became White* (New York: Routledge, 1996), 126; Graham Russell Hodges, *Root and Branch: African Americans in New York and East Jersey, 1613–1863* (Chapel Hill: University of North Carolina Press, 1999), 231.

33 Gilje, *The Road to Mobocracy*, 135.

34 *Subterranean*, June 7, 1845, August 16, 1845; on Walsh, see Roediger, *The Wages of Whiteness*, 77–80; Sean Wilentz, *Chants Democratic: New York City and the Rise of the American Working Class, 1788–1850* (New York: Oxford University Press, 2004), 328–329; Ignatiev, *How the Irish Became White*, 82–84; Tyler Anbinder, *Five Points: The 19th Century New York City Neighborhood that Invented Tap Dance, Stole Elections and Became the World's Most Notorious Slum* (New York: Plume, 2001), 156–58.

35 Edwin G. Burrows and Mike Wallace, *Gotham: A History of New York City to 1898* (New York: Oxford University Press, 2000), 823.

36 Ignatiev, *How the Irish Became White*, 148–76.

37 Jean H. Baker, *Affairs of Party: The Political Culture of Northern Democrats in the Mid-19th Century* (Ithaca: Cornell University Press, 1983), 159.

38 Burrows and Wallace, *Gotham*, 886.

39 Adrian Cook, *Armies of the Streets: The New York City Draft Riots of 1863* (Lexington: University Press of Kentucky, 1974), 177–80.

40 Edward Beecher, *Narrative of Riots at Alton: In Connection with the Death of Elijah Lovejoy* (Alton, Ill.: G. Holton, 1838), 9.

41 Gilje, *Rioting in America*, 83, 86; Brown, *Strain of Violence*, x.

42 Frank Browning and John Gerassi, *The American Way of Crime* (New York: Putnam, 1980), 142.

43 Anbinder, *Five Points*, 274–96; Ignatiev, *How the Irish Became White*, 154; Richard Schneirov, *Labor and Urban Politics: Class Conflict and the Origins of Modern Liberalism in Chicago, 1864–97* (Urbana: University of Illinois Press, 1998); Waldrep, *The Verdict of Judge Lynch*, 63–66.

44 Saxton, *The Rise and Fall of the White Republic*, 200, quoting from Bennett, *Leni Leoti; or, Adventures in the Far West* (Cincinnati: J. A. and U. P. James, 1853), 45.

45 Slotkin, *Regeneration through Violence*; idem, *The Fatal Environment*; idem, *Gunfighter Nation*.

46 Gronowicz, *Race and Class Politics in New York City before the Civil War*, 86–87; Ned Buntline, *The B'Hoys of New York* (New York: Dick and Fitzgerald, 1850); Anbinder, *Five Points*, 179–80.

47   Slotkin, *Regeneration through Violence*.

48   Ibid., July 11, 1834. On the history of New York's political newspapers, see Burrows and Wallace, *Gotham*, 455–87.

49   *Evening Post*, July 12, 1834.

50   Roediger, *The Wages of Whiteness*, 35, 59–60.

51   Stowe, *A Key to Uncle Tom's Cabin* (Boston and Cincinnati, 1835), 25, quoted in Fredrickson, *The Black Image in the White Mind*, 110–12.

52   Abraham Lincoln, "Cooper Union Address," February 27, 1860, available online at http://www.americanrhetoric.com/speeches/abelincoln-cooperunionaddress.htm (accessed February 16, 2008).

53   Bruce Dain, "A Hideous Monster of the Mind: American Race Theory, 1787–1859," Ph.D. diss., Princeton University, Princeton, 1996, 168.

54   Ibid., 175; Baker, *Affairs of Party*, 227–29; Roediger, *The Wages of Whiteness*, 101–102.

55   Michel-Rolph Trouillot, "Unthinkable History: The Haitian Revolution as a Non-Event," in *Silencing the Past: Power and the Production of History*, ed. Michel-Rolph Trouillot (Boston: Beacon Press, 1995).

56   Herbert Aptheker, *Nat Turner's Slave Rebellion: Together with the Full Text of the So-Called "Confessions" of Nat Turner Made in Prison in 1831* (New York: Humanities Press, 1966), 2, 35, 39, 128–130; Kenneth S. Greenberg, ed., *Nat Turner: A Slave Rebellion in History and Memory* (New York: Oxford University Press, 2003), 37.

57   E. Anthony Rotundo, *American Manhood: Transformations in Masculinity from the Revolution to the Modern Era* (New York: Basic Books, 1993); Sundquist, *To Wake the Nations*; Roberta J. Park, "Biological Thought, Athletics and the Formation of a Man of Character" and "Introduction," in *Manliness and Morality: Middle-Class Masculinity in Britain and America, 1800–1940*, ed. J. A. Mangan and James Walvin (New York: St. Martin's Press, 1987); Herbert Sussman, *Victorian Masculinities: Manhood and Masculine Poetics in Early Victorian Literature and Art* (Cambridge: Cambridge University Press, 1995).

58   *Richmond Compiler*, August 24, 1831, in Henry Irving Tragle, *The Southampton Slave Revolt of 1831: A Compilation of Source Material* (New York; Vintage, 1973), 37.

59   *Richmond Enquirer*, August 30, 1831, ibid., 43.

60   *Richmond Compiler*, September 3, 1831, *Richmond Constitutional Whig*, August 29, 1831, both ibid., 50, 59.

61   *Richmond Compiler*, August 24, 1831, ibid., 36.

62   Iver Bernstein, *The New York City Draft Riots: Their Significance for American Society and Politics in the Age of the Civil War* (New York: Oxford University Press, 1990); Cook, *Armies of the Streets*, 177–78; George Templeton Strong, *Diary of George Templeton Strong: Selections*, ed. Allan Nevins and Thomas J. Pressley (Seattle: University of Washington Press, 1988), 237–45, 261.

63 Greenberg, *Nat Turner*; Tragle, *The Southampton Slave Revolt of 1831*, esp. 17; Sally E. Hadden, *Slave Patrols: Law and Violence in Virginia and the Carolinas* (Cambridge, Mass.: Harvard University Press, 2001), 145–46.

64 *American Beacon* (Norfolk, Va.), August 26, 1831; *Richmond Compiler*, August 27, 1831; *Richmond Constitutional Whig*, August 29, 1831; *Edenton Gazette* (Edenton, N.C.), August 31, 1831, *Lynchburg Virginian*, September 8, 1831, all in Tragle, *The Southampton Slave Revolt of 1831*; see also Vincent Harding, *There Is a River: The Black Struggle for Freedom in America* (New York: Harcourt Brace Jovanovich, 1981), 75–100.

65 *Liberator*, September 3, 1831. David Reynolds argues that Brown's endorsement of slave rebellion "crystallized the difference" with Garrison: Reynolds, *John Brown, Abolitionist*, 51.

66 Benjamin Sillman, as quoted in Abzug, *Passionate Liberator*, 86.

67 *Workingman's Advocate*, October 1, 1831.

68 Ibid., August 29, 1831.

69 Ibid., September 10, 1831.

70 Ibid., October 1, 1831.

71 *Sentinel* (New York), n.d., in Tragle, *The Southampton Slave Revolt of 1831*, 104–105.

72 Harriet Beecher Stowe, *Dred: A Tale of the Great Dismal Swamp*, 1:320–21, available online at http://ibiblio.lsu.edu/main/Docsouth/nc/stowe2/illustr.html (accessed February 16, 2008).

73 Abzug, *Passionate Liberator*, 131.

74 Roediger, *The Wages of Whiteness*, 127.

75 On theories of white racial identity and the concept of projection, see Joel Kovel, *White Racism: A Psychohistory* (New York: Columbia University Press, 1970); George P. Rawick, *From Sundown to Sunup: The Making of the Black Community* (Westport, Conn.: Greenwood Press, 1972), 150–66; Roediger, *The Wages of Whiteness*; Eric Lott, *Love and Theft: Blackface Minstrelsy and the American Working Class* (New York: Oxford University Press, 1993).

76 *Atlantic Monthly*, December 1857, 290, February 1861, 252–54.

77 Thomas Wentworth Higginson, "Saints and Their Bodies," in idem, *Outdoor Papers* (Boston: Ticknor and Fields, 1863), 8–10.

78 Parker, as quoted in Littlefield, "Blacks, John Brown, and a Theory of Manhood," 94, fn. 46.

79 John L. Thomas, *The Liberator: William Lloyd Garrison, a Biography* (Boston: Little, Brown, 1963), 207.

80 Harriet Martineau, *The Martyr Age of the United States* (Boston: Weeks, Jordan, 1839).

81 The Lovejoy story has been disputed, but the most recent biography of Brown asserts its importance: Reynolds, *John Brown, Abolitionist*, 62, 65.

82 Harry Andrew Wright, "John Brown in Springfield," *New England Magazine*, May 1894, John Brown / Boyd Stutler Collection Database, no. PR 030008 AJ, West Virginia State Archives, Charleston, http://www.wvculture.org/history/wvmemeory/imlsintro.html (accessed February 19, 2008).

83 *Liberator*, November 24, 1837, as quoted in Thomas, *The Liberator*, 256; Merton Dillon, *Elijah P. Lovejoy, Abolitionist Editor* (Urbana: University of Illinois Press, 1961), 175–78.

84 Iyunolu Folayan Osagie, *The Amistad Revolt: Memory, Slavery, and the Politics of Identity in the United States and Sierra Leone* (Athens: University of Georgia Press, 2000), 12; Howard Jones, *Mutiny on the Amistad: The Saga of a Slave Revolt and Its Impact on American Law, Abolition, and Diplomacy* (New York: Oxford University Press, 1987), 45.

85 Ella Forbes, "'By My Own Right Arm': Redemptive Violence and the 1851 Christiana, Pennsylvania Resistance," *Journal of Negro History* 83, no. 3 (Summer 1998): 164, quoting Frederick Douglass, "Is It Right and Wise to Kill a Kidnapper?" *Frederick Douglass Paper*, June 2, 1854.

86 Ibid., 164.

87 For an article summing up continuing debates about the nature of slavery, see George Fredrickson, "The Skeleton in the Closet," *New York Review of Books*, vol. 47, no. 17, November 2, 2000, 61–66.

88 Matthew Jacobson, *Whiteness of a Different Color: European Immigrants and the Alchemy of Race* (Cambridge, Mass.: Harvard University Press, 1998), 35–44; Levin, *History as Romantic Art*.

89 Communipaw (James McCune Smith), *Frederick Douglass' Paper*, December 18, 1851; for pseudonym, see John K. Stauffer, "Advent among the Indians: The Revolutionary Ethos of Gerrit Smith, James McCune Smith, Frederick Douglass and John Brown," in *Antislavery Violence: Sectional, Racial, and Cultural Conflict in Antebellum America*, ed. John R. McKivigan and Stanley Harrold (Knoxville: University of Tennessee Press, 1999), 236–73.

90 Douglass, *Narrative of the life of Frederick Douglass*, 107, 111–13.

91 Paul Gilroy, *The Black Atlantic: Modernity and Double Consciousness* (Cambridge, Mass.: Harvard University Press, 1993), 60–63; Susan Buck-Morss, "Hegel and Haiti," *Critical Inquiry* 26, no. 4 (Summer 2000): 821–65.

92 Henry Highland Garnet, "Address to the Slaves of the United States," in Newman et al., *Pamphlets of Protest*, 161, 164.

93 James Redpath, *The Public Life of Capt. John Brown* (Boston: Thayer and Eldridge, 1860), 267, 298.

94 Nat Brandt, *The Town That Started the Civil War* (New York: Bantam Dell, 1991); Frederick J. Blue, *No Taint of Compromise: Crusaders in Antislavery Politics* (Baton Rouge: Louisiana State University Press, 2006); Jacob R. Shipherd, *History of the Oberlin–Wellington Rescue* (1859), reprint. ed. (New York: Da Capo Press, 1972).

95 Leslie M. Harris, *In the Shadow of Slavery: African Americans in New York City, 1626–1863* (Chicago: University of Chicago Press, 2003), 172–73.

96 William Wells Brown, "John Brown and the Fugitive Slave Law," *Independent*, March 10, 1870; Lewis Hayden to Mary E. Stearns, letter, April 8, 1878, in John Brown / Boyd Stutler Collection, no. MS07–0003 A-C, West Virginia State Archives, Charleston, http://www.wvculture.org/history/wvmemeory/imlsintro.html (accessed February 19, 2008).

97 John Brown, "Words of Advice," in *A John Brown Reader: The Story of John Brown In His Own Words, in the Words of Those Who Knew Him, and in the Poetry and Prose of the Literary Heritage*, ed. Louis Ruchames (London: Abelard-Schuman, 1959), 76–78.

98 Shipherd, *The Oberlin-Wellington Rescue*, 7. The rescuers also spoke of John Brown's son who had been killed in Kansas at their "felon's feast" before the trial: ibid., 10.

99 Ibid., 46.

100 Ibid., 175, 177.

101 John Brown, "Dear Wife," Springfield, Mass., January 17, 1851, in Ruchames, *A John Brown Reader*, 75.

102 Saidiya V. Hartman, *Scenes of Subjection: Terror, Slavery, and Self-Making in Nineteenth Century America* (New York: Oxford University Press, 1997), 17–22; Maryann Noble, "Ecstasy of Apprehension: Gothic Pleasure of Sentimental Fiction," in *Frontier Gothic: Terror and Wonder at the Frontier in American Literature*, ed. David Mogen, Scott Sanders, and Joanne Karpinski (Rutherford, N.J.: Farleigh Dickinson University Press, 1993); Brown, "Dear Wife," 75.

103 Redpath, *The Public Life of Capt. John Brown*, 206. Brown advocated holding land in common and thus demonstrated a similarity to English dissenters: W. A. Phillips, "Three Interviews with Old John Brown," *Atlantic Monthly*, December 1879, 741; Christopher Hill, *The World Turned Upside Down: Radical Voices during the English Revolution* (London: Temple Smith, 1972), 111.

104 On Brown's relationship with Gerrit Smith and James McCune Smith, see Stauffer, *The Black Hearts of Men*; on the relationship between Jonathan Edwards, Calvinism, and Republican theory, see James Cooper, *Tenacious of Their Liberties: The Congregationalists of Colonial Massachusetts* (New York: Oxford University Press, 1999); Leo Hirrel, *Children of Wrath: New School Calvinism and Antebellum Reform* (Lexington: University Press of Kentucky, 1998); Joseph Conforti, *Jonathan Edwards: Religious Tradition and American Culture* (Chapel Hill: University of North Carolina Press, 1995); Daniel J. McInerney, *Fortunate Heirs of Freedom* (Lincoln: University Of Nebraska Press, 1994).

105 Conforti, *Jonathan Edwards*, 25. On Brown's methods of prayer, see Osborne Perry Anderson, *A Voice from Harper's Ferry: A Narrative of Events*

at *Harper's Ferry with Incidents Prior and Subsequent to Its Capture by Captain Brown and His Men* (Boston: for the author, 1861), 24, 28; Redpath, *The Public Life of Capt. John Brown*, 111–14. There are significant differences of opinion about John Brown's religious beliefs. Most of those who are critical of Brown refer to him either as a "strict Calvinist," as does Stephen Oates, or an "antinomian," as does John Stauffer. Louis De Caro Jr., the only theologian who has studied Brown, refers to him as a "post-millennial Calvinist": De Caro, *Fire from the Midst of You: A Religious Life of Captain Brown* (New York: New York University Press, 2002).

106 Frederick Douglass, *The Life and Times of Frederick Douglass*, reprint. ed. (New York: Macmillan, 1962), 271. On Garnet, see Benjamin Quarles, *Black Abolitionists* (New York: Oxford University Press, 1969); Sterling Stuckey, *Slave Culture: Nationalist Theory and the Foundations of Black America* (New York: Oxford University Press, 1987).

107 Douglass, *The Life and Times of Frederick Douglass*, 327.

108 John Brown to Mary Brown, letter, January 9, 1856, John Brown Papers, Chicago Historical Society, Chicago.

109 Philip Foner, *The Life and Writings of Frederick Douglass* (New York: International Publishers, 1950), 87, fn. 3; Douglass, *The Life and Times of Frederick Douglass*, 274.

110 John Brown Jr., speech at J. Sella Martin's church, Boston, as published in *Weekly Anglo African*, December 22, 1860.

111 Letter from John Brown, dated December 15, 1851, *Frederick Douglass' Paper*, December 25, 1851, 3.

112 John Brown to Mary, letter, Boston, December 22, 1851, in Ruchames, *A John Brown Reader*, 78.

113 S. L. Blumenson, "He Was John Brown's Right Hand Man: August Bondi, Fighter for Freedom," *National Jewish Monthly*, June 1952. Bondi's mother had told him that "as a Jew it was his duty to defend institutions which give equal rights to all beliefs." Brown's willingness to fight with Bondi and two other Jewish men is further evidence that his religious sectarianism has been exaggerated in many historical accounts. On Brown's trip to Chicago, see the Ernst Schmidt scrapbook in Ernst Schmidt Papers, Chicago Historical Society, and Frederick Schmidt, trans. and ed., *He Chose: The Other Was a Treadmill Thing*, Santa Fe, 1968, from a scrapbook of articles, poems, essays, and tales collected by R. Ernest Schmidt, Paul Avrich Collection, Chicago Historical Society.

114 On the theory of the "slave power," see Foner, *Free Soil, Free Labor, Free Men*; Leonard Richards, *The Slave Power: The Free North and Southern Domination, 1780–1860* (Baton Rouge: Louisiana State University Press, 2000).

115 Frederick Douglass, "Lecture on Slavery," December 8, 1850, in Foner, *The Life and Writings of Frederick Douglass*, 139, 146.

116 Anderson, *A Voice from Harper's Ferry*, 5.

117 Littlefield, "Blacks, John Brown, and a Theory of Manhood," 67–97.

118 Reynolds, *John Brown, Abolitionist*, 139.

119 Slotkin, *The Fatal Environment*, esp. 242–47, 262, on the filibuster William Walker.

120 George Collison, *Shadrach Minkins: From Fugitive Slave to Citizen* (Cambridge, Mass.: Harvard University Press, 1998); Albert Von Frank, *The Trials of Anthony Burns: Freedom and Slavery and Emerson's Boston* (Cambridge, Mass.: Harvard University Press, 1998); Jeffery Rossbach, *Ambivalent Conspirators: John Brown, the Secret Six and a Theory of Slave Violence* (Philadelphia: University of Pennsylvania Press, 1983); Edward J. Renehan, *The Secret Six: The Men Who Conspired with John Brown* (New York: Crown Publishing, 1995).

121 Brown to Andrew Hunter, November 22, 1859, in Ruchames, *A John Brown Reader*, 144.

122 Allies for Freedom, *John Brown Mysteries* (Missoula, Mont.: Pictorial Histories Publishing, 1999).

123 Descriptions of events leading up to Brown's raid can be found in Boyd Stutler, *Preface to a Provisional Constitution of the United States* (Providence, R.I.: M and S Press, 1969); Louis Ruchames, ed., *A John Brown Reader: The Story of John Brown In His Own Words, in the Words of Those Who Knew Him, and in the Poetry and Prose of the Literary Heritage* (London: Abelard-Schuman, 1959); Finkelman, *His Soul Goes Marching On*; Anderson, *A Voice from Harper's Ferry*.

124 John Brown, *Provisional Constitution and Ordinances for People of the United States* (Weston, Mass.: M and S Press, 1969).

125 *Chicago Press and Tribune*, December 3, 1859.

126 *Chicago Tribune*, November 12, 1859.

127 American Anti-Slavery Society, *The Anti-Slavery History of the John Brown Year*, reprint. ed. (New York: Negro University Press, 1969), 90.

128 James N. Gloucester to John Brown, February 19, 1858, and March 9, 1858, in *The Black Abolitionist Papers*, 5 vols., ed. Peter Ripley, Roy E. Finkenbine, and Michael F. Hembree (Chapel Hill: University of North Carolina Press, 1985–1992), 377–82.

129 Bertram Brown-Wyatt, as quoted in Paul Finkelman, "Manufacturing Martyrdom," in idem, *His Soul Goes Marching On*, 56.

130 Strong, *Diary, Volume 2: The Turbulent Fifties*, 465.

131 Daniel C. Littlefield, "Blacks, John Brown, and a Theory of Manhood," in Finkelman, *His Soul Goes Marching On*, 76.

132 Charles H. Robinson to John Brown, September 14, 1856, copied from original by Oswald Garrison Villard, in John Brown / Boyd Stutler Collection Database, no. MS09–0019 AB, West Virginia State Archives, Charleston, http://www.wvculture.org/history/wvmemeory/imlsintro.html (accessed February 19, 2008). See also Thomas Wentworth Higginson, *A Ride through Kansas*, 1857, no. PR09–0001 A-X, ibid.; William A. Phillips, *The Conquest of Kansas*

(Boston: Phillips, Sampson, 1856); and Gunja SenGupta, *For God and Mammon: Evangelicals and Entrepreneurs, Master and Slaves in Territorial Kansas, 1854–1860* (Athens: University of Georgia Press, 1996), 113.

133   David M. Potter, *The Impending Crisis, 1848–1861* (New York: Harper and Row, 1976), 219–21.

134   On the relationship between Know-Nothingism and Free Soilism, see Stephen Maizlish, "The Know Nothing Movement in the Antebellum North," in Gienapp, *Essays on Antebellum Politics*, 96; see also Slotkin, *The Fatal Environment*; Saxton, *The Rise and Fall of the White Republic*; Streeby, *American Sensations*.

135   SenGupta, *For God and Mammon*.

136   "Defending Beecher" in the *New York Tribune*, April 4, 1856: "Men should carry with them the means of physical defense as well as of spiritual illumination. These principles are such that any honest, Christian, freedom-loving man might be proud to avow," 4.

137   Thomas Wentworth Higginson, *A Ride through Kanzas: Letters Originally Published with the Signature of Worcester, in the New York Tribune* (New York: Anti-Slavery Society, c. 1856), and *New York Tribune*, May 26, 1856, 6.

138   Mrs. J. C. Swayze, *Osawatomie Brown* (New York: Samuel French, 1856, 1859). Swayze was Kate Edwards Swayze, a young playwright from New York. See "An Old Play on John Brown by Kate Edwards," *Kansas Historical Quarterly* 6 (February 1937): 34–59.

139   *New York Tribune*, November 16, 1859.

140   Slotkin, *The Fatal Environment*, 269.

141   On nineteenth-century critiques of perfectionism, see James H. Moorhead, "Perry Miller's Jeremiad against Nineteenth Century Protestantism," *South Atlantic Quarterly* 86 (Summer 1987): 312–26; Perry Miller, *The Life of the Mind in America from the Revolution to the Civil War* (New York: Harcourt, Brace, 1965); Ann Douglas, *The Feminization of American Culture* (New York: Alfred A. Knopf, 1977).

142   "Carlyle," *Atlantic Monthly*, December 1857, 185, 193. On the Congregational, Unitarian, and Presbyterian reformers; their origins; and their theological differences from Methodists and other perfectionists, see Cooper, *Tenacious of Their Liberties*; Paul Goodman, *Of One Blood: Abolitionism and the Origins of Racial Equality* (Berkeley: University of California Press, 1998), 83, 90–93, 113, 114–15; Hirrel, *Children of Wrath*; Conforti, *Jonathan Edwards*; Randall Balmer and Lauren F. Winner, *Protestantism in America* (New York: Columbia University Press, 2002), 14, 39, 46, 58.

143   Kerby Miller, *Emigrants and Exiles: Ireland and the Irish Exodus to North America* (New York: Oxford University Press, 1988).

144   Margaret Fuller on Carlyle, *Dial*, July 2, 1841, 131–33; Henry David Thoreau, "Thomas Carlyle and His Works," in idem, *A Yankee in Canada, with Anti-Slavery and Reform Papers* (New York: Haskell House, 1969).

145   Charles Lane, "Cromwell," *Dial*, October 1842, 258.

146 Carlyle to Emerson, in *The Correspondence of Thomas Carlyle and Ralph Waldo Emerson*, 2 vols., ed. C. E. Norton (Boston: Ticknor, 1886), 2:10. On Thoreau, see Michael T. Gilmore, *American Romanticism and the Marketplace* (Chicago: University of Chicago Press, 1985); Slotkin, *Regeneration through Violence*, 518–37; David Leverenz, *Manhood and the American Renaissance* (Ithaca: Cornell University Press, 1989), 90.

147 Thomas Carlyle, *On Heroes, Hero-Worship and the Heroic in History* (Berkeley: University of California Press, 1993), 109.

148 Carlyle, *Oliver Cromwell's Letters and Speeches: With Elucidations* (London: Methuen, 1904), 186, 192.

149 Franklin Sanborn, speech to Concord School, March 1857, John Brown Papers, Chicago Historical Society.

150 Ibid.

151 Anne C. Rose, *Transcendentalism as a Social Movement, 1830–1850* (New Haven: Yale University Press, 1981), 209.

152 Henry David Thoreau, "A Plea for Captain Brown," in James Redpath, ed., *Echoes of Harper's Ferry* (New York: Arno Press, 1969), 17–42, quotations on 18–19. For a lengthy discussion of Thoreau's use of western tropes to define Brown, see Slotkin, *The Fatal Environment*, 262–77; Lucy Maddox, *Removals: Nineteenth-Century American Literature and the Politics of Indian Affairs* (New York: Oxford University Press, 1991), 133–57.

153 Henry David Thoreau, entry dated December 3, 1859, in Bradford Torrey and Francis H. Allen, eds., *The Journal of Henry D. Thoreau*, 14 vols. (1906; Salt Lake City: G. M. Smith, 1984), 13:4.

154 Stephen B. Oates, *To Purge This Land with Blood* (New York: Harper & Row, 1970), 233.

155 Richard Ellis, *The Dark Side of the Left: Illiberal Egalitarianism in America* (Lawrence: University Press of Kansas, 1998), 36, 43.

156 Thomas Wyatt Brown, "A Volcano beneath a Mountain of Snow: John Brown and the Problem of Interpretation," in Finkelman, *His Soul Goes Marching On*, 10–38. See also Wyatt Brown, *Lewis Tappan and the Evangelical War against Slavery* (Cleveland: Case Western Reserve University Press, 1969).

157 Stauffer, *The Black Hearts of Men*, 58.

158 Robert Burckholder, as quoted in Victor Vincent Verney, "John Brown: Cultural Icon in American Mythos," Ph.D. diss., State University of New York, Buffalo, 1996, 177.

159 Ken Chowder, "The Father of American Terrorism," *American Heritage*, vol. 51, no. 1, February–March 2000, 1.

160 Peter Linebaugh and Marcus Rediker, *The Many-Headed Hydra: Sailors, Slaves, Commoners and the Hidden History of the Revolutionary Atlantic* (Boston: Beacon Press, 2000), 81; Hill, *The World Turned Upside Down*.

161 James L. Huston, "The Experiential Basis of the Northern Anti-Slavery Impulse," *Journal of Southern History* 56, no.4 (November 1990):

609–40; Merton Dillon, *Slavery Attacked: Southern Slaves and Their Allies, 1619–1865* (Baton Rouge: Louisiana State University Press, 1990).

162 De Caro, *Fire from the Midst of You*, 4.

163 Wendell Phillips, "The Lesson of the Hour," in Redpath, *Echoes of Harper's Ferry*, 43–66.

164 Ibid., 60.

165 Brown, "Dear Wife," 75. On Thomas Thomas, see Wright, "John Brown in Springfield."

166 De Caro, *Fire from the Midst of You*, 137–54; Wright, "John Brown in Springfield."

167 Reynolds, *John Brown, Abolitionist*, 164.

168 John Foxe, *Actes and Monuments* (Boston: Little, Brown, 1966), 110; David Loades, *John Foxe and the English Reformation* (Aldershot and Hants: Scolar Press, 1997).

169 Letter to Annie Brown, March 1, 1860, John Brown Papers, Chicago Historical Society.

170 Aaron D. Stevens to Annie Brown, letter, January 5, 1860, ibid.

171 Letters of John Copeland, in Ripley et al., *Black Abolitionist Papers*, 5:43–50.

172 Redpath, *The Public Life of Capt. John Brown*, 376.

173 Brown, ibid., 293.

174 Ibid., 342.

175 *New York Tribune*, December 17, 1859.

176 American Anti-Slavery Society, *The Anti-Slavery History of the John Brown Year*, 93.

177 Ibid., 138; Anderson, *A Voice from Harper's Ferry*, 40, 45, 50, 59–60.

178 A. Smith, "Remember Harper's Ferry," *Weekly Anglo-African*, December 22, 1860.

179 Elijah Lovejoy, who was killed while defending his abolitionist printing press from an anti-abolitionist mob, has also been the subject of this claim. The interest in Brown rather than Lovejoy as the first martyr hinges partly on the fact that Lovejoy was killed by a Northern mob rather than by a Southern court.

180 *Liberator*, November 21, 1859.

181 Ibid., November ?, 1859.

182 Ibid., January 11, 1860.

183 William Wells Brown, "John Brown and the Fugitive Slave Law," *Independent*, March 10, 1870; "John Brown's Fugitives," *Springfield Daily Republican*, June 12, 1909; correspondence between Ernest Gayden and Boyd Stutler on the history of the Quindaro, Kansas, monument, no. RP 08010G; J. Max Barber, "A Pilgrimage to John Brown's Grave," *Crisis*, August 1922; Barbara Easterwood, "John Brown Historical Group Tours Osawatomie Park," *Call* (Kansas City, Mo.), April 30, 1965, all in John Brown / Boyd Stutler

Collection Database, West Virginia State Archives, Charleston, http://www
.wvculture.org/history/wvmemeory/imlsintro.html (accessed February 19,
2008).

184 Finkelman, "Manufacturing Martyrdom," 55–58.

185 Redpath, *The Public Life of Capt. John Brown*, 60.

186 Idem, *The Roving Editor; or Talks with Slaves in the Southern States*,
ed. John McKivigan (University Park: Pennsylvania State University Press,
1996), 8, 55.

187 Redpath, *The Public Life of Capt. John Brown*, 14.

188 Ibid., 103.

189 James Newton Gloucester, February 19, 1858, in Benjamin Quarles,
Blacks on John Brown (Urbana: University of Illinois Press, 1972), 3–4.

190 T. Thomas Fortune, as quoted ibid., 75.

191 Eugene Debs, "John Brown: History's Greatest Hero," *Appeal to Reason*, November 23 1907, in *Debs: His Life, Writings, and Speeches* (Chicago:
Charles Kerr, 1908), 272.

192 Merrill D. Peterson, *John Brown: The Legend Revisited* (Charlottesville: University of Virginia Press, 2002), 172.

2 Haymarket

1 The Haymarket "riot" occurred during massive strikes for the eight-hour
day in Chicago. Chicago police charged on a demonstration while speakers
were finishing. Someone—no one has ever proved who—threw a bomb into
the ranks of the police, killing one officer. During the melee that followed, eight
police died or received mortal wounds. Thirty-five people were arrested. Eight
were eventually tried and convicted: Four were hanged; one committed suicide
in jail the night before the executions; and three signed a clemency plea and
had their sentences commuted to life in prison. Those three eventually were
released through a governor's pardon. For details about the case and the anarchists, see James Green, *Death in the Haymarket: A Story of Chicago, the First
Labor Movement and the Bombing That Divided Gilded Age America* (New York:
Pantheon, 2006); David R. Roediger and Franklin Rosemont, eds., *The Haymarket Scrapbook* (Chicago: Charles H. Kerr, 1986); Henry David, *The Haymarket Affair: A Study of the American Social-Revolutionary and Labor Movements*
(1936; New York: Collier, 1963); Bruce Nelson, *Beyond the Martyrs: A Social
History of Chicago's Anarchists, 1870–1900* (New Brunswick, N.J.: Rutgers University Press, 1988); Paul Avrich, *The Haymarket Tragedy* (Princeton: Princeton
University Press, 1984).

2 Most recently, a piece of the speech was used as the title of a new book:
Sharon Smith, *Subterranean Fire: A History of Working-Class Radicalism in the
United States* (New York: Haymarket Books, 2006).

3 "Address of August Spies," *The Accused and the Accusers: The Famous Speeches of the Eight Chicago Anarchists in Court* (New York: Arno, 1969), 10.

4 Green, *Death in the Haymarket*, 291, 299.

5 Bakhtin, *Rabelais and His World*, 322, 327.

6 Linebaugh and Rediker, *The Many-Headed Hydra*, 3–6, 229, 233–34; August Reinsdorf, as quoted in *Alarm*, April 4, 1885, April 18, 1885.

7 Michel Foucault, *Discipline and Punish: The Birth of the Prison*, trans. Alan Sheridan (1977; New York: Vintage, 1995), 59–69; Peter Linebaugh, *The London Hanged: Crime and Civil Society in the Eighteenth Century* (New York: Verso, 2006), 7–8, 15, 25–37; idem, "The Tyburn Riot against the Surgeons," in *Albion's Fatal Tree: Crime and Society in Eighteenth-Century England*, ed. Douglas Hey et al. (New York: Pantheon, 1975), 65–117.

8 Pauline Gregg, *Free-Born John: The Biography of John Lilburne* (London: Phoenix Press, 2000), 78, 103, 292–302.

9 Gilje, *Rioting in America*, 25–26, 28; Woody Holton, *Forced Founders: Indians, Debtors, Slaves, and the Making of the American Revolution in Virginia* (Chapel Hill: University of North Carolina Press, 1999).

10 Linebaugh, *The London Hanged*, 7–8. On James, see T. J. Stiles, *Jesse James: Last Rebel of the Civil War* (New York: Vintage, 2003). On James's self-conscious production of his legend, see ibid., 207–26, 224–26, 236. Stiles notes that when James quoted from his "Jack Shepherd" letter during an Iowa train robbery, he and his gang were dressed in Ku Klux Klan outfits. Jesse James is still popular, if PBS's poll of viewers of the "American Experience" documentary series is any indication: On July 8, 2006, 66 percent of those who responded to the poll said that James's "life of crime" was justified. Results of the poll are available online at http://www.pbs.org/wgbh/amex/james/sfeature/sf_poll.html (accessed July 8, 2006).

PBS did not take a similar poll to correspond with the documentary *John Brown's Holy War*. American Heritage, however, has taken a poll in which 46 percent of respondents found John Brown to be a "madman" and only 13 percent considered him a hero. This poll is available online at http://www.americanheritage.com/polls/?page=listPollVotes&pollID=208&startRow=0 (accessed February 18, 2008).

11 Leon Fink, *Workingmen's Democracy: The Knights of Labor in American Politics* (Urbana: University of Illinois Press, 1985); idem, *In Search of the Working Class: Essays in American Labor History and Political Culture* (Urbana: University of Illinois Press, 1994); Peter Rachleff, *Black Labor in Richmond, 1865–1890* (Urbana: University of Illinois Press, 1989), 124–57.

12 There is a debate about the actual affiliation of the Chicago anarchists with Bakunin's international. According to Paul Avrich, the Chicago group was close to the London social-revolutionary club: Avrich, *The Haymarket Tragedy*, 55–56. James Green tends to agree: Green, *Death in the Haymarket*, 93–95. Bruce Nelson, however, devotes an entire chapter to arguing that the Chicago group

were not anarchists, asserting, "Bakunin Never Slept in Chicago": Nelson, *Beyond the Martyrs*, 153–73.

13 Karl Marx, *The Communist Manifesto: A Modern Edition* (New York: Verso, 1998), 61.

14 Schneirov, *Labor and Urban Politics*, 25.

15 Alan Trachtenburg, *The Incorporation of America: Culture and Society in the Gilded Age* (New York: Hill and Wang, 1982); Nell Irvin Painter, *Standing at Armageddon: The United States, 1877–1919* (New York: W. W. Norton, 1987); White, *"It's Your Misfortune and None of My Own"*; Stephen Skowronek, *Building a New American State: The Expansion of Administrative Capacities* (Cambridge: Cambridge University Press, 1982); Christopher Tomlins, *The State and the Unions: Labor Relations, Law and the Organized Labor Movement in America, 1880–1960* (Cambridge: Cambridge University Press, 1985), esp. 35; William E. Forbath, *Law and the Shaping of the American Labor Movement* (Cambridge, Mass.: Harvard University Press, 1991); Peter Irons, *A People's History of the Supreme Court* (New York: Penguin, 1999); Joel Bakan, *The Corporation: The Pathological Pursuit of Profit and Power* (New York: Free Press, 2005). See also an old classic: Matthew Josephson, *The Robber Barons: The Great American Capitalists* (1934; New York: Harcourt Brace Jovanovich, 1962).

16 Philip M. Katz, *From Appomattox to Montmartre: Americans and the Paris Commune* (Cambridge, Mass.: Harvard University Press, 1998), 38.

17 Timothy Messer-Kruse, *The Yankee International: Marxism and the American Reform Tradition 1848–1876* (Chapel Hill: University of North Carolina Press, 1998).

18 Green, *Death in the Haymarket*, 43; Jeremy Brecher, *Strike: Revised and Updated Edition* (Boston: South End Press, 1998); Painter, *Standing at Armageddon*; David Stowell, *Streets, Railroads, and the Great Strike of 1877* (Chicago: University of Chicago Press, 1999); Paul Boyer, *Urban Masses and Moral Order in America, 1820–1920* (Cambridge, Mass.: Harvard University Press, 1978).

19 Herman Melville, *Billy Budd: An Inside Story in Billy Budd and Other Stories* (New York: Penguin, 1986). For two radically different interpretations of the story, see Franklin, *Prison Literature in America*, 67–68; Hannah Arendt, *On Violence* (New York: Harcourt Brace, 1970), 64.

20 *Alarm*, November 1, 1884 (quoting the *Indianapolis Journal*) following the 1877 railroad strikes.

21 George Frederick Parsons, "On the Labor Question," *Atlantic Monthly*, July 1886, 97–113, see 112.

22 Boyer, *Urban Masses and Moral Order in America*, 127.

23 J. J. Ingalls, "John Brown's Place in History," *North American Review* 138 (1885): 138–50.

24 National Prison Association (NPA), *Annual Proceedings*, 1885, 167; Sidney Harring, *Policing a Class Society: The Experience of American Cities, 1865–1915* (New Brunswick, N.J.: Rutgers University Press, 1983); Samuel Walker, *A*

Critical History of Police Reform: The Emergence of Police Professionalism (Lexington, Mass.: Lexington Books, 1977); Frank Donner, *Protectors of Privilege: Red Squads and Police Repression in Urban America* (Berkeley: University of California Press, 1992); Nelson, *Beyond the Martyrs*; Schneirov, *Labor and Urban Politics*; Erik Olin Wright, *The Politics of Punishment: A Critical Analysis of Prisons in America* (New York: Harper and Row, 1973); Norval Morris and David J. Rothman, *The Oxford History of the Prison: The Practice of Punishment in Western Society* (New York: Oxford University Press, 1997); David J. Rothman, *Conscience and Convenience: The Asylum and Its Alternatives in Progressive America* (Boston: Little, Brown, 1980); Mark Colvin, *Penitentiaries, Reformatories and Chain Gangs: Social Theory and the History of Punishment in Nineteenth Century America* (New York: St. Martin's Press, 1997); Thomas G. Blomberg and Karol Lucken, *American Penology: A History of Control* (Hawthorne, N.Y.: Aldine de Gruyter, 2000); Alex Lichtenstein, *Twice the Work of Free Labor: The Political Economy of Convict Labor in the New South* (New York: Verso, 1997).

25 Nelson, *Beyond the Martyrs*, 185–86.

26 *Chicago Tribune*, July 1, 1877. On vagrancy laws more generally, see John Irwin, *The Jail: Managing the Underclass in American Society* (Berkeley: University of California Press, 1985).

27 *Chicago Tribune*, July 26, 1877.

28 Charles E. Felton, in NPA, *Annual Proceedings*, 1874, 404; ibid., 1884, 63.

29 President Rutherford B. Hayes, ibid., 1884, 139.

30 Governor Charles P. Johnson of Missouri, May 13–16, 1874, ibid., 1874, 18.

31 Rawick, *From Sundown to Sunup*, 127–40; Roediger, *The Wages of Whiteness*, 95–111; Lott, *Love and Theft*.

32 The Du Bois quote and the description of the strike committee are both in David R. Roediger, "'Not Only the Ruling-Classes to Overcome but also the So-Called Mob': Class Skill and Community in the St. Louis General Strike of 1877," *Journal of Social History* 19 (Winter 1985): 213–39; Jacobson, *Whiteness of a Different Color*.

33 Morgan, *American Slavery, American Freedom*, 320.

34 Ibid., 321.

35 David R. Roediger and James Barrett, "In Between People," in David R. Roediger *Colored White: Transcending the Racial Past* (Berkeley: University of California Press, 2002); David R. Roediger, *Working toward Whiteness: How America's Immigrants Became White, the Strange Journey from Ellis Island to the Suburbs* (New York: Basic Books, 2005); Jacobson, *Whiteness of a Different Color*.

36 Thomas Morn, *The Eye That Never Sleeps: A History of the Pinkerton National Detective Agency* (Bloomington: University of Indiana Press, 1982); Walker, *A Critical History of Police Reform*; Donner, *Protectors of Privilege*.

37 Frederic Jameson describes how narrative works to resolve class conflict in Frederic Jameson, *The Political Unconscious: Narrative as a Socially Symbolic Act* (Ithaca: Cornell University Press, 1981).

38 Michael Denning, *Mechanic Accents: Dime Novels and Working-Class Culture in America* (London: Verso, 1987), 125–26; Slotkin, *Gunfighter Nation*, 217–23; Kevin Kenny, *Making Sense of the Molly Maguires* (New York: Oxford University Press, 1998); Kevin Klein, *Easterns, Westerns and Private Eyes: American Matters, 1870–1900* (Madison: University of Wisconsin Press, 1994).

39 The anarchists frequently mentioned Hugo in their paper, commenting that, while capitalists might honor the great man, it was unlikely that they had read any of his books. Upon Hugo's death, the *Alarm* printed the full text of his addresses to the rich and to the poor: *Alarm*, May 30, 1885.

40 In the more than one thousand pages of Hugo's *Les Miserables*, there is only one character who works in a factory or at any sort of trade: Fantine, who has a job in Jean Valjean's jet-bead factory. This is described as a benevolent institution.

41 *Alarm*, November 8, 1884.

42 Ibid., October 4, 1884.

43 Ibid., October 18, 1884.

44 Ibid., February 7, 1885.

45 Ibid., November 15, 1884.

46 Ibid., November 8, 1884.

47 Ibid., October 11, 1884.

48 Lucy Parsons, "A Word to Tramps," *Alarm*, October 4, 1884.

49 Idem, *The Life of Albert Parsons* (Chicago: Lucy E. Parsons, 1903), 125–26.

50 Kenny, *Making Sense of the Molly Maguires*, 281.

51 Messer-Kruse, *The Yankee International*; James Joll, *The Anarchists* (New York: Dell, 1964).

52 NPA, *Standing Committee on Police*, 1874, 127, 132–35.

53 *Alarm*, May 16, 1885.

54 Ibid., September 19, 1885.

55 On the Republican critique of "hireling" workers and soldiers, see Roediger, *The Wages of Whiteness*, 45.

56 Alarm, May 2, and June 13, 1885; Peter Brooks, *The Melodramatic Imagination: Balzac, Henry James, Melodrama, and the Mode of Excess* (New Haven: Yale University Press, 1976), 40–41.

57 August Spies, "August Spies' Autobiography: His Speeches in Court and General Notes," ed. Nina Van Zandt-Spies, MS, Chicago Historical Society, 24–25; Avrich, *The Haymarket Tragedy*, 93, 126.

58 Carolyn Ashbaugh, *Lucy Parsons: American Revolutionary* (Chicago: Charles Kerr, 1976), 60, n. 13. On the importance of Captain John Bonfield's

actions as leading to increased conflict between the police and workers, see Schneirov, *Labor and Urban Politics*, 170–73.

59   *Alarm*, November 15, 1884.

60   Ibid., February 21, 1885. Spies speculated that it was because of his exposé of the Seidel rape that the police swore revenge against him: see Spies, *Autobiography*, 25.

61   "Address of Oscar Neebe," in *The Accused and the Accusers*, 35.

62   Raymond C. Sun, "Misguided Martyrdom," *International Labor and Working-Class History* 29 (Spring 1986): 57.

63   Avrich, *The Haymarket Tragedy*, 147, 160–77; Floyd Dell, "Bomb Talking," in Roediger and Rosemont, *The Haymarket Scrapbook*, 74; Green, *Death in the Haymarket*, 141.

64   *Alarm*, November 26, 1885.

65   *Labor Leaf*, May 12, 1886.

66   *Labor Enquirer*, May 15, 1886.

67   *Labor Leaf*, May 12, 1886.

68   "Cato," in *Labor Enquirer*, May 15, 1886.

69   "Chapman, a Lawyer," *Labor Leaf*, June 2, 1886.

70   *Labor Enquirer*, June 12, 1886.

71   Ibid., October 2, 1886.

72   *Alarm*, October 11, 1884.

73   Ibid., May 30, 1885; Avrich, *The Haymarket Tragedy*, 138–39.

74   *Alarm*, December 27, 1884; Avrich, *The Haymarket Tragedy*, 138.

75   *Alarm*, April 4, 1885, April 18, 1885.

76   Ibid., February 21, 1885.

77   William Holmes, "Speech on the Paris Commune," ibid., April 4, 1885.

78   For a more detailed discussion of French coverage of the anarchists, see Marjorie Murphy, "And They Sang the Marseilles: A Look at the Left French Press as It Responded to the Haymarket," *International Labor and Working-Class History* 29 (Spring 1986): 28–37.

79   Ernst Schmidt, "The Defense and Amnesty Campaigns," in Roediger and Rosemont, *The Haymarket Scrapbook*, 112–13.

80   The defense and the appeal addressed the credibility of witnesses, bias in the choosing of the jury, possible bribery of jurors, judicial bias, prosecutorial misconduct, and the use of newspaper quotations as evidence, as well as the questionable legality of using "conspiracy" to charge people for the act of someone unknown to them.

81   "Address of Albert Parsons," in *The Accused and the Accusers*, 120.

82   Ibid., 107.

83   "Address of August Spies," in *The Accused and the Accusers*, 7–8.

84   Samuel Gompers, as quoted in Bernard Mandel, *Samuel Gompers: A Biography* (Yellow Springs, Ohio: Antioch Press, 1963), 56–57.

85 "Address of Louis Lingg," in *The Accused and the Accusers,* 42.

86 Schmidt, "The Defense and Amnesty Campaigns," 112.

87 Karl Marx, as quoted in Sender Garlin, *Three American Radicals: John Swinton, Charles Steinmetz, and William Dean Howells* (Boulder: Westview Press, 1991), 19.

88 Avrich, *The Haymarket Tragedy,* 355–59. Engel, Fischer, Lingg, and Albert Parsons demanded "liberty or death," arguing that requests for commutation were admissions of guilt and that advocating revolution was a free speech right guaranteed by the Constitution. Oglesby commuted Fielden's and Schwab's sentences to life imprisonment on November 10, 1887. Both were released in 1893, along with Neebe. Fielden lived until 1922, and Schwab died in 1898 of a respiratory disease he had contracted in prison. Blaine McKinley, "Samuel Fielden," 57, and David Roediger, "Michael Schwab," 65, in the *Haymarket Scrapbook,* Roediger and Rosemont, eds.

89 Dyer Lum, *The Great Trial of the Chicago Anarchists* (New York: Arno, 1969), 107.

90 General Matthew Trumbull, "The Life of Albert Parsons," in Roediger and Rosemont, *The Haymarket Scrapbook,* 29.

91 Carolyn Ashbaugh has concluded that Lucy Parsons was a former African American slave: Ashbaugh, *Lucy Parsons,* 99–100, 267–68, n. 4. Parsons claimed that she was a Mexican Indian, and she could easily have had both Indian and Black heritage. However, many at the time saw her as Black. Dyer Lum, Terence Powderly, and the *New York Times* all referred to her as a "Negress." The *New York Times* in particular argued that proof of Albert Parsons's insanity could be founding the fact that he was "a proud Southern man who married a Negress": *New York Times,* November 10, 1887. Powderly cited Lucy Parsons's race as one of many reasons he would not support the anarchists during the clemency campaign: see Roediger and Rosemont, "Low Points," in idem, *The Haymarket Scrapbook,* 136.

92 Miscellaneous defense-committee pamphlets, Albert Parsons Papers, Wisconsin State Historical Society, Madison.

93 On Parsons's history, see Green, *Death in the Haymarket;* Avrich, *The Haymarket Tragedy;* Ashbaugh, *Lucy Parsons;* and Parsons, *The Life of Albert Parsons.*

94 George Schilling, biography of Ernst Schmidt, MS, Ernst Schimdt Papers, Chicago Historical Society.

95 William Black, Moses Salomon, and Sigmund Zeisler, *In the Supreme Court of Illinois* (Chicago: Barnard and Gunthorp, 1887), 260, 266–67.

96 Albert Parsons Papers, Wisconsin State Historical Society, Madison.

97 Samuel Gompers, "Why the AFL Defended the Chicago Anarchists," in Roediger and Rosemont, *The Haymarket Scrapbook,* 134; Green, *Death in the Haymarket,* 248, 262–63. On Powderly, see Roediger and Rosemont, *The Haymarket Scrapbook,* 135.

98 William B. Shaw, "Social and Economic Legislation of the States in 1892," *Quarterly Journal of Economics* 7 (January 1893): 187–92; Populist Party Platform, 1892, Omaha, Neb., in George Brown Tindall, ed., *A Populist Reader: Selections from the Works of America's Populist Leaders* (New York: Harper & Row, 1966), 90–96; *Omaha Morning World-Herald*, July 5, 1892.

99 John Peter Altgeld, *Live Questions: Including Our Penal Machinery and Its Victims* (Chicago: Donohue and Heneberry, 1890), 196.

100 References to the bomb thrower as a member of a police conspiracy appear in "Address of Albert Parsons," in *The Accused and the Accusers*, 111; General Matthew Trumbull, *Was It a Fair Trial? An Appeal to the Governor of Illinois* (Chicago: Health and Home Publishers, 1887); Emma Goldman, *Living My Life* (1930; New York: Dover, 1970), 8.

101 Edward Bellamy, *Looking Backward* (1887; Garden City, N.Y.: Doubleday, 1959), 177. For another dramatic example of revolutionary action as chaos, see Ignatius Donnelly, *Caesar's Column* (1890; Cambridge, Mass.: Harvard University Press, 1960).

102 Henry Demarest Lloyd, "Free Speech and Assemblage," in Lloyd, *Mazzini and Other Essays* (New York: Putnam, 1910), 125–46.

103 On Lombroso's ties to the Italian Socialist Party, see Carlo Levy, *Gramsci and the Anarchists* (Oxford: Berg, 1999), 21–22.

104 For a discussion of Freud's authoritarianism, see Jose Brunner, "Oedipus Politicus: Freud's Paradigm of Social Relations," in *Freud: Conflict and Culture*, ed, Michael S. Roth (New York: Alfred A. Knopf, 1998), 80–93.

105 Gustave Le Bon, *The Crowd: A Study of the Popular Mind* (1895; Dunwoody, Ga.: N. S. Berg, 1968); Sigmund Freud, *Group Psychology and the Analysis of the Ego* (New York: W. W. Norton, 1989), 62.

106 "Address of Samuel Fielden," in *The Accused and the Accusers*, 57.

107 Lucy Parsons, publisher's note, in Albert R. Parsons, *Anarchism: Its Philosophy and Scientific Basis as Defended by Some of Its Apostles* (Chicago: Mrs. A. R. Parsons, 1887), 8.

108 "Address of Albert Parsons," ibid., 90.

109 Trumbull, *Was It a Fair Trial?* 60.

110 Avrich, *The Haymarket Tragedy*, 383.

111 Alexander Berkman, ed., *Selected Works of Voltairine de Cleyre* (New York: Mother Earth Publishers, 1914), 34, 166.

112 "Address of Samuel Fielden," in *The Accused and the Accusers*, 60.

113 John Brown Jr., letter, in Roediger and Rosemont, *The Haymarket Scrapbook*, 143.

114 "Address if George Engel," in *The Accused and the Accusers*, 45–46; Kopelkof, "John Brown: Anarchist," *Mother Earth*, February 1907, 34.

115 Eugene Debs, "The Martyred Apostles of Labor," in Debs, *Debs*, 266.

116 *Alarm*, November 19, 1887, 1.

117 *Chicago Tribune*, July 23, 1877.

118 *Alarm*, November 10, 1887.

119 Lum became the editor of the *Alarm* during the trial and after the hangings: Nelson, *Beyond the Martyrs*, 214–15; Avrich, *The Haymarket Tragedy*, 320.

120 *New York Times*, November 10, 1887, August Spies, "Foreword," in Spies, *Autobiography*; Frank Beck, *Hobohemia: Emma Goldman, Lucy Parsons, Ben Reitman and Other Agitators and Outsiders in 1920s/30s Chicago* (Chicago: Charles Kerr, 2000).

121 Schmidt scrapbook, Ernst Schmidt Collection, Chicago Historical Society.

122 Franklin Rosemont, "The Most Dangerous Anarchist in All Chicago: The Legend and Legacy of Louis Lingg," in Roediger and Rosemont, *The Haymarket Scrapbook*, 51–56.

123 Frank Harris, "1920 Introduction," in Harris, *The Bomb* (Portland, Ore.: Feral House, 1996), 17.

124 Ibid., 113.

125 See Karen Halttunen, *Confidence Men and Painted Women: A Study of Middle-Class Culture in America, 1830–1870* (New Haven: Yale University Press, 1986); Brooks, *The Melodramatic Imagination*, 4, 12–14.

126 Seward Mitchell to Lucy Parsons, letter, December 1886, Albert Parsons Papers, Wisconsin State Historical Society, Madison.

127 Jack London, *The Iron Heel* (Westport, Conn.: Lawrence Hill, 1980), 5.

128 IBG to Lucy Parsons, *Alarm*, November 11, 1887.

129 Voltairine de Cleyre, "The Gods and the People," in Berkman, *Selected Works of Voltairine de Cleyre*, 54.

130 *Arbeiter Zeitung*, November 14, 1887, in *German Workers in Chicago: A Documentary History of Working-Class Culture from 1850 to World War I*, trans. Hartmut Keil (Urbana: University of Illinois Press, 1988), 190.

131 Nelson, *Beyond the Martyrs*, 195–200.

132 The ACLU, for instance, would not be organized until the First World War, in response to the jailing of draft resisters by a combination of anarchists, socialists, and liberals.

133 William Fielden in *Alarm*, December 26, 1885.

134 J. Allen Evans in *Alarm*, November 22, 1885.

135 Hartman, *Scenes of Subjection*. I will discuss this dynamic further in chapter 3.

136 Schmidt, *He Chose*; Spies, *Autobiography*, 27.

137 *Huntsville Gazette*, October 1, 1887, November 12, 1887; "Chinamen and Anarchists," *New York Freeman*, May 15, 1888.

138 David R. Roediger, "Strange Legacies: The Black International and Black America," in Roediger and Rosemont, *The Haymarket Scrapbook*, 95; Roediger, *The Wages of Whiteness*, esp. 8–10; Hartman, *Scenes of Subjection*.

139 As Jacques Derrida suggests, the rejection of writing as "artificial" and unnatural is based not in radical democracy, but in a philosophy of the

primitive as a source of "presence" that cannot exercise power without being violated and impure: see Jacques Derrida, "The Violence of the Letter: From Levi-Strauss to Rousseau," in Derrida, *Of Grammatology*, trans. Gayatri Chakravorty Spivak (Baltimore: Johns Hopkins University Press, 1969),101–40.

140 T. Thomas Fortune, "Bloody Murder Rampant," *New York Age*, May 15, 1886.

141 See, e.g., *Washington Bee*, November 12, 1887; *Huntsville Gazette*, September 24, 1887; *New York Freeman*, May 15, 1888.

142 Lucy Parsons, *Alarm*, April 8, 1885. See also C. S. Griffin, "Murderers: Can Statute Law Prevent Crime and Punish the Criminal?" *Alarm*, October 17, 1885; "Zeno," "Law and Lawyers," *Alarm*, January 24, 1885, November 28, 1885. See also Roediger, "Strange Legacies: The Black International and Black America," in Roediger and Rosemont, *The Haymarket Scrapbook*, 93.

143 Michael Moore, "Is the Left Nuts? (Or Is It Me?)," *Nation*, November 17, 1997.

144 Ien Ang, *Watching Dallas: Soap Opera and the Melodramatic Imagination* (New York: Methuen, 1985); Janice Radway, *Reading the Romance: Women, Patriarchy and Popular Literature* (Chapel Hill: University of North Carolina Press, 1984); Annalee Newitz, *White Trash* (New York: Routledge, 1997).

3 Anti-Lynching and Labor Defense

1 U.S. Circuit Court, *The Great Ku Klux Klan Trials: Official Report of the Proceedings* (Columbia, S.C, 1872), 459, 499, 603–5, 799.

2 Robert Charles, who will be discussed later in the chapter, shot and killed two policemen in New Orleans in 1900. The Jelly Roll Morton quote is in Courtney Patterson Cerney, "Jazz and the Cultural Transformation of America in the 1920s," Ph.D. diss., Louisiana State Agricultural and Mechanical College, Baton Rouge, 2003, 56. Charles Crowe, "Southern Repression and Black Resistance, 1900, 1917, and 1932," *Reviews in American History* 5, no. 3 (September 1977): 379–90. Cecil Brown, *Stagolee Shot Billy* (Cambridge, Mass.: Harvard University Press, 2003); David M. Oshinsky, *Worse than Slavery: Parchman and the Ideal of Jim Crow Justice* (New York: Free Press, 1996); Slotkin, *Gunfighter Nation*; Frank Richard Prassel, *The Great American Outlaw: A Legacy of Fact and Fiction* (Norman: University of Oklahoma Press, 1993).

3 Rayford Logan, *The Negro in American Life and Thought: The Nadir, 1877–1901* (New York: Dial Press, 1954); Robert Wiebe, *The Search for Order* (New York: Hill and Wang, 1966). For general studies on lynching, see W. Fitzhugh Brundage, *Lynching in the New South: Georgia and Virginia, 1880–1930* (Urbana: University of Illinois Press, 1993); idem, *Under Sentence of Death*; Stew-

art E. Tolnay and E. M. Beck, *Festival of Violence: An Analysis of the Lynching of African Americans in the American South, 1882–1930* (Urbana: University of Illinois Press, 1995); Waldrep, *The Many Faces of Judge Lynch*, 2002.

4   Berry, *Black Resistance, White Law*, esp. 22–26.

5   The NAACP and the IWW were multiracial organizations. However, the NAACP's central focus was on African American rights, and while the IWW was unique in the broader labor movement for its antiracist ideals and had particular locals in which African American, Mexican, and Chinese workers played an important role, its national leadership was largely white. Similarly, although some local chapters of the NAACP featured a high level of membership among the working class (such as the one in Galveston, Texas, described in Steven A. Reich, "Soldiers of Democracy: Black Texans and the Fight for Citizenship, 1917–1921," *Journal of American History* 82 [March 1996]: 1478–1504), the leadership of the organization favored middle-class uplift.

6   From I. Gustavus R. Ford, in the *Washington Bee*, about the lynching of Jesse Washington in 1916, quoted in Patricia Bernstein, *The First Waco Horror: The Lynching of Jesse Washington and the Rise of the NAACP* (College Station: University of Texas A&M Press, 2005), 131.

7   Booker T. Washington, as quoted in Eric Rauchway, *Murdering McKinley: The Making of Theodore Roosevelt's America* (New York: Hill and Wang, 2003), 77–78.

8   Walter White, as quoted in Philip Dray, *At the Hands of Persons Unknown: The Lynching of Black America* (New York: Modern Library, 2003), 268.

9   Papers of the National Association for the Advancement of Colored People (hereafter, NAACP Papers), Part 7, microfilm, reel 2.

10   Ibid.

11   I refer to anarchists who followed the general ideas of anarcho-communism and who clustered around Emma Goldman as the Berkman–Goldman anarchists. Goldman probably did more than any other American to popularize anarchism, and in the twentieth century self-identified anarchists from Italy, Russia, Spain, and elsewhere in central Europe and eastern Europe tended to identify themselves not only with the "Martyrs of Chicago" but with the second-generation group led by Goldman and Alexander Berkman. On the history of these anarchists, see Paul Avrich, *Anarchist Portraits* (Princeton: Princeton University Press, 1990); idem, *Anarchist Voices* (Princeton: Princeton University Press, 1996); Candace Falk, *Love, Anarchy and Emma Goldman* (New Brunswick, N.J.: Rutgers University Press, 1984); Joll, *The Anarchists*.

12   Goldman, *Living My Life*, 87.

13   Ibid., 312.

14   David M. Rabban, *Free Speech in Its Forgotten Years, 1870–1920* (Cambridge: Cambridge University Press, 1997); Mari Jo Buhle, *Women and Ameri-*

can Socialism, 1870–1920 (Urbana: University of Illinois Press, 1983), 276–79; Linda Gordon, *Women's Body, Woman's Right: Birth Control in America* (New York: Penguin, 1990).

15 For a concise discussion of conflicts between industrial unions and business unions over issues of control, see James Green, *The World of the Worker: Labor in Twentieth Century America* (Chicago: University of Illinois Press, 1998). For a general discussion of the rise of corporate–labor collusion, see David Montgomery, *The Fall of the House of Labor: The Workplace, the State, and American Labor Activism, 1865–1925* (Cambridge: Cambridge University Press, 1987).

16 *Agitator*, January 1, 1911, June 15, 1911.

17 Nancy McLean, *Behind the Mask of Chivalry: The Making of the Second Ku Klux Klan* (New York: Oxford University Press, 1994); Chip Berlet and Matthew N. Lyons, *Right-Wing Populism in America: Too Close for Comfort* (New York: Guilford Press, 2000); Theodore Kornweibel, *Seeing Red: Federal Campaigns against Black Militancy, 1919–1925* (Bloomington: Indiana University Press, 1998); Mark Ellis, *Race, War and Surveillance: African Americans and the United States Government during World War I* (Bloomington: Indiana University Press, 2001).

18 Gilmore, *Gender and Jim Crow*, 3–4.

19 Waldrep, *The Verdict of Judge Lynch*, 90–91.

20 On the role of literary representations of lynching in the formation of Black nationalism, see Trudier Harris, *Exorcising Blackness: Historical and Literary Lynching and Burning Rituals* (Bloomington: Indiana University Press, 1984).

21 On Wells's influence on the NAACP, see Patricia Schecter, *Ida B. Wells Barnett and American Reform, 1880–1930* (Chapel Hill: University of North Carolina Press, 2001); Mary Brown, *Eradicating This Evil: Women in the American Anti-Lynching Movement, 1892–1940* (New York: Garland, 2000); Charles Kellogg, *The NAACP, Volume I: 1909–1920* (Baltimore: Johns Hopkins University Press, 1968); Jonas, *Freedom's Sword*; Waldrep, *The Many Faces of Judge Lynch*.

22 Ida B. Wells, "Mob Rule in New Orleans" (1900), in *Southern Horrors and Other Writings: The Anti-Lynching Campaign of Ida B. Wells*, ed. Jacqueline Jones Royster (Boston: Bedford Books, 1997), 166.

23 Ida B. Wells, "Southern Horrors," in *On Lynchings: Southern Horrors, a Red Record, Mob Rule in New Orleans* (New York: Arno, 1969), 18–19.

24 Brown, *Strain of Violence*; Richard Maxwell Brown, *No Duty to Retreat: Violence and Values in American History and Society* (New York: Oxford University Press, 1991).

25 Ida B. Wells, *Crusade for Justice: The Autobiography of Ida B. Wells* (Chicago: University of Chicago Press, 1977), 84.

26 Ibid., 70.

27 Ibid., 137.

28 Leon Litwack, *Been in the Storm So Long: The Aftermath of Slavery* (New York: Vintage, 1980); Tera Hunter, *To 'Joy My Freedom: Southern Black Women's Lives and Labors after the Civil War* (Cambridge, Mass.: Harvard University Press, 1997).

29 Wells, *Crusade for Justice*, 72. On Wells's success in changing African Americans' attitudes toward lynching, see Waldrep, *The Many Faces of Judge Lynch*.

30 Wells, *Crusade for Justice*, 64.

31 Ibid., 220.

32 Ibid., 50.

33 Fredrickson, *The Black Image in the White Mind*, 256–82.

34 Wells, "Southern Horrors," 17.

35 Wells, *Crusade for Justice*, 140–41.

36 *Springfield Weekly Republican*, April 28, 1899, as quoted in, *One Hundred Years of Lynchings*, ed. Ralph Ginzburg (Baltimore: Black Classic Press, 1988), 15. This account records Hose's name as Holt, as many papers did: Leon Litwack, "Hellhounds," in *Without Sanctuary: Lynching Photography in America*, ed. James Allen (Santa Fe, N.M.: Twin Palms, 2000), 35, fn. 1.

37 Wells, "Southern Horrors," 19.

38 Hazel Carby argues that this tendency was a general trend in the late nineteenth century, making post-Reconstruction America part of a "woman's era": Hazel Carby, *Reconstructing Womanhood: The Emergence of the Afro-American Woman Novelist* (New York: Oxford University Press, 1989); see also Deborah Gray White, *Too Heavy a Load: Black Women in Defense of Themselves, 1894–1994* (New York: W. W. Norton, 1999).

39 Wells, "Mob Rule in New Orleans," 165–67.

40 Wells, "A Red Record," 31–32.

41 Ibid., 34.

42 Wells, "Southern Horrors," 23.

43 Wells, "Mob Rule in New Orleans," 175.

44 Wells, "A Red Record," 40.

45 David Levering Lewis, *W. E. B. Du Bois: The Biography of a Race, 1868–1919* (New York: Henry Holt, 1993), 471; Kellogg, *The NAACP*, 94.

46 Ray Stannard Baker in *American Magazine*, February 1907, 517–20, April 1907, 567, June 1907, 146.

47 Wells, *Crusade for Justice*, 201–12; Linda McMurry, *To Keep the Waters Troubled: The Life of Ida B. Wells* (New York: Oxford University Press, 2000); Dray, *At the Hands of Persons Unknown*, 106–10; Brown, *Eradicating This Evil*, 81.

48 Wells, *Crusade for Justice*, 284.

49 Gail Bederman, *Manliness and Civilization: A Cultural History of Gender and Race in the United States, 1880–1917* (Chicago: University of Chicago Press, 1996).

50 Michel Foucault, *Discipline and Punish: The Birth of the Prison*, trans. Alan Sheridan (New York: Pantheon, 1977); David J. Rothman, *The Discovery of the Asylum: Social Order and Disorder in the New Republic* (Boston: Back Bay Books, 1990); Philip English Mackey, ed., *Voices against Death: American Opposition to Capital Punishment, 1787–1975* (New York: B. Franklin, 1976); Hugo Adam Bedau, *The Death Penalty in America: Current Controversies* (New York: Oxford University Press, 1997).

51 Wells, *Crusade for Justice*, 85.

52 Idem, "Mob Rule in New Orleans," 173.

53 Bederman, *Manliness and Civilization*.

54 See Hartman, *Scenes of Subjection*, 145–48.

55 Kellogg, *The NAACP*, 111.

56 Ibid., 121.

57 Frank Moss, "Persecution of Negroes by Roughs and Policemen in the City of New York, August 1900," in *Police Brutality: An Anthology*, ed. Jill Nelson (New York: W. W. Norton, 2000).

58 *Crisis*, March 1913, 233.

59 "Along the Color Line," *Crisis*, December 1912, 43.

60 Ibid., June 1910, 57.

61 *Crisis*, August 1921, 149.

62 Ibid., January 1913, 125.

63 Alex Lichtenstein, *Twice the Work of Free Labor: Convict Leasing in the New South* (New York: Verso, 1996).

64 *Crisis*, April 1913, 299.

65 Ibid., December 1912, 92.

66 Ibid., December 1915.

67 Ibid., September 1913, 221.

68 Some examples of organizing against police and resistance to police can be found ibid., January 1912, 144, June 1912, 164, August 1913, 170, December 1919, 148.

69 NAACP Papers, Part 7, microfilm, reel 1, April 1914.

70 *Crisis*, July 1916; Bernstein, *The First Waco Horror*.

71 *Black Topeka*, as quoted in Litwack, "Hellhounds," 11. See also Dora Apel, *Imagery of Lynching: Black Men, White Women and the Mob* (New Brunswick, N.J.: Rutgers University Press, 2004).

72 Letter to May Childs Nerney, April 15, 1914, then to Mrs. E. W. Anderson, Friday Club, April 22, 1914, NAACP Papers, Part 7, microfilm, reel 1.

73 J. H. Coleman to Mabelle White, letter, May 15, 1914, NAACP Papers, Part 7, microfilm, reel 1. On the anti-lynching crusaders, see Brown, *Eradicating This Evil*, 146. See also Bernstein, *The First Waco Horror*, 57–58. Information about Marie Scott is available online at http://womhist.alexanderstreet.com/lynch/doc7.htm (accessed March 1, 2008) and at http://www.strangefruit.org/marie_scott.htm (accessed March 1, 2008).

74   W. Fitzhugh Brundage, "The Roar on the Other Side of Silence: Black Resistance and White Violence in the American South, 1880–1940," in Brundage, *Under Sentence of Death*, 277.

75   "Negroes in Protest March," *New York Times*, July 29, 1917, 12. On middle-class efforts and the working class, see Hunter, *To 'Joy My Freedom*; Kevin Gaines *Uplifting the Race: Black Leadership, Politics and Culture in the Twentieth Century* (Chapel Hill: University of North Carolina Press, 1996); Joe William Trotter Jr., *Black Milwaukee: The Making of an Industrial Proletariat, 1915–1945* (Urbana: University of Illinois Press, 1985), 80–114.

76   Susan D. Carle, "Race, Class and Legal Ethics in the Early NAACP, 1910–1920," *Law and History Review* 20, no. 1 (Spring 2002): 97–146.

77   For a survey of white sociologists' views on lynching, see W. Fitzhugh Brundage, "Introduction," in idem, *Under Sentence of Death*, 1–16.

78   On James K. Vardaman, see Oshinsky, *Worse than Slavery*, 102. On Tom Watson, see C. Vann Woodward, *Tom Watson: Agrarian Rebel* (New York: Oxford University Press, 1963), 320, 327–28.

79   Ray Stannard Baker, *Following the Color Line: American Negro Citizenship in the Progressive Era* (New York: Harper Torch Books, 1964), 17.

80   Fenton Johnson, "Call of the Patriot," *Crisis*, February 1917, 171–73.

81   Gomez, *Exchanging Our Country Marks*, 186–243.

82   Waldrep, *The Verdict of Judge Lynch*, 99, fn. 72.

83   Terence Finnegan, "Lynching and Political Power," in Brundage, *Under Sentence of Death*, 194–97.

84   Brundage, *Lynching in the New South*, 133–34.

85   Stewart E. Tolnay and E. M. Beck conclude that in the majority of these cases, groups of Blacks murdered Blacks who were not punished by the court for "serious offenses" because of non-prosecution of cases involving Black victims. Some examples were rape and murder of Black women or children, gross fraud perpetrated on a Black community, and crimes against family members, particularly incest. They found that a similar portion of white victims of white mobs were killed for "family-related" offenses: Tolnay and Beck, "When Race Didn't Matter: Black and White Mob Violence against Their Own Color," in Brundage, *Under Sentence of Death*, 147.

86   Ibid., 140.

87   Brown, *Stagolee Shot Billy*, 84.

88   Ibid., 42.

89   Oshinsky, *Worse than Slavery*, 223–24.; John Roberts, *From Trickster to Badman: The Black Folk Hero in Slavery and Freedom* (Philadelphia: University of Pennsylvania Press, 1989), 177–80; Brown, *Stagolee Shot Billy*, 121.

90   Eugene Barnett transcript of radio program recorded in the early 1940s, Oral History of the American Left, Tamiment Library / Robert F. Wagner Labor Archives, Elmer Holmes Bobst Library, New York University.

91   *Mother Earth*, July 1907, 211.

92   Elizabeth Jameson, *All That Glitters: Class, Conflict, and Community in Cripple Creek* (Urbana: University of Illinois Press, 1998), 151.

93   Preston, *Aliens and Dissenters*, 30–32.

94   On the reference to Frank Steunenberg as a martyr, see J. Anthony Lukas, *Big Trouble: A Murder in a Small Western Town Sets Off a Struggle for the Soul of America* (New York: Simon and Schuster, 1997), 91.

95   Elliot Gorn, *Mother Jones: The Most Dangerous Woman in America* (New York: Hill and Wang, 2003); Edward Steele, ed., *The Court-Martial of Mother Jones* (Lexington: University Press of Kentucky, 1995); David Alan Corbin, *Life, Work, and Rebellion in the Coal Fields: The Southern West Virginia Miners, 1880–1922* (Urbana: University of Illinois Press, 1989).

96   On the Ludlow massacre, see Montgomery, *The Fall of the House of Labor*, 346–48; James Green, "Crime against History at Ludlow," *Labor: Studies in Working-Class History of the Americas* 1, no. 1 (Spring 2004): 9–16, and *Taking History to Heart: The Power of the Past in Building Social Movements* (Amherst: University of Massachusetts Press, 2000), 122; Gorn, *Mother Jones*, 212–18. For an example of a contemporary memorial to Ludlow, see the Web page at http://www.rebelgraphics.org/ludlow.html (accessed March 1, 2008).

97   On the IWW's many run-ins with the law, see Preston, *Aliens and Dissenters*; Rabban, *Free Speech in Its Forgotten Years*; Clemens Work, *Darkest before Dawn: Sedition and Free Speech in the American West* (Albuquerque: University of New Mexico Press, 2005); Nigel Anthony Sellars, *Oil, Wheat and Wobblies: The Industrial Workers of the World in Oklahoma, 1905–1930s* (Norman: University of Oklahoma Pres, 1998); Greg Hall, *Harvest Wobblies: The Industrial Workers of the World and Agricultural Laborers in the American West, 1905–1930* (Corvallis: Oregon State University Press, 2001); Philip S. Foner, ed., *Fellow Workers and Friends: The IWW Free Speech Fights as Told by Participants* (Westport, Conn.: Greenwood Press, 1981).

98   Geoffrey Cowan, *The People v. Clarence Darrow: The Bribery Trial of America's Greatest Lawyer* (New York: Times Books, 1993), 34; David Ray Papke, *The Pullman Case: The Clash of Labor and Capital in Industrial America* (Lawrence: University of Kansas Press, 1999).

99   Clarence Darrow, "Somewhere There Is a Conspiracy: The Kidd Case, Oshkosh Wisconsin," in idem, *Attorney for the Damned*, ed. Arthur Weinberg (New York: Simon and Schuster, 1957), 282, 303.

100   The events of the Haywood–Moyer–Pettibone trial were that the governor of Idaho, Frank Steunenberg, was murdered by an exploding bomb at his home. When the Pinkerton detective James McParland, who notoriously had been involved in the Molly Maguires case in the 1870s, got involved, he argued that the bombing was a conspiracy cooked up in the inner circle of the Western Federation of Miners. Haywood, Moyer, and Pettibone had been abducted from Colorado and sent by train to Idaho, where they were charged

with the murder. The jury did not believe the testimony of Harry Orchard, the confessed killer, and Haywood, Moyer, and Pettibone were acquitted. On the trial and surrounding events, see Jameson, *All That Glitters*; Lukas, *Big Trouble*; David Grover, *Debaters and Dynamiters: The Story of the Haywood Trial* (Corvallis: Oregon State University Press, 1964).

101 Bill Haywood, *Bill Haywood's Book* (New York: International Publishers, 1928), 211.

102 Grover, *Debaters and Dynamiters*, 111.

103 Eugene Debs, "Arouse, Ye Slaves!" in Debs, *Debs*, 309–10.

104 Statements from Charles Moyer, Bill Haywood, and George Pettibone originally published in *Appeal to Reason* and reprinted in *Industrial Worker*, April 1906.

105 *Mother Earth*, February 1907, March 1907; *La Questione Sociale*, February–March 1907.

106 *Mother Earth*, June 1907, April 1907, July 1907.

107 J. T. Doran, as quoted in Grover, *Debaters and Dynamiters*, 77–79.

108 "The Battle of Boise," *International Socialist Review*, May 1907, 687.

109 Clarence Darrow, closing arguments, as quoted in *Chicago Tribune*, June 25, 1907.

110 *Chicago Tribune*, July 29, 1907; *New York Post*, July 29, 1907.

111 *Mother Earth*, August 1907. The anarchists may have been right. Newspaper reports about the trial indicated a general disgust with Orchard's character as he confessed to crime after crime without showing remorse. The picture for which he posed, "The End of the Poker Game," which depicted him with a jovial smile and a smoking gun, did not help: See *Chicago Tribune*, June–July 1907. The photograph was published in the *Chicago Tribune*, July 5, 1907.

112 Cowan, *The People v. Clarence Darrow*, 121.

113 Bill Haywood, "Get Ready," *International Socialist Review*, June 1911, 725–26.

114 Eugene Debs, "The McNamara Case and the Labor Movement," *International Socialist Review*, December 1912, 397, 399.

115 Frank Boehn, "The Passing of the McNamaras," *International Socialist Review*, December 1912, 403–404.

116 *International Socialist Review*, December 1911, 467.

117 Lincoln Steffens, "Making of a Fighter," *American Magazine*, August 1907; Lindsay Dennison, "The Reverend Billy Sunday and His War with the Devil," *American Magazine*, September 1907; "The Meaning of Insurgency," *American Magazine*, April 1911.

118 Hall, *Harvest Wobblies*; Frank Tobias Higbie, *Indispensable Outcasts: Hobo Workers and Community in the American Midwest, 1880–1930* (Urbana: University of Illinois Press, 2003); Sellars, *Oil, Wheat and Wobblies*; Fred Thompson, *The IWW: Its First Seventy Years, 1905–1975* (Chicago: Charles Kerr,

1976); Covington Hall, *Labor Struggles in the Deep South* (Chicago: Charles Kerr, 1999).

119 Rabban, *Free Speech in Its Forgotten Years*, 85.

120 Franklin Rosemont, *Joe Hill: The IWW and the Making of a Revolutionary Working-Class Counter Culture* (Chicago: Charles Kerr, 2003).

121 Interview with Lucy Ann Cloud by Tom Copeland, in Oral History of the American Left, Tamiment Library / Robert F. Wagner Labor Archives, Elmer Holmes Bobst Library, New York University.

122 Rabban, *Free Speech in Its Forgotten Years*, 93.

123 Gibbs M. Smith, *Joe Hill* (Salt Lake City: University of Utah Press, 1969), 90, 121.

124 Joe Hill, as quoted in Rosemont, *Joe Hill*, 209.

125 For more on Hill as an IWW hero, see Ralph Chaplin, *Wobbly: The Rough and Tumble Story of an American Radical* (Chapel Hill: University of North Carolina Press,1948); Philip Foner, *The Case of Joe Hill* (New York: International Publishers, 1965); Archie Green, *Wobblies, Pile Butts and Other Heroes: Laborlore Explorations* (Urbana: University of Illinois Press, 1993); Smith, *Joe Hill*; Melvyn Dubofsky, *We Shall Be All: A History of the Industrial Workers of the World* (Urbana: University of Illinois Press, 1988; Donald Winter, *Soul of the Wobblies: The IWW, Religion and American Culture in the Progressive Era* (Westport, Conn.: Greenwood Press, 1985); Wendy Ellen Waisala, "To Bring Forth a Note of One's Worth: Contested Memory and the Labor Literature of the Haymarket, the Triangle Fire, and Joe Hill," Ph.D. diss., New York University, 1997.

126 Elizabeth Gurley Flynn, *The Rebel Girl: An Autobiography* (New York: International Publishers, 1955), 192–93.

127 Cartoon, *Industrial Worker*, April 15, 1916, cover.

128 The best description of the distribution and scattering of the ash is in Rosemont, *Joe Hill*.

129 Ella Reeve Bloor to Elizabeth Gurley Flynn, letter, December 26, 1917, and Frank Walsh to Ella Reeve Bloor, letter, July 8, 1919, June 10, 1919, all in Workers Defense Union Correspondence, Elizabeth Gurley Flynn papers.

130 IWW Defense News Service, *Daily Bulletin*, April 26, 1918.

131 Carl Haessler, "The Fort Leavenworth General Strike of Prisoners: An Experiment in the Radical Guidance of Mass Discontent," *Labor Defender*, January 1927, 10–11; Stephen M. Kohn, *American Political Prisoners: Prosecutions under the Espionage and Sedition Acts* (Wesport, Conn.: Praeger, 1994), 56.

132 Jones, although a promising organizer, met a tragic end, killing his landlady and himself in November 1919 following continuing harassment by the federal government: Kornweibel, *Seeing Red*, 157–64.

133 Class War Prisoner 13104, "A Little Rebel Speaks," *One Big Union Monthly*, March 1919, 15; Garey, *Defending Everybody*, 62–63.

134 *Industrial Worker*, November 18, 1916.

135 Ibid., November 25, 1916.

136 John McClelland, *Wobbly War: The Centralia Story* (Tacoma: Washington State Historical Society, 1987), 12–13.

137 Ibid., 14.

138 Ibid.; Tom Copeland, *The Centralia Tragedy of 1919: Elmer Smith and the Wobblies* (Seattle: University of Washington Press, 1993).

139 Covington Hall, "Most Cruel Crime in History of Peonage and Slaughter," *Industrial Worker*, July 28, 1917.

140 Charles Ashleigh, *Defense News Bulletin*, November 17, 1917.

141 Ralph Chaplin, *The Centralia Conspiracy* (Austin: Workplace Publishers, 1971), 4.

142 William Jones, *The Tribe of Black Ulysses: African-American Lumber Workers in the Jim Crow South* (Urbana: University of Illinois Press, 2005).

143 Chaplin, *The Centralia Conspiracy*, 10.

144 Chaplin, "The West Is Dead," *Industrial Pioneer*, October 1923; Vera Moher, "Martyrs (Suggested by a Painting by Remington)," *Industrial Pioneer*, December 1923, 37.

145 David Karsner, *Talks with Debs in Terre Haute* (New York: New York Call, 1922), 52–54.

146 As Sal Salerno persuasively argues, European syndicalism played an important role in defining the IWW's goals, and the organization has been represented incorrectly as being "western." However, the IWW's representation of itself in internal documents, and in foreign-language papers, was different from how it presented itself during major political trials: Salerno, *Red November, Black November: Culture and Community in the Industrial Workers of the World* (Albany: SUNY Press, 1989).

147 Dubofsky, *We Shall Be All*, 24.

148 Beck, *Hobohemia*.

149 *Agitator*, January 1, 1912, January 15, 1912.

150 Rosemont, *Joe Hill*.

151 Michael Miller Topp, *Those without a Country: The Political Culture of Italian-American Syndicalists* (Minneapolis: University of Minnesota Press, 2001), 3; Flynn, *The Rebel Girl*, 148–49; Sellars, *Oil, Wheat and Wobblies*.

152 Ardis Cameron, *Radicals of the Worst Sort: Laboring Women in Lawrence, Massachusetts, 1860–1912* (Urbana: University of Illinois Press, 1993), 130, 133.

153 Max Eastman, "Niggers and Night Riders," *Masses*, January 1913.

154 Forrest Edwards, "The Merits of Legal Defense," *One Big Union Monthly*, September 1919, 10–11.

155 Garey, *Defending Everybody*; Samuel Walker, *In Defense of American Liberties: A History of the ACLU* (New York: Oxford University Press, 1991).

156 Preston, *Aliens and Dissenters*, 141.

157   Covington Hall (writing as "Ami"), "Race Riots," *Industrial Worker*, July 21, 1917.

158   Covington Hall, "Riots and Race Wars, Lynchings and Massacres, Military Law, Terrorism and Great Strikes," *One Big Union Monthly*, November 1919, 9.

159   Kornweibel, *Seeing Red*, 101.

160   Marcus Garvey, "The Negro, Communism, Trade Unionism, and His Friend: Beware of Greeks Bearing Gifts," in *The Philosophy and Opinions of Marcus Garvey*, ed. Amy Jacques-Garvey (1923; New York: Athaenum, 1969), 70.

161   NAACP Papers, Part 7, microfilm, reel 8, Arkansas; Group 1 series D on Houston defense; Grif Stockley, *Blood in Their Eyes: The Elaine Race Massacres of 1919* (Fayetteville: University of Arkansas Press, 2004); Richard Cortner, *A Mob Intent on Death: The NAACP and Arkansas Riot Cases* (Middletown, Conn.: Wesleyan University Press, 1988); Kevin Boyle, *The Arc of Justice: A Saga of Race, Civil Rights and Murder in the Jazz Age* (New York: Henry Holt, 2004); Phyllis Vine, *One Man's Castle: Clarence Darrow in Defense of the American Dream* (New York: HarperCollins, 2004); Scott Ellsworth, *Death in the Promised Land: The Tulsa Race Riot of 1921* (Baton Rouge: Louisiana State University Press, 1992); James Hirsch, *Riot and Remembrance: The Tulsa Riot and Its Legacy* (New York: Houghton Mifflin, 2002).

162   NAACP Papers, Part 7, microfilm, reel 8, January 24, 1924, Shepperson to Mr. Bagnell.

163   "Justice for the Negro: How He Can Get It," IWW leaflet, 1919, Labor History and Urban Affairs Collection, Reuther Library, Wayne State University, Detroit; also in Kornweibel, ed., *Federal Surveillance of Afro-Americans (1917– 1925): The First World War, the Red Scare, and the Garvey Movement* (Frederick, Md.: University Publications of America, 1986), reel 12.

164   "Colored Workers of America: Why You Should Join the I.W.W.," IWW pamphlet, folder A11, Reuther Library archives, Wayne State University, De- troit. I thank Sal Salerno for giving me a copy of this pamphlet, which also ap- pears in Philip S. Foner and Ronald L. Lewis, *Black Workers: A Documentary History from Colonial Times to the Present* (Philadelphia: Temple University Press, 1989).

165   Frederick A. Blossom, "Justice for the Negro," *One Big Union Monthly*, October 1919, 30–31.

166   "Emigration," *One Big Union, Monthly*, June 1919, 8.

167   On the Farmers' union, see Covington Hall, "Another Letter to the Edi- tor," *One Big Union Monthly*, December 1919, 61; "Riots and Race Wars, Lynch- ings and Massacres, Military Law, Terrorism and Great Strikes," *One Big Union Monthly*, November 1919, 9; "People's Freedom Union," *One Big Union Monthly*, December 1919, 44–45; *Crisis*, March 1920, June 1920, September 1920; Cortner, *A Mob Intent on Death*; Stockley, *Blood in Their Eyes*.

168 Tulsa pamphlet of Communist Party, in Kornweibel, ed., *Federal Surveillance of Afro-Americans (1917–1925)*.

169 Ellsworth, *Death in the Promised Land*, 24–25; Kornweibel, *Seeing Red*; Ellis, *Race, War and Surveillance*.

170 George Vanderveer, "Opening Address," in Harrison George, *The IWW Trial: Story of the Greatest Trial in Labor's History by One of the Defendants* (New York: Arno Press, 1969), 65; *One Big Union Monthly*, November 1919, 9–11.

171 *L'Adunata dei Refrattari*, May 26, 1923.

172 Papers of Elizabeth Gurley Flynn, Microfilm edition.

173 Al Wesibord, "A Negro Chamber of Labor," *Crisis*, July 1934, 198–99.

174 Haessler, "The Fort Leavenworth General Strike of Prisoners," 10–11.

175 Wells, *Crusade for Justice*, 157.

176 W. E. B. Du Bois, *The Autobiography of W. E. B. Du Bois: A Soliloquy on Viewing My Life from the First Decade of Its Last Century* (New York: International Publishers, 1968), 305.

177 Len S. Nembhard, *Trials and Triumphs of Marcus Garvey* (Millwood, N.Y.: Kraus Reprint, 1978), 64, 66–67.

178 See, e.g., Ben Fletcher, "The Negro and Organized Labor," *Messenger*, vol. 5, no. 7, June 1923, 759–60.

4 Sacco and Vanzetti

1 Paul Avrich, *Sacco and Vanzetti: The Anarchist Background* (Princeton: Princeton University Press, 1991), 97–162. According to Michael Miller Topp, Galleani's presence in America "guaranteed the anti-organizationalists would dominate the Italian American Anarchist movement": Topp, *Those without a Country*, 30.

2 "Per Sacco e Vanzetti: Recriminazione Colposo," *L'Adunata dei Refrattari*, September 15, 1922.

3 Nunzio Pernicone, "Carlo Tresca and The Sacco–Vanzetti Case," *Journal of American History* 66, no. 3 (December 1979): 540.

4 According to Nigel Anthony Sellars, Moore was a good lawyer who was dedicated to the IWW, but he was also "an emotionally unpredictable man who too often argued with defense committees or his clients, suffered a series of psychological problems, and even simply vanished for weeks on end": Sellars, *Oil, Wheat and Wobblies*, 125.

5 Flynn, *The Rebel Girl*, 129–30; Dorothy Gallagher, *All the Right Enemies: The Life and Murder of Carlo Tresca* (New Brunswick, N.J.: Rutgers University Press, 1988), 37. Michael Miller Topp argues that the trial was seen as a "test of strength" by the Italian syndicalists: Topp, *Those without a Country*, 104.

6 Topp, *Those without a Country*, 148, fn. 72.

7 Ibid., 106.

8   John Higham, *Strangers in the Land: Patterns of American Nativism, 1860–1925* (New York: Atheneum, 1977), 321–24.

9   McLean, *Behind the Mask of Chivalry.*

10   David M. Schmitz, *Thank God They're on Our Side: The United States and Right-Wing Dictatorships, 1921–1965* (Chapel Hill: University of North Carolina Press, 1999), 11, 32–45 (the Mussolini quote is on 41).

11   "Cronstadt," *L'Adunata dei Refrattari,* April 30, 1922.

12   "Il Movimento Makhnovista e L'Antisemitismo," *L'Adunata dei Refrattari,* October 30, 1922. The article referred to the Makhno movement as a "spontaneous revolutionary movement of the masses" that combatted both the "violence of the communist party" and the right wing Deniken reaction that sought to reassert Russian officers' authority at the same time, and it argued that Makhno dealt severely with anti-Semitic acts.

13   For Berkman and Goldman about Russian communism, see Alexander Berkman, *The Bolshevik Myth* (New York: Boni and Liveright, 1925), and Emma Goldman, *My Disillusionment in Russia* (New York: Doubleday, 1923). On Italians' relief work on behalf of Russian prisoners, see *L'Adunata dei Refrattari,* April 30, 1922; see also Roger Baldwin et al., "Political Persecution Today," pamphlet published by the International Committee for Political Prisoners, 1925, at the Tamiment Library, New York University. On Makhno, see Alexandra Skirda, *Nestor Makhno, Anarchy's Cossack: The Struggle for Free Soviets in the Ukraine, 1917–1921,* trans. Paul Sharkey (New York: AK Press, 2003).

14   Zeev Sternhell and David Maisel, *The Birth of Fascist Ideology* (Princeton: Princeton University Press, 1995); Stephen Whitaker, *The Anarchist-Individualist Origins of Italian Fascism* (New York: Peter Lang, 2002). Some of the syndicalists who became fascists were Edmondo Rossoni, Giovanni Baldazzi, Massimo Rocca, Libero Tancredi, and Ada Negri. Those who stayed on the left included Pedro Esteve, the editor of *La Question Sociale*: Topp, *Those without a Country,* 7–8, 14, 39.

15   On the IWW split, see Thompson, *The IWW*; David R. Roediger, ed., *Fellow Worker: The Life of Fred Thompson* (Chicago: Charles Kerr, 1993).

16   Nicola Sacco, "Ai Rivoluzionari . . . Christiani," *L'Adunata dei Refrattari,* December 15, 1922.

17   Michael Miller Topp, *The Sacco–Vanzetti Case: A Brief History in Documents* (New York: Palgrave Macmillan, 2005), 9–10; Avrich, *Sacco and Vanzetti,* 99–102; *La Questione Sociale,* July 29, 1905.

18   Bartolomeo Vanzetti to Elizabeth Glendower Evans, December 18, 1920, Herbert B. Ehrmann Papers, Law School Library, Harvard University, Cambridge, Massachusetts.

19   T. R. Ravindranathan, *Bakunin and the Italians* (Kingston: McGill/Queens University Press, 1988), 14, 43–44, 182–84, 222; Mikhail Bakunin, *Statism and Anarchy,* trans. Marshall S. Shatz (Cambridge: Cambridge University

Press, 1990), esp. 32, 39, 46, 90, 204, 216–17; Gustave Le Bon, *The Crowd: A Study of the Popular Mind* (1896; Mineola, N.Y.: Dover Publications, 2002).

20 Levy, *Gramsci and the Anarchists*, 226, n. 99.

21 Ibid, 3.

22 Salvatore Salerno, "No God, No Master: Italian Anarchists and the Industrial Workers of the World," in *The Lost World of Italian American Radicals: Labor, Politics, and Culture*, ed. Phillip Cannistraro (Westport, Conn.: Praeger, 2003), 171–88; Topp, *Those without a Country*.

23 On Galleani in Italy, see Levy, *Gramsci and the Anarchists*, 33–35,125–26; Nunzio Pernicone, *Italian Anarchism 1864–1892* (Princeton: Princeton University Press, 1993).

24 *"Crumiro"* originated as a term for Algerian "brigands" who attacked the French in 1882. It was later adopted as a term for scabs. This derivation appears in *Novissimo Melzi: Completo Dizionario Italiano in due parti* (Milan: Antonio Vallardi, 1935).

25 Tom Guglielmo, "White on Arrival," in *Are Italians White? How Race Is Made in America*, ed. Jennifer Guglielmo and Salvatore Salerno (New York: Routledge, 2003); Roediger, *Working toward Whiteness*, 12–13.

26 Topp, *Those without a Country*, 111.

27 Salvatore Salerno, *"L'Odio di Razza*? (Race Hatred?): The Beginnings of a Racial Discourse in the Italian American Community," in *Italian American Politics: Local, Global/Cultural, Personal*, ed. Jerome Krase, Phillip Cannistraro, and Joseph Scelsa (New York: American Italian Historical Association, Hunter College, 1998). Sacco's and Vanzetti's history is an example of the Italians as part of an Italian-Latin alliance. One of the most important members of the defense committee was Frank Lopez, who built the Sacco and Vanzetti movement in South America.

28 Topp, *Those without a Country*, 98.

29 "Marat," "Sulle Razze," *L'Adunata dei Refrattari*, October 31, 1926; "The Strike of the Coal Miners," *L'Adunata dei Refrattari*, April 15, 1922; "Sono Crumiri Gli Operai," *L'Adunata dei Refrattari*, April 15, 1922; "Patria ed Umanita," *L'Adunata dei Refrattari*, March 17, 1923.

30 *The Sacco and Vanzetti Case: Transcript of the Record of the Trial of Nicola Sacco and Bartolomeo Vanzetti in the Courts of Massachusetts and Subsequent Proceedings 1920–27* (5 vols.; Mamaroneck, N.Y.: P. P. Appel, 1969), 1877.

31 *L'Adunata dei Refrattari*, May 24, 1924.

32 Salerno, *"L'Odio di Razza."*

33 Avrich, *Sacco and Vanzetti*, 137–62.

34 *One Big Union Monthly*, August 1920.

35 Kate Richards O'Hare, *In Prison* (New York: Alfred A. Knopf, 1923), 144–45.

36 "Intorno All Tragica Fine Di Salsedo, Un Memorandum di Palmer— Chi E L'informatore?" *Il Martello*, May 1920; Gallagher, *All the Right Enemies*.

37 Gallagher, *All the Right Enemies*, 52–53.

38 See George Carey, "*La Questione Sociale*, an Anarchist Newspaper in Paterson, New Jersey, 1895–1908," in *Italian Americans: New Perspectives in Italian Immigration and Ethnicity*, ed. Lydio Tomasi (Staten Island, N.Y.: Center for Migration Studies, 1983); Avrich, *Sacco and Vanzetti. L'Adunara dei Refrattari* contains numerous examples endorsing revolutionary violence: see, e.g., Sacco, "Ai Rivoluzioniari . . . Christiani."

39 *L'Adunata dei Refrattari*, February 10, 1921; *L'Agitazione*, February 8, 1921.

40 *L'Agitazione*, December 1, 1920. *L'Agitazione* was the newspaper dedicated to Sacco's and Vanzetti's defense.

41 Carey, "*La Questione Sociale*," 293.

42 Topp, *Those without a Country*, 89.

43 *L'Adunata dei Refrattari*, July 7, 1923.

44 "Valorizziamo l'individuo in Rivolta," *L'Adunata dei Refrattari*, April 7, 1923; "Gli Individualisti, L'Atentato Individuale, ed Azione Revoluzionaria," *L'Adunata dei Refrattari*, May 12, 1923.

45 Nicola Sacco to Aldino Felicani, February 1927, Aldino Felicani Collection, Rare Books and Manuscripts, Boston Public Library, Boston (hereafter, AFC).

46 On the term *muliebre* as the preferred term for feminine among Fascist writers, see Barbara Spackman, "Fascist Women and the Rhetoric of Virility," in *Mothers of Invention: Women, Italian Fascism and Culture*, ed. Robin Pickering-Lazzi (Minneapolis: University of Minnesota Press, 1995), 100–120.

47 Tina Cacici, "Profile Muliebre," *Rinascimento*, May 1920.

48 Arendt, *On Revolution*, 69–70; idem, *The Origins of Totalitarianism*, 324, 473–79.

49 Topp, *Sacco and Vanzetti*, 37; Tina Cacici to the defense committee, December 19, 1924, AFC.

50 *L'Adunata dei Refrattari*, November 13, 1926.

51 Ibid., April 7, 1923.

52 Ibid., October 30, 1926.

53 Ibid., July 30, 1927, August 6, 1927.

54 Fred Moore to Eugene Lyons, August 29, 1921, AFC; *New York Daily News*, August 25, 1921. For speculation on Galleanist involvement, see Avrich, *Sacco and Vanzetti*, 205–207.

55 The FBI file on the Sacco and Vanzetti case is now available online at http://foia.fbi.gov/foiaindex/vanzetti.htm (accessed February 22, 2008).

56 *L'Adunata dei Refrattari*, May 5, 1923.

57 Nicola Sacco to Aldino Felicani, "For the International Proletariat," May 6, 1927, AFC.

58 Nicola Sacco to the international proletariat, February 1927, AFC.

59 "Castroni," *L'Adunata dei Refrattari*, May 12, 1923; "Per Sacco e Vanzetti: Una Canaglia che Vorrebbe Farsi Onore," *L'Adunata dei Refrattari*, September 2, 1926.

60 *L'Adunata dei Refrattari*, June 14, 1924.

61 "Parliamoci Chiaro," *L'Adunata dei Refrattari*, October 30, 1922.

62 "Congressomania," *L'Adunta dei Refrattari*, August 15, 1922; editorial, *L'Adunta dei Refrattari*, September 15, 1922.

63 Fred Moore to Elizabeth Gurley Flynn, August 26, 1920, AFC, series 4A.

64 Ibid., August 18, 1920.

65 Ibid., September 21, 1920.

66 Ibid., November 5, 1920.

67 Elizabeth Gurley Flynn to Fred Moore, December 20, 1920, AFC, series 4A.

68 Ibid., December 17, 1920.

69 Elizabeth Gurley Flynn and Big Bill Haywood took opposite sides when Flynn pled several miners guilty during the trial of 1917 following the strike at the Mesabi iron range, which Haywood argued was a political fiasco. In a letter to the attorney general, Flynn severed herself from the rest of the IWW during the First World War resister trials and said that she supported the war. For two views on Flynn's role, see Gallagher, *All the Right Enemies*, 67–70; Thompson, *The IWW: The First Fifty Years*, 103.

70 Fred Moore to Elizabeth Gurley Flynn, December 20, 1920, AFC.

71 Fred Moore to Art Shields, July 21, 1921, AFC.

72 Art Shields, "War on the Alien in New England," *One Big Union Monthly*, January 1921, 41.

73 Topp, *Those without a Country*, 48. On the IWW generally, see Elizabeth Faue, *Community of Suffering and Struggle: Women, Men, and the Labor Movement in Minneapolis, 1915–1945* (Chapel Hill: University of North Carolina Press, 1991).

74 Fred Moore to Eugene Lyons, May 3, 1924, AFC, 2030-4A.

75 Mary Heaton Vorse, *Footnote to Folly: Reminiscences of Mary Heaton Vorse* (New York: Arno Press, 1980), 335; *Il Martello*, January 1921.

76 "Can Women Stop the War?" *One Big Union Monthly*, July 1920, 54–55.

77 Enrico Albertini, "L'Ora Stringe," *Il Martello*, November 1, 1920.

78 Arturo Giovannitti, "When the Cock Crows: To the Memory of Frank Little, Hanged at Midnight," in Giovannitti, *Collected Poems* (Chicago: Clemente and Sons, 1962), 26.

79 *The Sacco and Vanzetti Case*, 1877; Bartolomeo Vanzetti to Virginia MacMechan, August 26, 1923, in *The Letters of Sacco and Vanzetti*, ed. Marion Denman Frankfurter and Gardner Jackson (New York: Viking, 1928; New York: Penguin, 1997), 99.

80 "Communicati," April 16, 1921, May 28, 1921, July 16, 1921, August 13, 1921, November 12, 1921, November 19, 1921, November 26, 1921, all in *Il Martello*.

81 Nicola Sacco to Mrs. Ehrmann, April 10, 1927, Herbert B. Ehrmann Papers, Law School Library, Harvard University, Cambridge, Massachusetts.

82 Fred Moore to Elizabeth Gurley Flynn, December 15, 1921, AFC.

83 Elizabeth Gurley Flynn to Fred Moore, December 19, 1921, AFC.

84 Ibid., Kansas City, February 5, 1922, AFC.

85 Ibid. Luigi Quintiliano had a similar experience while on tour and spent hours discussing Sacco's possible guilt with Carlo Tresca: see Gallagher, *All the Right Enemies*, 86.

86 Bartolomeo Vanzetti to Fred Moore, 1922, box 13, folder 12, Herbert B. Ehrmann Papers, Law School Library, Harvard University, Cambridge, Massachusetts.

87 While he found Frank Lopez willing to cooperate, he was less favorable to the rest of the committee—that is, Felice Guadagni, Constantino Zonchello, Ermanno Bianchini, and Aldino Felicani.

88 Aldino Felicani, circular, n.d. (ca. 1922); Felicani, letter to International Hod Carriers, July 20, 1922, AFC.

89 Gallagher, *All the Right Enemies*; Constantino Zonchello to Bartolomeo Vanzetti, July 31, 1923, AFC; Bartolomeo Vanzetti to Alice Stone Blackwell, June 18, 1927, AFC. This part of the letter was edited out of the published *Letters of Sacco and Vanzetti*.

90 Fred Moore to Elizabeth Gurley Flynn, November 22, 1922, AFC.

91 "Parliamoci Chiaro," *L'Adunata dei Refrattari*, October 30, 1922. There is a suggestion here, as there is in Vanzetti's letter to Moore, that his friends could free him if they had the courage to say it.

92 On the split in the U.S. Federazione Socialista Italiana (FSI), see Topp, *Those without a Country*, 128–29, 137. On Giovannitti's speeches, see ibid., 222: "By linking Gompers natvisim and anti-radicalism with anti-radical elements in Italy, the mission unified Italian American leftist opposition to the post-war reaction in the US."

93 Files on Sacco and Vanzetti Defense, October 15, 1921, FBI Files, sec. 4a, 7, FOIA.FBI.gov, 2189 pages (accessed August 2006).

94 Elizabeth Gurley Flynn to Fred Moore, January 27, 1923, AFC.

95 "Hiri Hiri Hiri: God Saves the Commonwealth of Massachusetts," *L'Adunata dei Refrattari*, April 21, 1923.

96 Elizabeth Gurley Flynn to Fred Moore, March 14, 1923, AFC.

97 Bartolomeo Vanzetti to Elizabeth Glendower Evans, April 14, 1923, in Frankfurter and Jackson, eds., *The Letters of Sacco and Vanzetti*, 91, 128, 131.

98 Galleani, "Fronte Unico," *L'Adunata dei Refrattari*, September 4, 1926.

99 *Sacco and Vanzetti Defense Committee Official Bulletin*, vol. 1, no. 1, January 6, 1924.

100 Rosa Zamboni and Felice Guadagni to Fred Moore, April 5, 1924, AFC.

101 Fred Moore to Matilda Robbins, May 6, 1924, AFC.

102   Constantino Zonchello to Bartolomeo Vanzetti, July 31, 1923, AFC. In the letter, Zonchello alludes to Carlo Tresca's complaints about Moore, as well.

103   Fred Moore to SVDC, July 7, 1924, AFC.

104   Elizabeth Gurley Flynn to Fred Moore, August 15, 1924, AFC.

105   Elizabeth Gurley Flynn to John Codman, August 15, 1924, AFC.

106   Nick Sacco, August 18, 1924, in Frankfurter and Jackson, eds., *Letters of Sacco and Vanzetti*, 21.

107   Emilio Coda to Aldino Felicani, September 26, 1924, AFC.

108   Osmond Fraenkel, *The Sacco and Vanzetti Case* (1931; New York: Russell and Russell, 1969), 5.

109   Clarence Darrow, "The Immigration Question," in *Verdicts out of Court*, ed. Arthur and Lila Weinberg (Chicago: Quadrangle Books, 1963); see also Vernon Parrington, *Main Currents in American Thought: The Colonial Mind* (New York: Harcourt Brace Jovanovich, 1927).

110   Bartolomeo Vanzetti, June 13, 1926, in Frankfurter and Jackson, eds., *Letters of Sacco and Vanzetti*, 201.

111   Flynn, *The Rebel Girl*, 135.

112   Vorse, *Footnote to Folly*, 12.

113   Ray Stannard Baker, "The Revolutionary Strike," *American Magazine*, May 1912, 24, as cited in Joyce L. Kornbluh, *Rebel Voices: An IWW Anthology* (Ann Arbor: University of Michigan Press, 1965), 158.

114   John Sayles, dir., *Matewan* (Red Dog Films/Cinecom International, 1987).

115   In *Whiteness of a Different Color*, Matthew Jacobson makes a persuasive argument that many European immigrants were not entirely "white" because they were described as "races" in the 1920s and that this did not end until the Second World War. Southern Italians, as Jacobson shows, were defined as a race because they were seen as Saracen or African. Northern Italians, by contrast, were defined as Aryans. See also Cesare Lombroso, *Crime: Its Causes and Remedies*, trans. Henry P. Horton (c. 1911; Montclair, N.J.: Patterson Smith, 1968), 23–29.

116   See, e.g., *The Sacco and Vanzetti Case*, 273, when a white worker fails to identify the other workers in his crew because "they were all Italian fellows."

117   Thomas Dabney, "A Negro Looks at Sacco's America," *Nation*, November 21, 1927.

118   NPA, *Annual Proceedings*, 1927, 25. On eugenics in prison reform in the 1920s, see Colvin, *Penitentiaries, Reformatories and Chain Gangs*.

119   *Boston Globe*, February 22, 1927.

120   Felix Frankfurter, "The Case of Sacco and Vanzetti," *Atlantic Monthly*, March 1927, 409–32.

121   Bartolomeo Vanzetti to Virginia MacMahon, May 15, 1926, in Frankfurter and Jackson, eds., *Letters of Sacco and Vanzetti*, 194.

122   Bruce Bliven, "In Dedham Jail: A Visit to Sacco and Vanzetti," *New Republic*, June 22, 1927, 120–21.

123   Jim Seymour, "They're Only a Couple of God-Damn Dagoes," *Industrial Pioneer*, December 1921, 21.

124   Elizabeth Glendower Evans, *Outstanding Features of the Sacco–Vanzetti Case* (Boston: New England Civil Liberties Union, 1924), 19.

125   Edward J. Larson, *Summer for the Gods: The Scopes Trial and America's Continuing Debate over Science and Religion* (Cambridge, Mass.: Harvard University Press, 1998).

126   George Kirchwey, "Sacco-Vanzetti," *Nation*, April 20, 1927.

127   Editorial, *Nation*, August 10, 1927.

128   Nicola Sacco and Bartolomeo Vanzetti to New Trial League, July 23, 1924, Sacco–Vanzetti Defense Committee file, Tamiment Library / Robert F. Wagner Labor Archives, Elmer Holmes Bobst Library, New York University.

129   Evans, *Outstanding Features of the Sacco–Vanzetti Case*, 28.

130   Ibid, 25–26.

131   Bartolomeo Vanzetti to Elizabeth Glendower Evans, October 1923, Herbert B. Ehrmann Papers, Law School Library, Harvard University, Cambridge, Massachusetts.

132   NPA, *Proceedings*, 1923, 204.

133   Felix Frankfurter Papers, Law Library, Harvard University, Cambridge, Mass. (hereafter, FFP).

134   *New Republic*, August 24, 1927.

135   Herbert Ehrmann, *The Case That Will Not Die: The Commonwealth v. Sacco and Vanzetti* (Boston: Little, Brown, 1969), 159.

136   *Nation*, August 17, 1927.

137   Felix Frankfurter to Herbert Ehrmann, July 14, 1927, FFP.

138   "Justice Underfoot" (editorial), *The Nation*, August 17, 1927, 147; Paul Kellogg, *The Lantern*, 4, FFP.

139   James Cannon, "Free Sacco and Vanzetti," *Labor Defender*, May 1927, 63.

140   Sam Marcus in *L'Adunata dei Refrattari*, May 28, 1927.

141   In Baldwin letter and in letter to Elizabeth Glendower Evans, June 17, 1926, Herbert B. Ehrmann Papers, Law School Library, Harvard University, Cambridge, Massachusetts.

142   Bartolomeo Vanzetti to Roger Baldwin, February 15, 1926, AFC.

143   Idem to Roger Baldwin, September 30, 1926, AFC. For a critique of the ILD, see *L'Adunata dei Refrattari*, July 18, 1927.

144   Bartolomeo Vanzetti to Elizabeth Glendower Evans, November 2, 1926, AFC.

145   Bartolomeo Vanzetti to Mary Donovan, March 21, 1927, AFC. Vanzetti reiterated that he meant "the great cause" of socialist anarchism, not the great cause of his own case.

146   Bartolomeo Vanzetti to Alice Stone Blackwell, November 13, 1925, in Frankfurter and Jackson, eds., *Letters of Sacco and Vanzetti*, 181.

147   Theodore Draper, *American Communism and Soviet Russia* (New York: Viking Press, 1960), 262–67; minutes of Political Committee (Pol Com) meeting, August 4, 1927; files of the CPUSA in the Comintern, Russian State Archive of Socio-Political History (hereafter, RGASPI), fond 515, delo 983.

148   *Labor Defender,* June 1927, 89.

149   James Cannon, "Sacco and Vanzetti Must Not Burn in the Electric Chair" *Labor Defender,* May 1927, 38.

150   James Cannon, "Friends of Sacco and Vanzetti," *Labor Defender,* September 1927.

151   Ibid.; James Cannon, "Death or Commutation?," *Labor Defender,* July 1927, 99–100.

152   Eugene Lyons, *The Life and Death of Sacco and Vanzetti* (1927; New York: Da Capo, 1970), 73.

153   *Labor Defender,* October 1927, 149, 152–53, 171–72.

154   Daniel Aaron, *Writers on the Left* (New York: Oxford University Press, 1977).

155   *Nation,* August 17, 1927.

156   Thomas Dewey in *New Republic,* November 23, 1927.

157   *New Republic,* August 31, 1927; excerpt from the *Waterbury Republican* in "Press Comment on the Saco-Vanzetti Execution," *Nation* 125, no. 3245, 252.

158   Mike Gold, "Thirteen Thoughts in Sacco–Vanzetti: A Symposium," *New Masses,* October 1927.

159   *Lantern,* August 1929, FFP.

160   Sidney Sutherland, "The Mystery of Sacco–Vanzetti," *Liberty Magazine,* March 8, 1930.

161   Alfred Hitchcock, dir., *The Wrong Man,* written by Maxwell Anderson and Angus McPhail (Warner Brothers, 1956).

162   Henry Ward Dana to Felix Frankfurter, January 6, 1930, FFP.

163   "Una Lettera di Rosina Sacco," *L'Adunata dei Refrattari,* January 7, 1928.

164   On Tina Cacici, see *Rinascimento,* May 1920; Tina Cacici to the SVDC, letter, December 19, 1924, AFC. On "Linda J." in Detroit, see correspondence in *L'Agitazione,* 1920–27; and Avrich, *Sacco and Vanzetti.* On Selma Maximon, see Fred Moore to John Beffel, May 8, 1922, AFC; FBI FOIA, Sacco, Nicola/Vanzetti, part 6a, p. 54. On Auroro D'Angelo, see *L'Adunata dei Refrattari,* ca. late September 1927.

165   Candace Falk, *Love, Anarchy and Emma Goldman,* 225.

166   Bartolomeo Vanzetti to Mary Donovan, May 24, 1926, in Frankfurter and Jackson, eds., *The Letters of Sacco and Vanzetti,* 200.

167   Upton Sinclair, *Boston* (New York: A. and C. Boni, 1928), 37.

168 Ibid., 261.

169 Rosa Sacco, testimony, in *The Sacco and Vanzetti Case*, 2062.

170 Felice Guadagni, testimony, *The Sacco and Vanzetti Case*, 5091.

171 Avrich, *Sacco and Vanzetti*, 216–17.

172 Sinclair, *Boston*, 309.

173 John Dos Passos, *The Big Money* (1946; New York: Washington Square Press, Inc., 1961), 620.

174 Dos Passos, *The Big Money*, 621; Dos Passos, *Facing the Chair: The Story of the Americanization of Two Foreignborn Workingmen* (1927; New York: Da Capo, 1970), 45.

175 Lyons, *The Life and Death of Sacco and Vanzetti*, 25–26.

176 There are several possible parallel characters for Jake. Powers Hapgood was an organizer for the mine workers in Colorado who later married Mary Donovan, a working-class socialist on the defense committee, and eventually became an alcoholic. Elizabeth Gurley Flynn, who toured the country as the principal English-speaking labor organizer on the case for several years finally had a physical and mental breakdown when her relationship with Carlo Tresca ended. In the middle of the case, she left to spend the next six years convalescing with the birth-control activist Mari Equi in Portland, Oregon, with whom many contemporary historians speculate she had a lesbian relationship. On Flynn, see Rosalyn Baxandall, *Words on Fire: The Life and Writing of Elizabeth Gurley Flynn* (New Brunswick, N.J.: Rutgers University Press, 1987). On Hapgood, see Aldino Felicani to Powers Hapgood, July 18, 1938, AFC.

177 Flynn, *The Rebel Girl*, 335.

178 Paolo Schicchi, "L' Africa," *L'Adunata dei Refrattari*, August 11, 1923. For more on similar uses of Africa to represent the degeneration of Italy, see Topp, *Those without a Country*, 71.

5 Scottsboro to the Rosenbergs

Epigraphs: Joseph Stalin, as quoted in Nikita Khrushchev, "Secret Report to the 20th Party Congress of the CPSU," in *The Stalinist Legacy*, ed. Tariq Ali (Middlesex: Penguin, 1984), 257; Clarence Norris in *New York Times*, October 26, 1976, as quoted in James Goodman, *Stories of Scottsboro* (New York: Vintage, 1994), 388.

1 He was also known as Sol Auerbach.

2 James Allen, *Organizing in the Depression South: A Communist's Memoir* (Minneapolis: MEP Publications, 2001).

3 Michael Belknap, *Cold War Political Justice: The Smith Act, the Communist Party and American Civil Liberties* (Westport, Conn.: Greenwood Press, 1977), 38; Ellen Schrecker, *Many Are the Crimes: McCarthyism in America* (Princeton: Princeton University Press, 1998), 104–5.

4 John Earl Haynes and Harvey Klehr, *Venona: Decoding Soviet Espionage in America* (New Haven: Yale University Press, 2000); Harvey Klehr, *The Secret World of American Communism: Harvey Klehr, John Earl Haynes, and Fridrikh Igorevich Firsov* (New Haven: Yale University Press, 1995); Vernon Pedersen, *The Communist Party in Maryland, 1919–1957* (Urbana: University of Illinois Press, 2000); Allen Weinstein and Victor Vassilev, *The Haunted Wood: Soviet Espionage in America—The Stalin Era* (New York: Modern Library, 2000); John Earl Haynes and Harvey Klehr, *In Denial: Historians, Communism and Espionage* (San Francisco: Encounter Books, 2005).

5 Robin D. G. Kelley, *Hammer and Hoe: Alabama Communists during the Great Depression* (Chapel Hill: University of North Carolina Press, 1990); Michael E. Brown, *Studies in the Politics and Culture of U.S. Communism* (New York: Monthly Review Press, 1993); Josie Fowler, "To Be Red and 'Oriental': The Experiences of Japanese and Chinese Immigrant Communists in the American and International Communist Movements, 1919–1934," Ph.D. diss., University of Minnesota, Minneapolis, 2003; James Barrett, *William Z. Foster and the Tragedy of American Radicalism* (Chicago: University of Chicago Press, 1999); Bryan Palmer, "Rethinking the Historiography of U.S. Communism," *American Communist History* 2 (December 2003): 139–73.

6 Michael Denning, *The Cultural Front: The Laboring of American Culture in the Twentieth Century* (New York: Verso, 1996), 13.

7 Draper, *American Communism and Soviet Russia*, 180–81.

8 Edward Hallett Carr, *Twilight of the Comintern, 1930–1935* (New York: Pantheon Books, 1982), 125–30; Jonathan Haslam, "The Comintern and the Origins of the Popular Front: 1934–1935," *Historical Journal* 22, no. 3 (September 1979): 673–91.

9 Belknap, *Cold War Political Justice*, 10; Barrett, *William Z. Foster and the Tragedy of American Radicalism*, 131; Irons, *A People's History of the Supreme Court*, 285–88; *Gitlow v. People of the State of New York*, 268 U.S. 652 (1925). More generally, see Patricia Cayo Sexton, *The War on Labor and the Left: Understanding America's Unique Conservatism* (Boulder: Westview Press, 1991); Schrecker, *Many Are the Crimes*; Preston, *Aliens and Dissenters*.

10 RGASPI, fond 515, delo 202, 60–61.

11 Barrett, *William Z. Foster and the Tragedy of American Communism*, 133.

12 Edward P. Johanningsmeier, *Forging American Communism: The Life of William Z. Foster* (Princeton: Princeton University Press, 1998), 165, fn. 40.

13 RGASPI, fond 515, delo 202.

14 Frank Walsh, December 21, 1921, RGASPI, fond 515, delo 80; Harry Feinberg to Communist Party re bail jumping, IWW General Defense Committee, RGASPI, fond 515, delo 81.

15 Roger Baldwin to Bill Haywood, October 21, 1921, RGASPI, fond 515, delo 39. According to Johanningsmeier's account, *Forging American Commu-*

nism, Haywood's bail was included in the request to the Comintern for defense money.

16 Draper, *American Communism and Soviet Russia*, 180–81.

17 Chaplin, *Wobbly*, 333.

18 James Cannon, "The Second Annual Conference of the International Labor Defense," *Labor Defender*, October 1926, 167.

19 Ralph Chaplin, "In the Shadow of the Electric Chair," *Labor Defender*, January 1926, 2–3.

20 "Report on the First ILD Conference," *Labor Defender*, January 1926, 7.

21 Cannon, "The Second Annual Conference of the International Labor Defense," 168.

22 ILD, "Under Arrest: Workers' Self-Defense in the Courts," 1928, pamphlet no. 5, Tamiment Library, New York University.

23 James Cannon, "A Living Monument to Sacco and Vanzetti," *Labor Defender*, August 1927.

24 RGASPI, March 3, 1925, fond 515, delo 510.

25 Roger Baldwin to Earl Browder, March 3, 1925, RGASPI, fond 515, delo 510. On Browder's position in the party in the spring of 1925, see Theodore Draper, *American Communism and Soviet Russia*; James G. Akerman, *Earl Browder: The Failure of American Communism* (Tuscaloosa: University of Alabama Press, 1997), 25–26.

26 Earl Browder to Roger Baldwin, April 2, 1925, RGASPI, fond 515, delo 504.

27 Roger Baldwin to Earl Browder, March 19, 1925, RGASPI, fond 515, delo 510.

28 Earl Browder to Roger Baldwin, March 31, 1925, RGASPI, fond 515, delo 510.

29 Roger Baldwin, as quoted in Garey, *Defending Everybody*, 93.

30 Upton Sinclair to Ida Rothstein, April 4, 1931, RGASPI, fond 515, delo 2573.

31 March 5, 1930, RGASPI, fond 515, delo 2190.

32 Forrest Bailey to the editor of the *Daily Worker* (labeled "Personal, not for publication"), August 23, 1923, RGASPI, fond 515, delo 207.

33 Chaplin, *Wobbly*, 348; Hammer, Stanton, and Evans, "Confidential Report on the IWW," RGASPI, fond 515, delo 81 (see also delo 246); report by Walter Bates, Joe Carvel, Alan B. Cobbs, and Harrison George. On the IWW's takeover of the ILD, see Harry Glickson to Louis Engdahl, RGASPI, fond 515, delo 1838.

34 John Patrick Diggins, "Italo-American Anti-Fascist Opposition," *Journal of American History* 54, no. 3 (December 1967), 579–98.

35 Resolution on organization, and resolution on old class-war-prisoners cases, both ILD Third Conference, November 1927, RGASPI, fond 515, delo 1206.

36 Colegore Greco and Donato Corrillo, "Smash the Frame Up System!" RGASPI, fond 515, delo 1531, 65–66.

37 RGASPI, fond 515, delo 1837.

38 Resolution on organization, ILD Third Conference, RGASPI, fond 515, delo 1206, 16.

39 George Maurer to Rose Karsner, January 24, 1926, January 29, 1926, RGASPI, fond 515, delo 915.

40 District organizers' reports, 1934, RGASPI fond 515, delo 3692.

41 The WIR was an organization dedicated to supporting strikers in the Communist Party's independent unions of the 1920s.

42 Secretary to William Weinstone, May 20, 1926, RGASPI, fond 515, delo 715.

43 Cleveland conference call to action, RGASPI, fond 515, delo 3013. "Orphan Jones" was "Euel Lee," a Black agricultural worker who was convicted of killing a landowner and his family in Snow Hill, Md., in 1932. Despite the ILD's efforts, Lee was executed in 1933. See Solomon, *The Cry Was Unity*, 187–88; Vernon L. Pederson, *The Communist Party in Maryland 1919–1957* (Champaign: University of Illinois, 2000), 57–61. The Imperial Valley defendants were communists and strikers imprisoned on criminal syndicalism charges following an effort to organize agricultural workers in Southern California in 1930. The last of these defendants was released in 1933. See Dorothy Healey and Maurice Isserman, *Dorothy Healey Remembers: A Life in the American Communist Party* (New York: Oxford University Press, 1990,) 42–54; Carey McWilliams, *Factories in the Field: The Story of Migratory Farm Labor in California* (1939; Berkeley: University of California, 2000), 213.

44 Directive letter to the ILD of the United States, RGASPI, fond 515, delo 3012, 6. Although the date on the document is 1921, it must refer to 1931, as everything else in the folder is dated 1932, and the ILD did not exist in 1921.

45 Cleveland conference call to action.

46 George Maurer to all ILD district organizers, February 6, 1930, RGASPI, fond 515, delo 2194.

47 Rough draft of letter to district organizers, unsigned, n.d., RGASPI, fond 515, delo. 2194.

48 Martin Abern to the Political Committee of the Workers (Communist) Party, September 18, 1928, RGASPI, fond 515, delo 1530, 8–10.

49 Vern Smith, "The Negro—A Subject Race," *Industrial Pioneer*, April 1924, 5–6.

50 William Patterson and Fort Whitman, RGASPI, fond 515, delo 1212; Mark Solomon, *The Cry Was Unity: Communists and African-Americans, 1917–1936* (Oxford: University Press of Mississippi, 1998), 64.

51 RGASPI, fond 515, delo 983. On the "Black Belt" thesis and the 1928 conference, see Kelley, *Hammer and Hoe*; Mark Naison, *Communists in Harlem during the Depression* (New York: Grove, 1985); Nell Irvin Painter, *The*

Narrative of Hoseah Hudson: The Life and Times of a Black Radical (1979; New York: W. W. Norton, 1994); Solomon, *The Cry Was Unity*; Harry Haywood, *Black Bolshevik: Autobiography of an Afro-American Communist* (Chicago: Liberator Press, 1978).

52 John A. Salmond, *Gastonia 1929: The Story of the Loray Mill Strike* (Chapel Hill: University of North Carolina Press, 1995).

53 On the impact of the split, see ibid., 105; Lucy Parsons, "The Haymarket Martyrs and Gastonia," *Labor Defender*, July 1929, 139.

54 Field fraction meeting of the ILD, with Reid, Walter Trumbull, Juliette Stuart Poyntz, Ellen Dawson, Fred Wagenacht, Joseph Brodsky, Bill Dunne, Al Weisbord present, June 10, 1929, RGASPI, fond 515, delo 1837.

55 Salmond, *Gastonia*, 128–34.

56 Robert Korstad, *Civil Rights Unionism: Tobacco Workers and the Struggle for Democracy in the Mid-Twentieth Century South* (Chapel Hill: University of North Carolina Press, 2003), 124–25.

57 National Convention, ILD, December 29–31, 1929, RGASPI, fond 515, delo 1835.

58 Fraction National Executive Committee (NEC), May 16, 1930, RGASPI, fond 515, delo 2191. On Beal's story of the bail skipping and his views of the Soviet Union, see Salmond, *Gastonia*, 167–72; Fred Beal, *Proletarian Journey: New England, Gastonia, Moscow* (New York: Hillman Curl, 1937).

59 Karl Reeve to all party editors, July 15, 1929, RGASPI, fond 515, delo 1832.

60 From national fraction to comrade Ross in Birmingham, RGASPI, fond 515, delo 3017.

61 Salmond, *Gastonia*, 36, 49, 66–67.

62 RGASPI, fond 515, delo 1835.

63 George Maurer, report on the Southern ILD conference, December 11, 1929, RGASPI, fond 515, delo 1807.

64 Ibid., delo 1835.

65 Ibid., delo 1839, 42.

66 Ibid., May 22, 1930, delo 2190. Kelley, *Hammer and Hoe*, 39–43; Sasha Small, *20,000 Unknown Soldiers* (New York: International Labor Defense, 1936); Gerald Horne, *Black Liberation / Red Scare: Ben Davis and the Communist Party* (Newark: University of Delaware Press, 1994).

67 Angelo Herndon, *Let Me Live* (New York: Random House, 1937); Kelley, *Hammer and Hoe*; Theodore Rosengarten, *All God's Dangers: The Life of Nate Shaw* (New York: Vintage, 1989).

68 Kelley, *Hammer and Hoe*, 76 (see also 39–43, 48–52); Sasha Small, *Hell in Georgia: What Angelo Herndon Faces* (New York: International Labor Defense, 1935).

69 "Factual Information on the ILD" (anonymous document with "Browder" handwritten in the top left corner), February 23, 1935, RGASPI, fond 515, delo 3928.

70 Robert L. Zangrando, *The NAACP Crusade against Lynching, 1909–1950* (Philadelphia: Temple University Press, 1980), 115–16; Minutes of the All Southern Conference for Civil and Trade Union Rights, Nocteagle, Tenn., May 26, 1935, RGASPI, fond 515, delo 3951, 5.

71 George Maurer, "Five ILD Years," *Labor Defender*, July 1930, 121.

72 National Bureau ILD fraction meeting, February 24, 1931, RGASPI, fond 515, delo 2572; Maurer report, February 25, 1931, fond 515, delo 2572.

73 Cyril Briggs to George Padmore, March 14, 1930, RGASPI, fond 515, delo 2023.

74 Ibid.

75 Minutes of the meeting of July 25, 1930, RGASPI, fond 515, delo 2022, 20. Harry Haywood says the removal was due to Otto Huiswood's article against the line decided at the Sixth Congress: Haywood, *Black Bolshevik*, 321.

76 Kratov's identity is a mystery.

77 RGASPI, fond 515, delo 2222.

78 National Bureau meeting, ILD, January 24, 1931, RGASPI, fond 515, d. 2572.

79 RGASPI, fond 515, delo 2572.

80 April 9, 1931, RGASPI, fond 515, delo 2572.

81 Letter to George Chamlee, July 9, 1932, RGASPI, fond 515, delo 3017.

82 Max Bedacht, 1931, RGASPI, fond 515, delo 2266. On Bedacht's history, see Draper, *American Communism and Soviet Russia*, 431, 435.

83 On Ralph Gray, see *Liberator*, November 21, 1931, as quoted in Robin D. G. Kelley, "Afric's Sons with Banner Red: African-American Communists and the Politics of Culture, 1919–1934," in Kelley, *Race Rebels: Culture Politics and the Black Working Class* (New York: Free Press, 1994), 112.

84 R. A. S., "The Halter around the Negro's Neck," *Labor Defender*, March 1928, 58; Nora West, "Fascism—Southern Style," *Labor Defender*, November 1930, 220; Jim Allen, "Voice from the South," *Labor Defender*, November 1930, 221; Myra Page, "Lynching and Pay Checks," *Labor Defender*, October 1930, 196; Louis Engdahl, "No Death, No Prison!" *Labor Defender*, July 1930, 134; "Five Lynchings in Five Days as Unemployment Grows Worse," *Southern Worker*, September 20, 1930; miscellaneous fliers, RGASPI, fond 515, delo 1807.

85 A. Jakira, "As if to Slaughter," *Labor Defender*, March 1930; Joseph North, "Unemployment and the Noose," *Labor Defender*, March 1930, 48; Otto Hall, "Gastonia and the Negro," *Labor Defender*, August 1929, 153; calls to demonstrate by the LSNR, April 2, 1931, April 19, 1931, fond 515, delo 2589.

86 Allen, *Organizing in the Depression South*, 27.

87 Minutes of the ILD National Bureau, June 4, 1930, RGASPI, fond 515, delo 2190.

88 Elizabeth Lawson, *They Shall Not Die: The Story of Scottsboro in Pictures* (New York: Workers' Library, 1932).

89 James Allen, "Smash the Scottsboro Lynch Verdict," 1931, ILD vertical file, Tamiment Library / Robert F. Wagner Labor Archives, Elmer Holmes Bobst Library, New York University.

90 See James Allen (Aurbach), "The Knights of Fascism," *Labor Defender*, April 1920, 78; Theodore Dreiser, "Mr. President: Free the Scottsboro Boys," ILD vertical file, Tamiment Library / Robert F. Wagner Labor Archives, Elmer Holmes Bobst Library, New York University.

91 Ibid, 15.

92 Isidore Schneider, *Story of Scottsboro* (New York: International Labor Defense, 1933), pamphlet available in the Michigan State University digital library at http://archive.lib.msu.edu/AFS/dmc/radicalism/public/all/storyscottsboro/ALS.pdf?CFID=8309338&CFTOKEN=62675693 (accessed March 5, 2008).

93 Goodman, *Stories of Scottsboro*. The infantilization of the Scottsboro Boys was more likely among liberal and socialist supporters than among communists: see Allan Knight Chalmers, *They Shall Be Free* (New York: Doubleday, 1951), 237–38.

94 Jane Dillon to Gertrude Akerman,, August 14, 1931, RGASPI, fond 515, delo 2573.

95 Kelley, *Hammer and Hoe*, 42–43.

96 John Hammond Moore, "The Angelo Herndon Case, 1932–1937," *Phylon* 32, no. 1 (1960): 60; Gerald Horne, *Black Liberation / Red Scare: Ben Davis and the Communist Party* (Newark: University of Delaware Press, 1994); Charles H. Martin, *The Angelo Herndon Case and Southern Justice* (Baton Rouge: Louisiana State University Press, 1976); Herndon, *Let Me Live*.

97 Kelley, *Hammer and Hoe*, 134.

98 Scottsboro Defense Committee, "Scottsboro: A Record of a Broken Promise" (New York: Scottsboro Defense Committee, 1938), 11, pamphlet available in the Michigan State University digital library at http://archive.lib.msu.edu/AFS/dmc/radicalism/public/all/scottsbororecordbroken/ALT.pdf?CFID=8309338&CFTOKEN=62675693 (accessed March 5, 2008).

99 William Patterson, RGASPI, fond 515, delo 3928.

100 On legal-defense work among Negroes, see ILD newsletter, December 29, 1931, 3–4, ILD vertical file, Tamiment Library / Robert F. Wagner Labor Archives, Elmer Holmes Bobst Library, New York University.

101 Rebecca Hill, "'Dry Your Tears and Speak Your Mind': Black Feminism as Anti-Fascism," in Nikhil Pal Singh et al, eds., *Rethinking Black Marxism* (Durham, N.C.: Duke University Press, forthcoming); Horne, *Black Liberation/Red Scare*, 48.

102 ILD National Bureau meeting, January 16, 1930, RGASPI, fond 515, delo 2190.

103 William Patterson, June 6, 1934, RGASPI, fond 515, delo 3692; see also June 7–8, 1934.

104 "Patronati," February 8, 1930, RGASPI, fond 515, delo 2194.

105 On the interrogation of Marinus van der Lubbe during the Reichstag Fire trial, see Georgi Dimitrov, *Selected Works*, vols, 1, 9 (Sofia:Foreign Language Press, 1960), 313–99; available online at http://www.marxists.org/reference/archive/dimitrov/works/1933/reich/index.htm (accessed May 12, 2006).

106 Ibid.

107 Maurer, "Five ILD Years," 120.

108 Young Communist League, *Clarity*, 1940, 54; Penny von Eschen, *Race against Empire: Black Americans and Anti-Colonialism, 1937–1957* (Ithaca: Cornell University Press, 2001).

109 Louis Engdahl, speech to the New York District of the ILD, December 15, 1929, RGASP, fond 515, delo 1835.

110 Herndon, *Let Me Live*, 261, 287–96.

111 Kevin McDermott and Jeremy Agnew, Dimitrov diary, Nov. 1937, *The Comintern: A History of the International from Lenin to Stalin* (New York: St Martin's Press, 1997), 35.

112 Maurer, "Five ILD Years," 121.

113 Edward Hallett Carr, *The Bolshevik Revolution, 1917–1923* (1951; New York: Norton, 1985), 1:142.

114 Robert Bussel, *From Harvard to the Ranks of Labor: Powers Hapgood and the American Working Class* (Pittsburgh: Pennsylvania State University Press, 1999).

115 Alan Wald, *The New York Intellectuals: The Rise and Decline of the Anti-Stalinist Left from the 1930s–1980s* (Chapel Hill: University of North Carolina Press, 1987), 128–29.

116 Chafee, *Freedom of Speech in the United States*.

117 Max Shachtman, *Behind the Moscow Trial* (New York: Pioneer Press, 1936).

118 Earl Browder, as quoted in Joseph Clark, "Fifth Column of 1776," review of Carl Van Doren's *Secret History*, *Clarity*, Summer 1942, 84.

119 D. Zaslawasky, "A Trial in a Soviet Prison," *Labor Defender*, November 1929, 234.

120 Stephen M. Kohn, *American Political Prisoners: Prosecutions under the Espionage and Sedition Acts* (New York: Praeger, 1994).

121 Henry Hall, "The Trial of the Plotters against the USSR," *Labor Defender*, January 1931, 6.

122 Johanningsmeier, *Forging American Communism*, 285.

123 James Barrett, *Steve Nelson: American Radical* (Pittsburgh: University of Pittsburgh Press, 1992), 132.

124 Ibid., 242, 248.

125 Rebecca Hill, "Fosterites and Feminists," *New Left Review*, March–April 1998.

126 Oakley Johnson, "New Women Fight for a Better World," *Sunday Worker*, July 6, 1941, 6.

127 Women's page, *Sunday Worker*, January 21, 1945, 4.

128 *Sunday Worker*, November 9, 1941, 6.

129 See, e.g., Elizabeth Gurley Flynn, 'Doris Nelson, Canadian MP, Writes on New World for Women," *Daily Worker*, January 13, 1945, 11.

130 Sheila Fitzpatrick, *Everyday Stalinism Ordinary Life in Extraordinary Times: Soviet Russia in the 1930s* (New York: Oxford University Press, 1999), 73.

131 *Daily Worker*, November 12, 1937.

132 Allan Knight Chalmers, "Haymarket 1887–1937," *New Masses*, May 1937.

133 Howard Fast, *The American: A Middle Western Legend* (New York: Duell, Sloan and Pearce, 1946), 74–75.

134 Morris Hillquit, *Loose Leaves from a Busy Life* (New York: Rand School Press, 1934), 4–5; idem, *A History of Socialism in the United States* (New York: Funk and Wagnalls, 1910), 174.

135 Eugene Gordon, "The Great Tradition of John Brown," *Daily Worker*, October 16, 1942, 8.

136 Minutes of the ILD National Executive Board, February 23, 1940, October 21, 1941, at the New York Public Library, Science Industry and Business Library.

137 Minutes of the ILD National Committee, January 30, 1942, February 13, 1942, March 4, 1942, in the Science, Industry, and Business Library at the New York Public Library.

138 Ann Fagan Ginger and Eugene Tobin, *The National Lawyers Guild from Roosevelt to Reagan* (Philadelphia: Temple University Press, 1988), 52–53; see also Kenneth O'Reilly, "A New Deal for the FBI: The Roosevelt Administration, Crime Control and National Security," *Journal of American History* 69, no. 3 (1982): 638–58.

139 Dana Frank, *Buy American: The Untold Story of American Nationalism* (Boston: Beacon Press, 1999); Kim Moody, *An Injury to All: The Decline of American Unionism* (New York: Routledge, 1997); ILD, *Equal Justice and Democracy In the Service of Victory: Continuing the Work of Anna Damon* (New York: International Labor Defense, 1944).

140 Schrecker, *Many Are the Crimes*, 119–53.

141 William W. Keller, *The Liberals and J. Edgar Hoover: The Rise and Fall of a Domestic Intelligence State* (Princeton: Princeton University Press, 1989); see also Richard W. Steele, "Fear of the Mob and Faith in Government in Free Speech Discourse, 1919–1941," *American Journal of Legal History* 38, no. 1 (January 1994): 55–83.

142 Gardiner Jackson to Aldino Felicani, letter, March 17, 1942, AFC. On Morris Ernst's relationship with the FBI, see Schrecker, *Many Are the Crimes*, 82–85; Garey, *Defending Everybody*, 129–42; Keller, *The Liberals and J. Edgar Hoover*.

For an example of Ernst's anticommunist writing, see Morris L. Ernst and David Loth, *Report on the American Communist* (New York: Henry Holt, 1952).

143 Keller, *The Liberals and J. Edgar Hoover*, 28.

144 Leo Ribuffo, *The Old Christian Right* (Philadelphia: Temple University Press, 1988); Phillip Jenkins, *Hoods and Shirts: The Extreme Right in Pennsylvania, 1925–1950* (Chapel Hill: University of North Carolina Press, 1997).

145 For a discussion of this aspect of the 1930s left, the most comprehensive source is Denning, *The Cultural Front*.

146 Martin Dies, *The Trojan Horse in America* (New York: Dodd, Mead, 1940).

147 Ribuffo, *The Old Christian Right*, 57.

148 Cedric Belfrage, *The American Inquisition, 1945–1960: A Profile of the McCarthy Era* (New York: Thunder's Mouth Press, 1989).

149 For more on U.S. government and far-right collaboration, see David Schmitz, *Thank God They're on Our Side: The U.S. and Right-Wing Dictatorships, 1921–1965* (Chapel Hill: University of North Carolina Press, 1999); Albert Kahn, *High Treason: The Plot against the People* (New York: Lear Publishers, 1950).

150 Sasha Small, *You've Got a Right: Defending Democracy* (New York: International Labor Defense, 1938).

151 Hill, "Fosterites and Feminists."

152 William Patterson, report of the National Executive Secretary of the CRC, July 7, 1952, 20, CRC vertical file, Tamiment Library / Robert F. Wagner Labor Archives, Elmer Holmes Bobst Library, New York University, 26.

153 Jessica Mitford, *It's a Fine Old Conflict* (New York: Alfred A. Knopf, 1977); Gerald Horne, *Communist Front? The Civil Rights Congress, 1946–1956* (Rutherford, N.J.: Fairleigh Dickinson University Press, 1988).

154 Angela Davis Defense Committee Papers, NAARPR Papers, Schomburg Library.

155 Patterson, report of the National Executive Secretary of the CRC.

156 Hill, "Dry Your Tears and Speak Your Mind"; Mary Louise Patterson, "Black and Red All Over," in Linn Shapiro, ed., *Red Diapers: Growing up in the Communist Left* (Urbana: University of Illinois Press, 1998), 110–15.

157 CRC, pamphlet, CRC vertical file, Tamiment Library / Robert F. Wagner Labor Archives, Elmer Holmes Bobst Library, New York University.

158 Elizabeth Gurley Flynn, "Sacco and Vanzetti," *Labor Defender*, August 1928, 163.

159 "Lawyers under Fire," May 1952, 4, CRC organization file, Tamiment Library / Robert F. Wagner Labor Archives, Elmer Holmes Bobst Library, New York University.

160 Elizabeth Gurley Flynn, "A Better World" column, *Daily Worker*, 23 August 1951, 5. The files of the ILD reveal that the Smith Act was not a target of any kind of civil-liberties campaign following the Soviet Union's entry into the Second World War in 1941, although the ILD was actively critical of repressive

legislation during the period of the Hitler–Stalin Pact: ILD, National Meeting minutes, 1938–1942, Science, Industry, and Business Library, New York Public Library.

161 Elizabeth Gurley Flynn, "A Fateful Day," *Daily Worker*, May 8, 1951.

162 "Aptheker Tells McCarran Board of Marxism's Stand against Conspiracy," *Daily Worker*, June 19, 1952, 5.

163 "Membership Clause Still a Threat," *Smith Act Bulletin*, 1958–1959, 10, Elizabeth Gurley Flynn Papers, microfilm edition, Tamiment Library / Robert F. Wagner Labor Archives, Elmer Holmes Bobst Library, New York University. The previous case in California had resulted in the release of several communists on the grounds that the CPUSA did not meet the definition of an "action inciting organization," because its arguments placed revolution in the far future rather than in the immediate present. For a discussion of the legal basis of this decision, see Chafee, *Free Speech in the United States*.

164 Barrett, *Steve Nelson*, 335–37.

165 Ibid., 368, 384.

166 Elizabeth Gurley Flynn, official stenographic report of remarks on August 6, 1948, Elizabeth Gurley Flynn Papers.

167 Ibid, 1.

168 For more thorough discussion of communist community organizing and its influence on women, see Rosalyn Fraad Baxandall, "The Question Seldom Asked: Women in the CPUSA," in *New Studies in the Politics and Culture of U.S. Communism*, ed. Michael Brown (New York: Monthly Review Press, 1993), 141–61. For a discussion of women in communist literature, see Paula Rabinowitz, *Labor and Desire: Women's Revolutionary Fiction in Depression America* (Chapel Hill: University of North Carolina Press, 1991).

169 Rebecca Hill, "Nothing Personal? The CPUSA's Answer to the Woman Question, 1929–1956," senior thesis, Wesleyan University, Middletown, Conn., 1991; Kate Weigand, *Red Feminism: American Communism and the Making of Women's Liberation* (Baltimore: Johns Hopkins University Press, 2001).

170 *Daily Worker*, November 8, 1953. On the Families Committee, see Peggy Dennis, *The Autobiography of an American Communist: A Personal View of a Political Life* (Westport, Conn.: Lawrence Hill, 1977).

171 Elizabeth Gurley Flynn, *The Twelve and You* (New York: International Publishers, 1948), 14.

172 Defense committee pamphlet for Peggy Wellman, exhibit 288c, in U.S. Congress. House Committee on Un-American Activities (HUAC). Communist Political Subversion, Part 2; Appendix to Hearings. Eighty-fourth Congress, Second Session (Washington: U.S. Government Printing Office, 1957), 7598.

173 Kahn, *High Treason*, 167.

174 "Some Remarks on the Role of Review Commissions," CRC Papers, Schomburg Center for Research in Black Culture, New York Public Library.

175 Nikita Khrushchev, "Secret Report to the Twentieth Party Congress of the CPSU," in Ali, *The Stalinist Legacy*, 236.

176 Ibid, 27.

177 Walter and Miriam Schneir, "Cryptic Answers," *Nation*, August 14, 1995. The furor over the CIA's decoded transcripts of Soviet intelligence reports, the Venona cables, is surprising given the fact that the cables reveal that the defense committee for the Rosenbergs was largely correct. The cables prove that Ethel Rosenberg was not involved in espionage and that her husband had engaged in non-atomic espionage while the United States and Soviet Union were allies. Neither of these was a capital offense. Similarly, the cables reveal that the evidence used in the trial was not the major evidence used to convict them; the Rosenberg trial itself was a show trial. This, however, did not stop Ronald Radosh and Joyce Milton from blaming Ethel Rosenberg for her execution and the orphaning of her children: Radosh and Milton, *The Rosenberg File: Second Edition* (New Haven: Yale University Press, 1997).

178 William Z. Foster, "The Communist Fighting Spirit," *Daily Worker*, August 11, 1950.

179 Some of Bloch's detractors argue that he was incompetent and that the CPUSA assigned him to the case for that reason.

180 A transcript of the Rosenberg trial is available online at http://www.law.umkc.edu/faculty/projects/FTrials/Rosenberg/RosenbergTrial.pdf (accessed February 28, 2008).

181 *Daily Worker*, April 2, 1951.

182 Ibid., April 9, 1951.

183 William A. Reuben, *The Atom Spy Hoax* (New York: Action Books, 1955).

184 Advertisements for meetings and rallies in the *Daily Worker*, 1951–52.

185 Carl Bernstein, *Loyalties: A Son's Memoir* (New York: Simon and Schuster, 1989).

186 Jack Aronson and Cedric Belfrage, *Something to Guard: The Stormy Life of the National Guardian, 1948–1967* (New York: Columbia University Press, 1978), 166, 170–71, 175.

187 John Wexley, *The Judgment of Julius and Ethel Rosenberg* (New York: Ballantine Books, 1977), 9.

188 NCSJR, editorial, *Daily Worker*, October 13, 1952, 5.

189 "They Wouldn't Let Mrs. Rosenberg Have Flowers," *Daily Worker*, May 12, 1952, 3.

190 Julius Rosenberg quoted in "Father in Death Cell Heartened by His Child's Letter," *Daily Worker*, January 13, 1953, 2.

191 *Daily Worker*, January 12, 1953, 1.

192 Ibid., April 1951–June 19, 1953.

193 Harap exhibit 1, in HUAC Investigation into Communist Activities (Committee to Secure Justice in the Rosenberg Case), *Jewish Daily Forward*,

April 6, 1951; "A Fact Sheet on Anti-Semitism in the Case: Newspaper Comment," in HUAC, *Trial by Treason: National Committee to Secure Justice for the Rosenbergs* (Washington: Government Printing Office, 1956), 2251.

194 Aronson and Belfrage, *Something to Guard,* 94; George Hodos, *Show Trials: Stalinist Purges in Eastern Europe, 1948–1954* (New York: Praeger, 1987); Isaac Deutscher, *Stalin: A Political Biography* (New York: Oxford University Press, 1966), 618–19.

195 Julius Rosenberg to Michael Rosenberg, August 15, 1950, in Robbie Meeropol and Michael Meeropol, *We Are Your Sons: The Legacy of Julius and Ethel Rosenberg Written by Their Children* (Boston: Houghton Mifflin, 1975), 17–18.

196 All the accounts of the Rosenberg case, right and left, agree on this point.

197 Speech by Robbie Meeropol at Sabathani Community Center, Minneapolis, May 1995, author's personal notes; Meeropol and Meeropol, *We Are Your Sons*; Robert Meeropol, *An Execution in the Family: One Son's Journey* (New York: St. Martin's Press, 2003).

198 On the family connections in the Rosenberg case, see Meeropol and Meeropol, *We Are Your Sons*; Eileen Phillipson, *Ethel Rosenberg beyond the Myths* (New York: F. Watts, 1988); Ivy Meeropol, dir., *Heir to an Execution* (HBO Films, 2004); Walter Schneir and Miriam Schneir, *Invitation to an Inquest: Reopening the Rosenberg Case* (New York: Viking, 1973); Sam Roberts, *The Brother: The Untold Story of Atomic Spy David Greenglass and How He Sent His Sister, Ethel Rosenberg, to the Electric Chair* (New York: Random House, 2001).

199 Virginia Gardner, *The Rosenberg Story* (New York: Masses and Mainstream, 1954, 42).

200 This letter by Julius to "My Fair Flower of Ossining Manor," August 30, 1951, which appears in the Schneirs' *Invitation to an Inquest* (New York: Pantheon, 1983), 221, was not published in the 1950s.

201 *Daily Worker,* December 15, 1952, 7.

202 National Committee to Re-Open the Rosenberg Case (NCRRC) report, 1975, NCRRC Papers, Tamiment Library / Robert F. Wagner Labor Archives, Elmer Holmes Bobst Library, New York University.

203 HUAC, *Trial by Treason.*

204 David Alman, ibid., 3-B, 2221.

205 Edith Segal, "Give Us Your Hand," *Daily Worker,* December 12, 1952, 4.

206 Ann Rivington, "A Woman Walks: For Ethel and Julius Rosenberg," *Daily Worker,* January 1952.

207 Matthew Hall, "Personal (for the Rosenbergs)," *Daily Worker,* December 2, 1952, 7.

208 Paul Carter, "Don't Let the Stars Get in Your Eyes," *Daily Worker,* January 29, 1953, 7.

209 Ibid, 8.

210 James Glatis, friendly witness, HUAC, *Trial by Treason,* 2054.

211 Rothenberg, ibid, 2073, 2076.

212 Testimony of Phil Koritz, ibid, 2067–69.

213 Gilman, ibid, 2092.

214 Ibid, 2197, 2180.

215 Julius and Ethel Rosenberg, plea for executive clemency, in Ethel Rosenberg, *Death House Letters of Ethel and Julius Rosenberg* (New York: Jero, 1953), 155.

216 On the multiethnic ideals of the Communist Party during the Popular-Front era, see Denning, *The Cultural Front*; Naison, *Communists in Harlem during the Great Depression*; Brown, *New Studies in the Politics and Culture of U.S. Communism*.

217 Fernando Claudin, "Stalin and the Second World War," in Ali, *The Stalinist Legacy*, 210; and, generally, Claudin, *The Communist Movement: From Comintern to Cominform*, vol. 2 (New York: Monthly Review Press, 1975), 307–437.

218 Andrew Ross, "Reading the Rosenberg Letters," in Ross, ed., *No Respect: Intellectuals and Popular Culture* (New York: Routledge, 1989).

219 *New Republic*, January 19, 1953.

220 *Nation*, April 7, 1953.

221 George Morris, "What the Rosenberg Case Means to Labor," *Daily Worker*, January 16, 1953.

222 Morris, "Some Frank Thoughts on the Rosenberg Fight," *Daily Worker*, June 22, 1953.

223 Meeropol and Meeropol, *We Are Your Sons*, 233–34.

224 W. E. B. Du Bois, "To the Rosenbergs: Ethel and Michael, Robert and Julius," *Masses and Mainstream*, June 1953.

6 Born Guilty

1 James Baldwin in *Black Panther*, September 4, 1971.

2 Malcolm X, *Malcolm X Speaks* (London: Sacker and Warburg, 1966), 222.

3 Harold Jacobs, *Weatherman* (Berkeley: Ramparts Press, 1971), 44, 189, 450.

4 Noel Ignatiev, "Learn the Lessons of U.S. History," *New Left Notes*, March 25, 1968.

5 "The Fire Next Time," *New Left Notes*, September 20, 1969.

6 The faction of Ann Arbor's sds that would become the Weather Underground referred to itself as the "Jesse James Gang" and signed some early "weather" statements that way in *New Left Notes*. See also David Herreshoff, "Teaching Mark Twain in the 1960s, 1970s, and 1980s," *Monthly Review* 107, no. 6 (June 1984): 38–45.

7 "Declaration of War," in Dan Berger, *Outlaws of America: The Weather Underground and the Politics of Solidarity* (Oakland, Calif.: AK Press, 2006), 108; Green, *Death in the Haymarket*, 314–16; Bill Ayers, *Fugitive Days* (New York: Penguin,

2003), 164; William J. Adelman, "The True Story behind the Haymarket Police Statue," in Roediger and Rosemont, *The Haymarket Scrapbook*, 167–68.

8   Brown, *Stagolee Shot Billy*, 178, 185.

9   On views of police see John Houston, "What Did You Do in the Riots, Daddy?" *National Lawyers Guild Practitioner* 26, no. 4 (Fall 1967):119–23; Kerner Commission, *Report of the National Advisory Commission on Civil Disorders* (New York: Dutton, 1968); Claude Brown, *Manchild in the Promised Land* (New York: Signet, 1965); Gerald Horne, *The Fire This Time: Watts and the Uprising of the 1960s* (Charlottesville: University of Virginia Press, 1995), 54.

10   Min. S. Yee, *The Melancholy History of Soledad Prison, in which a Utopian Scheme Turns Bedlam* (New York: Harper's Magazine Press, 1973), 6; Mike Davis, *City of Quartz: Excavating the Future in Los Angeles* (New York: Vintage, 1992); Robin D. G. Kelley, "Kickin' Reality, Kickin' Ballistics: Gangsta Rap and Postindustrial Los Angeles," in Kelley, *Race Rebels*, 183–227; Ruth Wilson Gilmore, "Globalisation and U.S. Prison Growth: From Military Keynesianism to Post-Keynesian Militarism," *Race and Class* 401, nos. 2–3 (October 1998): 171–88; Horne, *The Fire This Time*.

11   *California Youth Authority Quarterly*, Spring 1962.

12   Karl Marx, *The German Ideology* (Moscow: Progress Publishers, 1976), 216–18.

13   Karl Marx, *Class Struggles in France, 1848–1850* (1850; New York: International Publishers, 1934), 142; see also Marx, *The Eighteenth Brumaire of Louis Bonaparte* (1869; New York: International Publishers, 1981), 74–75.

14   Edna Bonacich, "A Theory of Ethnic Antagonism: The Split Labor Market," *American Sociological Review* 37, no. 5 (October 1972): 547–59.

15   Vladimir Lenin, "Imperialism, the Highest Stage of Capitalism" (1917), in *The Lenin Anthology*, ed. Robert C. Tucker (New York: W. W. Norton, 1975), 257.

16   Fanon, *The Wretched of the Earth*, 122–23, 130; Catherine Coquery-Vidrovitch, *Africa: Endurance and Change South of the Sahara* (Berkeley; University of California Press, 1988). The British Communist Party leader Jack Woddis critiques Fanon's writing as celebrating the petit bourgeoisie and as characterized by "over grand exaggeration": Jack Woddis, *New Theories of Revolution: A Commentary on the Views of Frantz Fanon, Regis Debray, and Herbert Marcuse* (London: Lawrence and Wishart, 1972), 25–26, 40–41.

17   For this reason, most orthodox Marxists have dismissed the Black Panther Party's analysis of the lumpen proletariat as the product of popular culture stereotypes of African Americans as criminal or as the flawed thinking of Bakunin. For a primary example of this analysis, see Gil Green, *The New Radicalism: Anarchist or Marxist* (New York: International Publishers, 1971), 11, 18–19, 37, 114–19, who dismissively writes that the alliance between students and the lumpen proletariat was the fantasy of a group of kids whose lives could be summed up as "sponging off the old man." As Green's book

(and a number of other critiques) demonstrates, in the 1970s, the CPUSA was both hostile to the New Left, referring to its cultural politics as individualistic and bourgeois, and excited about the resurgence of activism following the 1950s. For their part, New Left activists, including the Black Panther Party's members, ridiculed the Old Left of the late Stalinist era for its rejection of revolution and its embrace of collaboration with capitalist democracies and the Democratic Party. I will discuss this issue further, as it became important to George Jackson's defense campaign.

18   Black Panther Party, Ten Point Program, point no. 8, in *The Black Panthers Speak*, ed. Philip S. Foner (1970; New York: Da Capo, 1995), 3.

19   Fanon, *The Wretched of the Earth*, 53.

20   Lance Hill, *Deacons of Defense: Armed Resistance and the Civil Rights Movement* (Chapel Hill: University of North Carolina Press, 2006); Jack Olsen, *Last Man Standing: The Tragedy and Triumph of Geronimo Pratt* (New York: Anchor Books, 2000); Timothy B. Tyson, *Radio Free Dixie: Robert F. Williams and the Roots of Black Power* (Chapel Hill: University of North Carolina Press, 1999); Akinyele Omowale Umoja, "Repression Breeds Resistance: The Black Liberation Army and the Radical Legacy of the Black Panther Party," in *Liberation, Imagination, and the Black Panther Party*, ed. Kathleen Cleaver and George Katsiaficas (New York: Routledge, 2001), 3–6.

21   According to the U.S. House of Representatives, the Black Panthers were a "subversive criminal group using a facade of Marxism Leninism": *New York Times*, August 24, 1971. Other contemporary accounts that described the Black Panthers as criminals who had "conned" the New Left were Sheehy, *Panthermania*, and Tom Wolfe, *Radical Chic and Mau-Mauing the Flak Catchers* (New York: Bantam Books, 1983). Two more recent works that make this argument are Hugh Pearson, *Shadow of the Panther: Huey Newton and the Price of Black Power in America* (Reading, Mass.: Addison-Wesley, 1994), and Peter Collier and David Horowitz, *Destructive Generation: Second Thoughts about the Sixties* (New York: Summit Books, 1989).

22   Angela Davis, *An Autobiography* (1974; New York: International Publishers, 1988), 317.

23   I could, of course, have chosen to focus on any number of Black Panther martyrs. Fred Hampton's and Bobby Hutton's tragic deaths were both legally and historically important events. However, Jackson's case was the most controversial and the longest lasting. It also included a legal-defense strategy that was not available to Hampton or Hutton.

24   Yee, *The Melancholy History of Soledad Prison*, 24, 26.

25   Ronald Berkman, *Opening the Gates: The Rise of the Prisoners' Movement* (Lexington, Mass.: Lexington Books, 1979), 48–53; Geoffrey O. G. Ogbar, *Black Power: Radical Politics and African American Identity* (Baltimore: Johns Hopkins University Press, 2004).

26   Malcolm X, *Malcolm X Speaks*, 66.

27 On Communist Party campaigns against police brutality and defense campaigns for Black men such as the Martinsville Seven and Willie McGee, see Jessica Mitford, *It's a Fine Old Conflict*; Eric Rise, "Race, Rape and Radicalism: The Case of the Martinsville Seven, 1949–1951," *Journal of Southern History* 58, no. 3 (August 1992): 461–90; Horne, *Communist Front?*; Haywood Patterson and Earl Conrad, *Scottsboro Boy* (1950; New York: Collier, 1969).

28 Ginger and Tobin, *The National Lawyers Guild from Roosevelt to Reagan*; Houston, "What Did You Do in the Riots, Daddy?"; Mitford, *It's a Fine Old Confllict*; Len Holt, *The Summer That Didn't End: The Story of the Mississippi Civil Rights Project of 1964* (New York: Da Capo Press, 1992).

29 Truman Nelson, *Torture of the Mothers* (Boston: Beacon Press, 1968).

30 Ron Rosenbaum, "Angela and George: Origins of a Myth," *Esquire* July 1972; Wiiliam L. Patterson, National Board Meeting, Civil Rights Congress, June 10–12, 1950, 9, CRC organization file, Tamiment Library / Robert F. Wagner Labor Archives, Elmer Holmes Bobst Library, New York University.

31 I use the word "racial" for the Nation of Islam's theories of the origins of social conflict in the evil of white people as a biologically defined racial group created by the demon Yakub: see C. Eric Lincoln, *Black Muslims in America* (Grand Rapids, Mich.: W. B. Eerdmans, 1994; Malcolm X with Alex Haley, *Autobiography of Malcolm X* (New York: Grove, 1965); Mattias Gardell, *In the Name of Elijah Muhammad: Louis Farrakhan and the Nation of Islam* (Durham: Duke University Press, 1996); Ogbar, *Black Power*.

32 Judson L. Jeffries, *Huey Newton, the Radical Theorist* (Jackson: University Press of Mississippi, 2002), 15.

33 Bobby Seale, *Seize the Time: The Story of the Black Panther Party and Huey Newton* (Baltimore: Black Classic Press, 1991), 132, 269.

34 Foner, *The Black Panthers Speak*, 28.

35 Huey Newton, ibid., 41–42.

36 All the quotations are from Eldridge Cleaver, "The Ideology of the Black Panther Party," *Black Panther*, June 6, 1970.

37 Nikhil Pal Singh, *Black Is a Country: Race and the Unfinished Struggle for Democracy* (Cambridge, Mass.: Harvard University Press, 2004), 203–5.

38 Brown, *Manchild in the Promised Land*, 8, 293. See also Jay MacLeod, *Ain't No Makin' It: Aspirations and Attainment in a Low Income Neighborhood* (Boulder: Westview Press, 1995).

39 Huey Newton, *Revolutionary Suicide* (New York: Harcourt Brace Jovanovich, 1973), 39–40.

40 MacLeod, *Ain't No Making It*, 227; Philippe Bourgois, *In Search of Respect: Selling Crack in El Barrio* (Cambridge: Cambridge University Press, 1995), 114–73.

41 Marvin Surkin and Dan Georgakis, *Detroit: I Do Mind Dying: A Study in Urban Revolution* (Boston: South End Press, 1998); Bruce Nelson, *Divided*

We Stand: American Workers and the Struggle for Black Equality (Princeton: Princeton University Press, 2001), esp. 103–35.

42 Seale, *Seize the Time,* 4.

43 Ibid., 248–49.

44 Robin D. G. Kelley, "The Riddle of the Zoot," in *Malcolm X: In Our Own Image,* ed. Joe Wood (New York: St. Martin's Press, 1992).

45 Brother Jimmy, East Oakland Community Center, in *Black Panther,* January 9, 1971.

46 Arna Bontemps, "Why I Returned," *Harper's,* April 1965, reprinted in *Black Literature Criticism: Excerpts of Criticism of the Most Significant Works of Black Authors over the Past 200 Years,* vol. 1, ed. James J. Draper (Detroit: Thomas Gale, 1992).

47 *Black Panther,* June 20, 1970.

48 Ibid., April 11, 1970.

49 "Message from the L.A. 18" and "L.A. Pigs Brutalize Unarmed Students," *Black Panther,* February 7, 1970, 2.

50 On Edwards, see Yohuru Williams, *Black Politics/White Power: Civil Rights, Black Power and the Black Panthers in New Haven* (St. James, N.Y.: Brandywine Press, 2000); Alan Bisbove, "The Night of the Panthers: The Murder of Alex Rackley and the Arrest of the New Haven Panthers," *Hartford Advocate,* November 20, 2003.

51 George Edwards, "State Pig Sty Runs Amuck," *Black Panther,* April 11, 1970.

52 Eldridge Cleaver, "On the Ideology of the Black Panther Party," *Black Panther,* June 6, 1970, 13–15.

53 Ward Churchill and Jim Vanderwall, *The Cointelpro Papers: Documents from the FBI's Secret Wars against Domestic Dissent* (Boston: South End Press, 1990), 126; David Cunningham, *There's Something Happening Here: The New Left, the Klan, and FBI Counterintelligence* (Berkeley: University of California Press, 2005).

54 FBI memos from J. Edgar Hoover dated October 12, 1961, September 2, 1964, August 25, 1967, Law Library, University of Minnesota, Minneapolis. For more on COINTELPRO, see Ward Churchill and Jim Vanderwall, *Agents of Repression: The FBI's Secret War against the Black Panther Party and the American Indian Movement* (Boston: South End Press, 1988); Churchill and Vanderwall, *The COINTELPRO Papers*; Kenneth O'Reilly, *Racial Matters: The FBI and Black Americans* (New York: Free Press, 1991); Richard Gid Powers, *Secrecy and Power: The Private Life of J. Edgar Hoover* (New York: Free Press, 1987); Clayborne Carson, *Malcolm X: The FBI File* (New York: Carroll and Graff, 1992); David Garrow, *The FBI and Martin Luther King: From Solo to Memphis* (New York: W. W. Norton, 1981).

55 Huey Newton at Bobby Hutton memorial and at a fund raiser for Bobby Seale, Angela Davis, and Ericka Huggins: *Black Panther,* February 13, 1971; Sonia Sanchez, "Death Poem," *Black Panther,* September 14, 1968.

56 Churchill and Vanderwall, *The COINTELPRO Papers*, 130–31.

57 Paul Bass and Douglas Rae, *Murder in the Model City: The Black Panthers, Yale, and the Redemption of a Killer* (New York: Perseus, 2006), makes sensational claims about Rackley's murder and argues that George Sams has been wrongly accused of being a police agent. The evidence presented for this claim is based on police interviews and the testimony of Warren Kimbro, the Black Panther who shot Rackley and who turned state's evidence during the original trial. The account of the New Haven party by Yohuru Williams (*Black Politics / White Power*) is more balanced in approaching the available evidence. It concludes that Sams was likely an informant.

58 Jeffries, *Huey Newton*, 68–69.

59 Jennifer Smith, *An International History of the Black Panther Party* (New York: Garland, 1999), 41.

60 Leigh Raiford, "Restaging Revolution: Black Power, *Vibe* Magazine, and Photographic Memory," in *The Civil Rights Movement in American Memory*, ed. Renee C. Romano and Leigh Raiford (Athens: University of Georgia Press, 2006), 226–30; Stew Albert, "White Radicals, Black Panthers and a Sense of Fulfillment," in Cleaver and Katsiaficas, *Liberation, Imagination, and the Black Panther Party*, 188–94.

61 Huey Newton, "Message to the Free Huey Rally," Oakland Auditorium, February 17, 1968, in Foner, *The Black Panthers Speak*, 47–48.

62 For a discussion of how George Jackson understood this phenomenon see George Jackson, *Blood in My Eye* (Baltimore: Black Classic Press, 1990), esp. 63–64. Communist Party members scoffed at this alliance; they referred to white student radicals who "didn't need to work" and defined the students' alliance with Black radicals of the era as "slumming": see Green, *The New Radicalism*, 11, 18–19, 37, 114–19. In contrast, the sociologist Elijah Anderson's empirical study of Philadelphia suggests that the presence of the counter-culture in low-income African American neighborhoods in the 1970s contributed to the building of interracial community projects and that former counter-culturalists, despite middle-class mobility and professionalization, played a role in community resistance to gentrifying "Yuppies": Elijah Anderson, *Streetwise: Race, Class and Change in an Urban Community* (Chicago: University of Chicago Press, 1990), 7–55.

63 Herbert Marcuse, *One Dimensional Man* (Boston: Beacon Press, 1964), xii, 24–36; Jeremy Varon, *Bringing the War Home: The Weather Underground, the Red Army Faction, and Revolutionary Violence in the 1960s and 1970s* (Berkeley: University of California Press, 2004), 45; Students for a Democratic Society, Port Huron Statement, 1962, available online at http://lists.village.virginia.edu/sixties/HTML_docs/Resources/Primary/Manifestos/SDS_Port_Huron.html (accessed February 23, 2008). See also Kirkpatrick Sale, *SDS* (New York: Vintage Books, 1974); James Miller, *Democracy Is in the Streets: From Port Huron to the Siege of Chicago* (Cambridge, Mass.: Harvard University Press, 1994).

64 *Black Panther*, May 9, 1970.

65 Although William Patterson and Ben Davis played very significant roles in leading Communist Party defense campaigns, it does not make sense to refer to the CPUSA as a "Black-led" organization. On Jean Seaberg, see Ward Churchill, "To Disrupt, Discredit and Destroy": The FBI's Secret War against the Black Panther Party," in Cleaver and Katsiaficas, *Liberation, Imagination, and the Black Panther Party*, 78–117, esp. 92.

66 Bass and Rae, *Murder in the Model City*, 130. The same argument can be found in the context of the "Free Huey" campaign in Cummins, *The Rise and Fall of the California's Radical Prison Movement*.

67 Jeffries, *Huey Newton*, 124. Ironically, while Jeffries faults Newton for underestimating Pan-Africanism, he does not address the East Coast Black Panthers, who were closer to Eldridge Cleaver and who were sympathetic to Pan-Africanism and Black cultural nationalism: Williams, *Black Politics/White Power*, 153.

68 Lott, *Love and Theft*.

69 George Lipsitz, "Against the Wind: Dialogic Aspects of Rock and Roll," in Lipsitz, *Time Passages: Collective Memory and American Popular* Culture (Minneapolis: University of Minnesota Press, 1990), 99–132; Brian C. Ward, *Just My Soul Responding: Rhythm and Blues, Black Consciousness and Race Relations* (London: UCL Press, 1998), 37–39, 128–30; Alice Echols, *Scars of Sweet Paradise: The Life and Times of Janis Joplin* (New York: Owl Books, 1999).

70 Jeffries, *Huey Newton*, 139; Kai Erickson quoted in Williams, *Black Politics / White Power*, 160. The original quotation is in Erickson, *In Search of Common Ground: Conversations with Erik H. Erickson and Huey P. Newton* (New York: Norton, 1973), 18.

71 Katsiaficas, "Organization and Movement: The Case of the Black Panther Party and the Revolutionary People's Constitutional Convention of 1970," in Cleaver and Katsiaficas, *Liberation, Imagination, and the Black Panther Party*, 147–48; David Hilliard, *This Side of Glory: The Autobiography of David Hilliard and the Story of the Black Panther Party* (Boston: Little, Brown, 1993), 319–21.

72 Don Cox, "The Split in the Party," in Cleaver and Katsiaficas, *Liberation, Imagination, and the Black Panther Party*, 119, 121.

73 Michelle Wallace, *Black Macho and the Myth of the Superwoman* (New York: Warner, 1980); Charles Jones, ed., *The Black Panther Party Reconsidered* (Baltimore: Black Classic Press, 1998).

74 Charles Garry Interview, *National Lawyers Guild Practioner*, 28, no. 2 (May 1969).

75 *Newsweek*, June 7, 1971, 27, 28.

76 Afeni Shakur, "To Our Black Brothers in Prison, Black Panther Party, USA," *Black Panther*, August 1, 1970.

77 Charles Bursey, "Jails Are the First Black Concentration Camps," *Black Panther*, May 18, 1968.

78 "Rory and Landon Shackled Like Slaves," *Black Panther*, January 3, 1970, 15.

79 Afeni Shakur, "The Prisons and Jails Are Filled with Political Prisoners," *Black Panther*, July 18, 1970.

80 Liberation News Service, September 26, 1970, October 2, 1970.

81 Sam Melville, *Letters from Attica* (New York: William Morrow, 1972).

82 *Berkeley Barb*, April 3, 1970.

83 "The Dope Bust," *Newsweek*, May 11, 1970, 95.

84 *Nation*, July 28, 1969.

85 James S. Kunen, quoted in Robert A. Jones, "Panthers Conference," *Nation*, August 11, 1969, 102. See also "Where It's at in the Streets," *Berkeley Barb*, July 5–11, 1968: "Now we whites know what it means to be Black. This is the lesson of Berkeley."

86 Cummins, *The Rise and Fall of California's Radical Prison Movement*, is the only full-length academic study of the white left's participation in the prisoner's movement. Cummins argues that the statement "We are all outlaws," which appeared immediately after the explosion of the Weather Underground town house in New York, was a shallow statement of the "outlaw" cult of the 1950s transmogrified into New Left politics.

87 John Irwin, *Prisons in Turmoil* (Boston: Little, Brown, 1980), 55–56.

88 Anonymous California State Corrections guard, as quoted in *Youth Authority Bulletin*, Spring 1957, 42–43; Donald Cressey, introduction, ibid., 40.

89 Irwin, *Prisons in Turmoil*. 50, 53, 70–72.

90 Brown, *Manchild in the Promised Land*, 249.

91 Ed Sanders, *The Family: The Manson Group and Its Aftermath* (New York: New American Library, 1990).

92 *Black Panther*, April 3, 1971, 6.

93 Horne, *The Fire This Time*, 90–91, 139.

94 On parole statistics, see *Summary Statistics of Felon Prisoners and Parolees* (Sacramento: California Department of Corrections Research Division, Administrative Statistics Section, 1960–63, 1967–73). Available online at http://www.cdcr.ca.gov/Reports_Research/Offender_Information_Services_Branch/Annual/CalPrisArchive.html (accessed February 23, 2008). On racial discrimination in the practice of discipline and job assignment, see Yee, *The Melancholy History of Soledad Prison*, 63; Berkman, *Opening the Gates*; Eve Pell, ed., *Maximum Security: Letters from California's Prisons* (New York: Dutton, 1972).

95 On the creation of riots caused by informal hierarchies of convicts and the corruption of guards, see Roger Morris, *The Devil's Butcher Shop: The New Mexico Prison Uprising* (Albuquerque: University of New Mexico Press, 1988); Thomas Murton and Joe Hyams, *Accomplices to the Crime* (New York: Grove, 1969).

96 See Berkman, *Opening the Gates*, 59–60.

97 George Jackson, "A Tribute to Three Slain Brothers," *Black Panther*, January 16, 1970.

98 Jackson, *Blood in My Eye*, 44–45.

99 Jackson, "A Tribute to Three Slain Brothers."

100 Johny Spain with Laurie Andrews, *Black Power, White Blood: The Life and Times of Johnny Spain* (New York: Pantheon, 1996), 95–97.

101 Yee, *The Melancholy History of Soledad Prison*, 81.

102 Ibid., 30, 32.

103 Ibid., 83.

104 Davis, *An Autobiography*, 252–57.

105 Faye Stender, "Introduction," in Pell, *Maximum Security*, 13.

106 For a representation of the English defense committee, see Jo Durden-Smith, *Who Killed George Jackson?* (New York: Alfred A. Knopf, 1976).

107 Yee, *The Melancholy History of Soledad Prison*, 81, 126, 256.

108 George Jackson to Fay Stender, letter, April 1970, in Jackson, *Soledad Brother: The Prison Letters of George Jackson* (Chicago: Lawrence Hill, 1994), 20–21.

109 For a more complete and thorough analysis of the role of contemporary prisons in the global economy and U.S. history, see Gilmore, "Globalisation and U.S. Prison Growth," 171–88.

110 George Jackson to "Mama," March 1967, in Jackson, *Soledad Brother*, 108–9.

111 Jackson and Foucault both discuss the role of confession as a tool for prisoners' submission in their analyses of the prison system.

112 Didier Eribon, *Michel Foucault* (Cambridge, Mass.: Harvard University Press, 1991), 77.

113 George Jackson to Greg Armstrong, June 1970, in Jackson, *Soledad Brother*, 3–16; Lester Jackson, "Dialogue with My Soledad Son," *Ebony*, November 1971, 72.

114 Endesha Ida Mae Holland, *From the Mississippi Delta* (New York: Simon and Schuster, 1997); Anne Moody, *Coming of Age if Mississippi* (New York: Laurel, 1968); Angela Davis to George Jackson, letters, Angela Davis Defense Committee Papers, Schomburg Center for Research in Black Culture, New York Public Library.

115 Jackson, *Soledad Brother*, 65.

116 Greg Armstrong, *The Dragon Has Come* (New York: Harper and Row, 1974), 167.

117 Georgia Jackson, as quoted in *New York Times*, August 30, 1971, 59.

118 Michael "Cetawayo" Tabor, Shakur, Ali Bey Hassan, all three in *Look for Me in the Whirlwind: The Collective Autobiography of the New York 21*, ed. Kuwasi Balagoon (New York: Random House, 1971), 69–84, 287–95, 67–79.

119 *Black Panther*, June 6, 1970. See also Wendell Wade, ibid., January 30, 1971; George Jackson, "PS. on Discipline," ibid., March 27, 1971.

120 Robert Williams in *Crusader*, February 1964; *Black Scholar*, November 1970. Williams went to Cuba in 1960 and to Beijing in 1965, saying that the Cuban revolution had "turned reactionary": Tyson, *Radio Free Dixie*, 294.

121 Robert Williams in *Crusader*, 1967, collection of Roger Peet, Minneapolis, for "Jericho '98" political activist committee.

122 Sam Greenlee, *The Spook Who Sat by the Door* (1969; Chicago: Lushina Books, 2002).

123 Tracye Matthews, "No One Ever Asks"; Regina Jennings, "Why I Joined the Party"; and Angela D. LeBlanc-Ernest, "The Most Qualified Person to Handle the Job, Black Panther Party Women 1966–1982," all in Jones, *The Black Panther Party Reconsidered*.

124 For examples of fights over centralized authority, see James Forman, *The Making of Black Revolutionaries* (New York: Macmillan, 1971); Cleveland Sellers, *The River of No Return: The Autobiography of a Black Militant* (Jackson: University Press of Mississippi, 1990); Jackson, "PS. on Discipline"; Mary King, *Freedom Song: A Personal History of the 1960s Civil Rights Movement* (New York: William Morrow, 1988).

125 On Kent State and Jackson State, see esp. Bill Whitaker, "The Big Chill: The Stifling Effect of the Official Response to the Kent State Killings," *Viet Nam Generation* 2, no. 2 (May 1990): 139–46.

126 Weather Underground, communiqué, Liberation News Service, May 27, 1970.

127 Based on a memo between Spiro Agnew and the CIA published in *Scanlan's Monthly*, July 1970, and quoted in Philip Foner, *U.S. Labor and the Vietnam War* (New York; International Publishers, 1989), 105–6.

128 Dan Baum, *Smoke and Mirrors: The War on Drugs and the Politics of Failure* (Boston: Little, Brown, 1996).

129 Erika Doss, "Revolutionary Art is a Tool for Liberation: Emory Douglas and Protest Aesthetics at the *Black Panther*," in Cleaver and Katsiaficas, *Liberation, Imagination, and the Black Panther Party*, 175–87.

130 *Ann Arbor Argus*, June 10–19, 1970.

131 Tackwood and Citizens Research and Investigating Committee, *The Glass House Tapes* (New York: Avon, 1973); Durden-Smith, *Who Killed George Jackson?*

132 San Quentin Black Panther Party, "Eulogy to Three Murdered Revolutionaries," *Black Panther*, August 29, 1970.

133 Tom Hayden, "We Are the Revolution," Liberation News Service, August 15, 1970.

134 Henry Winston, *The Meaning of San Rafael* (New York: New Outlook Publishers, 1971).

135 George Jackson, "From the Soledad Brothers," *Black Panther*, July 24, 1971.

136 Armstrong, *The Dragon Has Come*, 209.

137 Angela Davis, *If They Come in the Morning* (New York: Signet, 1972), 134.

138 Hilliard, *This Side of Glory*, 379–80.

139 Eldridge Cleaver, "Angela Davis" *Black Panther*, January 23, 1971, 5; George Jackson in *Black Panther*, March 13, 1971.

140 August 7 Movement to Eldridge Cleaver, *Black Panther*, March 13, 1971.

141 Jackson, *Blood in My Eye*, 3.

142 Tom Wicker, "The Death of a Brother," *New York Times*, August 24, 1971; Roger Wilkins, "My Brother George," *New York Times*, August 27, 1971, 33.

143 August 7th Movement, "Comrades, Brothers and Sisters," *Black Panther*, September 5, 1971, E.

144 Folsom Cadre, "Open Letter to Mr. and Mrs. Jackson," *Black Panther*, September 4, 1971.

145 Spain with Andrews, *Black Power, White Blood*; Tackwood, *The Glasshouse Tapes*; Safiya Bukhari, interview by the author, Minneapolis, 1998. Earlier, when I met her at Berkeley's Critical Resistance Conference in 1998, with tears in her eyes, Bukhari told me that "he was trying to draw the fire."

146 Folsom Cadre, "Open Letter to Mr. and Mrs. Jackson," *Black Panther*, September 4, 1971.

147 Bert Small, "Message to Mrs. Georgia Jackson, Read at Jackson's Memorial Service," supplement to *Black Panther*, September 4, 1971, A; Angela Davis, "Comrade George Jackson," *Black Panther*, August 28, 1971.

148 Frank "Big Black" Smith, interview by the author, Minneapolis, spring 1999.

149 Robert Minton, ed., *Inside Prison, American Style* (New York: Random House, 1971), 170, 206–8, 212, 227–28.

150 Joyce King, *Hate Crime: The Story of a Dragging in Jasper, Texas* (New York: Pantheon, 2002).

151 David Ward, *Confinement in Maximum Custody: The New Last Resort Prisons in the U.S. and Western Europe* (Lexington, Mass.: Lexington Books, 1981).

152 The most famous work to do this is Horowitz and Collier, *Destructive Generation: Second Thoughts about the Sixties* (New York: Summit Books, 1989). See also David Horowitz, ed., *Second Thoughts: Former Radicals Look back on the Sixties* (Lanham, Md.: Madison Books, 1989); Paul Liberatore, *The Road to Hell: The True Story of George Jackson, Stephen Bingham and the San Quentin Massacre* (New York: Atlantic Monthly Press, 1996); Cummins, *The Rise and Fall of California's Radical Prison Movement*.

153 Betsy Carr, "Afterword" to James Carr, *Bad: The Autobiography of James Carr* (New York: Carrol and Graf, 1994), 222. For a more general discussion of the use of dubious sources, see Reginald Major, "Stealth History: A Political

Process, a Review Essay of *The Shadow of the Panther* by Hugh Pearson and *The Rise and Fall of California's Radical Prison Movement* by Eric Cummins," *Black Scholar* 24 (Fall 1994): 39. For a new historiography of the Black Panthers, see Charles E. Jones and Judson L. Jeffries, "Don't Believe the Hype: Debunking the Panther Mythology," and Nikhil Pal Singh, "The Black Panthers and the Underdeveloped Country of the Left," both in Jones, *The Black Panther Party Reconsidered*, 25–56, 57–105; Cleaver and Katsiaficas, *Liberation, Imagination, and the Black Panther Party*; Ogbar, *Black Power*.

154 See esp. Cummins, *The Rise and Fall of California's Radical Prison Movement*. For an earlier version, see Durden-Smith, *Who Killed George Jackson?*

155 Frank "Big Black" Smith, telephone interview by the author, Minneapolis, February 1999.

156 See Singh, "The Black Panthers and the Undeveloped Country of the Left."

157 Of course, the argument that the Panthers did not sustain a single legal conviction is false in spirit and in fact. Huey Newton spent three years in prison on a manslaughter charge for shooting the police officer John Frey, despite a national campaign to defend him—an average prison term for a manslaughter conviction. Geronimo Pratt spent twenty-six years in prison for a crime he did not commit; Dhorbua Bin Wahad spent nineteen years in prison; Mumia Abu-Jamal remains in prison today, as do Black Panther Party members Herman Wallace, Albert Woodfox, Robert Wilkerson, Russell "Maroon" Shoats, Jalil Abdul Muntaqim (Anthony Bottom), and Albert Nuh Washington, to name just a few. It is more true to argue, as Ward Churchill does, that "not one cop or intelligence agent has spent a minute of time in prison" for the murders orchestrated by COINTELPRO: Churchill, "To Disrupt, Discredit and Destroy," 113.

158 David Horowitz, "Why I Am No Longer a Leftist," in Horowitz, ed., *Second Thoughts*, 6, 55.

159 "Free the Land" is the slogan of the Black Liberation Army.

160 Tupac Shakur, "White Man's World," on Shakur, *Makaveli: The Seven Day Theory* (CD, Death Row Records, 1996); Digable Planets, "Jettin,'" on *Blowout Comb* (CD, Pendulum Records/Columbia, 1994); Sanyika Shakur, "Flowing in File: The George Jackson Phenomenon," available online at http://www.anarchistblackcross.org/content/essays/shakur.html (accessed February 23, 2008). For a critique of Shakur, see Kali Tal, "From Panther to Monster: Black Popular Culture Representations of Resistance from the Black Power Movement of the 1960s to *Boyz in the Hood*," in Elaine Richardson and Ronald Jackson, eds., *Innovations in African-American Rhetoric* (Champaign: University of Illinois Press, 2003).

161 "Men against Sexism," an interview with Ed Mead by Daniel Burton-Rose, unpublished, loaned to me by Burton-Rose in the fall of 1999. See also, "The Anti-Exploits of Men against Sexism in which Mead is Horrified by Conditions in 'Concrete Mama' and Joins with New Companions to Improve Them,"

at the George Jackson Brigade Information Project, at http://www.gjbip.org (February 23, 2008). For "We Are Armed and Dangerous" quote, see George Jackson Brigade, Communiqué #6, "Celebrate International Women's Day, Celebrate the Role of Women in Struggle," at http://www.gjbip.org (accessed March 7, 2008).

162 Rita "Bo" Brown, interview by the author, Berkeley, Calif., September 1998.

Conclusion

1 Rachel Corrie, e-mail message, March 1, 2003, in *My Name Is Rachel Corrie*, ed. Alan Rickman and Katharine Viner (London: Nick Hern Books, 2005), 38.

2 Ibid., March 9, 2003, 49.

3 See the chapter on Chaney, Goodman, Schwerner, and SNCC in Rebecca Hill, "Men, Mobs, and Law," Ph.D. diss., University of Minnesota, Minneapolis, 2000.

4 Bernard Chazanow, interview by Jon Bloom, May 31, 1978, Oral History of the American Left, Tamiment Library / Robert F. Wagner Labor Archives, Elmer Holmes Bobst Library, New York University.

5 Rachel Corrie, journal entry, February 7, 2003, in Rickman and Viner, *My Name Is Rachel Corrie*, 31.

6 Dennis Prager, "Who Killed Rachel Corrie?" *WorldNetDaily*, March 25, 2003, available online at http://www.worldnetdaily.com/news/article .asp?ARTICLE_ID=31705 (August 2006).

7 Here I am referring to Ward Churchill, whose comment that the victims in the World Trade Center attack were "little Eichmanns" (Ward Churchill, "Some People Push Back: On the Justice of Roosting Chickens," *Pockets of Resistance*, September 2001) has led to his being fired from a tenured position at the University of Colorado, Boulder. Although I disagreed with Churchill's argument in discussions immediately following the attack, it is hard not to notice the widely different perceptions about which victims and martyrs are open to criticism and which victims are seen as sacrosanct. While the reason for his dismissal was plagiarism, not the essay, it was public reaction to the 9/11 essay that led to the investigation.

8 Joshua Hammer, "The Death of Rachel Corrie," *Mother Jones*, September–October 2003; Phan Nguyen, "Specious Journalism in Defense of Killers," *Counterpunch*, September 20, 2003.

9 Timothy Messer-Kruse, James O. Eckert Jr., Pannee Burckel, and Jeffrey Dunn, "The Haymarket Bomb: Reassessing the Evidence," *Labor: Studies in Working-Class History of the Americas* 2, no. 2 (Summer 2005): 39–51; Timothy Messer-Kruse, "Response to Bryan Palmer," *Labor: Studies in Working-Class History of the Americas* 3, no. 1 (Spring 2006): 37–40.

10 Nathan Schwerner, "Schwerner Letter," SNCC papers, 1959–72, UMI microfilm edition, reel 56, 149, series 1: Administrative Files; full-page ad and "mobe" speech, in SNCC papers, reel 47, n. 208, 111.

11 Arendt, *The Origins of Totalitarianism*, 451–52.

12 Herman Melville, "Billy Budd, an Inside Narrative," in Melville, *Billy Budd*, 359.

13 Franklin, *Prison Literature in America*, 67.

14 Melville, "Billy Budd, an Inside Narrative," 355.

15 Ibid., 382–83.

16 Ibid., 383.

17 Ibid, 384.

18 Ibid, 291–92.

19 David Feige, *Indefensible: One Lawyer's Journey into the Inferno of American Justice* (Boston: Little, Brown, 2006), 53.

Index

Abolitionists, 11, 60; comparison of, to Jacobins, 31, 33; defense of use of violence by, 27–29; fugitive slave defense by, 21, 43–46; Harper's Ferry raid described by, 50; idealization of slaves by, 294; mob violence and, 31–35; nonresistance and, 52; slave rebellions and, 37–42, 337n136. *See also under names of individual abolitionists*

Abromovich, Rafail, 217–18

Abu-Jamal, Mumia, 19, 111, 316

Adams, John Quincy, 41–42

African Blood Brotherhood (ABB): 153–54, 157, 160, 228

Agnew, Spiro, 301

Alcohol, representations of, 19, 66, 69, 76–77, 79–82, 92, 96, 147, 206, 277, 369n176

Allen, James, 209, 231–33

Alman, David, and Emily Alman, 259, 261

Altgeld, John Peter, 92, 109, 242

American Civil Liberties Union (ACLU), 2, 25, 348n132; Communist Party and, 213, 216–18; expulsion of Flynn and, 249; on FBI during New Deal, 245; IWW and, 115, 153, 160; Sacco-Vanzetti defense and, 164, 179, 188–89, 196

American exceptionalism, 6, 16, 108, 115

American Federation of Labor (AFL), 81, 87, 92, 101, 110, 179, 244; business unionism and, 116, 170; critiques of, by left, 139, 170, 230; Darrow's defense of Kidd for, 136–37; ILD defense of members of, 214; McNamara defense by, 138–39; in St. Louis Race Riot, 154

American Legion, 157, 237, 246, 301; killing of Everest and, 147; Sacco and Vanzetti vs., 192

American Negro Labor Congress (ANLC), 222, 225–28

American Revolution, 4–9; abolitionists and memory of, 27–29; anarchists' self-comparison to, 84, 87, 97–98; Communist Party's self-comparison to, 242; Darrow's defendants and, 135–36; Haywood and, 138; John Brown and, 48, 65; Parsons and, 90, 242

Amistad revolt, 41–42

Anarchism: anarcho-communism and, 115–16, 137–38, 159, 350n11; Communists' repudiation of, 205–7, 239, 242–43, 250; counterculture and, 148; definition of, by liberals, 193–95, 201, 208; gender and, 181, 201–2; in "Haymarket" group, 72, 79, 81, 83, 85, 101–2, 109–10; individualist, 81, 172; Italian, 149, 157, 208; lynching defined as, 112–14, 126–27, 131; media

Anarchism (*cont.*)
    representations of, 93–94, 112; in New Left, 301; in Reichstag Fire trial, 237; Sacco's and Vanzetti's beliefs in, 163–72; Sacco-Vanzetti defense strategy of, 174–78, 185–86, 193–95, 197, 201–2, 208
Anderson, Elijah, 387n62
Anderson, Osborne Perry, 49, 52, 64
Anderson, Maxwell, 200, 255
Anthony, Earl, 280
Anticommunism: in Cold War, 244–46; fascism and, 244; in Sacco-Vanzetti defense, 189, 197, 207–8
Anti-Fascist Alliance of North America (AFANA), 218–19; Greco-Carillo defense and, 215
Antinomianism: Edwards and, 46; John Brown and, 58–60
Anti-racism: in anti-lynching activism, 118, 121–22, 156; Communist Party and, 235, 237, 253; defense campaigns' advocacy of, 146–47, 157, 190–92, 200; of Italian anarchists, 169–70; John Brown and, 65; in labor movement, 222–24; in New Left, 283–84; prison organizing and, 292. *See also* Brown, John; National Association for the Advancement of Colored People; Wells, Ida B.
Antistatism, 25, 159; IWW and, 116
Antolini, Ella, 171, 202
Aptheker, Herbert, 250
Arendt, Hannah, 1, 7, 9–10, 22, 174, 319
Armed self-defense: defense campaigns' arguments for, 86, 133, 216, 223; against lynching, 109, 118, 125, 154–55; national arguments for, 5, 12; against prison rape, 314; repudiation of, 242; slaves' right to, 41, 65. *See also* Violence
Armstrong, Greg, 295, 298
Aronson, Jack, 253
Atlanta Six, defense of, 225–26

Attica rebellion, 287, 309
August 7th Movement, 306–8

Bailey, Forrest, 218
Bail skipping, 224
Baker, Ray Stannard, 126, 131, 190
Bakhtin, Mikail, 4, 19, 70
Bakunin, Mikhail, 72, 167, 169, 250, 274; Chicago anarchists and, 341n12
Baldwin, James, 266
Baldwin, Roger, 153, 166, 179, 186, 188, 197, 217
Beal, Fred, 221, 224
Bedacht, Max, 229–30
Beecher, Edward, 33
Beecher, Henry Ward, and "Beecher Bibles," 53, 337n136
Beffel, John, 180
Belfrage, Cedric, 253, 255, 264
Bellamy, Edward, *Looking Backward*, 92–93
Berkman, Alexander, 114–16, 165–66, 169, 172, 350n11
Bilbo, Senator Theodore, 234
Bill of Rights, 115, 216, 221, 247, 249; free-speech fights and, 141; right to bear arms and, 86
Bird, Joan, 286
"Bisbee Deportation," 146–47, 154
Black, Captain William, 91
Black Guerilla Family (BGF), 306, 310, 312
Black Liberation Army, (BLA), 299, 313
Black Panther Party (BPP): "Blackness" and, 283, 285; cartoons celebrating cop killing of, 302–3; as criminal conspiracy, 384n21, 311–12; defense campaigns for, 280–86, 294; definition of "political prisoner" and, 271; funeral for George Jackson and, 308–9; impact of repression on, 299, 304; on lumpen proletariat, 268, 273–77; merging of anti-lynching and labor defense

by, 33; ongoing incarceration of members of, 393n157; origins of, 272; Panther 21, 285; on police, 278; on prisons, 269, 286–87; Stagolee as model for, 267, 270; targeting of, by police and FBI, 279–80. *See also under names of individual members*

"Blackness," 10, 77, 265, 310; popular culture and, 283–85

Blackwell, Alice Stone, 189, 197, 201

"Bleeding Kansas," 11, 48–50, 53–55, 66, 71, 334n98

Bliven, Bruce, 193

Bloch, Emmanuel "Manny," 253, 264, 380n179. *See also* Rosenberg, Ethel, and Julius: defense of

Bloor, Ella Reeve "Mother," 144, 199

Blossom, Frederick A., 155

Bolsheviks, 165

Bombings: George Jackson Brigade and, 314; in Haymarket Square (1886), 69, 83–84, 86, 93, 242, 340n1; by Melville, 287; by Mooney, 143; of Palmer's House, 163, 171; Steunenberg assassination by, 135, 138, 355n100; of Wall Street (1921), 176; of World Trade Center, 23, 317, 325n33

Bondi, August, 48, 335n113

Bonfield, Captain John, 82

Bontemps, Arna, 277

Boston Massacre, 5, 8

Bourgeoise, Pierre, 276

Bowery B'hoy, 34

Bresci, Gaetano, 167–69, 176

Bridgeman, Michigan, trial, 213

Briggs, Cyril, 154, 160, 227–28, 243

Brinsmade, Chapin, 129

Brodsky, Joseph, 229

Brooks, Preston, 41

Browder, Earl, 217, 239; "Browderism" and, 247, 250

Brown, Annie, 62

Brown, Claude, 265, 289

Brown, Elaine, 284

Brown, H. Rap, 266

Brown, John, 3, 5, 75, 316, 341n10; on Black heroism, 49; Communist Party's representation of, 243; Cromwell and, 56–57, 62; economic views of, 46, 334n103; on French Revolution of 1848, 48; fugitive slaves and, 61; Harper's Ferry raid and, 47, 50–51, 54–55; Haymarket anarchists and, 85, 90, 97–98; heroic martyrdom and, 41; in Kansas, 49, 53–55; League of Gileadites and, 44–46; Malcolm X on, 266; McNamara brothers compared to, 139–40; religious views of, 48, 55, 58, 60, 335n105; remembrance of, by Black Americans, 64–65; Sacco and Vanzetti compared to, 199; slave rebellion and, 30, 43, 47, 50, 61; trial of, 62–63; Weather Underground compared to, 59, 266; as "white" hero, 49–52, 65–67

Brown, John, Jr., 47, 97–98

Brown, Rita "Bo," 314

Brown, William Wells, 44

Bukharin, Mikhail, 217

Burns, Anthony, 44

Bursey, Charles, 280

Byrd, James, lynching of, 310

Cacici, Tina, 173–74, 202

Cafiero, Carlo, 167, 169

Calley, Lieutenant William, 301

Calvinism, 55–58, 66–67, 189, 335n105

Cannon, James, 198, 214, 216, 219–20

Carlyle, Thomas, 5, 27, 55–57

Carillo, Donato, 215, 218–19

Carr, James, 289, 304–7, 311

Carter, Alprentice "Bunchy," 273, 280

Cellar, Emmanuel, 243

Centralia victims, 147; Wesley Everest, 147–48

Chalmers, Allan Knight, 234

Sacco-Vanzetti campaign and, 180, 188–90, 192–93, 205

Counter-culture: Black Panther Party and, 281–83; Goldman-Berkman anarchists and, 190; Haymarket anarchists, 97, 99, 102, 106, 110–11; IWW and, 148–49; race and, 283, 287

Counter-Intelligence Program (COINTELPRO), 278–80, 310; Tackwood and, 304, 307, 311

Courts martial: of African-American soldiers in Houston, 155; of Lieutenant Calley, 301; of Mother Jones, 135

Cowley, Malcolm, 239

Cox, Don, 285

Craft, William, and Ellen Craft, rescue of, 44

Crandall, Prudence, 41

Crime, crimes, 330; analysis of, by anti-lynching activists, 129–30; Black Panthers' view of, 276; as cause of lynching, 126, 131, 162; Chicago anarchists on causes of, 78–79; Communist Party and, 209, 215; criminology and, 76, 94; defense campaigns as parody of, 17, 82; definition of, as class warfare, 79, 171–72, 275, 277; against Jim Crow, 122; lynching as federal, 114; media representation of, 3–4, 11–14, 74–75, 120, 192; Nation of Islam against, 272; Sacco and Vanzetti and, 163, 191

Criminals: as class, 12, 76–77; Black Panthers as, 310–12, 384n21; Blacks as, 117–18, 121, 126–28, 269, 282; defense of, by anti-lynching activists, 129–30; as heroes, 34, 71–72, 133, 275–76, 285; immigrant workers as, 74–75; Italian anarchists as, 162, 190–92; moral codes of, 261, 289; political prisoners not, 88–89, 175,

183, 189; power of label of, 22, 76, 275–76. See also Lumpen-proletariat

Critical Resistance Organization, 313

Crockett, Davy, 34, 50, 66

Cromwell, Oliver, 55–57, 61–62, 67, 71

Croppers and Farm Workers Union (CFWU), 226

Czolgosz, Leon, 113–14, 135

Daily Worker, 197–98, 206, 241, 249, 251, 253–54, 257, 260

Damon, Anna: 244

Dana, Henry Ward, 201

D'Angelo, Aurora, 202

Darrow, Clarence, 113–14, 135–36, 138–39, 140, 189, 218

Davis, Angela, 271, 293, 298, 303, 305–8, 313, 322

Davis, Benjamin, 226, 247, 388n65

Deacons for Defense, 270

Death penalty: for lynchers, 227; movements against, 22–23, 127, 248

Death Wish, film, 312

Debray, Regis, 270

Debs, Eugene, 67, 98, 114, 135–37, 139, 148, 169

DeCaro, Louis, 60

Declaration of Independence, 4, 6, 28, 116, 141, 216

De Cleyre, Voltairine, 96–97, 103, 104, 137

Defense campaigns: definition of 1–3; as democratic, 20–21; as heroic, 21; as mothering, 20; as popular history, 21–22, 106. See also under names of specific defense campaigns

Derrida, Jacques, "Violence of the Letter," 348–49n139

Devi, Mahasweta, 18

Dewey, John, 199

Dickstein, Samuel, 243

Dies, Senator Martin, 234, 246

Dies committee, 246

Dillon, Jane, 229, 233

Dill Pickle Club, 148

French Revolution, 7–9; abolitionism compared to 31–32, 36, 66; Chicago anarchists and, 72–73; of 1848, 268
Freud, Sigmund, 94
Frey, John, 279
Frick, Henry Clay, 114
Friedel, Elsie, 100, 104
Fuchs, Klaus, 254
Fugitive Slave Act, rescues of victims of, 6, 21, 40–45, 71, 128
Fuller, Governor Alvin T., 194–95
Fuller, Margaret, 56, 57

Galleani, Luigi, 163, 169, 186; Italian anarchists and, 149, 157, 208
Gardner, Virginia, 256, 258
Garnet, Henry Highland, 27–28, 43
Garrison, William Lloyd, 29, 38, 41, 52, 60
Garry, Charles, 248, 280, 285, 293
Garvey, Marcus, 117, 153–54; trial of, 160
Gastonia defense, 208, 211, 215, 218, 223–25, 231
General Defense Committee. See Industrial Workers of the World
General strike: proposed as defense strategy, 115–16, 138–39, 145, 149, 165, 197, 205, 216; in St. Louis (1877), 76
Generational conflict, 298
Genet, Jean, 265, 281–82, 286, 314, 322
George Jackson Brigade, 314
Ghetto, 267–68; as internal colonies, 269, 285; as prison, 15, 286, 296
Giovannitti, Arturo, 171, 182, 185, 218; trial of, 149, 165
Gitlow, Benjamin, 212, 250
Gladstein, William, 244
Gloucester, James Newton, 51, 66
Gold, Mike, 200
Goldman, Emma, 102–3, 113–16, 134, 137, 165–66, 169, 172, 190, 203, 360n11
Gompers, Samuel, 87, 91–92, 137–40, 165
Gray, Ralph, 226, 233

Great Man theory of history, 53, 55, 61, 66
Greco and Carillo defense, 215, 218–19
Green, Gil, 383–84n17, 387n62
Green, Shields, 52
Greenglass, David, 253, 258
Greenglass, Ruth, 258
Greenlee, Sam, Spook Who Sat by the Door, 300
Griggs. Sutton E., Imperium in Imperio, 133, 270
Guevara, Ernesto "Che," 270

Hall, Covington, 147, 154, 157
Hall, Henry, 240
Hallie, Phillip, 13–14
Hampton, Fred, 280
Hapgood, Powers, 195, 239, 369n176
Harper's Ferry raid, 27, 43, 47, 50–52, 54–55
Harris, Frank, The Bomb, 102–3
Hayden, Louis, 44
Hayden, Tom, 305
Hayes, Arthur Garfield, 218
Haymarket affair, 48, 69, 71–72, 341n1; Communist Party histories of, 242–43; defense of bomb thrower of, 83–84; in left history, 110–11; legal arguments of lawyers in, 345n80; media's role in, 73–74, 79, 91, 95–97, 110–11; memorials to martyrs of, 100–106; New Left and, 266, 316, 317–18; trial of and clemency campaign and petition, 86–92, 346n88. See also under names of individual anarchists
Haywood, William (Big Bill), 23, 134, 136–40, 213–14, 322
Haywood-Moyer-Pettibone trial, 136–38, 355n100; celebrations after, 138
Hazlett, Andrew, 52, 62
Hecht, Ben, 255
Hegel, Georg Wilhelm Friedrich, 18, 43

International Labor Defense (ILD), 23, 164, 209–11; disbanding of, in Alabama, 234; Gastonia defense by, 223–24; influence of, on civil rights movement, 247; IWW vs., 213–16, 218, 222; lynching and, 229–31, 235; mass defense ideals and, 219–21, 233; membership in, 220; MOPR and, 236; popular history and, 241–42; Sacco-Vanzetti defense by, 186, 197–98; USSR and, 237–40. *See also* Communist Party, USA

International Red Aid. *See* International Society for Relief of Revolutionaries

International Society for Relief of Revolutionaries, (MOPR), 210, 214, 228, 236

International Solidarity Movement (ISM), 315, 317

International Working People's Association (IWPA), 72, 83, 85, 107, 341–42n12

Internment of Japanese Americans, 210, 240, 245

Irwin, John, 288–89

Jackson, Andrew, 29, 33

Jackson, Gardiner, 200, 245

Jackson, George, 17, 265–66, 269, 271, 275–76, 286; as criminal, 311–12; Davis and, 271, 293–94, 298, 305–8, 313–14; defense campaign for, 293–94, 306; defense of San Rafael Courthouse attempt by, 305; funeral of, 308–9; guerilla warfare and, 299–300; killing of, 307–8; killing of Soledad guard by, 293; prisoner organizing by, 289–93; on prison racism, 289–90, 295; Sacco compared to, 296; *Soledad Brother*, 294–99; Spies compared to, 296; Stender shooting blamed on, 310

Jackson, Georgia, 293, 298–99, 307–8

Jackson, Jonathan, 303–5

Jackson, "Popeye," 306

Jackson State, students killed at, 301

James, Jesse, 71, 112, 266; current status of, 341n10; Weathermen on, 382n6

Jefferson, Thomas, 4, 6, 8, 10, 116; on Shays, 6; slavery and, 8–9, 39; Jeffersonian tradition and, 136, 159; Vanzetti on, 170

Jerry (fugitive slave), 43–44

John Birch Society, 290

"John Brown's Body," 65, 71

Jones, Joseph J., 145, 357n131

Jones, Mary Harris ("Mother Jones"), 135, 143

Jones, "Orphan" (Euel Lee), 220, 372n43

Jordan, Robert, 272

"Judge Lynch," 107; Haymarket anarchists appeal to, 82, 110

Kahn, Albert, 251

Kansas Border Wars, 11, 48–50, 55, 66, 71, 334n98; media coverage of, 53–54

Karenga, Ron, 280

Karsner, Rose, 219–20

Keller, William, 245

Kent State, students killed at, 301

Kerner Commission (National Advisory Commission on Civil Disorders), 267–68

KGB (Committee for State Security), 210, 254

Killers, street gang, 33

King, Rev. Dr. Martin Luther, Jr., 279

Knights of Labor, 72, 80, 82–83, 87, 92, 99, 101

Know-Nothings (American political party), 34

Kossuth, Louis, 42, 47–48, 74; Kansas Free-Soilers compared to, 54

Krieger, Charles, 164

Kronstadt rebellion, 165, 216

Kruschev, Nikita, "secret speech" by, 252

Ku Klux Klan, 117, 165, 189, 192; Communist Party and, 227, 232, 237, 247; comparison of Haymarket defendants to, 91; comparison of Italian fascists to, 157–58, 232, 237; connections of, to U.S. government, 231, 247; Dies Committee on, 246; establishment violence by, 6–7; Jesse James as member of, 351n10; trials of, 112

Labor Defender, 197, 214, 239–40
LaGuardia, Fiorello, 207
Lane, Charles, 56
Langston, Charles H., 45, 71
Lawson, Elizabeth, 231, 235
League of Gileadites, 44
League of Revolutionary Black Workers, 276
Le Bon, Gustave, 94, 167
Lee, Euel, 220, 372n43
Legalism: criticism of, by anarchists, 173, criticism of, by communists, 212, 216; Dewey on, 199
Lenin, Vladimir "Ilyich," 268
Lewis, John, 221
Lilburne, John, 71
Lincoln, Abraham, 31, 35, 52
Linebaugh, Peter, 71
Lingg, Louis, 69, 85, 87, 90, 99–100, 102, 104; emulation of, by Berkman, 114; George Jackson compared to, 296; Stagolee compared to, 133, 270
Lippard, George, 31
Little, Frank, 147, 182
Littlefield, Daniel, 49
Lloyd, Henry Demarest, 93
Lombroso, Cesare, 93–94
London, Jack, 103
Love: concept of, in defense campaigns: 20–22, 71, 322; George Jackson and, 292, 306, 308–9; Haymarket anarchists and, 98–104; McNamaras and, 139–40; metaphor of, in anarchist movement,

182; Rosenbergs' relationship of, 256–57, 259; as self-sacrificing, 172–74; Stagolee and, 133
Lovejoy, Elijah, 33, 41, 339n179; IWW compared to, 147; John Brown and, 332n81
Lovestone, Jay, 222, 229
Lowell, A. Lawrence, 194
Ludlow Massacre, 135, 171
Lum, Dyer, 69, 98, 100, 110
Lumpen-proletariat: Black Panther Party and, 3, 268–69, 273–77, 284–85, 291; definition of, 83; definition of white and black poor and, 66–67; George Jackson and, 297; Haymarket anarchists and, 80; Marx's theories about, 268; New Left and, 281; police as, 83; the unemployed and, 75, 78–80, 291–92. *See also* Criminals
Lynching: abolitionists on, 42; anarchism compared to, 113–14 ; Black armed resistance to, 132–33, Black-on-Black, 354n85; class and, 131–32, 158, 226, 230–35, 237, 244; Communist Party and, 222–27, 230–31, 234; as European, 277; Haymarket anarchists and, 107, 109–10; Haywood on, 140; as irrational, 113, 118, 120, 125, 156; IWW and, 116, 134, 140, 147, 149, 154–55, 222; labor unions' response to, 153–56; legal, 16, 156, 226, 230; media responsibility for, 13–14, 119; NAACP campaign against 128–30, 162; as "popular justice," 26; social control and, 22; as "un-American," 234; victims of, as heroic, 15, 22, 122; Wells on, 117–22, 125–28; whiteness and, 10. *See also* Police-mob continuum; *and under names of individual lynching victims*
Lyons, Eugene, 181, 199

MacLeod, Douglas, 276
Madeiros, Celestino, 189, 192

Madison, James, 7
Makhno, Nestor, 166, 216, 361n12
Malatesta, Errico, 167, 169, 186
Malcolm X, 67, 266, 272, 274
Manhood: abolitionists' argument for, of slave, 42–47, 60, 64; anarchists' transformation of concept of, 80–82, 100, 102, 106; anti-lynching activists' argument for, of Blacks, 22, 113, 117, 121, 125–27; Black Panthers and, 273, 277, 297, 299–300; celebration of, by anarchists, 85, 107, 110; free labor ideal and, 76, 80; George Jackson and, 295–97, 308, 314; IWW and, 116, 136–37, 139, 142; John Brown and, 57, 63, 65, 67; Manson and, 290, 310; in 1960s, 266; in prison, 292, 295–96; republican heroism and, 7–8, 17, 265; Sacco and Vanzetti and, 195; Stagolee and, 267; whiteness and, 11, 34–35, 52–53, 107, 151
Marcuse, Herbert, 281
Martineau, Harriet, 41–42
Martyrs, martydom: abolitionists as, 30–31, 41; Corrie as example of, 315, 317; in critiques of leftism, 1, 263, 317–19; in folk belief, 19, 70, 104–5; Foxe's book of, 62–63; as heroic choice, 17–18, 24; Italian anarchists and, 167, 173–74; IWW and, 146–47, 159; legends of, for movements, 23–24, 98, 101; Soviet, 241; Williams's rejection of, 100
Marx, Karl, 21, 23, 72, 88, 268, 270, 292
Mass action in defense campaigns: for Black Panthers, 284–85, 293, 296, 303, 305–6, 313; for Chicago anarchists, 69–71, 99; for early communists, 209–11; ILD on, 215–21, 230; for IWW, 115–16, 142, 152, 160; against McCarthyism, 247; in Rosenberg case, 255; for Sacco and Vanzetti, 165–66, 172, 176–78, 182, 184, 189, 196–98; in Scottsboro case, 226–29,

233–35. *See also* Industrial Workers of the World; International Labor Defense; Masses; Mobs; *and under names of individual defense campaigns*
Masses: abstract concept of, 173–74; as deluded, 95–98, 167; as democratic, 25–26, 60, 134; heroic representation of, 2–3, 15, 17–18, 20–21, 24, 72, 87–88, 104–5, 153, 211, 230, 233, 300, 314; liberals' rejection of, 195–96, 202, 261; as source of terror, 9–10, 22, 31, 127, 243, 245; USSR as embodiment of, 240; as white, 158. *See also* Mass action in defense campaigns; Mobs
Maurer, George, 219, 220–21, 225, 227
Maximon, Selma, 202
McCarthyism, 246–47, 249–52, 258, 260–62, 264. *See also* Anticommunism; House Committee on Un-American Activities; Rosenberg, Ethel, and Julius; Smith Act
McKay, Claude, 151
McKenney, Ruth, 206, 369n176
McKinley, William, 113
McMullen, William, 33
McNamara, J. B., and J. J. McNamara: confession by, 139, 140; defense of, 138–39
Mead, Ed, 314
Melodrama, 12–13, 17, 74–75, 82
Melville, Herman, *Billy Budd*, 320–21
Melville, Sam, 287
Messer-Kruse, Timothy, 318
Miller, Alvin, 292–93
Minkins, Shadrach, rescue of, 44
Miserables, Les, 78, 275, 344n40
Mobs: anti-abolitionist, 31–32, 34–35, 37, 41; anti-black terror and, 110, 113, 117, 122, 125, 154, 159, 191, 226; as hero, 15, 72, 83, 99, 106, 167; as

Nietzsche, Friedrich, 82; Nietzschean heroism and, 169, 172, 313–14; *ressentiment* and, 5, 11, 16
Nixon, Richard, 301
Nolen, William, 290–91, 293
Nonresistance, 29–30

Oates, Stephen J., 58
O'Hare, Kate Richards, 146, 171
Oberlin-Wellington Rescue, 44–45
Orchard, Harry, 356n111

Palmer, A. Mitchell, 156; raids of, 160, 162, 164, 171, 191, 212
Paris Commune, 72–74, 79, 84, 85, 112
Parker, William, 44
Parsons, Albert, 69, 80, 89, 102, 107; Communist Party literature about, 242
Parsons, Lucy, 1, 20, 80, 87, 96, 99–100, 103–4; on Blacks, 108; Gastonia defense activism by, 223; at IWW founding convention, 115; racial background of, 89, 346n91
Patterson, Haywood, 272
Patterson, William, 191, 222, 228, 236, 247, 252, 272–73, 388n65
Patronati Societies, 236
Pavlichenko, Liudmilla, 241
Pettibone, Edward, 134, 136–37
Phillips, Wendell, 42, 60–61
Phillips, William, 53
Pieh, Sengbe (Cinque), 41–42
Pinkerton, Alan, 77
Pinkertons, 77, 82, 86, 92, 135
Police: 14, 21, 75, 290–91, 299, 303; anarchist descriptions of, 72, 78, 81–84, 86–87, 90, 105; Black Panther Party and, 3, 267, 270, 272–75, 277–80, 300, 303–6, 311; brutality of, 15, 128, 223, 287–88; communist campaigns against brutality by, 231, 248, 272–73; NAACP and, 123, 129–30; New Left and, 266; in popular fiction, 77–78; progressives call for reform of,

90–93; IWW and, 141–42, 148, 171; Wells on, 117–20, 122, 125. *See also* Police-mob continuum
Police-mob continuum, 15–16, 117–20, 126, 128–30, 156, 191, 230, 248, 271–72
Popular fiction, 3, 11–12, 34, 77–78, 82, 100–102, 133, 147–48, 255, 300
Popular Front, the. *See* Communist Party, USA
Popular history: defense campaign as, 21, 215; ILD as source of, 241–43
Populist Party, 92
Pottawatomie Massacre, 53, 63, 66
Powderly, Terrence, 81, 92
Powells, William A., killing of, in Soledad prison, 292
Poyntz, Juliette Stewart, 217
Prager, Dennis, 317
Pratt, Elmer "Geronimo," 273, 299
Prejean, Sister Helen, 22
Preston, William, 153
Price, John (fugitive), 44
Prison: as apex of capitalism, 15, 79; Black Panthers' theory of, 267–69; as destroyer of men and families, 24, 116, 143–44, 176, 182–83, 248; as fascist, 295; gangs in, 309–10; growth of, 81, 267; IWW protest inside, 141, 145, 159; labor control in, 76–77, 79; segregation in, 75, 247, 288, 290, 309; as slavery, 21–23, 129, 272, 285–86; Soviets' held up as models, 239–40
Prisoners: early activism for, 70–72; organizing of, 285–87, 290–93; political vs. criminal, 158–59, 175–76, 191–92, 271, 287; Russian anarchists as, 166, 197
Prohibition, 191–92
Propaganda of the deed, 149, 167, 169, 171, 175–76, 201, 273
Prosser, Gabriel, 27
Puritanism, 54, 55–59, 64, 67, 89, 97, 189, 193, 266, 300

Quintiliano, Luigi, 182

Rabinowitz, Abraham, death of, 146–47

Racial theories, 30, 36, 66; on abolitionists, 31; on Anglo-Saxons, 3, 40, 65, 77, 157; on Blacks, 35, 40, 76–77, 118, 151; on Germans or "Teutonic," 77; on guilt and innocence, 12–15, 23, 26, 117, 119, 127, 265, 269; on Italians, 94, 149, 170, 194–95; on Jews, 108; on mobs, 76–77; on violence, 8. *See also* Whiteness

Rackley, Alex, 280, 300, 387n57

Rakosi, Mathias, 237

Randolph, A. Phillip, 117, 154

Rankin, John, 246

Reagan, Ronald, 290

Redpath, James, 43, 50, 52, 55, 65

Reichstag fire trial, 212, 236–67

Reinsdorf, August, 70, 84

Republicanism: Chicago anarchists, and 70, 72, 81–82, 84, 86, 89, 109, 111, 116; Darrow and, 136, 138; John Brown and, 50–56, 63; manhood and, 21, 30–31, 35, 42, 46–48, 76, 87; race and, 5–11, 25, 35, 49, 76. *See also* Manhood; Nationalism

Ressentiment, 5, 11, 16

Reuben, William, 254

Revolutionary Action Movement (RAM), 300

Riddle, Albert G., 45

Riots, 31–35, 37; in Atlanta (1906), 126; in Attica, 287, 309; Berkeley, 288; at Democratic National Convention (Chicago 1968), 279; in Elaine, Arkansas, 154, 157; "hard hat," 301; Newark (1967), 300; New York Draft Riots, 33; in prisons, 290; in St. Louis (1917), 130, 154; in Tulsa, 154–55, 157; in Watts, 267

Rivington, Ann, 260

Robespierre, Maximilien, 9

Robinson, Charles, and Pottawatomie Massacre, 53

Roediger, David, 7, 35

Roosevelt, Franklin Delano, 211, 232; wiretapping bills and, 243

Roosevelt, Theodore, 127

Rosenberg, Ethel, 253, 255–56, 258. *See also* Rosenberg, Ethel, and Julius

Rosenberg, Ethel, and Julius: defense of, 249, 253–64; espionage evidence against, 380n177; execution of, 252; letters of, 256–57, 262; liberal attacks on, 263

Rosenberg, Julius, 256, 258–59. *See also* Rosenberg, Ethel, and Julius

Rubin, Jerry, 279

Sacco, Nicola, 166–67, 172, 177, 179–80, 182, 198; appeal of, to dynamite, 177; death threat of, against Fred Moore, 188; hunger strike of, 176; in mental institution, 186; racial depictions of, 194, 201, 204; son of (Dante), 203

Sacco, Rosina, 202, 204

Sacco-Vanzetti defense, 20, 156, 162–63, 174–99; African Americans and, 191; alliance of anarchists and liberals in, 189–96; communists' identification of, as symbols of working class, 180, 183; ILD and, 197–99; issue of racist prosecution in, 190–92, 362n27; literary representation of, 204–7; multi-ethnic version of American working class created by, 246; Sacco and Vanzetti as symbols of anarchism and, 175–76

Salem witch trials, 70, 193, 264

Salomon, Moses, 86

Salsedo, Andrea, 163–64, 175

Sams, George, 280, 387n57

Sanborn, Franklin, 56, 66, 75

Sanchez, Sonia, 279

San Francisco Vigilance Committee, 32

Strikes (cont.)
135; of Fort Leavenworth prisoners,
145; in Lawrence, Massachusetts
(1912), 148–49, 190, 208; in
Paterson, N.J. (1913), 149, 190; in
Passaic, N.J. (1927), 220
Strong, George Templeton, 32, 52
Sue, Eugene, 268
Sumner, Charles, 41
Supreme Court of the United States,
41, 73, 135, 141, 212, 264
Surveillance, by U.S. government, 243
Swayze, Kate Edwards ("Osawatomie
Brown"), 54
Sweet, Ossian, 155
Syndicalism, 172

Tackwood, Louis, 304, 307, 311
Taft, William Howard, 127
Temperance, 80
Thalman, Ernst, 215, 236
Thaw, Harry, 136
Thayer, Judge Webster, 187, 198
Third Period of Communist theory of
crisis, 211–12, 238
Thomas, Norman, 186, 214, 218
Thomas, Thomas (fugitive), 61
Thompson, William, 188
Thoreau, Henry David, 57, 61
Torture, 18
Totalitarianism, 1, 9, 22, 25, 174,
245, 319
Toussaint L'Ouverture, 40, 42; evoca-
tion of, by Max Eastman, 151
Trade Union Education League
(TUEL), 166, 221, 223
Transcendentalism, 56
Tresca, Carl, 164, 171, 175, 178, 196, 208,
214, 218
Trotsky, Leon, 217
Trotskyists, 210, 245
Trumbull, General Matthew, 89
Tubman, Harriet, 50
Turner, Nathaniel, 11, 14, 27–29, 36–37;
comparison of, to John Brown,

51–52, 67; in media, 37–39; as
model, 300, 311; rebellion of, 38–39
Turpin, Dick, 71
Tweed, William "Boss," 33

Unemployed, the, 75, 78–80, 291–92.
See also Lumpen-proletariat
Union of Soviet Socialist Republics
(USSR), 209, 212, 213, 224, 238–40
United Mine Workers of America
(UMWA), 179
Urban guerilla warfare in United
States, 302, 305
United States war with Mexico, 30–31
USS Creole rebellion, 327n1

Van der Lubbe, Marinus, 236–37. See
also Dimitrov, Georgi; Reichstag
fire trial
Vanderveer, George, 147, 157
Van Zandt-Spies, Nina, 100–101
Vanzetti, Bartolomeo, 152, 163–64,
167, 170, 177, 181–82, 186, 189, 192;
on Communist Party and ILD, 197,
219; criticism of defense committee
by, 183, 189–90, 195; on Moore, 184;
"Story of a Proletarian Life," 201
Vardaman, Governor James, 131
Vesey, Denmark, 27
Vigilantism, 31, 33–34, 25, 116;
Communist Party and, 211, 222;
against IWW, 146–48, 157; against
labor, 134; in San Francisco, 32. See
also Lynching; Mobs
Vigilance Committee: New York, 44;
of NAACP, 128
Villard, Oswald Garrison, 126
Violence: against slaves, 29, 60;
historians' concerns about, 58–59;
justification of, by abolitionists,
27–28, 42–43, 53; justification of,
by left, 83–86, 89, 109, 114, 116, 139,
148–49, 170, 176–78, 188, 216, 266,
275, 277, 302–3; justification of, by
state, 5, 17, 23, 39, 57, 85, 143, 155,
162, 196, 252, 316–17, 340, 372n43,